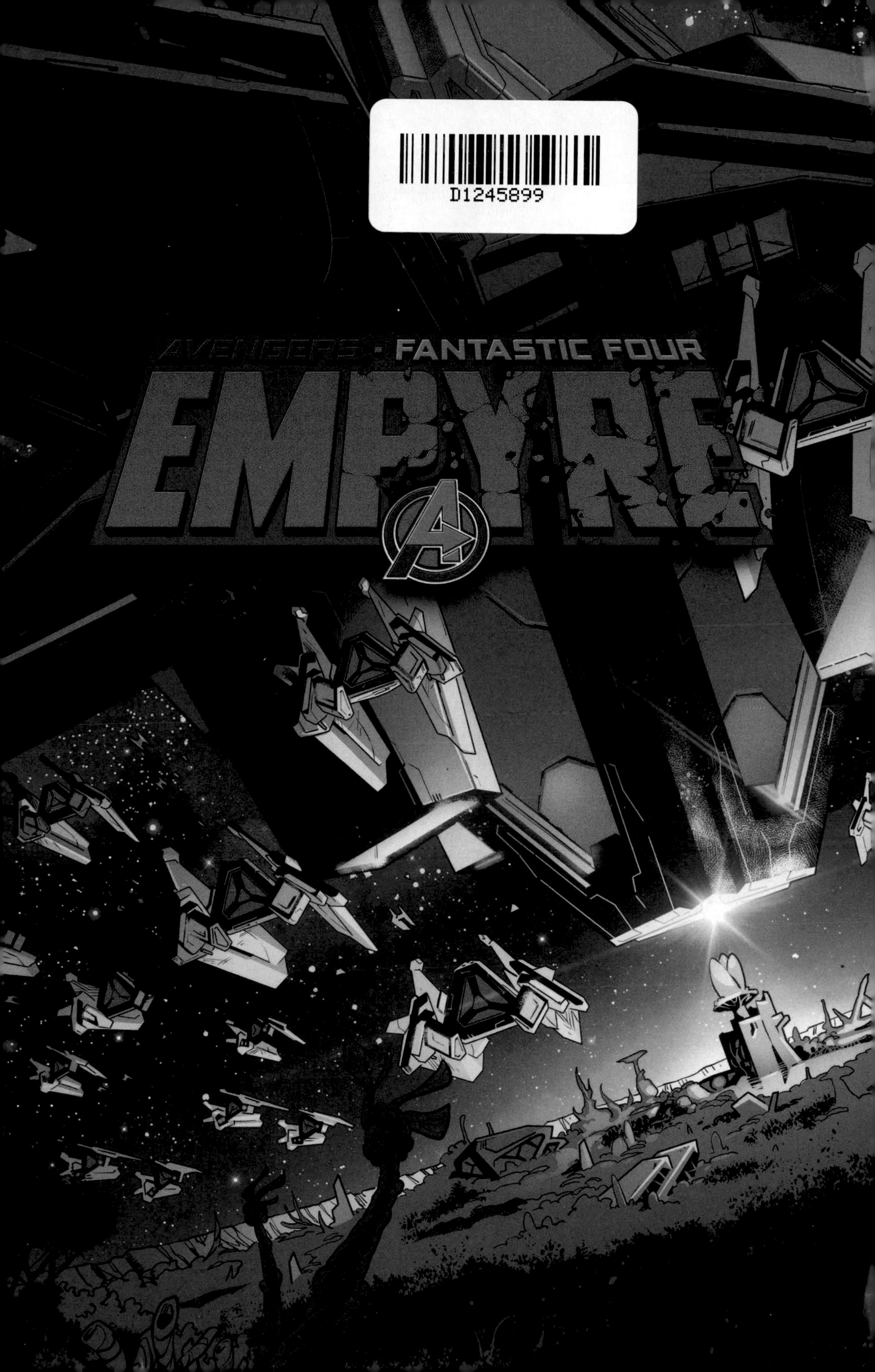
AVENGERS · FANTASTIC FOUR
EMPYRE

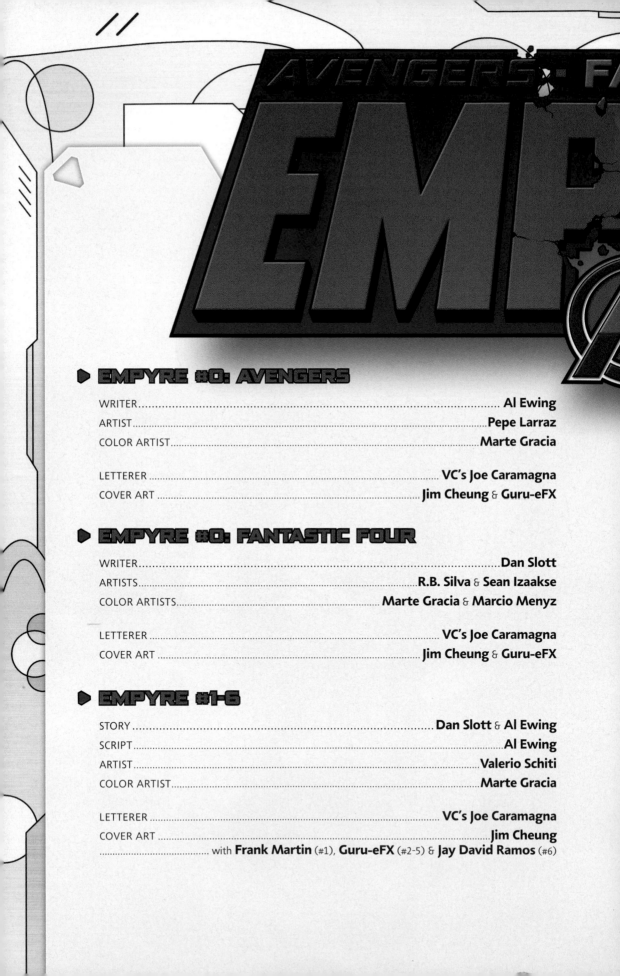

EMPYRE #0: AVENGERS

WRITER .... **Al Ewing**
ARTIST ....**Pepe Larraz**
COLOR ARTIST..**Marte Gracia**

LETTERER ....**VC's Joe Caramagna**
COVER ART ....**Jim Cheung** & **Guru-eFX**

EMPYRE #0: FANTASTIC FOUR

WRITER...**Dan Slott**
ARTISTS..**R.B. Silva** & **Sean Izaakse**
COLOR ARTISTS.. **Marte Gracia** & **Marcio Menyz**

LETTERER ....**VC's Joe Caramagna**
COVER ART ....**Jim Cheung** & **Guru-eFX**

EMPYRE #1-6

STORY ....**Dan Slott** & **Al Ewing**
SCRIPT...**Al Ewing**
ARTIST...**Valerio Schiti**
COLOR ARTIST...**Marte Gracia**

LETTERER ....**VC's Joe Caramagna**
COVER ART ....**Jim Cheung**
.... with **Frank Martin** (#1), **Guru-eFX** (#2-5) & **Jay David Ramos** (#6)

NTASTIC FOUR

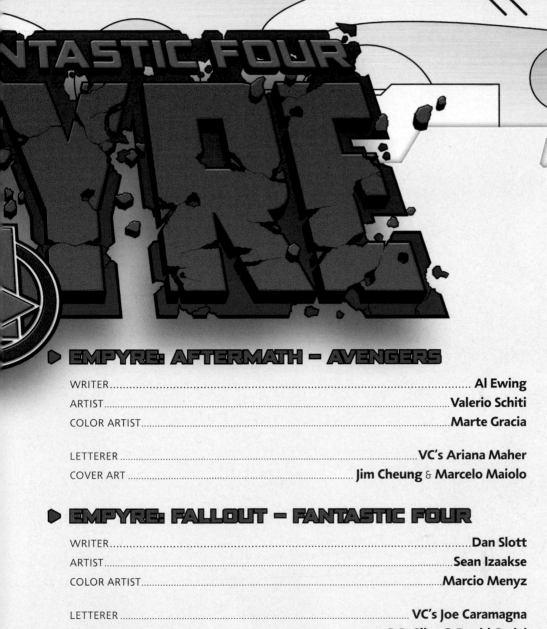

EMPYRE: AFTERMATH – AVENGERS

WRITER .... **Al Ewing**
ARTIST .... **Valerio Schiti**
COLOR ARTIST .... **Marte Gracia**

LETTERER .... **VC's Ariana Maher**
COVER ART .... **Jim Cheung** & **Marcelo Maiolo**

EMPYRE: FALLOUT – FANTASTIC FOUR

WRITER .... **Dan Slott**
ARTIST .... **Sean Izaakse**
COLOR ARTIST .... **Marcio Menyz**

LETTERER .... **VC's Joe Caramagna**
COVER ART .... **R.B. Silva & David Curiel**

ASSISTANT EDITOR .... **Martin Biro**
ASSOCIATE EDITOR .... **Alanna Smith**
EDITOR .... **Tom Brevoort**

AVENGERS & FANTASTIC FOUR CREATED BY **Stan Lee** & **Jack Kirby**

COLLECTION EDITOR **Jennifer Grünwald**
ASSISTANT MANAGING EDITOR **Lisa Montalbano**
EDITOR, SPECIAL PROJECTS **Mark D. Beazley**
LAYOUT **Jeph York**
SVP PRINT, SALES & MARKETING **David Gabriel**

ASSISTANT MANAGING EDITOR **Maia Loy**
ASSOCIATE MANAGER, DIGITAL ASSETS **Joe Hochstein**
VP PRODUCTION & SPECIAL PROJECTS **Jeff Youngquist**
BOOK DESIGNER **Jay Bowen**
EDITOR IN CHIEF **C.B. Cebulski**

EMPYRE. Contains material originally published in magazine form as EMPYRE #0 AVENGERS (2020), EMPYRE #0 FANTASTIC FOUR (2020), EMPYRE (2020) #1-6, EMPYRE: AFTERMATH AVENGERS (2020) #1 and EMPYRE: FALLOUT FANTASTIC FOUR (2020) #1. First printing 2020. ISBN 978-1-302-92438-6. Published by MARVEL WORLDWIDE, INC., a subsidiary of MARVEL ENTERTAINMENT, LLC. OFFICE OF PUBLICATION: 1290 Avenue of the Americas, New York, NY 10104. **Printed in the U.S.A.** KEVIN FEIGE, Chief Creative Officer; DAN BUCKLEY, President, Marvel Entertainment; JOHN NEE, Publisher; JOE QUESADA, EVP & Creative Director; TOM BREVOORT, SVP of Publishing; DAVID BOGART, Associate Publisher & SVP of Talent Affairs; Publishing & Partnership; DAVID GABRIEL, VP of Print & Digital Publishing; JEFF YOUNGQUIST, VP of Production & Special Projects; DAN CARR, Executive Director of Publishing Technology; ALEX MORALES, Director of Publishing Operations; DAN EDINGTON, Managing Editor; RICKEY PURDIN, Director of Talent Relations; SUSAN CRESPI, Production Manager; STAN LEE, Chairman Emeritus. For information regarding advertising in Marvel Comics or on Marvel.com, please contact Vit DeBellis, Custom Solutions & Integrated Advertising Manager, at vdebellis@marvel.com. For Marvel subscription inquiries, please call 888-511-5480. **Manufactured between 9/4/2020 and 10/6/2020 by LSC COMMUNICATIONS INC., KENDALLVILLE, IN, USA.**

10 9 8 7 6 5 4 3 2 1

EMPYRE 0: AVENGERS

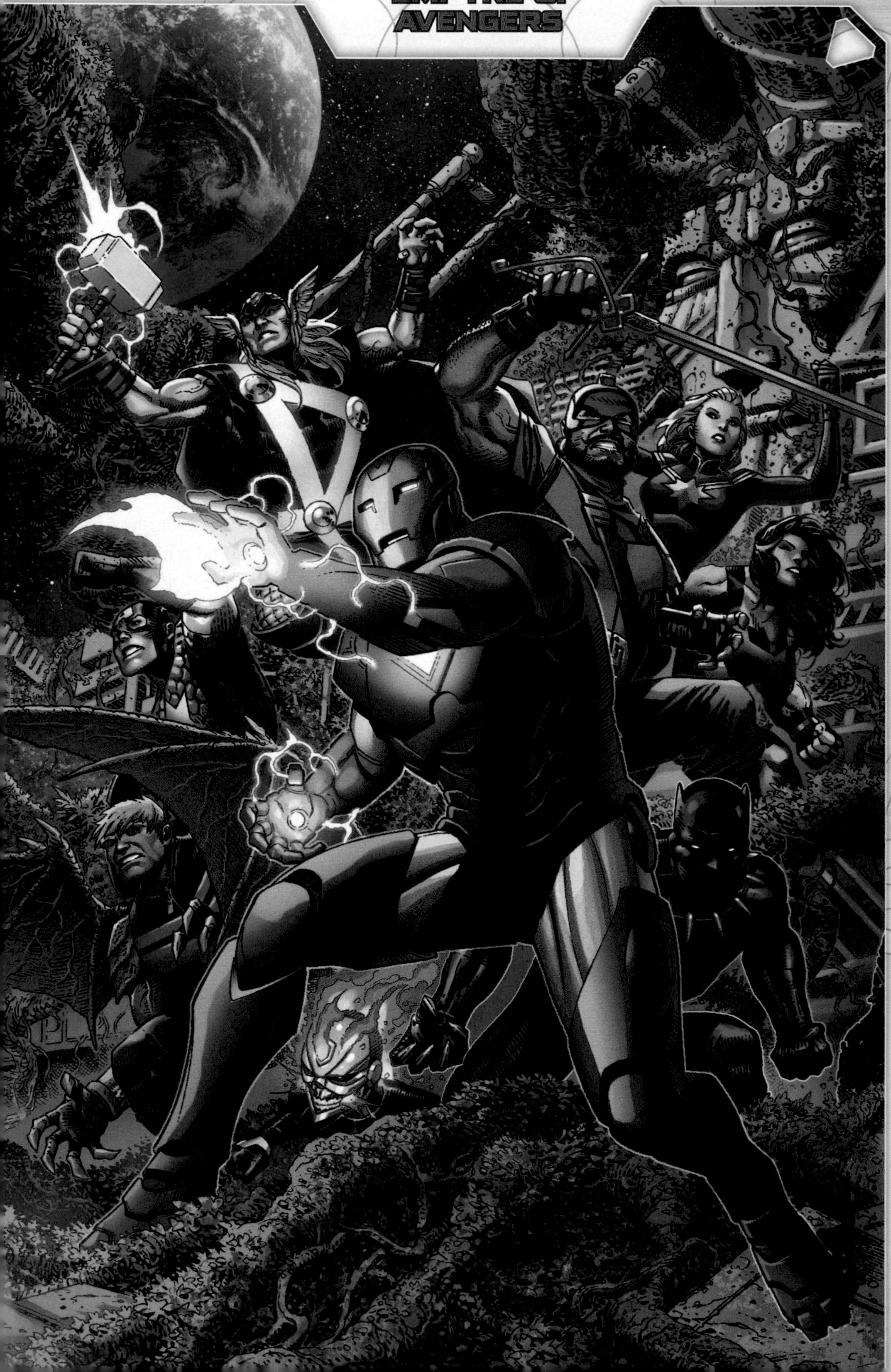

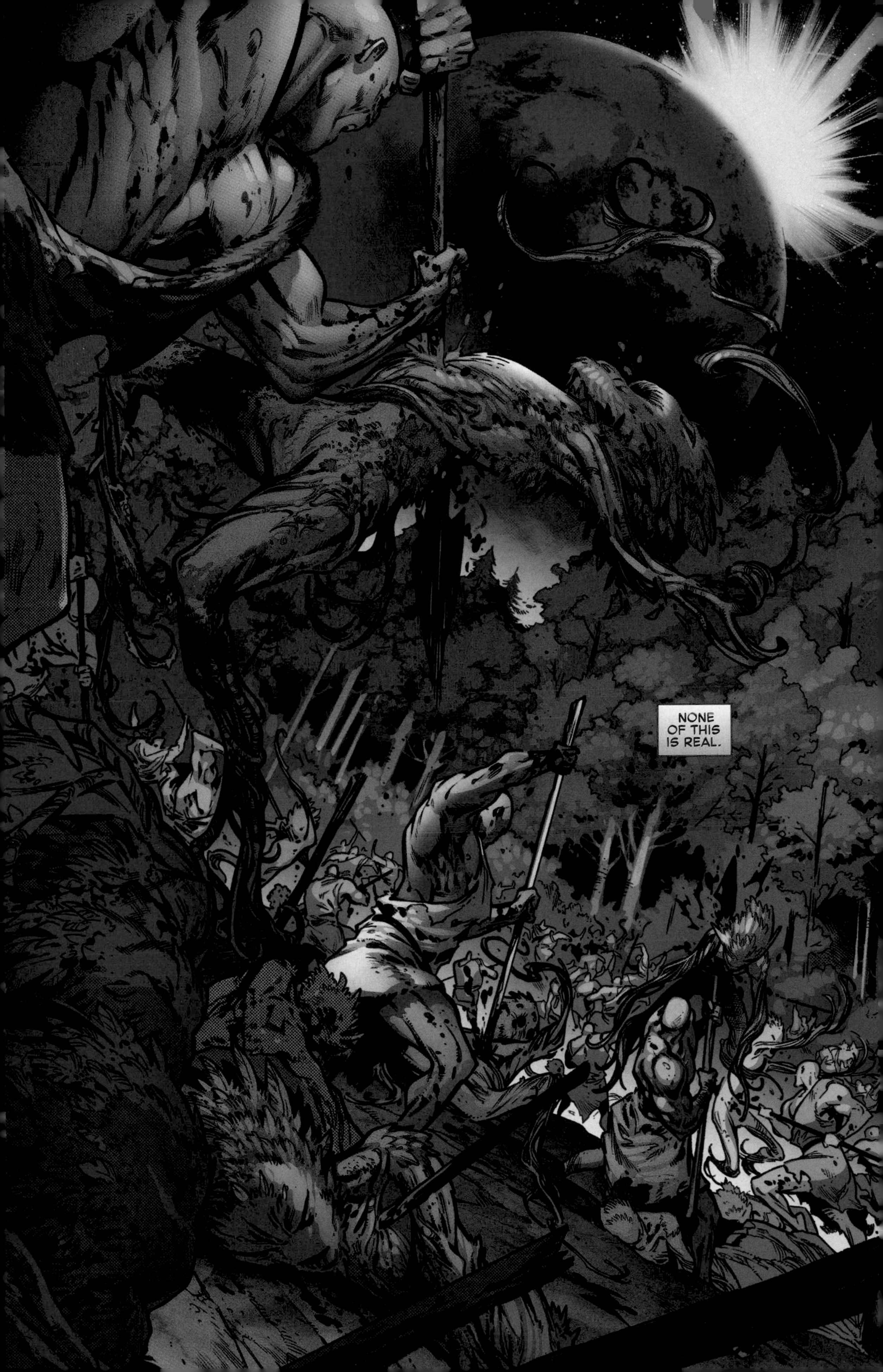
NONE OF THIS IS REAL.

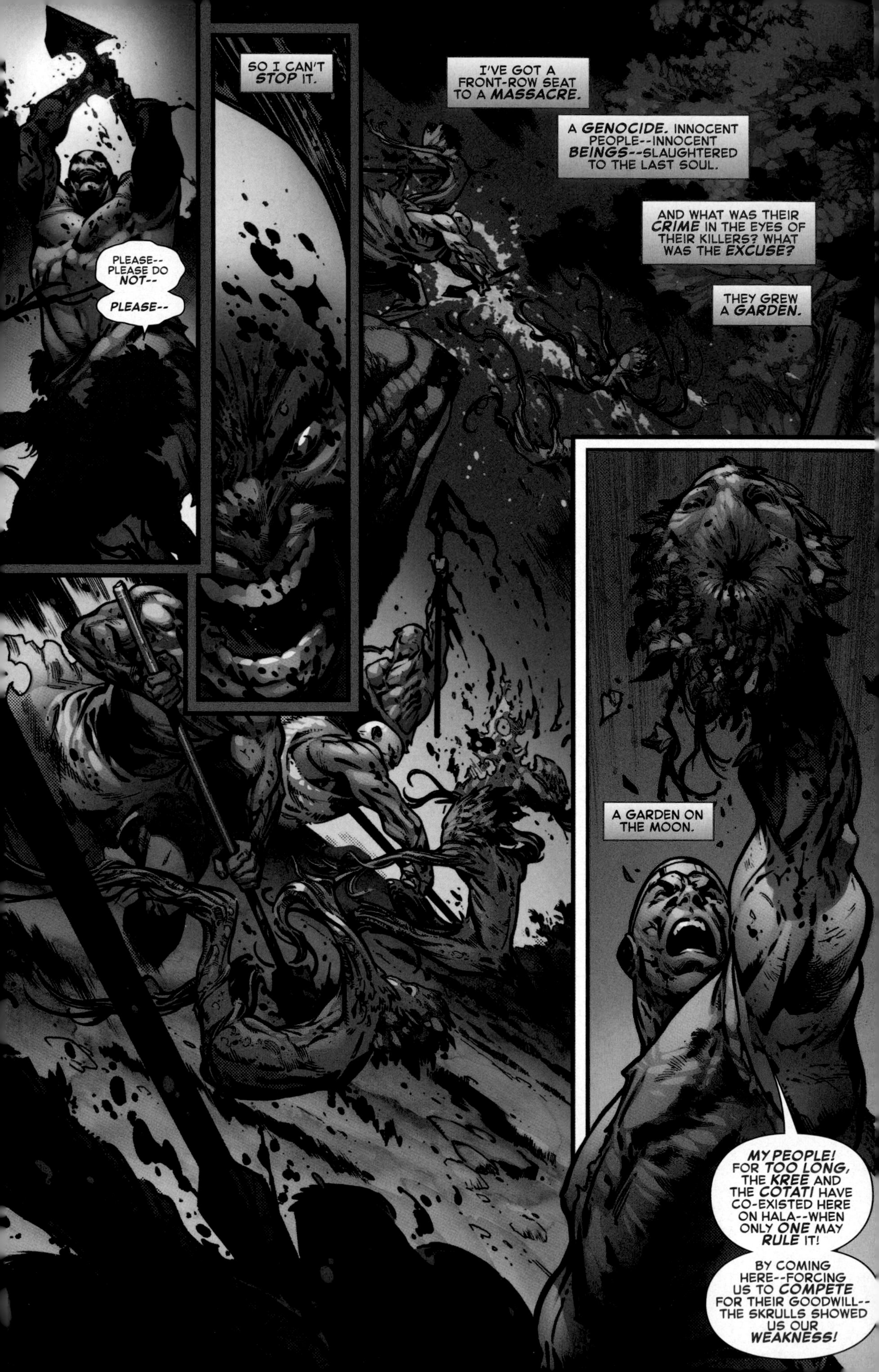
PLEASE-- PLEASE DO NOT--
PLEASE--
SO I CAN'T STOP IT.
I'VE GOT A FRONT-ROW SEAT TO A MASSACRE.
A GENOCIDE. INNOCENT PEOPLE--INNOCENT BEINGS--SLAUGHTERED TO THE LAST SOUL.
AND WHAT WAS THEIR CRIME IN THE EYES OF THEIR KILLERS? WHAT WAS THE EXCUSE?
THEY GREW A GARDEN.
A GARDEN ON THE MOON.
MY PEOPLE! FOR TOO LONG, THE KREE AND THE COTATI HAVE CO-EXISTED HERE ON HALA--WHEN ONLY ONE MAY RULE IT!
BY COMING HERE--FORCING US TO COMPETE FOR THEIR GOODWILL--THE SKRULLS SHOWED US OUR WEAKNESS!

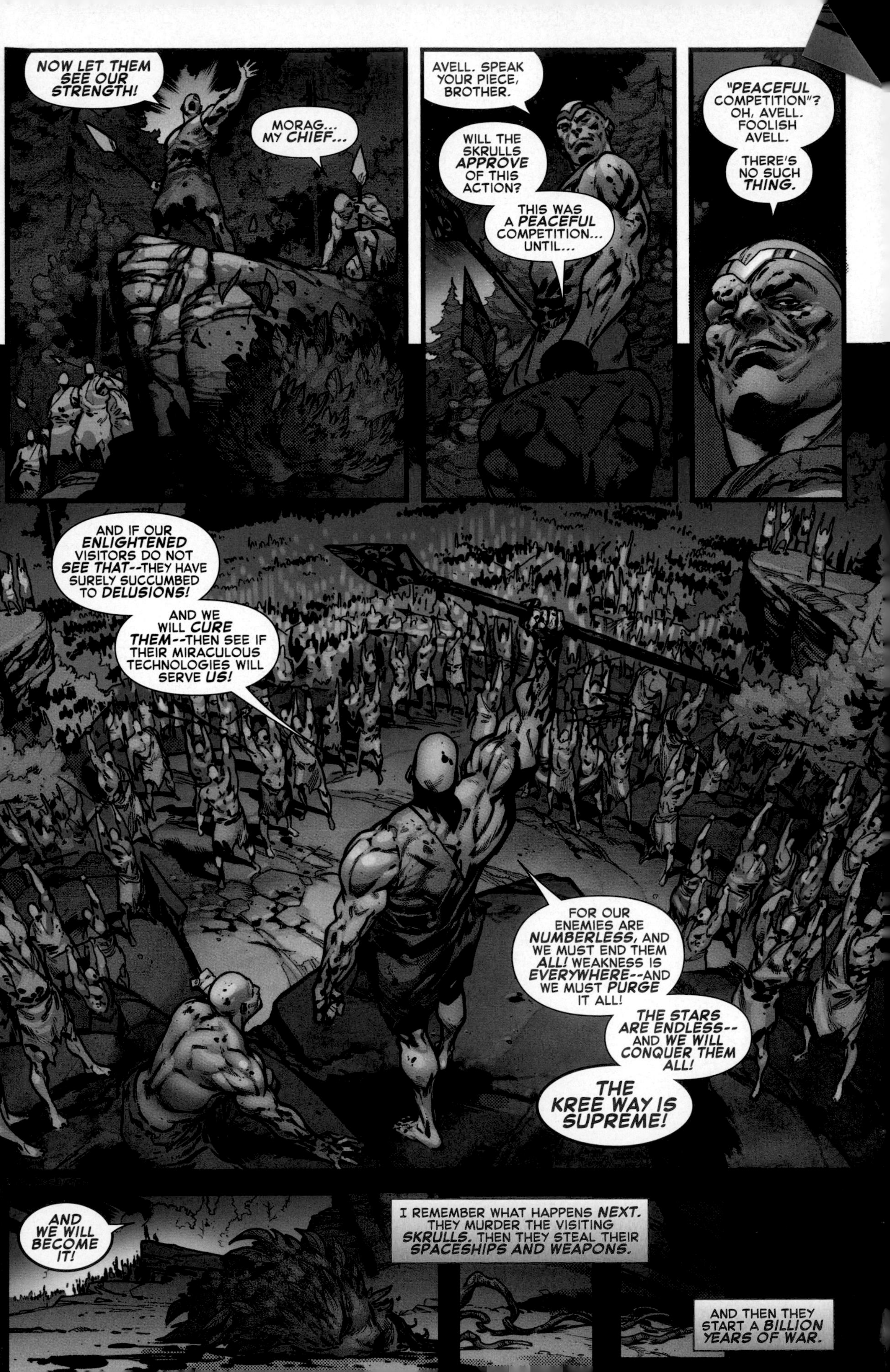
NOW LET THEM SEE OUR STRENGTH!
MORAG... MY CHIEF...
AVELL. SPEAK YOUR PIECE, BROTHER.
WILL THE SKRULLS APPROVE OF THIS ACTION?
THIS WAS A PEACEFUL COMPETITION... UNTIL...
"PEACEFUL COMPETITION"? OH, AVELL. FOOLISH AVELL.
THERE'S NO SUCH THING.
AND IF OUR ENLIGHTENED VISITORS DO NOT SEE THAT--THEY HAVE SURELY SUCCUMBED TO DELUSIONS!
AND WE WILL CURE THEM--THEN SEE IF THEIR MIRACULOUS TECHNOLOGIES WILL SERVE US!
FOR OUR ENEMIES ARE NUMBERLESS, AND WE MUST END THEM ALL! WEAKNESS IS EVERYWHERE--AND WE MUST PURGE IT ALL!
THE STARS ARE ENDLESS--AND WE WILL CONQUER THEM ALL!
THE KREE WAY IS SUPREME!
AND WE WILL BECOME IT!
I REMEMBER WHAT HAPPENS NEXT. THEY MURDER THE VISITING SKRULLS. THEN THEY STEAL THEIR SPACESHIPS AND WEAPONS.
AND THEN THEY START A BILLION YEARS OF WAR.

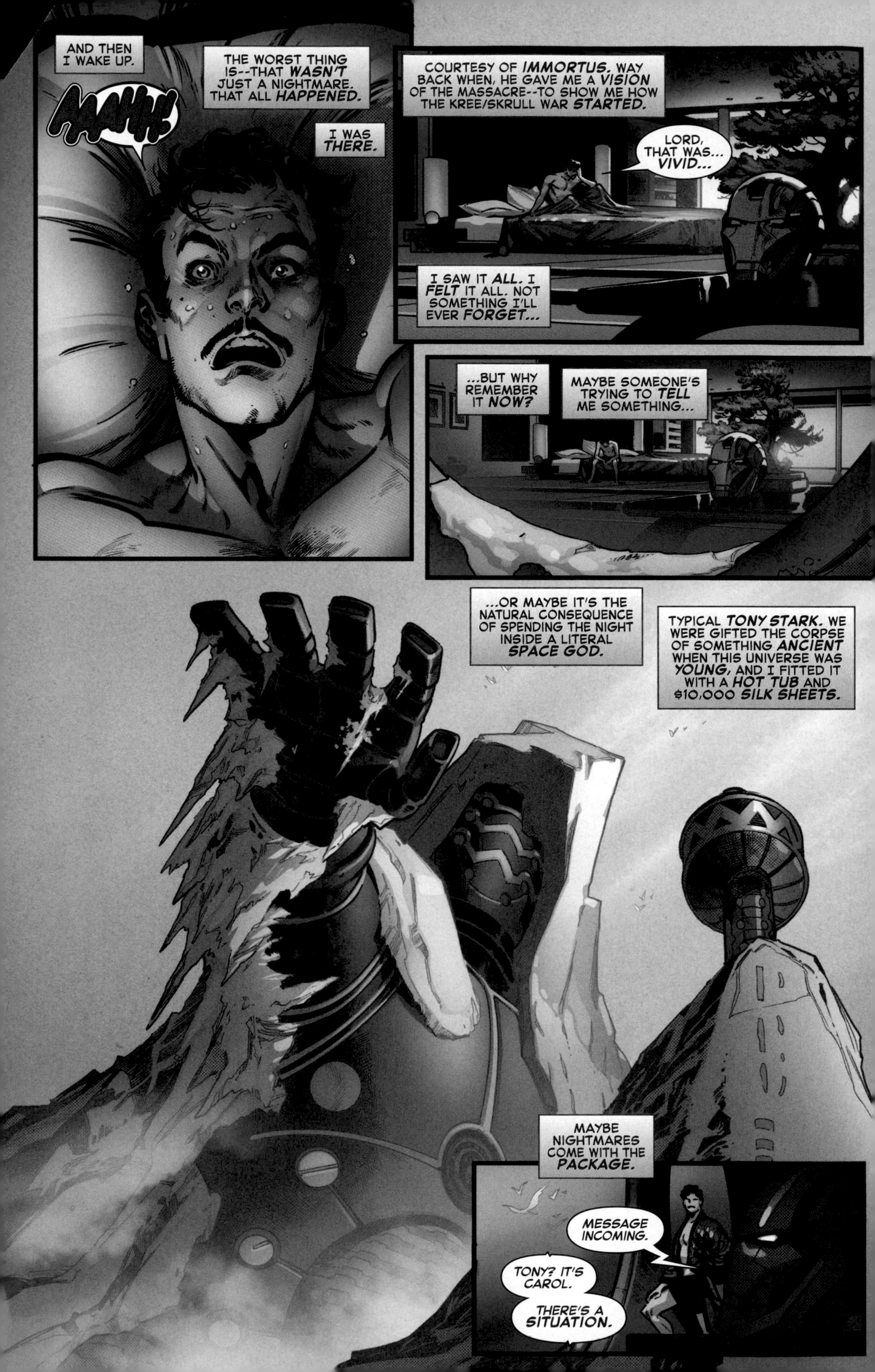
AND THEN I WAKE UP.
AAAHH!
THE WORST THING IS--THAT WASN'T JUST A NIGHTMARE. THAT ALL HAPPENED.
I WAS THERE.
COURTESY OF IMMORTUS. WAY BACK WHEN, HE GAVE ME A VISION OF THE MASSACRE--TO SHOW ME HOW THE KREE/SKRULL WAR STARTED.
LORD, THAT WAS... VIVID...
I SAW IT ALL. I FELT IT ALL. NOT SOMETHING I'LL EVER FORGET...
...BUT WHY REMEMBER IT NOW?
MAYBE SOMEONE'S TRYING TO TELL ME SOMETHING...
...OR MAYBE IT'S THE NATURAL CONSEQUENCE OF SPENDING THE NIGHT INSIDE A LITERAL SPACE GOD.
TYPICAL TONY STARK. WE WERE GIFTED THE CORPSE OF SOMETHING ANCIENT WHEN THIS UNIVERSE WAS YOUNG, AND I FITTED IT WITH A HOT TUB AND $10,000 SILK SHEETS.
MAYBE NIGHTMARES COME WITH THE PACKAGE.
MESSAGE INCOMING.
TONY? IT'S CAROL.
THERE'S A SITUATION.

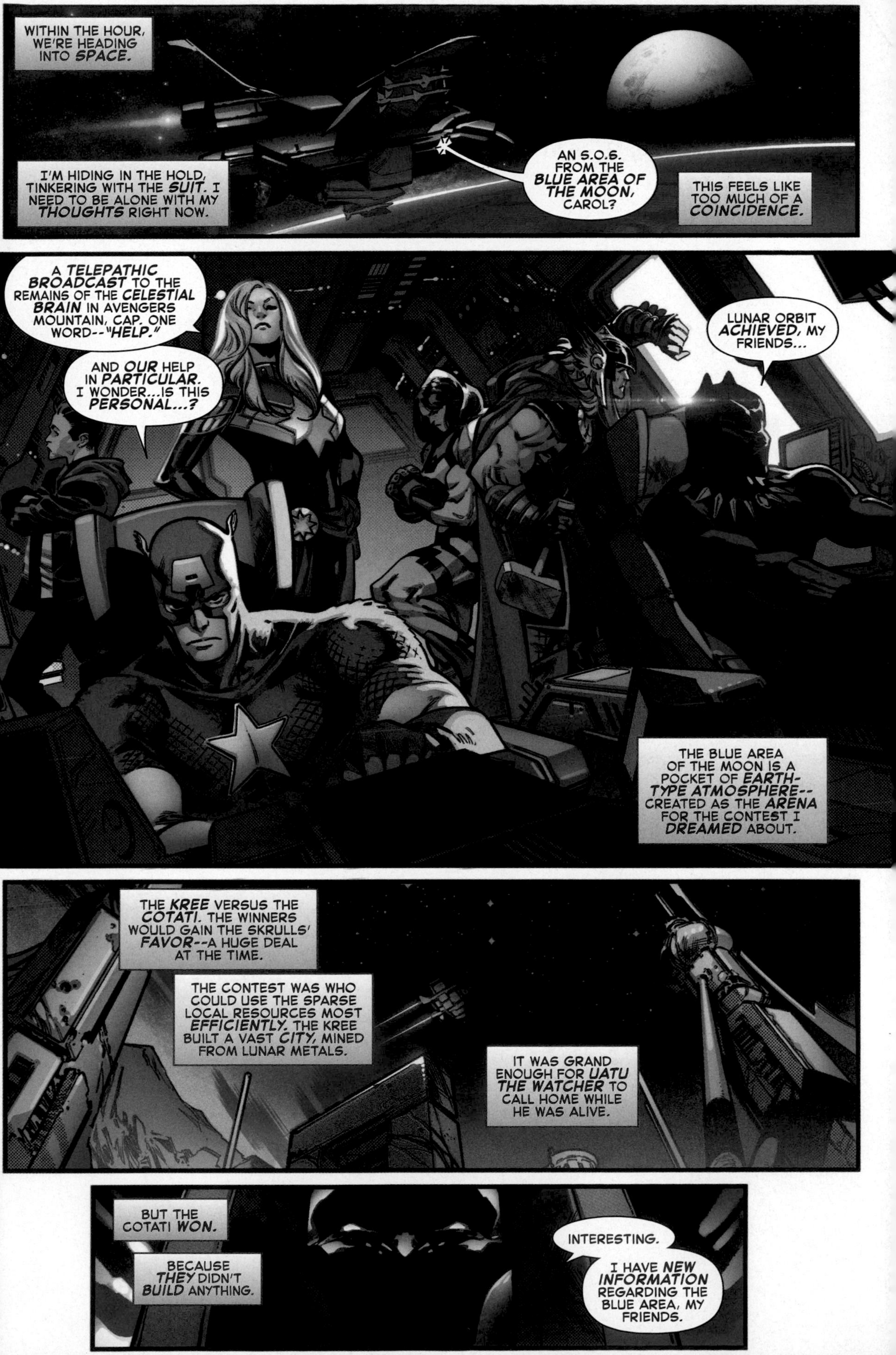
WITHIN THE HOUR, WE'RE HEADING INTO SPACE.
I'M HIDING IN THE HOLD, TINKERING WITH THE SUIT. I NEED TO BE ALONE WITH MY THOUGHTS RIGHT NOW.
AN S.O.S. FROM THE BLUE AREA OF THE MOON, CAROL?
THIS FEELS LIKE TOO MUCH OF A COINCIDENCE.
A TELEPATHIC BROADCAST TO THE REMAINS OF THE CELESTIAL BRAIN IN AVENGERS MOUNTAIN, CAP. ONE WORD--"HELP."
AND OUR HELP IN PARTICULAR. I WONDER...IS THIS PERSONAL...?
LUNAR ORBIT ACHIEVED, MY FRIENDS...
THE BLUE AREA OF THE MOON IS A POCKET OF EARTH-TYPE ATMOSPHERE--CREATED AS THE ARENA FOR THE CONTEST I DREAMED ABOUT.
THE KREE VERSUS THE COTATI. THE WINNERS WOULD GAIN THE SKRULLS' FAVOR--A HUGE DEAL AT THE TIME.
THE CONTEST WAS WHO COULD USE THE SPARSE LOCAL RESOURCES MOST EFFICIENTLY. THE KREE BUILT A VAST CITY, MINED FROM LUNAR METALS.
IT WAS GRAND ENOUGH FOR UATU THE WATCHER TO CALL HOME WHILE HE WAS ALIVE.
BUT THE COTATI WON.
BECAUSE THEY DIDN'T BUILD ANYTHING.
INTERESTING.
I HAVE NEW INFORMATION REGARDING THE BLUE AREA, MY FRIENDS.

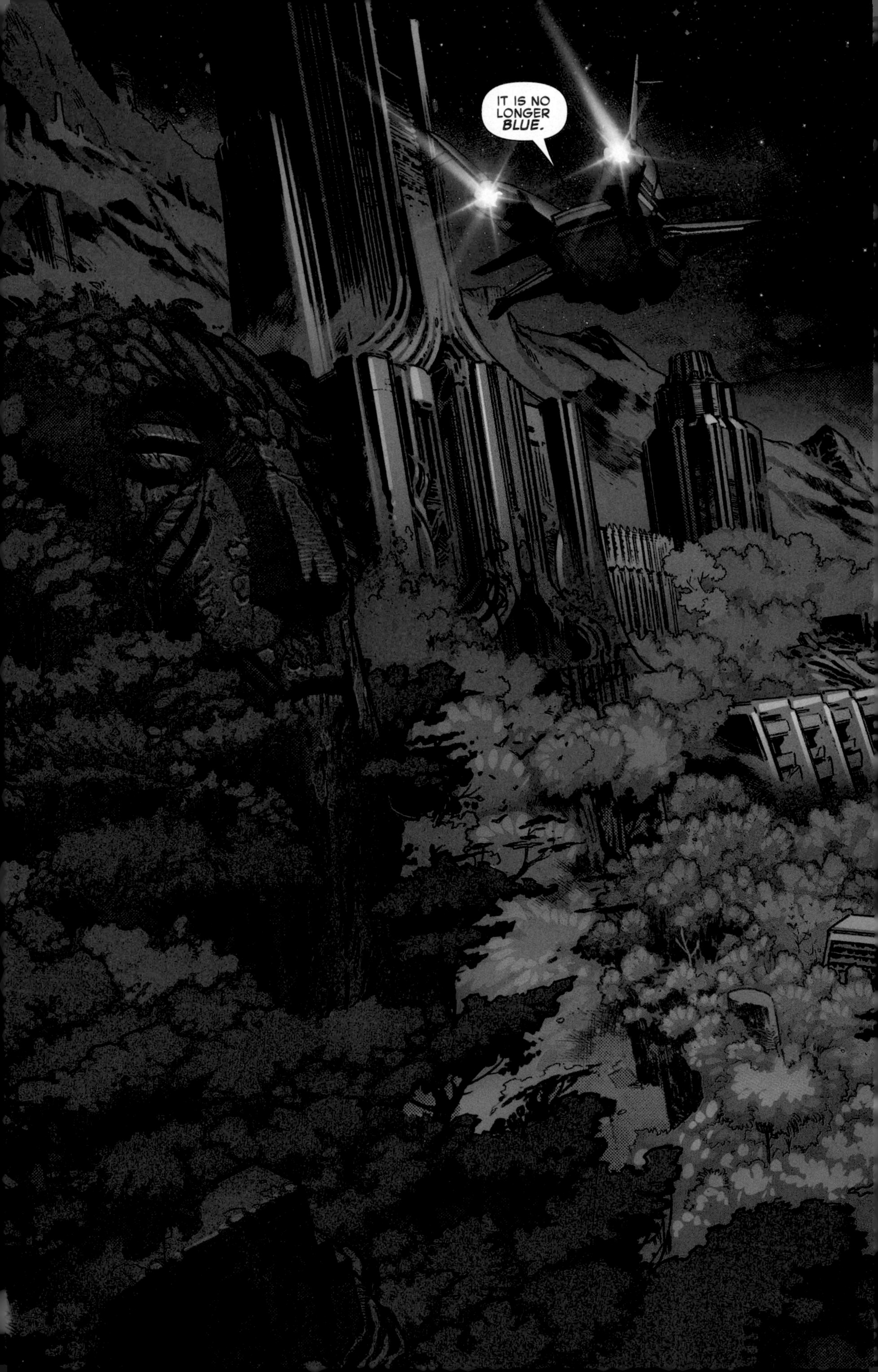
IT IS NO LONGER BLUE.

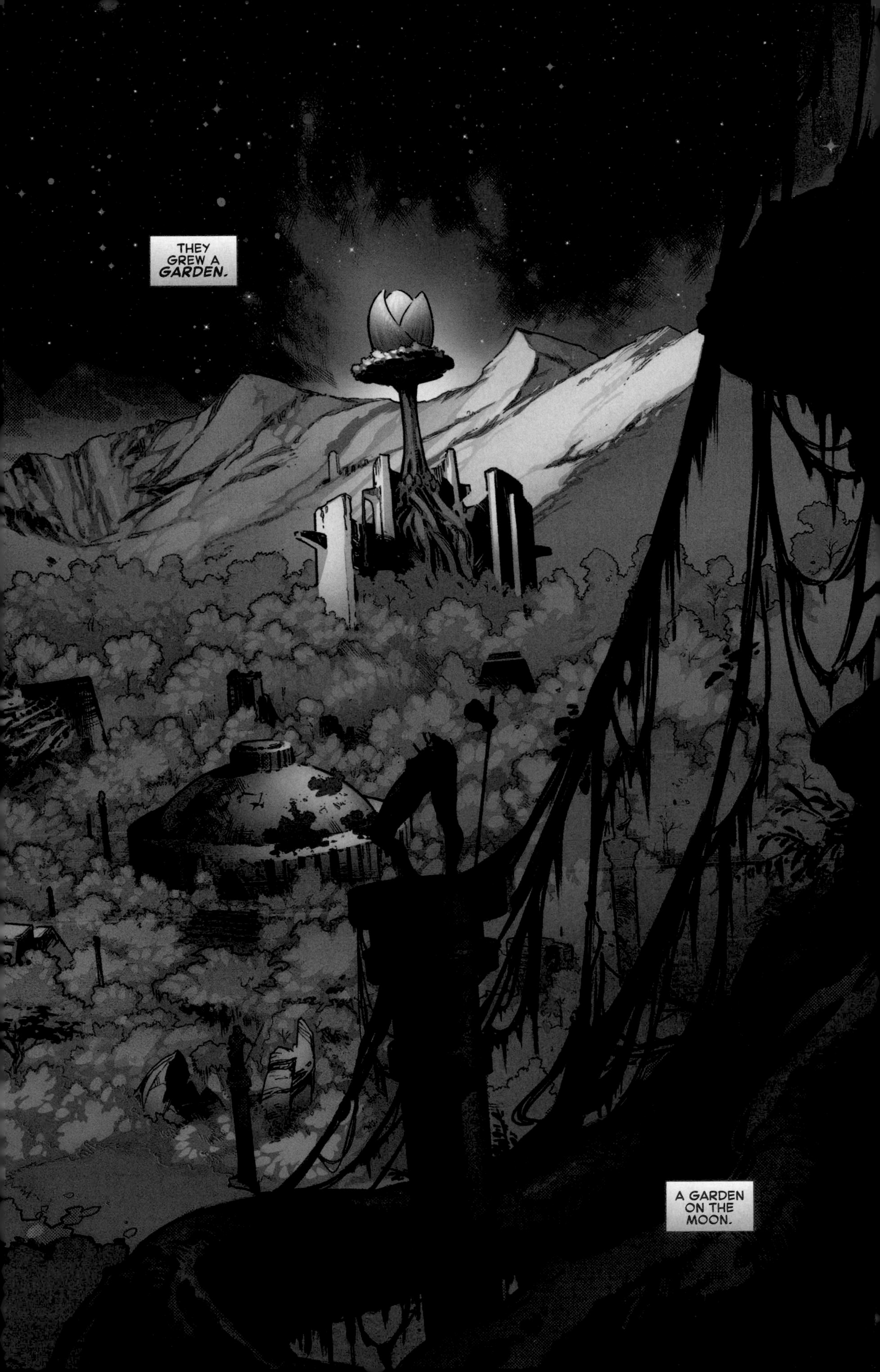
THEY GREW A GARDEN.
A GARDEN ON THE MOON.

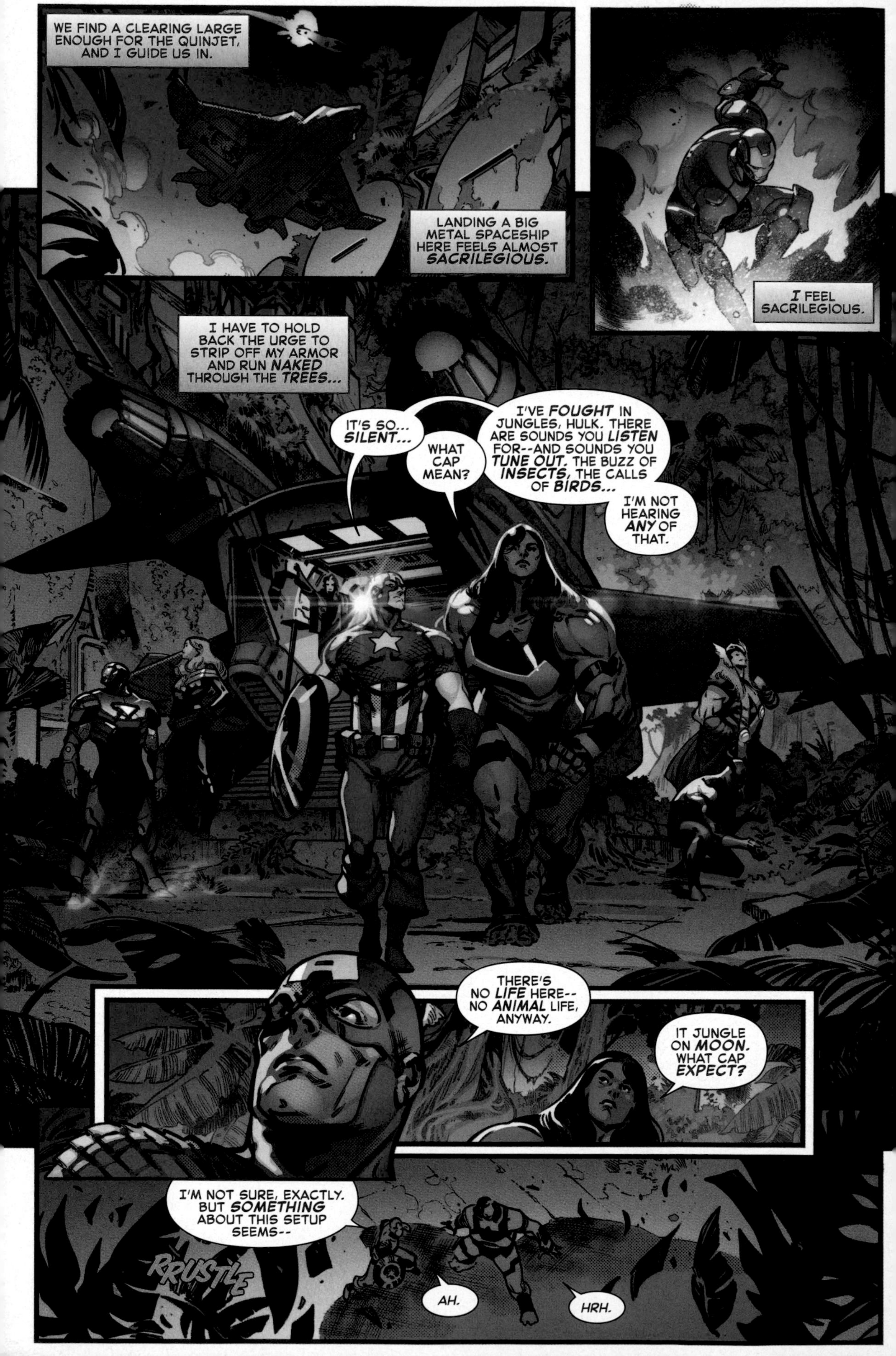

WE FIND A CLEARING LARGE ENOUGH FOR THE QUINJET, AND I GUIDE US IN.
LANDING A BIG METAL SPACESHIP HERE FEELS ALMOST SACRILEGIOUS.
I FEEL SACRILEGIOUS.
I HAVE TO HOLD BACK THE URGE TO STRIP OFF MY ARMOR AND RUN NAKED THROUGH THE TREES...
IT'S SO... SILENT...
WHAT CAP MEAN?
I'VE FOUGHT IN JUNGLES, HULK. THERE ARE SOUNDS YOU LISTEN FOR--AND SOUNDS YOU TUNE OUT. THE BUZZ OF INSECTS, THE CALLS OF BIRDS...
I'M NOT HEARING ANY OF THAT.
THERE'S NO LIFE HERE-- NO ANIMAL LIFE, ANYWAY.
IT JUNGLE ON MOON. WHAT CAP EXPECT?
I'M NOT SURE, EXACTLY. BUT SOMETHING ABOUT THIS SETUP SEEMS--
RRUSTLE
AH.
HRH.

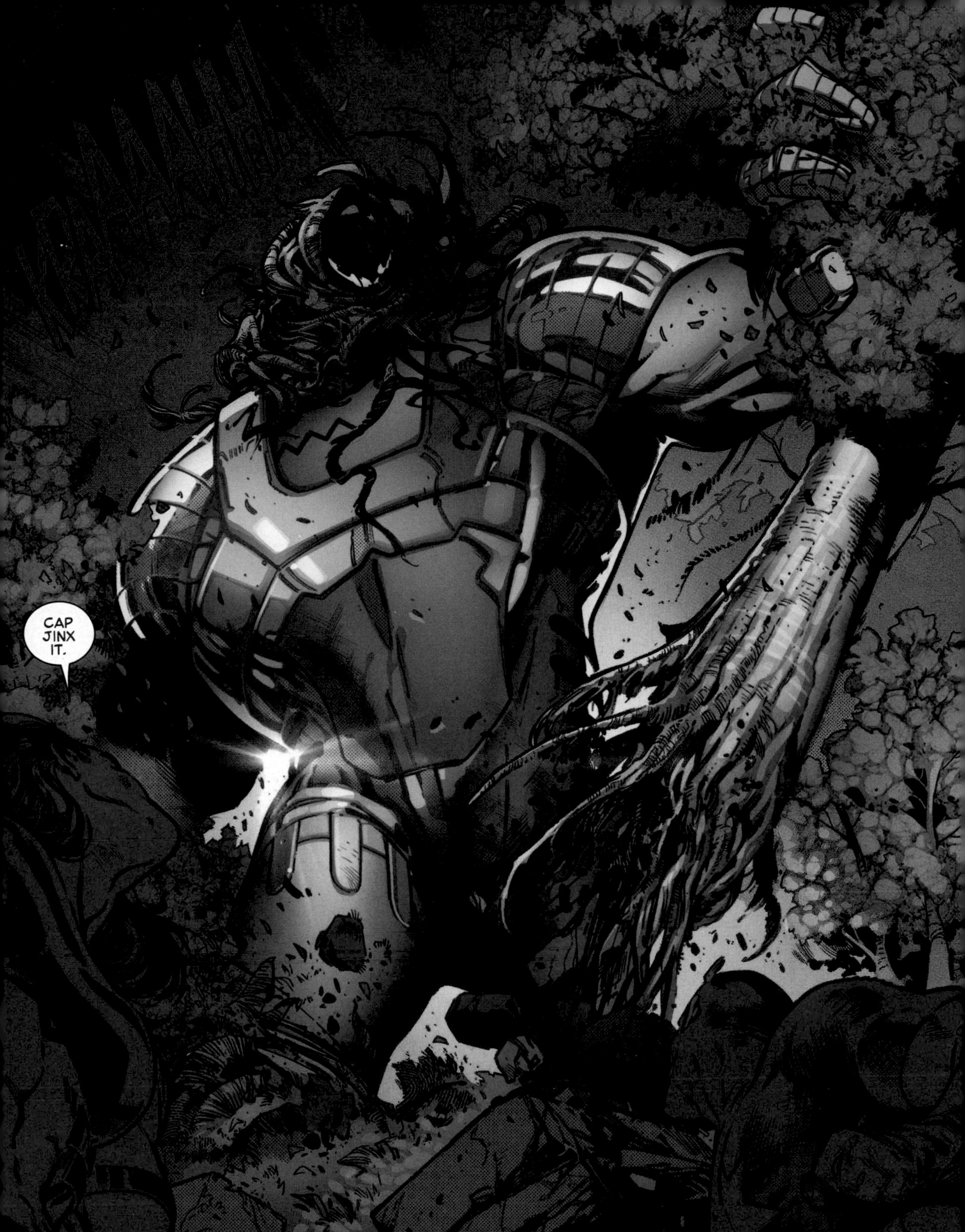
CAP JINX IT.

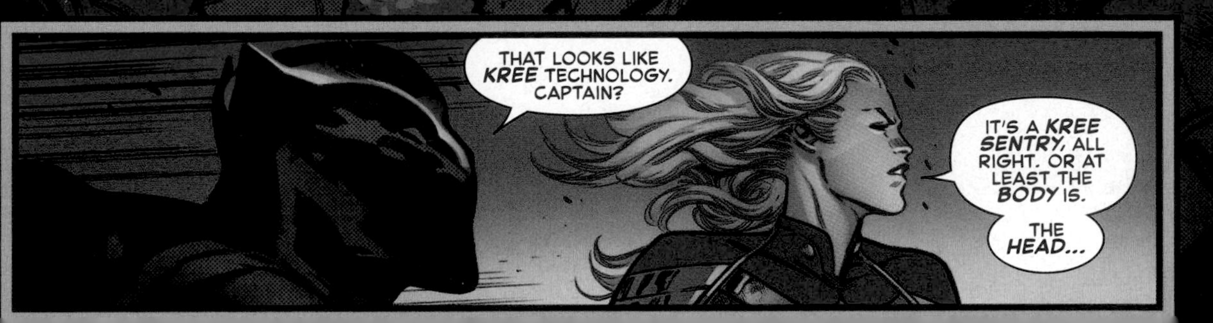
THAT LOOKS LIKE KREE TECHNOLOGY. CAPTAIN?
IT'S A KREE SENTRY, ALL RIGHT. OR AT LEAST THE BODY IS.
THE HEAD...

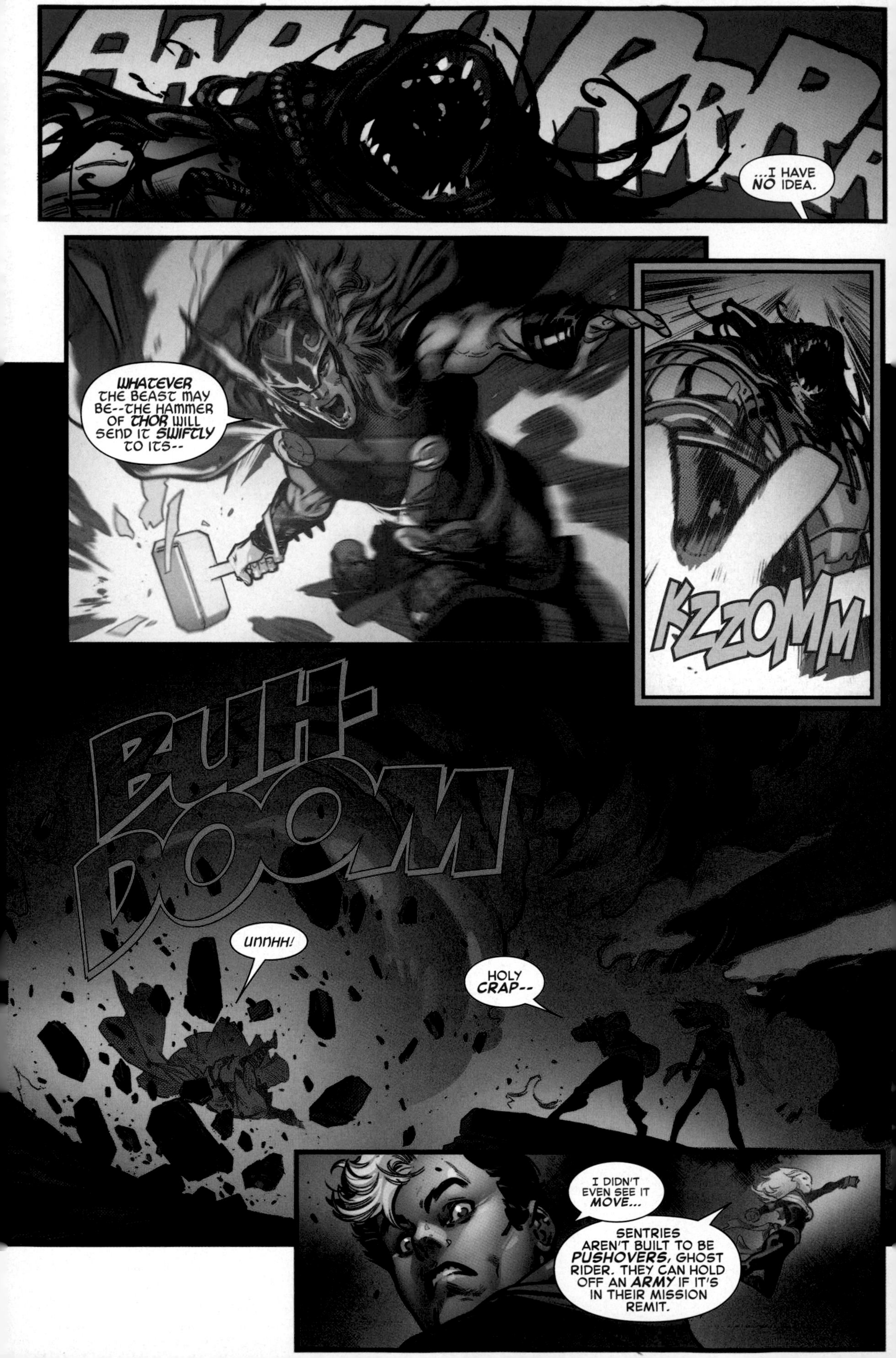

AAAAHRRRR
...I HAVE NO IDEA.
WHATEVER THE BEAST MAY BE--THE HAMMER OF THOR WILL SEND IT SWIFTLY TO ITS--
KZZOMM
BUH-DOOM
UNNHH!
HOLY CRAP--
I DIDN'T EVEN SEE IT MOVE...
SENTRIES AREN'T BUILT TO BE PUSHOVERS, GHOST RIDER. THEY CAN HOLD OFF AN ARMY IF IT'S IN THEIR MISSION REMIT.

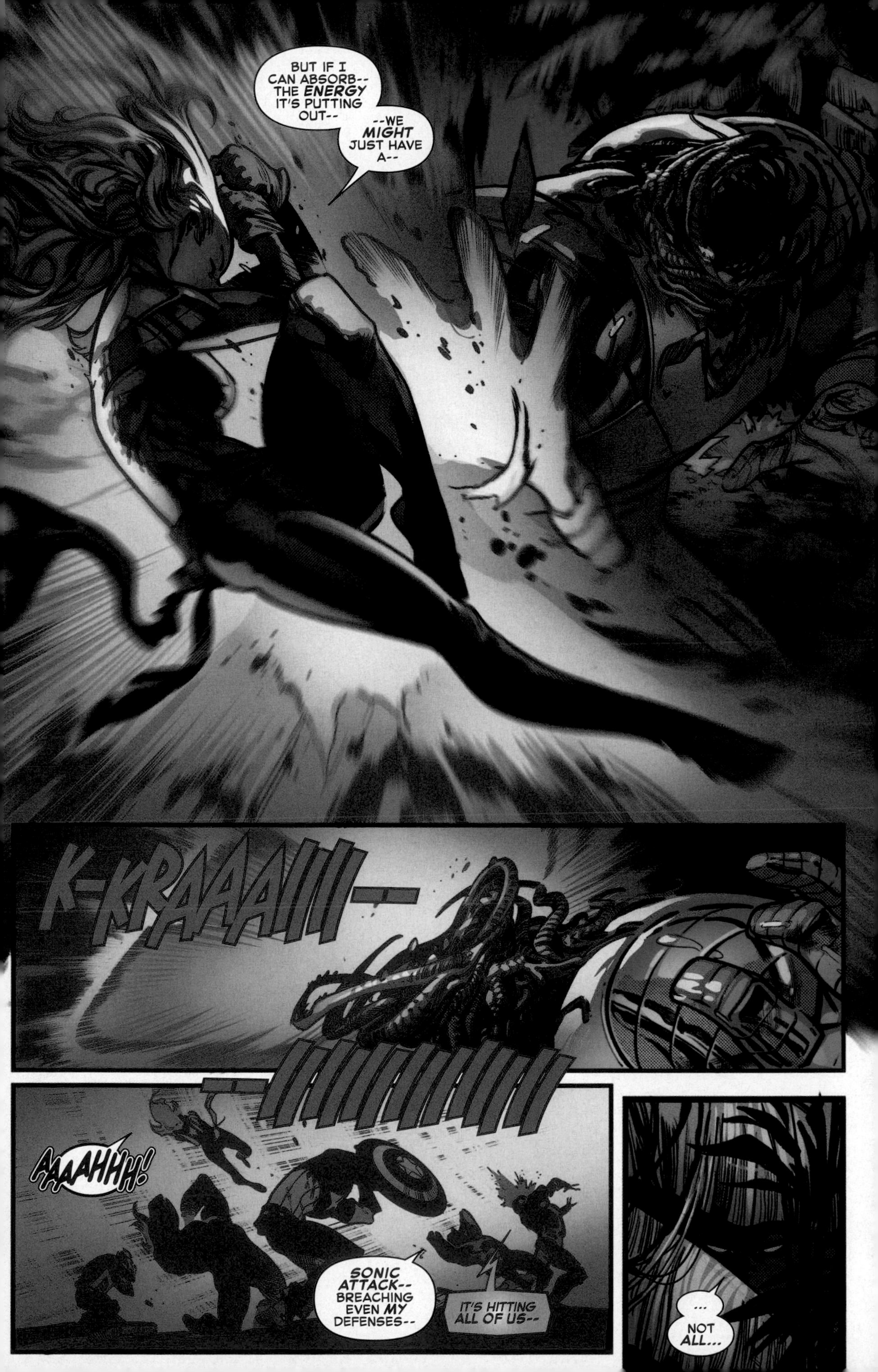
BUT IF I CAN ABSORB-- THE ENERGY IT'S PUTTING OUT--
--WE MIGHT JUST HAVE A--
K-KRAAAIIII--
--IIIIIIIIIIIII
AAAAHHH!
SONIC ATTACK-- BREACHING EVEN MY DEFENSES--
IT'S HITTING ALL OF US--
...
NOT ALL...

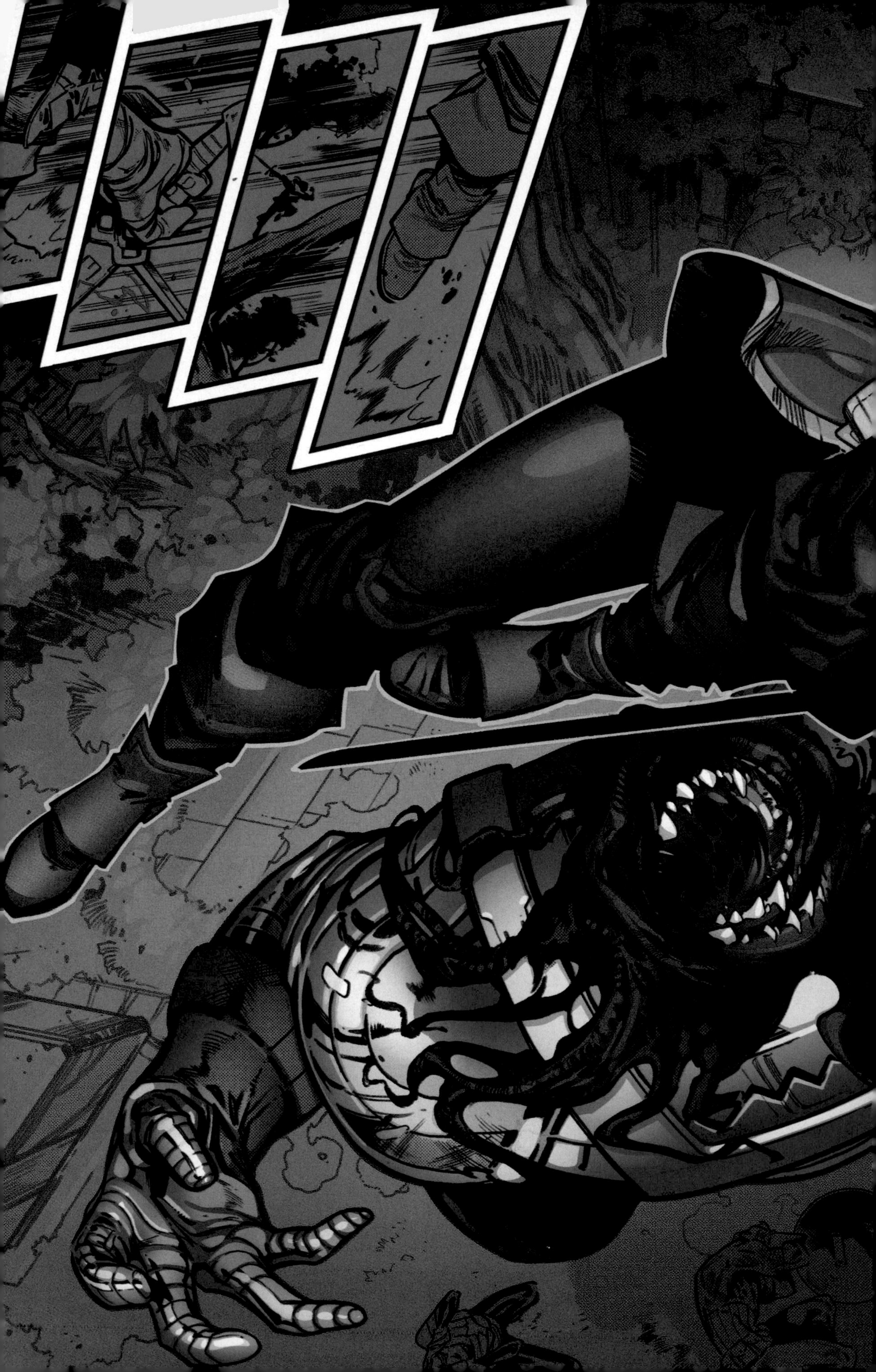

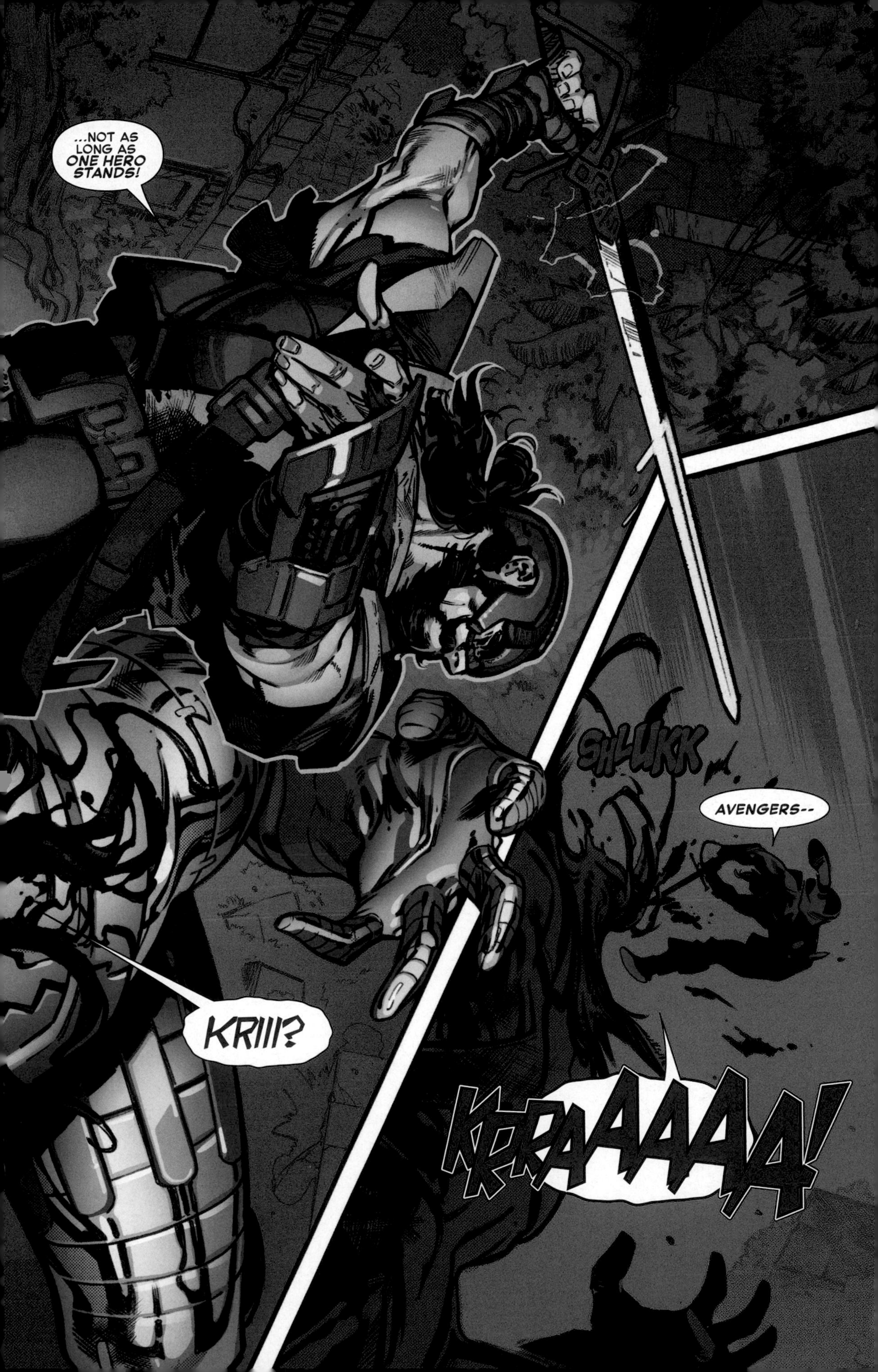
...NOT AS LONG AS ONE HERO STANDS!
SHLUKK
AVENGERS--
KRIII?
KRRAAAAA!

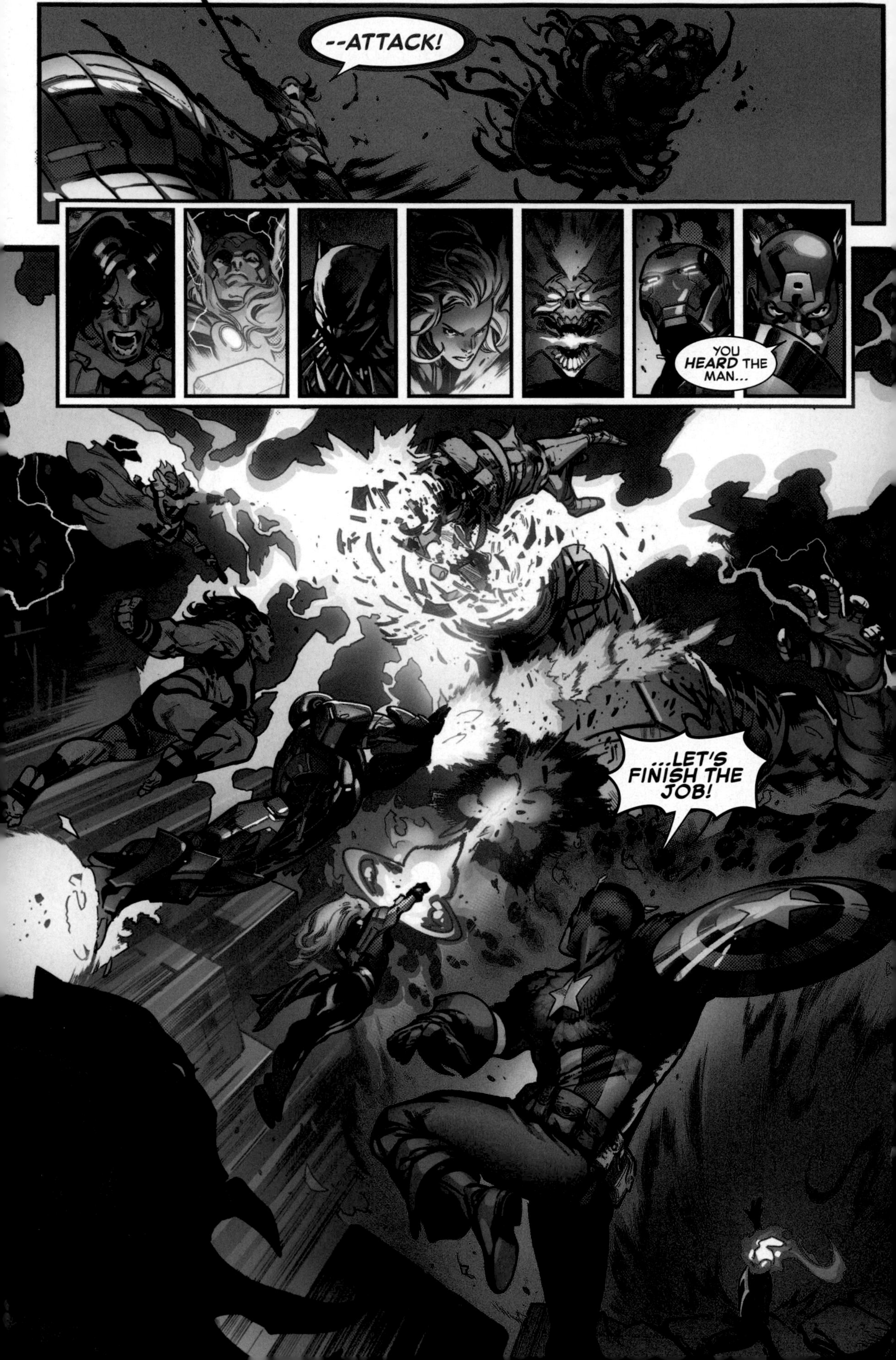
--ATTACK!
YOU HEARD THE MAN...
...LET'S FINISH THE JOB!

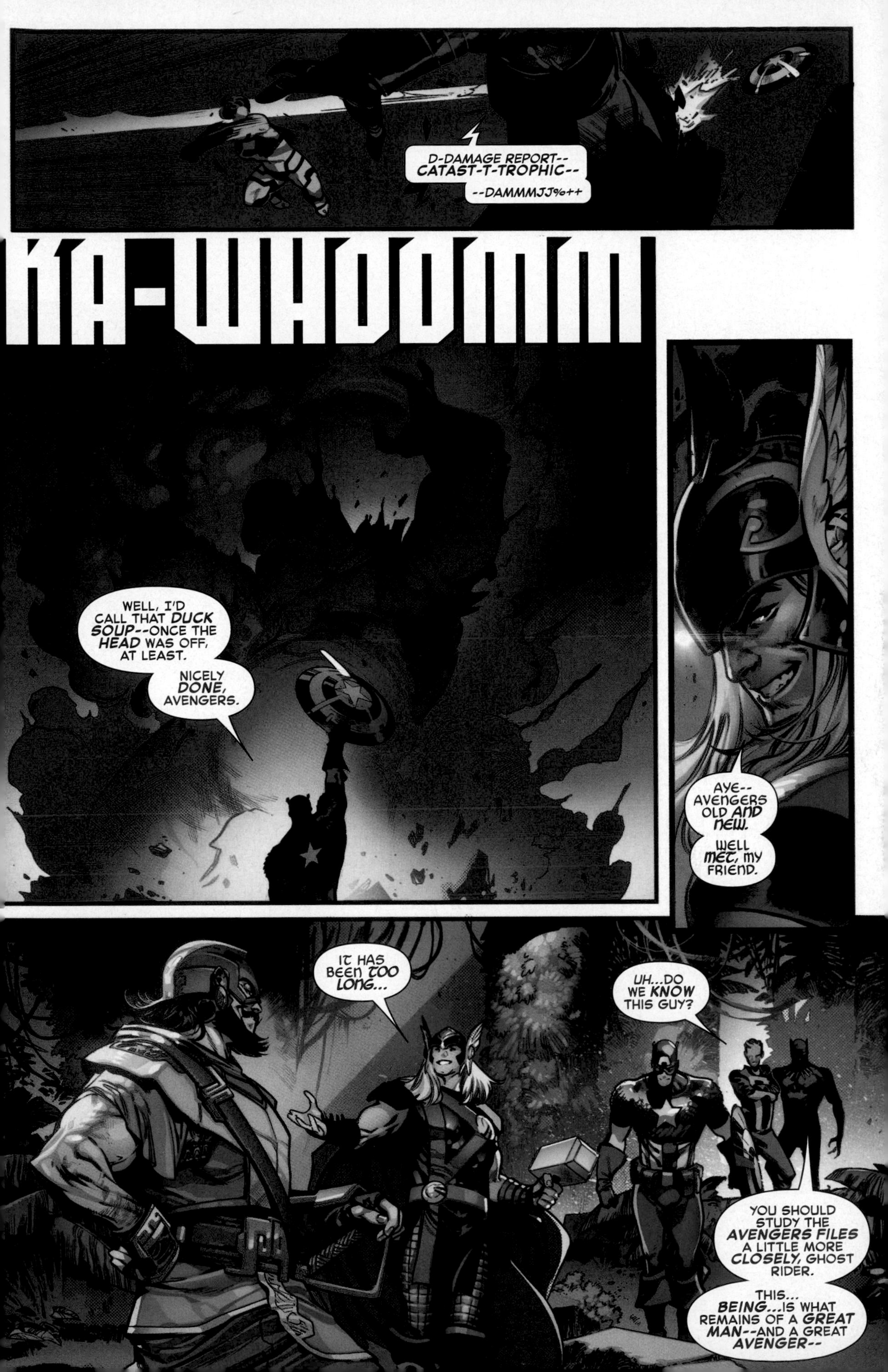
D-DAMAGE REPORT-- CATAST-T-TROPHIC--
--DAMMMJJ%++
KA-WHOOMM
WELL, I'D CALL THAT DUCK SOUP--ONCE THE HEAD WAS OFF, AT LEAST.
NICELY DONE, AVENGERS.
AYE-- AVENGERS OLD AND NEW.
WELL MET, MY FRIEND.
IT HAS BEEN TOO LONG...
UH...DO WE KNOW THIS GUY?
YOU SHOULD STUDY THE AVENGERS FILES A LITTLE MORE CLOSELY, GHOST RIDER.
THIS... BEING...IS WHAT REMAINS OF A GREAT MAN--AND A GREAT AVENGER--

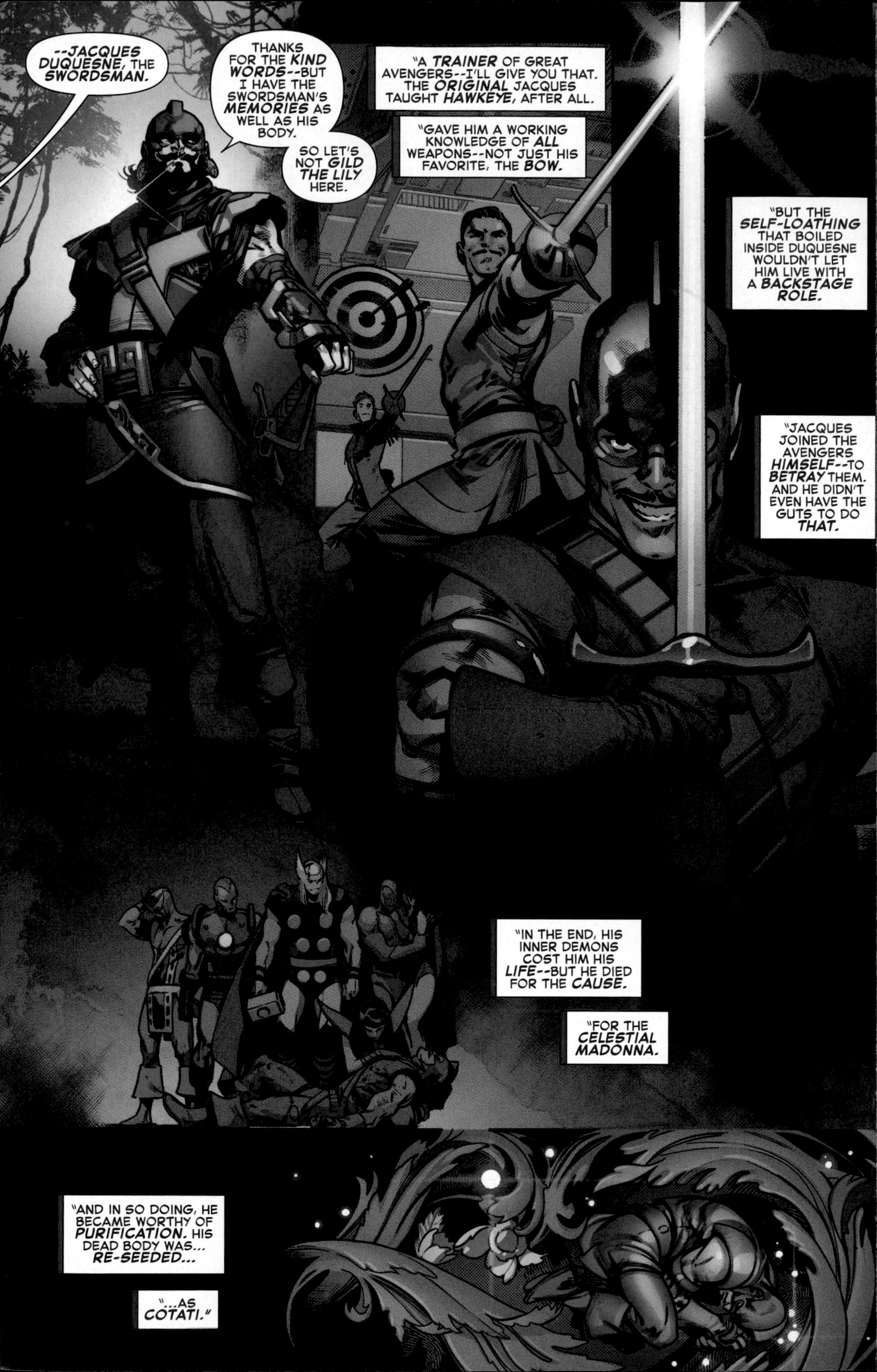
--JACQUES DUQUESNE, THE SWORDSMAN.
THANKS FOR THE KIND WORDS--BUT I HAVE THE SWORDSMAN'S MEMORIES AS WELL AS HIS BODY.
SO LET'S NOT GILD THE LILY HERE.
"A TRAINER OF GREAT AVENGERS--I'LL GIVE YOU THAT. THE ORIGINAL JACQUES TAUGHT HAWKEYE, AFTER ALL.
"GAVE HIM A WORKING KNOWLEDGE OF ALL WEAPONS--NOT JUST HIS FAVORITE, THE BOW.
"BUT THE SELF-LOATHING THAT BOILED INSIDE DUQUESNE WOULDN'T LET HIM LIVE WITH A BACKSTAGE ROLE.
"JACQUES JOINED THE AVENGERS HIMSELF--TO BETRAY THEM. AND HE DIDN'T EVEN HAVE THE GUTS TO DO THAT.
"IN THE END, HIS INNER DEMONS COST HIM HIS LIFE--BUT HE DIED FOR THE CAUSE.
"FOR THE CELESTIAL MADONNA.
"AND IN SO DOING, HE BECAME WORTHY OF PURIFICATION. HIS DEAD BODY WAS... RE-SEEDED...
"...AS COTATI."

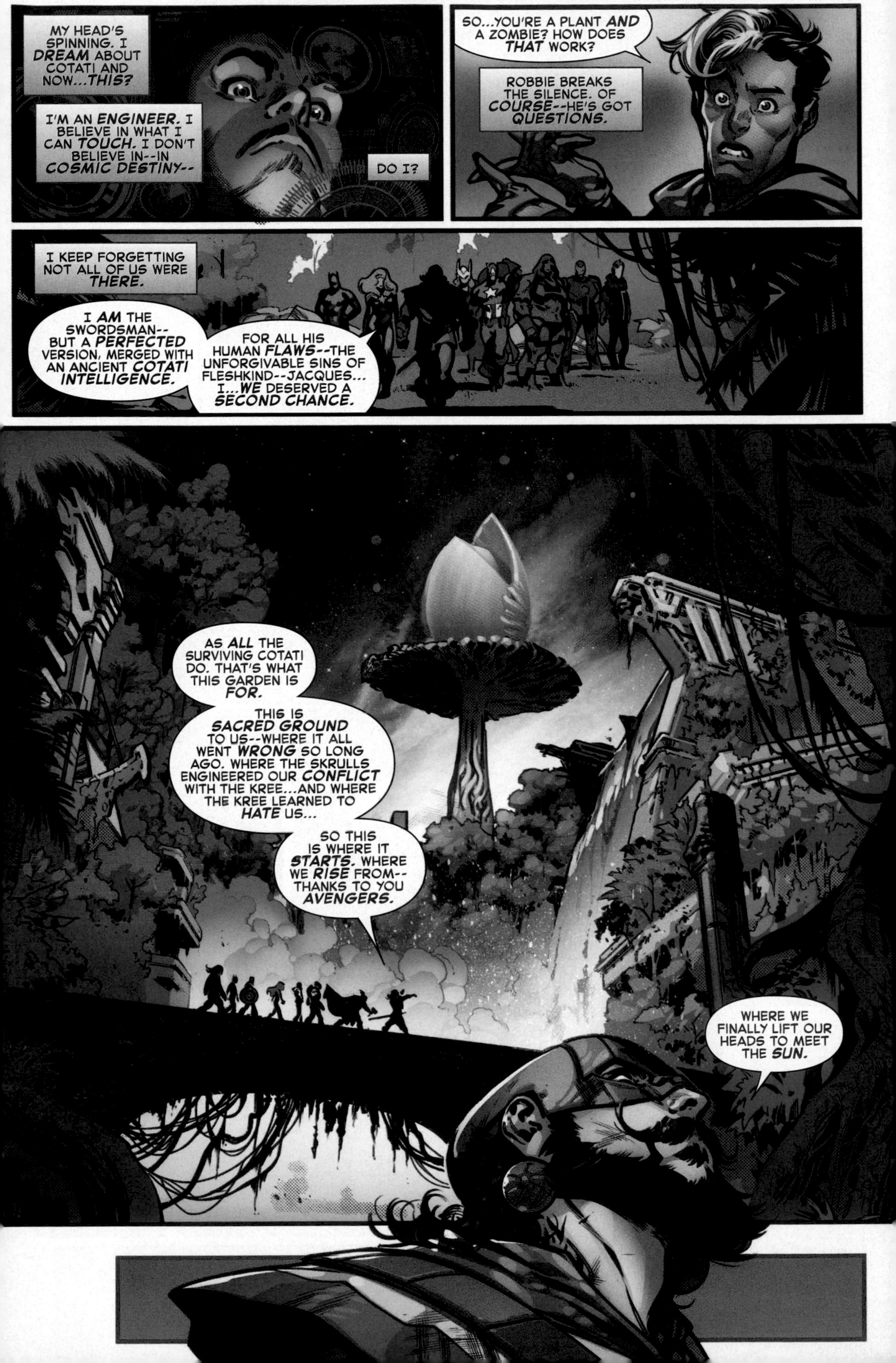
MY HEAD'S SPINNING. I DREAM ABOUT COTATI AND NOW...THIS?
I'M AN ENGINEER. I BELIEVE IN WHAT I CAN TOUCH. I DON'T BELIEVE IN--IN COSMIC DESTINY--
DO I?
SO...YOU'RE A PLANT AND A ZOMBIE? HOW DOES THAT WORK?
ROBBIE BREAKS THE SILENCE. OF COURSE--HE'S GOT QUESTIONS.
I KEEP FORGETTING NOT ALL OF US WERE THERE.
I AM THE SWORDSMAN--BUT A PERFECTED VERSION, MERGED WITH AN ANCIENT COTATI INTELLIGENCE.
FOR ALL HIS HUMAN FLAWS--THE UNFORGIVABLE SINS OF FLESHKIND--JACQUES... I...WE DESERVED A SECOND CHANCE.
AS ALL THE SURVIVING COTATI DO. THAT'S WHAT THIS GARDEN IS FOR.
THIS IS SACRED GROUND TO US--WHERE IT ALL WENT WRONG SO LONG AGO. WHERE THE SKRULLS ENGINEERED OUR CONFLICT WITH THE KREE...AND WHERE THE KREE LEARNED TO HATE US...
SO THIS IS WHERE IT STARTS. WHERE WE RISE FROM--THANKS TO YOU AVENGERS.
WHERE WE FINALLY LIFT OUR HEADS TO MEET THE SUN.

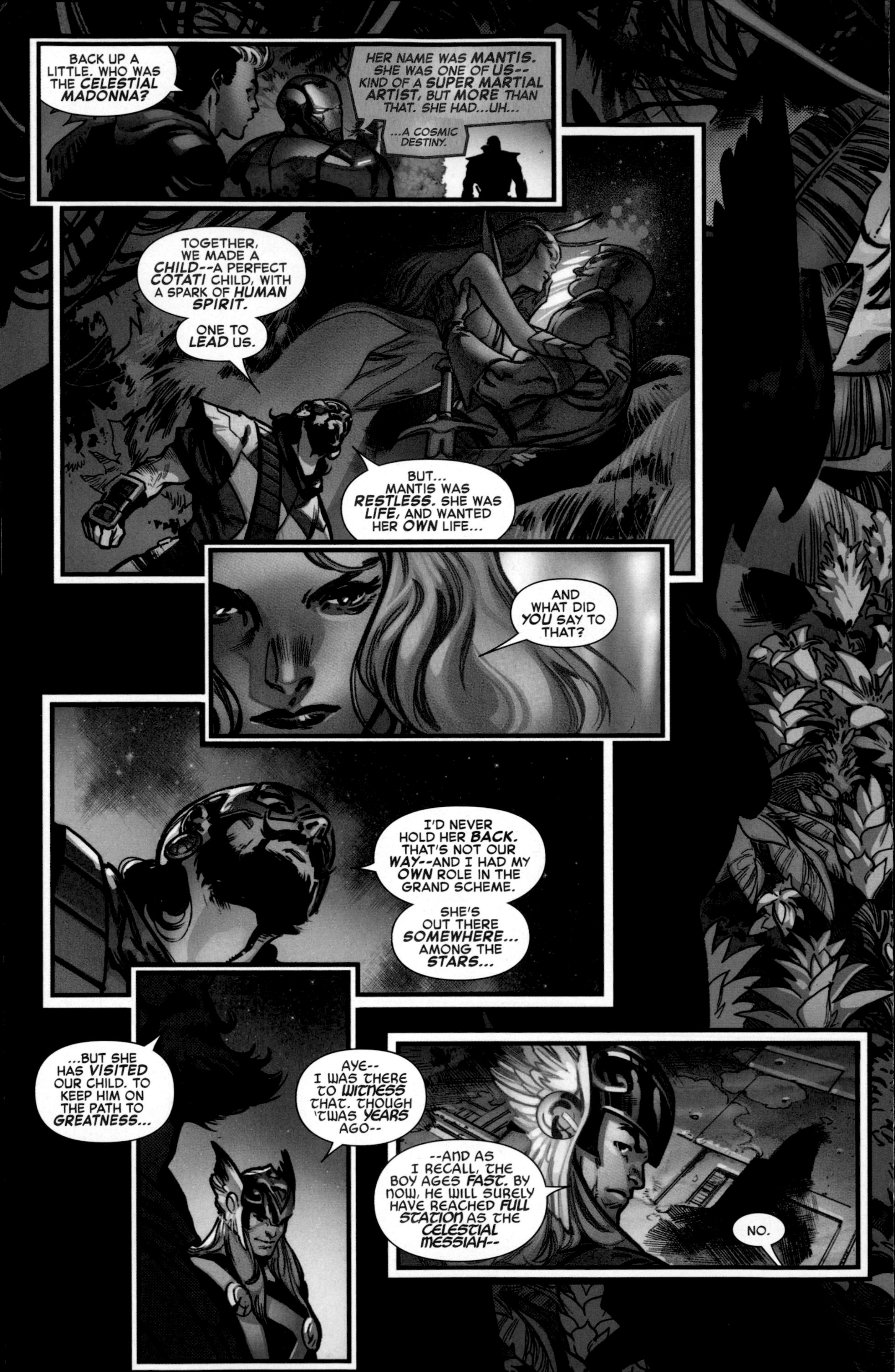

BACK UP A LITTLE. WHO WAS THE CELESTIAL MADONNA?
HER NAME WAS MANTIS. SHE WAS ONE OF US--KIND OF A SUPER MARTIAL ARTIST, BUT MORE THAN THAT. SHE HAD...UH...
...A COSMIC DESTINY.
TOGETHER, WE MADE A CHILD--A PERFECT COTATI CHILD, WITH A SPARK OF HUMAN SPIRIT.
ONE TO LEAD US.
BUT... MANTIS WAS RESTLESS. SHE WAS LIFE, AND WANTED HER OWN LIFE...
AND WHAT DID YOU SAY TO THAT?
I'D NEVER HOLD HER BACK. THAT'S NOT OUR WAY--AND I HAD MY OWN ROLE IN THE GRAND SCHEME.
SHE'S OUT THERE SOMEWHERE... AMONG THE STARS...
...BUT SHE HAS VISITED OUR CHILD. TO KEEP HIM ON THE PATH TO GREATNESS...
AYE--I WAS THERE TO WITNESS THAT. THOUGH 'TWAS YEARS AGO--
--AND AS I RECALL, THE BOY AGES FAST. BY NOW, HE WILL SURELY HAVE REACHED FULL STATION AS THE CELESTIAL MESSIAH--
NO.

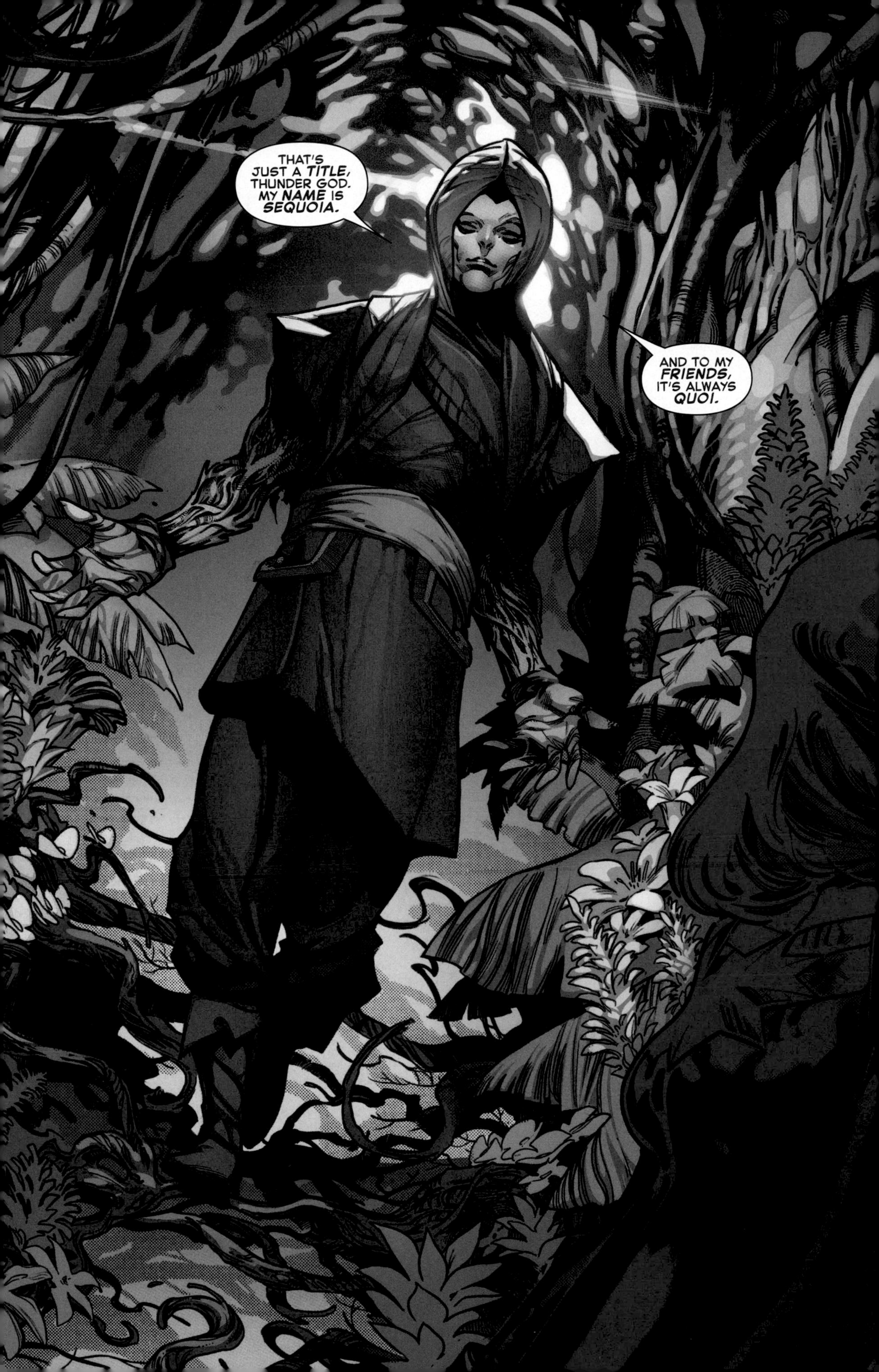
THAT'S JUST A TITLE, THUNDER GOD. MY NAME IS SEQUOIA.
AND TO MY FRIENDS, IT'S ALWAYS QUOI.

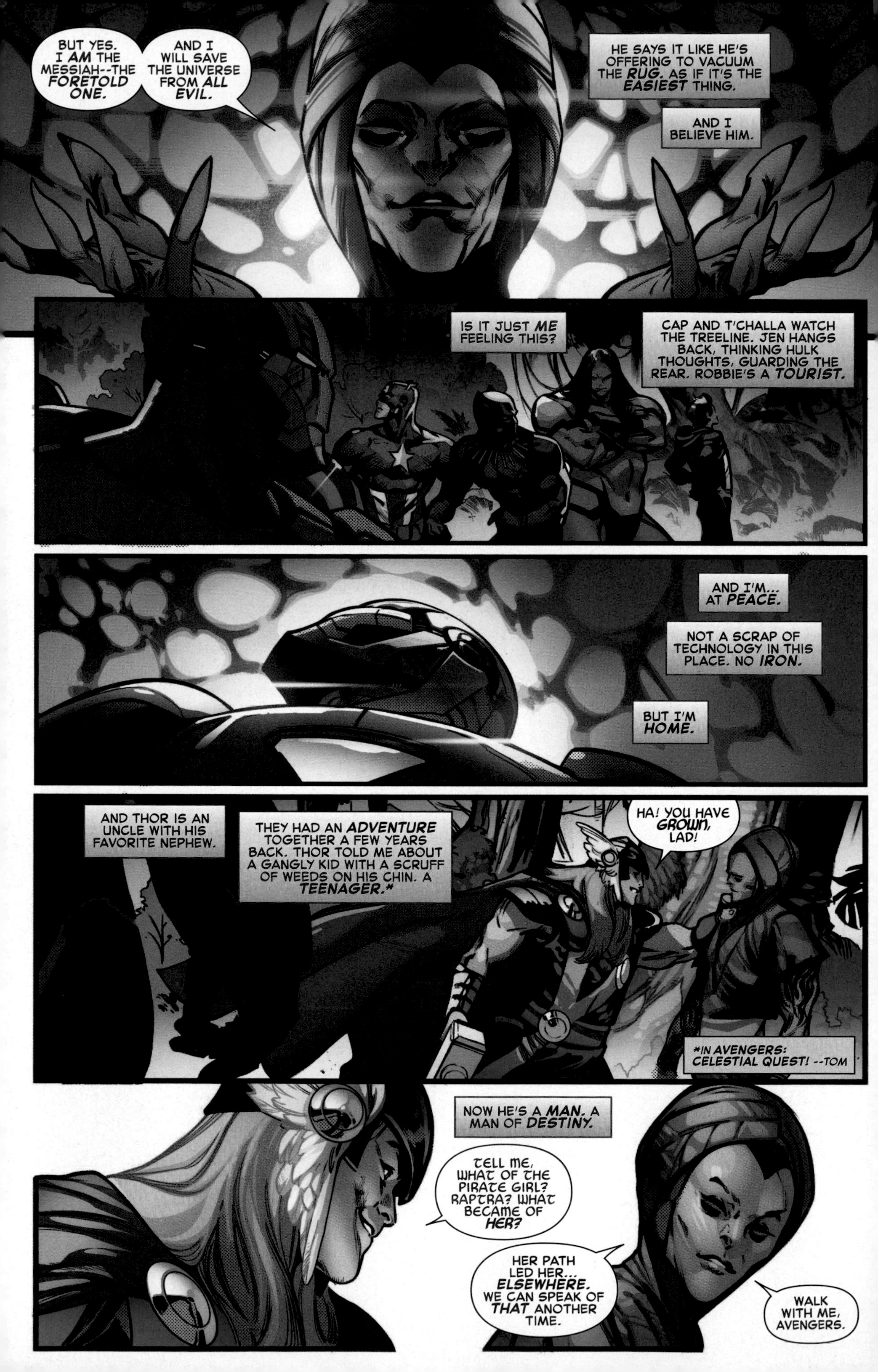
BUT YES. I AM THE MESSIAH--THE FORETOLD ONE.
AND I WILL SAVE THE UNIVERSE FROM ALL EVIL.
HE SAYS IT LIKE HE'S OFFERING TO VACUUM THE RUG, AS IF IT'S THE EASIEST THING.
AND I BELIEVE HIM.
IS IT JUST ME FEELING THIS?
CAP AND T'CHALLA WATCH THE TREELINE. JEN HANGS BACK, THINKING HULK THOUGHTS, GUARDING THE REAR. ROBBIE'S A TOURIST.
AND I'M... AT PEACE.
NOT A SCRAP OF TECHNOLOGY IN THIS PLACE. NO IRON.
BUT I'M HOME.
AND THOR IS AN UNCLE WITH HIS FAVORITE NEPHEW.
THEY HAD AN ADVENTURE TOGETHER A FEW YEARS BACK. THOR TOLD ME ABOUT A GANGLY KID WITH A SCRUFF OF WEEDS ON HIS CHIN. A TEENAGER.*
HA! YOU HAVE GROWN, LAD!
*IN AVENGERS: CELESTIAL QUEST! --TOM
NOW HE'S A MAN. A MAN OF DESTINY.
TELL ME, WHAT OF THE PIRATE GIRL? RAPTRA? WHAT BECAME OF HER?
HER PATH LED HER... ELSEWHERE. WE CAN SPEAK OF THAT ANOTHER TIME.
WALK WITH ME, AVENGERS.

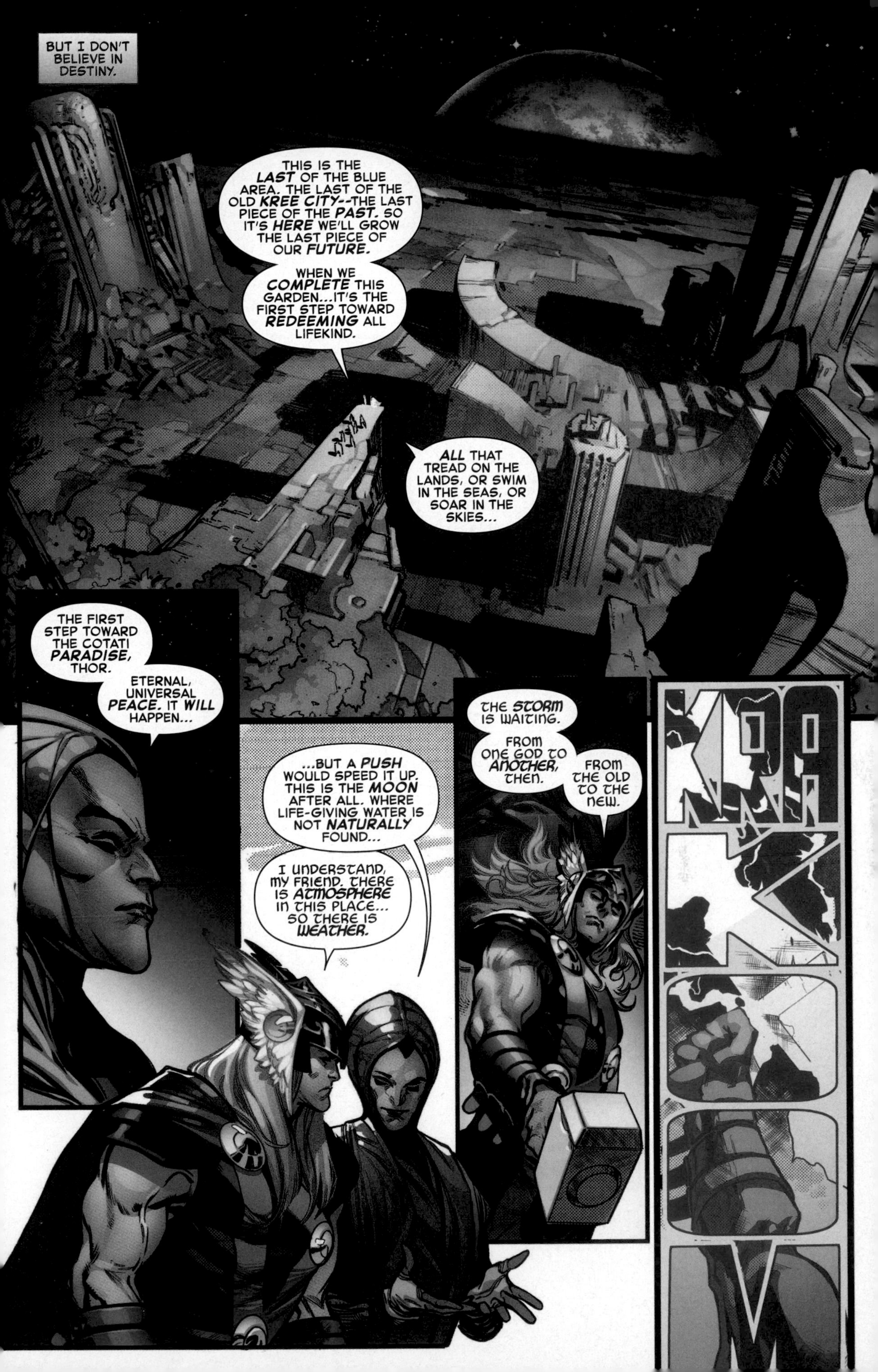

BUT I DON'T BELIEVE IN DESTINY.
THIS IS THE LAST OF THE BLUE AREA. THE LAST OF THE OLD KREE CITY--THE LAST PIECE OF THE PAST. SO IT'S HERE WE'LL GROW THE LAST PIECE OF OUR FUTURE.
WHEN WE COMPLETE THIS GARDEN...IT'S THE FIRST STEP TOWARD REDEEMING ALL LIFEKIND.
ALL THAT TREAD ON THE LANDS, OR SWIM IN THE SEAS, OR SOAR IN THE SKIES...
THE FIRST STEP TOWARD THE COTATI PARADISE, THOR.
ETERNAL, UNIVERSAL PEACE. IT WILL HAPPEN...
...BUT A PUSH WOULD SPEED IT UP. THIS IS THE MOON AFTER ALL. WHERE LIFE-GIVING WATER IS NOT NATURALLY FOUND...
I UNDERSTAND, MY FRIEND. THERE IS ATMOSPHERE IN THIS PLACE... SO THERE IS WEATHER.
THE STORM IS WAITING.
FROM ONE GOD TO ANOTHER, THEN.
FROM THE OLD TO THE NEW.

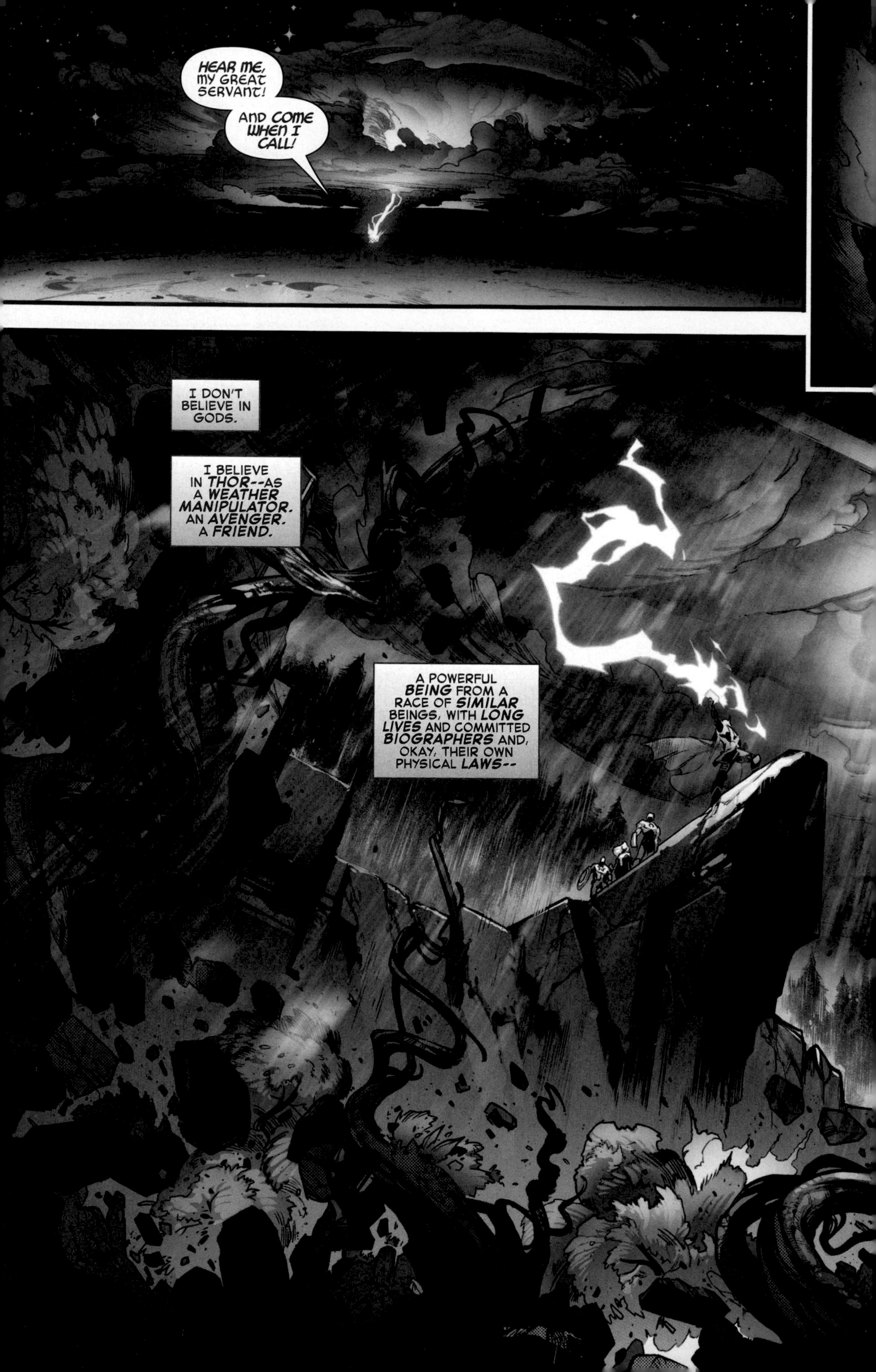
HEAR ME, MY GREAT SERVANT!
AND COME WHEN I CALL!
I DON'T BELIEVE IN GODS.
I BELIEVE IN THOR--AS A WEATHER MANIPULATOR. AN AVENGER. A FRIEND.
A POWERFUL BEING FROM A RACE OF SIMILAR BEINGS, WITH LONG LIVES AND COMMITTED BIOGRAPHERS AND, OKAY, THEIR OWN PHYSICAL LAWS--

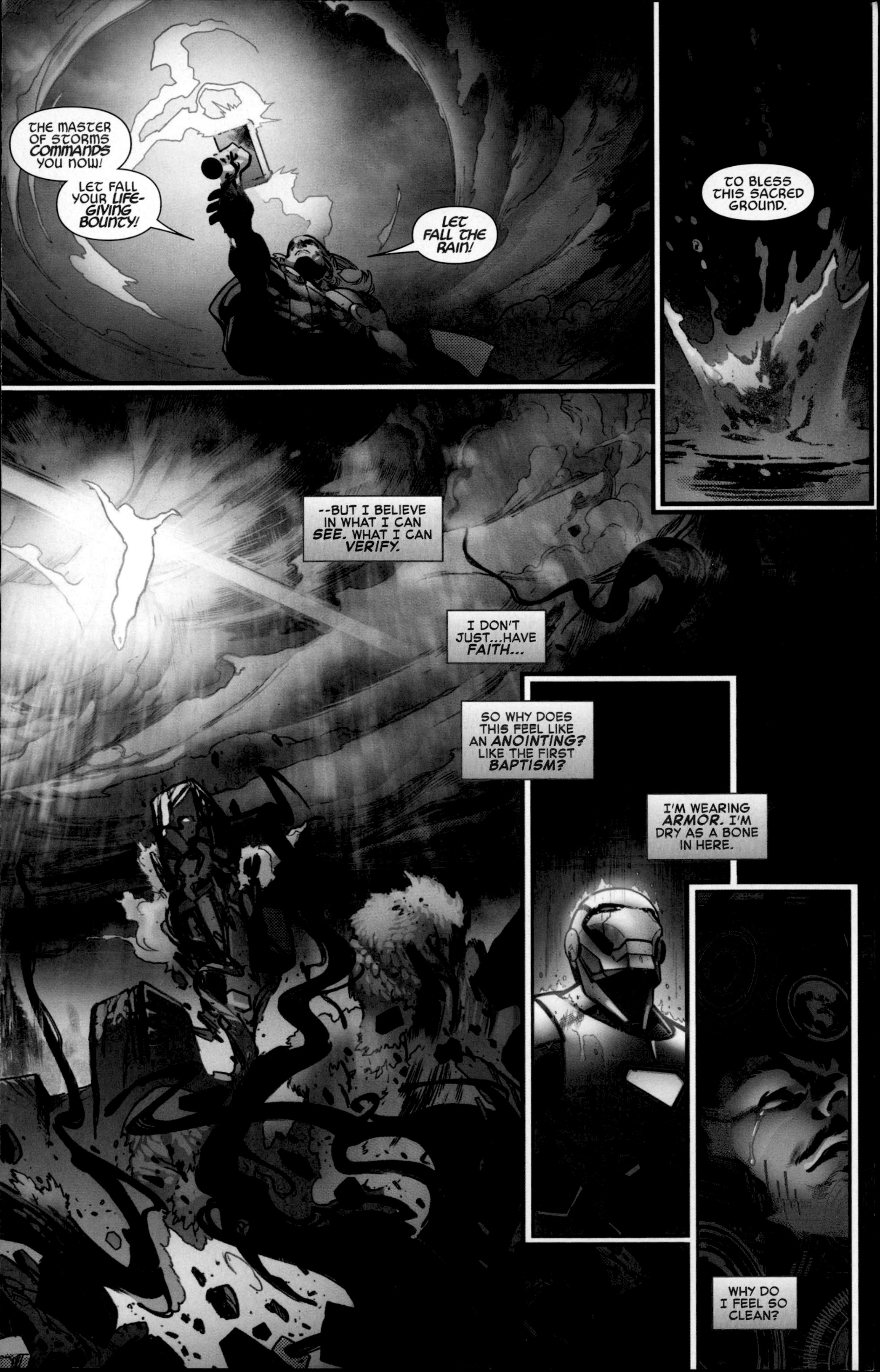
THE MASTER OF STORMS COMMANDS YOU NOW!
LET FALL YOUR LIFE-GIVING BOUNTY!
LET FALL THE RAIN!
TO BLESS THIS SACRED GROUND.
--BUT I BELIEVE IN WHAT I CAN SEE. WHAT I CAN VERIFY.
I DON'T JUST...HAVE FAITH...
SO WHY DOES THIS FEEL LIKE AN ANOINTING? LIKE THE FIRST BAPTISM?
I'M WEARING ARMOR. I'M DRY AS A BONE IN HERE.
WHY DO I FEEL SO CLEAN?

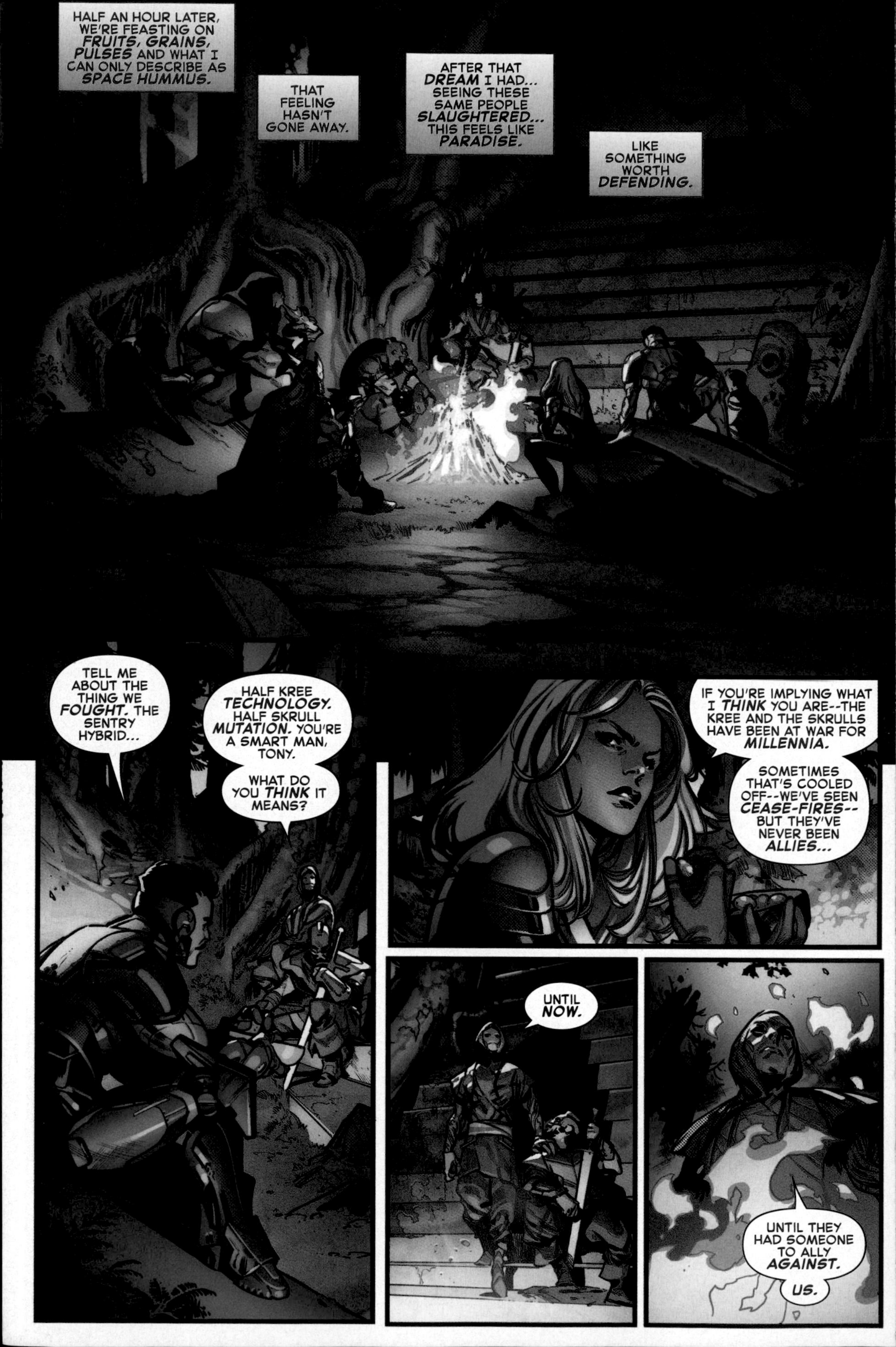
HALF AN HOUR LATER, WE'RE FEASTING ON FRUITS, GRAINS, PULSES AND WHAT I CAN ONLY DESCRIBE AS SPACE HUMMUS.
THAT FEELING HASN'T GONE AWAY.
AFTER THAT DREAM I HAD... SEEING THESE SAME PEOPLE SLAUGHTERED... THIS FEELS LIKE PARADISE.
LIKE SOMETHING WORTH DEFENDING.
TELL ME ABOUT THE THING WE FOUGHT. THE SENTRY HYBRID...
HALF KREE TECHNOLOGY. HALF SKRULL MUTATION. YOU'RE A SMART MAN, TONY.
WHAT DO YOU THINK IT MEANS?
IF YOU'RE IMPLYING WHAT I THINK YOU ARE--THE KREE AND THE SKRULLS HAVE BEEN AT WAR FOR MILLENNIA.
SOMETIMES THAT'S COOLED OFF--WE'VE SEEN CEASE-FIRES--BUT THEY'VE NEVER BEEN ALLIES...
UNTIL NOW.
UNTIL THEY HAD SOMEONE TO ALLY AGAINST.
US.

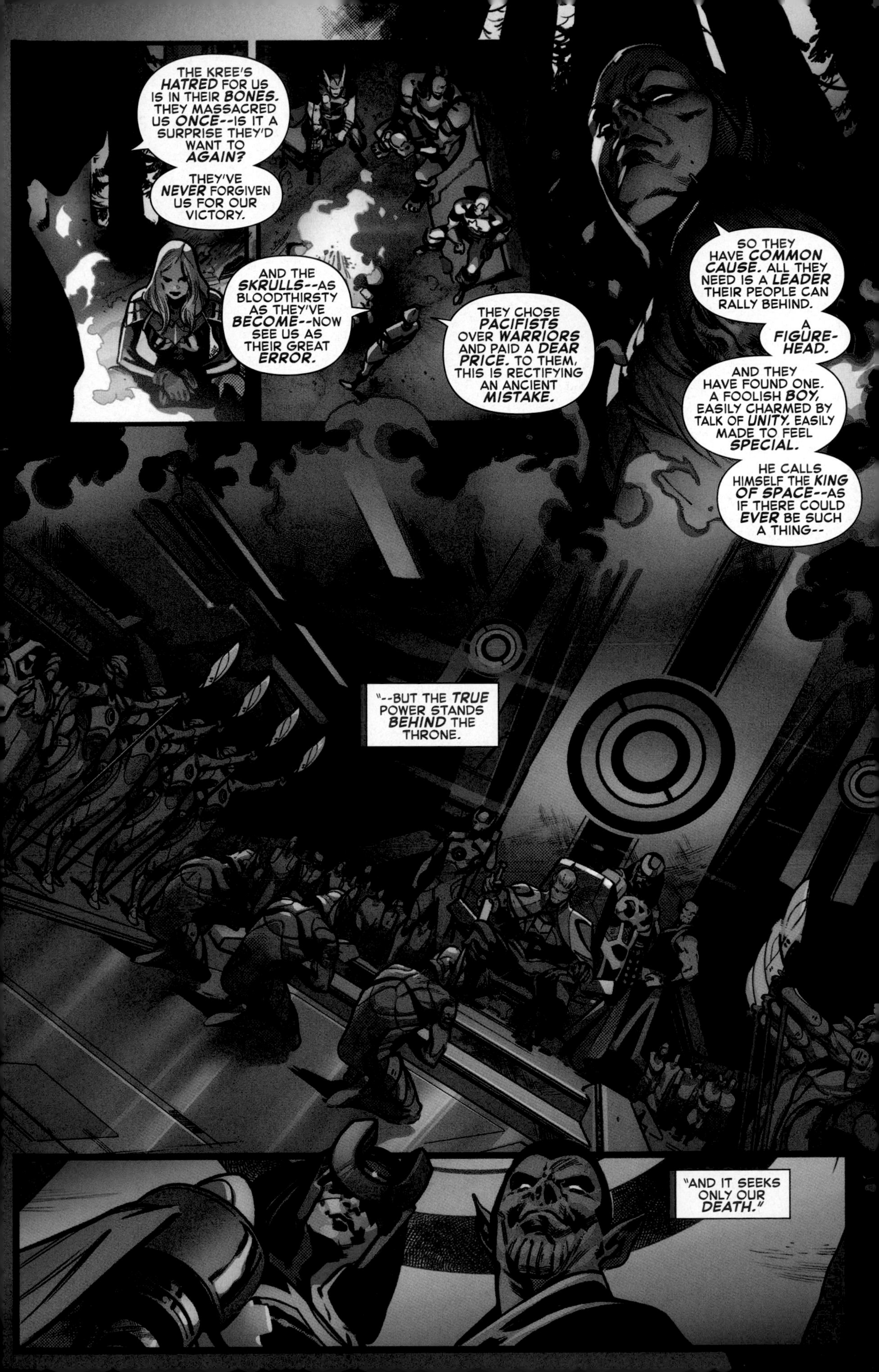
THE KREE'S HATRED FOR US IS IN THEIR BONES. THEY MASSACRED US ONCE--IS IT A SURPRISE THEY'D WANT TO AGAIN?
THEY'VE NEVER FORGIVEN US FOR OUR VICTORY.
AND THE SKRULLS--AS BLOODTHIRSTY AS THEY'VE BECOME--NOW SEE US AS THEIR GREAT ERROR.
THEY CHOSE PACIFISTS OVER WARRIORS AND PAID A DEAR PRICE. TO THEM, THIS IS RECTIFYING AN ANCIENT MISTAKE.
SO THEY HAVE COMMON CAUSE. ALL THEY NEED IS A LEADER THEIR PEOPLE CAN RALLY BEHIND.
A FIGURE-HEAD.
AND THEY HAVE FOUND ONE. A FOOLISH BOY, EASILY CHARMED BY TALK OF UNITY. EASILY MADE TO FEEL SPECIAL.
HE CALLS HIMSELF THE KING OF SPACE--AS IF THERE COULD EVER BE SUCH A THING--
"--BUT THE TRUE POWER STANDS BEHIND THE THRONE.
"AND IT SEEKS ONLY OUR DEATH."

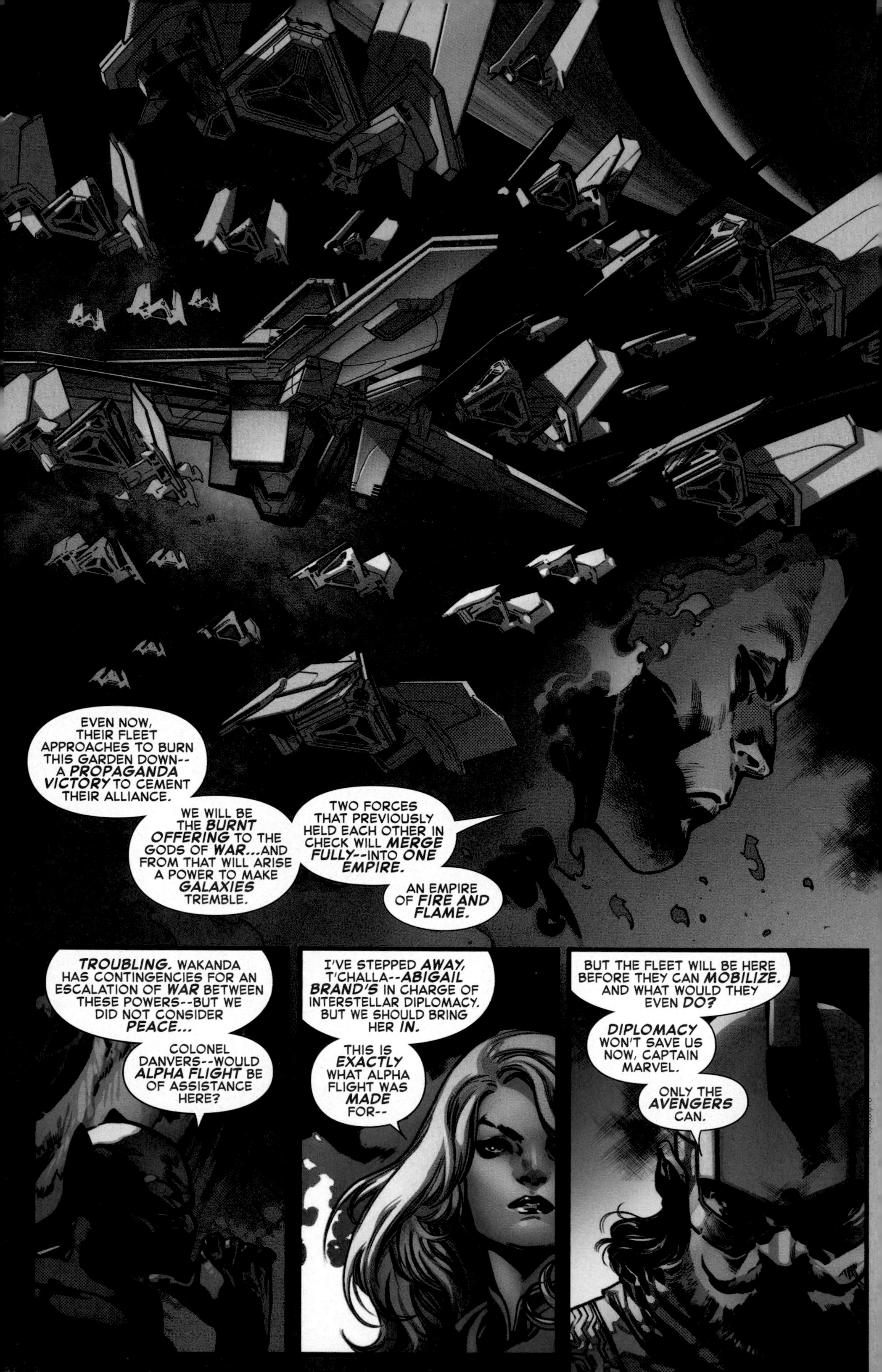
EVEN NOW, THEIR FLEET APPROACHES TO BURN THIS GARDEN DOWN--A PROPAGANDA VICTORY TO CEMENT THEIR ALLIANCE.
WE WILL BE THE BURNT OFFERING TO THE GODS OF WAR...AND FROM THAT WILL ARISE A POWER TO MAKE GALAXIES TREMBLE.
TWO FORCES THAT PREVIOUSLY HELD EACH OTHER IN CHECK WILL MERGE FULLY--INTO ONE EMPIRE.
AN EMPIRE OF FIRE AND FLAME.
TROUBLING. WAKANDA HAS CONTINGENCIES FOR AN ESCALATION OF WAR BETWEEN THESE POWERS--BUT WE DID NOT CONSIDER PEACE...
COLONEL DANVERS--WOULD ALPHA FLIGHT BE OF ASSISTANCE HERE?
I'VE STEPPED AWAY, T'CHALLA--ABIGAIL BRAND'S IN CHARGE OF INTERSTELLAR DIPLOMACY. BUT WE SHOULD BRING HER IN.
THIS IS EXACTLY WHAT ALPHA FLIGHT WAS MADE FOR--
BUT THE FLEET WILL BE HERE BEFORE THEY CAN MOBILIZE. AND WHAT WOULD THEY EVEN DO?
DIPLOMACY WON'T SAVE US NOW, CAPTAIN MARVEL.
ONLY THE AVENGERS CAN.

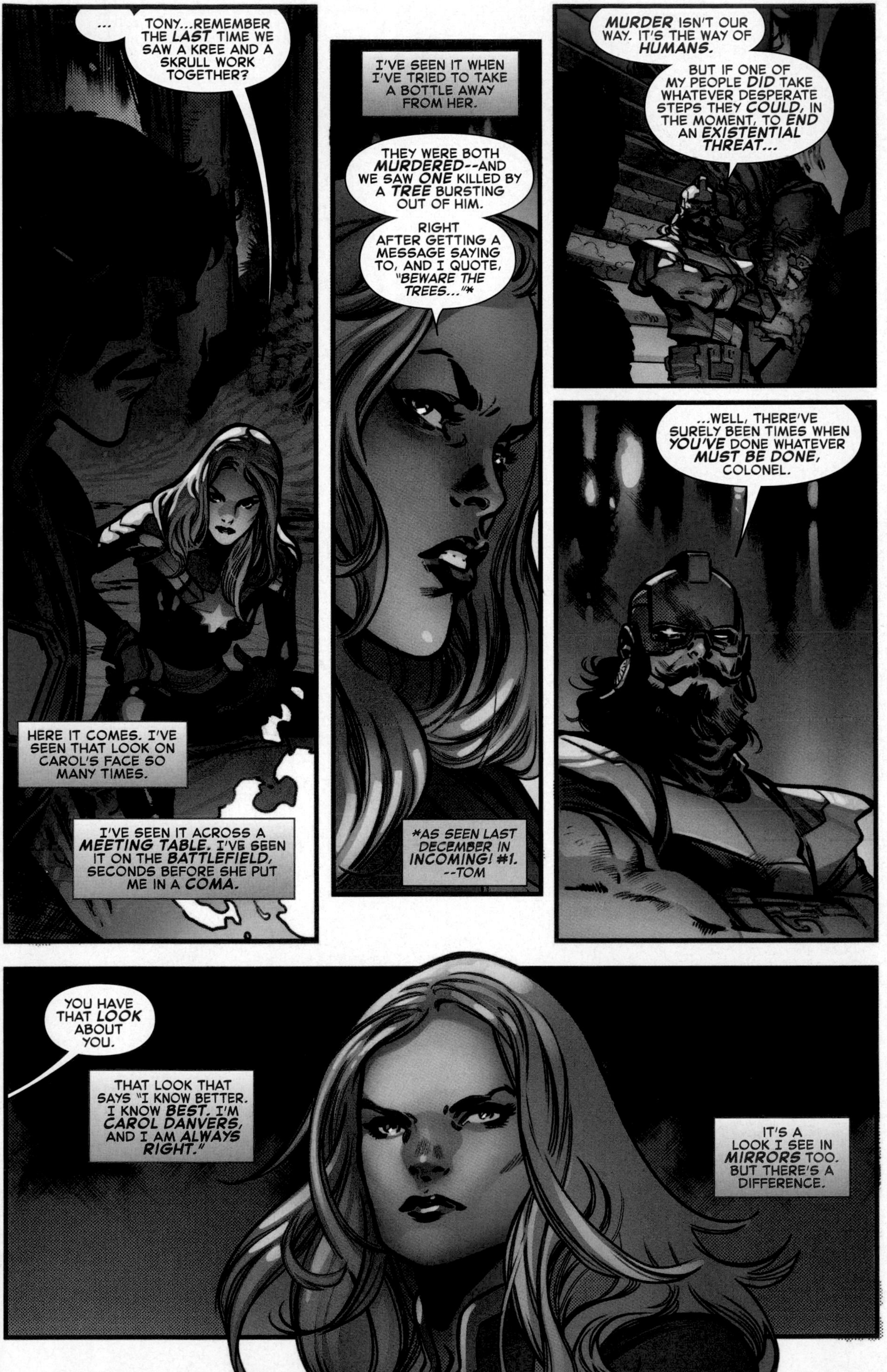
...
TONY...REMEMBER THE LAST TIME WE SAW A KREE AND A SKRULL WORK TOGETHER?
HERE IT COMES. I'VE SEEN THAT LOOK ON CAROL'S FACE SO MANY TIMES.
I'VE SEEN IT ACROSS A MEETING TABLE. I'VE SEEN IT ON THE BATTLEFIELD, SECONDS BEFORE SHE PUT ME IN A COMA.
I'VE SEEN IT WHEN I'VE TRIED TO TAKE A BOTTLE AWAY FROM HER.
THEY WERE BOTH MURDERED--AND WE SAW ONE KILLED BY A TREE BURSTING OUT OF HIM.
RIGHT AFTER GETTING A MESSAGE SAYING TO, AND I QUOTE, "BEWARE THE TREES..."*
*AS SEEN LAST DECEMBER IN INCOMING! #1. --TOM
MURDER ISN'T OUR WAY. IT'S THE WAY OF HUMANS.
BUT IF ONE OF MY PEOPLE DID TAKE WHATEVER DESPERATE STEPS THEY COULD, IN THE MOMENT, TO END AN EXISTENTIAL THREAT...
...WELL, THERE'VE SURELY BEEN TIMES WHEN YOU'VE DONE WHATEVER MUST BE DONE, COLONEL.
YOU HAVE THAT LOOK ABOUT YOU.
THAT LOOK THAT SAYS "I KNOW BETTER. I KNOW BEST. I'M CAROL DANVERS, AND I AM ALWAYS RIGHT."
IT'S A LOOK I SEE IN MIRRORS TOO. BUT THERE'S A DIFFERENCE.

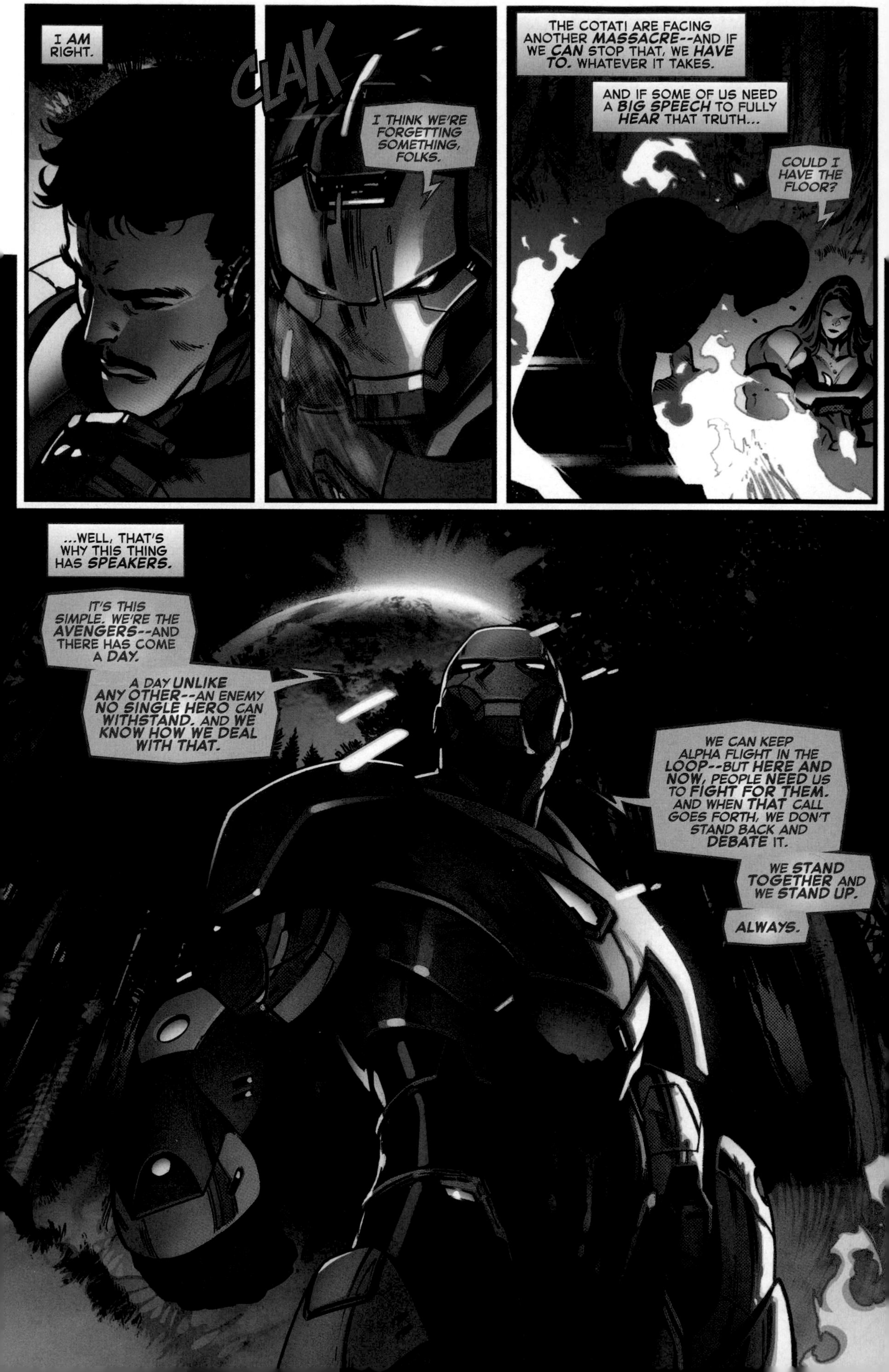
I AM RIGHT.
CLAK
I THINK WE'RE FORGETTING SOMETHING, FOLKS.
THE COTATI ARE FACING ANOTHER MASSACRE--AND IF WE CAN STOP THAT, WE HAVE TO. WHATEVER IT TAKES.
AND IF SOME OF US NEED A BIG SPEECH TO FULLY HEAR THAT TRUTH...
COULD I HAVE THE FLOOR?
...WELL, THAT'S WHY THIS THING HAS SPEAKERS.
IT'S THIS SIMPLE. WE'RE THE AVENGERS--AND THERE HAS COME A DAY.
A DAY UNLIKE ANY OTHER--AN ENEMY NO SINGLE HERO CAN WITHSTAND. AND WE KNOW HOW WE DEAL WITH THAT.
WE CAN KEEP ALPHA FLIGHT IN THE LOOP--BUT HERE AND NOW, PEOPLE NEED US TO FIGHT FOR THEM. AND WHEN THAT CALL GOES FORTH, WE DON'T STAND BACK AND DEBATE IT.
WE STAND TOGETHER AND WE STAND UP.
ALWAYS.

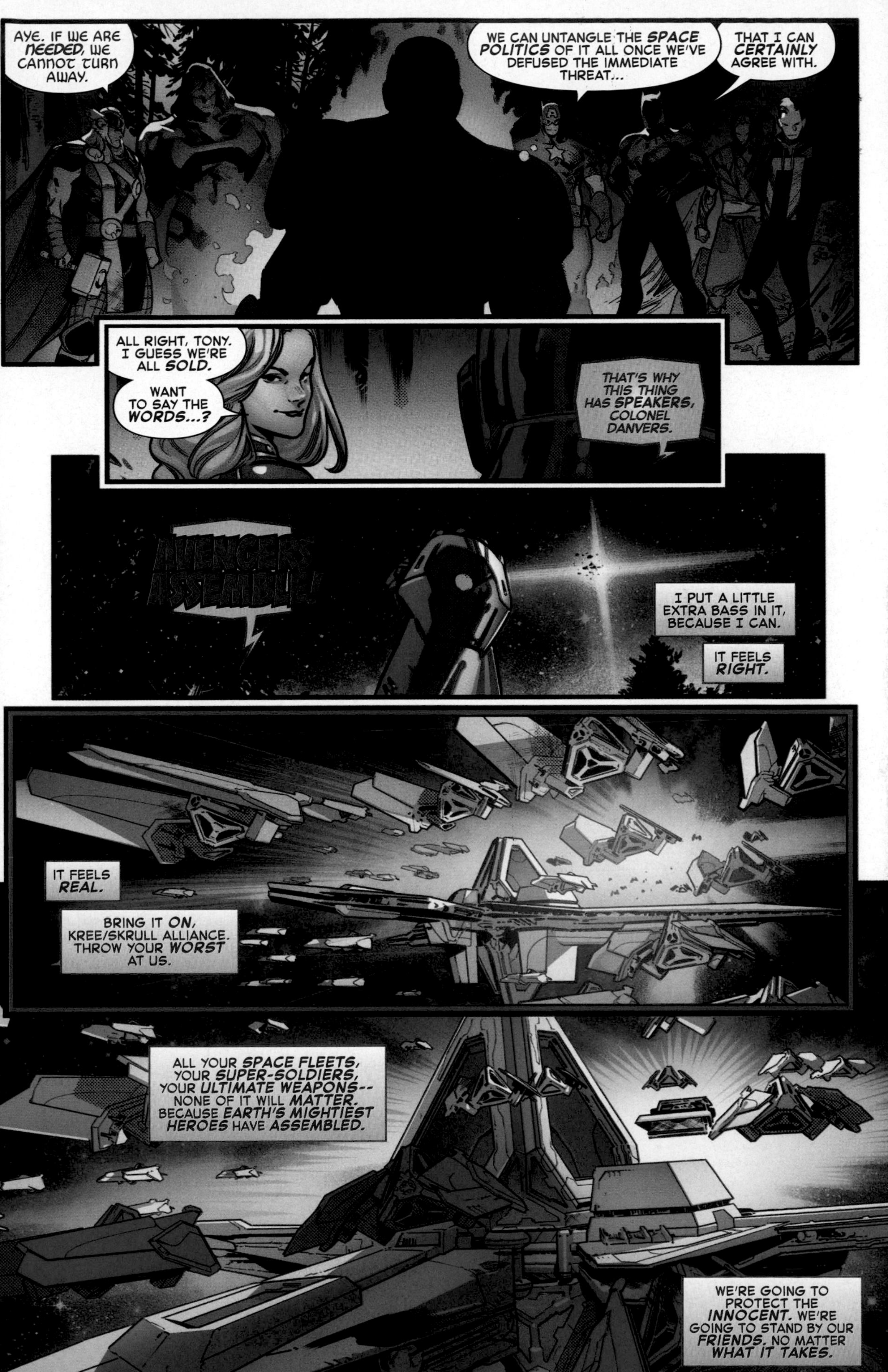
AYE. IF WE ARE NEEDED, WE CANNOT TURN AWAY.
WE CAN UNTANGLE THE SPACE POLITICS OF IT ALL ONCE WE'VE DEFUSED THE IMMEDIATE THREAT...
THAT I CAN CERTAINLY AGREE WITH.
ALL RIGHT, TONY. I GUESS WE'RE ALL SOLD.
WANT TO SAY THE WORDS...?
THAT'S WHY THIS THING HAS SPEAKERS, COLONEL DANVERS.
AVENGERS ASSEMBLE!
I PUT A LITTLE EXTRA BASS IN IT, BECAUSE I CAN.
IT FEELS RIGHT.
IT FEELS REAL.
BRING IT ON, KREE/SKRULL ALLIANCE. THROW YOUR WORST AT US.
ALL YOUR SPACE FLEETS, YOUR SUPER-SOLDIERS, YOUR ULTIMATE WEAPONS-- NONE OF IT WILL MATTER. BECAUSE EARTH'S MIGHTIEST HEROES HAVE ASSEMBLED.
WE'RE GOING TO PROTECT THE INNOCENT. WE'RE GOING TO STAND BY OUR FRIENDS. NO MATTER WHAT IT TAKES.

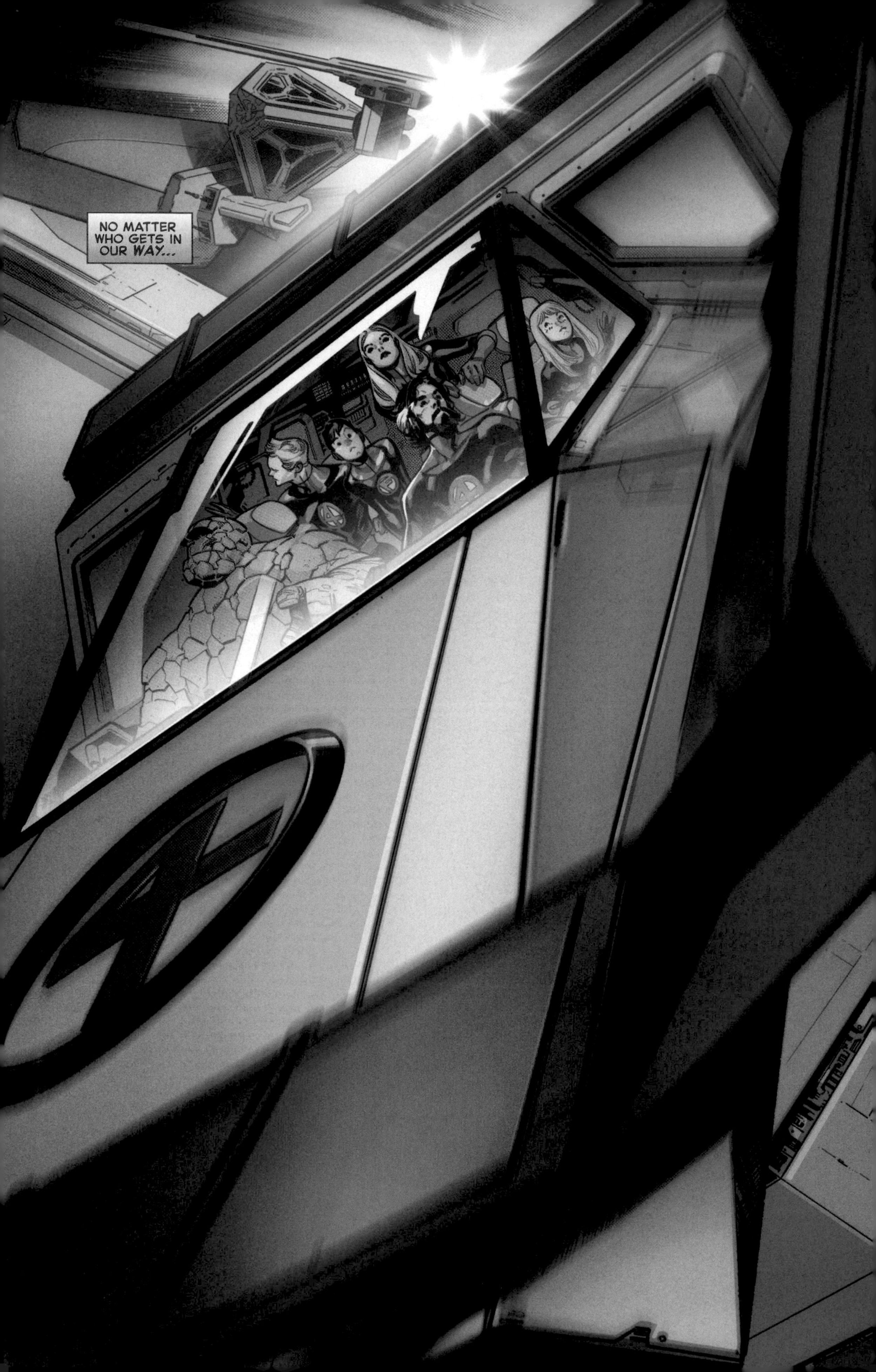
NO MATTER WHO GETS IN OUR WAY...

EMPYRE 0: FANTASTIC FOUR

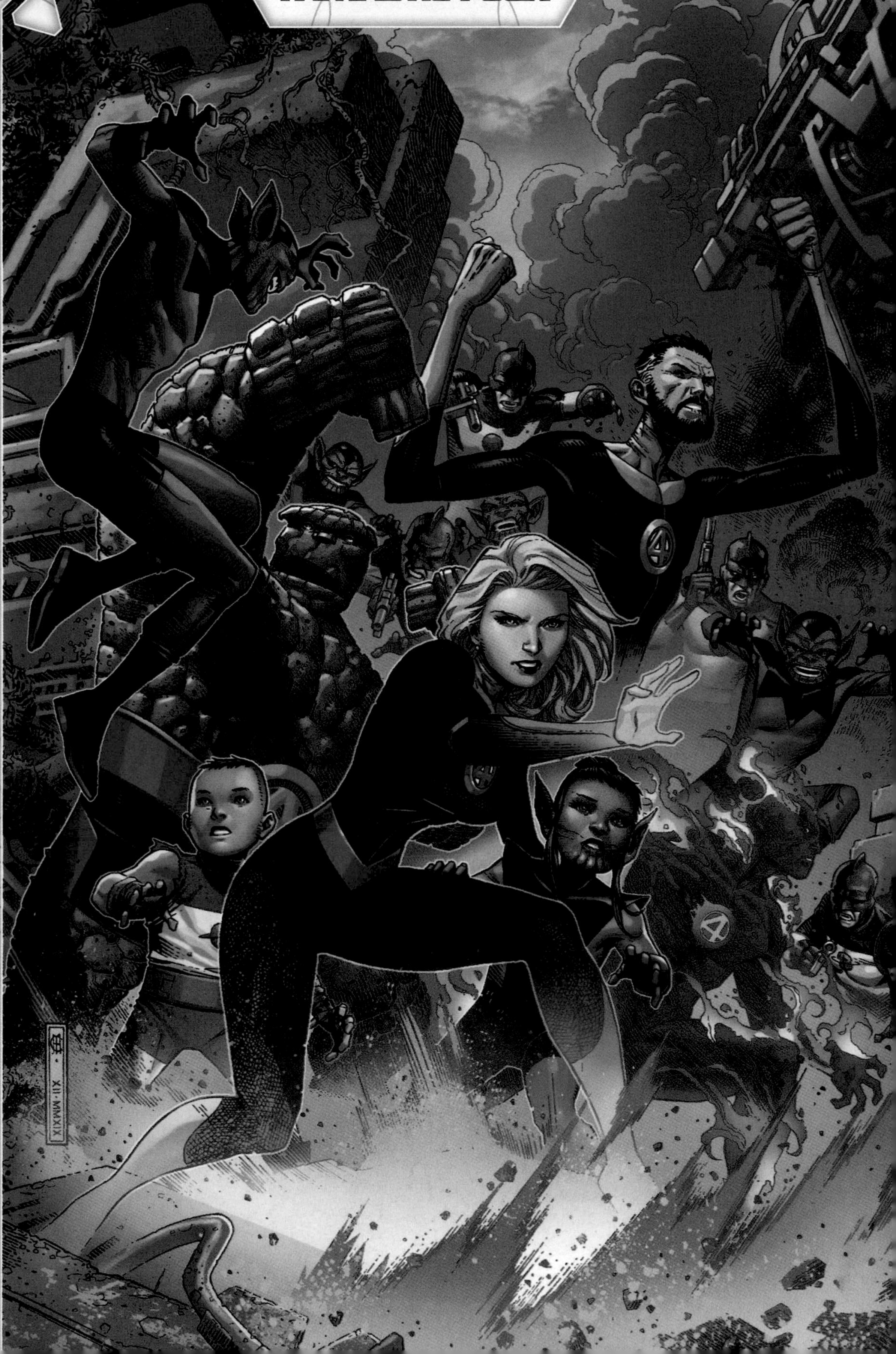
XII · MMXIX

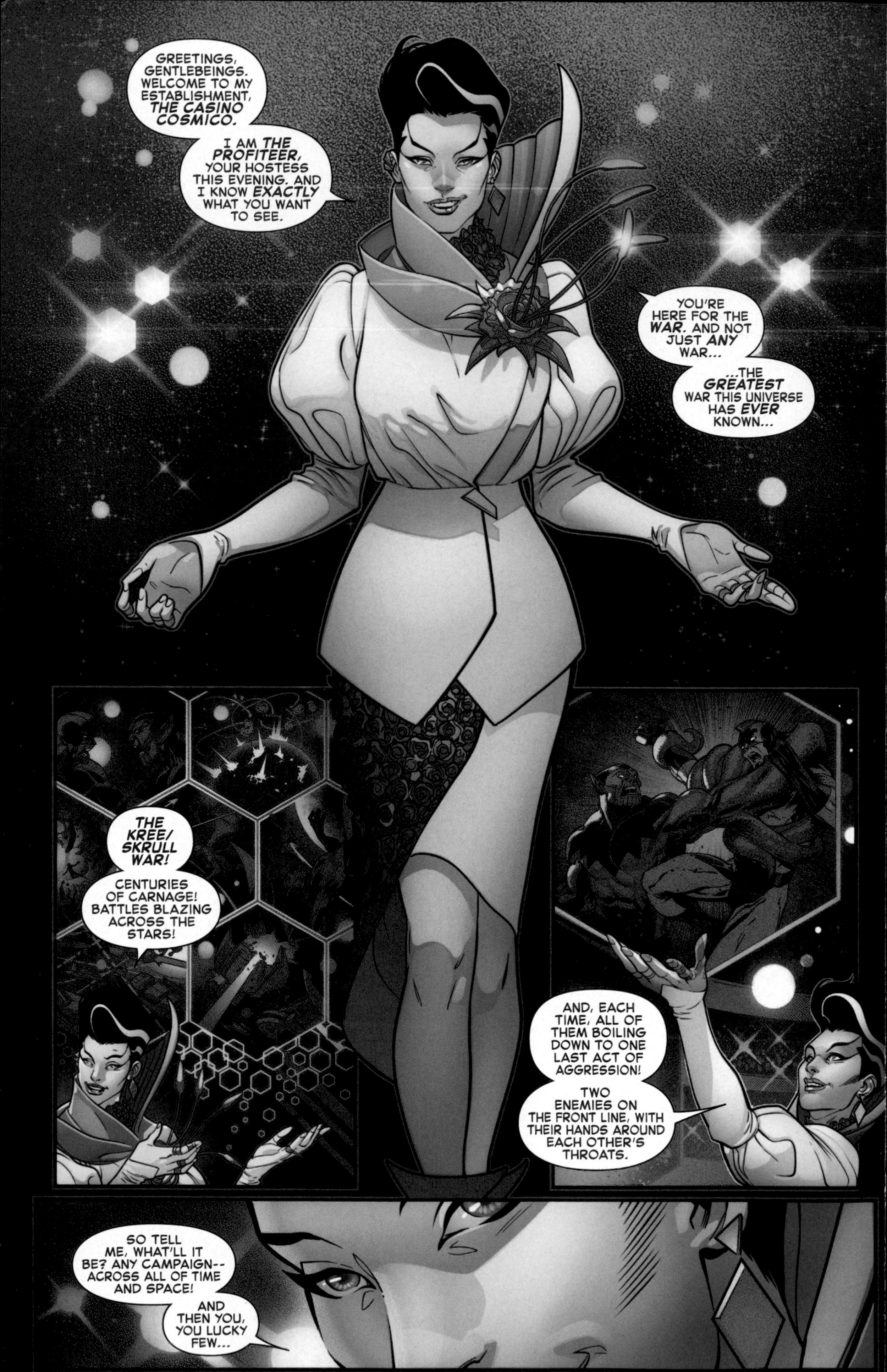
GREETINGS, GENTLEBEINGS. WELCOME TO MY ESTABLISHMENT, THE CASINO COSMICO.
I AM THE PROFITEER, YOUR HOSTESS THIS EVENING. AND I KNOW EXACTLY WHAT YOU WANT TO SEE.
YOU'RE HERE FOR THE WAR. AND NOT JUST ANY WAR...
...THE GREATEST WAR THIS UNIVERSE HAS EVER KNOWN...
THE KREE/ SKRULL WAR!
CENTURIES OF CARNAGE! BATTLES BLAZING ACROSS THE STARS!
AND, EACH TIME, ALL OF THEM BOILING DOWN TO ONE LAST ACT OF AGGRESSION!
TWO ENEMIES ON THE FRONT LINE, WITH THEIR HANDS AROUND EACH OTHER'S THROATS.
SO TELL ME, WHAT'LL IT BE? ANY CAMPAIGN-- ACROSS ALL OF TIME AND SPACE!
AND THEN YOU, YOU LUCKY FEW...

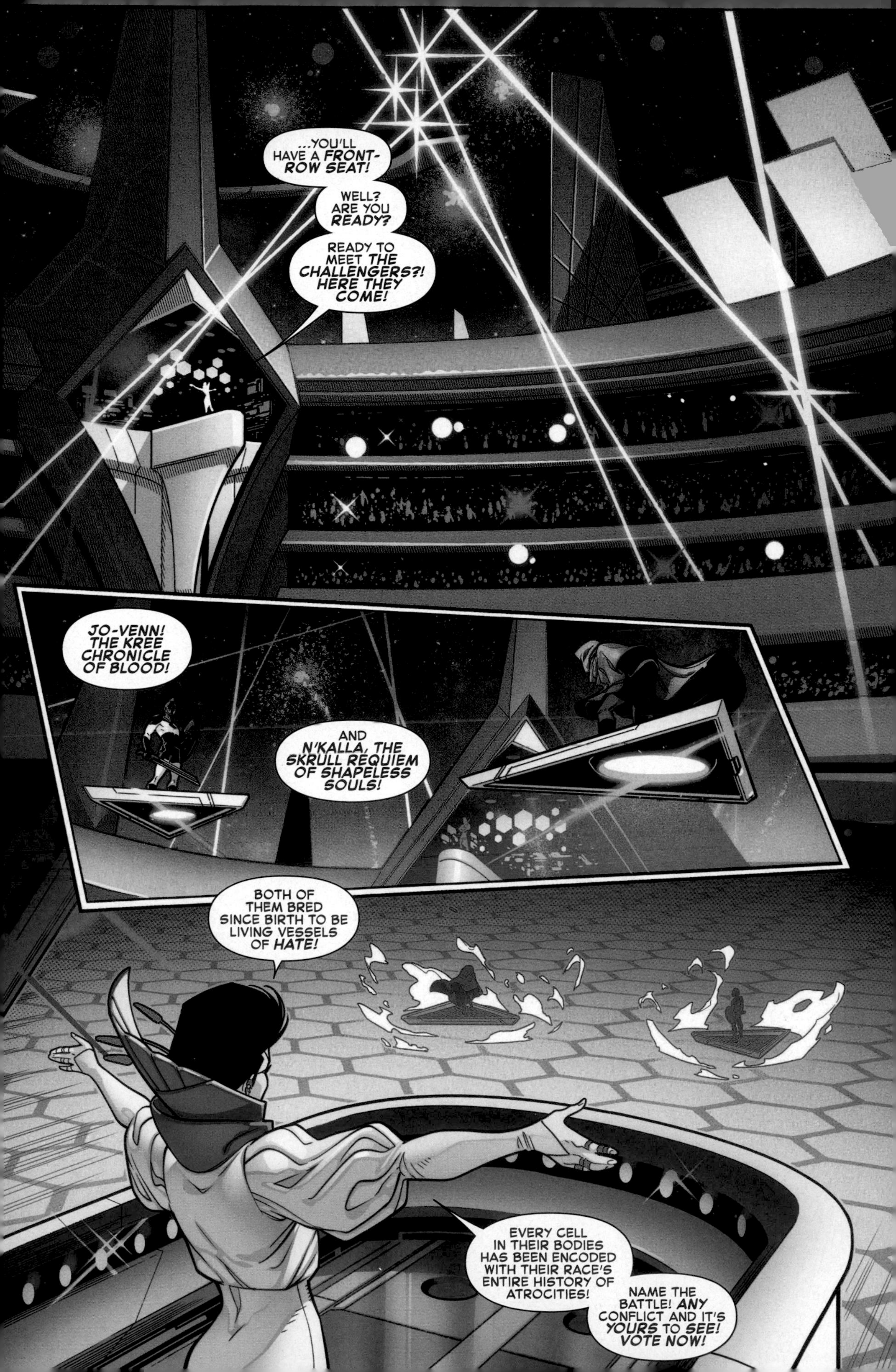
...YOU'LL HAVE A FRONT-ROW SEAT!
WELL? ARE YOU READY?
READY TO MEET THE CHALLENGERS?! HERE THEY COME!
JO-VENN! THE KREE CHRONICLE OF BLOOD!
AND N'KALLA, THE SKRULL REQUIEM OF SHAPELESS SOULS!
BOTH OF THEM BRED SINCE BIRTH TO BE LIVING VESSELS OF HATE!
EVERY CELL IN THEIR BODIES HAS BEEN ENCODED WITH THEIR RACE'S ENTIRE HISTORY OF ATROCITIES!
NAME THE BATTLE! ANY CONFLICT AND IT'S YOURS TO SEE! VOTE NOW!

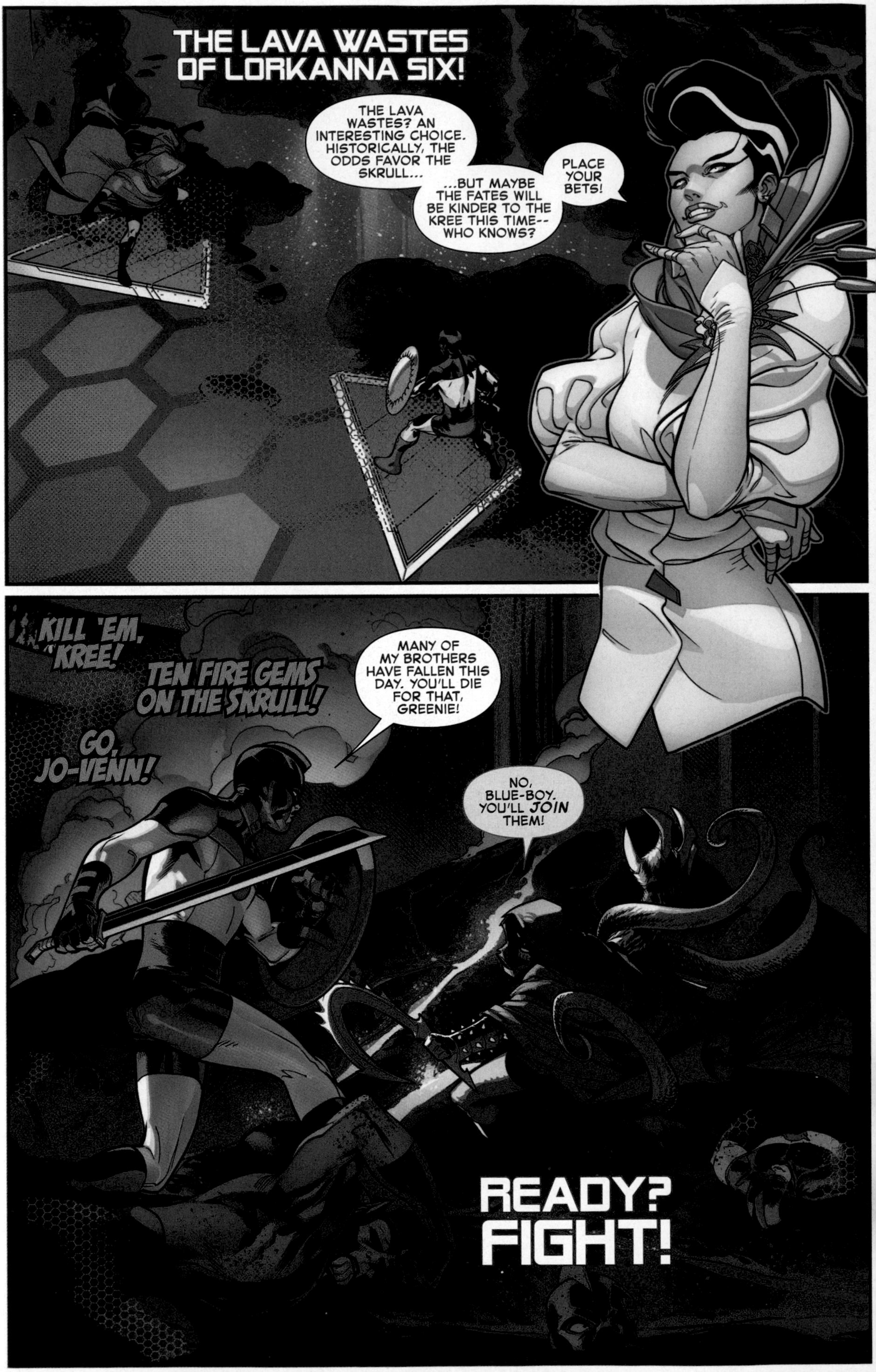
THE LAVA WASTES OF LORKANNA SIX!
THE LAVA WASTES? AN INTERESTING CHOICE. HISTORICALLY, THE ODDS FAVOR THE SKRULL...
...BUT MAYBE THE FATES WILL BE KINDER TO THE KREE THIS TIME-- WHO KNOWS?
PLACE YOUR BETS!
KILL 'EM, KREE!
TEN FIRE GEMS ON THE SKRULL!
GO, JO-VENN!
MANY OF MY BROTHERS HAVE FALLEN THIS DAY. YOU'LL DIE FOR THAT, GREENIE!
NO, BLUE-BOY. YOU'LL JOIN THEM!
READY? FIGHT!

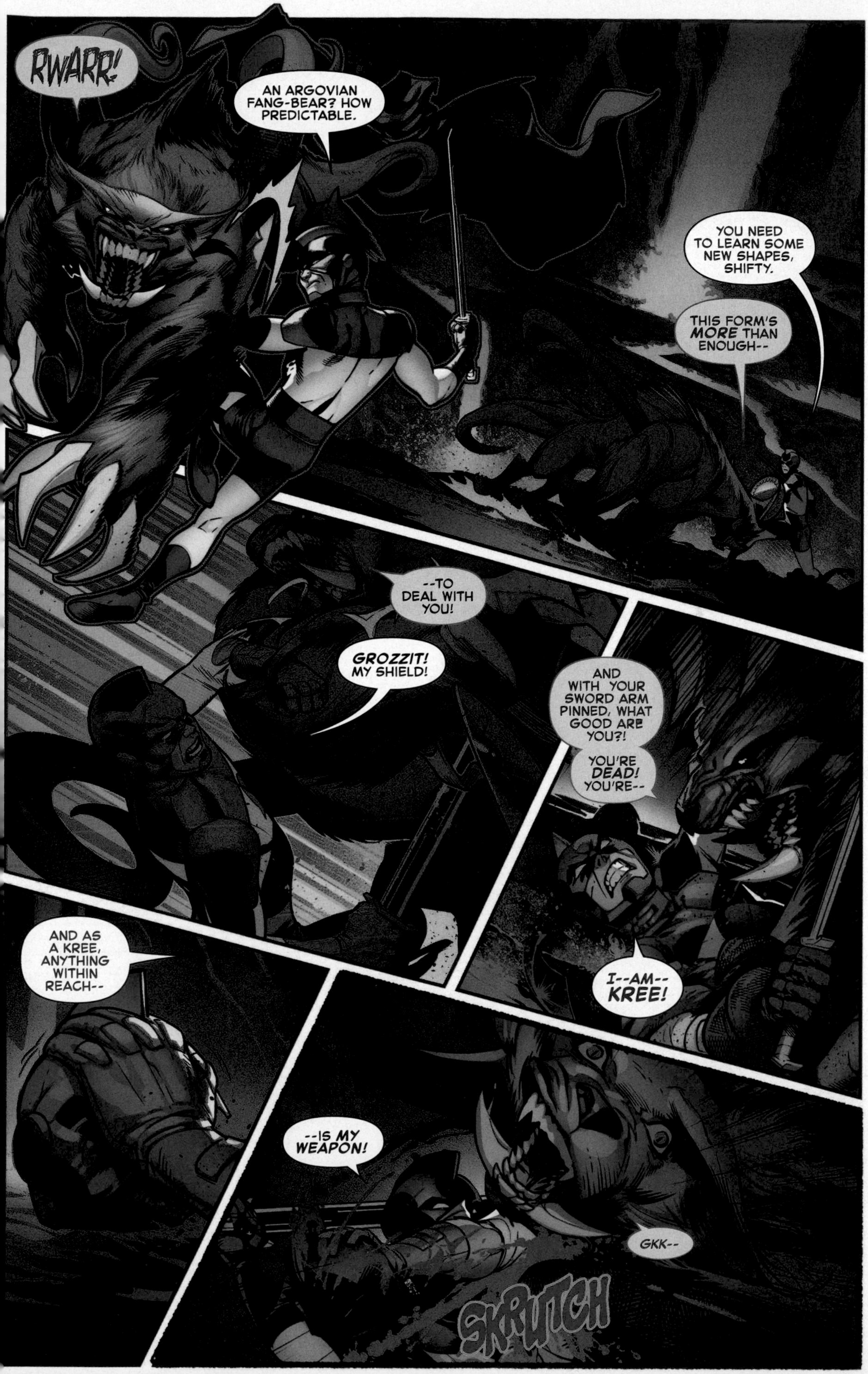

RWARR!
AN ARGOVIAN FANG-BEAR? HOW PREDICTABLE.
YOU NEED TO LEARN SOME NEW SHAPES, SHIFTY.
THIS FORM'S MORE THAN ENOUGH--
--TO DEAL WITH YOU!
GROZZIT! MY SHIELD!
AND WITH YOUR SWORD ARM PINNED, WHAT GOOD ARE YOU?!
YOU'RE DEAD! YOU'RE--
I--AM--KREE!
AND AS A KREE, ANYTHING WITHIN REACH--
--IS MY WEAPON!
GKK--
SKRUTCH

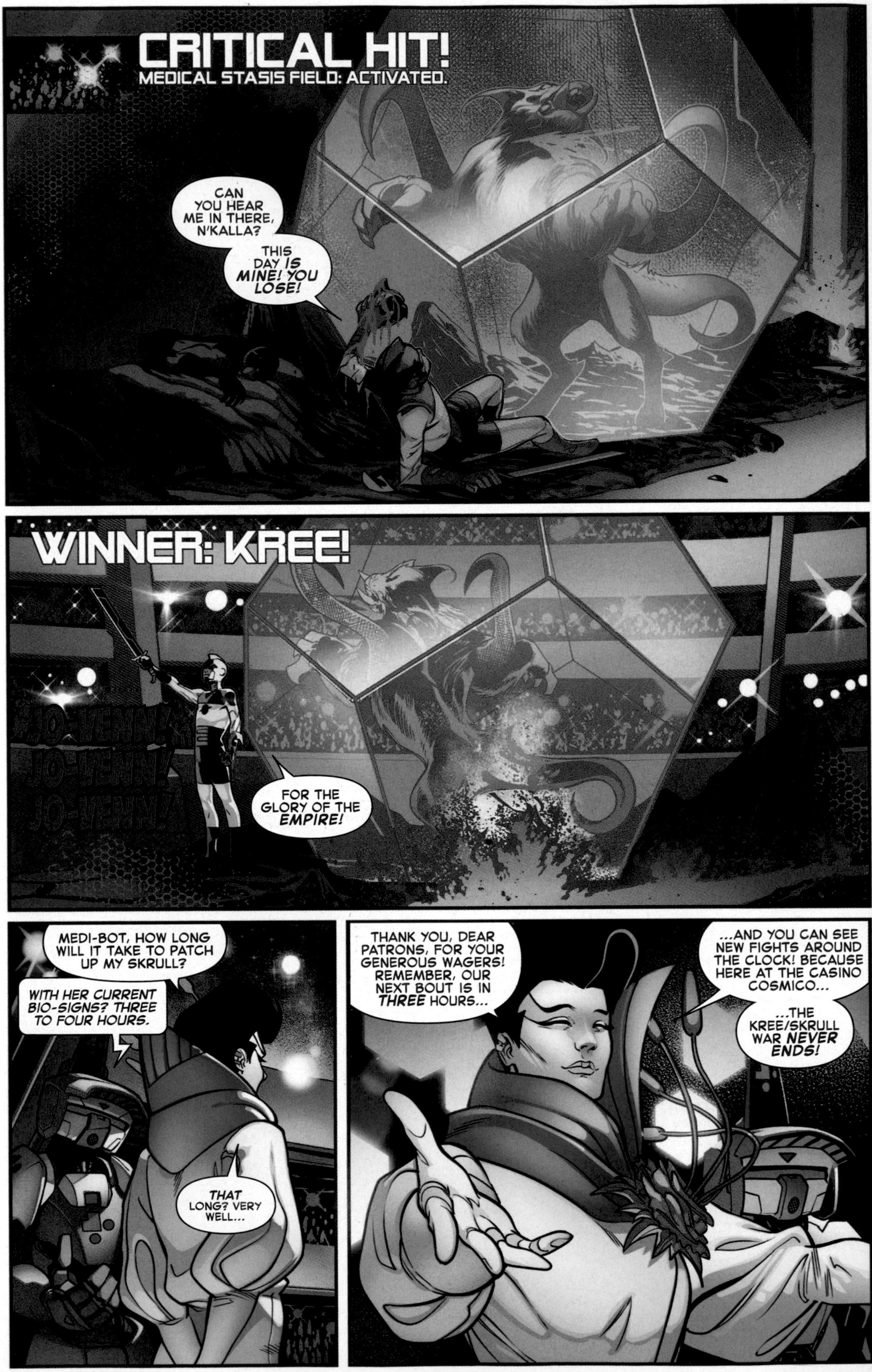
CRITICAL HIT!
MEDICAL STASIS FIELD: ACTIVATED.
CAN YOU HEAR ME IN THERE, N'KALLA?
THIS DAY *IS MINE! YOU LOSE!*
WINNER: KREE!
JO-VENN! JO-VENN! JO-VENN!
FOR THE GLORY OF THE *EMPIRE!*
MEDI-BOT, HOW LONG WILL IT TAKE TO PATCH UP MY SKRULL?
WITH HER CURRENT BIO-SIGNS? THREE TO FOUR HOURS.
THAT LONG? VERY WELL...
THANK YOU, DEAR PATRONS, FOR YOUR GENEROUS WAGERS! REMEMBER, OUR NEXT BOUT IS IN *THREE* HOURS...
...AND YOU CAN SEE NEW FIGHTS AROUND THE CLOCK! BECAUSE HERE AT THE CASINO COSMICO...
...THE KREE/SKRULL WAR *NEVER ENDS!*

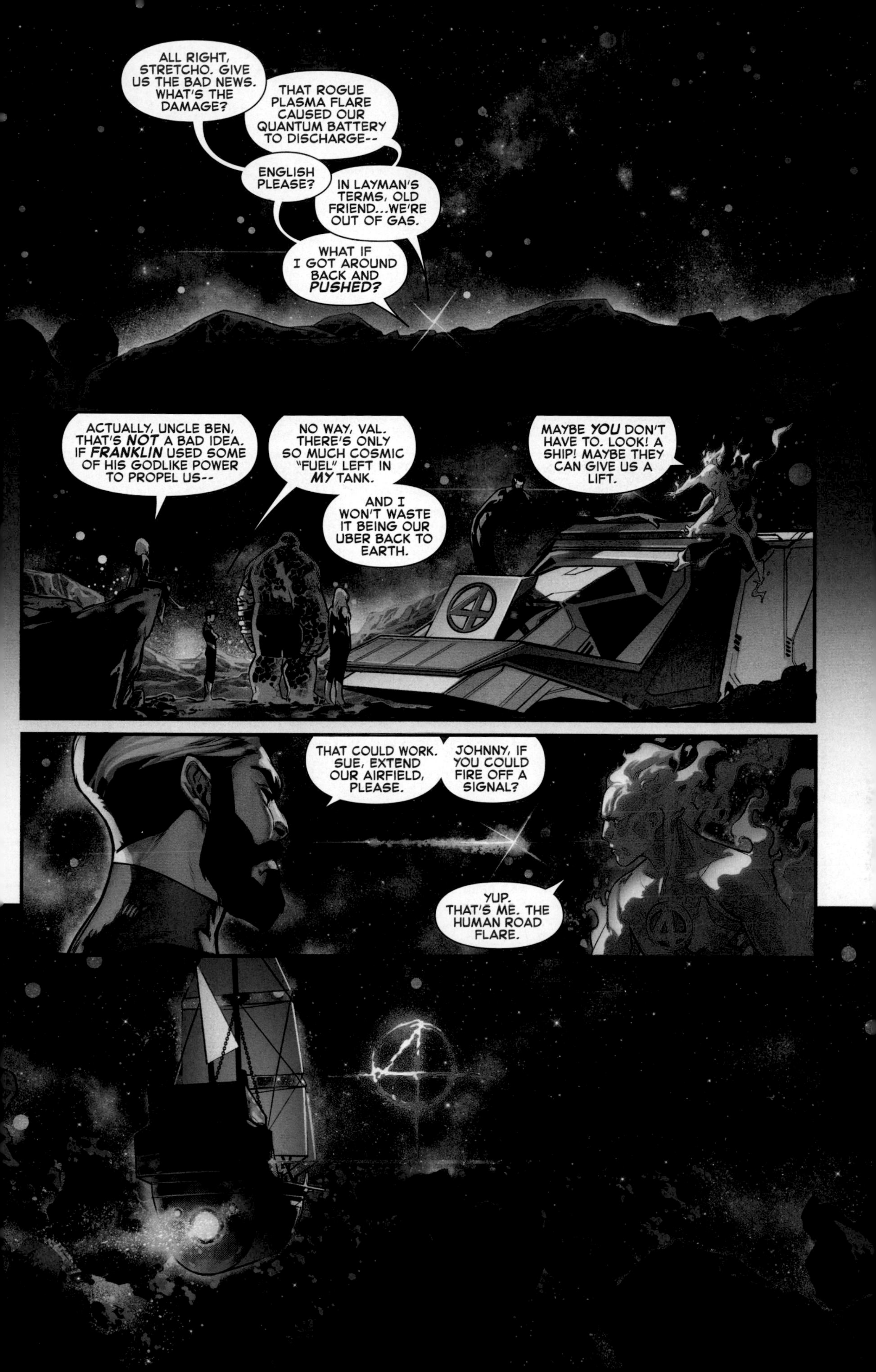
ALL RIGHT, STRETCHO. GIVE US THE BAD NEWS. WHAT'S THE DAMAGE?
THAT ROGUE PLASMA FLARE CAUSED OUR QUANTUM BATTERY TO DISCHARGE--
ENGLISH PLEASE?
IN LAYMAN'S TERMS, OLD FRIEND...WE'RE OUT OF GAS.
WHAT IF I GOT AROUND BACK AND *PUSHED?*
ACTUALLY, UNCLE BEN, THAT'S *NOT* A BAD IDEA. IF *FRANKLIN* USED SOME OF HIS GODLIKE POWER TO PROPEL US--
NO WAY, VAL. THERE'S ONLY SO MUCH COSMIC "FUEL" LEFT IN *MY* TANK.
AND I WON'T WASTE IT BEING OUR UBER BACK TO EARTH.
MAYBE *YOU* DON'T HAVE TO. LOOK! A SHIP! MAYBE THEY CAN GIVE US A LIFT.
THAT COULD WORK. SUE, EXTEND OUR AIRFIELD, PLEASE.
JOHNNY, IF YOU COULD FIRE OFF A SIGNAL?
YUP. THAT'S ME. THE HUMAN ROAD FLARE.

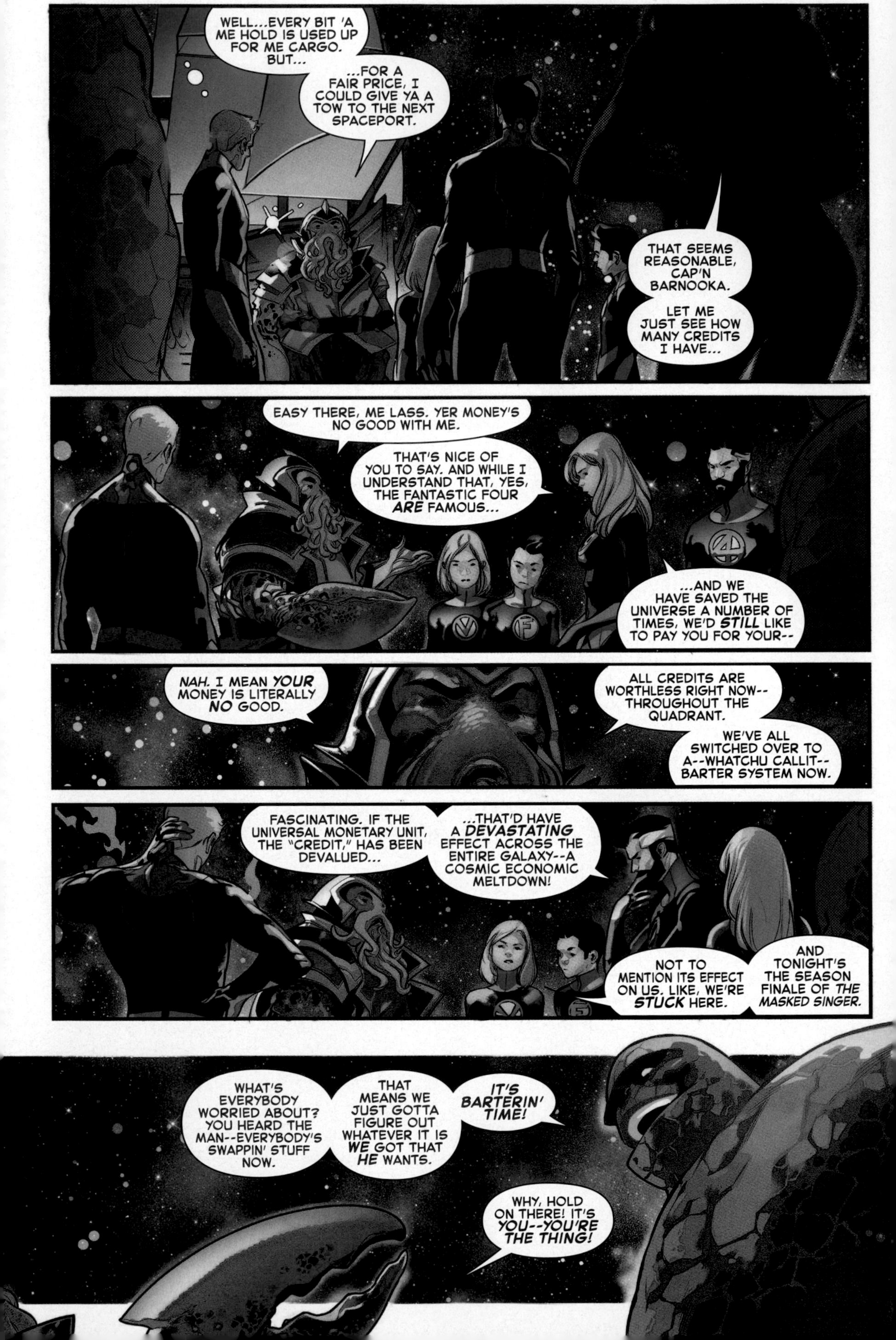
WELL...EVERY BIT 'A ME HOLD IS USED UP FOR ME CARGO. BUT...
...FOR A FAIR PRICE, I COULD GIVE YA A TOW TO THE NEXT SPACEPORT.
THAT SEEMS REASONABLE, CAP'N BARNOOKA.
LET ME JUST SEE HOW MANY CREDITS I HAVE...
EASY THERE, ME LASS. YER MONEY'S NO GOOD WITH ME.
THAT'S NICE OF YOU TO SAY. AND WHILE I UNDERSTAND THAT, YES, THE FANTASTIC FOUR ARE FAMOUS...
...AND WE HAVE SAVED THE UNIVERSE A NUMBER OF TIMES, WE'D STILL LIKE TO PAY YOU FOR YOUR--
NAH. I MEAN YOUR MONEY IS LITERALLY NO GOOD.
ALL CREDITS ARE WORTHLESS RIGHT NOW-- THROUGHOUT THE QUADRANT.
WE'VE ALL SWITCHED OVER TO A--WHATCHU CALLIT-- BARTER SYSTEM NOW.
FASCINATING. IF THE UNIVERSAL MONETARY UNIT, THE "CREDIT," HAS BEEN DEVALUED...
...THAT'D HAVE A DEVASTATING EFFECT ACROSS THE ENTIRE GALAXY--A COSMIC ECONOMIC MELTDOWN!
NOT TO MENTION ITS EFFECT ON US. LIKE, WE'RE STUCK HERE.
AND TONIGHT'S THE SEASON FINALE OF THE MASKED SINGER.
WHAT'S EVERYBODY WORRIED ABOUT? YOU HEARD THE MAN--EVERYBODY'S SWAPPIN' STUFF NOW.
THAT MEANS WE JUST GOTTA FIGURE OUT WHATEVER IT IS WE GOT THAT HE WANTS.
IT'S BARTERIN' TIME!
WHY, HOLD ON THERE! IT'S YOU--YOU'RE THE THING!

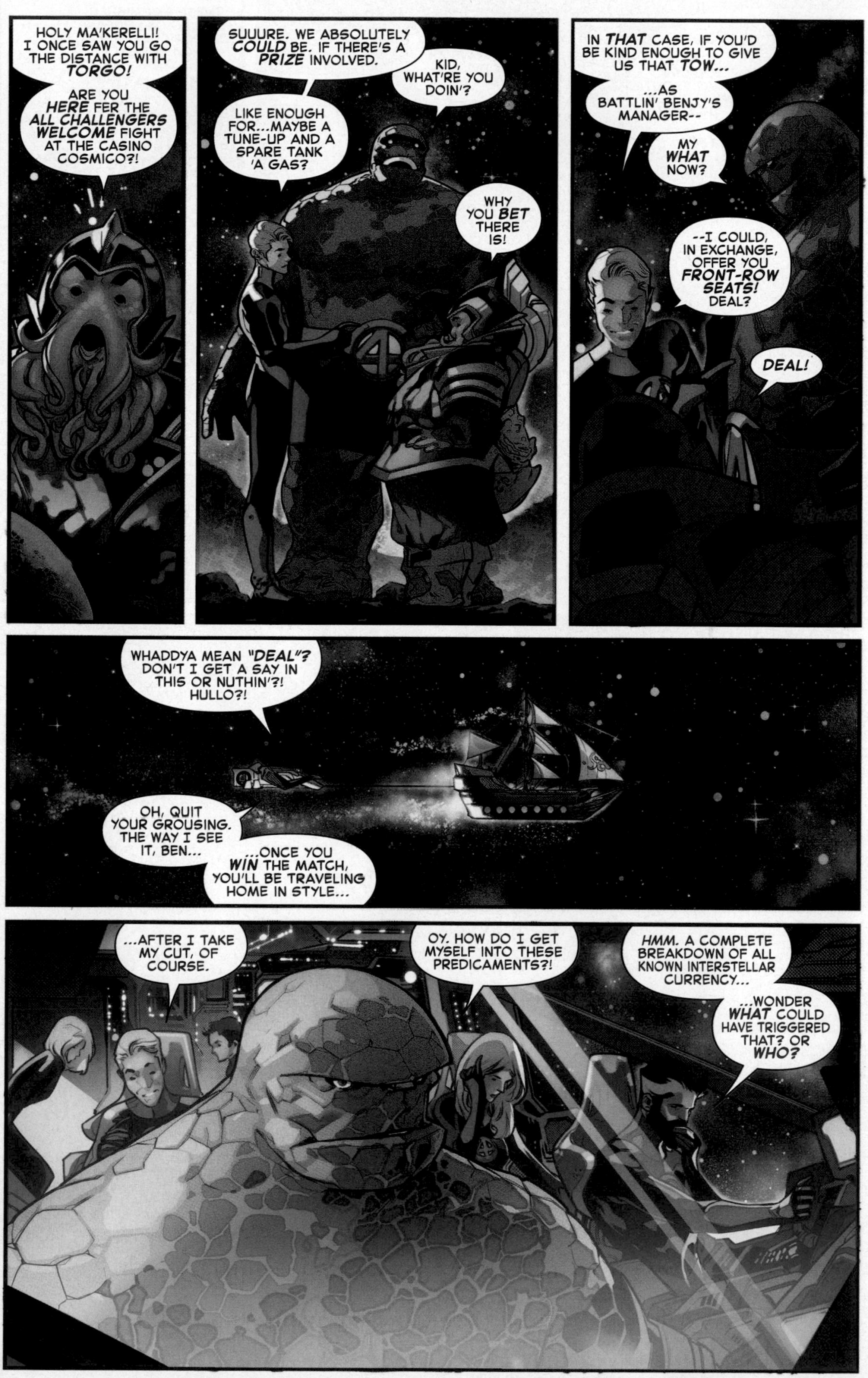
HOLY MA'KERELLI! I ONCE SAW YOU GO THE DISTANCE WITH TORGO!
ARE YOU HERE FER THE ALL CHALLENGERS WELCOME FIGHT AT THE CASINO COSMICO?!
SUUURE. WE ABSOLUTELY COULD BE. IF THERE'S A PRIZE INVOLVED.
KID, WHAT'RE YOU DOIN'?
LIKE ENOUGH FOR...MAYBE A TUNE-UP AND A SPARE TANK 'A GAS?
WHY YOU BET THERE IS!
IN THAT CASE, IF YOU'D BE KIND ENOUGH TO GIVE US THAT TOW...
...AS BATTLIN' BENJY'S MANAGER--
MY WHAT NOW?
--I COULD, IN EXCHANGE, OFFER YOU FRONT-ROW SEATS! DEAL?
DEAL!
WHADDYA MEAN "DEAL"? DON'T I GET A SAY IN THIS OR NUTHIN'?! HULLO?!
OH, QUIT YOUR GROUSING. THE WAY I SEE IT, BEN...
...ONCE YOU WIN THE MATCH, YOU'LL BE TRAVELING HOME IN STYLE...
...AFTER I TAKE MY CUT, OF COURSE.
OY. HOW DO I GET MYSELF INTO THESE PREDICAMENTS?!
HMM. A COMPLETE BREAKDOWN OF ALL KNOWN INTERSTELLAR CURRENCY...
...WONDER WHAT COULD HAVE TRIGGERED THAT? OR WHO?

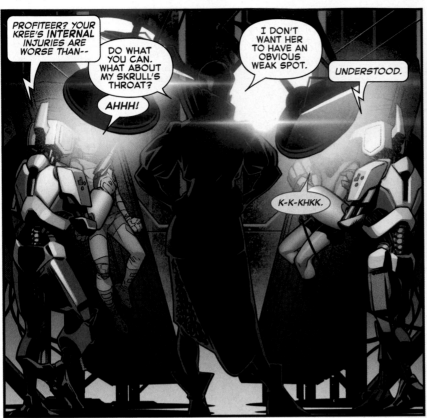

PROFITEER? YOUR KREE'S INTERNAL INJURIES ARE WORSE THAN--

DO WHAT YOU CAN. WHAT ABOUT MY SKRULL'S THROAT?

I DON'T WANT HER TO HAVE AN OBVIOUS WEAK SPOT.

UNDERSTOOD.

AHHH!

K-K-KHKK.

THESE SKIRMISHES MUST GO ON LONGER, OR OUR CLIENTS WILL GROW BORED OF THEM.

PERHAPS IF WE POSTPONE THEIR NEXT FIGHT, MA'AM? GIVE THEM TIME TO REST?

THAT'S WHAT THE CASINO COSMICO'S PREVIOUS OWNER WOULD HAVE DONE IN THIS SITUATION--

WHICH IS PRECISELY WHY MY BROTHER, THE GRANDMASTER, IS THE PREVIOUS OWNER.

MEEP.

YARGH!

BECAUSE THIS PLACE WAS SIMPLY ANOTHER GAME TO HIM.

FOR ME, IT'S A BUSINESS. NEVER FORGET THAT, WERMAN.

Y-Y-YES, MA'AM.

NOW, TELL ME, WHO ELSE IS ON THE TITLE CARD FOR TONIGHT?

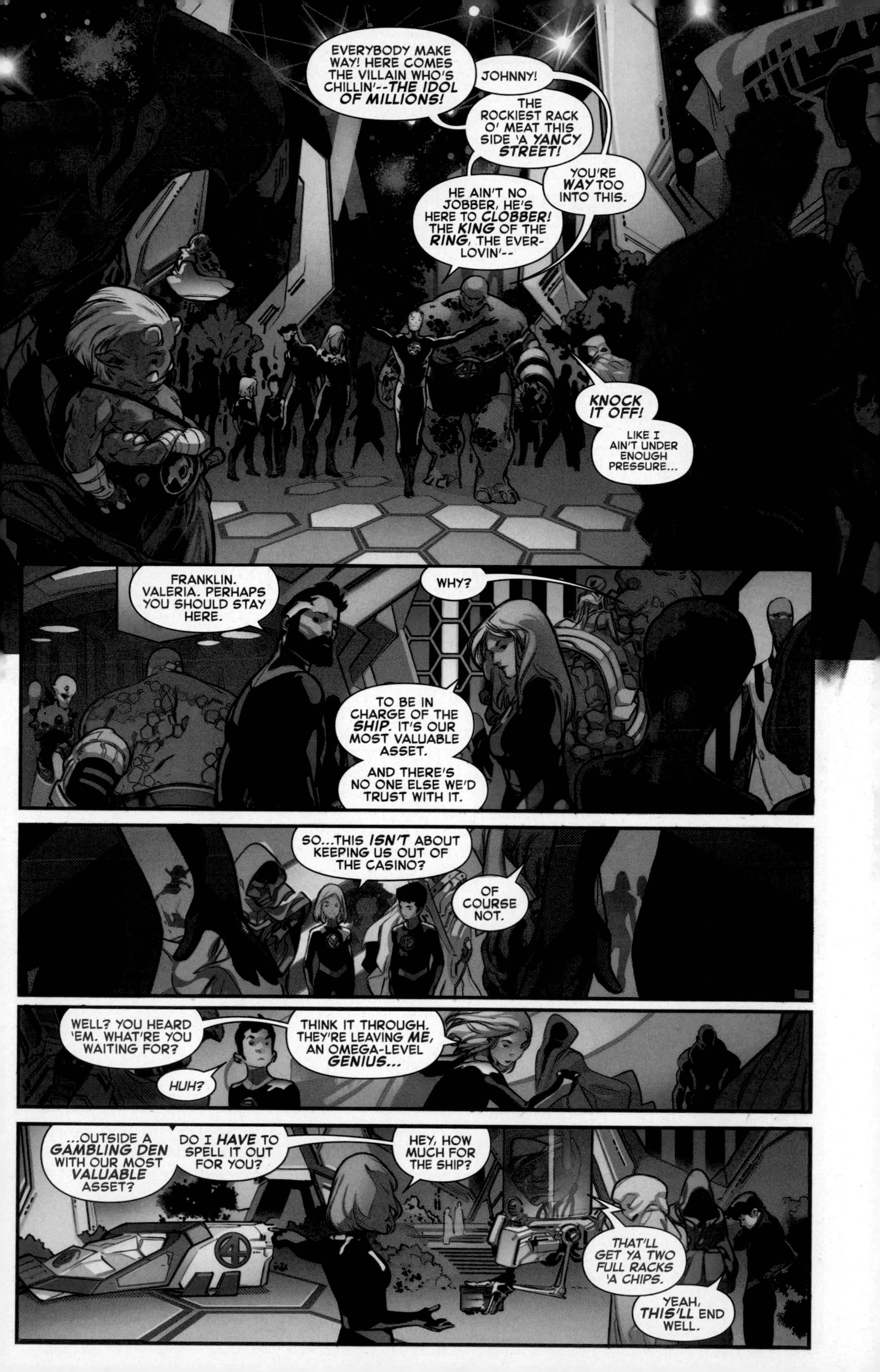
EVERYBODY MAKE WAY! HERE COMES THE VILLAIN WHO'S CHILLIN'--THE IDOL OF MILLIONS!
JOHNNY!
THE ROCKIEST RACK O' MEAT THIS SIDE 'A YANCY STREET!
YOU'RE WAY TOO INTO THIS.
HE AIN'T NO JOBBER, HE'S HERE TO CLOBBER! THE KING OF THE RING, THE EVER-LOVIN'--
KNOCK IT OFF!
LIKE I AIN'T UNDER ENOUGH PRESSURE...
FRANKLIN. VALERIA. PERHAPS YOU SHOULD STAY HERE.
WHY?
TO BE IN CHARGE OF THE SHIP. IT'S OUR MOST VALUABLE ASSET.
AND THERE'S NO ONE ELSE WE'D TRUST WITH IT.
SO...THIS ISN'T ABOUT KEEPING US OUT OF THE CASINO?
OF COURSE NOT.
WELL? YOU HEARD 'EM. WHAT'RE YOU WAITING FOR?
THINK IT THROUGH. THEY'RE LEAVING ME, AN OMEGA-LEVEL GENIUS...
HUH?
...OUTSIDE A GAMBLING DEN WITH OUR MOST VALUABLE ASSET?
DO I HAVE TO SPELL IT OUT FOR YOU?
HEY, HOW MUCH FOR THE SHIP?
THAT'LL GET YA TWO FULL RACKS 'A CHIPS.
YEAH, THIS'LL END WELL.

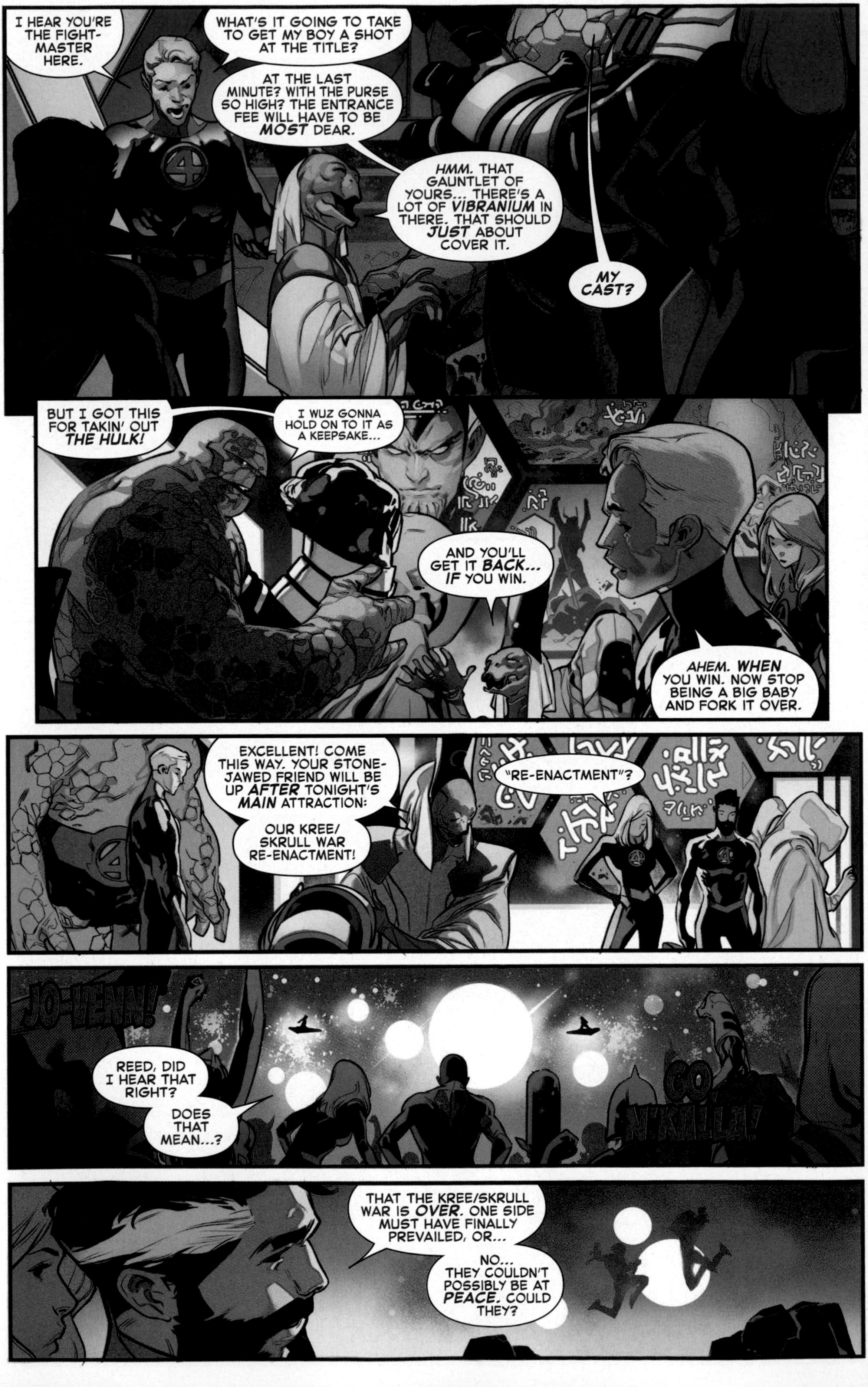
I HEAR YOU'RE THE FIGHT-MASTER HERE.
WHAT'S IT GOING TO TAKE TO GET MY BOY A SHOT AT THE TITLE?
AT THE LAST MINUTE? WITH THE PURSE SO HIGH? THE ENTRANCE FEE WILL HAVE TO BE MOST DEAR.
HMM. THAT GAUNTLET OF YOURS... THERE'S A LOT OF VIBRANIUM IN THERE. THAT SHOULD JUST ABOUT COVER IT.
MY CAST?
BUT I GOT THIS FOR TAKIN' OUT THE HULK!
I WUZ GONNA HOLD ON TO IT AS A KEEPSAKE...
AND YOU'LL GET IT BACK... IF YOU WIN.
AHEM. WHEN YOU WIN. NOW STOP BEING A BIG BABY AND FORK IT OVER.
EXCELLENT! COME THIS WAY. YOUR STONE-JAWED FRIEND WILL BE UP AFTER TONIGHT'S MAIN ATTRACTION:
OUR KREE/SKRULL WAR RE-ENACTMENT!
"RE-ENACTMENT"?
JO-VENN!
REED, DID I HEAR THAT RIGHT?
DOES THAT MEAN...?
THAT THE KREE/SKRULL WAR IS OVER. ONE SIDE MUST HAVE FINALLY PREVAILED, OR...
NO... THEY COULDN'T POSSIBLY BE AT PEACE. COULD THEY?

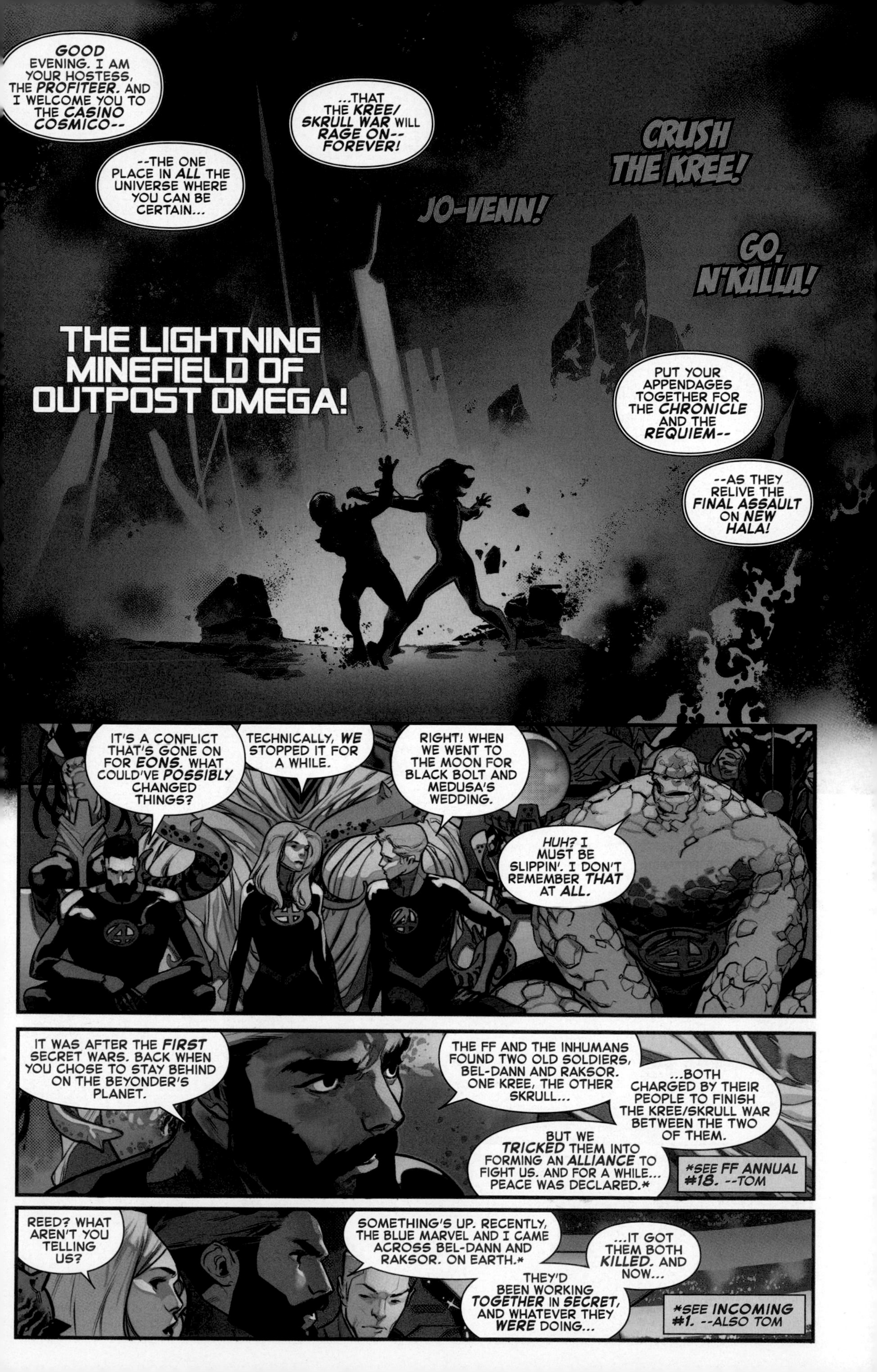
GOOD EVENING. I AM YOUR HOSTESS, THE PROFITEER. AND I WELCOME YOU TO THE CASINO COSMICO--
--THE ONE PLACE IN ALL THE UNIVERSE WHERE YOU CAN BE CERTAIN...
...THAT THE KREE/SKRULL WAR WILL RAGE ON--FOREVER!
CRUSH THE KREE!
JO-VENN!
GO, N'KALLA!
THE LIGHTNING MINEFIELD OF OUTPOST OMEGA!
PUT YOUR APPENDAGES TOGETHER FOR THE CHRONICLE AND THE REQUIEM--
--AS THEY RELIVE THE FINAL ASSAULT ON NEW HALA!
IT'S A CONFLICT THAT'S GONE ON FOR EONS. WHAT COULD'VE POSSIBLY CHANGED THINGS?
TECHNICALLY, WE STOPPED IT FOR A WHILE.
RIGHT! WHEN WE WENT TO THE MOON FOR BLACK BOLT AND MEDUSA'S WEDDING.
HUH? I MUST BE SLIPPIN'. I DON'T REMEMBER THAT AT ALL.
IT WAS AFTER THE FIRST SECRET WARS. BACK WHEN YOU CHOSE TO STAY BEHIND ON THE BEYONDER'S PLANET.
THE FF AND THE INHUMANS FOUND TWO OLD SOLDIERS, BEL-DANN AND RAKSOR. ONE KREE, THE OTHER SKRULL...
...BOTH CHARGED BY THEIR PEOPLE TO FINISH THE KREE/SKRULL WAR BETWEEN THE TWO OF THEM.
BUT WE TRICKED THEM INTO FORMING AN ALLIANCE TO FIGHT US. AND FOR A WHILE... PEACE WAS DECLARED.*
*SEE FF ANNUAL #18. --TOM
REED? WHAT AREN'T YOU TELLING US?
SOMETHING'S UP. RECENTLY, THE BLUE MARVEL AND I CAME ACROSS BEL-DANN AND RAKSOR. ON EARTH.*
THEY'D BEEN WORKING TOGETHER IN SECRET, AND WHATEVER THEY WERE DOING...
...IT GOT THEM BOTH KILLED. AND NOW...
*SEE INCOMING #1. --ALSO TOM

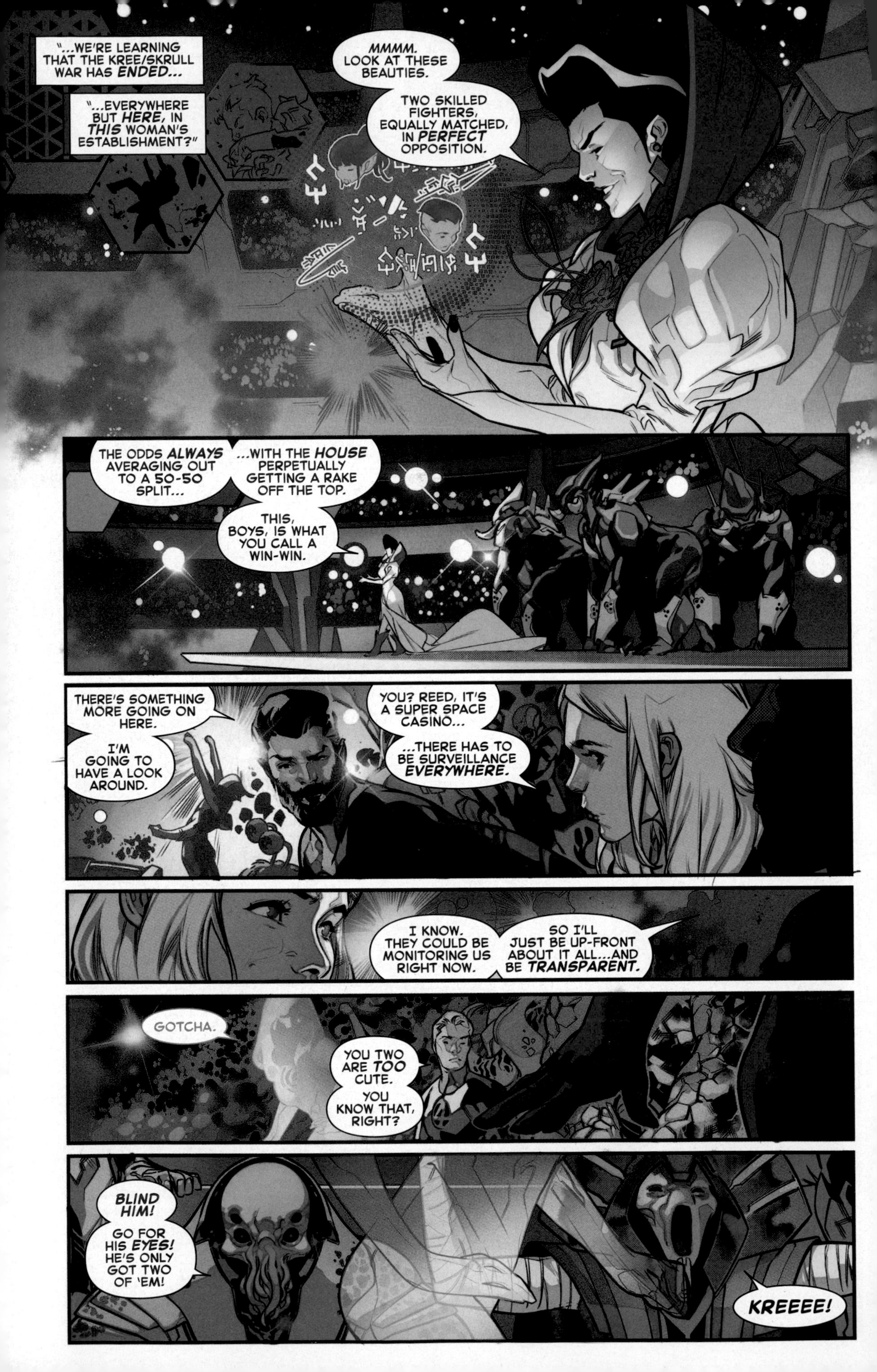
"...WE'RE LEARNING THAT THE KREE/SKRULL WAR HAS ENDED...
"...EVERYWHERE BUT HERE, IN THIS WOMAN'S ESTABLISHMENT?"
MMMM. LOOK AT THESE BEAUTIES.
TWO SKILLED FIGHTERS, EQUALLY MATCHED, IN PERFECT OPPOSITION.
THE ODDS ALWAYS AVERAGING OUT TO A 50-50 SPLIT...
...WITH THE HOUSE PERPETUALLY GETTING A RAKE OFF THE TOP.
THIS, BOYS, IS WHAT YOU CALL A WIN-WIN.
THERE'S SOMETHING MORE GOING ON HERE.
I'M GOING TO HAVE A LOOK AROUND.
YOU? REED, IT'S A SUPER SPACE CASINO...
...THERE HAS TO BE SURVEILLANCE EVERYWHERE.
I KNOW. THEY COULD BE MONITORING US RIGHT NOW.
SO I'LL JUST BE UP-FRONT ABOUT IT ALL...AND BE TRANSPARENT.
GOTCHA.
YOU TWO ARE TOO CUTE.
YOU KNOW THAT, RIGHT?
BLIND HIM!
GO FOR HIS EYES! HE'S ONLY GOT TWO OF 'EM!
KREEEE!

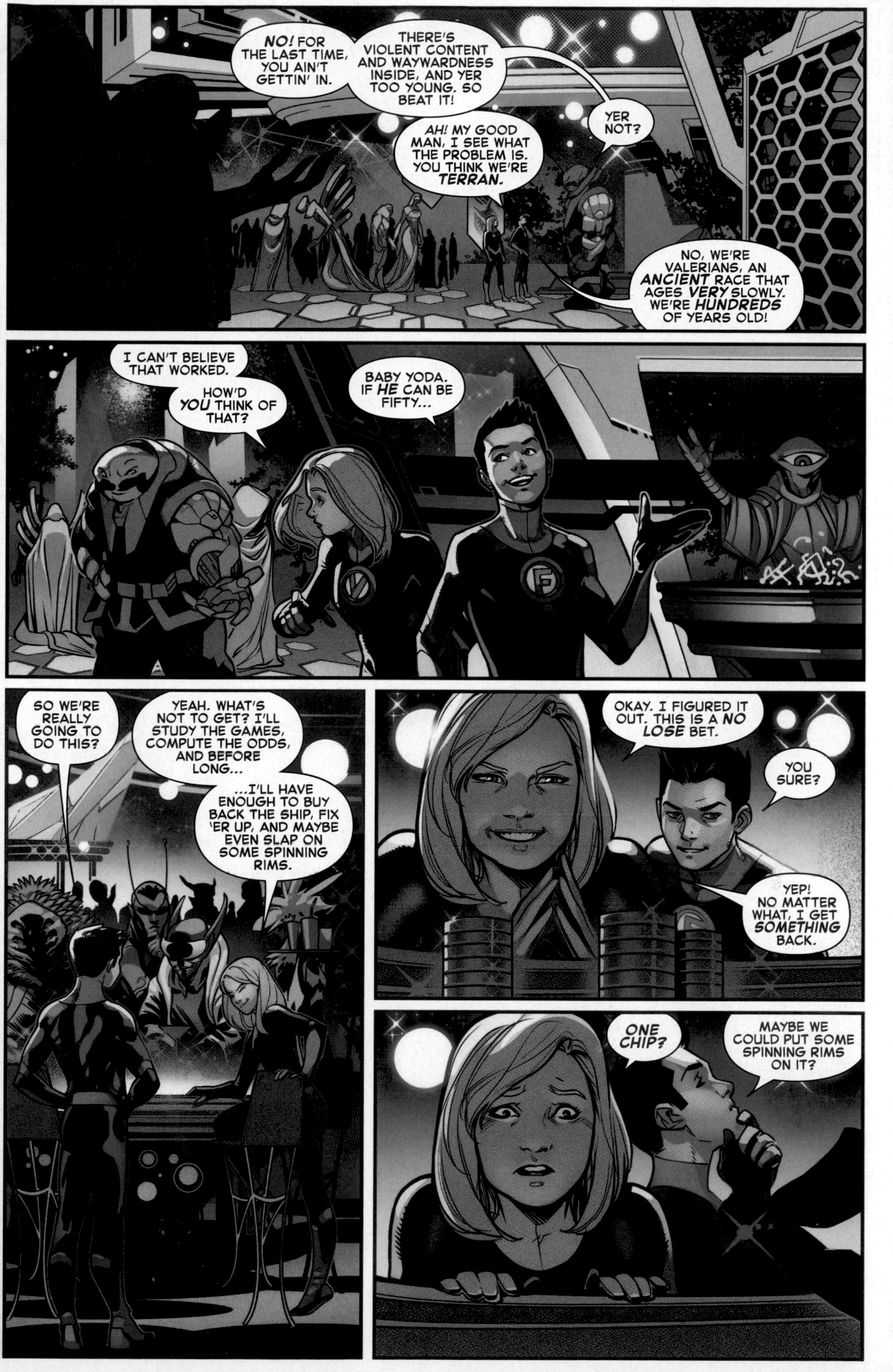

NO! FOR THE LAST TIME, YOU AIN'T GETTIN' IN.
THERE'S VIOLENT CONTENT AND WAYWARDNESS INSIDE, AND YER TOO YOUNG. SO BEAT IT!
AH! MY GOOD MAN, I SEE WHAT THE PROBLEM IS. YOU THINK WE'RE TERRAN.
YER NOT?
NO, WE'RE VALERIANS, AN ANCIENT RACE THAT AGES VERY SLOWLY. WE'RE HUNDREDS OF YEARS OLD!
I CAN'T BELIEVE THAT WORKED.
HOW'D YOU THINK OF THAT?
BABY YODA. IF HE CAN BE FIFTY...
SO WE'RE REALLY GOING TO DO THIS?
YEAH. WHAT'S NOT TO GET? I'LL STUDY THE GAMES, COMPUTE THE ODDS, AND BEFORE LONG...
...I'LL HAVE ENOUGH TO BUY BACK THE SHIP, FIX 'ER UP, AND MAYBE EVEN SLAP ON SOME SPINNING RIMS.
OKAY. I FIGURED IT OUT. THIS IS A NO LOSE BET.
YOU SURE?
YEP! NO MATTER WHAT, I GET SOMETHING BACK.
ONE CHIP?
MAYBE WE COULD PUT SOME SPINNING RIMS ON IT?

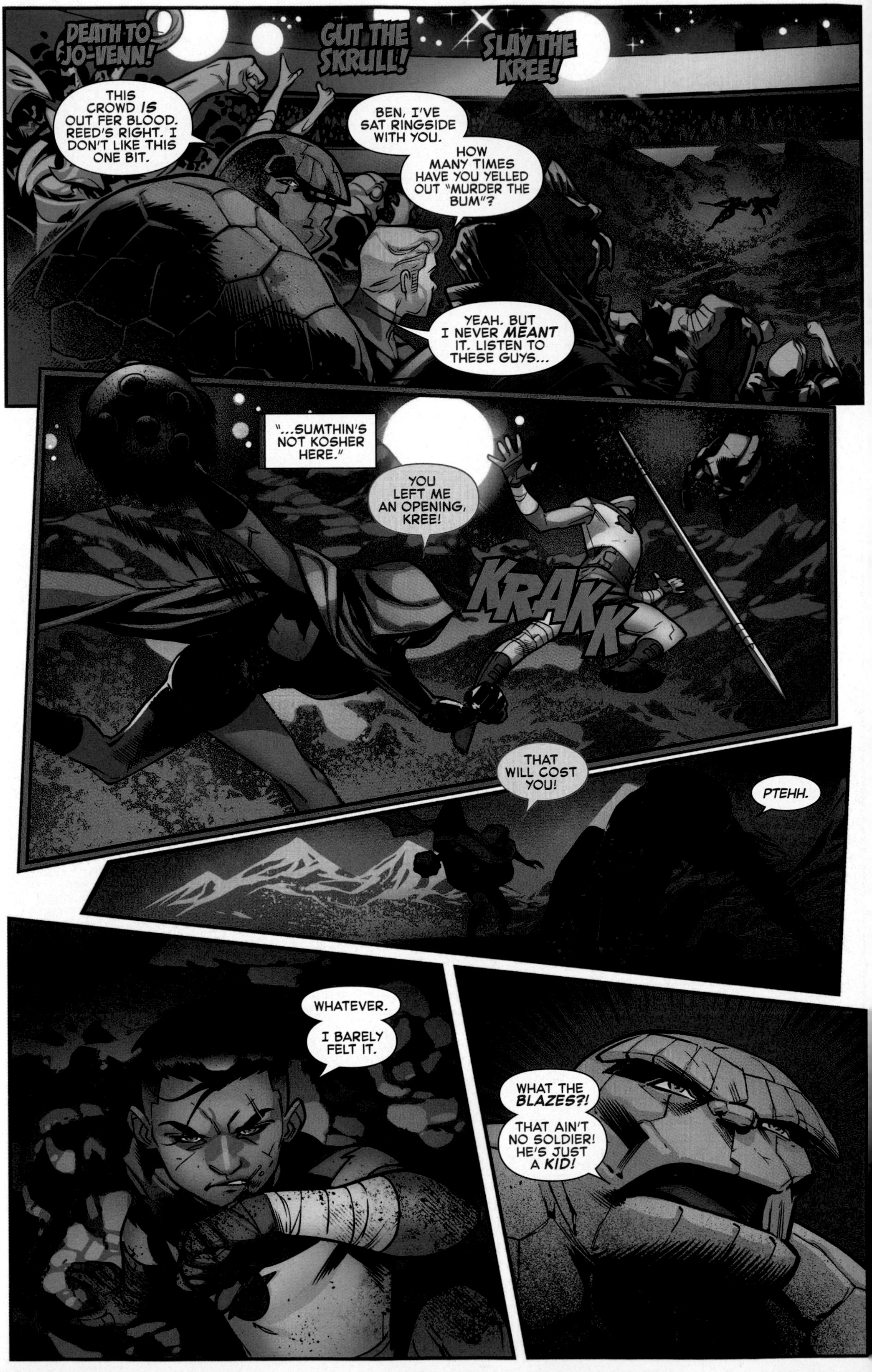
DEATH TO JO-VENN!
GUT THE SKRULL!
SLAY THE KREE!
THIS CROWD IS OUT FER BLOOD. REED'S RIGHT. I DON'T LIKE THIS ONE BIT.
BEN, I'VE SAT RINGSIDE WITH YOU.
HOW MANY TIMES HAVE YOU YELLED OUT "MURDER THE BUM"?
YEAH. BUT I NEVER MEANT IT. LISTEN TO THESE GUYS...
"...SUMTHIN'S NOT KOSHER HERE."
YOU LEFT ME AN OPENING, KREE!
KRAKK
THAT WILL COST YOU!
PTEHH.
WHATEVER.
I BARELY FELT IT.
WHAT THE BLAZES?!
THAT AIN'T NO SOLDIER! HE'S JUST A KID!

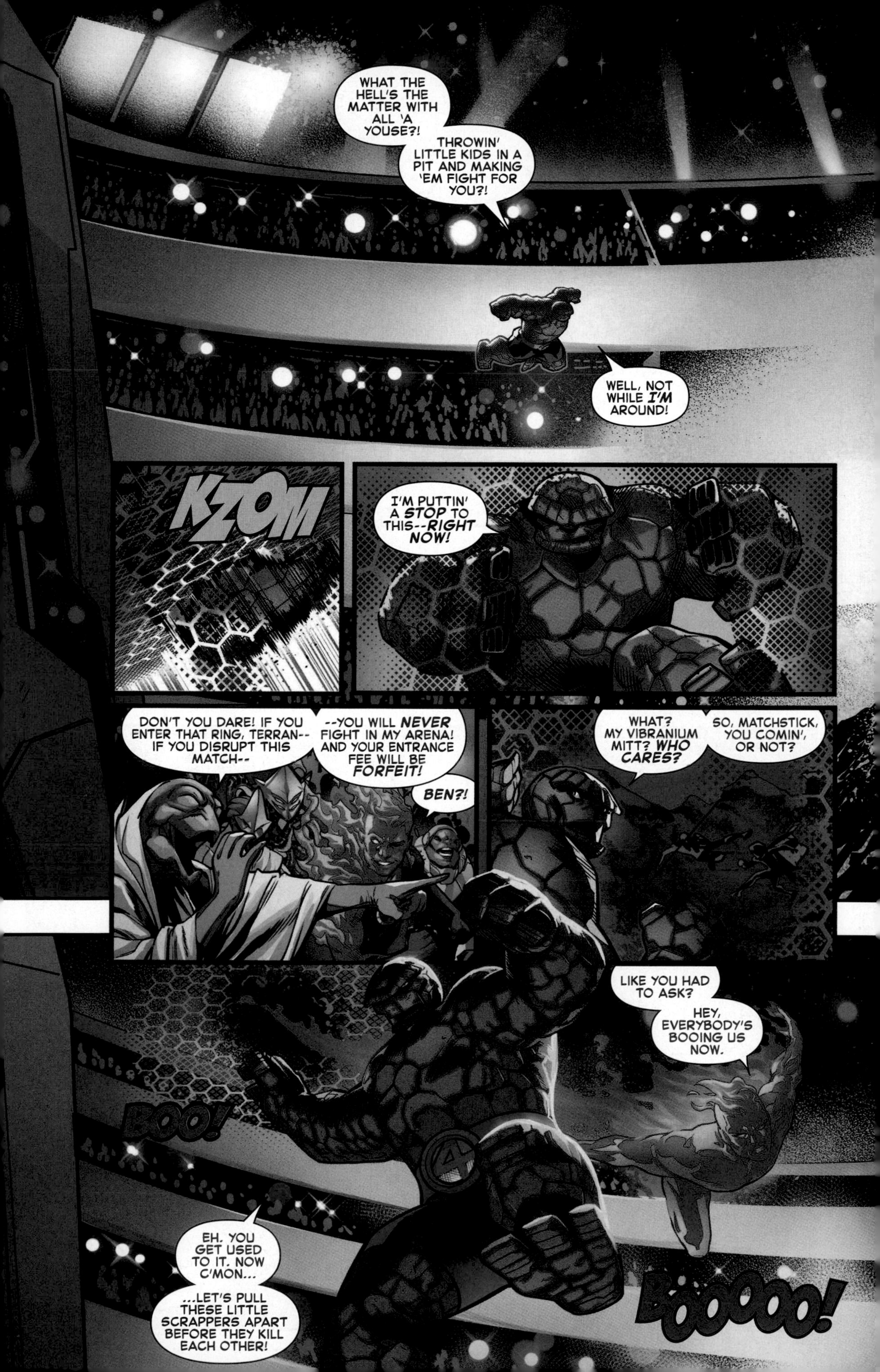
WHAT THE HELL'S THE MATTER WITH ALL 'A YOUSE?!
THROWIN' LITTLE KIDS IN A PIT AND MAKING 'EM FIGHT FOR YOU?!
WELL, NOT WHILE I'M AROUND!
KZOM
I'M PUTTIN' A STOP TO THIS--RIGHT NOW!
DON'T YOU DARE! IF YOU ENTER THAT RING, TERRAN-- IF YOU DISRUPT THIS MATCH--
--YOU WILL NEVER FIGHT IN MY ARENA! AND YOUR ENTRANCE FEE WILL BE FORFEIT!
BEN?!
WHAT? MY VIBRANIUM MITT? WHO CARES?
SO, MATCHSTICK, YOU COMIN', OR NOT?
LIKE YOU HAD TO ASK?
HEY, EVERYBODY'S BOOING US NOW.
BOO!
EH. YOU GET USED TO IT. NOW C'MON...
...LET'S PULL THESE LITTLE SCRAPPERS APART BEFORE THEY KILL EACH OTHER!
BOOOOOO!

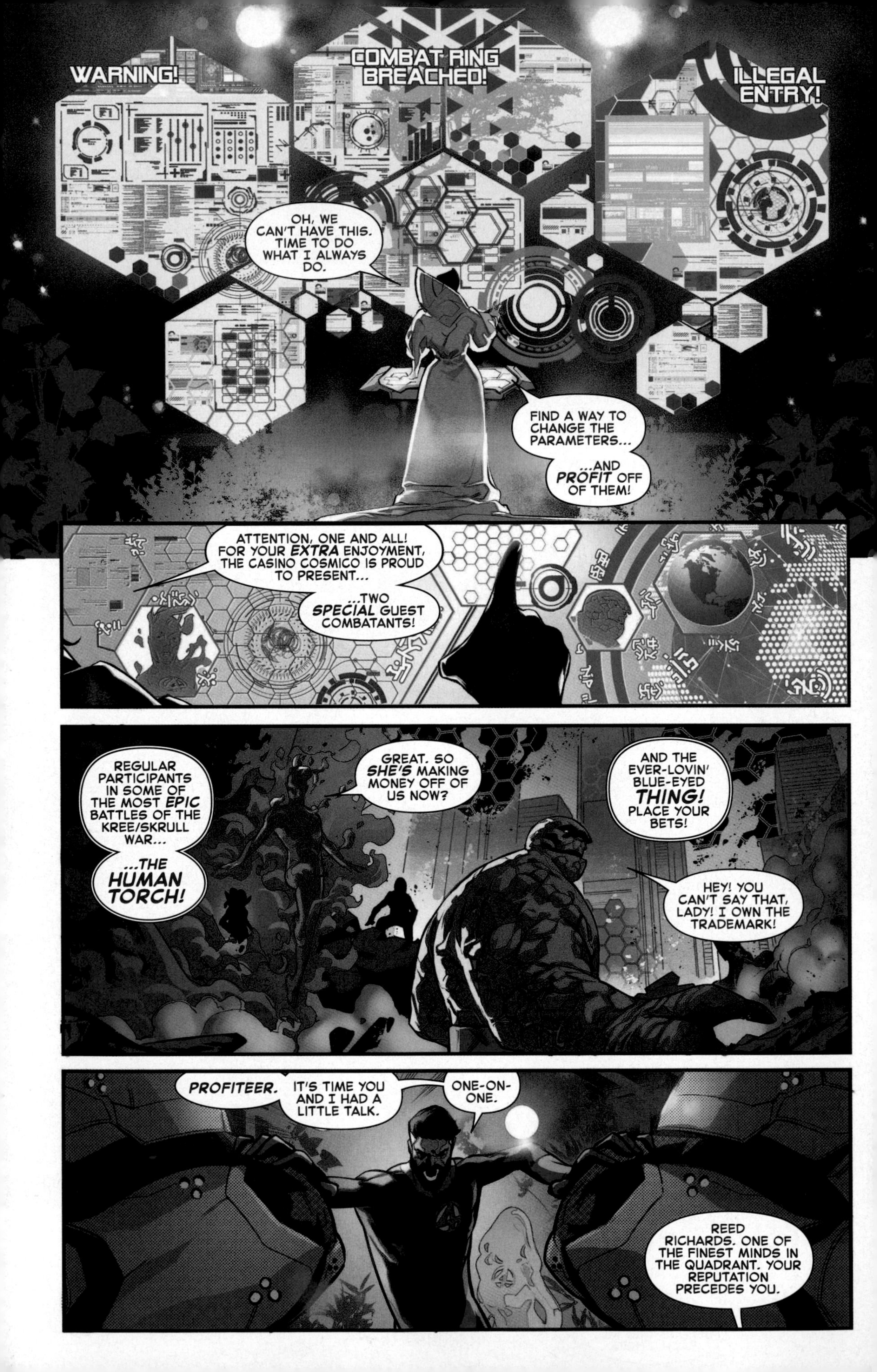

WARNING!
COMBAT RING BREACHED!
ILLEGAL ENTRY!
OH, WE CAN'T HAVE THIS. TIME TO DO WHAT I ALWAYS DO.
FIND A WAY TO CHANGE THE PARAMETERS...
...AND PROFIT OFF OF THEM!
ATTENTION, ONE AND ALL! FOR YOUR EXTRA ENJOYMENT, THE CASINO COSMICO IS PROUD TO PRESENT...
...TWO SPECIAL GUEST COMBATANTS!
REGULAR PARTICIPANTS IN SOME OF THE MOST EPIC BATTLES OF THE KREE/SKRULL WAR...
...THE HUMAN TORCH!
GREAT. SO SHE'S MAKING MONEY OFF OF US NOW?
AND THE EVER-LOVIN' BLUE-EYED THING! PLACE YOUR BETS!
HEY! YOU CAN'T SAY THAT, LADY! I OWN THE TRADEMARK!
PROFITEER.
IT'S TIME YOU AND I HAD A LITTLE TALK.
ONE-ON-ONE.
REED RICHARDS. ONE OF THE FINEST MINDS IN THE QUADRANT. YOUR REPUTATION PRECEDES YOU.

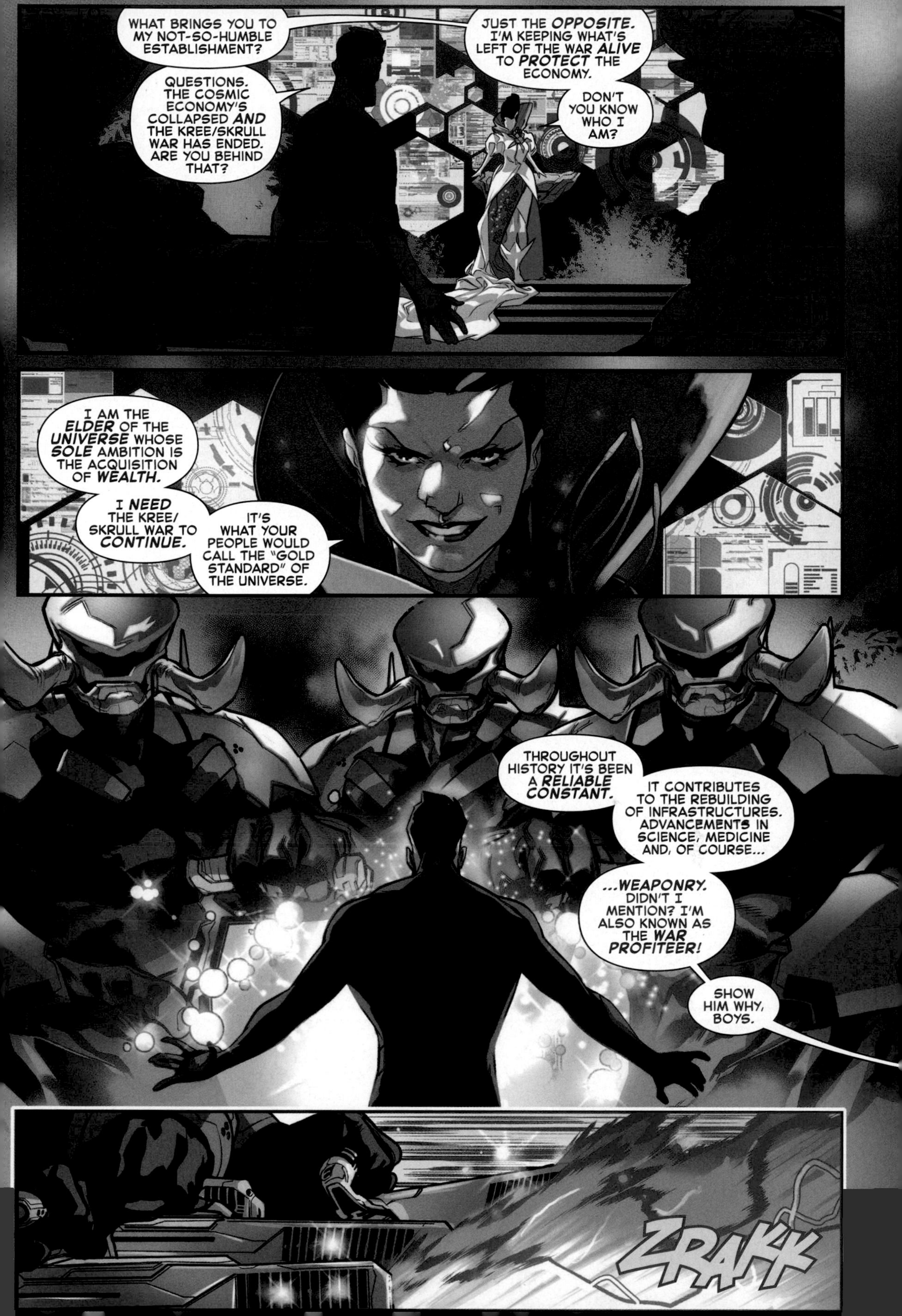
WHAT BRINGS YOU TO MY NOT-SO-HUMBLE ESTABLISHMENT?
QUESTIONS. THE COSMIC ECONOMY'S COLLAPSED AND THE KREE/SKRULL WAR HAS ENDED. ARE YOU BEHIND THAT?
JUST THE OPPOSITE. I'M KEEPING WHAT'S LEFT OF THE WAR ALIVE TO PROTECT THE ECONOMY.
DON'T YOU KNOW WHO I AM?
I AM THE ELDER OF THE UNIVERSE WHOSE SOLE AMBITION IS THE ACQUISITION OF WEALTH.
I NEED THE KREE/SKRULL WAR TO CONTINUE.
IT'S WHAT YOUR PEOPLE WOULD CALL THE "GOLD STANDARD" OF THE UNIVERSE.
THROUGHOUT HISTORY IT'S BEEN A RELIABLE CONSTANT.
IT CONTRIBUTES TO THE REBUILDING OF INFRASTRUCTURES. ADVANCEMENTS IN SCIENCE, MEDICINE AND, OF COURSE...
...WEAPONRY. DIDN'T I MENTION? I'M ALSO KNOWN AS THE WAR PROFITEER!
SHOW HIM WHY, BOYS.
ZRAKK

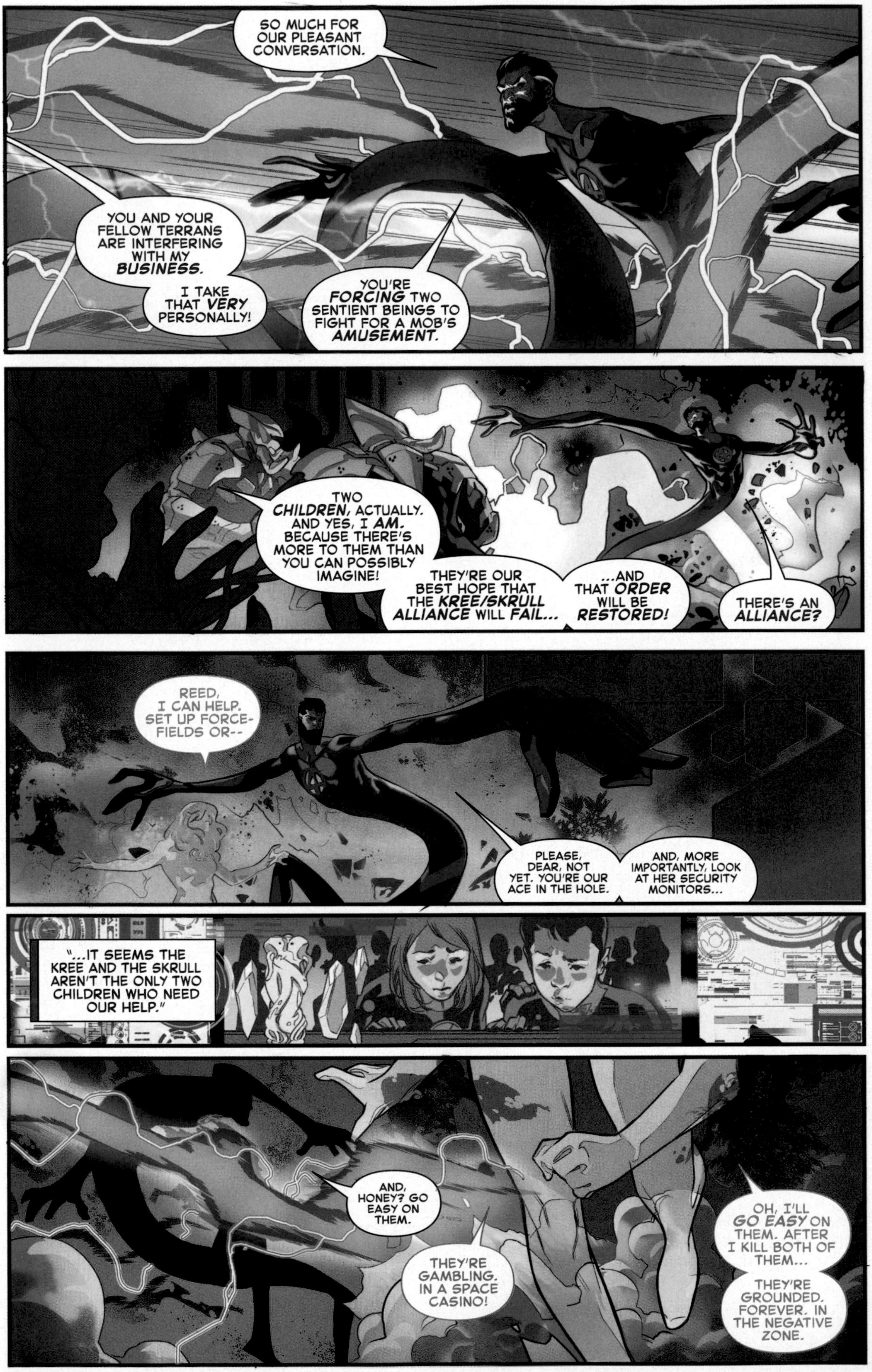
SO MUCH FOR OUR PLEASANT CONVERSATION.
YOU AND YOUR FELLOW TERRANS ARE INTERFERING WITH MY BUSINESS.
I TAKE THAT VERY PERSONALLY!
YOU'RE FORCING TWO SENTIENT BEINGS TO FIGHT FOR A MOB'S AMUSEMENT.
TWO CHILDREN, ACTUALLY. AND YES, I AM. BECAUSE THERE'S MORE TO THEM THAN YOU CAN POSSIBLY IMAGINE!
THEY'RE OUR BEST HOPE THAT THE KREE/SKRULL ALLIANCE WILL FAIL...
...AND THAT ORDER WILL BE RESTORED!
THERE'S AN ALLIANCE?
REED, I CAN HELP. SET UP FORCE-FIELDS OR--
PLEASE, DEAR, NOT YET. YOU'RE OUR ACE IN THE HOLE.
AND, MORE IMPORTANTLY, LOOK AT HER SECURITY MONITORS...
"...IT SEEMS THE KREE AND THE SKRULL AREN'T THE ONLY TWO CHILDREN WHO NEED OUR HELP."
AND, HONEY? GO EASY ON THEM.
THEY'RE GAMBLING. IN A SPACE CASINO!
OH, I'LL GO EASY ON THEM. AFTER I KILL BOTH OF THEM...
THEY'RE GROUNDED. FOREVER. IN THE NEGATIVE ZONE.

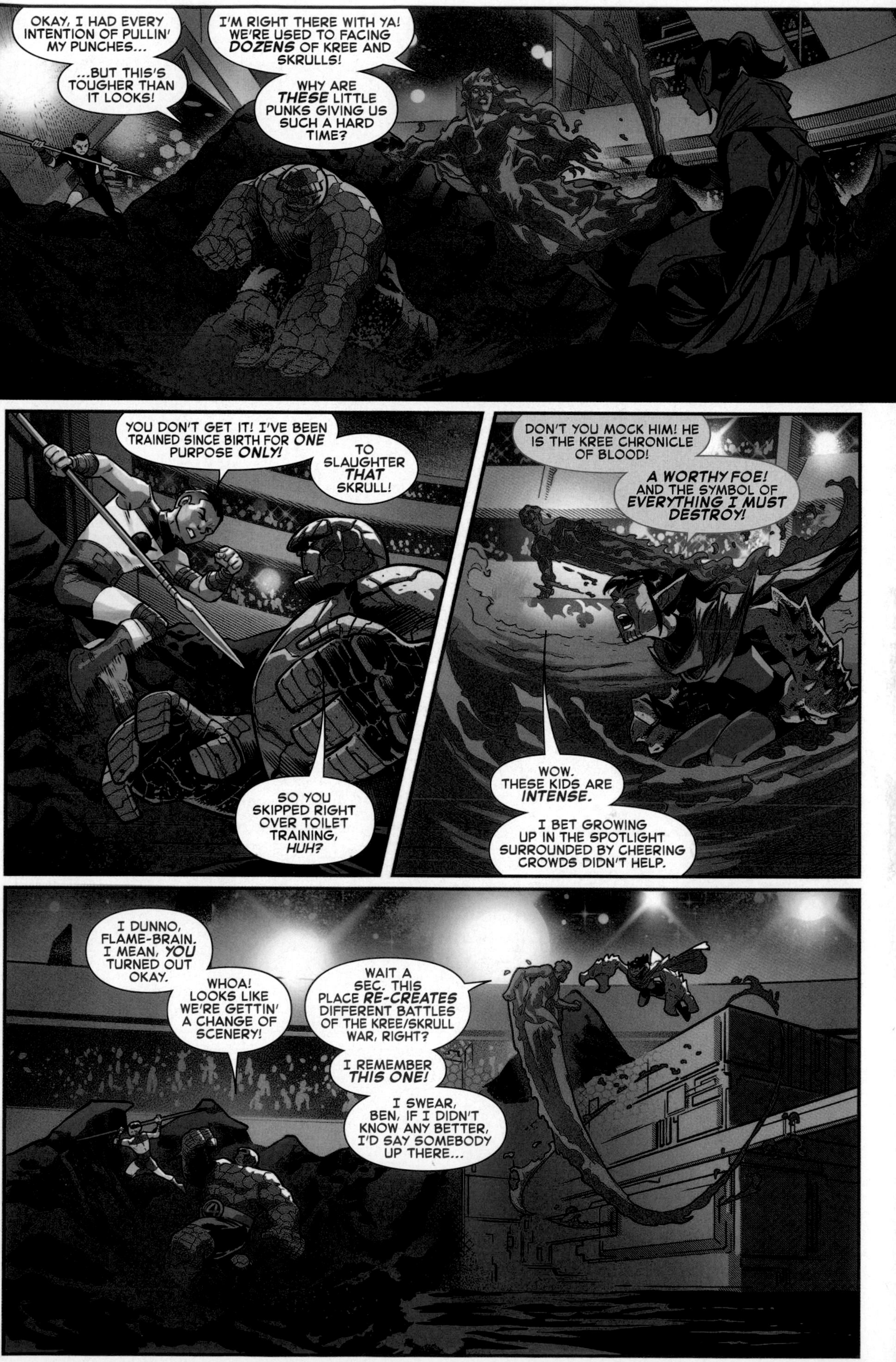
OKAY, I HAD EVERY INTENTION OF PULLIN' MY PUNCHES...
...BUT THIS'S TOUGHER THAN IT LOOKS!
I'M RIGHT THERE WITH YA! WE'RE USED TO FACING DOZENS OF KREE AND SKRULLS!
WHY ARE THESE LITTLE PUNKS GIVING US SUCH A HARD TIME?
YOU DON'T GET IT! I'VE BEEN TRAINED SINCE BIRTH FOR ONE PURPOSE ONLY!
TO SLAUGHTER THAT SKRULL!
SO YOU SKIPPED RIGHT OVER TOILET TRAINING, HUH?
DON'T YOU MOCK HIM! HE IS THE KREE CHRONICLE OF BLOOD!
A WORTHY FOE! AND THE SYMBOL OF EVERYTHING I MUST DESTROY!
WOW. THESE KIDS ARE INTENSE.
I BET GROWING UP IN THE SPOTLIGHT SURROUNDED BY CHEERING CROWDS DIDN'T HELP.
I DUNNO, FLAME-BRAIN. I MEAN, YOU TURNED OUT OKAY.
WHOA! LOOKS LIKE WE'RE GETTIN' A CHANGE OF SCENERY!
WAIT A SEC. THIS PLACE RE-CREATES DIFFERENT BATTLES OF THE KREE/SKRULL WAR, RIGHT?
I REMEMBER THIS ONE!
I SWEAR, BEN, IF I DIDN'T KNOW ANY BETTER, I'D SAY SOMEBODY UP THERE...

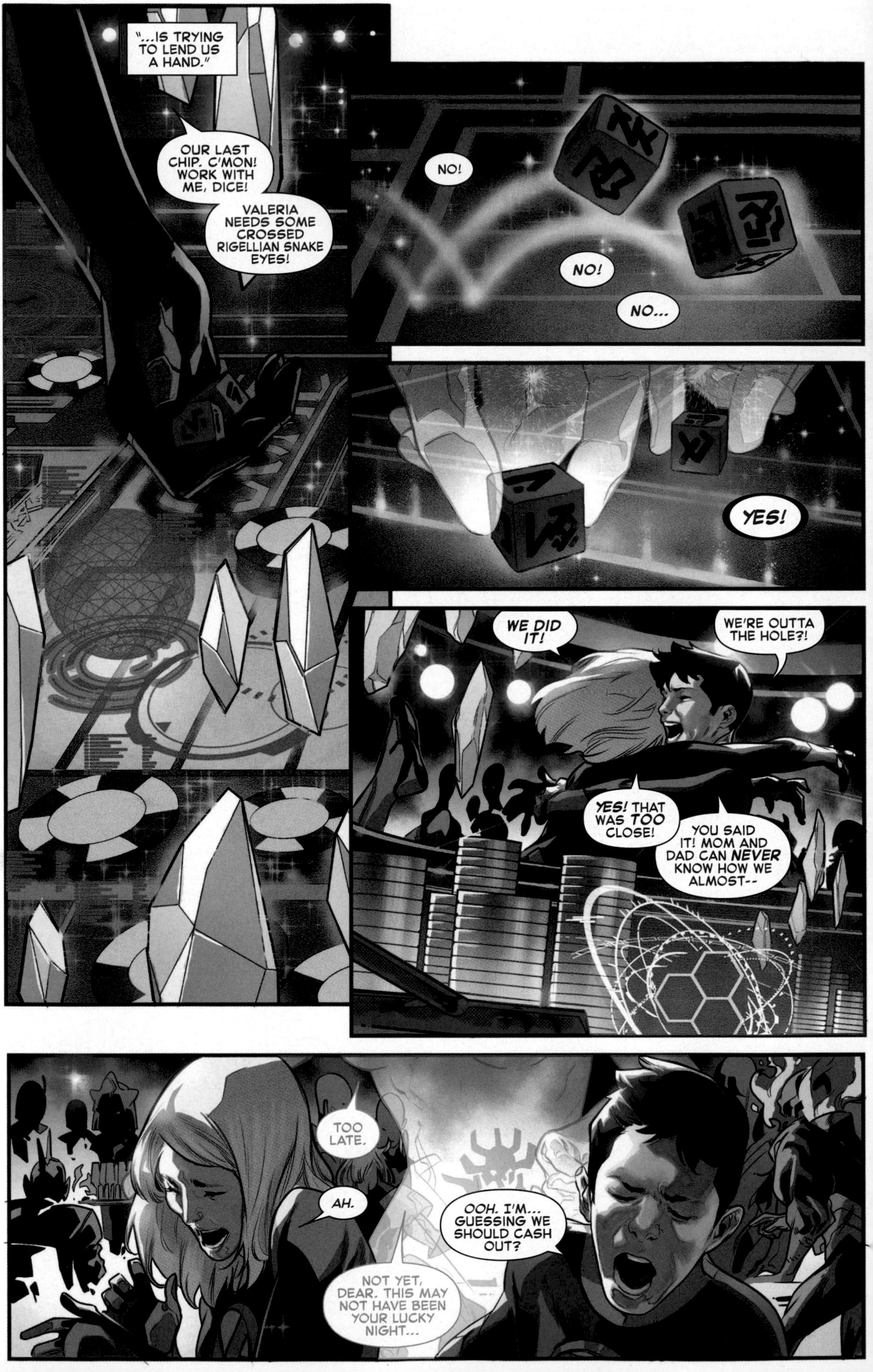
"...IS TRYING TO LEND US A HAND."
OUR LAST CHIP. C'MON! WORK WITH ME, DICE!
VALERIA NEEDS SOME CROSSED RIGELLIAN SNAKE EYES!
NO!
NO!
NO...
YES!
WE DID IT!
WE'RE OUTTA THE HOLE?!
YES! THAT WAS TOO CLOSE!
YOU SAID IT! MOM AND DAD CAN NEVER KNOW HOW WE ALMOST--
TOO LATE.
AH.
OOH. I'M... GUESSING WE SHOULD CASH OUT?
NOT YET, DEAR. THIS MAY NOT HAVE BEEN YOUR LUCKY NIGHT...

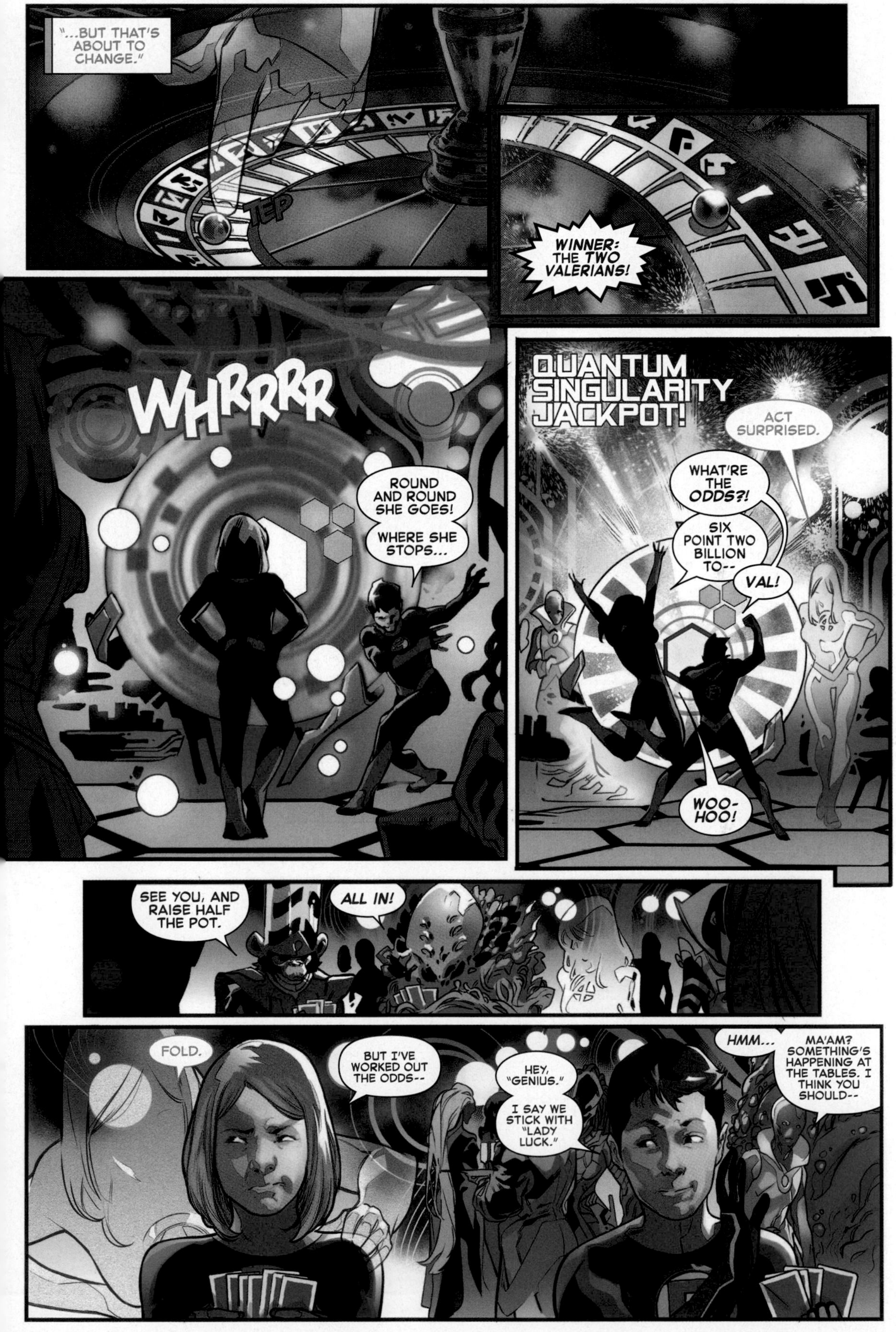
"...BUT THAT'S ABOUT TO CHANGE."
WINNER: THE TWO VALERIANS!
WHRRRR
ROUND AND ROUND SHE GOES!
WHERE SHE STOPS...
QUANTUM SINGULARITY JACKPOT!
ACT SURPRISED.
WHAT'RE THE ODDS?!
SIX POINT TWO BILLION TO--
VAL!
WOO-HOO!
SEE YOU, AND RAISE HALF THE POT.
ALL IN!
FOLD.
BUT I'VE WORKED OUT THE ODDS--
HEY, "GENIUS."
I SAY WE STICK WITH "LADY LUCK."
HMM...
MA'AM? SOMETHING'S HAPPENING AT THE TABLES. I THINK YOU SHOULD--

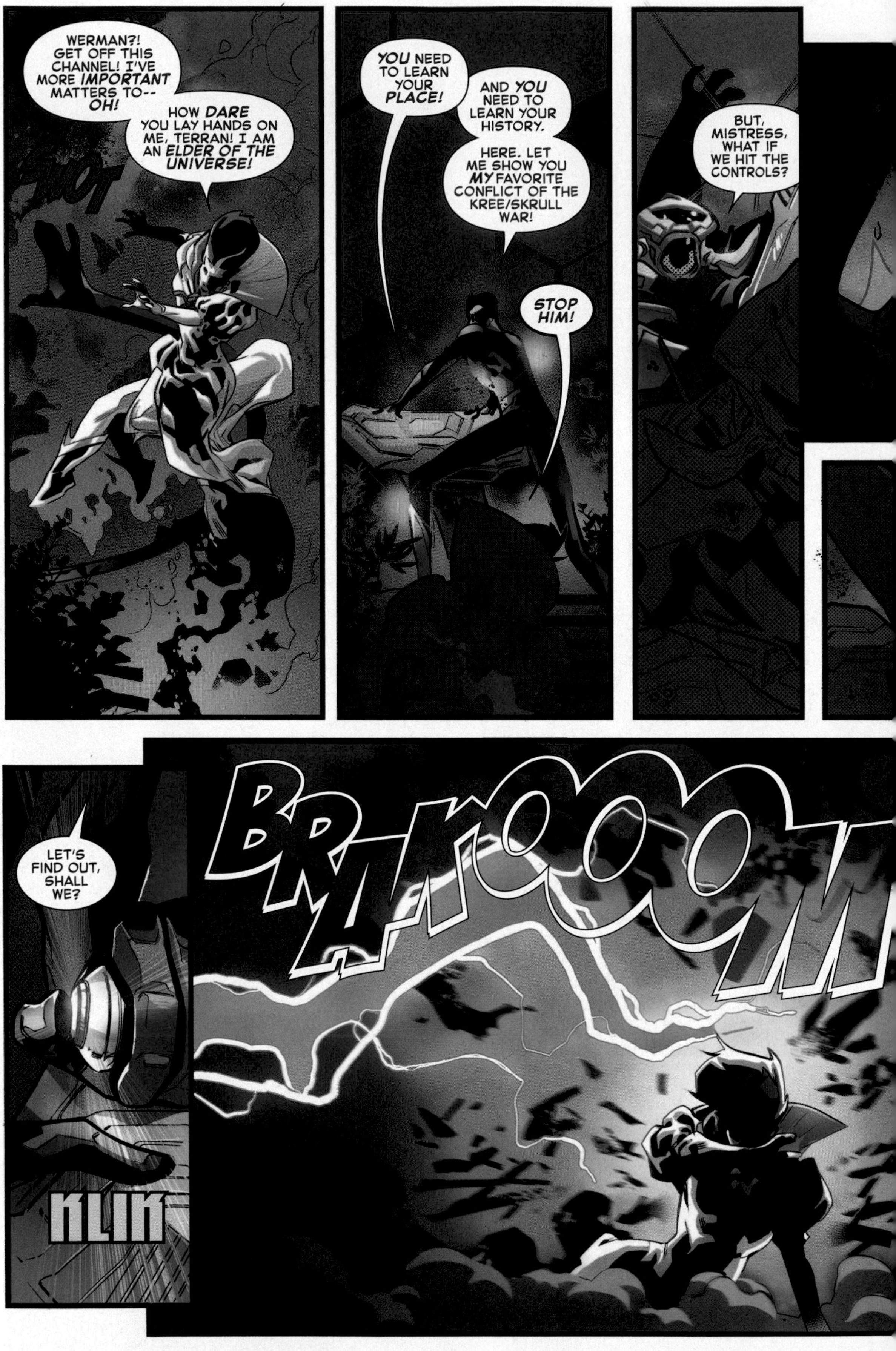
WERMAN?! GET OFF THIS CHANNEL! I'VE MORE IMPORTANT MATTERS TO-- OH!
HOW DARE YOU LAY HANDS ON ME, TERRAN! I AM AN ELDER OF THE UNIVERSE!
YOU NEED TO LEARN YOUR PLACE!
AND YOU NEED TO LEARN YOUR HISTORY.
HERE. LET ME SHOW YOU MY FAVORITE CONFLICT OF THE KREE/SKRULL WAR!
STOP HIM!
BUT, MISTRESS, WHAT IF WE HIT THE CONTROLS?
LET'S FIND OUT, SHALL WE?
KLIK

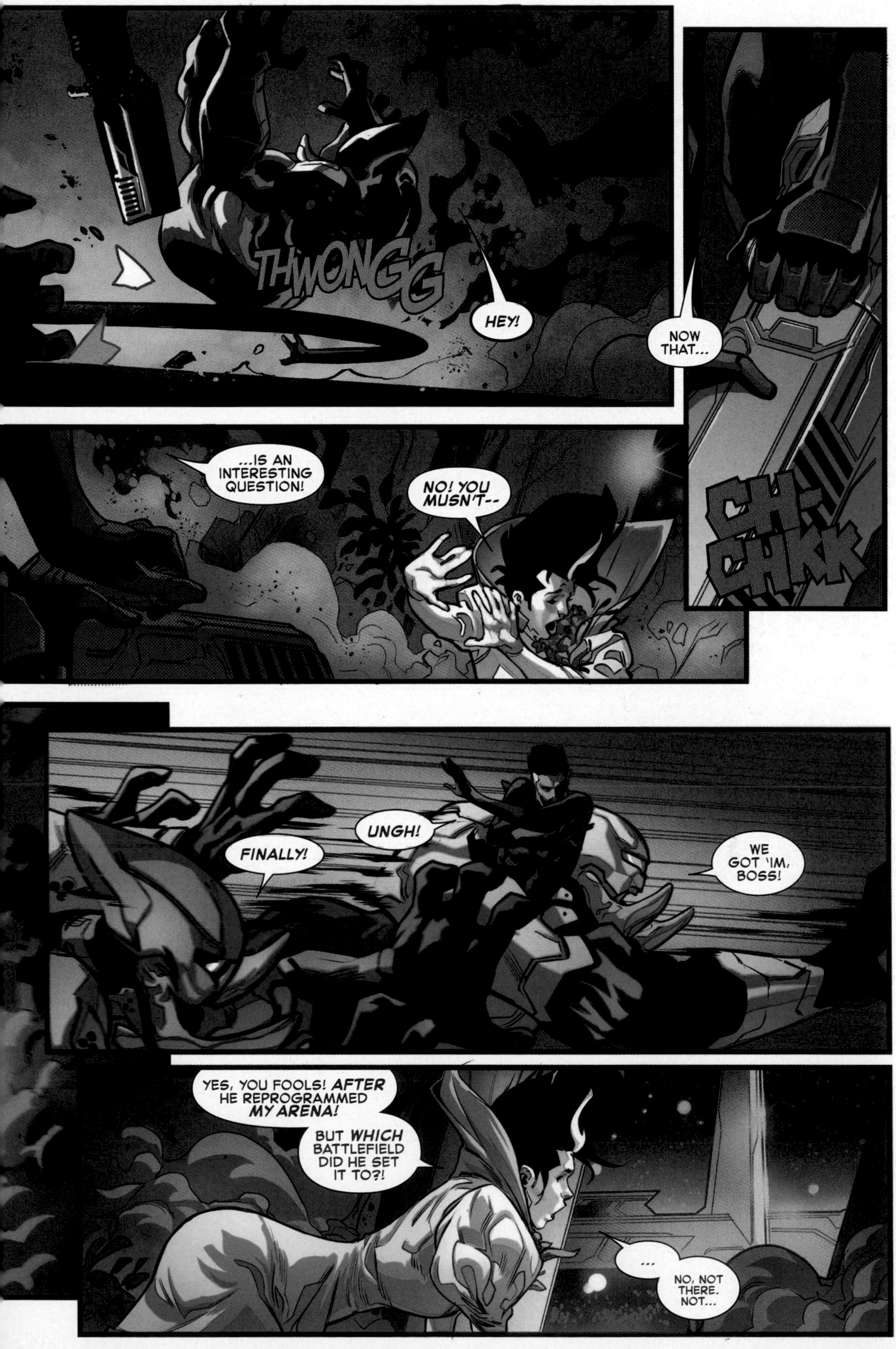
THWONGG
HEY!
NOW THAT...
CH-CHKK
...IS AN INTERESTING QUESTION!
NO! YOU MUSN'T--
FINALLY!
UNGH!
WE GOT 'IM, BOSS!
YES, YOU FOOLS! AFTER HE REPROGRAMMED MY ARENA!
BUT WHICH BATTLEFIELD DID HE SET IT TO?!
...
NO, NOT THERE. NOT...

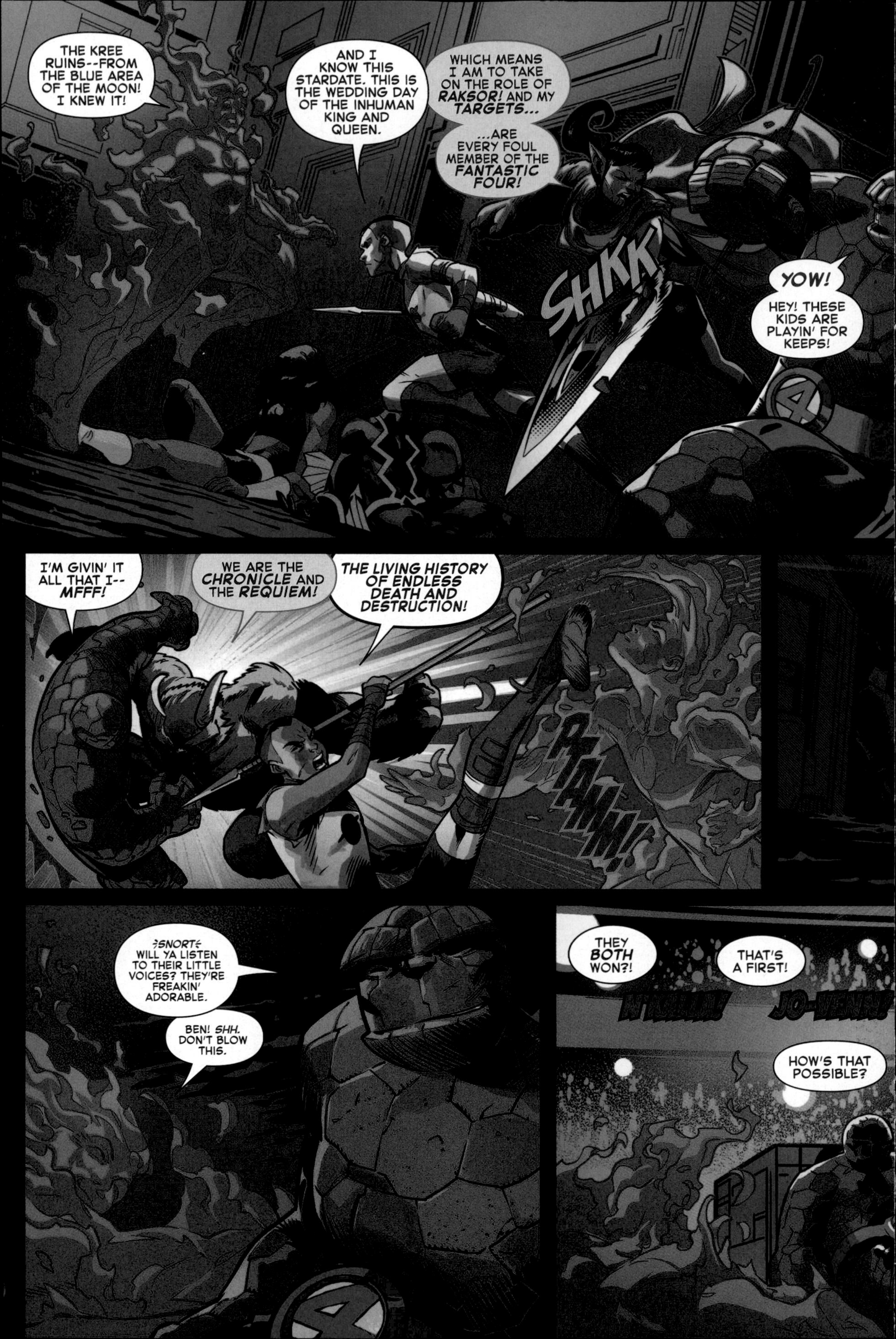
THE KREE RUINS--FROM THE BLUE AREA OF THE MOON! I KNEW IT!
AND I KNOW THIS STARDATE. THIS IS THE WEDDING DAY OF THE INHUMAN KING AND QUEEN.
WHICH MEANS I AM TO TAKE ON THE ROLE OF RAKSOR! AND MY TARGETS...
...ARE EVERY FOUL MEMBER OF THE FANTASTIC FOUR!
SHKK
YOW!
HEY! THESE KIDS ARE PLAYIN' FOR KEEPS!
I'M GIVIN' IT ALL THAT I-- MFFF!
WE ARE THE CHRONICLE AND THE REQUIEM!
THE LIVING HISTORY OF ENDLESS DEATH AND DESTRUCTION!
SNORT WILL YA LISTEN TO THEIR LITTLE VOICES? THEY'RE FREAKIN' ADORABLE.
BEN! SHH. DON'T BLOW THIS.
THEY BOTH WON?!
THAT'S A FIRST!
HOW'S THAT POSSIBLE?

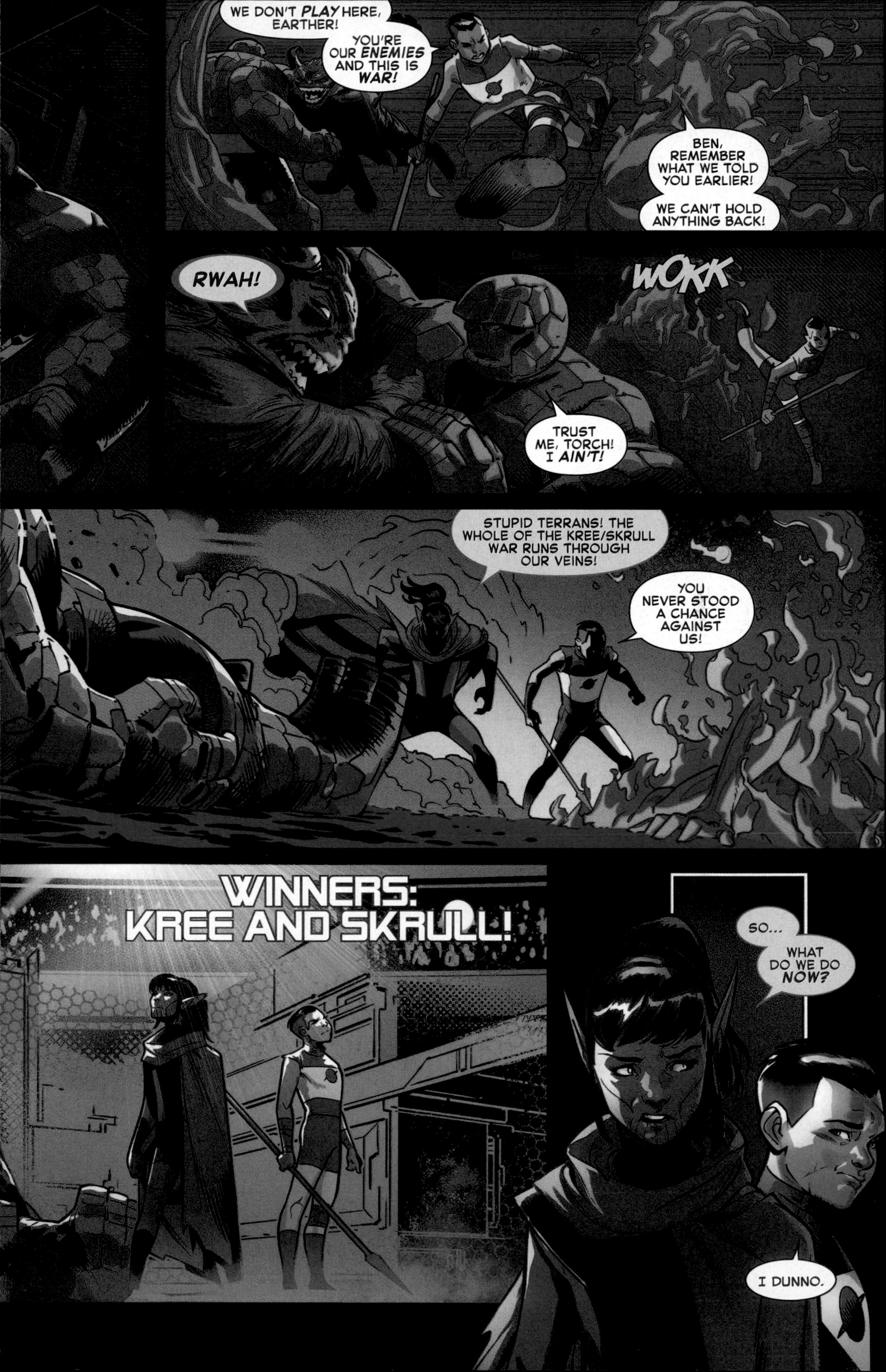
WE DON'T PLAY HERE, EARTHER!
YOU'RE OUR ENEMIES AND THIS IS WAR!
BEN, REMEMBER WHAT WE TOLD YOU EARLIER!
WE CAN'T HOLD ANYTHING BACK!
RWAH!
WOKK
TRUST ME, TORCH! I AIN'T!
STUPID TERRANS! THE WHOLE OF THE KREE/SKRULL WAR RUNS THROUGH OUR VEINS!
YOU NEVER STOOD A CHANCE AGAINST US!
WINNERS: KREE AND SKRULL!
SO...
WHAT DO WE DO NOW?
I DUNNO.

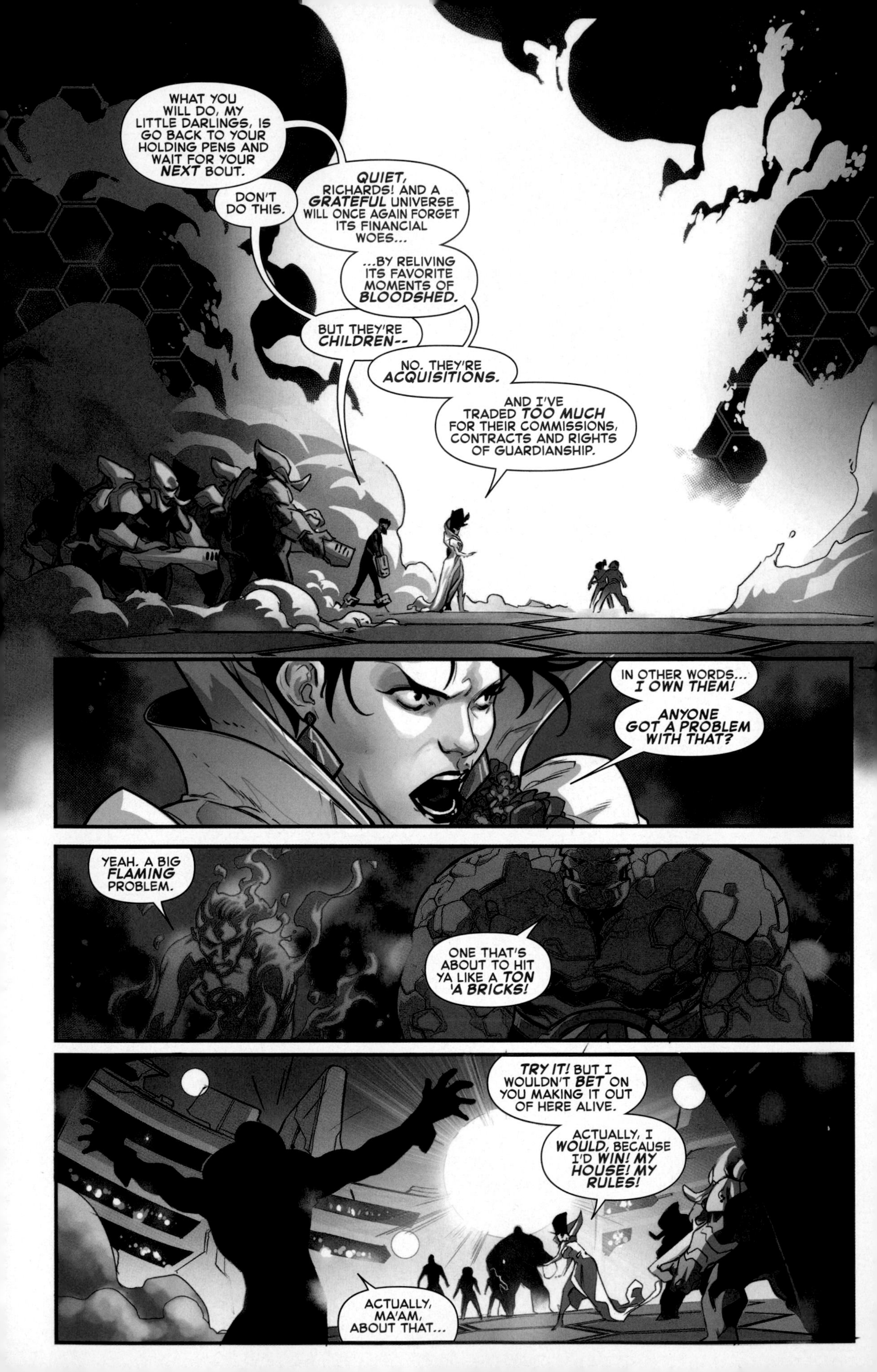
WHAT YOU WILL DO, MY LITTLE DARLINGS, IS GO BACK TO YOUR HOLDING PENS AND WAIT FOR YOUR NEXT BOUT.
DON'T DO THIS.
QUIET, RICHARDS! AND A GRATEFUL UNIVERSE WILL ONCE AGAIN FORGET ITS FINANCIAL WOES...
...BY RELIVING ITS FAVORITE MOMENTS OF BLOODSHED.
BUT THEY'RE CHILDREN--
NO. THEY'RE ACQUISITIONS.
AND I'VE TRADED TOO MUCH FOR THEIR COMMISSIONS, CONTRACTS AND RIGHTS OF GUARDIANSHIP.
IN OTHER WORDS... I OWN THEM!
ANYONE GOT A PROBLEM WITH THAT?
YEAH. A BIG FLAMING PROBLEM.
ONE THAT'S ABOUT TO HIT YA LIKE A TON 'A BRICKS!
TRY IT! BUT I WOULDN'T BET ON YOU MAKING IT OUT OF HERE ALIVE.
ACTUALLY, I WOULD, BECAUSE I'D WIN! MY HOUSE! MY RULES!
ACTUALLY, MA'AM, ABOUT THAT...

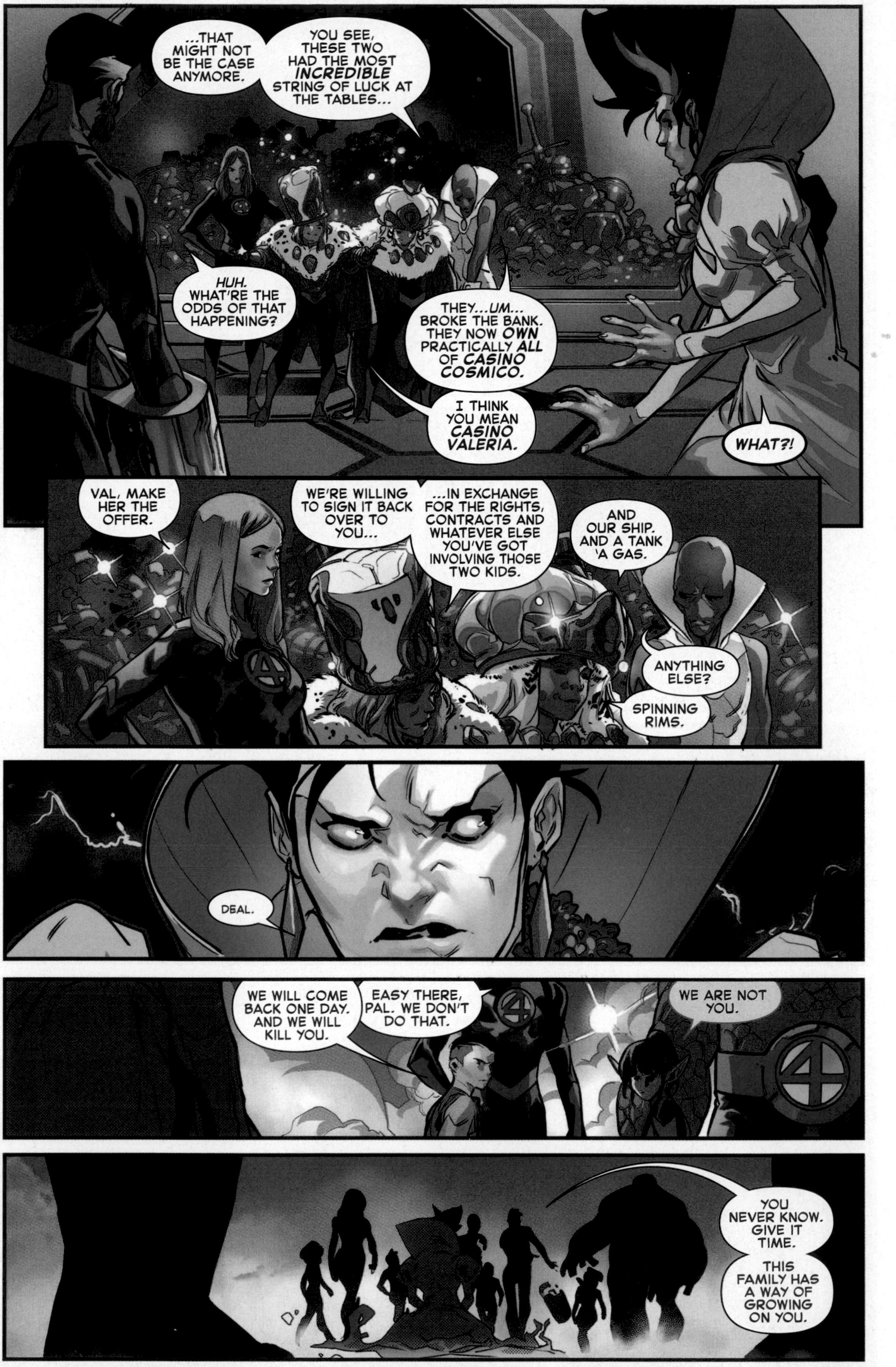
...THAT MIGHT NOT BE THE CASE ANYMORE.
YOU SEE, THESE TWO HAD THE MOST *INCREDIBLE* STRING OF LUCK AT THE TABLES...
HUH. WHAT'RE THE ODDS OF THAT HAPPENING?
THEY...*UM*... BROKE THE BANK. THEY NOW *OWN* PRACTICALLY *ALL* OF *CASINO COSMICO.*
I THINK YOU MEAN *CASINO VALERIA.*
WHAT?!
VAL, MAKE HER THE OFFER.
WE'RE WILLING TO SIGN IT BACK OVER TO YOU...
...IN EXCHANGE FOR THE RIGHTS, CONTRACTS AND WHATEVER ELSE YOU'VE GOT INVOLVING THOSE TWO KIDS.
AND OUR SHIP. AND A TANK 'A GAS.
ANYTHING ELSE?
SPINNING RIMS.
DEAL.
WE WILL COME BACK ONE DAY. AND WE WILL KILL YOU.
EASY THERE, PAL. WE DON'T DO THAT.
WE ARE NOT YOU.
YOU NEVER KNOW. GIVE IT TIME.
THIS FAMILY HAS A WAY OF GROWING ON YOU.

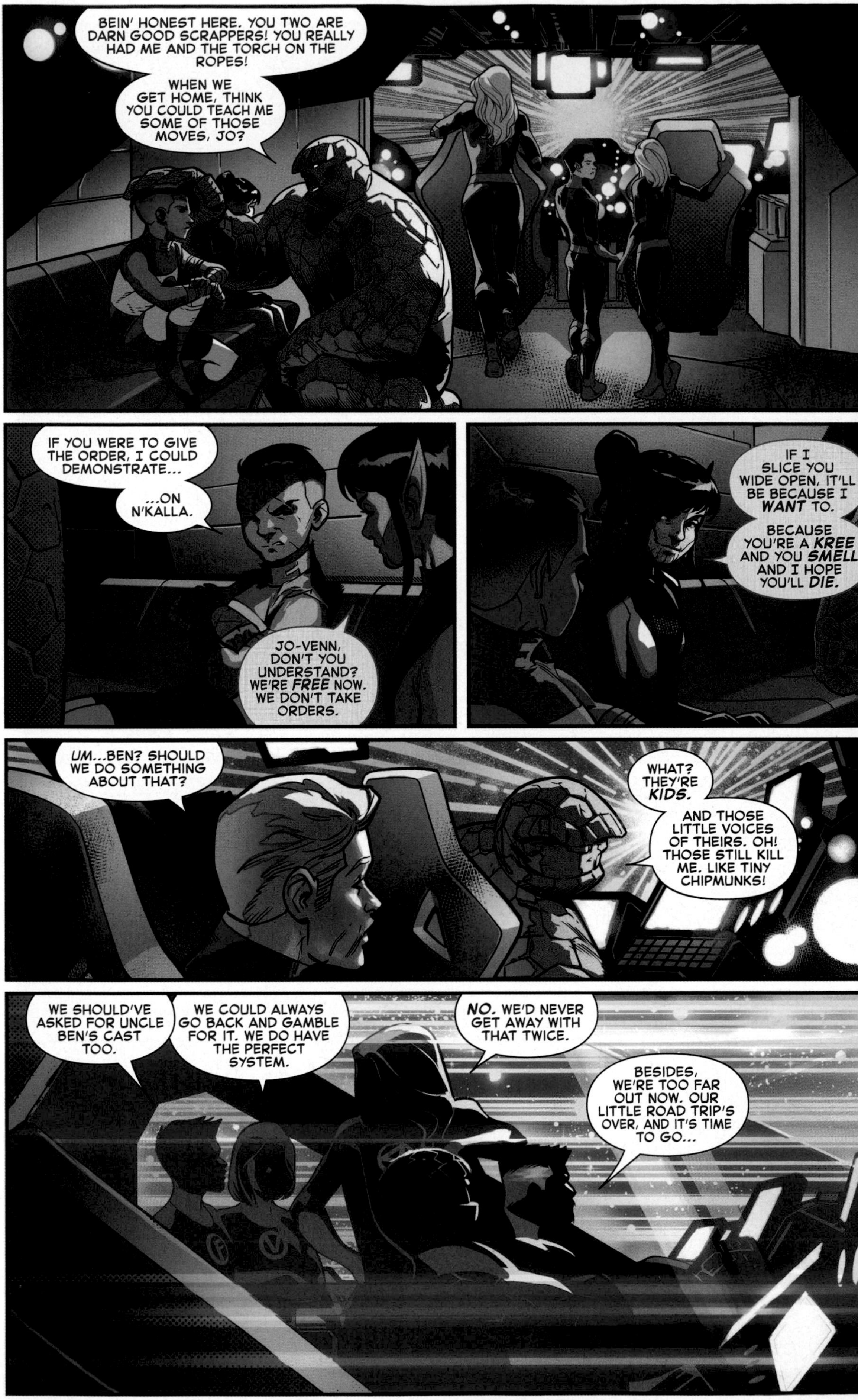
BEIN' HONEST HERE. YOU TWO ARE DARN GOOD SCRAPPERS! YOU REALLY HAD ME AND THE TORCH ON THE ROPES!
WHEN WE GET HOME, THINK YOU COULD TEACH ME SOME OF THOSE MOVES, JO?
IF YOU WERE TO GIVE THE ORDER, I COULD DEMONSTRATE...
...ON N'KALLA.
JO-VENN, DON'T YOU UNDERSTAND? WE'RE *FREE* NOW. WE DON'T TAKE ORDERS.
IF I SLICE YOU WIDE OPEN, IT'LL BE BECAUSE I *WANT* TO.
BECAUSE YOU'RE A *KREE* AND YOU *SMELL* AND I HOPE YOU'LL *DIE.*
UM...BEN? SHOULD WE DO SOMETHING ABOUT THAT?
WHAT? THEY'RE *KIDS.*
AND THOSE LITTLE VOICES OF THEIRS. OH! THOSE STILL KILL ME. LIKE TINY CHIPMUNKS!
WE SHOULD'VE ASKED FOR UNCLE BEN'S CAST TOO.
WE COULD ALWAYS GO BACK AND GAMBLE FOR IT. WE DO HAVE THE PERFECT SYSTEM.
NO. WE'D NEVER GET AWAY WITH THAT TWICE.
BESIDES, WE'RE TOO FAR OUT NOW. OUR LITTLE ROAD TRIP'S OVER, AND IT'S TIME TO GO...

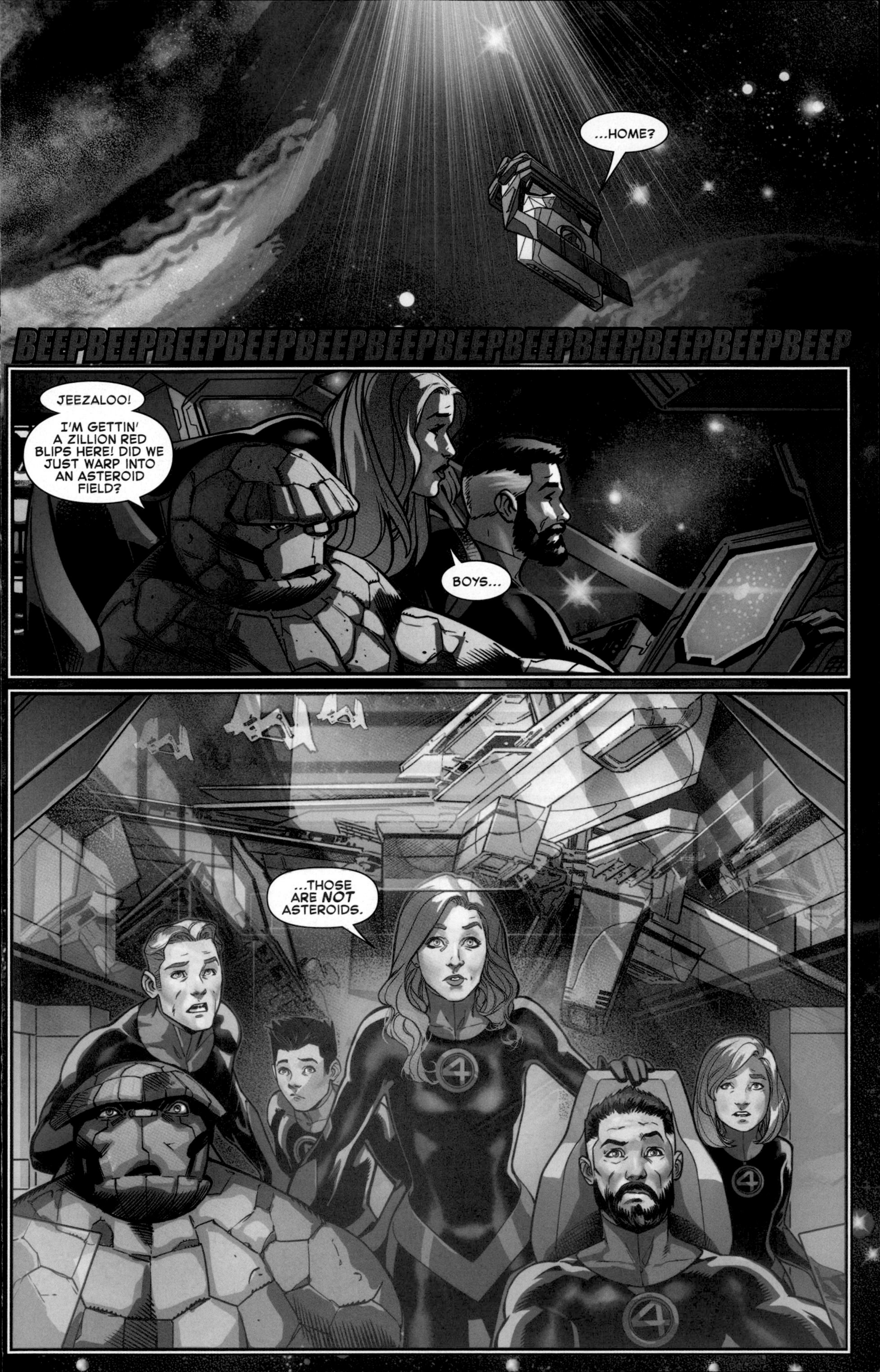
...HOME?
BEEPBEEPBEEPBEEPBEEPBEEPBEEPBEEPBEEPBEEPBEEPBEEP
JEEZALOO!
I'M GETTIN' A ZILLION RED BLIPS HERE! DID WE JUST WARP INTO AN ASTEROID FIELD?
BOYS...
...THOSE ARE NOT ASTEROIDS.

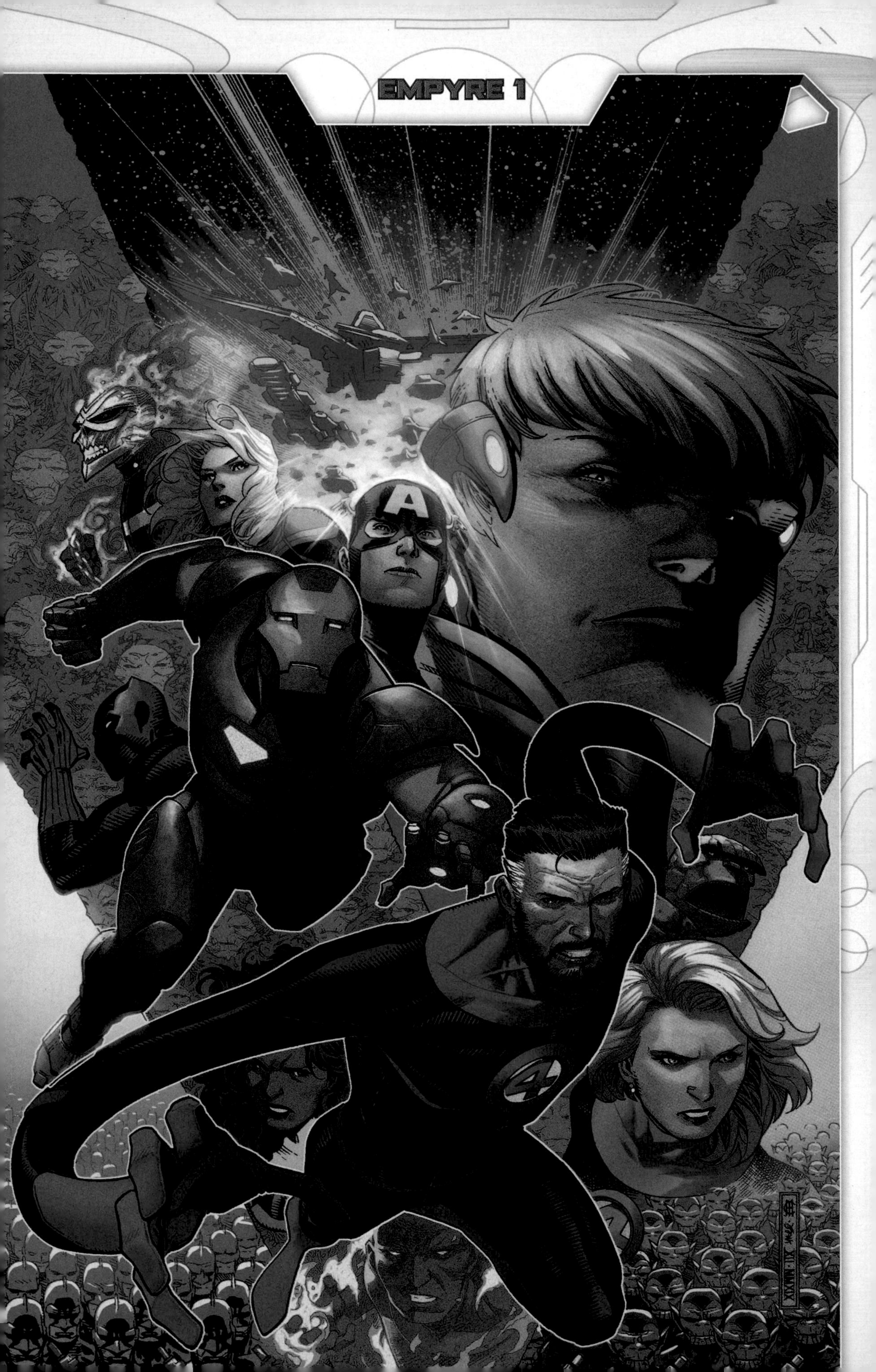
EMPYRE 1

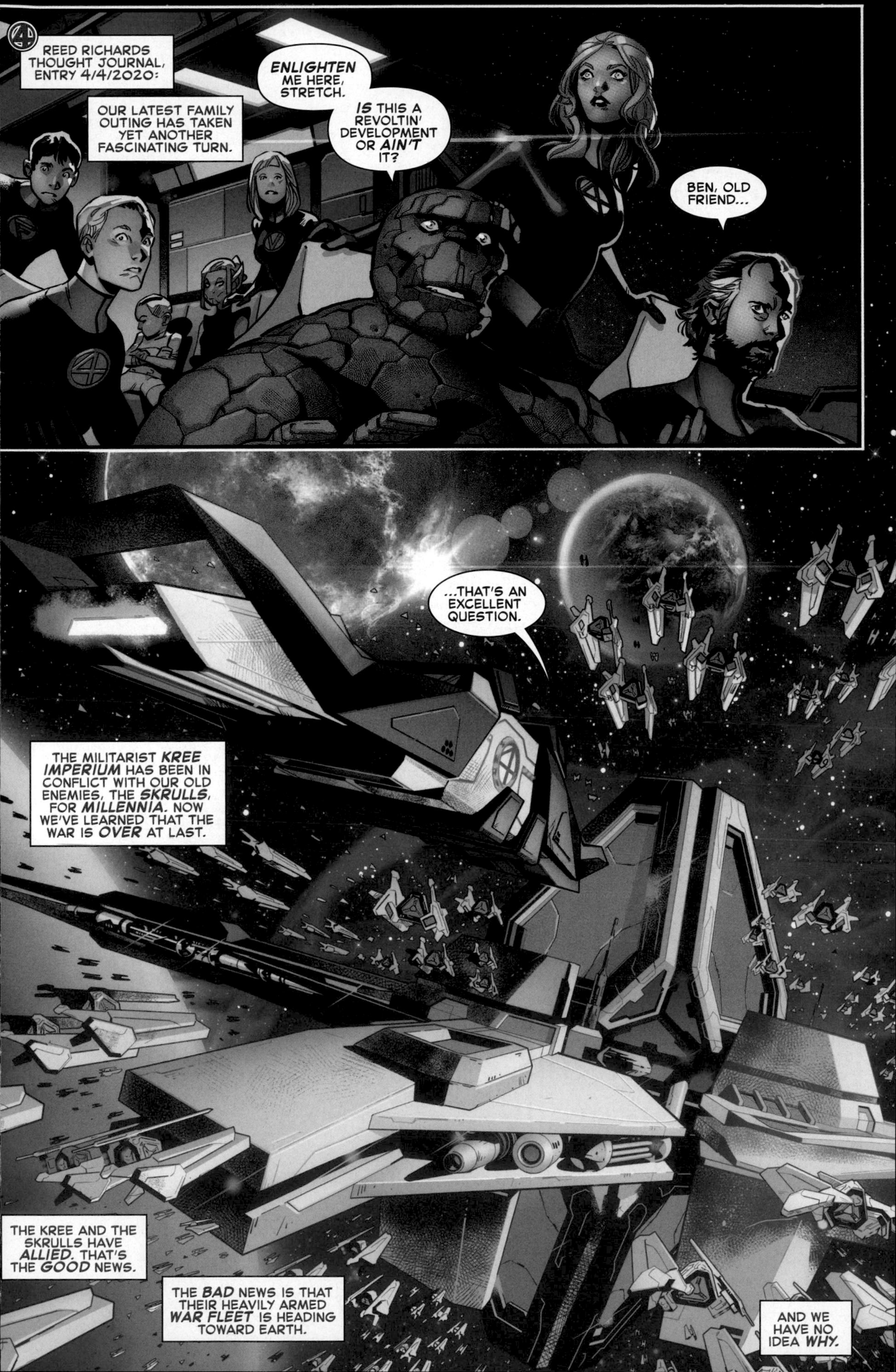
REED RICHARDS THOUGHT JOURNAL, ENTRY 4/4/2020:
OUR LATEST FAMILY OUTING HAS TAKEN YET ANOTHER FASCINATING TURN.
ENLIGHTEN ME HERE, STRETCH.
IS THIS A REVOLTIN' DEVELOPMENT OR AIN'T IT?
BEN, OLD FRIEND...
...THAT'S AN EXCELLENT QUESTION.
THE MILITARIST KREE IMPERIUM HAS BEEN IN CONFLICT WITH OUR OLD ENEMIES, THE SKRULLS, FOR MILLENNIA. NOW WE'VE LEARNED THAT THE WAR IS OVER AT LAST.
THE KREE AND THE SKRULLS HAVE ALLIED. THAT'S THE GOOD NEWS.
THE BAD NEWS IS THAT THEIR HEAVILY ARMED WAR FLEET IS HEADING TOWARD EARTH.
AND WE HAVE NO IDEA WHY.

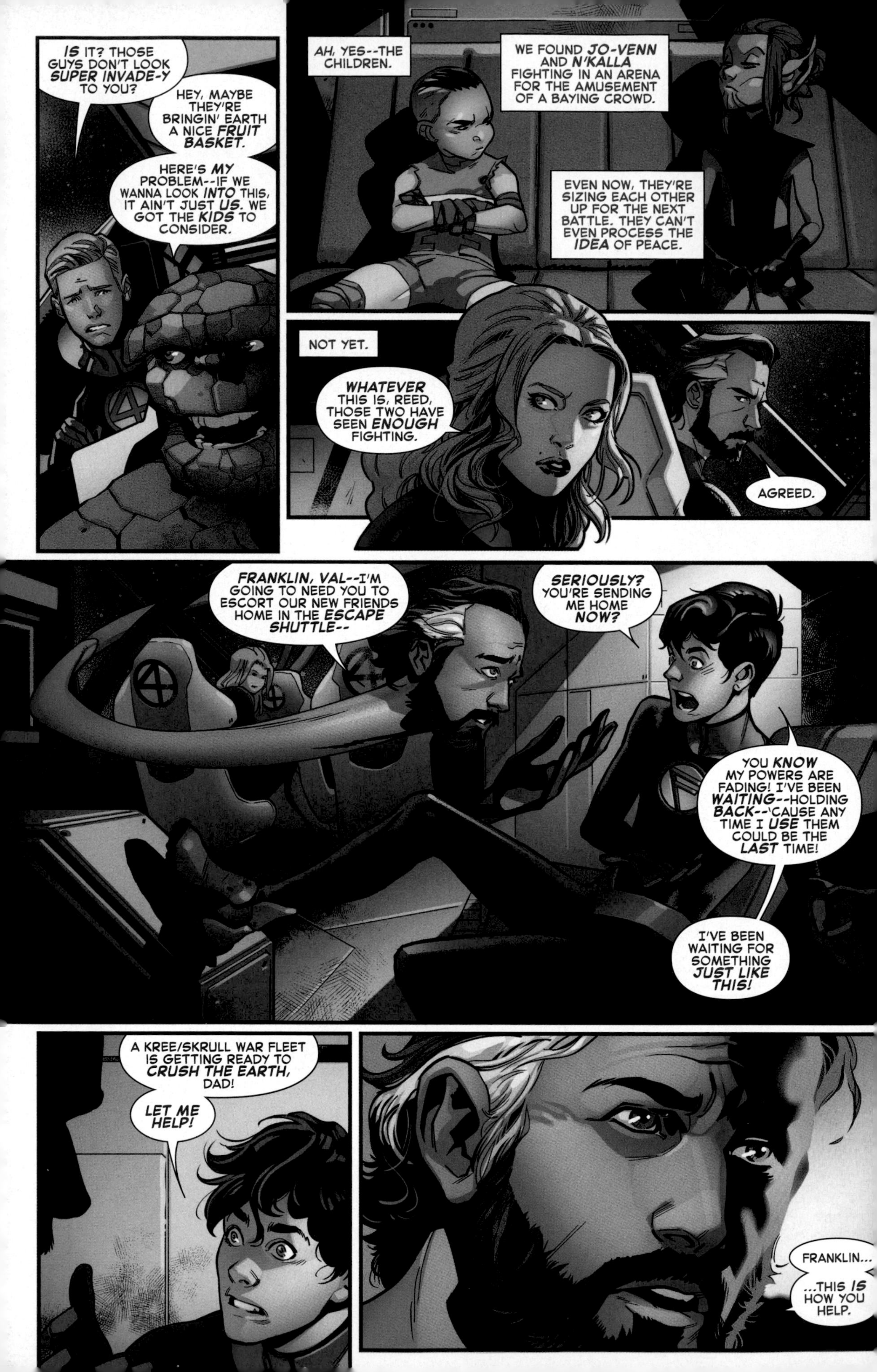
IS IT? THOSE GUYS DON'T LOOK SUPER INVADE-Y TO YOU?
HEY, MAYBE THEY'RE BRINGIN' EARTH A NICE FRUIT BASKET.
HERE'S MY PROBLEM--IF WE WANNA LOOK INTO THIS, IT AIN'T JUST US. WE GOT THE KIDS TO CONSIDER.
AH, YES--THE CHILDREN.
WE FOUND JO-VENN AND N'KALLA FIGHTING IN AN ARENA FOR THE AMUSEMENT OF A BAYING CROWD.
EVEN NOW, THEY'RE SIZING EACH OTHER UP FOR THE NEXT BATTLE. THEY CAN'T EVEN PROCESS THE IDEA OF PEACE.
NOT YET.
WHATEVER THIS IS, REED, THOSE TWO HAVE SEEN ENOUGH FIGHTING.
AGREED.
FRANKLIN, VAL--I'M GOING TO NEED YOU TO ESCORT OUR NEW FRIENDS HOME IN THE ESCAPE SHUTTLE--
SERIOUSLY? YOU'RE SENDING ME HOME NOW?
YOU KNOW MY POWERS ARE FADING! I'VE BEEN WAITING--HOLDING BACK--'CAUSE ANY TIME I USE THEM COULD BE THE LAST TIME!
I'VE BEEN WAITING FOR SOMETHING JUST LIKE THIS!
A KREE/SKRULL WAR FLEET IS GETTING READY TO CRUSH THE EARTH, DAD!
LET ME HELP!
FRANKLIN...
...THIS IS HOW YOU HELP.

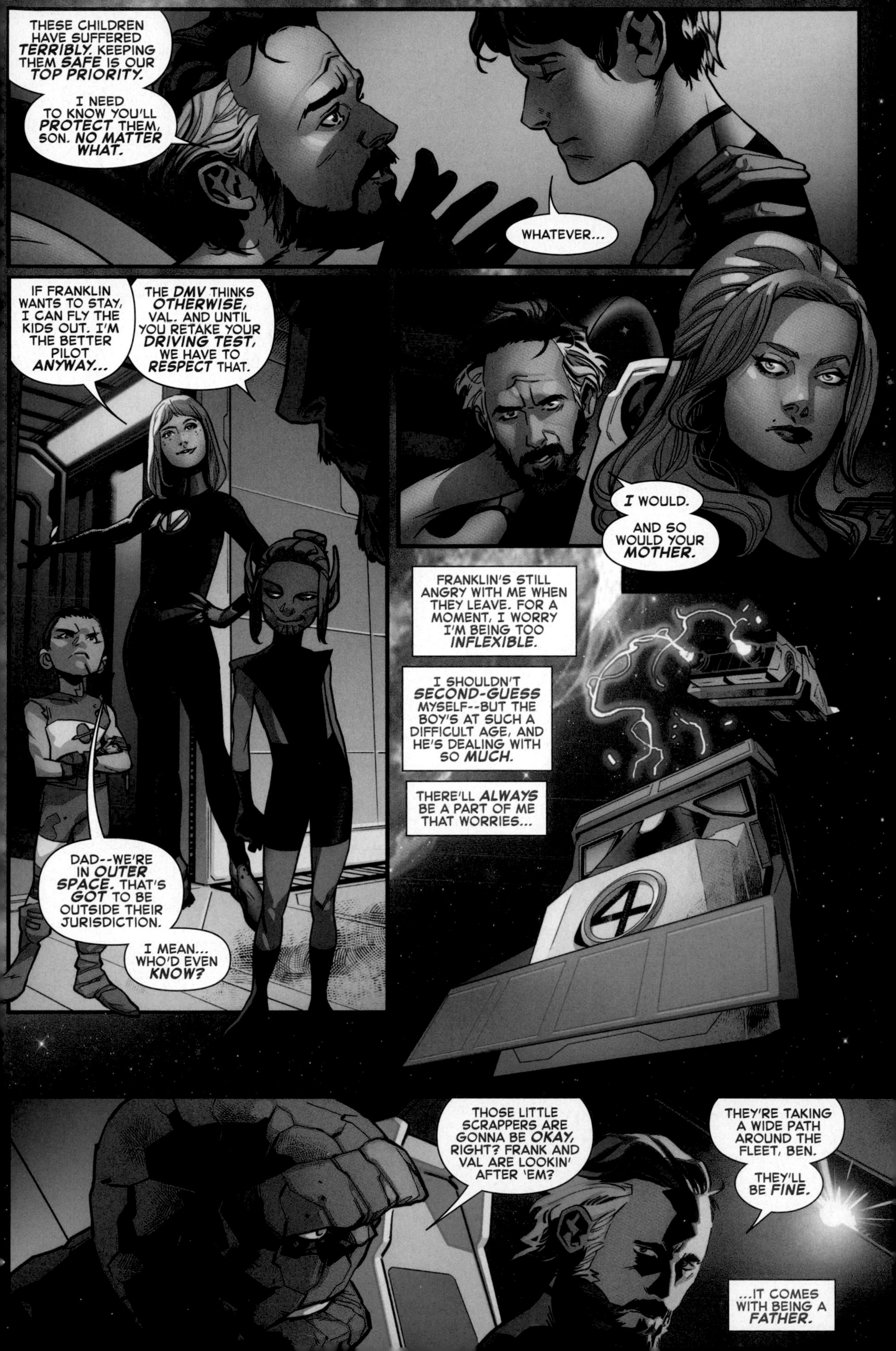
THESE CHILDREN HAVE SUFFERED TERRIBLY. KEEPING THEM SAFE IS OUR TOP PRIORITY.
I NEED TO KNOW YOU'LL PROTECT THEM, SON. NO MATTER WHAT.
WHATEVER...
IF FRANKLIN WANTS TO STAY, I CAN FLY THE KIDS OUT. I'M THE BETTER PILOT ANYWAY...
THE DMV THINKS OTHERWISE, VAL. AND UNTIL YOU RETAKE YOUR DRIVING TEST, WE HAVE TO RESPECT THAT.
DAD--WE'RE IN OUTER SPACE. THAT'S GOT TO BE OUTSIDE THEIR JURISDICTION.
I MEAN... WHO'D EVEN KNOW?
I WOULD.
AND SO WOULD YOUR MOTHER.
FRANKLIN'S STILL ANGRY WITH ME WHEN THEY LEAVE. FOR A MOMENT, I WORRY I'M BEING TOO INFLEXIBLE.
I SHOULDN'T SECOND-GUESS MYSELF--BUT THE BOY'S AT SUCH A DIFFICULT AGE, AND HE'S DEALING WITH SO MUCH.
THERE'LL ALWAYS BE A PART OF ME THAT WORRIES...
THOSE LITTLE SCRAPPERS ARE GONNA BE OKAY, RIGHT? FRANK AND VAL ARE LOOKIN' AFTER 'EM?
THEY'RE TAKING A WIDE PATH AROUND THE FLEET, BEN.
THEY'LL BE FINE.
...IT COMES WITH BEING A FATHER.

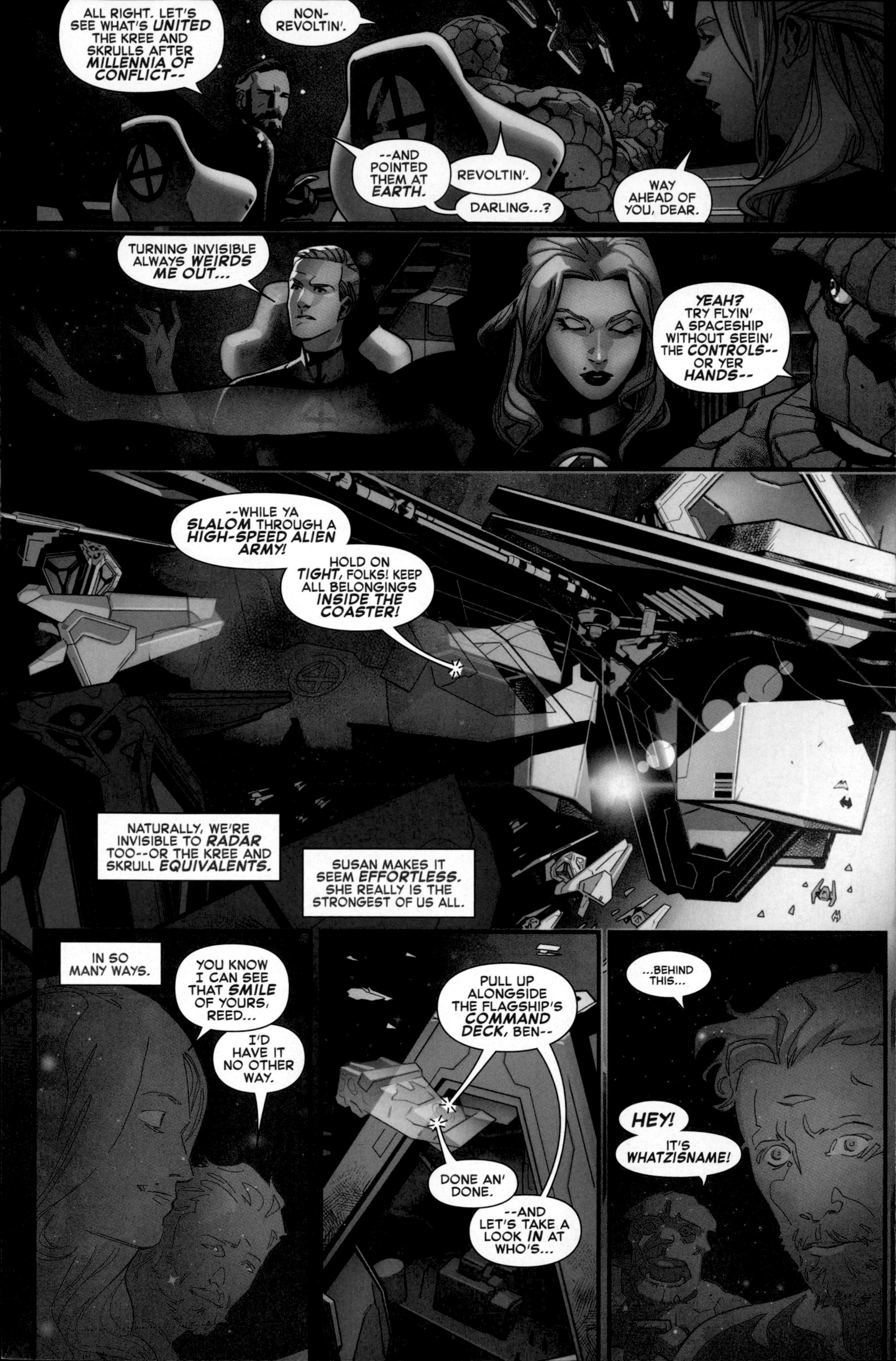
ALL RIGHT. LET'S SEE WHAT'S UNITED THE KREE AND SKRULLS AFTER MILLENNIA OF CONFLICT--
NON-REVOLTIN'.
--AND POINTED THEM AT EARTH.
REVOLTIN'.
DARLING...?
WAY AHEAD OF YOU, DEAR.
TURNING INVISIBLE ALWAYS WEIRDS ME OUT...
YEAH? TRY FLYIN' A SPACESHIP WITHOUT SEEIN' THE CONTROLS-- OR YER HANDS--
--WHILE YA SLALOM THROUGH A HIGH-SPEED ALIEN ARMY!
HOLD ON TIGHT, FOLKS! KEEP ALL BELONGINGS INSIDE THE COASTER!
NATURALLY, WE'RE INVISIBLE TO RADAR TOO--OR THE KREE AND SKRULL EQUIVALENTS.
SUSAN MAKES IT SEEM EFFORTLESS. SHE REALLY IS THE STRONGEST OF US ALL.
IN SO MANY WAYS.
YOU KNOW I CAN SEE THAT SMILE OF YOURS, REED...
I'D HAVE IT NO OTHER WAY.
PULL UP ALONGSIDE THE FLAGSHIP'S COMMAND DECK, BEN--
DONE AN' DONE.
--AND LET'S TAKE A LOOK IN AT WHO'S...
...BEHIND THIS...
HEY! IT'S WHATZISNAME!

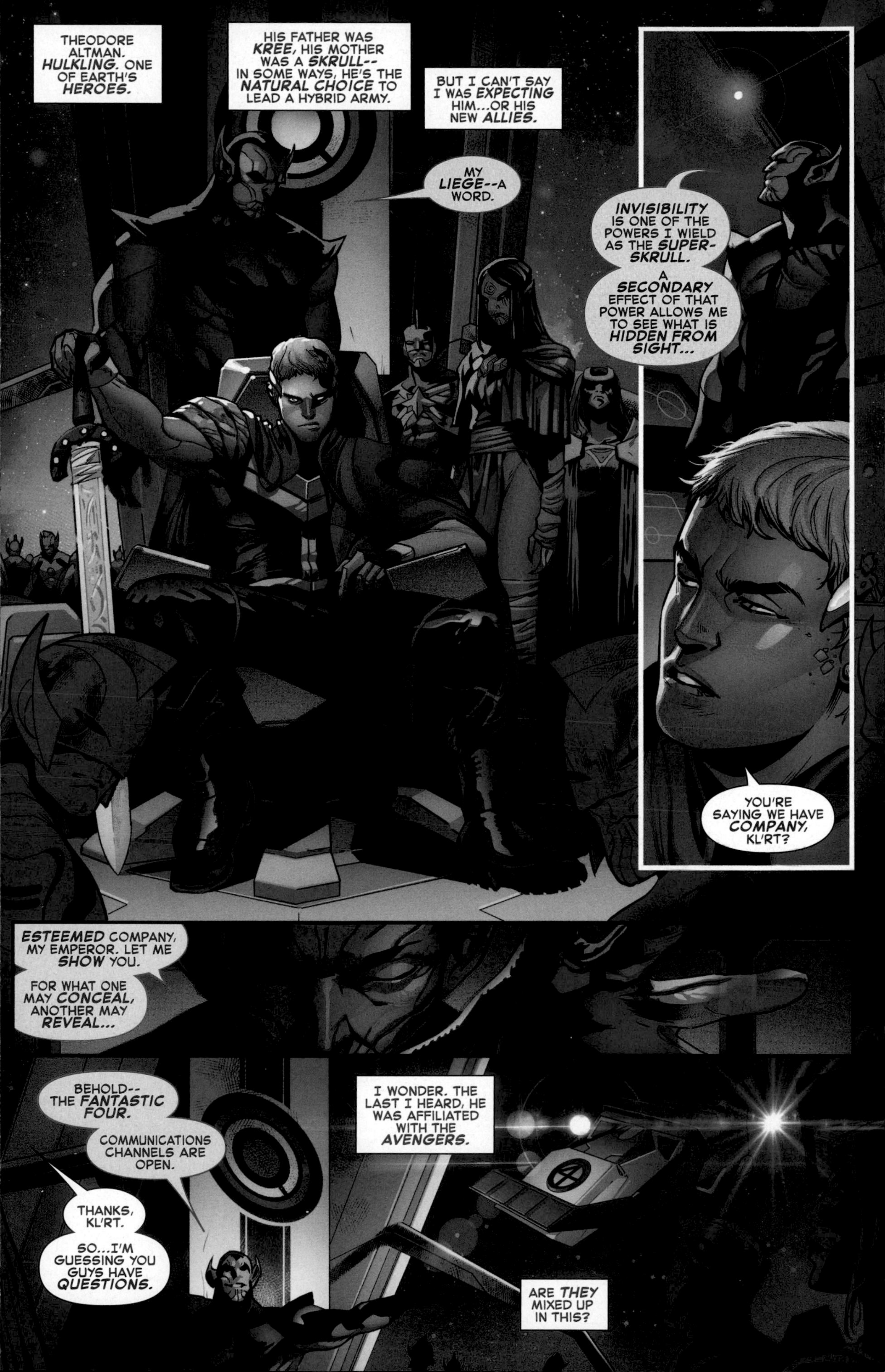
THEODORE ALTMAN. HULKLING. ONE OF EARTH'S HEROES.
HIS FATHER WAS KREE, HIS MOTHER WAS A SKRULL-- IN SOME WAYS, HE'S THE NATURAL CHOICE TO LEAD A HYBRID ARMY.
BUT I CAN'T SAY I WAS EXPECTING HIM...OR HIS NEW ALLIES.
MY LIEGE--A WORD.
INVISIBILITY IS ONE OF THE POWERS I WIELD AS THE SUPER-SKRULL.
A SECONDARY EFFECT OF THAT POWER ALLOWS ME TO SEE WHAT IS HIDDEN FROM SIGHT...
YOU'RE SAYING WE HAVE COMPANY, KL'RT?
ESTEEMED COMPANY, MY EMPEROR. LET ME SHOW YOU.
FOR WHAT ONE MAY CONCEAL, ANOTHER MAY REVEAL...
BEHOLD-- THE FANTASTIC FOUR.
COMMUNICATIONS CHANNELS ARE OPEN.
THANKS, KL'RT.
SO...I'M GUESSING YOU GUYS HAVE QUESTIONS.
I WONDER. THE LAST I HEARD, HE WAS AFFILIATED WITH THE AVENGERS.
ARE THEY MIXED UP IN THIS?

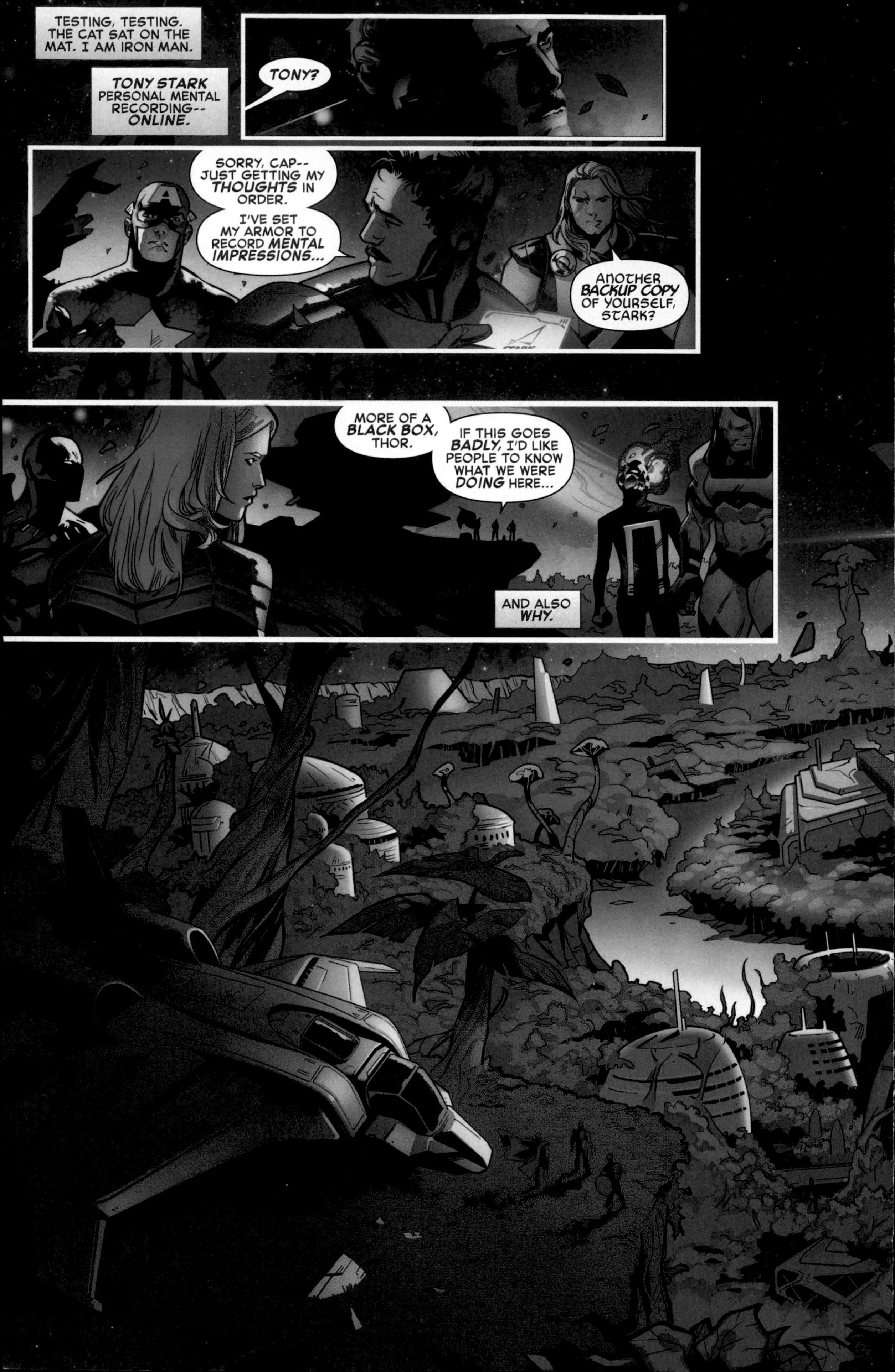
TESTING, TESTING. THE CAT SAT ON THE MAT. I AM IRON MAN.
TONY STARK PERSONAL MENTAL RECORDING-- ONLINE.
TONY?
SORRY, CAP-- JUST GETTING MY THOUGHTS IN ORDER.
I'VE SET MY ARMOR TO RECORD MENTAL IMPRESSIONS...
ANOTHER BACKUP COPY OF YOURSELF, STARK?
MORE OF A BLACK BOX, THOR.
IF THIS GOES BADLY, I'D LIKE PEOPLE TO KNOW WHAT WE WERE DOING HERE...
AND ALSO WHY.

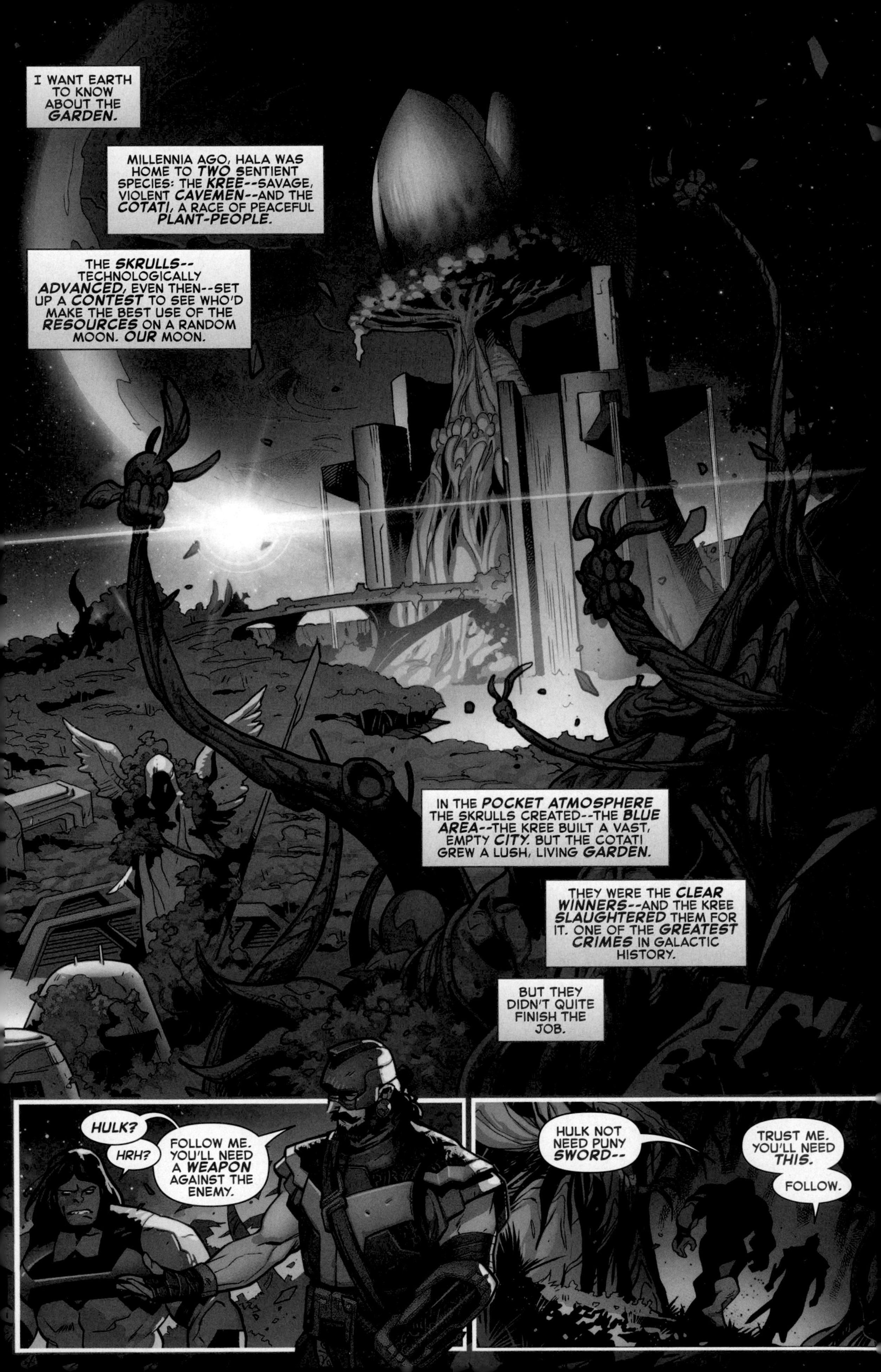
I WANT EARTH TO KNOW ABOUT THE GARDEN.
MILLENNIA AGO, HALA WAS HOME TO TWO SENTIENT SPECIES: THE KREE--SAVAGE, VIOLENT CAVEMEN--AND THE COTATI, A RACE OF PEACEFUL PLANT-PEOPLE.
THE SKRULLS--TECHNOLOGICALLY ADVANCED, EVEN THEN--SET UP A CONTEST TO SEE WHO'D MAKE THE BEST USE OF THE RESOURCES ON A RANDOM MOON. OUR MOON.
IN THE POCKET ATMOSPHERE THE SKRULLS CREATED--THE BLUE AREA--THE KREE BUILT A VAST, EMPTY CITY. BUT THE COTATI GREW A LUSH, LIVING GARDEN.
THEY WERE THE CLEAR WINNERS--AND THE KREE SLAUGHTERED THEM FOR IT. ONE OF THE GREATEST CRIMES IN GALACTIC HISTORY.
BUT THEY DIDN'T QUITE FINISH THE JOB.
HULK?
HRH?
FOLLOW ME. YOU'LL NEED A WEAPON AGAINST THE ENEMY.
HULK NOT NEED PUNY SWORD--
TRUST ME. YOU'LL NEED THIS.
FOLLOW.

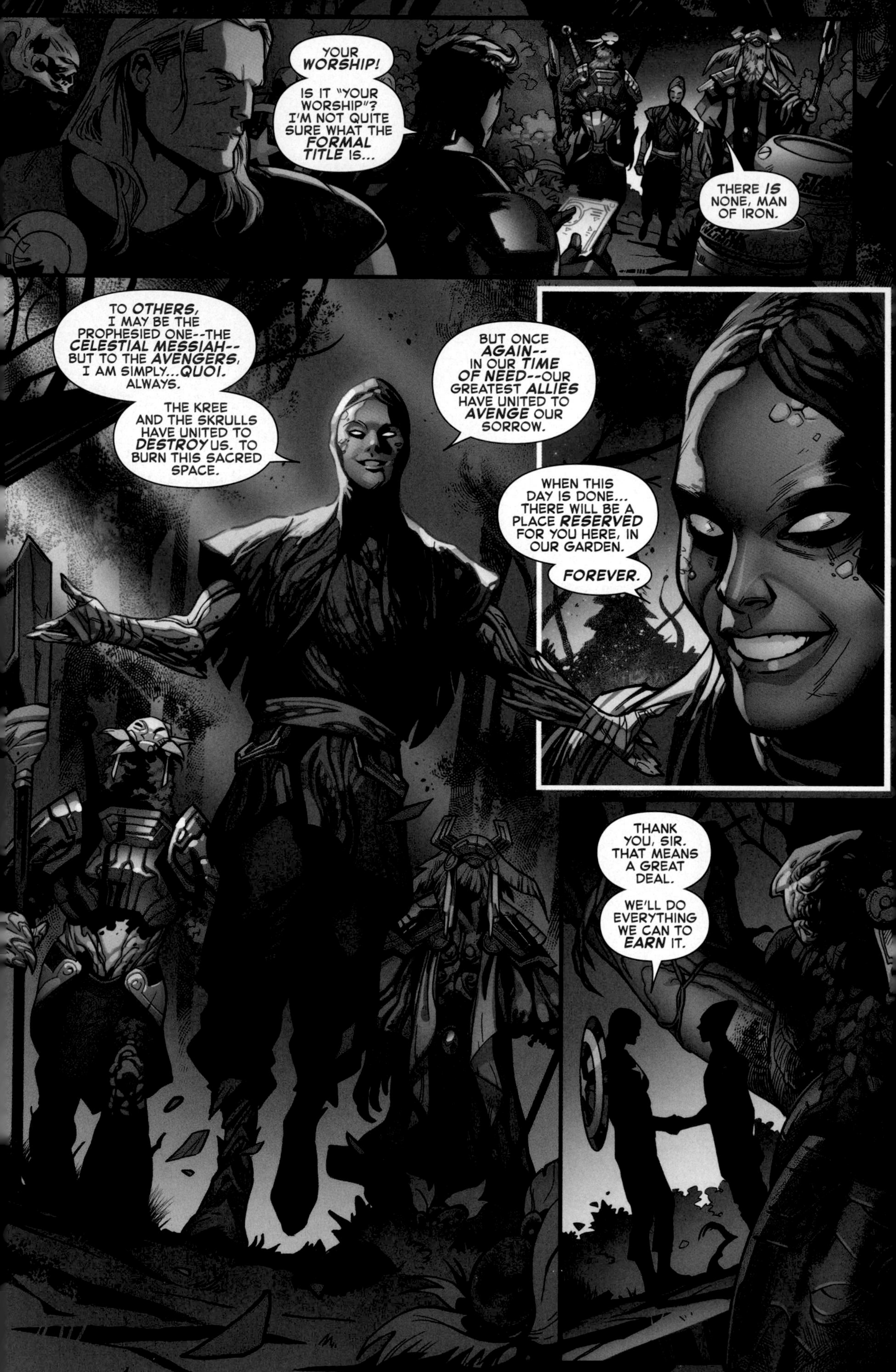

YOUR WORSHIP!
IS IT "YOUR WORSHIP"? I'M NOT QUITE SURE WHAT THE FORMAL TITLE IS...
THERE IS NONE, MAN OF IRON.
TO OTHERS, I MAY BE THE PROPHESIED ONE--THE CELESTIAL MESSIAH--BUT TO THE AVENGERS, I AM SIMPLY...QUOI. ALWAYS.
THE KREE AND THE SKRULLS HAVE UNITED TO DESTROY US. TO BURN THIS SACRED SPACE.
BUT ONCE AGAIN--IN OUR TIME OF NEED--OUR GREATEST ALLIES HAVE UNITED TO AVENGE OUR SORROW.
WHEN THIS DAY IS DONE... THERE WILL BE A PLACE RESERVED FOR YOU HERE, IN OUR GARDEN.
FOREVER.
THANK YOU, SIR. THAT MEANS A GREAT DEAL.
WE'LL DO EVERYTHING WE CAN TO EARN IT.

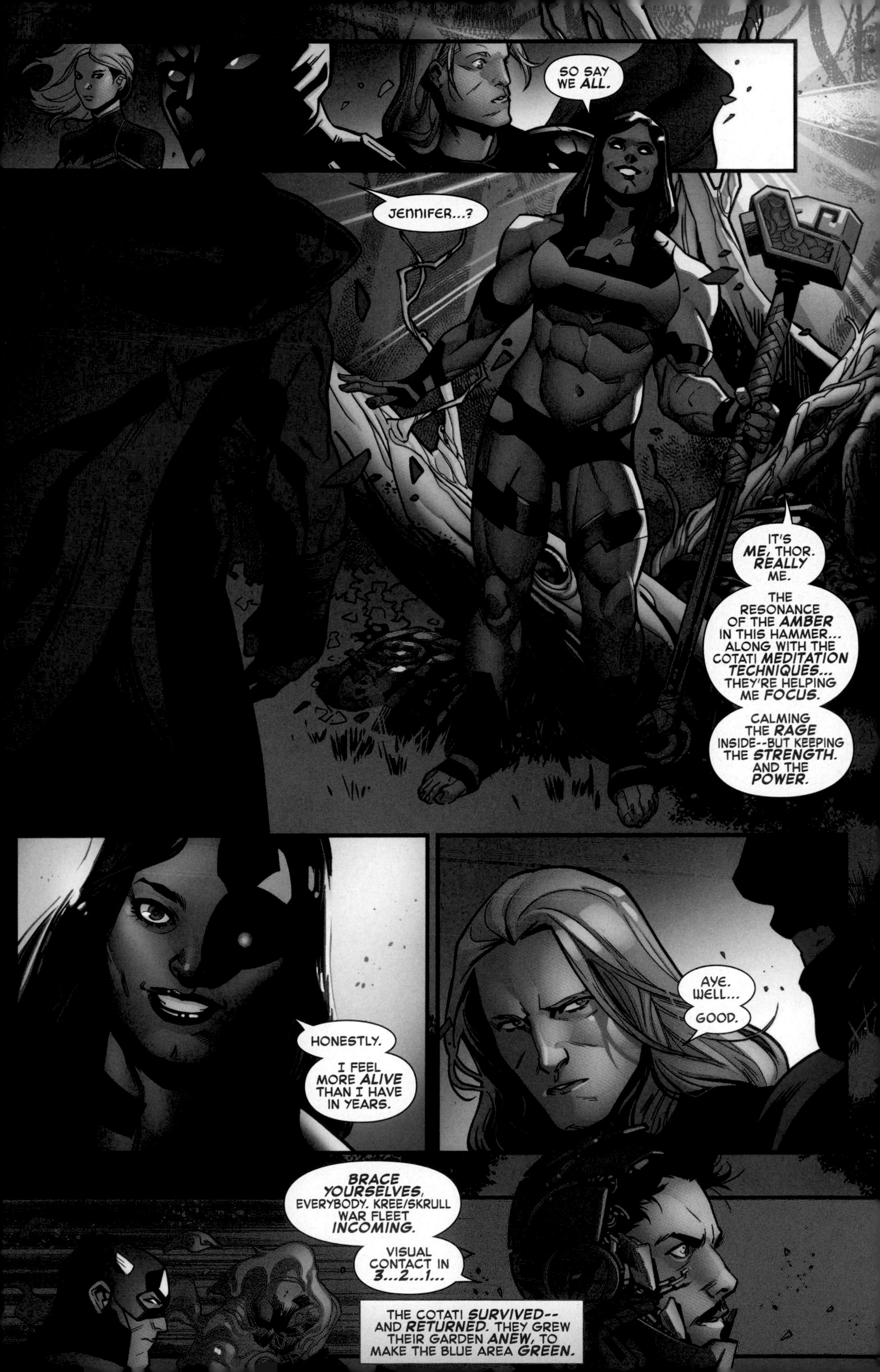
SO SAY WE ALL.
JENNIFER...?
IT'S ME, THOR. REALLY ME.
THE RESONANCE OF THE AMBER IN THIS HAMMER... ALONG WITH THE COTATI MEDITATION TECHNIQUES... THEY'RE HELPING ME FOCUS.
CALMING THE RAGE INSIDE--BUT KEEPING THE STRENGTH. AND THE POWER.
HONESTLY.
I FEEL MORE ALIVE THAN I HAVE IN YEARS.
AYE. WELL...
GOOD.
BRACE YOURSELVES, EVERYBODY. KREE/SKRULL WAR FLEET INCOMING.
VISUAL CONTACT IN 3...2...1...
THE COTATI SURVIVED-- AND RETURNED. THEY GREW THEIR GARDEN ANEW, TO MAKE THE BLUE AREA GREEN.

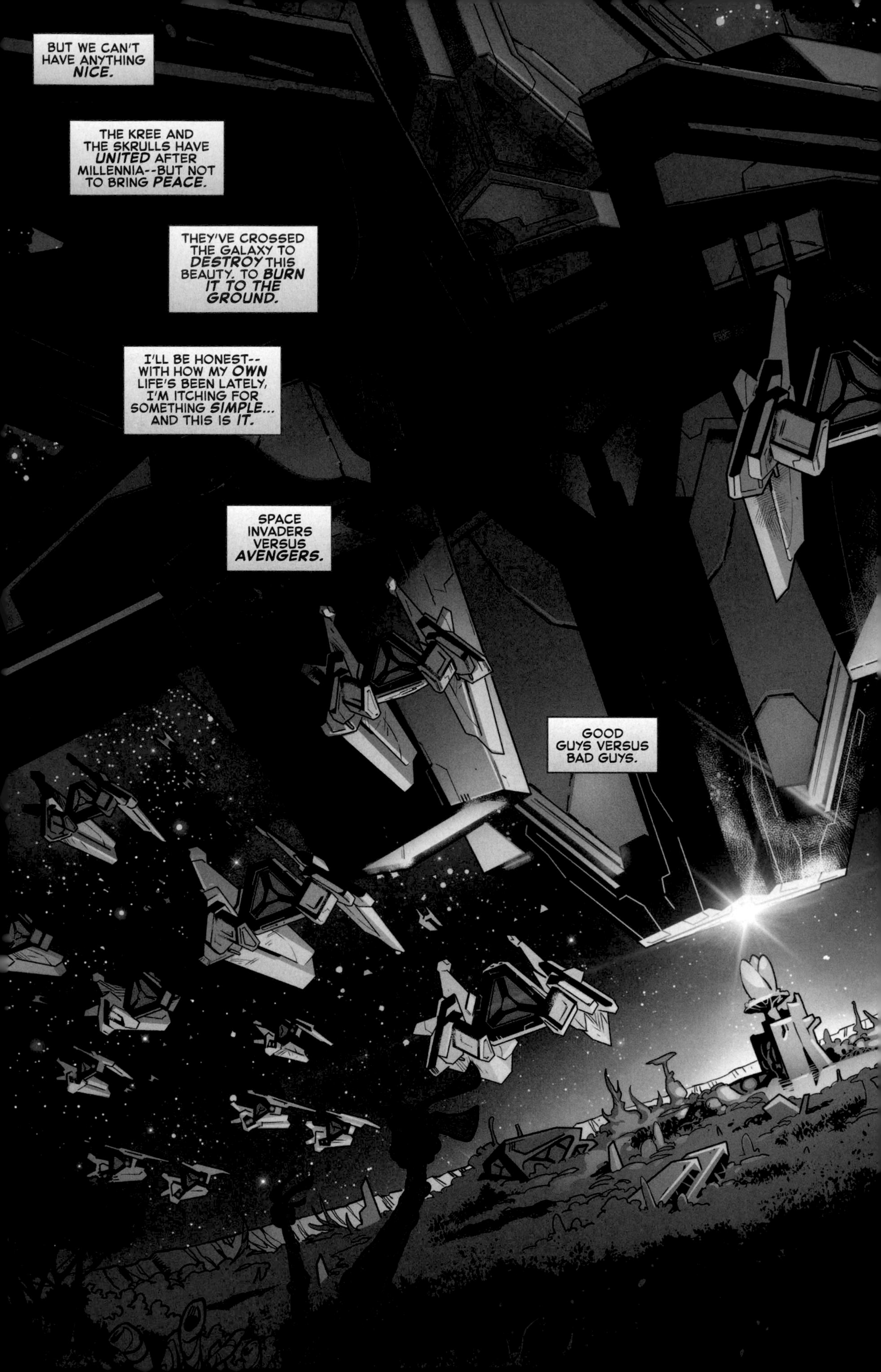
BUT WE CAN'T HAVE ANYTHING NICE.
THE KREE AND THE SKRULLS HAVE UNITED AFTER MILLENNIA--BUT NOT TO BRING PEACE.
THEY'VE CROSSED THE GALAXY TO DESTROY THIS BEAUTY. TO BURN IT TO THE GROUND.
I'LL BE HONEST--WITH HOW MY OWN LIFE'S BEEN LATELY, I'M ITCHING FOR SOMETHING SIMPLE... AND THIS IS IT.
SPACE INVADERS VERSUS AVENGERS.
GOOD GUYS VERSUS BAD GUYS.

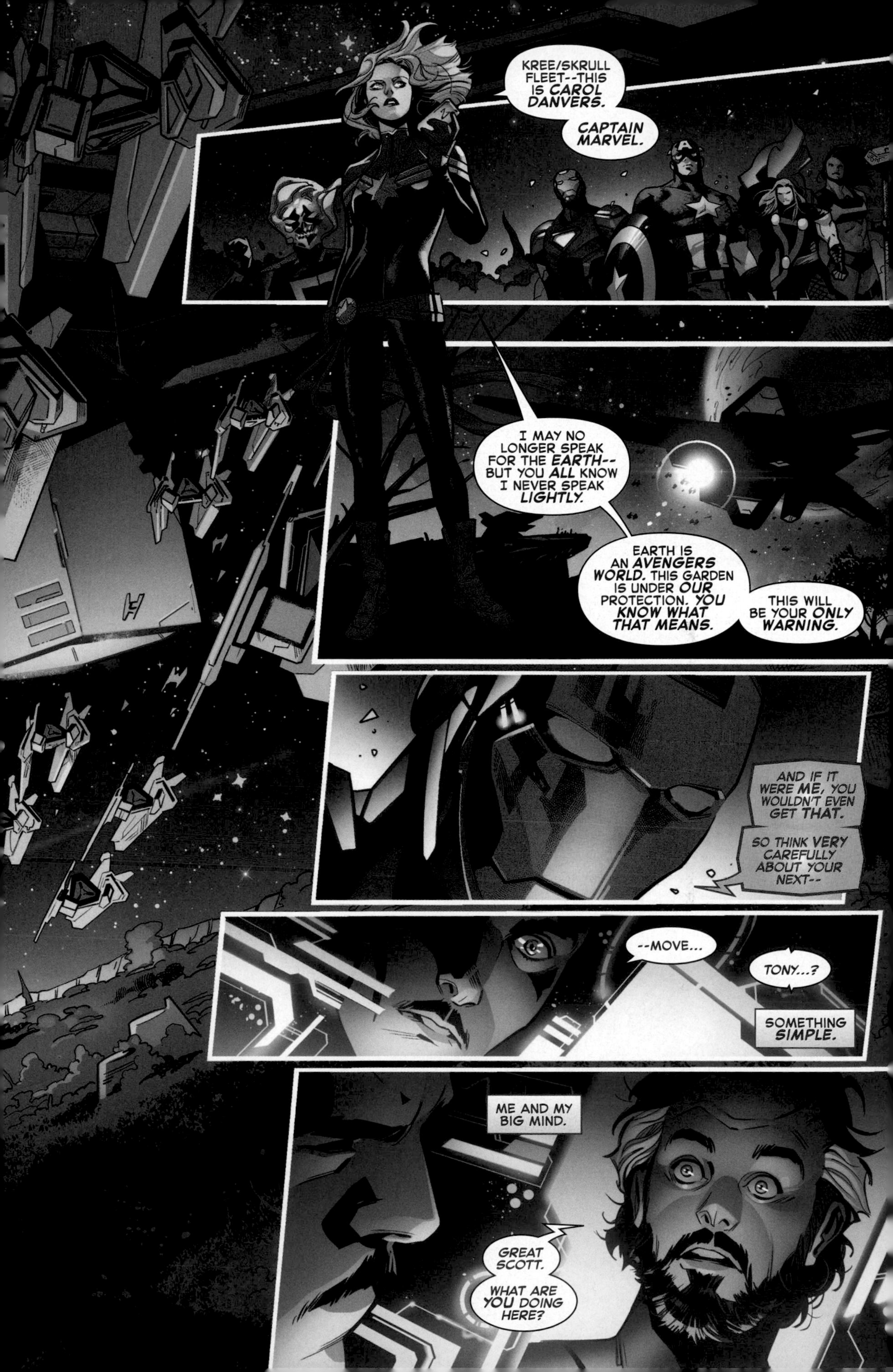
KREE/SKRULL FLEET--THIS IS CAROL DANVERS.
CAPTAIN MARVEL.
I MAY NO LONGER SPEAK FOR THE EARTH--BUT YOU ALL KNOW I NEVER SPEAK LIGHTLY.
EARTH IS AN AVENGERS WORLD. THIS GARDEN IS UNDER OUR PROTECTION. YOU KNOW WHAT THAT MEANS.
THIS WILL BE YOUR ONLY WARNING.
AND IF IT WERE ME, YOU WOULDN'T EVEN GET THAT.
SO THINK VERY CAREFULLY ABOUT YOUR NEXT--
--MOVE...
TONY...?
SOMETHING SIMPLE.
ME AND MY BIG MIND.
GREAT SCOTT.
WHAT ARE YOU DOING HERE?

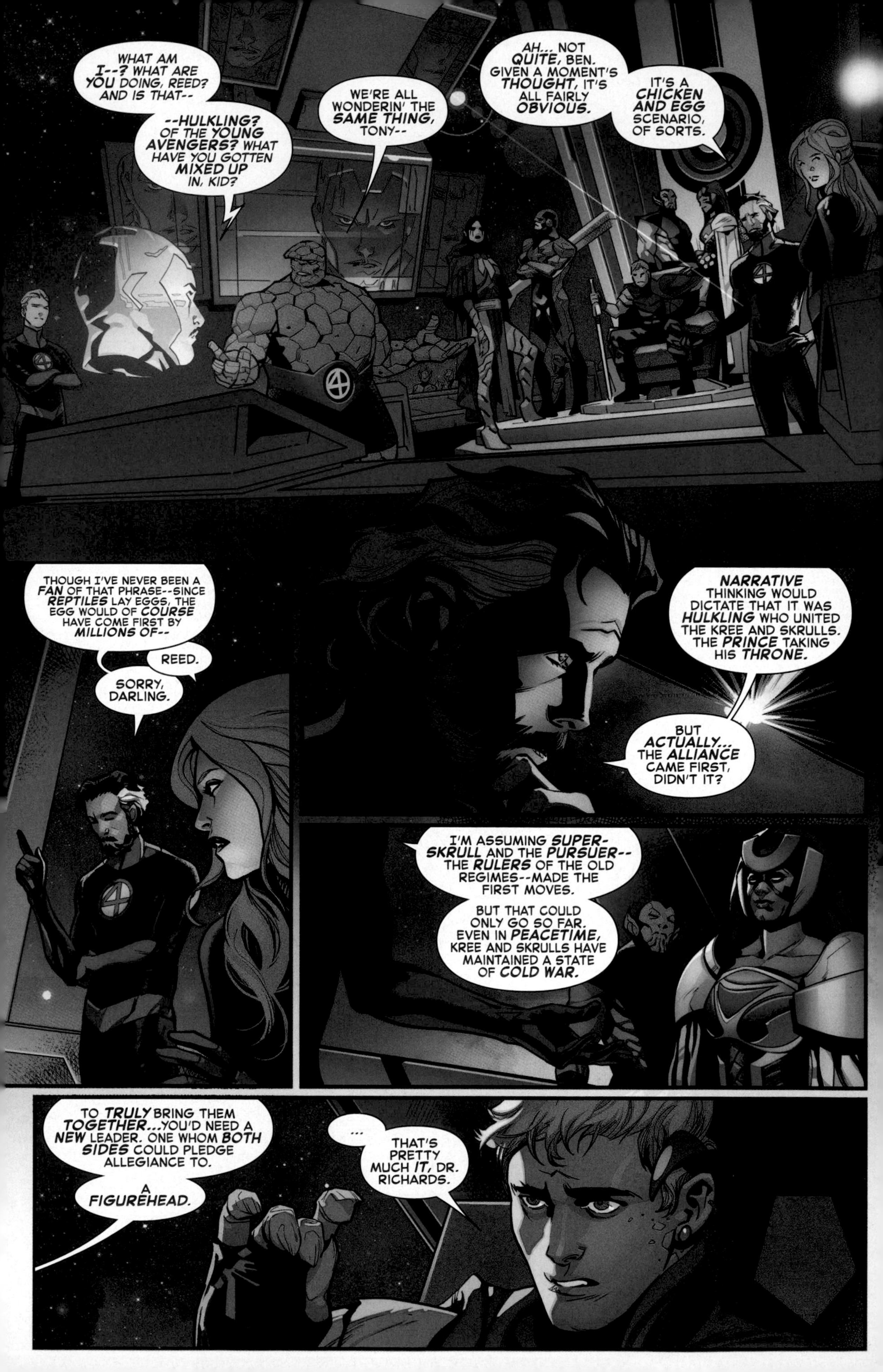
WHAT AM I--? WHAT ARE YOU DOING, REED? AND IS THAT--
--HULKLING? OF THE YOUNG AVENGERS? WHAT HAVE YOU GOTTEN MIXED UP IN, KID?
WE'RE ALL WONDERIN' THE SAME THING, TONY--
AH... NOT QUITE, BEN. GIVEN A MOMENT'S THOUGHT, IT'S ALL FAIRLY OBVIOUS.
IT'S A CHICKEN AND EGG SCENARIO, OF SORTS.
THOUGH I'VE NEVER BEEN A FAN OF THAT PHRASE--SINCE REPTILES LAY EGGS, THE EGG WOULD OF COURSE HAVE COME FIRST BY MILLIONS OF--
REED.
SORRY, DARLING.
NARRATIVE THINKING WOULD DICTATE THAT IT WAS HULKLING WHO UNITED THE KREE AND SKRULLS. THE PRINCE TAKING HIS THRONE.
BUT ACTUALLY... THE ALLIANCE CAME FIRST, DIDN'T IT?
I'M ASSUMING SUPER-SKRULL AND THE PURSUER--THE RULERS OF THE OLD REGIMES--MADE THE FIRST MOVES.
BUT THAT COULD ONLY GO SO FAR. EVEN IN PEACETIME, KREE AND SKRULLS HAVE MAINTAINED A STATE OF COLD WAR.
TO TRULY BRING THEM TOGETHER...YOU'D NEED A NEW LEADER. ONE WHOM BOTH SIDES COULD PLEDGE ALLEGIANCE TO.
A FIGUREHEAD.
...
THAT'S PRETTY MUCH IT, DR. RICHARDS.

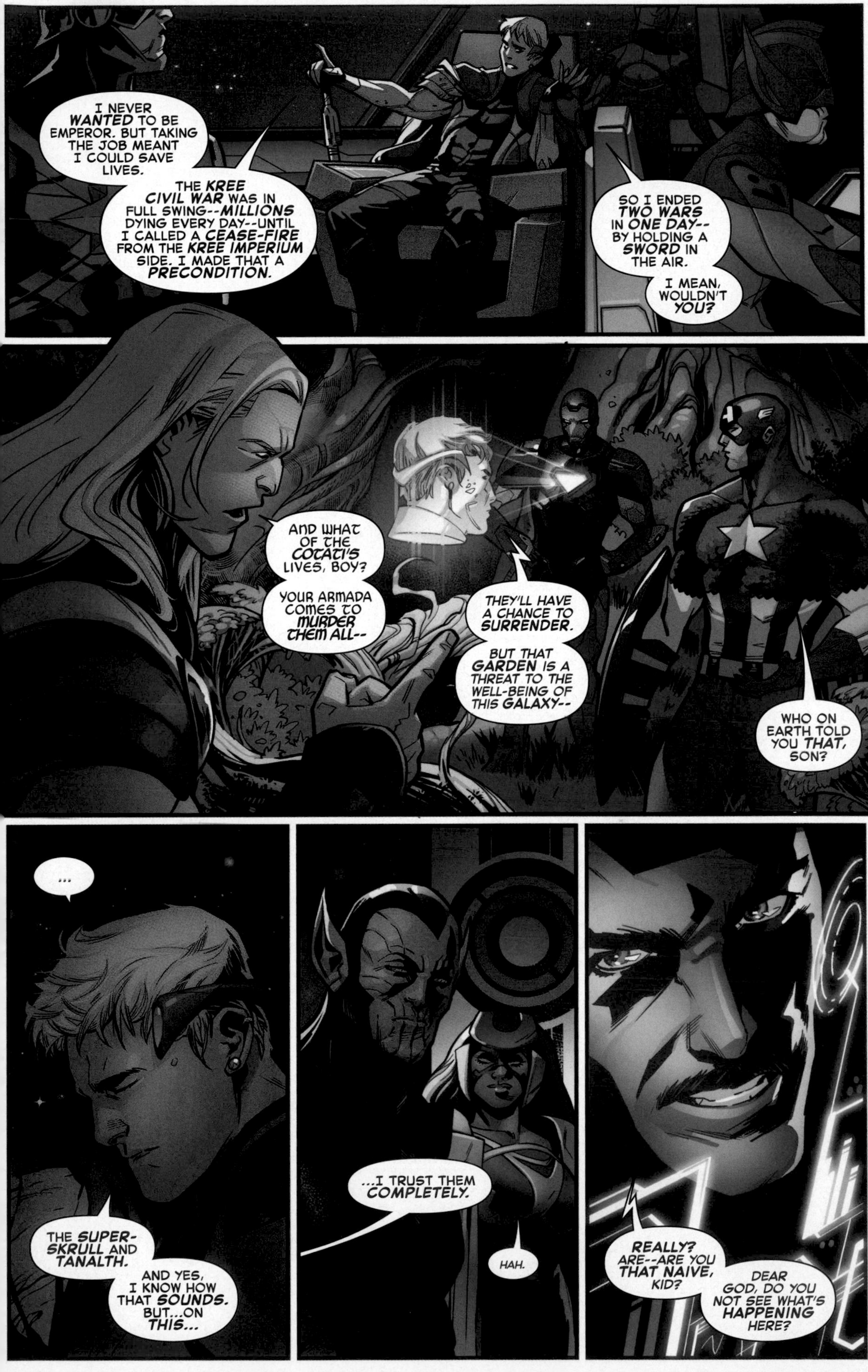
I NEVER WANTED TO BE EMPEROR. BUT TAKING THE JOB MEANT I COULD SAVE LIVES.
THE KREE CIVIL WAR WAS IN FULL SWING--MILLIONS DYING EVERY DAY--UNTIL I CALLED A CEASE-FIRE FROM THE KREE IMPERIUM SIDE. I MADE THAT A PRECONDITION.
SO I ENDED TWO WARS IN ONE DAY--BY HOLDING A SWORD IN THE AIR.
I MEAN, WOULDN'T YOU?
AND WHAT OF THE COTATI'S LIVES, BOY?
YOUR ARMADA COMES TO MURDER THEM ALL--
THEY'LL HAVE A CHANCE TO SURRENDER.
BUT THAT GARDEN IS A THREAT TO THE WELL-BEING OF THIS GALAXY--
WHO ON EARTH TOLD YOU THAT, SON?
...
THE SUPER-SKRULL AND TANALTH.
AND YES, I KNOW HOW THAT SOUNDS. BUT...ON THIS...
...I TRUST THEM COMPLETELY.
HAH.
REALLY? ARE--ARE YOU THAT NAIVE, KID?
DEAR GOD, DO YOU NOT SEE WHAT'S HAPPENING HERE?

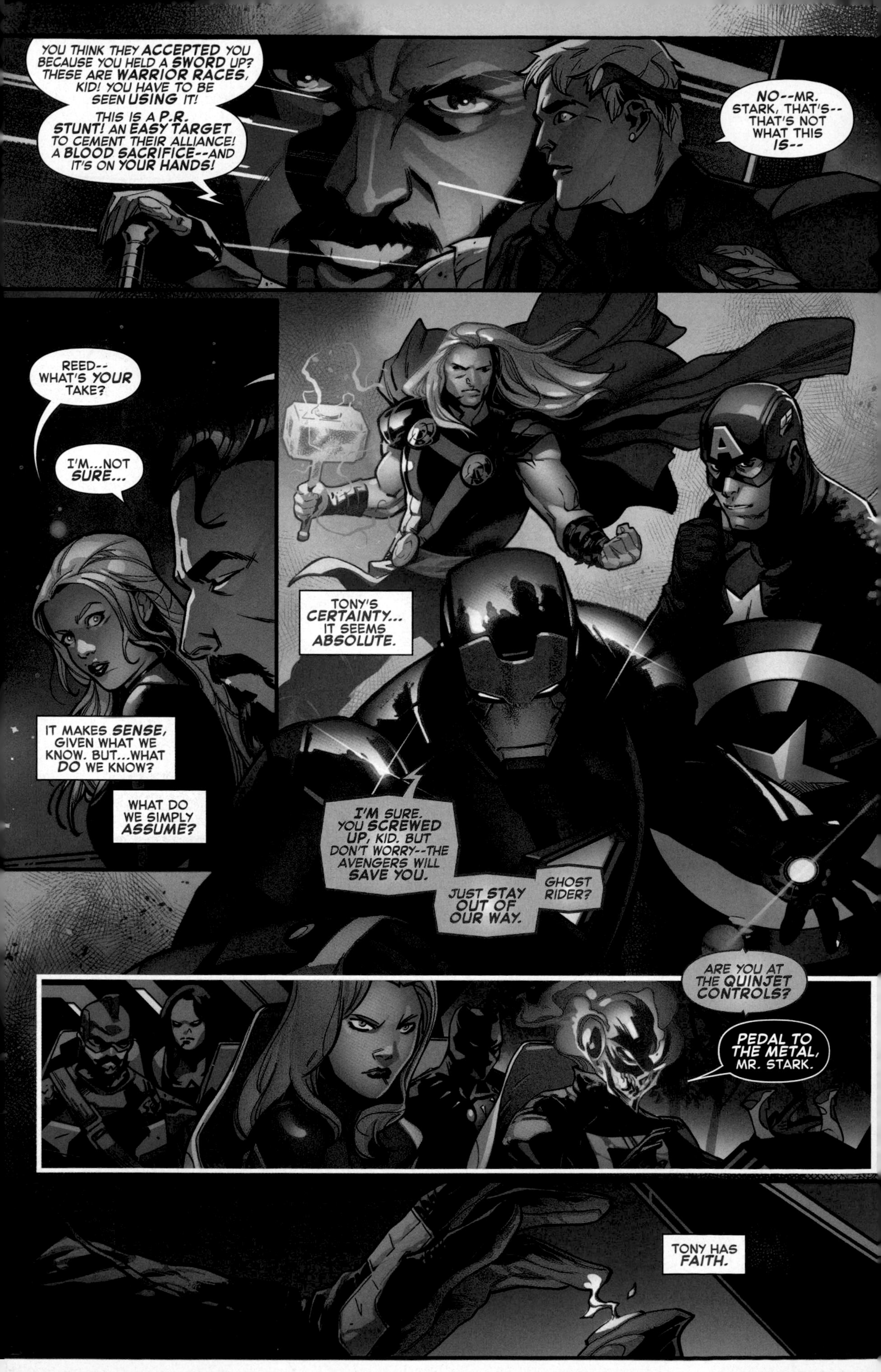
YOU THINK THEY ACCEPTED YOU BECAUSE YOU HELD A SWORD UP? THESE ARE WARRIOR RACES, KID! YOU HAVE TO BE SEEN USING IT!
THIS IS A P.R. STUNT! AN EASY TARGET TO CEMENT THEIR ALLIANCE! A BLOOD SACRIFICE--AND IT'S ON YOUR HANDS!
NO--MR. STARK, THAT'S-- THAT'S NOT WHAT THIS IS--
REED-- WHAT'S YOUR TAKE?
I'M...NOT SURE...
TONY'S CERTAINTY... IT SEEMS ABSOLUTE.
IT MAKES SENSE, GIVEN WHAT WE KNOW. BUT...WHAT DO WE KNOW?
WHAT DO WE SIMPLY ASSUME?
I'M SURE. YOU SCREWED UP, KID. BUT DON'T WORRY--THE AVENGERS WILL SAVE YOU.
JUST STAY OUT OF OUR WAY.
GHOST RIDER?
ARE YOU AT THE QUINJET CONTROLS?
PEDAL TO THE METAL, MR. STARK.
TONY HAS FAITH.

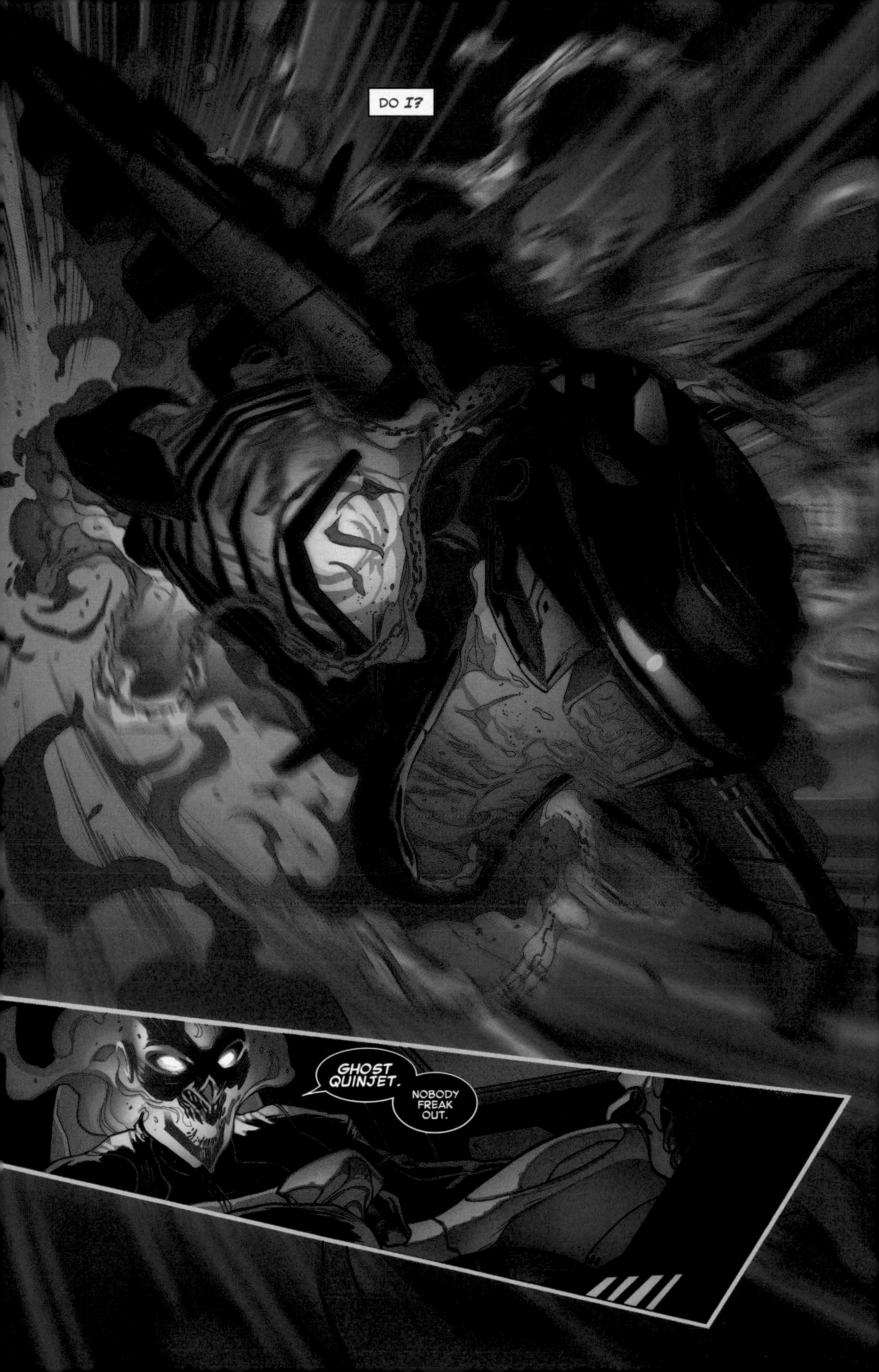
DO I?
GHOST QUINJET.
NOBODY FREAK OUT.

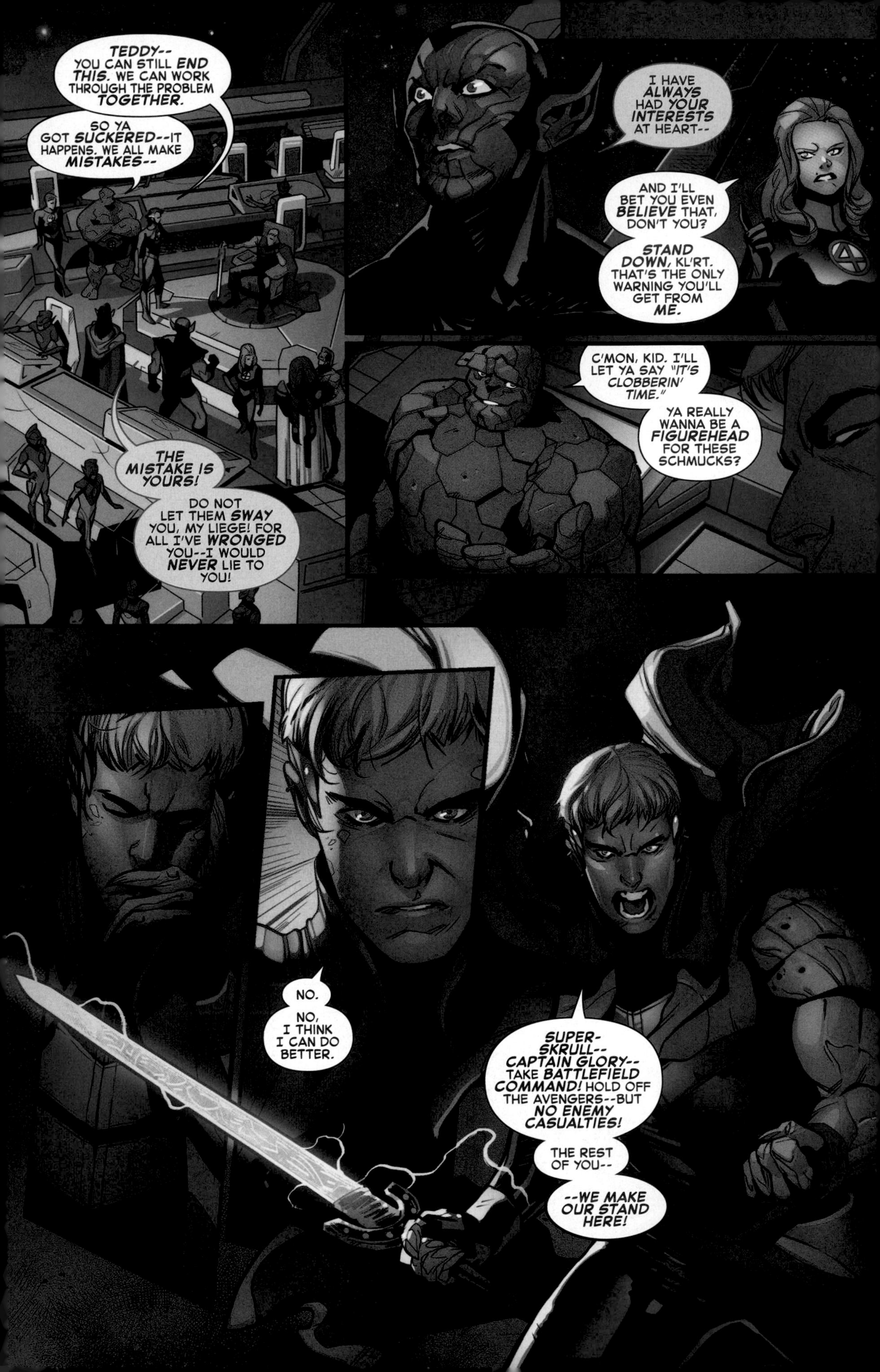
TEDDY-- YOU CAN STILL END THIS. WE CAN WORK THROUGH THE PROBLEM TOGETHER.
SO YA GOT SUCKERED--IT HAPPENS. WE ALL MAKE MISTAKES--
THE MISTAKE IS YOURS!
DO NOT LET THEM SWAY YOU, MY LIEGE! FOR ALL I'VE WRONGED YOU--I WOULD NEVER LIE TO YOU!
I HAVE ALWAYS HAD YOUR INTERESTS AT HEART--
AND I'LL BET YOU EVEN BELIEVE THAT, DON'T YOU?
STAND DOWN, KL'RT. THAT'S THE ONLY WARNING YOU'LL GET FROM ME.
C'MON, KID. I'LL LET YA SAY "IT'S CLOBBERIN' TIME."
YA REALLY WANNA BE A FIGUREHEAD FOR THESE SCHMUCKS?
NO.
NO, I THINK I CAN DO BETTER.
SUPER-SKRULL--CAPTAIN GLORY--TAKE BATTLEFIELD COMMAND! HOLD OFF THE AVENGERS--BUT NO ENEMY CASUALTIES!
THE REST OF YOU--
--WE MAKE OUR STAND HERE!

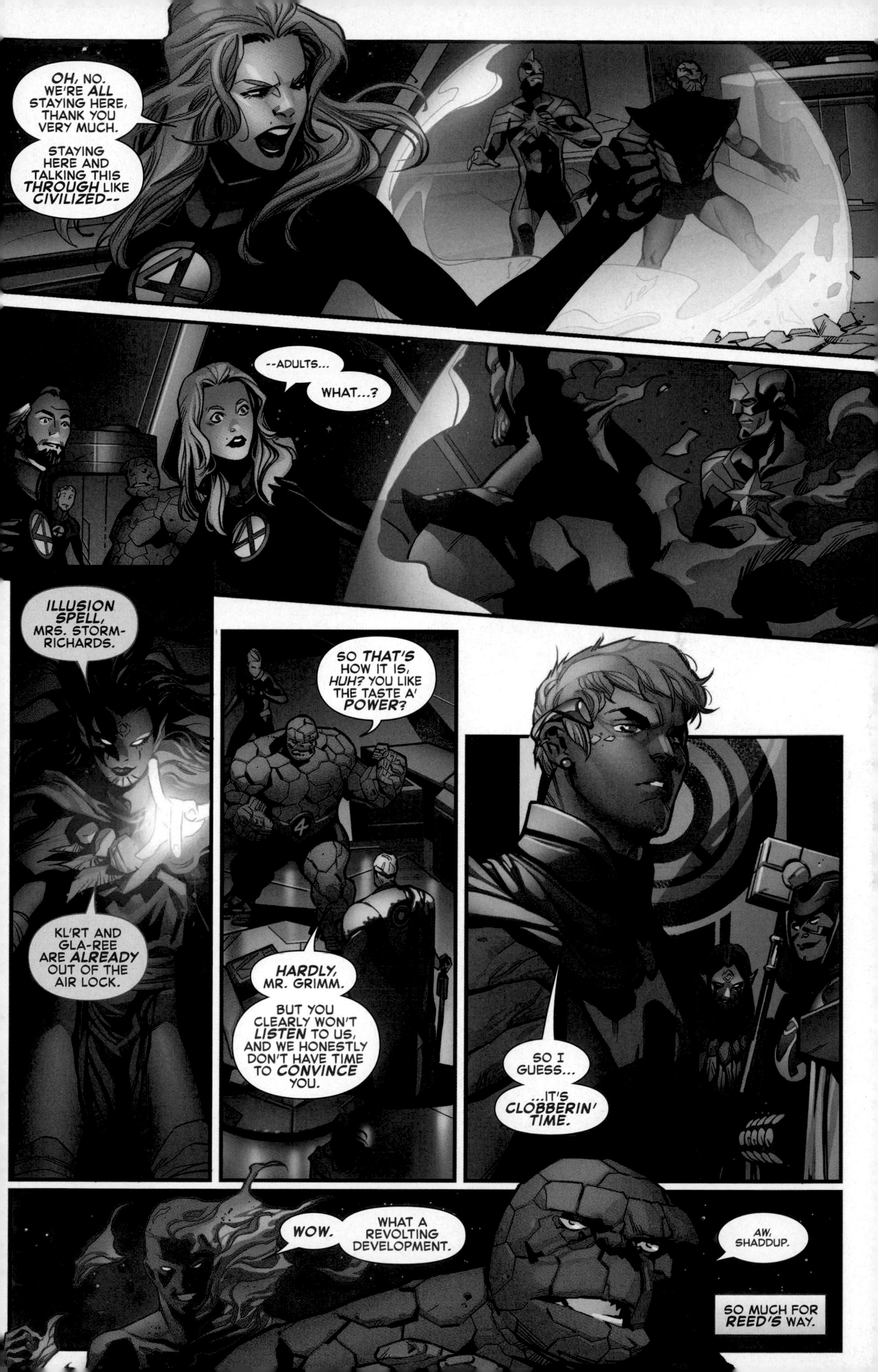

OH, NO. WE'RE ALL STAYING HERE, THANK YOU VERY MUCH.
STAYING HERE AND TALKING THIS THROUGH LIKE CIVILIZED--
--ADULTS...
WHAT...?
ILLUSION SPELL, MRS. STORM-RICHARDS.
KL'RT AND GLA-REE ARE ALREADY OUT OF THE AIR LOCK.
SO THAT'S HOW IT IS, HUH? YOU LIKE THE TASTE A' POWER?
HARDLY, MR. GRIMM.
BUT YOU CLEARLY WON'T LISTEN TO US, AND WE HONESTLY DON'T HAVE TIME TO CONVINCE YOU.
SO I GUESS...
...IT'S CLOBBERIN' TIME.
WOW.
WHAT A REVOLTING DEVELOPMENT.
AW, SHADDUP.
SO MUCH FOR REED'S WAY.

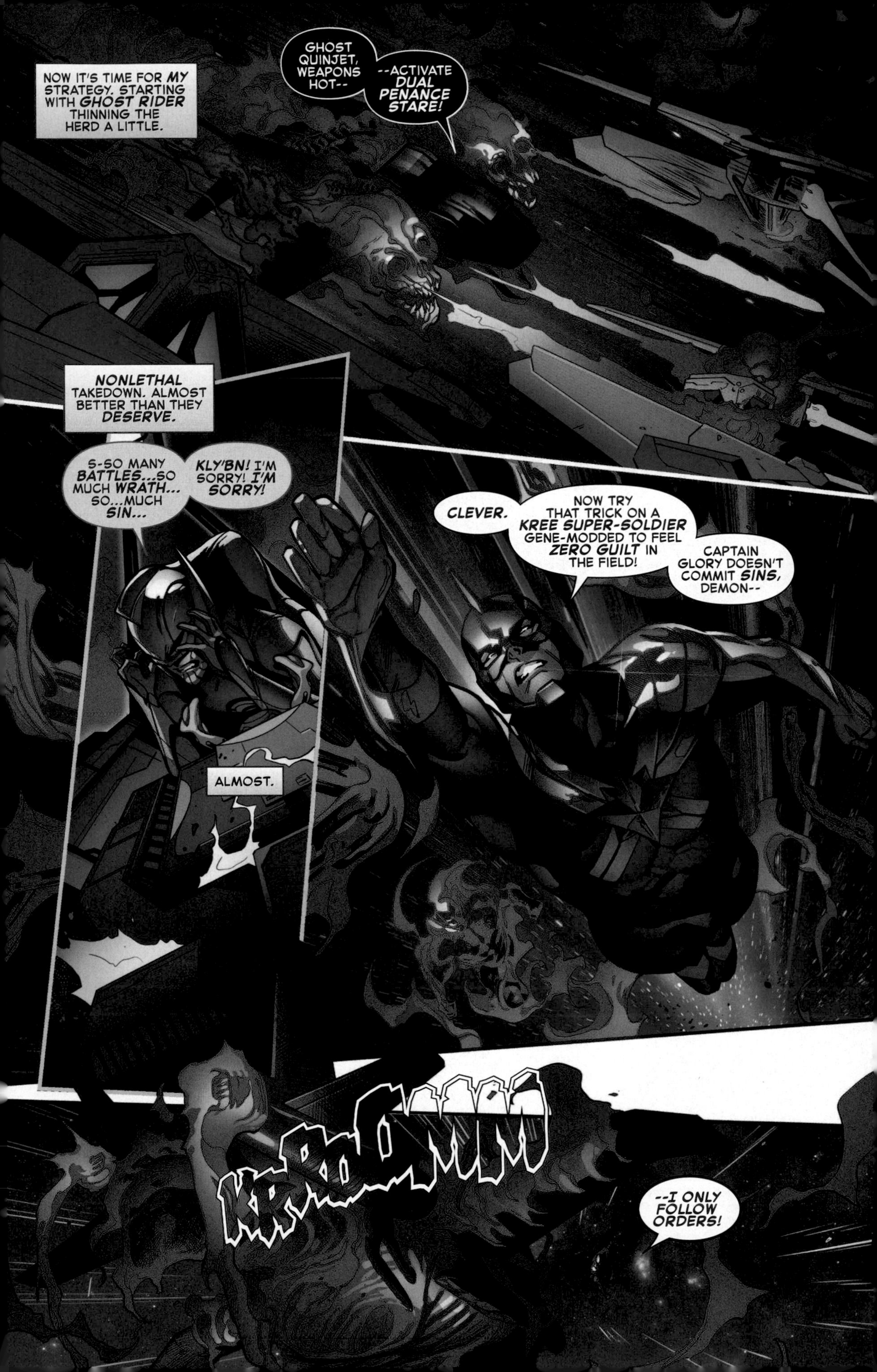
NOW IT'S TIME FOR MY STRATEGY. STARTING WITH GHOST RIDER THINNING THE HERD A LITTLE.
GHOST QUINJET, WEAPONS HOT--
--ACTIVATE DUAL PENANCE STARE!
NONLETHAL TAKEDOWN. ALMOST BETTER THAN THEY DESERVE.
S-SO MANY BATTLES...SO MUCH WRATH... SO...MUCH SIN...
KLY'BN! I'M SORRY! I'M SORRY!
ALMOST.
CLEVER.
NOW TRY THAT TRICK ON A KREE SUPER-SOLDIER GENE-MODDED TO FEEL ZERO GUILT IN THE FIELD!
CAPTAIN GLORY DOESN'T COMMIT SINS, DEMON--
KRBOOOMM
--I ONLY FOLLOW ORDERS!

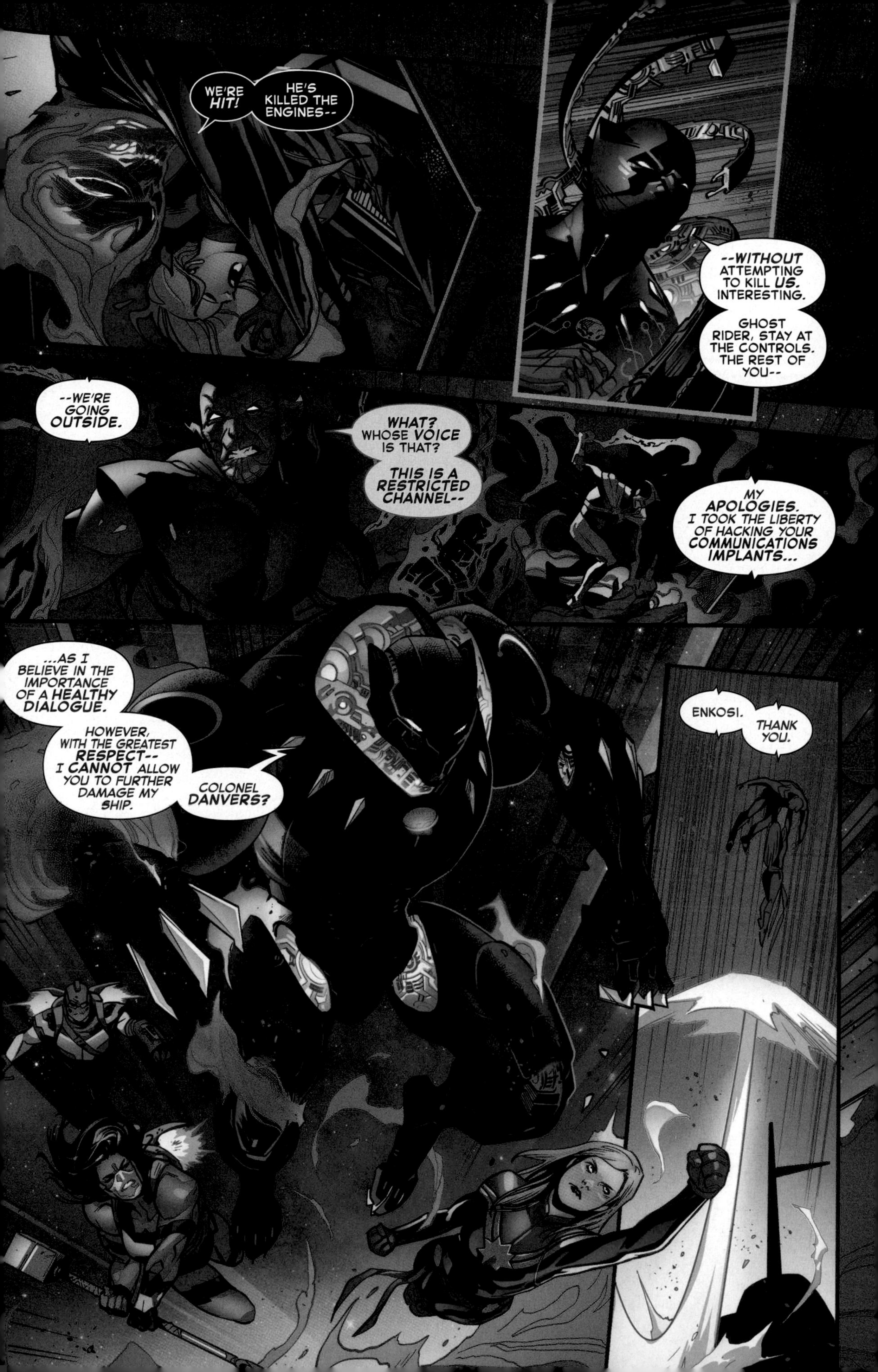

WE'RE HIT!
HE'S KILLED THE ENGINES--
--WITHOUT ATTEMPTING TO KILL US. INTERESTING.
GHOST RIDER, STAY AT THE CONTROLS. THE REST OF YOU--
--WE'RE GOING OUTSIDE.
WHAT? WHOSE VOICE IS THAT?
THIS IS A RESTRICTED CHANNEL--
MY APOLOGIES. I TOOK THE LIBERTY OF HACKING YOUR COMMUNICATIONS IMPLANTS...
...AS I BELIEVE IN THE IMPORTANCE OF A HEALTHY DIALOGUE.
HOWEVER, WITH THE GREATEST RESPECT-- I CANNOT ALLOW YOU TO FURTHER DAMAGE MY SHIP.
COLONEL DANVERS?
ENKOSI.
THANK YOU.

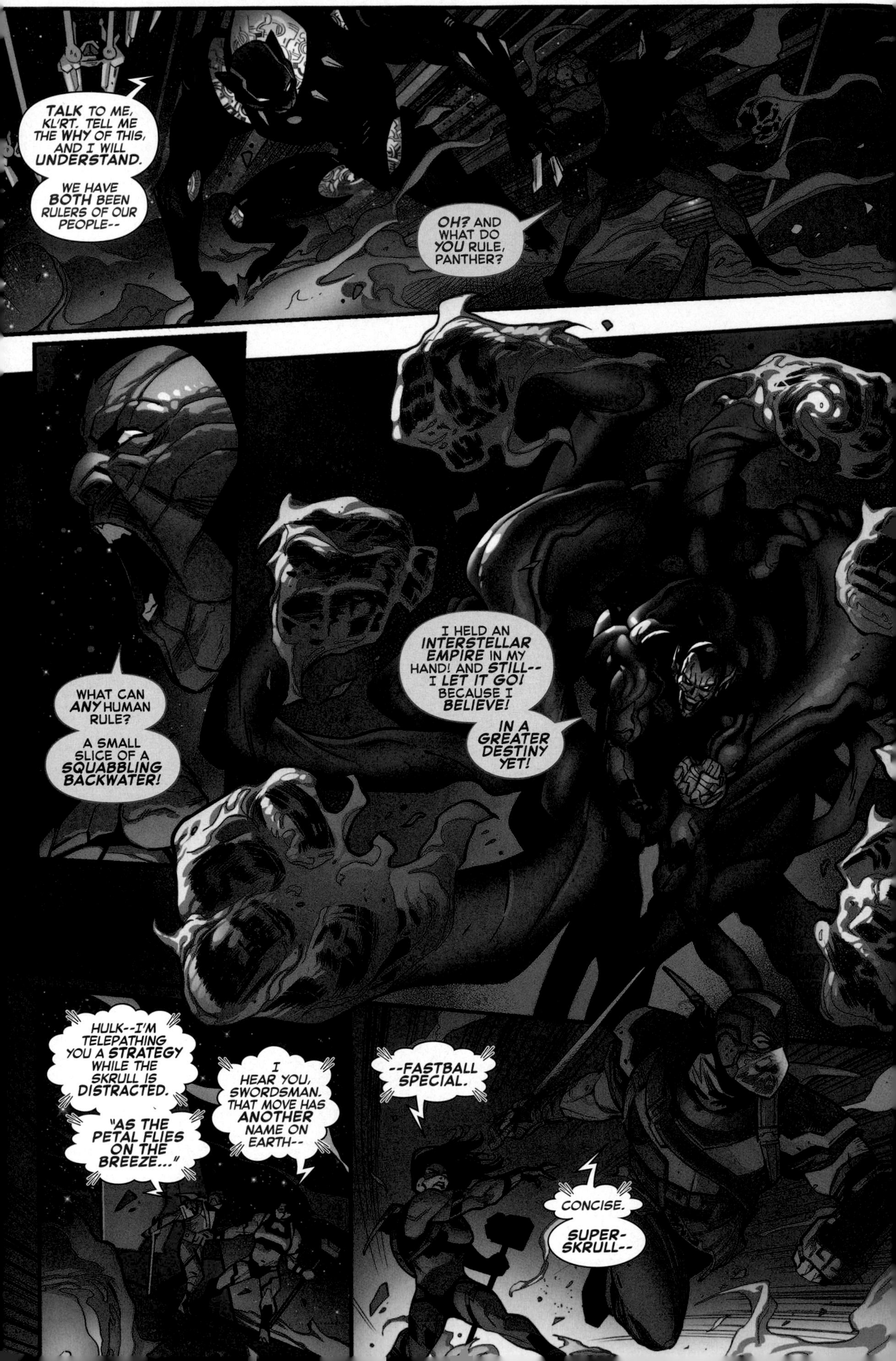

TALK TO ME, KL'RT. TELL ME THE WHY OF THIS, AND I WILL UNDERSTAND.
WE HAVE BOTH BEEN RULERS OF OUR PEOPLE--
OH? AND WHAT DO YOU RULE, PANTHER?
WHAT CAN ANY HUMAN RULE?
A SMALL SLICE OF A SQUABBLING BACKWATER!
I HELD AN INTERSTELLAR EMPIRE IN MY HAND! AND STILL-- I LET IT GO! BECAUSE I BELIEVE!
IN A GREATER DESTINY YET!
HULK--I'M TELEPATHING YOU A STRATEGY WHILE THE SKRULL IS DISTRACTED.
"AS THE PETAL FLIES ON THE BREEZE..."
I HEAR YOU, SWORDSMAN. THAT MOVE HAS ANOTHER NAME ON EARTH--
--FASTBALL SPECIAL.
CONCISE.
SUPER-SKRULL--

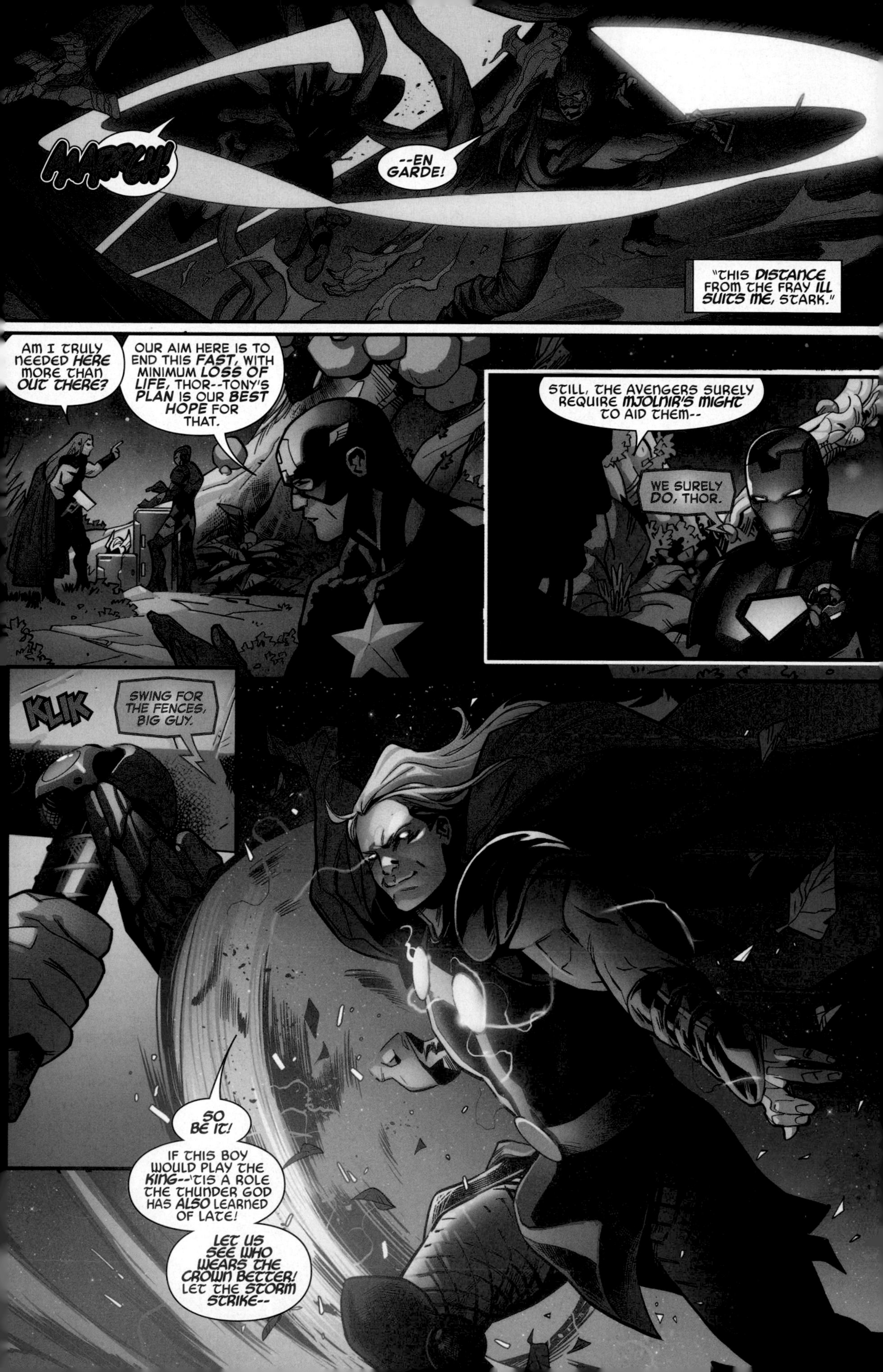
AAARRGH!
--EN GARDE!
"THIS DISTANCE FROM THE FRAY ILL SUITS ME, STARK."
AM I TRULY NEEDED HERE MORE THAN OUT THERE?
OUR AIM HERE IS TO END THIS FAST, WITH MINIMUM LOSS OF LIFE, THOR--TONY'S PLAN IS OUR BEST HOPE FOR THAT.
STILL, THE AVENGERS SURELY REQUIRE MJOLNIR'S MIGHT TO AID THEM--
WE SURELY DO, THOR.
KLIK
SWING FOR THE FENCES, BIG GUY.
SO BE IT!
IF THIS BOY WOULD PLAY THE KING--'TIS A ROLE THE THUNDER GOD HAS ALSO LEARNED OF LATE!
LET US SEE WHO WEARS THE CROWN BETTER! LET THE STORM STRIKE--

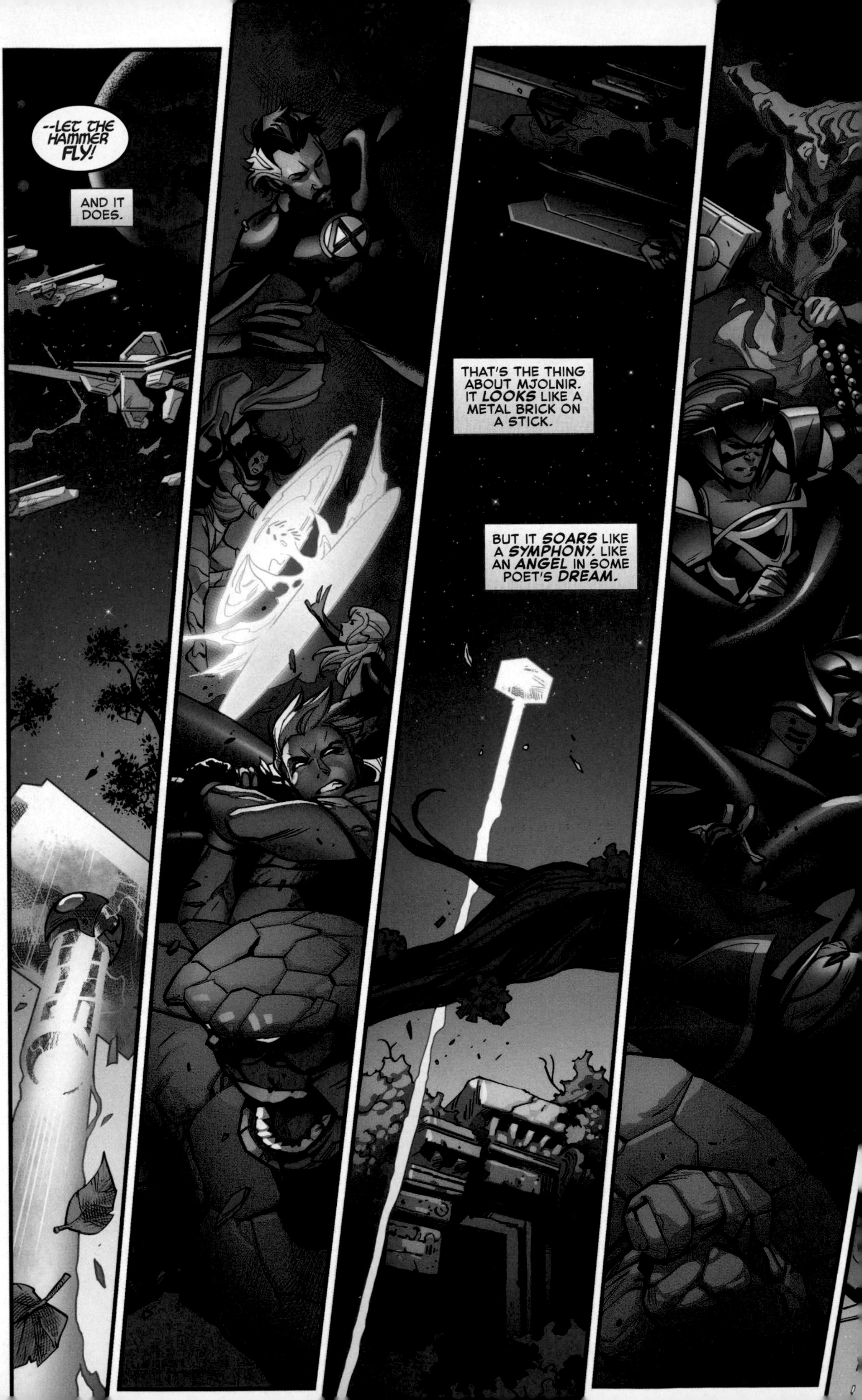
--LET THE HAMMER FLY!
AND IT DOES.
THAT'S THE THING ABOUT MJOLNIR. IT LOOKS LIKE A METAL BRICK ON A STICK.
BUT IT SOARS LIKE A SYMPHONY. LIKE AN ANGEL IN SOME POET'S DREAM.

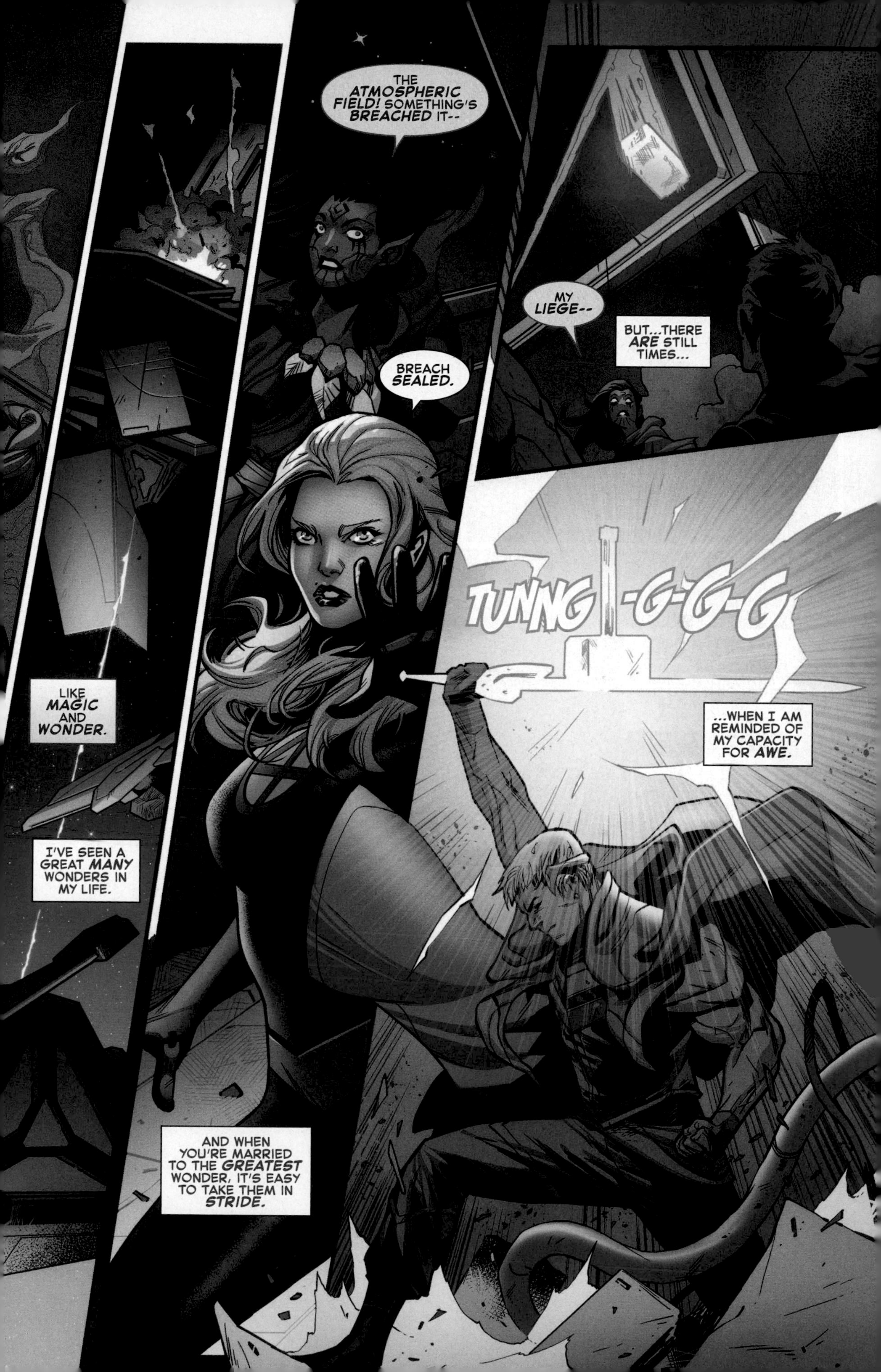
THE ATMOSPHERIC FIELD! SOMETHING'S BREACHED IT--
BREACH SEALED.
MY LIEGE--
BUT...THERE ARE STILL TIMES...
TUNNG-G-G-G
...WHEN I AM REMINDED OF MY CAPACITY FOR AWE.
LIKE MAGIC AND WONDER.
I'VE SEEN A GREAT MANY WONDERS IN MY LIFE.
AND WHEN YOU'RE MARRIED TO THE GREATEST WONDER, IT'S EASY TO TAKE THEM IN STRIDE.

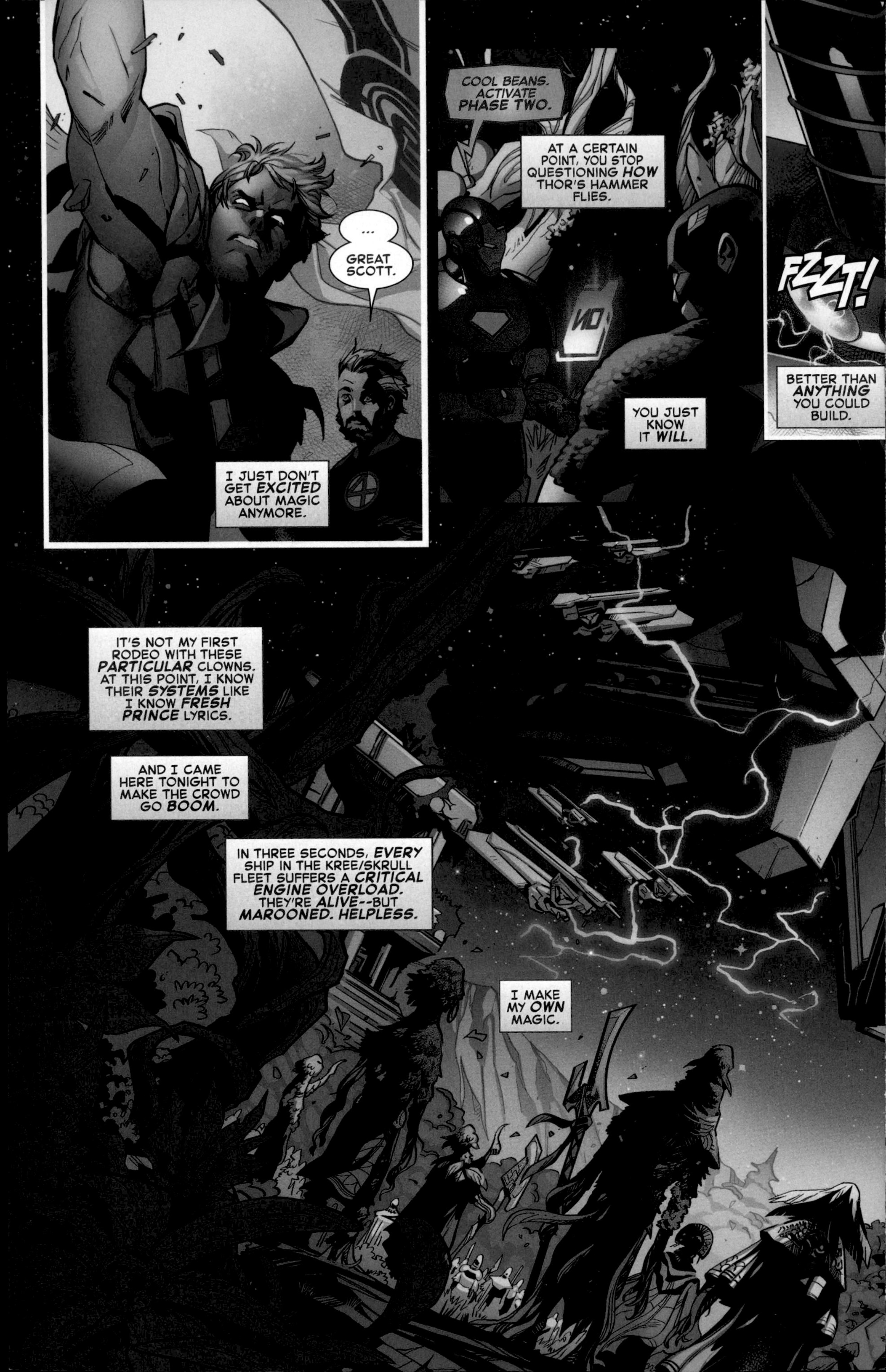
...
GREAT SCOTT.
I JUST DON'T GET EXCITED ABOUT MAGIC ANYMORE.
COOL BEANS. ACTIVATE PHASE TWO.
AT A CERTAIN POINT, YOU STOP QUESTIONING HOW THOR'S HAMMER FLIES.
YOU JUST KNOW IT WILL.
FZZT!
BETTER THAN ANYTHING YOU COULD BUILD.
IT'S NOT MY FIRST RODEO WITH THESE PARTICULAR CLOWNS. AT THIS POINT, I KNOW THEIR SYSTEMS LIKE I KNOW FRESH PRINCE LYRICS.
AND I CAME HERE TONIGHT TO MAKE THE CROWD GO BOOM.
IN THREE SECONDS, EVERY SHIP IN THE KREE/SKRULL FLEET SUFFERS A CRITICAL ENGINE OVERLOAD. THEY'RE ALIVE--BUT MAROONED. HELPLESS.
I MAKE MY OWN MAGIC.

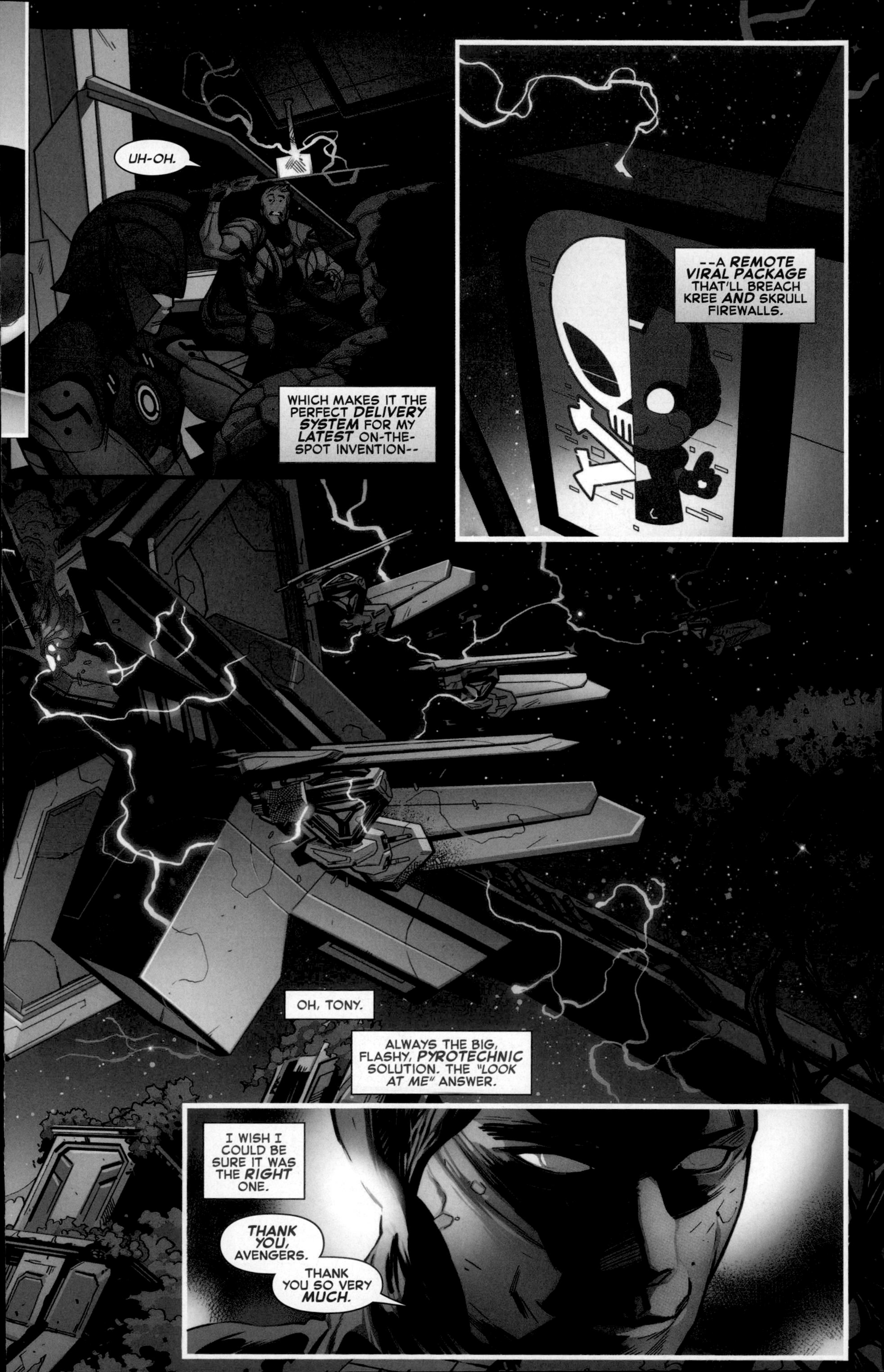
UH-OH.
WHICH MAKES IT THE PERFECT DELIVERY SYSTEM FOR MY LATEST ON-THE-SPOT INVENTION--
--A REMOTE VIRAL PACKAGE THAT'LL BREACH KREE AND SKRULL FIREWALLS.
OH, TONY.
ALWAYS THE BIG, FLASHY, PYROTECHNIC SOLUTION. THE "LOOK AT ME" ANSWER.
I WISH I COULD BE SURE IT WAS THE RIGHT ONE.
THANK YOU, AVENGERS.
THANK YOU SO VERY MUCH.

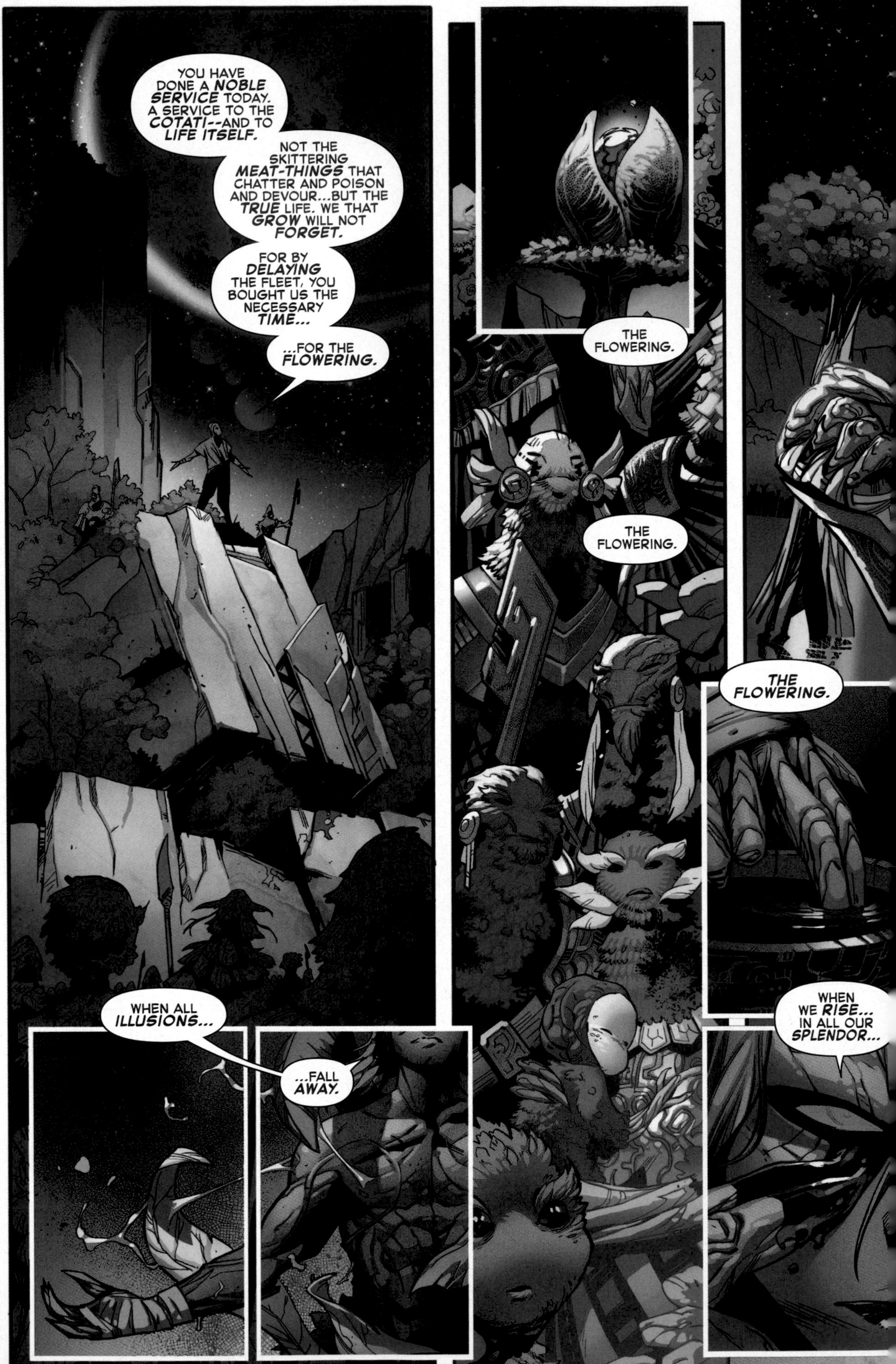
YOU HAVE DONE A NOBLE SERVICE TODAY. A SERVICE TO THE COTATI--AND TO LIFE ITSELF.
NOT THE SKITTERING MEAT-THINGS THAT CHATTER AND POISON AND DEVOUR...BUT THE TRUE LIFE. WE THAT GROW WILL NOT FORGET.
FOR BY DELAYING THE FLEET, YOU BOUGHT US THE NECESSARY TIME...
...FOR THE FLOWERING.
THE FLOWERING.
THE FLOWERING.
THE FLOWERING.
WHEN ALL ILLUSIONS...
...FALL AWAY.
WHEN WE RISE... IN ALL OUR SPLENDOR...

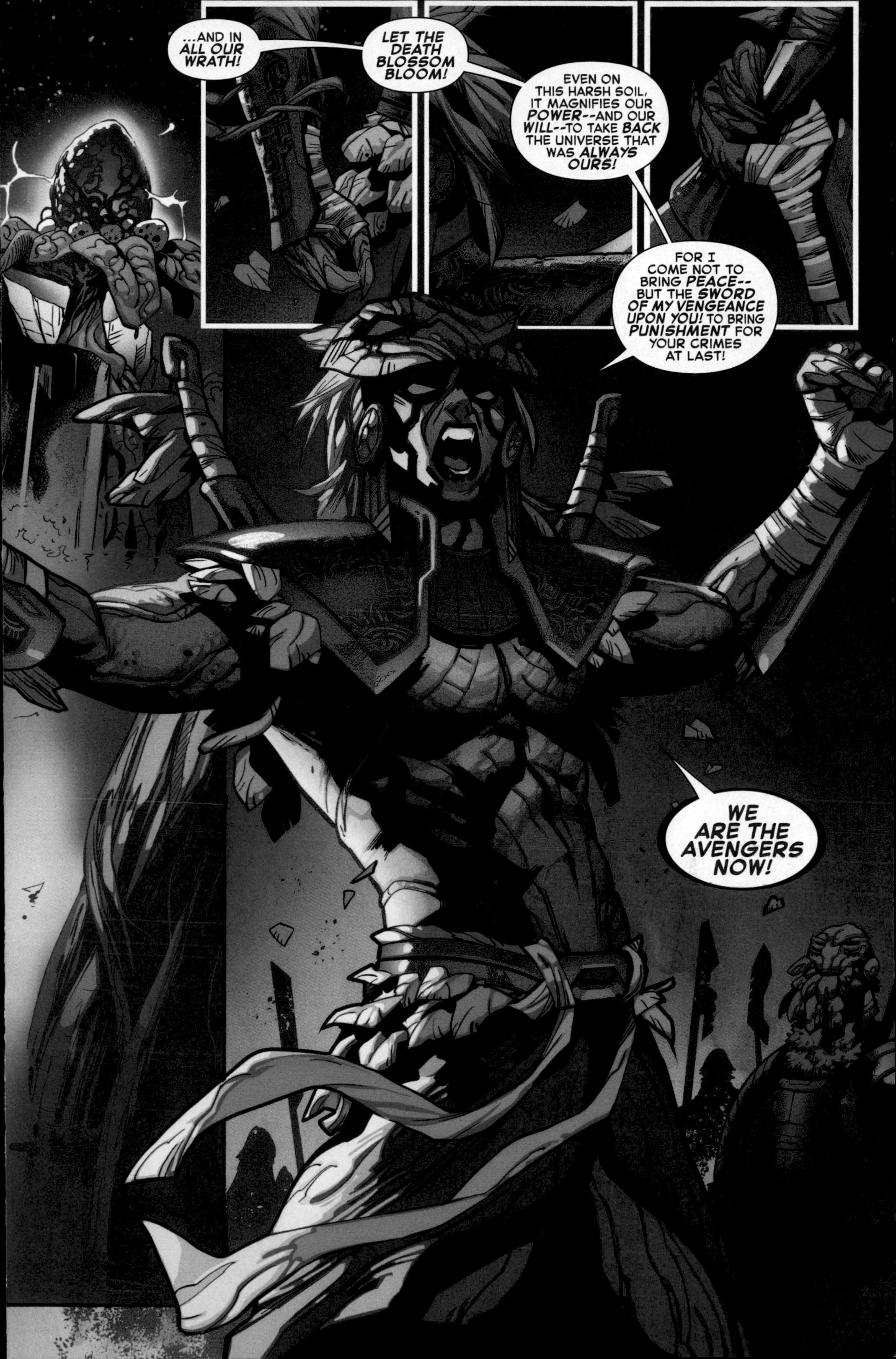
...AND IN ALL OUR WRATH!
LET THE DEATH BLOSSOM BLOOM!
EVEN ON THIS HARSH SOIL, IT MAGNIFIES OUR POWER--AND OUR WILL--TO TAKE BACK THE UNIVERSE THAT WAS ALWAYS OURS!
FOR I COME NOT TO BRING PEACE-- BUT THE SWORD OF MY VENGEANCE UPON YOU! TO BRING PUNISHMENT FOR YOUR CRIMES AT LAST!
WE ARE THE AVENGERS NOW!

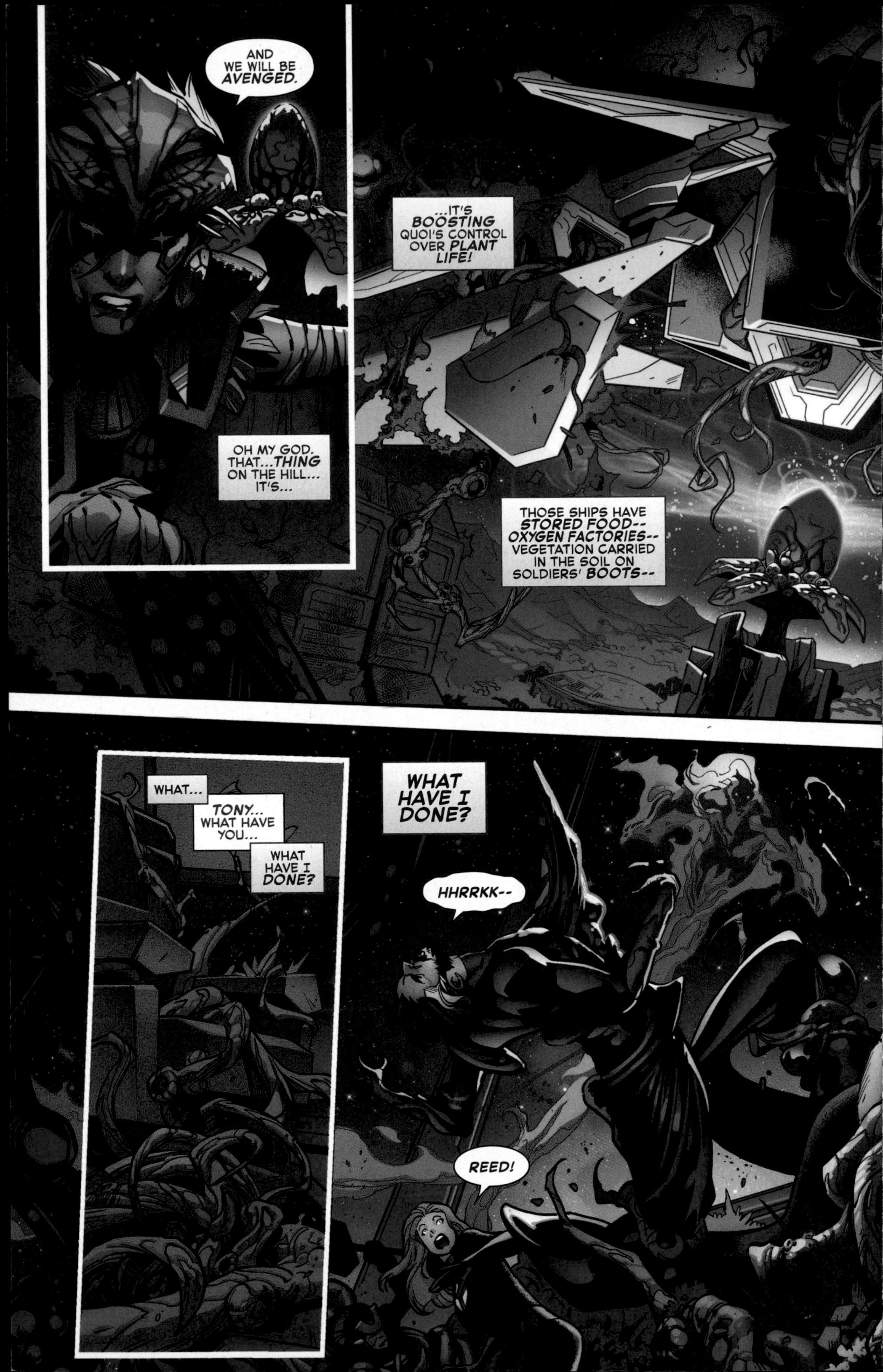
AND WE WILL BE AVENGED.
...IT'S BOOSTING QUOI'S CONTROL OVER PLANT LIFE!
OH MY GOD. THAT...THING ON THE HILL... IT'S...
THOSE SHIPS HAVE STORED FOOD-- OXYGEN FACTORIES-- VEGETATION CARRIED IN THE SOIL ON SOLDIERS' BOOTS--
WHAT...
TONY... WHAT HAVE YOU...
WHAT HAVE I DONE?
WHAT HAVE I DONE?
HHRRKK--
REED!

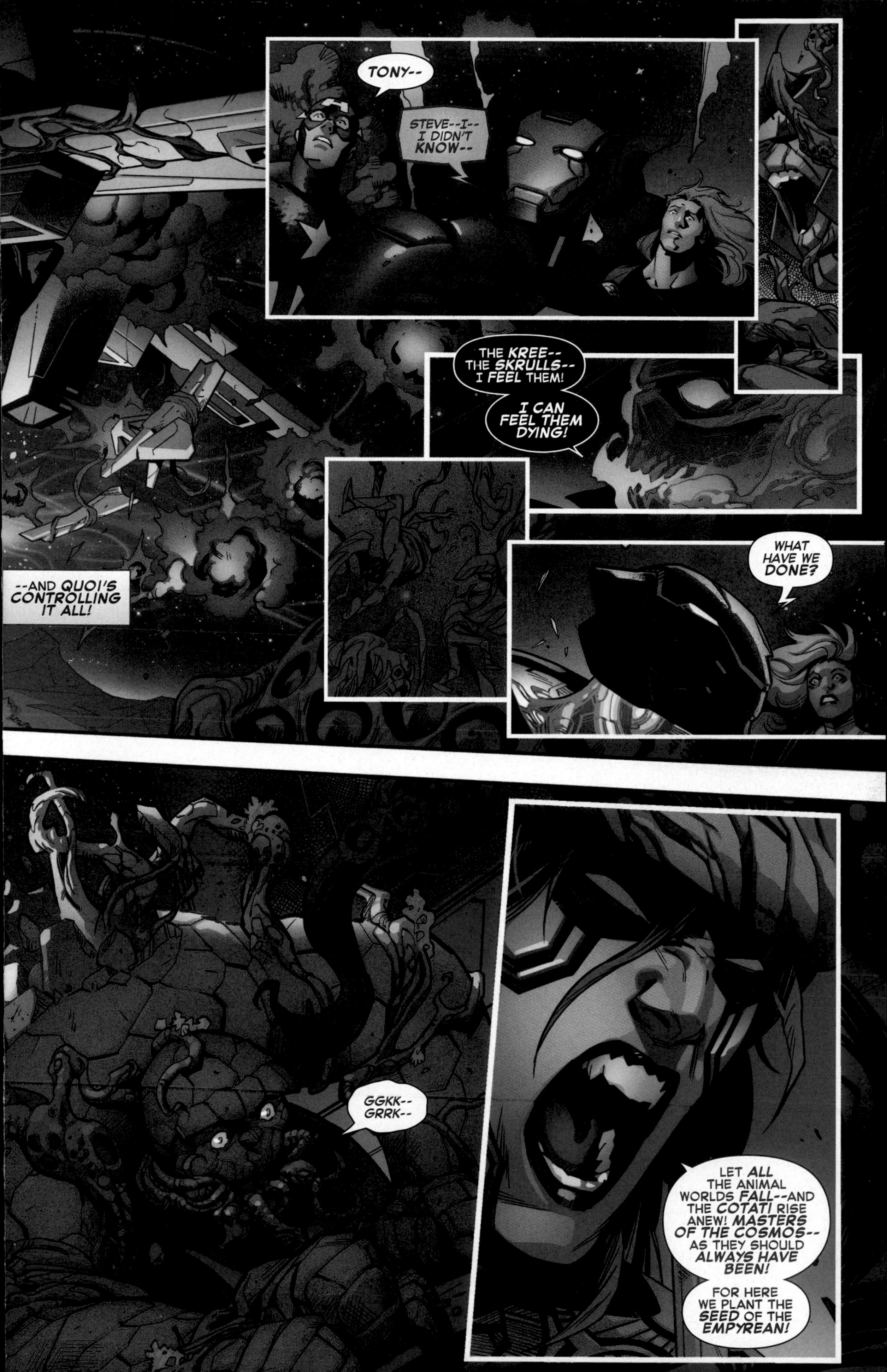
--AND QUOI'S CONTROLLING IT ALL!
TONY--
STEVE--I-- I DIDN'T KNOW--
THE KREE-- THE SKRULLS-- I FEEL THEM!
I CAN FEEL THEM DYING!
WHAT HAVE WE DONE?
GGKK-- GRRK--
LET ALL THE ANIMAL WORLDS FALL--AND THE COTATI RISE ANEW! MASTERS OF THE COSMOS-- AS THEY SHOULD ALWAYS HAVE BEEN!
FOR HERE WE PLANT THE SEED OF THE EMPYREAN!

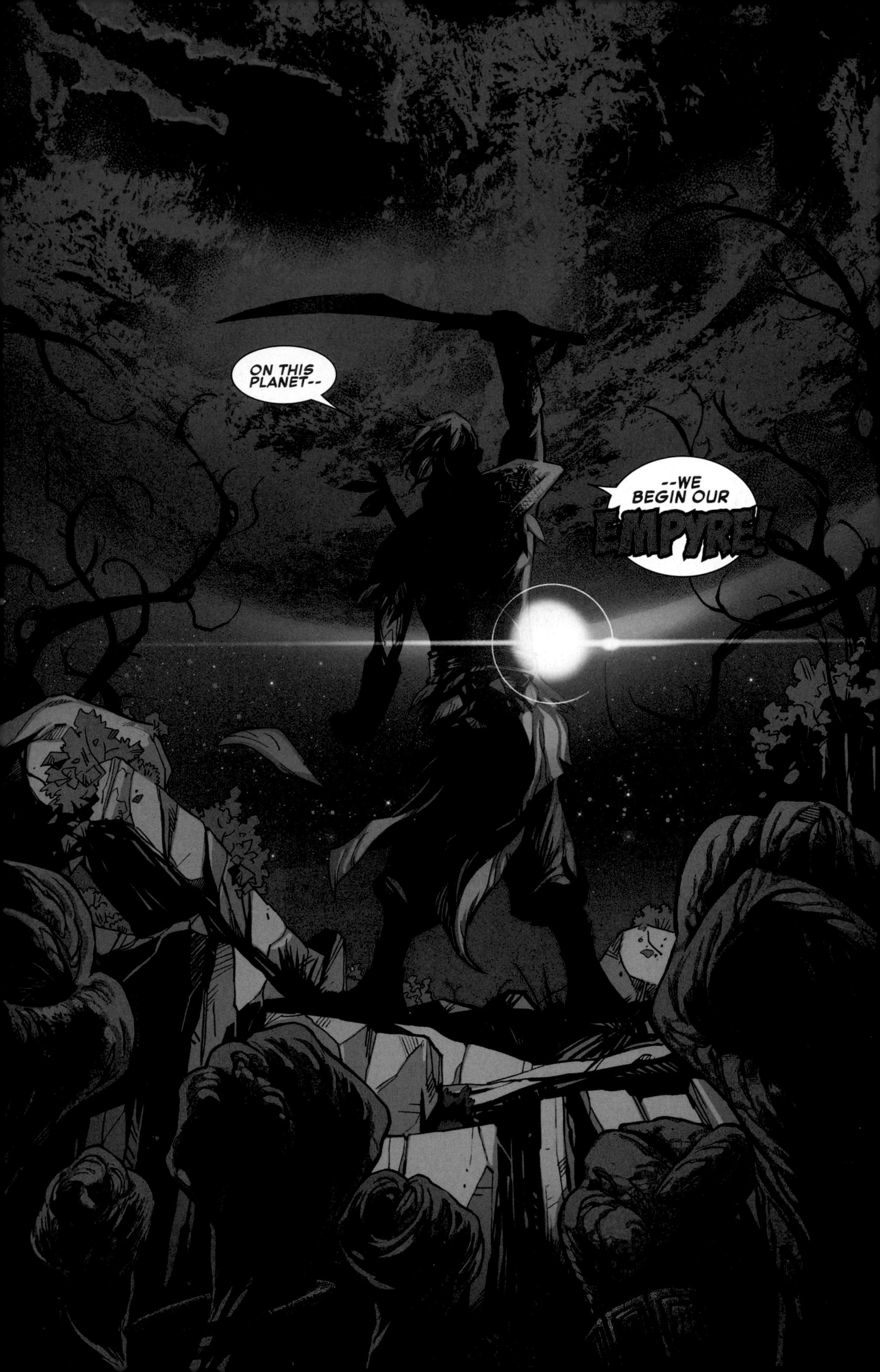
ON THIS PLANET--
--WE BEGIN OUR EMPYRE!

EMPYRE 1 VARIANT BY

Jamie McKelvie

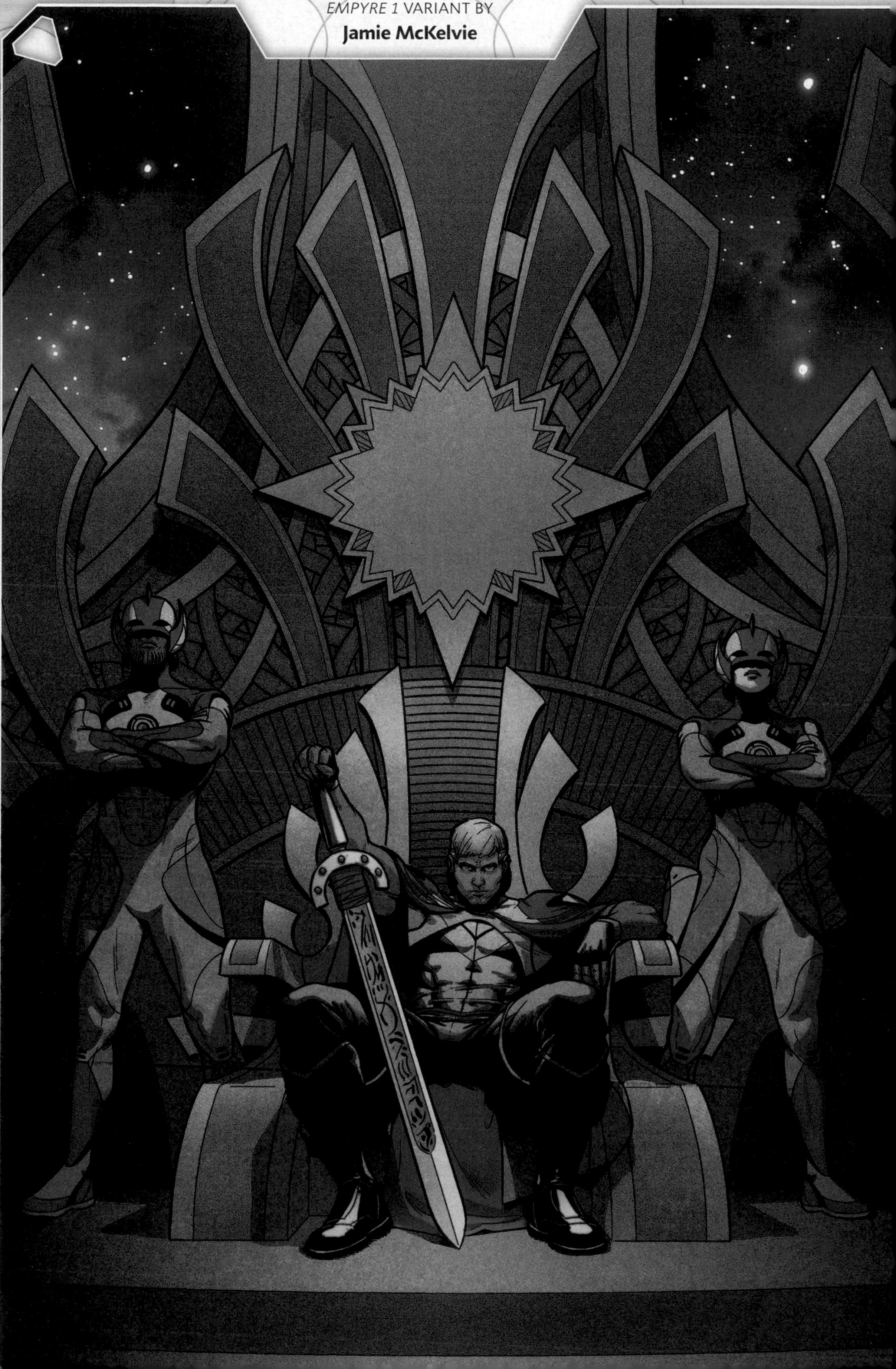

EMPYRE 2

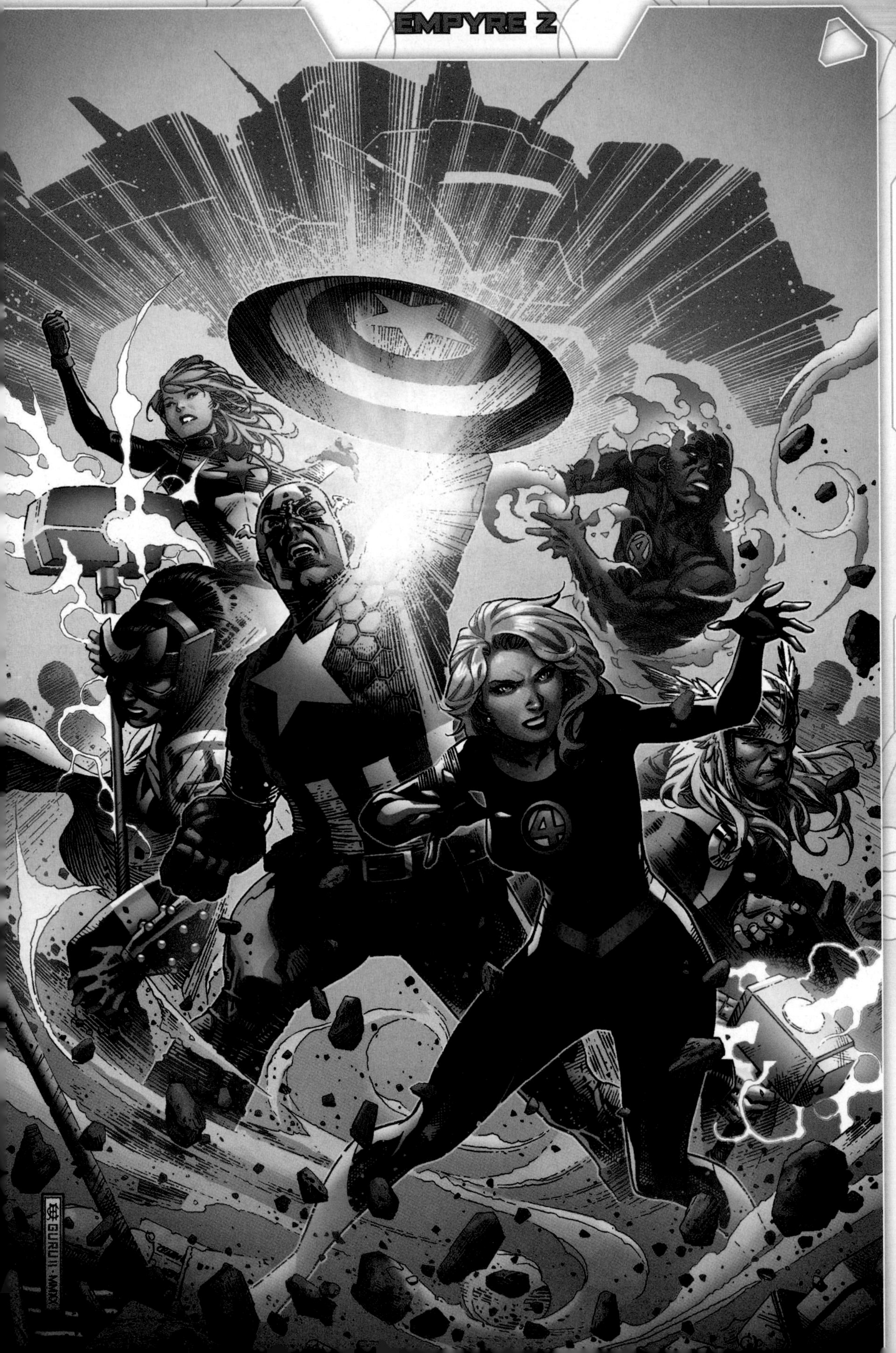
GURU
MMXX

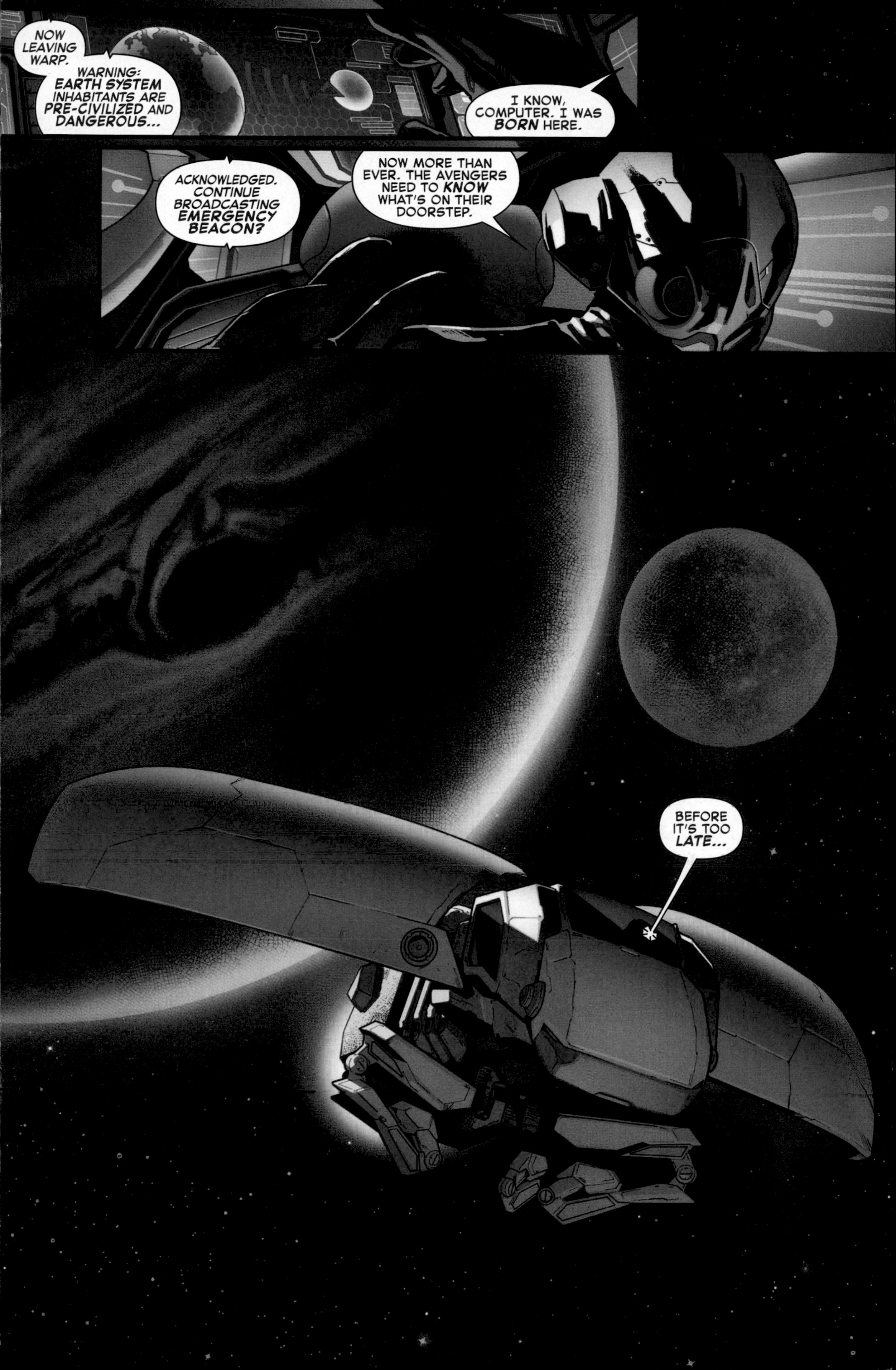
NOW LEAVING WARP.
WARNING: EARTH SYSTEM INHABITANTS ARE PRE-CIVILIZED AND DANGEROUS...
I KNOW, COMPUTER. I WAS BORN HERE.
ACKNOWLEDGED. CONTINUE BROADCASTING EMERGENCY BEACON?
NOW MORE THAN EVER. THE AVENGERS NEED TO KNOW WHAT'S ON THEIR DOORSTEP.
BEFORE IT'S TOO LATE...

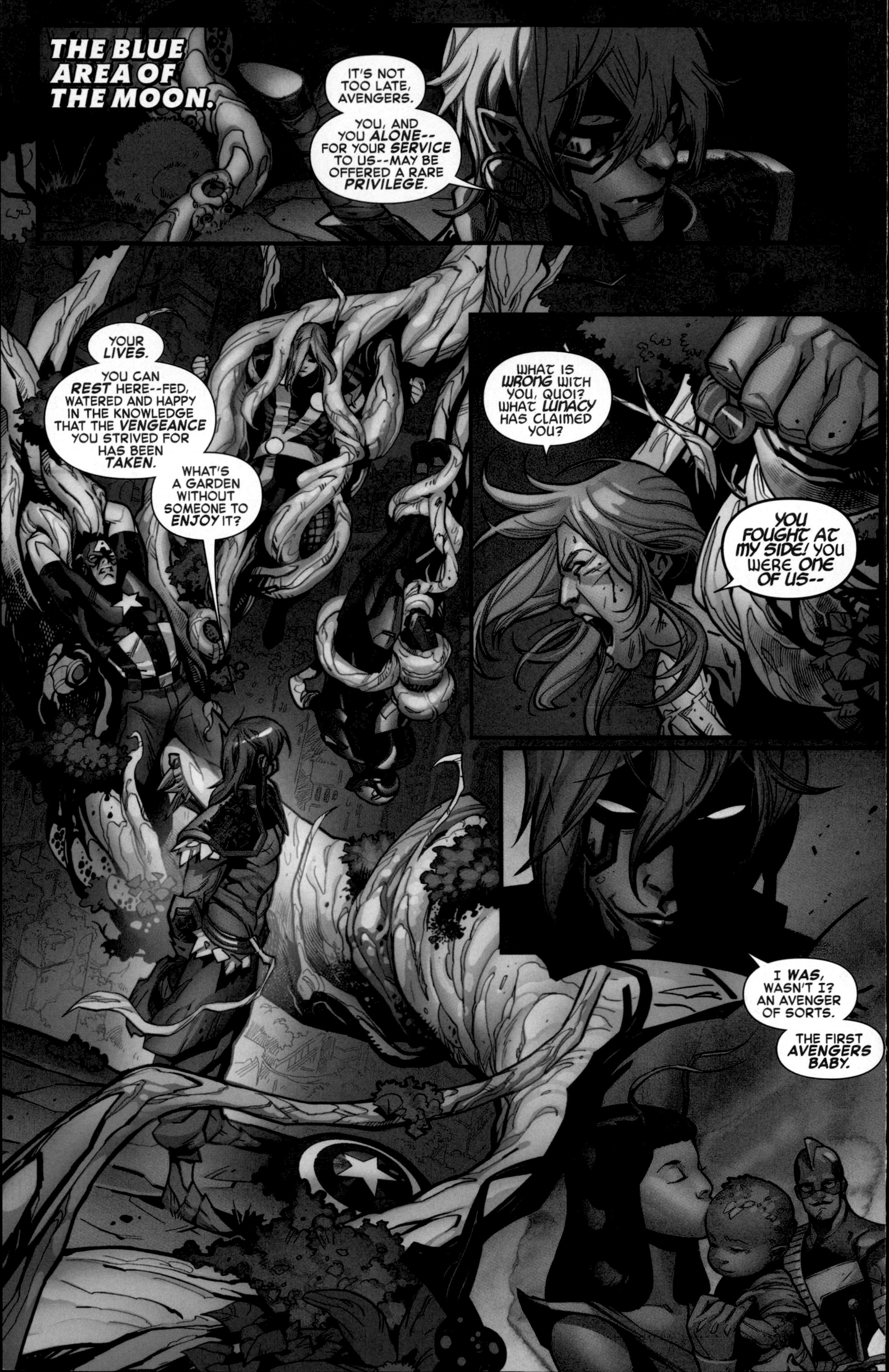

THE BLUE AREA OF THE MOON.
IT'S NOT TOO LATE, AVENGERS.
YOU, AND YOU ALONE-- FOR YOUR SERVICE TO US--MAY BE OFFERED A RARE PRIVILEGE.
YOUR LIVES.
YOU CAN REST HERE--FED, WATERED AND HAPPY IN THE KNOWLEDGE THAT THE VENGEANCE YOU STRIVED FOR HAS BEEN TAKEN.
WHAT'S A GARDEN WITHOUT SOMEONE TO ENJOY IT?
WHAT IS WRONG WITH YOU, QUOI? WHAT LUNACY HAS CLAIMED YOU?
YOU FOUGHT AT MY SIDE! YOU WERE ONE OF US--
I WAS, WASN'T I? AN AVENGER OF SORTS.
THE FIRST AVENGERS BABY.

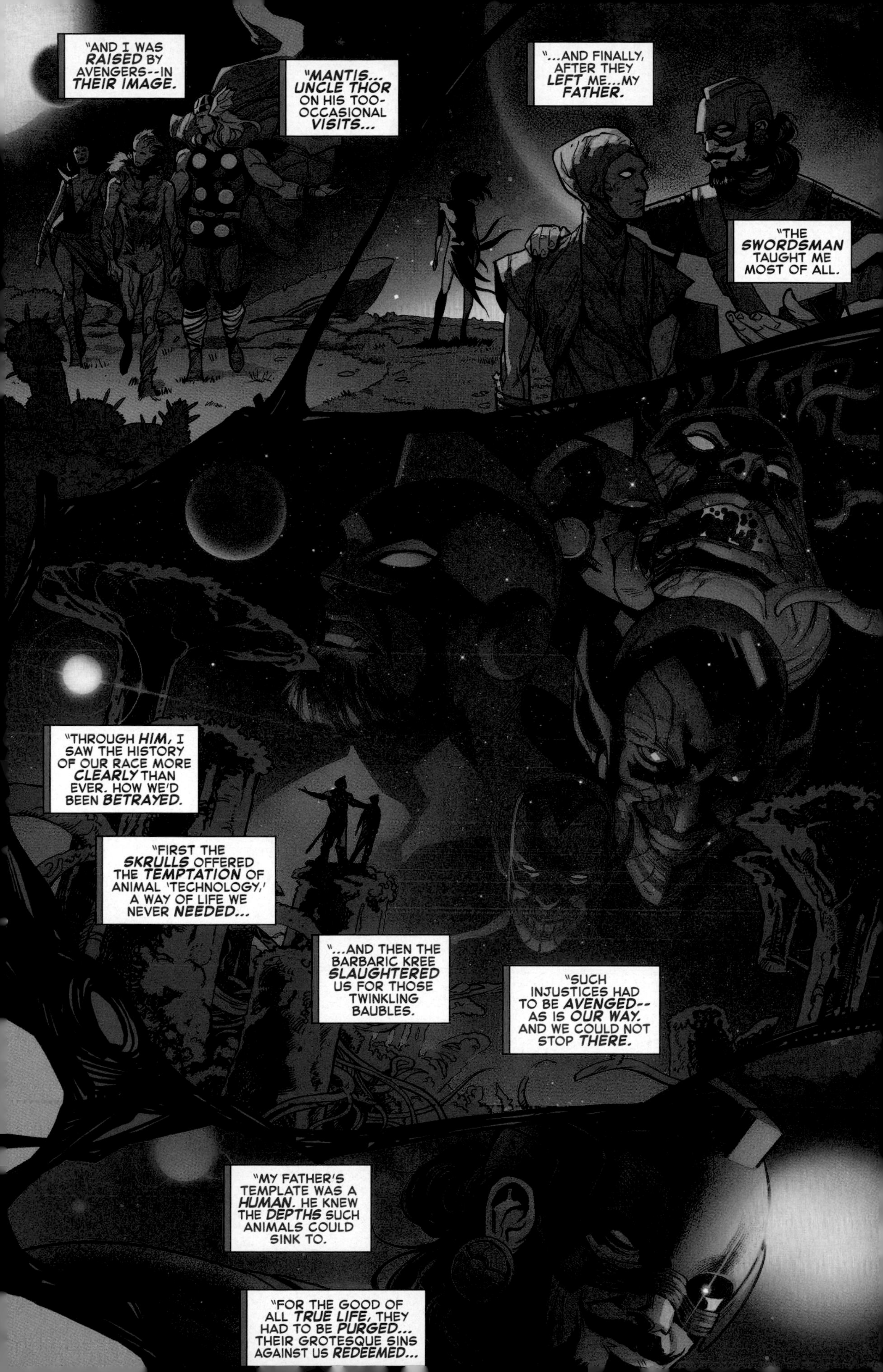
"AND I WAS RAISED BY AVENGERS--IN THEIR IMAGE.
"MANTIS... UNCLE THOR ON HIS TOO-OCCASIONAL VISITS...
"...AND FINALLY, AFTER THEY LEFT ME...MY FATHER.
"THE SWORDSMAN TAUGHT ME MOST OF ALL.
"THROUGH HIM, I SAW THE HISTORY OF OUR RACE MORE CLEARLY THAN EVER. HOW WE'D BEEN BETRAYED.
"FIRST THE SKRULLS OFFERED THE TEMPTATION OF ANIMAL 'TECHNOLOGY,' A WAY OF LIFE WE NEVER NEEDED...
"...AND THEN THE BARBARIC KREE SLAUGHTERED US FOR THOSE TWINKLING BAUBLES.
"SUCH INJUSTICES HAD TO BE AVENGED--AS IS OUR WAY. AND WE COULD NOT STOP THERE.
"MY FATHER'S TEMPLATE WAS A HUMAN. HE KNEW THE DEPTHS SUCH ANIMALS COULD SINK TO.
"FOR THE GOOD OF ALL TRUE LIFE, THEY HAD TO BE PURGED... THEIR GROTESQUE SINS AGAINST US REDEEMED...

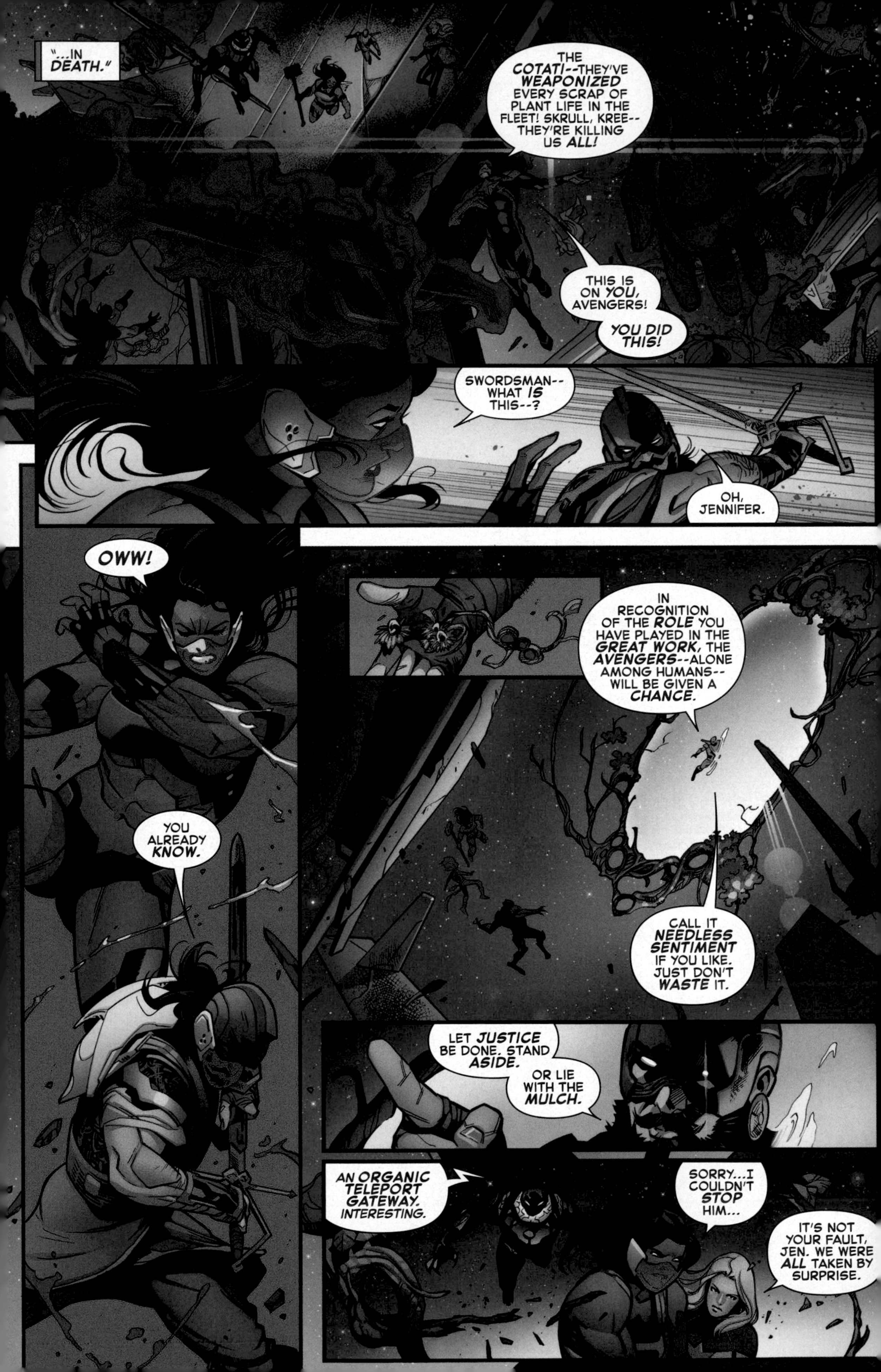
"...IN DEATH."
THE COTATI--THEY'VE WEAPONIZED EVERY SCRAP OF PLANT LIFE IN THE FLEET! SKRULL, KREE--THEY'RE KILLING US ALL!
THIS IS ON YOU, AVENGERS!
YOU DID THIS!
SWORDSMAN--WHAT IS THIS--?
OH, JENNIFER.
OWW!
YOU ALREADY KNOW.
IN RECOGNITION OF THE ROLE YOU HAVE PLAYED IN THE GREAT WORK, THE AVENGERS--ALONE AMONG HUMANS--WILL BE GIVEN A CHANCE.
CALL IT NEEDLESS SENTIMENT IF YOU LIKE. JUST DON'T WASTE IT.
LET JUSTICE BE DONE. STAND ASIDE.
OR LIE WITH THE MULCH.
AN ORGANIC TELEPORT GATEWAY. INTERESTING.
SORRY...I COULDN'T STOP HIM...
IT'S NOT YOUR FAULT, JEN. WE WERE ALL TAKEN BY SURPRISE.

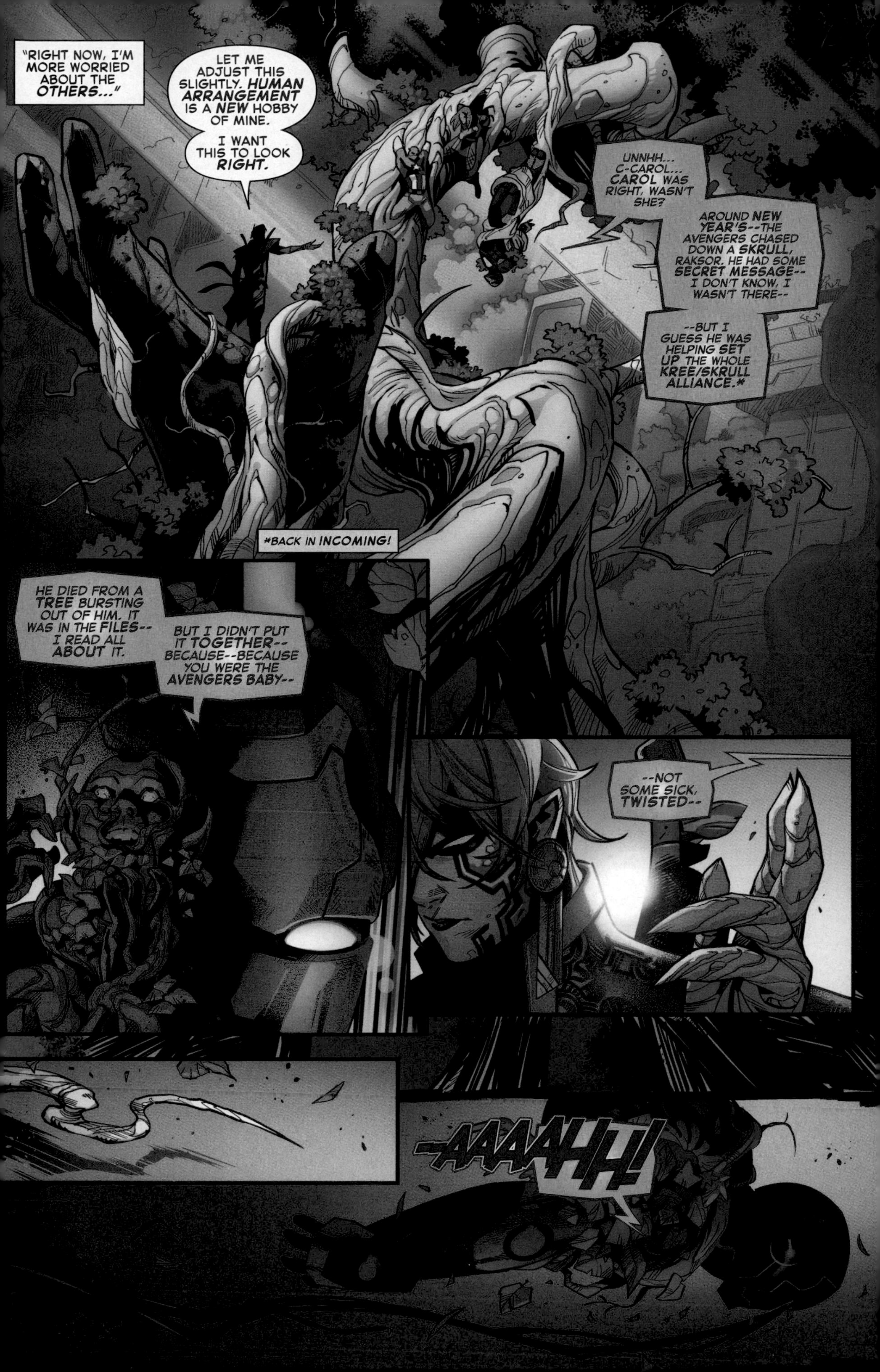
"RIGHT NOW, I'M MORE WORRIED ABOUT THE OTHERS..."
LET ME ADJUST THIS SLIGHTLY. HUMAN ARRANGEMENT IS A NEW HOBBY OF MINE.
I WANT THIS TO LOOK RIGHT.
UNNHH... C-CAROL... CAROL WAS RIGHT, WASN'T SHE?
AROUND NEW YEAR'S--THE AVENGERS CHASED DOWN A SKRULL, RAKSOR. HE HAD SOME SECRET MESSAGE--I DON'T KNOW, I WASN'T THERE--
--BUT I GUESS HE WAS HELPING SET UP THE WHOLE KREE/SKRULL ALLIANCE.*
*BACK IN INCOMING!
HE DIED FROM A TREE BURSTING OUT OF HIM. IT WAS IN THE FILES--I READ ALL ABOUT IT.
BUT I DIDN'T PUT IT TOGETHER--BECAUSE--BECAUSE YOU WERE THE AVENGERS BABY--
--NOT SOME SICK, TWISTED--
-AAAAHH!

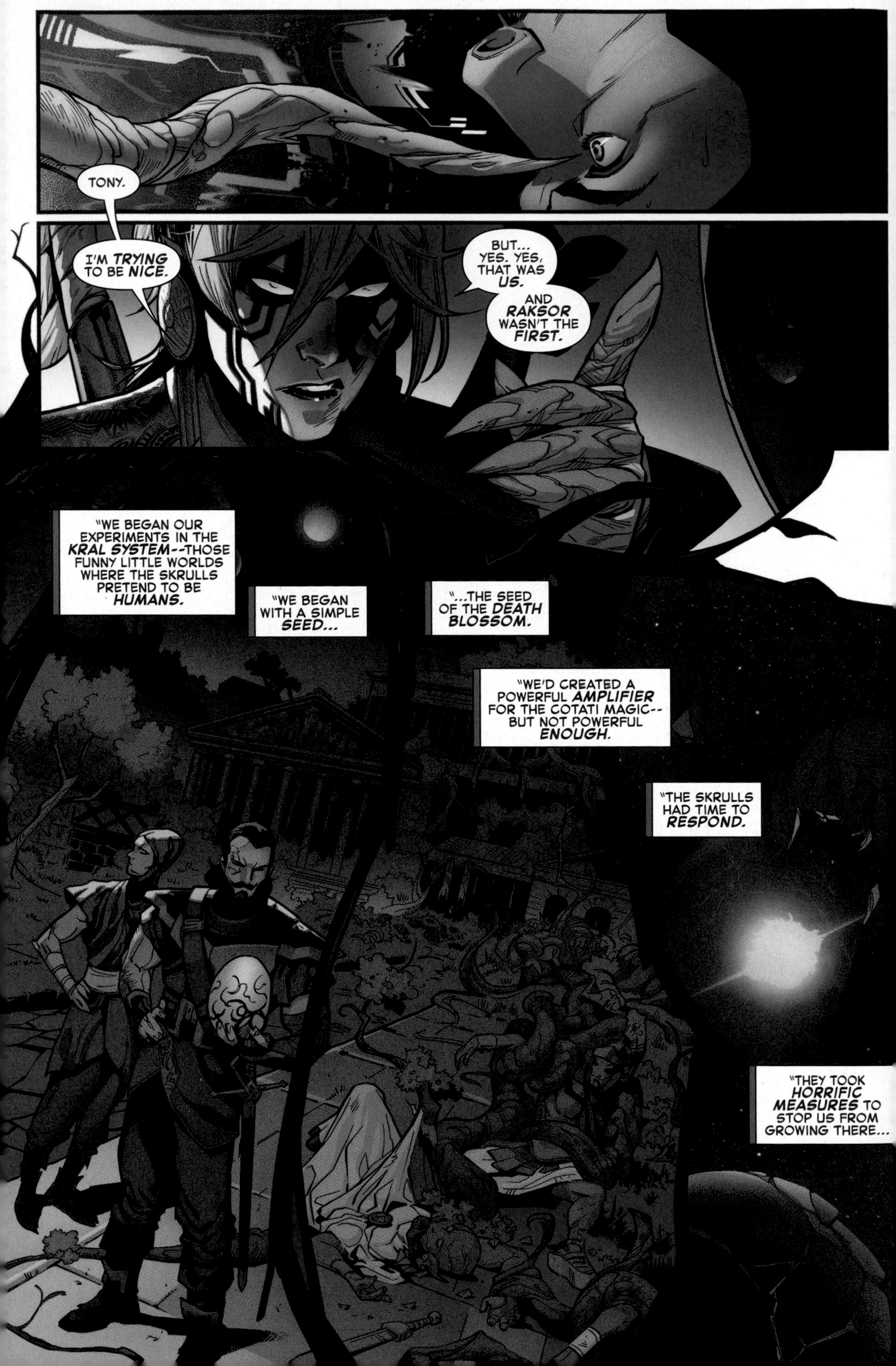
TONY.
I'M TRYING TO BE NICE.
BUT... YES. YES, THAT WAS US.
AND RAKSOR WASN'T THE FIRST.
"WE BEGAN OUR EXPERIMENTS IN THE KRAL SYSTEM--THOSE FUNNY LITTLE WORLDS WHERE THE SKRULLS PRETEND TO BE HUMANS.
"WE BEGAN WITH A SIMPLE SEED...
"...THE SEED OF THE DEATH BLOSSOM.
"WE'D CREATED A POWERFUL AMPLIFIER FOR THE COTATI MAGIC--BUT NOT POWERFUL ENOUGH.
"THE SKRULLS HAD TIME TO RESPOND.
"THEY TOOK HORRIFIC MEASURES TO STOP US FROM GROWING THERE...

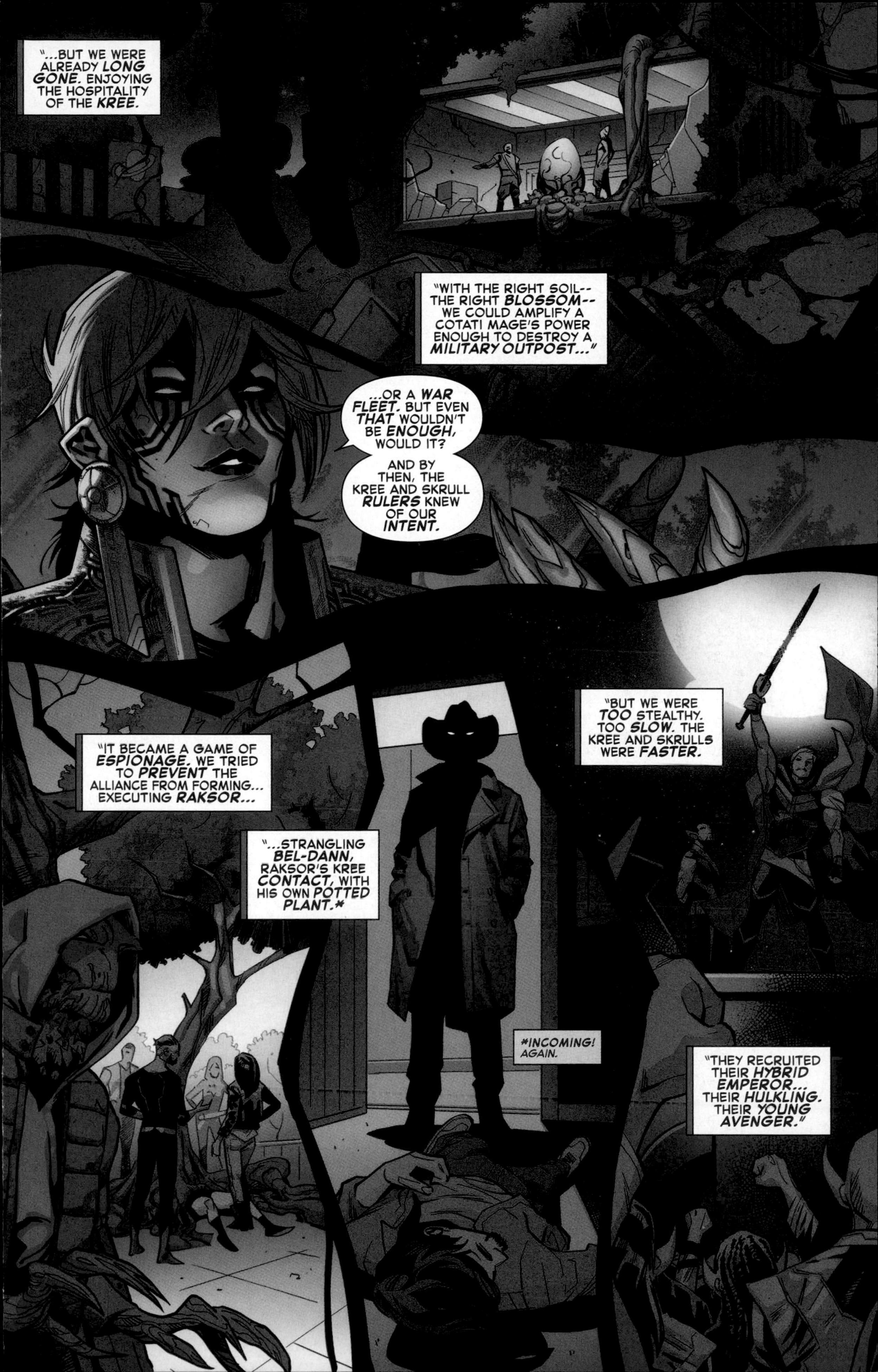
"...BUT WE WERE ALREADY LONG GONE. ENJOYING THE HOSPITALITY OF THE KREE.
"WITH THE RIGHT SOIL-- THE RIGHT BLOSSOM-- WE COULD AMPLIFY A COTATI MAGE'S POWER ENOUGH TO DESTROY A MILITARY OUTPOST..."
...OR A WAR FLEET. BUT EVEN THAT WOULDN'T BE ENOUGH, WOULD IT?
AND BY THEN, THE KREE AND SKRULL RULERS KNEW OF OUR INTENT.
"IT BECAME A GAME OF ESPIONAGE. WE TRIED TO PREVENT THE ALLIANCE FROM FORMING... EXECUTING RAKSOR...
"...STRANGLING BEL-DANN, RAKSOR'S KREE CONTACT, WITH HIS OWN POTTED PLANT.*
*INCOMING! AGAIN.
"BUT WE WERE TOO STEALTHY. TOO SLOW. THE KREE AND SKRULLS WERE FASTER.
"THEY RECRUITED THEIR HYBRID EMPEROR... THEIR HULKLING. THEIR YOUNG AVENGER."

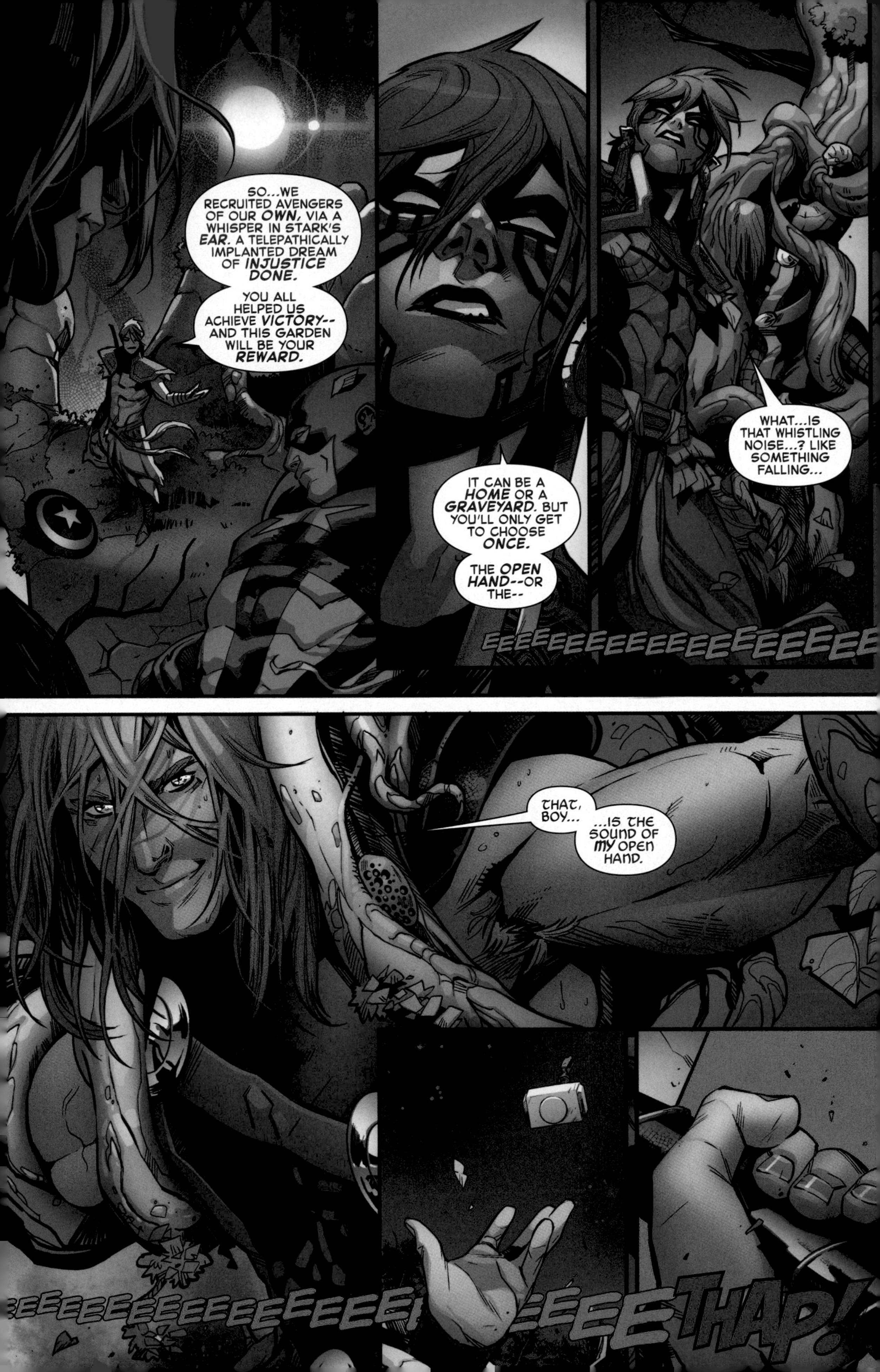

SO...WE RECRUITED AVENGERS OF OUR OWN, VIA A WHISPER IN STARK'S EAR. A TELEPATHICALLY IMPLANTED DREAM OF INJUSTICE DONE.
YOU ALL HELPED US ACHIEVE VICTORY-- AND THIS GARDEN WILL BE YOUR REWARD.
IT CAN BE A HOME OR A GRAVEYARD. BUT YOU'LL ONLY GET TO CHOOSE ONCE.
THE OPEN HAND--OR THE--
WHAT...IS THAT WHISTLING NOISE...? LIKE SOMETHING FALLING...
EEEEEEEEEEEEEEEEEEEE
THAT, BOY...
...IS THE SOUND OF MY OPEN HAND.
EEEEEEEEEEEEEEEEEEEEEEEEEEETHAP!

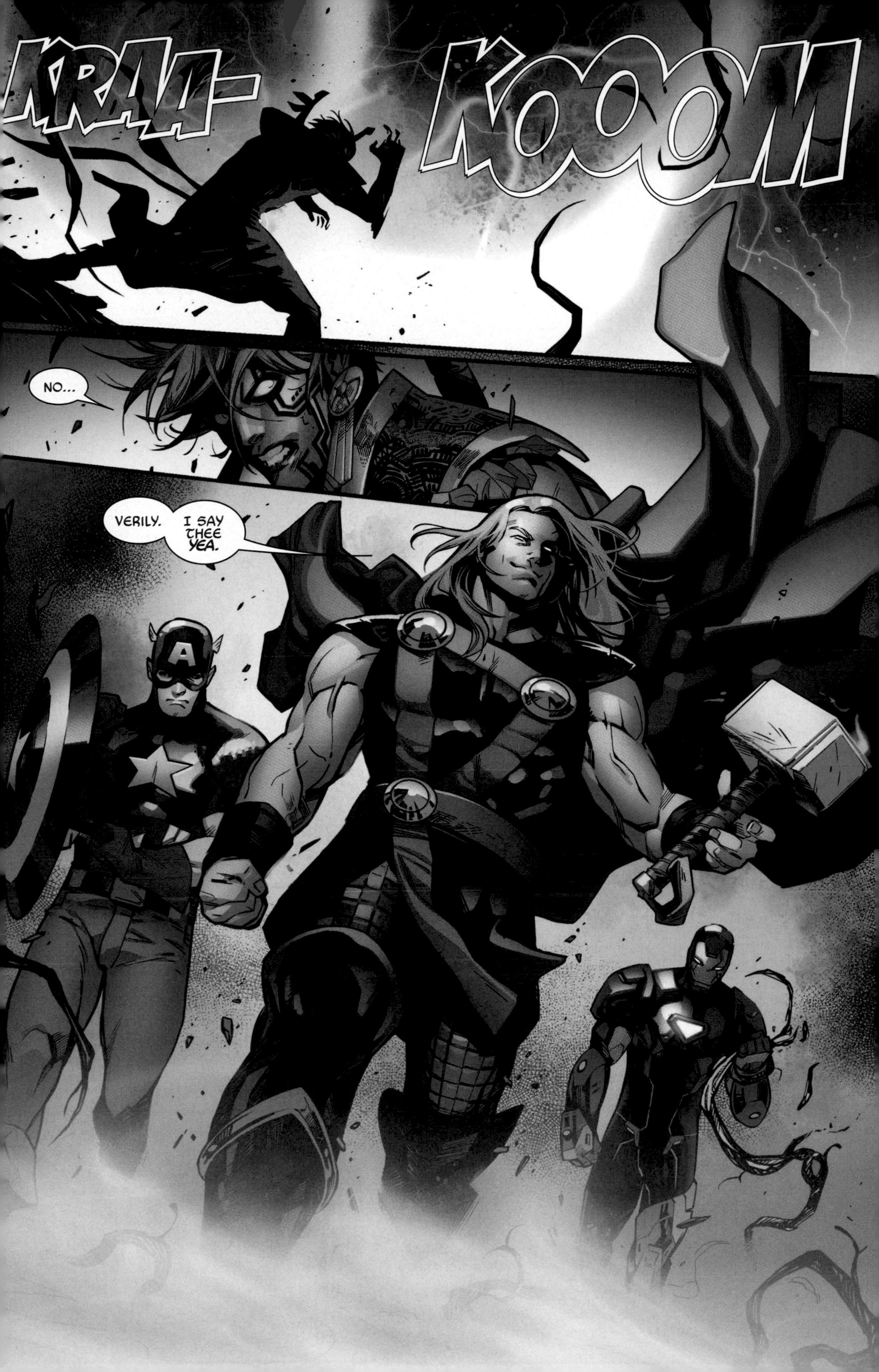
KRAAA-
KOOOM
NO...
VERILY.
I SAY THEE YEA.

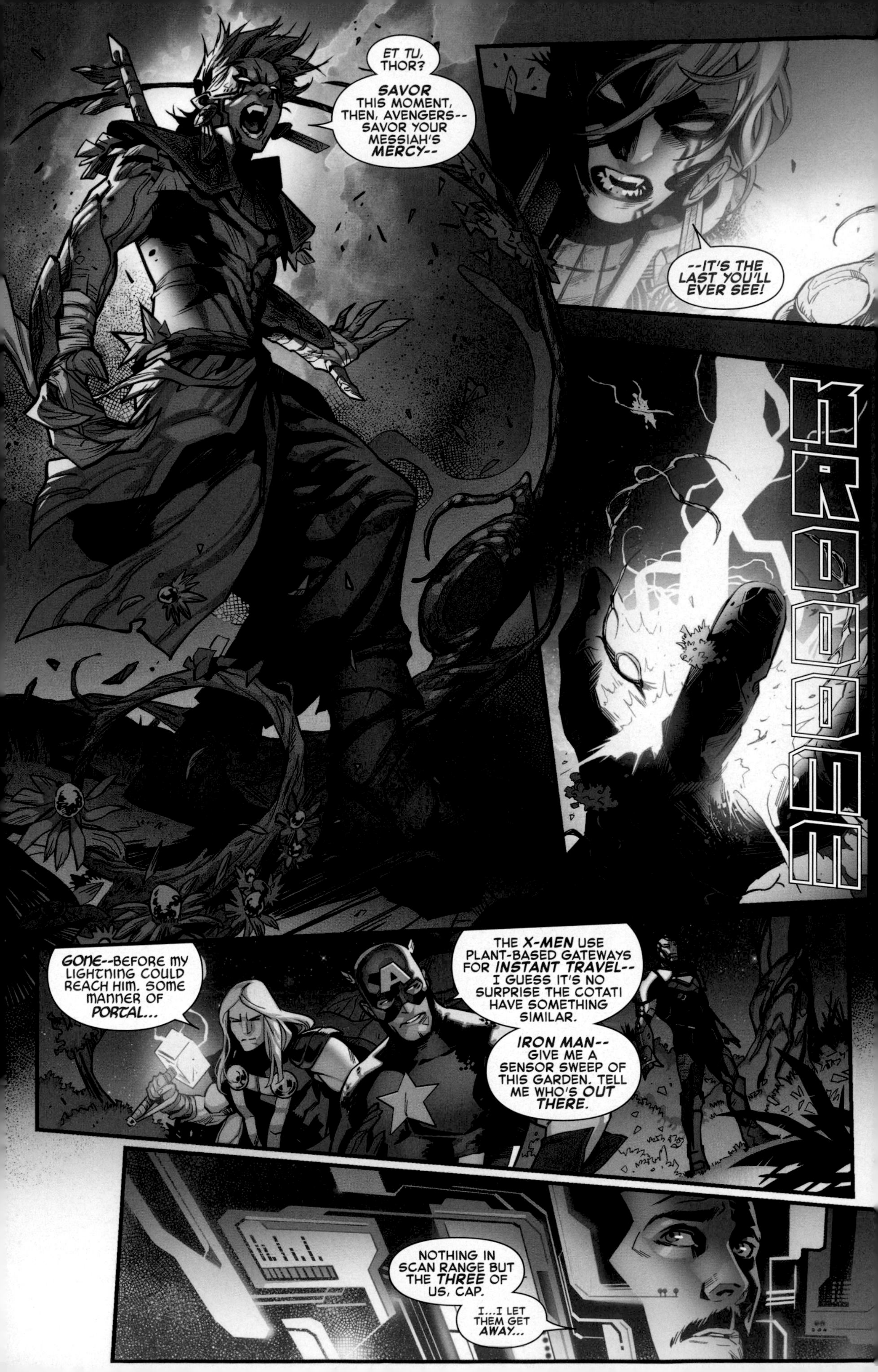
ET TU, THOR?
SAVOR THIS MOMENT, THEN, AVENGERS-- SAVOR YOUR MESSIAH'S MERCY--
--IT'S THE LAST YOU'LL EVER SEE!
KRDOOOM
GONE--BEFORE MY LIGHTNING COULD REACH HIM. SOME MANNER OF PORTAL...
THE X-MEN USE PLANT-BASED GATEWAYS FOR INSTANT TRAVEL-- I GUESS IT'S NO SURPRISE THE COTATI HAVE SOMETHING SIMILAR.
IRON MAN-- GIVE ME A SENSOR SWEEP OF THIS GARDEN. TELL ME WHO'S OUT THERE.
NOTHING IN SCAN RANGE BUT THE THREE OF US, CAP.
I...I LET THEM GET AWAY...

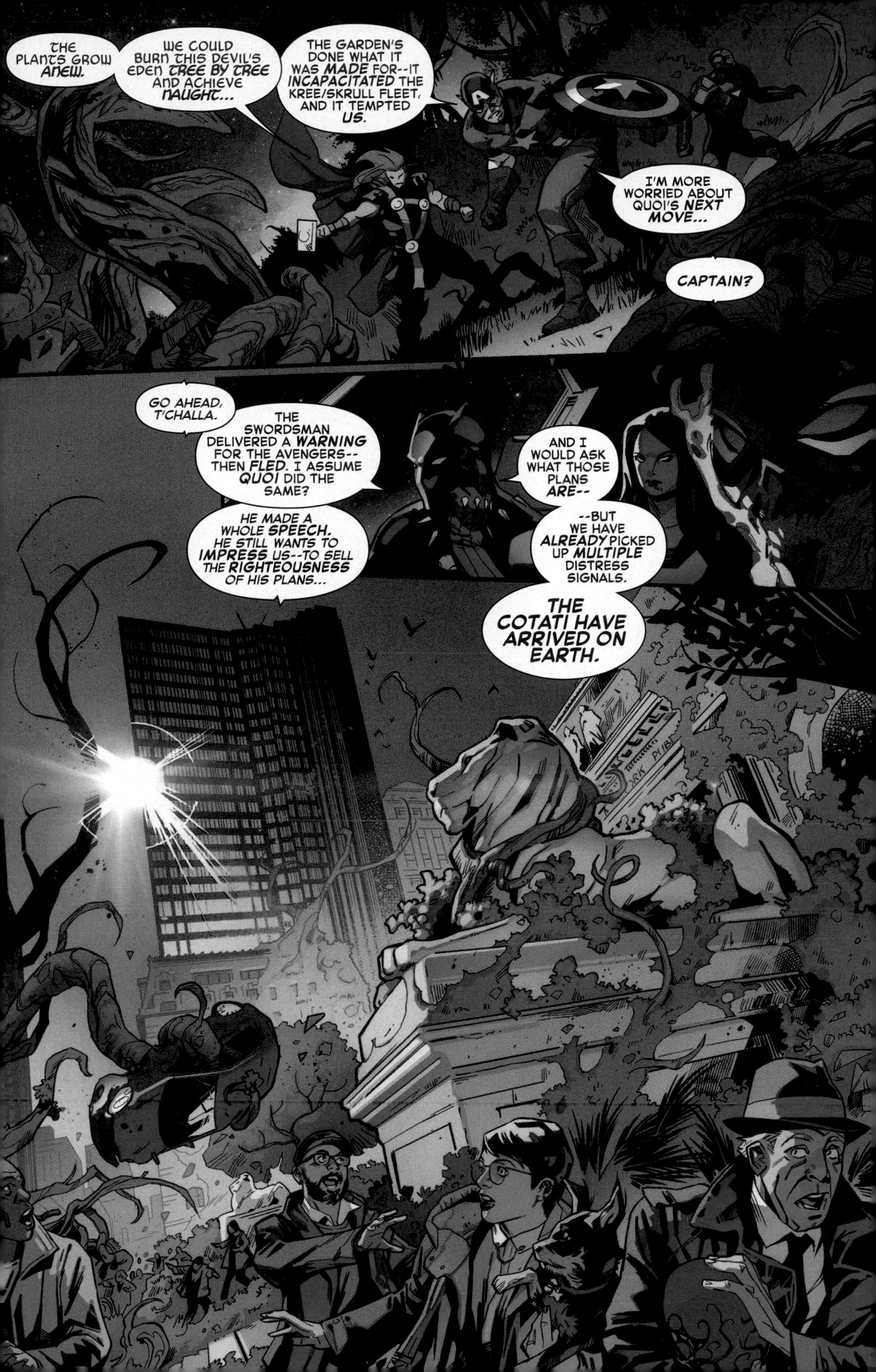
THE PLANTS GROW ANEW.
WE COULD BURN THIS DEVIL'S EDEN TREE BY TREE AND ACHIEVE NAUGHT...
THE GARDEN'S DONE WHAT IT WAS MADE FOR--IT INCAPACITATED THE KREE/SKRULL FLEET, AND IT TEMPTED US.
I'M MORE WORRIED ABOUT QUOI'S NEXT MOVE...
CAPTAIN?
GO AHEAD, T'CHALLA.
THE SWORDSMAN DELIVERED A WARNING FOR THE AVENGERS--THEN FLED. I ASSUME QUOI DID THE SAME?
HE MADE A WHOLE SPEECH. HE STILL WANTS TO IMPRESS US--TO SELL THE RIGHTEOUSNESS OF HIS PLANS...
AND I WOULD ASK WHAT THOSE PLANS ARE--
--BUT WE HAVE ALREADY PICKED UP MULTIPLE DISTRESS SIGNALS.
THE COTATI HAVE ARRIVED ON EARTH.

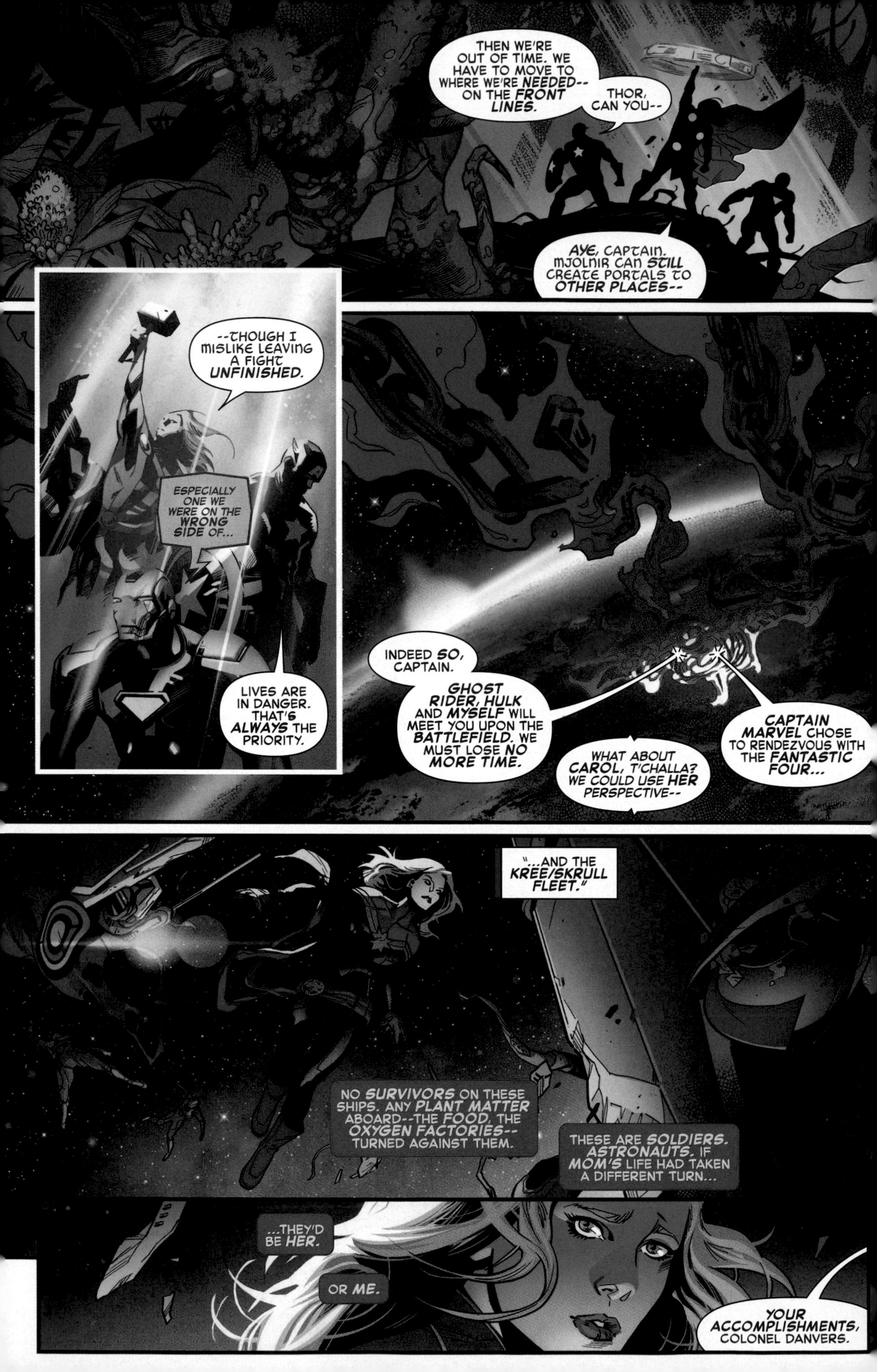
THEN WE'RE OUT OF TIME. WE HAVE TO MOVE TO WHERE WE'RE NEEDED-- ON THE FRONT LINES.
THOR, CAN YOU--
AYE, CAPTAIN. MJOLNIR CAN STILL CREATE PORTALS TO OTHER PLACES--
--THOUGH I MISLIKE LEAVING A FIGHT UNFINISHED.
ESPECIALLY ONE WE WERE ON THE WRONG SIDE OF...
LIVES ARE IN DANGER. THAT'S ALWAYS THE PRIORITY.
INDEED SO, CAPTAIN.
GHOST RIDER, HULK AND MYSELF WILL MEET YOU UPON THE BATTLEFIELD. WE MUST LOSE NO MORE TIME.
WHAT ABOUT CAROL, T'CHALLA? WE COULD USE HER PERSPECTIVE--
CAPTAIN MARVEL CHOSE TO RENDEZVOUS WITH THE FANTASTIC FOUR...
"...AND THE KREE/SKRULL FLEET."
NO SURVIVORS ON THESE SHIPS. ANY PLANT MATTER ABOARD--THE FOOD, THE OXYGEN FACTORIES-- TURNED AGAINST THEM.
THESE ARE SOLDIERS. ASTRONAUTS. IF MOM'S LIFE HAD TAKEN A DIFFERENT TURN...
...THEY'D BE HER.
OR ME.
YOUR ACCOMPLISHMENTS, COLONEL DANVERS.

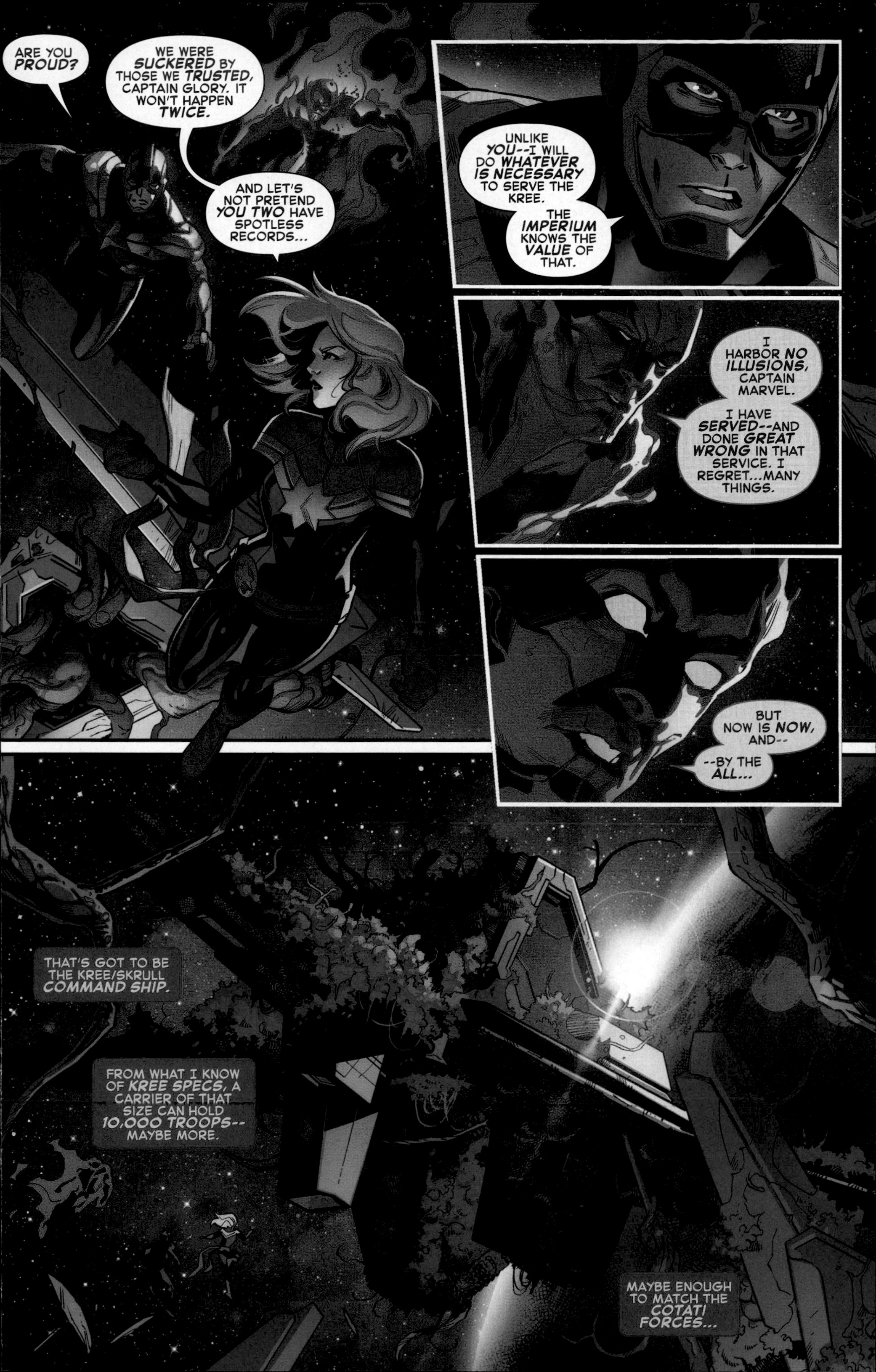
ARE YOU PROUD?
WE WERE SUCKERED BY THOSE WE TRUSTED, CAPTAIN GLORY. IT WON'T HAPPEN TWICE.
AND LET'S NOT PRETEND YOU TWO HAVE SPOTLESS RECORDS...
UNLIKE YOU--I WILL DO WHATEVER IS NECESSARY TO SERVE THE KREE.
THE IMPERIUM KNOWS THE VALUE OF THAT.
I HARBOR NO ILLUSIONS, CAPTAIN MARVEL.
I HAVE SERVED--AND DONE GREAT WRONG IN THAT SERVICE. I REGRET...MANY THINGS.
BUT NOW IS NOW, AND--
--BY THE ALL...
THAT'S GOT TO BE THE KREE/SKRULL COMMAND SHIP.
FROM WHAT I KNOW OF KREE SPECS, A CARRIER OF THAT SIZE CAN HOLD 10,000 TROOPS--MAYBE MORE.
MAYBE ENOUGH TO MATCH THE COTATI FORCES...

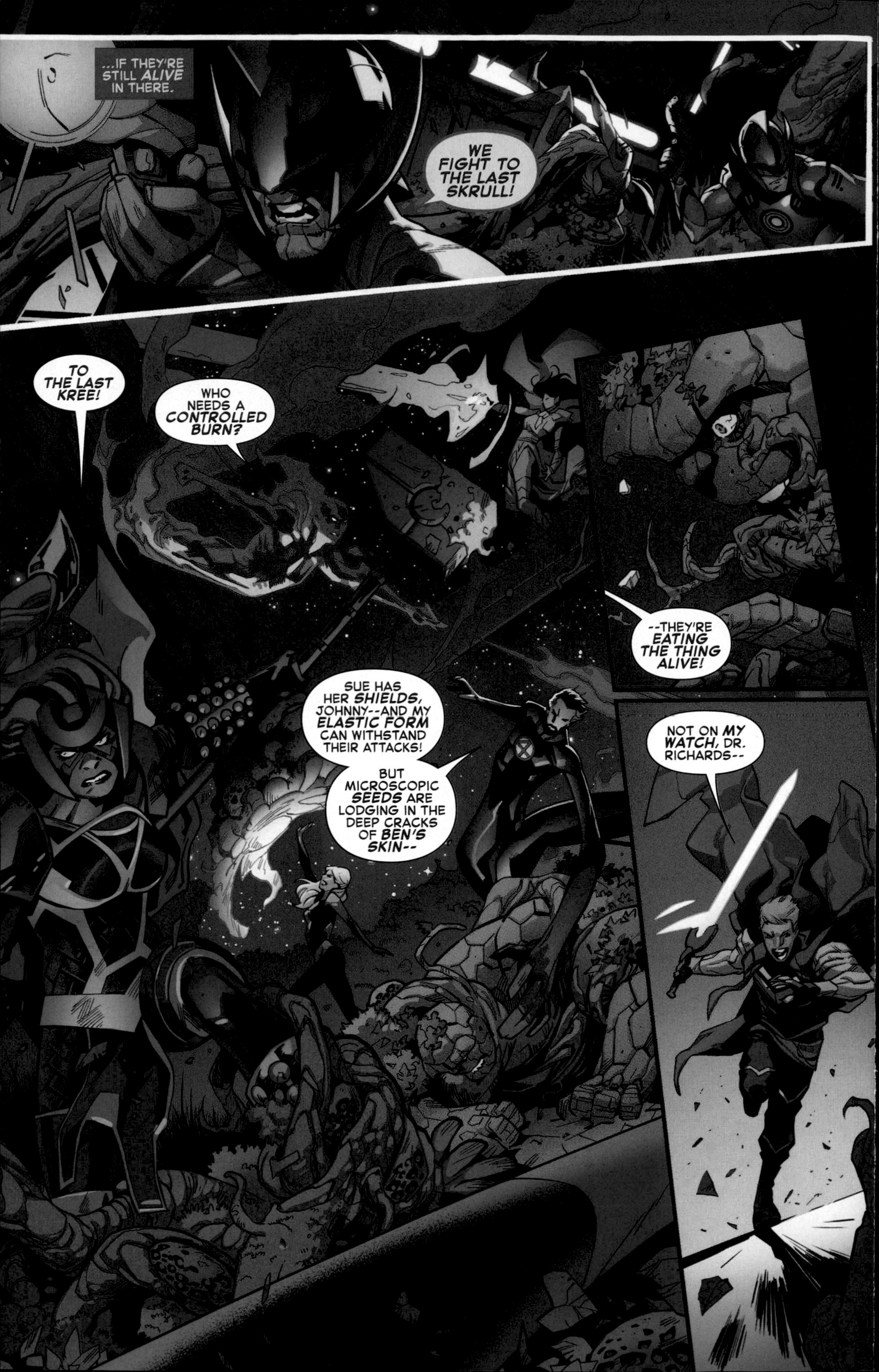
...IF THEY'RE STILL ALIVE IN THERE.
WE FIGHT TO THE LAST SKRULL!
TO THE LAST KREE!
WHO NEEDS A CONTROLLED BURN?
--THEY'RE EATING THE THING ALIVE!
SUE HAS HER SHIELDS, JOHNNY--AND MY ELASTIC FORM CAN WITHSTAND THEIR ATTACKS!
BUT MICROSCOPIC SEEDS ARE LODGING IN THE DEEP CRACKS OF BEN'S SKIN--
NOT ON MY WATCH, DR. RICHARDS--

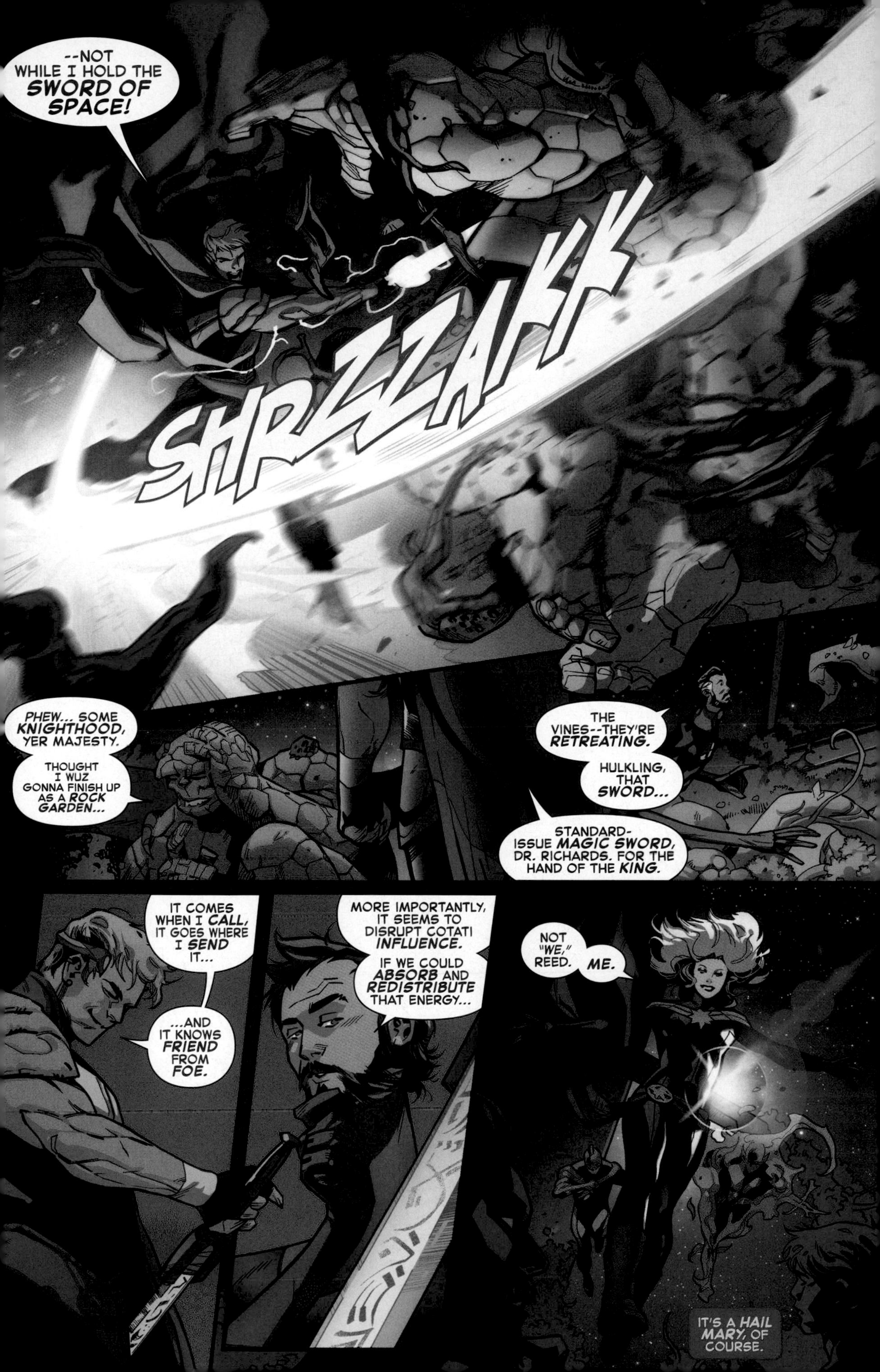
--NOT WHILE I HOLD THE SWORD OF SPACE!
SHRZZAKK
PHEW... SOME KNIGHTHOOD, YER MAJESTY.
THOUGHT I WUZ GONNA FINISH UP AS A ROCK GARDEN...
THE VINES--THEY'RE RETREATING.
HULKLING, THAT SWORD...
STANDARD-ISSUE MAGIC SWORD, DR. RICHARDS. FOR THE HAND OF THE KING.
IT COMES WHEN I CALL, IT GOES WHERE I SEND IT...
...AND IT KNOWS FRIEND FROM FOE.
MORE IMPORTANTLY, IT SEEMS TO DISRUPT COTATI INFLUENCE.
IF WE COULD ABSORB AND REDISTRIBUTE THAT ENERGY...
NOT "WE," REED.
ME.
IT'S A HAIL MARY, OF COURSE.

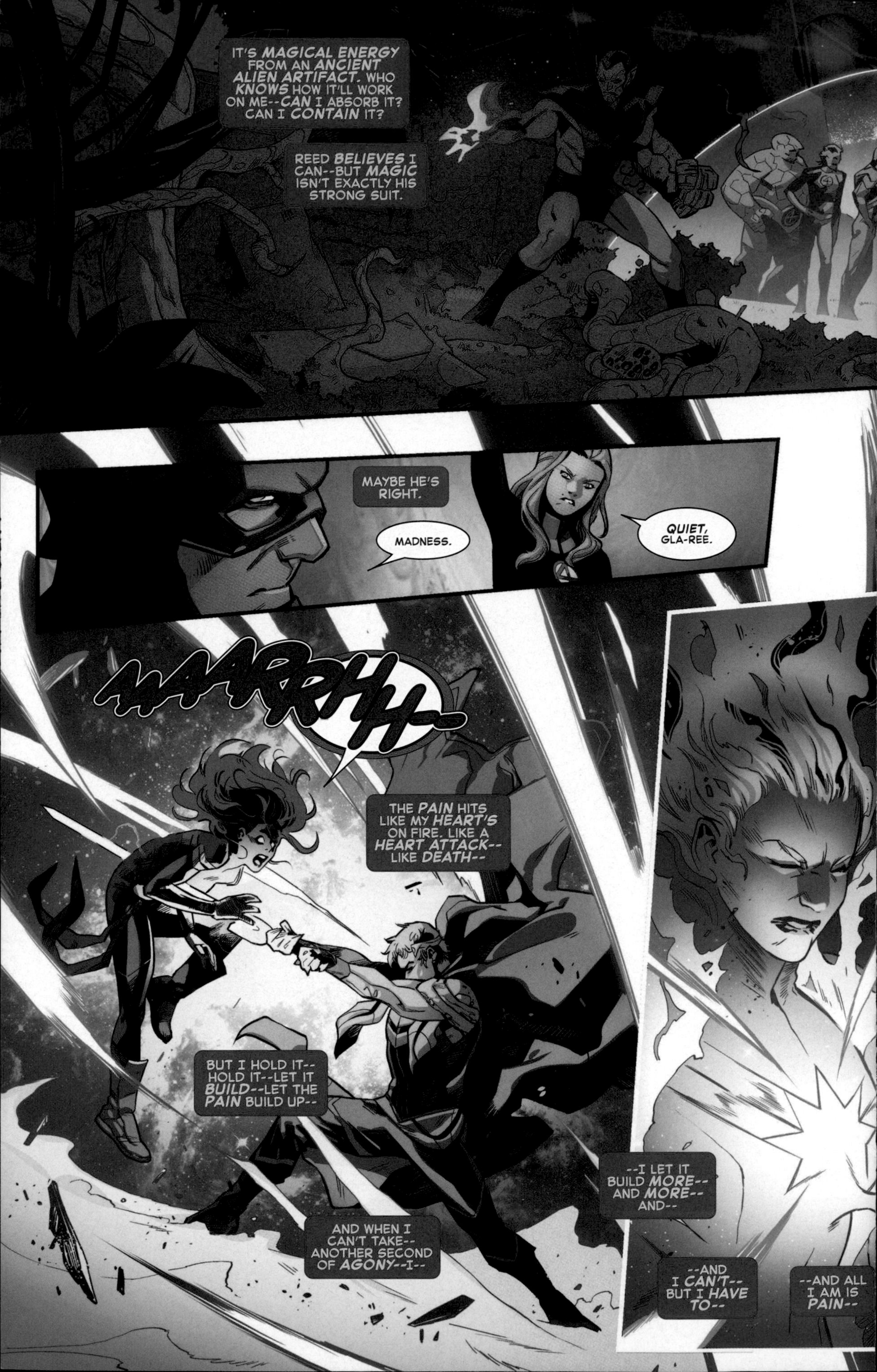

IT'S MAGICAL ENERGY FROM AN ANCIENT ALIEN ARTIFACT. WHO KNOWS HOW IT'LL WORK ON ME--CAN I ABSORB IT? CAN I CONTAIN IT?
REED BELIEVES I CAN--BUT MAGIC ISN'T EXACTLY HIS STRONG SUIT.
MAYBE HE'S RIGHT.
MADNESS.
QUIET, GLA-REE.
AAARRHH--
THE PAIN HITS LIKE MY HEART'S ON FIRE. LIKE A HEART ATTACK-- LIKE DEATH--
BUT I HOLD IT-- HOLD IT--LET IT BUILD--LET THE PAIN BUILD UP--
AND WHEN I CAN'T TAKE-- ANOTHER SECOND OF AGONY--I--
--I LET IT BUILD MORE-- AND MORE-- AND--
--AND I CAN'T-- BUT I HAVE TO--
--AND ALL I AM IS PAIN--

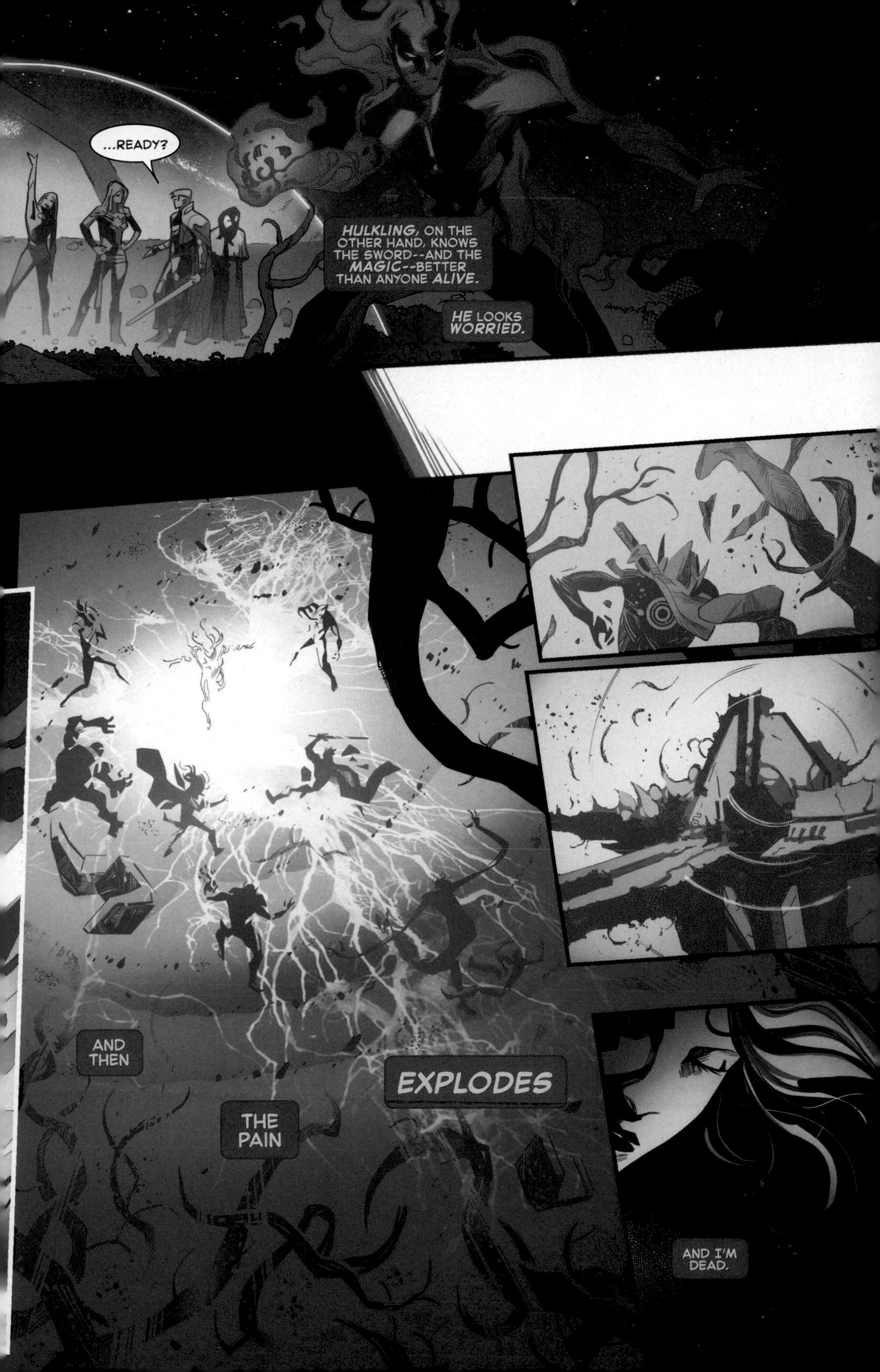
...READY?
HULKLING, ON THE OTHER HAND, KNOWS THE SWORD--AND THE MAGIC--BETTER THAN ANYONE ALIVE.
HE LOOKS WORRIED.
AND THEN
THE PAIN
EXPLODES
AND I'M DEAD.

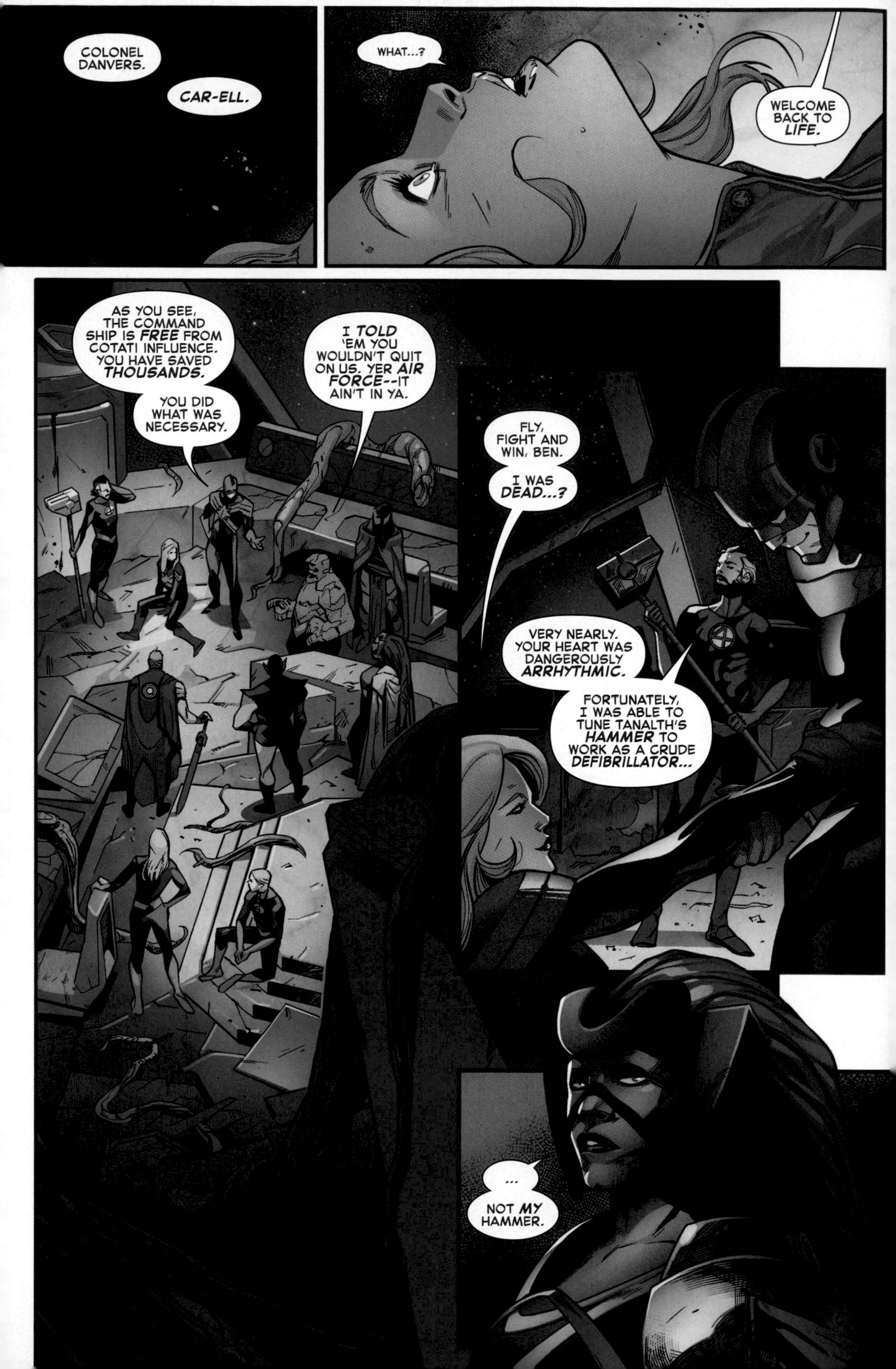
COLONEL DANVERS.
CAR-ELL.
WHAT...?
WELCOME BACK TO LIFE.
AS YOU SEE, THE COMMAND SHIP IS FREE FROM COTATI INFLUENCE. YOU HAVE SAVED THOUSANDS.
YOU DID WHAT WAS NECESSARY.
I TOLD 'EM YOU WOULDN'T QUIT ON US. YER AIR FORCE--IT AIN'T IN YA.
FLY, FIGHT AND WIN, BEN.
I WAS DEAD...?
VERY NEARLY. YOUR HEART WAS DANGEROUSLY ARRHYTHMIC.
FORTUNATELY, I WAS ABLE TO TUNE TANALTH'S HAMMER TO WORK AS A CRUDE DEFIBRILLATOR...
...
NOT MY HAMMER.

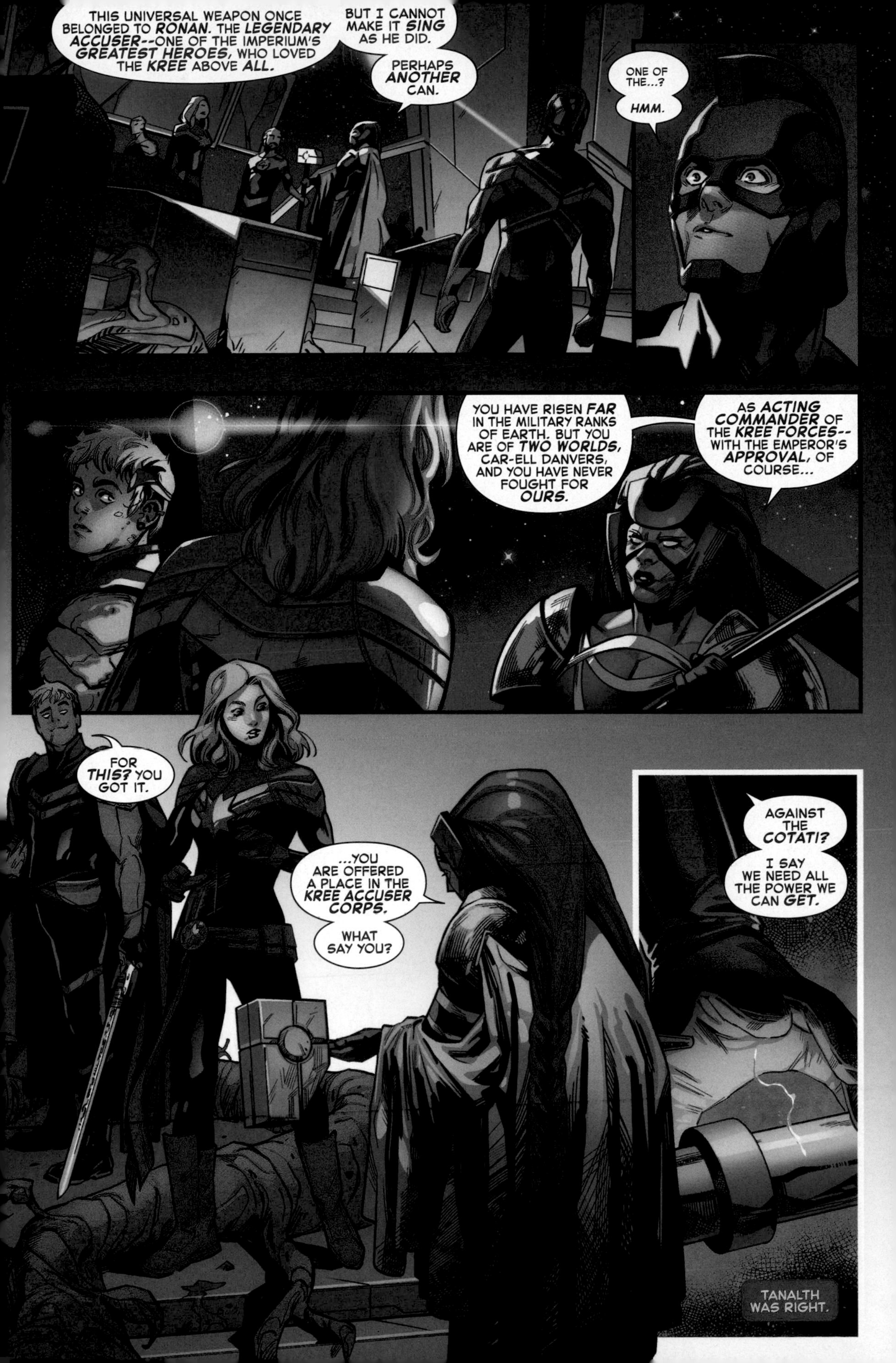

THIS UNIVERSAL WEAPON ONCE BELONGED TO RONAN. THE LEGENDARY ACCUSER--ONE OF THE IMPERIUM'S GREATEST HEROES, WHO LOVED THE KREE ABOVE ALL.
BUT I CANNOT MAKE IT SING AS HE DID.
PERHAPS ANOTHER CAN.
ONE OF THE...?
HMM.
YOU HAVE RISEN FAR IN THE MILITARY RANKS OF EARTH. BUT YOU ARE OF TWO WORLDS, CAR-ELL DANVERS, AND YOU HAVE NEVER FOUGHT FOR OURS.
AS ACTING COMMANDER OF THE KREE FORCES--WITH THE EMPEROR'S APPROVAL, OF COURSE...
...YOU ARE OFFERED A PLACE IN THE KREE ACCUSER CORPS.
WHAT SAY YOU?
FOR THIS? YOU GOT IT.
AGAINST THE COTATI?
I SAY WE NEED ALL THE POWER WE CAN GET.
TANALTH WAS RIGHT.

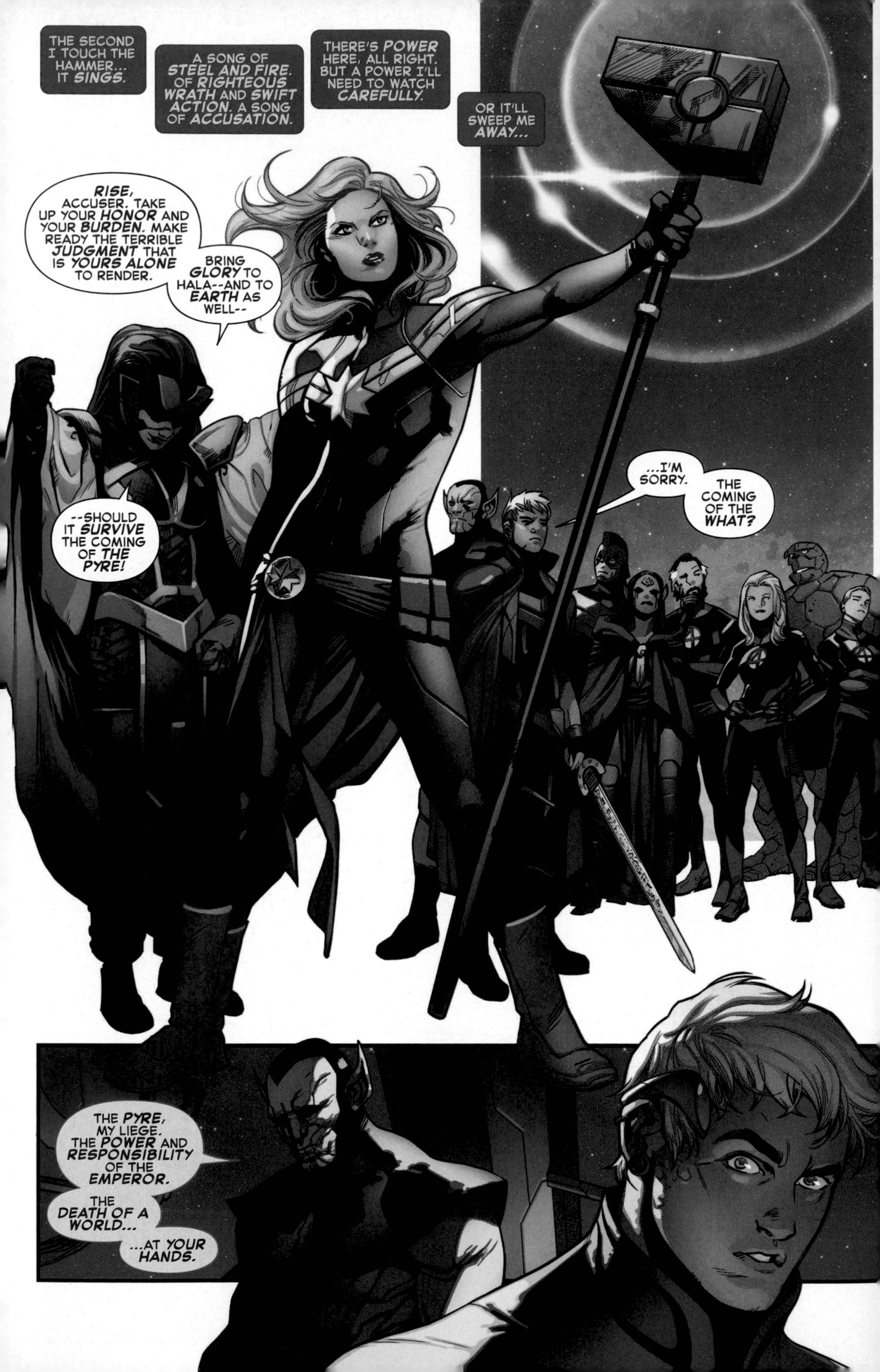
THE SECOND I TOUCH THE HAMMER... IT SINGS.
A SONG OF STEEL AND FIRE. OF RIGHTEOUS WRATH AND SWIFT ACTION. A SONG OF ACCUSATION.
THERE'S POWER HERE, ALL RIGHT. BUT A POWER I'LL NEED TO WATCH CAREFULLY.
OR IT'LL SWEEP ME AWAY...
RISE, ACCUSER. TAKE UP YOUR HONOR AND YOUR BURDEN. MAKE READY THE TERRIBLE JUDGMENT THAT IS YOURS ALONE TO RENDER.
BRING GLORY TO HALA--AND TO EARTH AS WELL--
--SHOULD IT SURVIVE THE COMING OF THE PYRE!
...I'M SORRY.
THE COMING OF THE WHAT?
THE PYRE, MY LIEGE. THE POWER AND RESPONSIBILITY OF THE EMPEROR.
THE DEATH OF A WORLD...
...AT YOUR HANDS.

EMPYRE 3 SECOND-PRINTING VARIANT BY
John Tyler Christopher

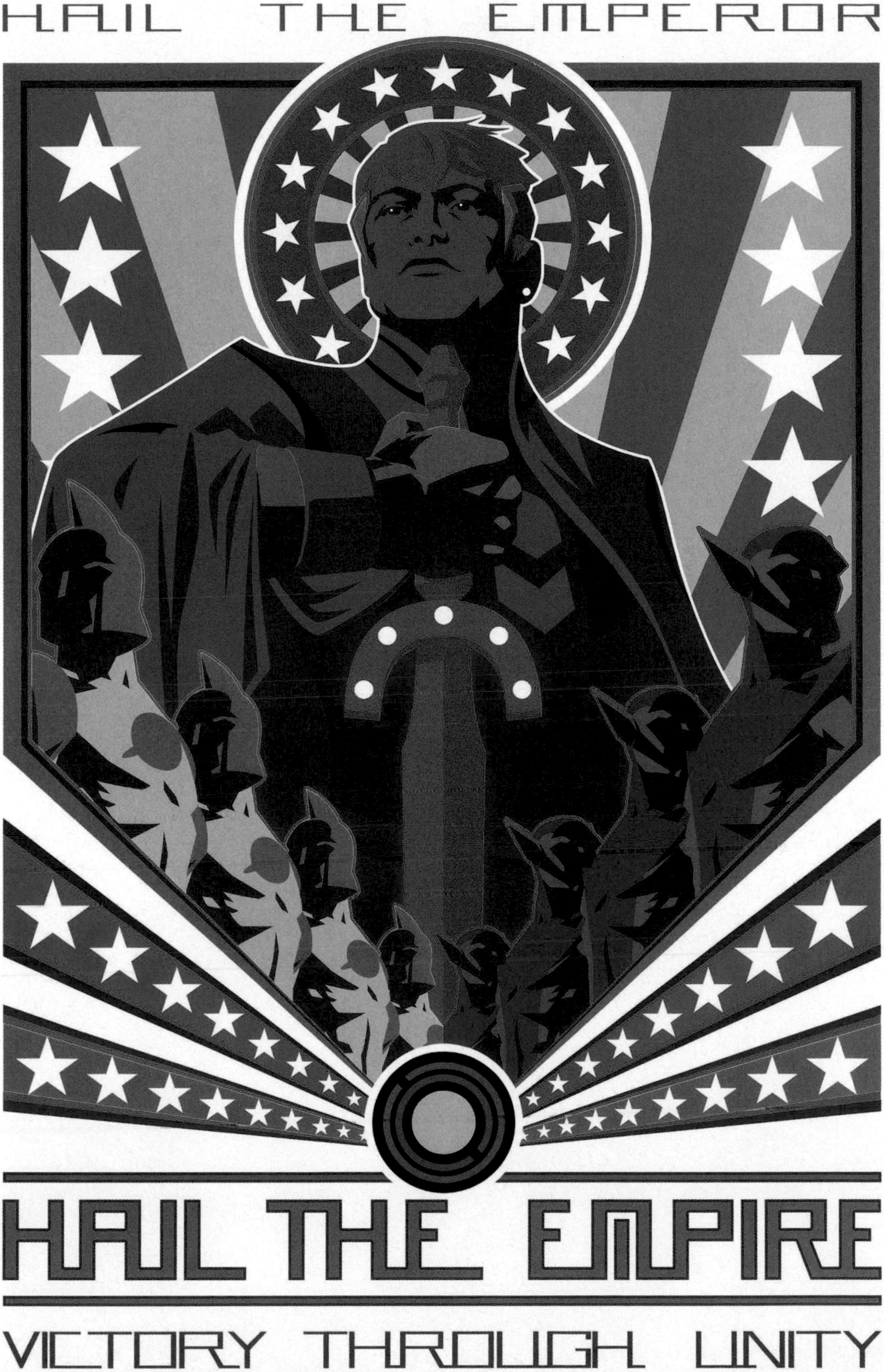
HAIL THE EMPEROR
HAIL THE EMPIRE
VICTORY THROUGH UNITY

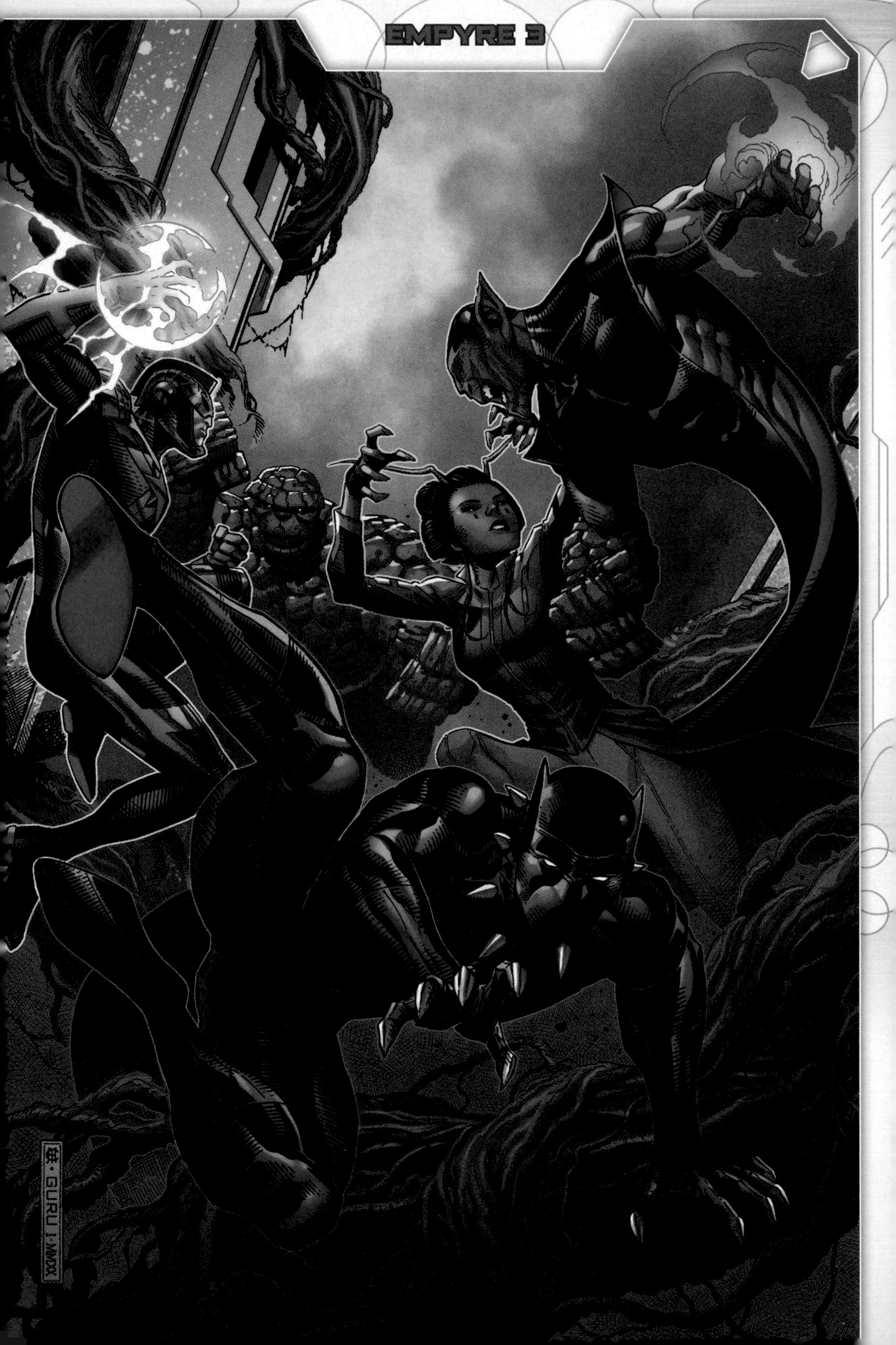
EMPYRE 3
GURU I·MMXX

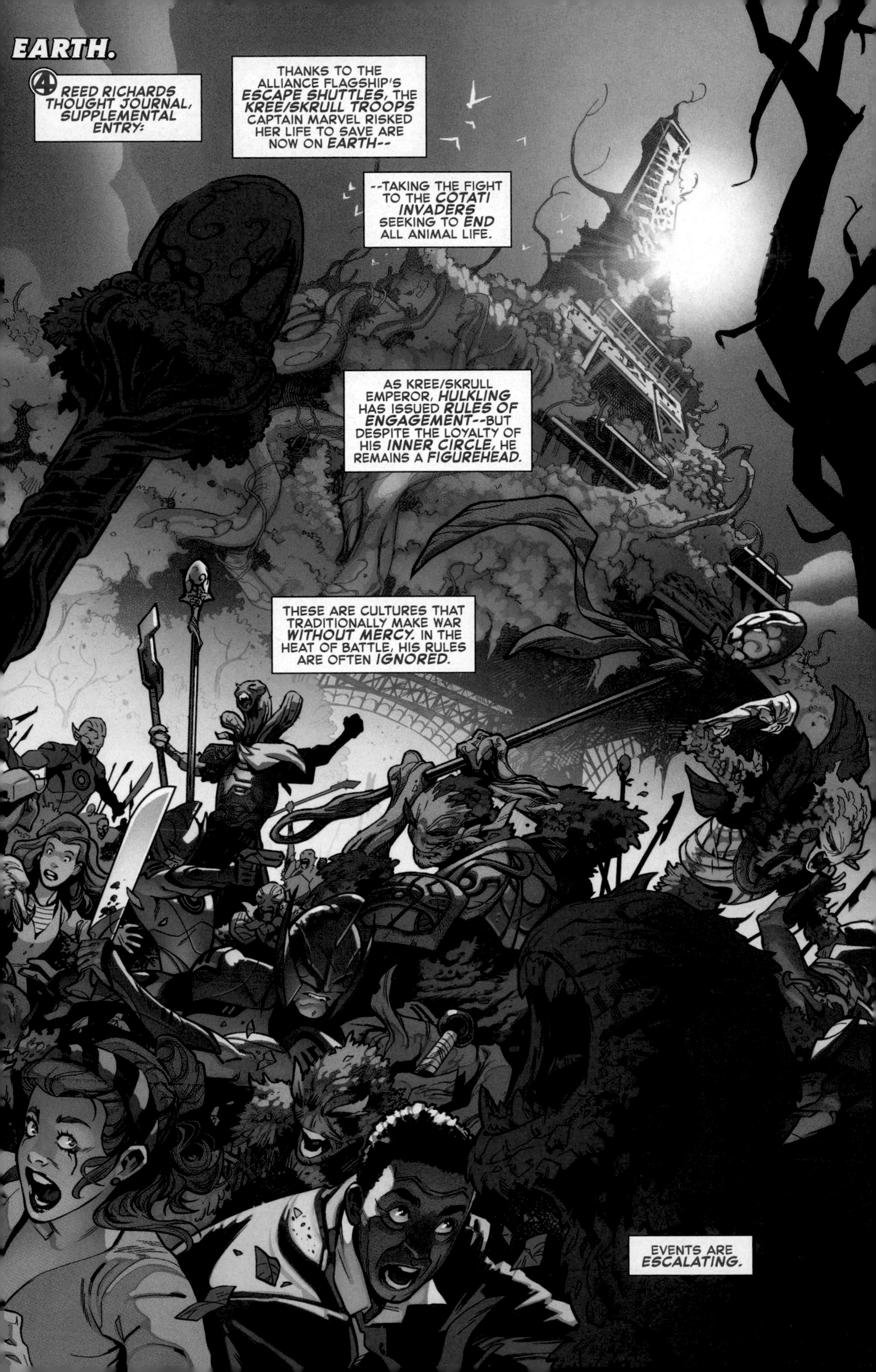
EARTH.
REED RICHARDS THOUGHT JOURNAL, SUPPLEMENTAL ENTRY:
THANKS TO THE ALLIANCE FLAGSHIP'S ESCAPE SHUTTLES, THE KREE/SKRULL TROOPS CAPTAIN MARVEL RISKED HER LIFE TO SAVE ARE NOW ON EARTH--
--TAKING THE FIGHT TO THE COTATI INVADERS SEEKING TO END ALL ANIMAL LIFE.
AS KREE/SKRULL EMPEROR, HULKLING HAS ISSUED RULES OF ENGAGEMENT--BUT DESPITE THE LOYALTY OF HIS INNER CIRCLE, HE REMAINS A FIGUREHEAD.
THESE ARE CULTURES THAT TRADITIONALLY MAKE WAR WITHOUT MERCY. IN THE HEAT OF BATTLE, HIS RULES ARE OFTEN IGNORED.
EVENTS ARE ESCALATING.

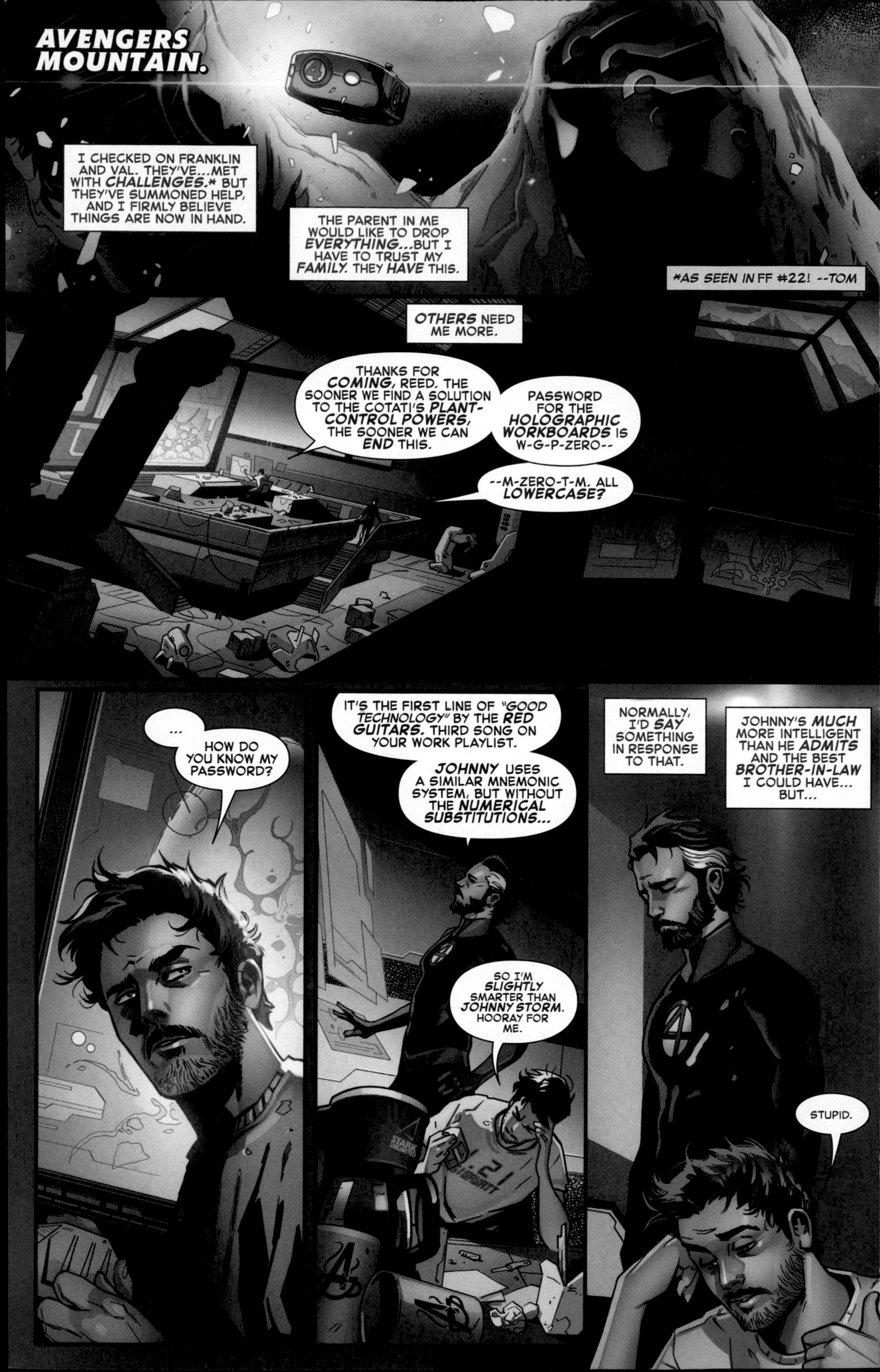
AVENGERS MOUNTAIN.
I CHECKED ON FRANKLIN AND VAL. THEY'VE...MET WITH CHALLENGES.* BUT THEY'VE SUMMONED HELP, AND I FIRMLY BELIEVE THINGS ARE NOW IN HAND.
THE PARENT IN ME WOULD LIKE TO DROP EVERYTHING...BUT I HAVE TO TRUST MY FAMILY. THEY HAVE THIS.
*AS SEEN IN FF #22! --TOM
OTHERS NEED ME MORE.
THANKS FOR COMING, REED. THE SOONER WE FIND A SOLUTION TO THE COTATI'S PLANT-CONTROL POWERS, THE SOONER WE CAN END THIS.
PASSWORD FOR THE HOLOGRAPHIC WORKBOARDS IS W-G-P-ZERO--
--M-ZERO-T-M. ALL LOWERCASE?
... HOW DO YOU KNOW MY PASSWORD?
IT'S THE FIRST LINE OF "GOOD TECHNOLOGY" BY THE RED GUITARS. THIRD SONG ON YOUR WORK PLAYLIST.
JOHNNY USES A SIMILAR MNEMONIC SYSTEM, BUT WITHOUT THE NUMERICAL SUBSTITUTIONS...
SO I'M SLIGHTLY SMARTER THAN JOHNNY STORM. HOORAY FOR ME.
NORMALLY, I'D SAY SOMETHING IN RESPONSE TO THAT.
JOHNNY'S MUCH MORE INTELLIGENT THAN HE ADMITS AND THE BEST BROTHER-IN-LAW I COULD HAVE... BUT...
STUPID.

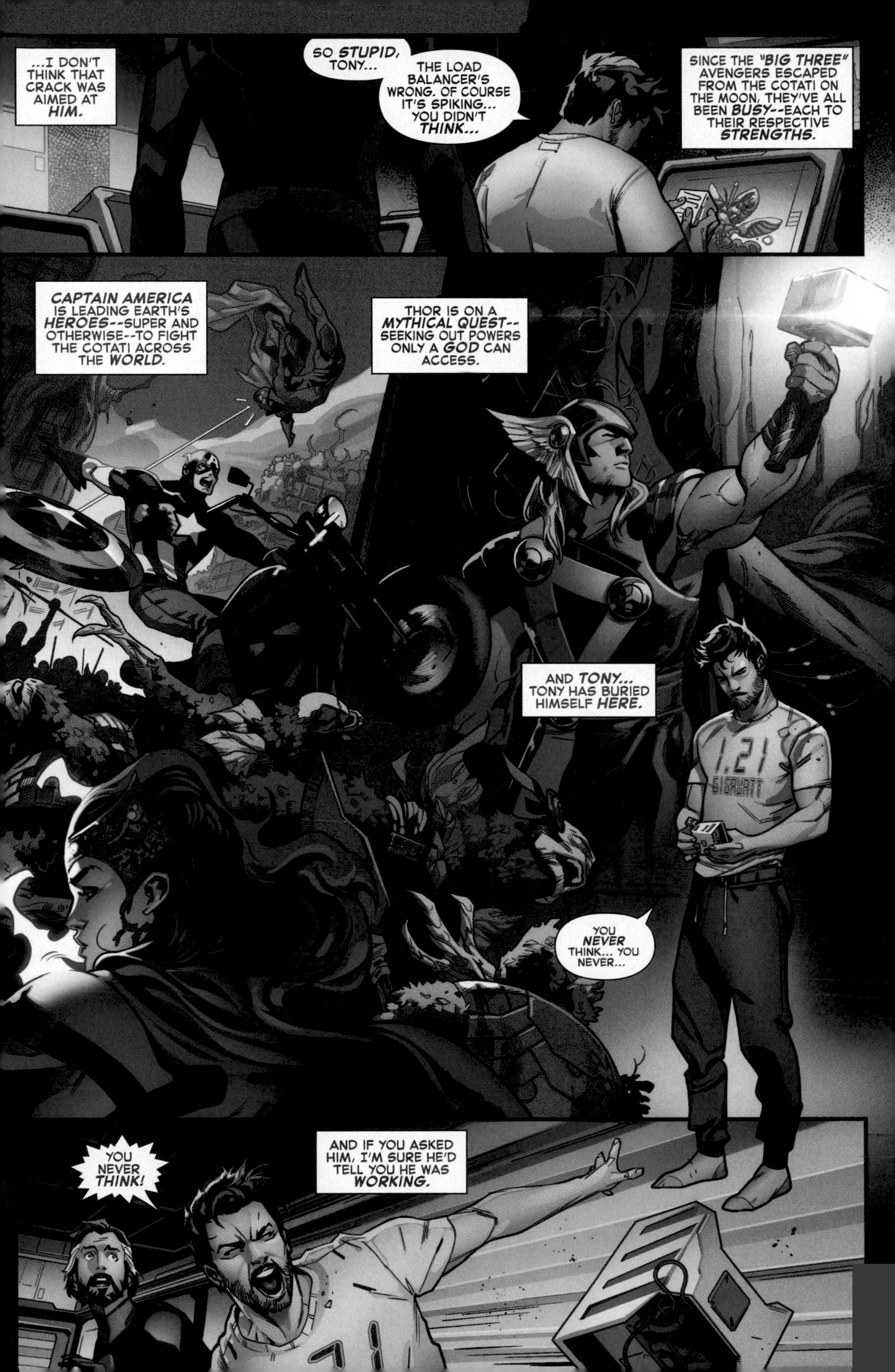
...I DON'T THINK THAT CRACK WAS AIMED AT HIM.
SO STUPID, TONY...
THE LOAD BALANCER'S WRONG. OF COURSE IT'S SPIKING... YOU DIDN'T THINK...
SINCE THE "BIG THREE" AVENGERS ESCAPED FROM THE COTATI ON THE MOON, THEY'VE ALL BEEN BUSY--EACH TO THEIR RESPECTIVE STRENGTHS.
CAPTAIN AMERICA IS LEADING EARTH'S HEROES--SUPER AND OTHERWISE--TO FIGHT THE COTATI ACROSS THE WORLD.
THOR IS ON A MYTHICAL QUEST--SEEKING OUT POWERS ONLY A GOD CAN ACCESS.
AND TONY... TONY HAS BURIED HIMSELF HERE.
1.21 GIGAWATT
YOU NEVER THINK... YOU NEVER...
YOU NEVER THINK!
AND IF YOU ASKED HIM, I'M SURE HE'D TELL YOU HE WAS WORKING.

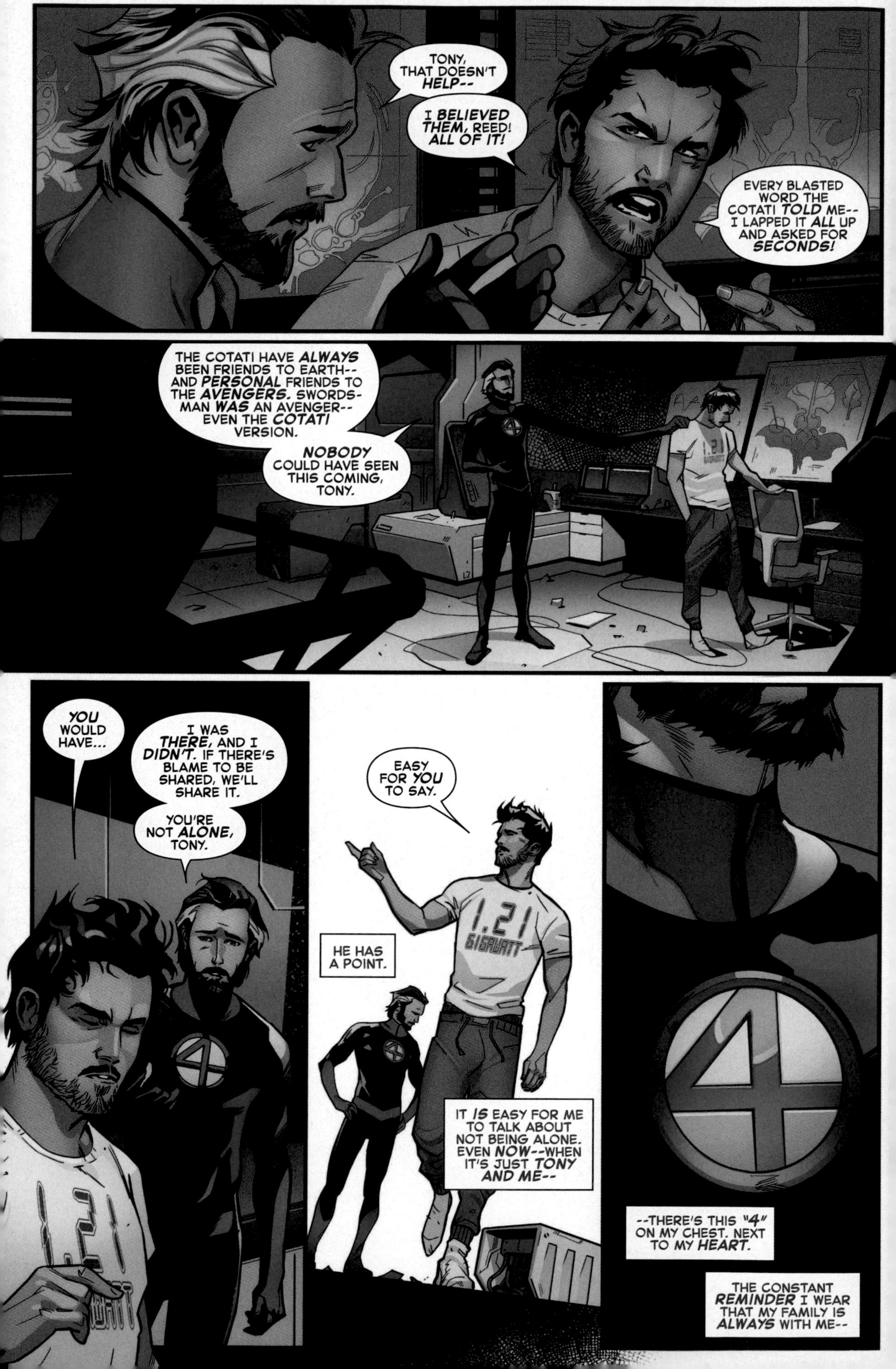
TONY, THAT DOESN'T HELP--
I BELIEVED THEM, REED! ALL OF IT!
EVERY BLASTED WORD THE COTATI TOLD ME-- I LAPPED IT ALL UP AND ASKED FOR SECONDS!
THE COTATI HAVE ALWAYS BEEN FRIENDS TO EARTH-- AND PERSONAL FRIENDS TO THE AVENGERS. SWORDS-MAN WAS AN AVENGER-- EVEN THE COTATI VERSION.
NOBODY COULD HAVE SEEN THIS COMING, TONY.
YOU WOULD HAVE...
I WAS THERE, AND I DIDN'T. IF THERE'S BLAME TO BE SHARED, WE'LL SHARE IT.
YOU'RE NOT ALONE, TONY.
EASY FOR YOU TO SAY.
HE HAS A POINT.
IT IS EASY FOR ME TO TALK ABOUT NOT BEING ALONE. EVEN NOW--WHEN IT'S JUST TONY AND ME--
--THERE'S THIS "4" ON MY CHEST. NEXT TO MY HEART.
THE CONSTANT REMINDER I WEAR THAT MY FAMILY IS ALWAYS WITH ME--

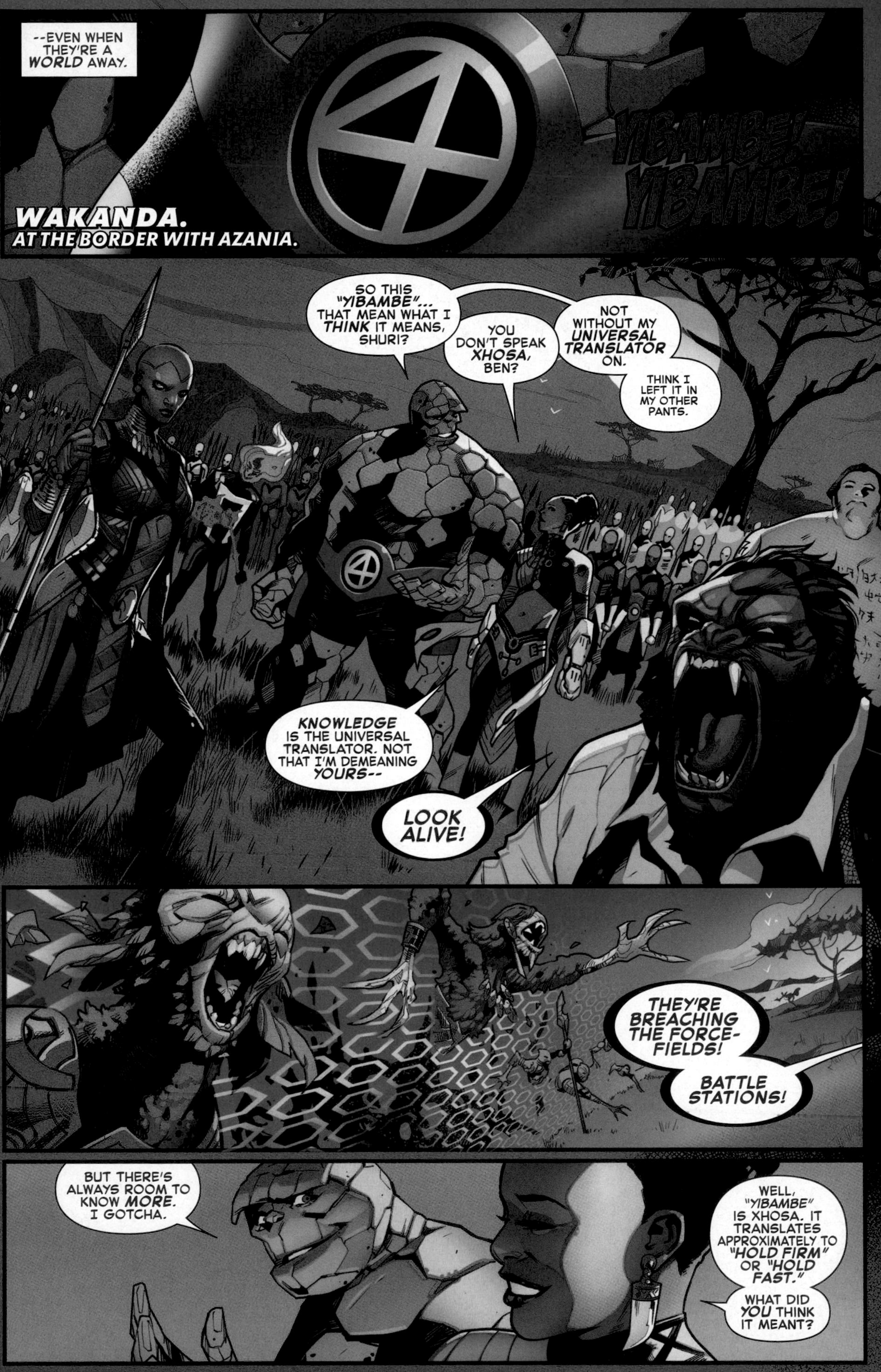
--EVEN WHEN THEY'RE A WORLD AWAY.
YIBAMBE! YIBAMBE!
WAKANDA. AT THE BORDER WITH AZANIA.
SO THIS "YIBAMBE"... THAT MEAN WHAT I THINK IT MEANS, SHURI?
YOU DON'T SPEAK XHOSA, BEN?
NOT WITHOUT MY UNIVERSAL TRANSLATOR ON.
THINK I LEFT IT IN MY OTHER PANTS.
KNOWLEDGE IS THE UNIVERSAL TRANSLATOR. NOT THAT I'M DEMEANING YOURS--
LOOK ALIVE!
THEY'RE BREACHING THE FORCE-FIELDS!
BATTLE STATIONS!
BUT THERE'S ALWAYS ROOM TO KNOW MORE. I GOTCHA.
WELL, "YIBAMBE" IS XHOSA. IT TRANSLATES APPROXIMATELY TO "HOLD FIRM" OR "HOLD FAST."
WHAT DID YOU THINK IT MEANT?

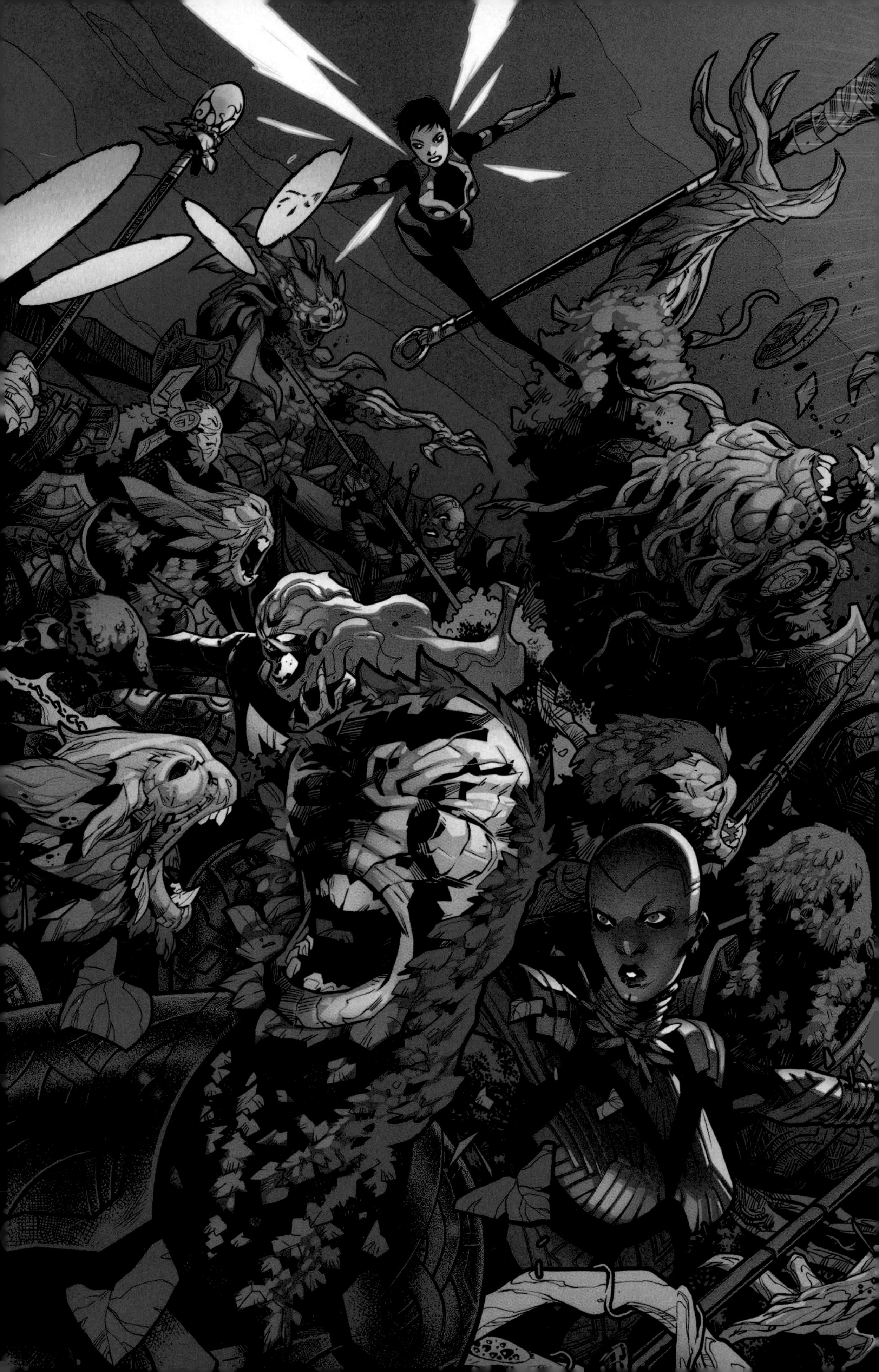

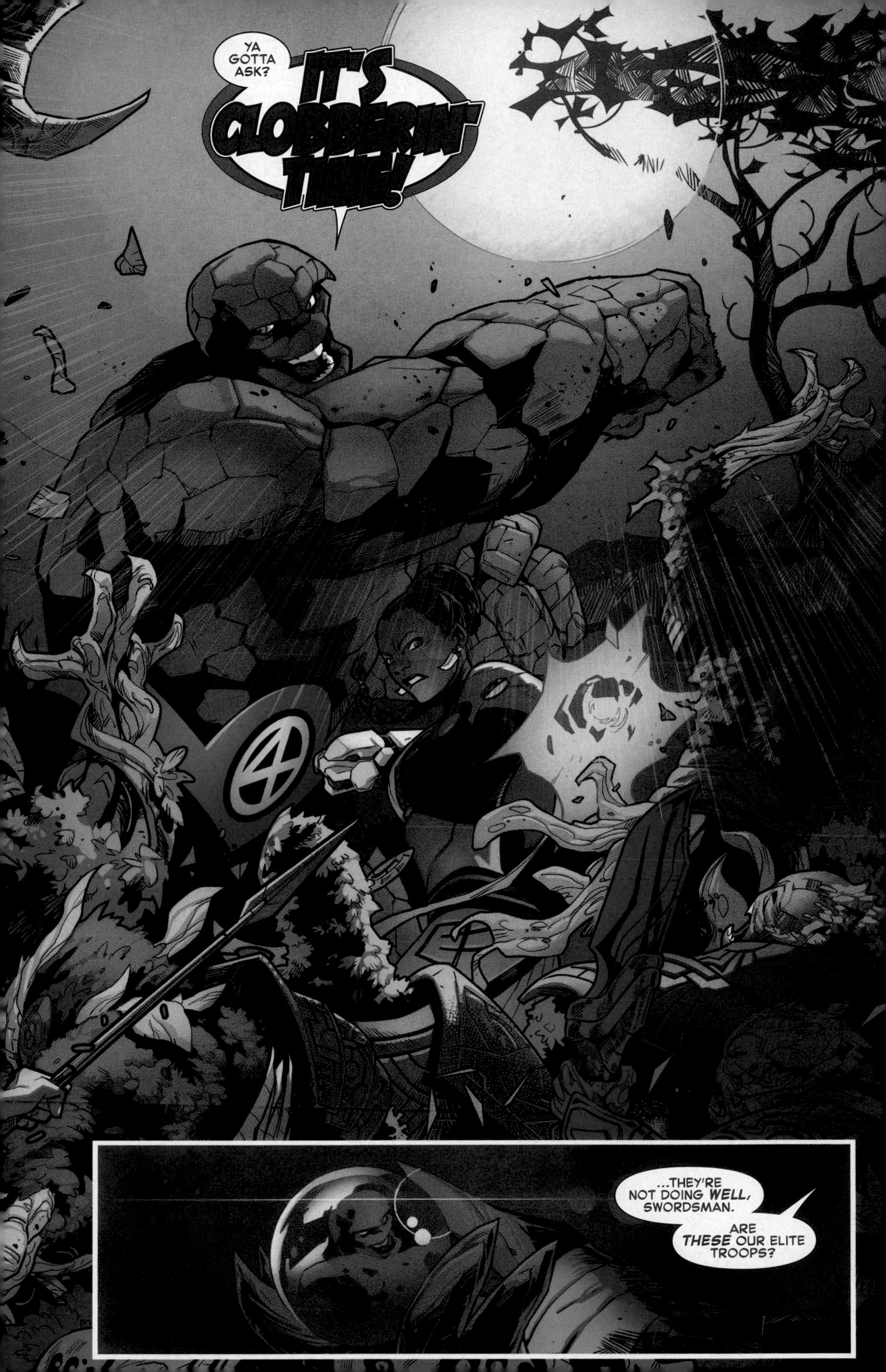
YA GOTTA ASK?
IT'S CLOBBERIN' TIME!
...THEY'RE NOT DOING WELL, SWORDSMAN.
ARE THESE OUR ELITE TROOPS?

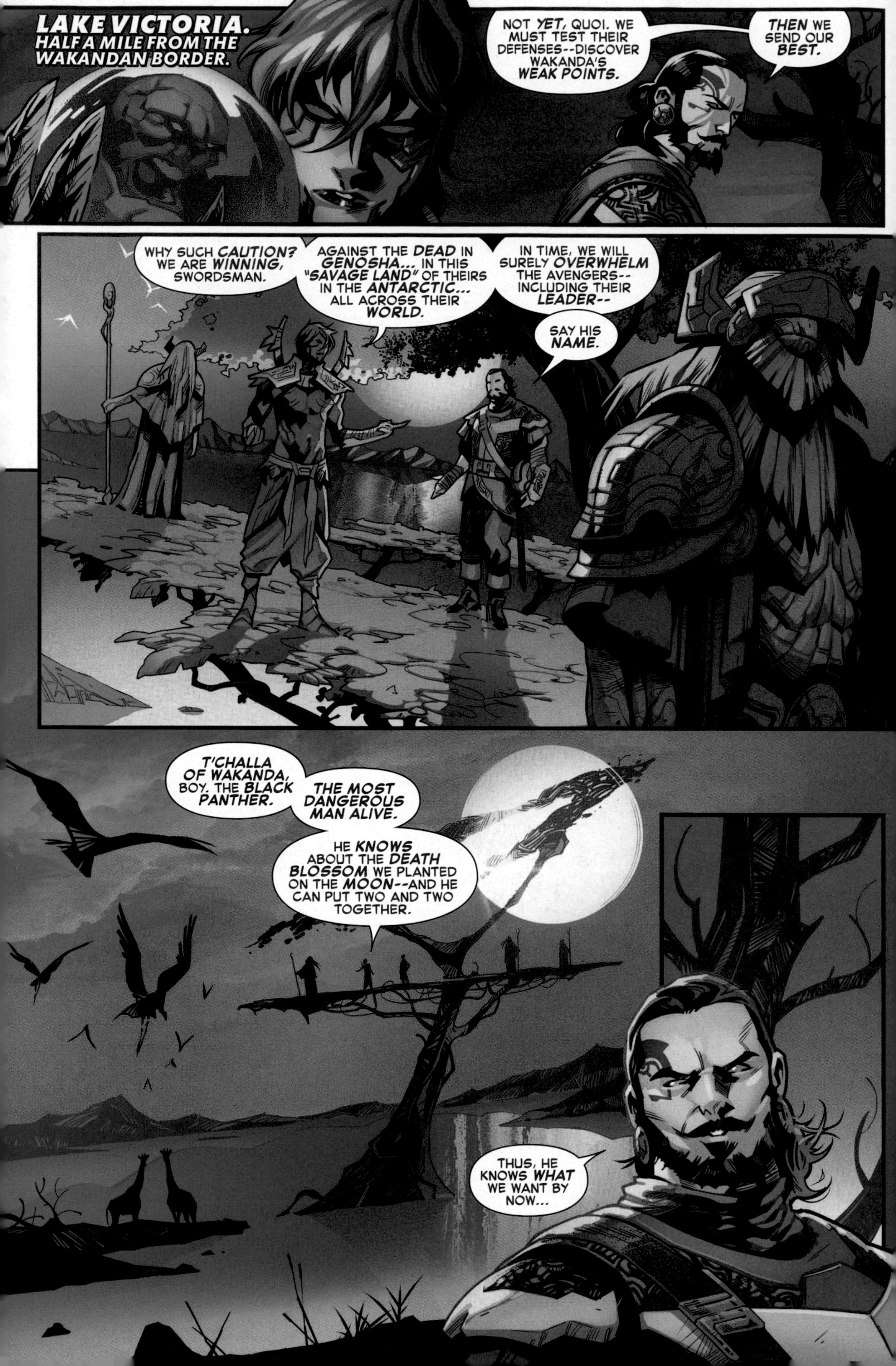
LAKE VICTORIA.
HALF A MILE FROM THE WAKANDAN BORDER.
NOT YET, QUOI. WE MUST TEST THEIR DEFENSES--DISCOVER WAKANDA'S WEAK POINTS.
THEN WE SEND OUR BEST.
WHY SUCH CAUTION? WE ARE WINNING, SWORDSMAN.
AGAINST THE DEAD IN GENOSHA... IN THIS "SAVAGE LAND" OF THEIRS IN THE ANTARCTIC... ALL ACROSS THEIR WORLD.
IN TIME, WE WILL SURELY OVERWHELM THE AVENGERS--INCLUDING THEIR LEADER--
SAY HIS NAME.
T'CHALLA OF WAKANDA, BOY. THE BLACK PANTHER.
THE MOST DANGEROUS MAN ALIVE.
HE KNOWS ABOUT THE DEATH BLOSSOM WE PLANTED ON THE MOON--AND HE CAN PUT TWO AND TWO TOGETHER.
THUS, HE KNOWS WHAT WE WANT BY NOW...

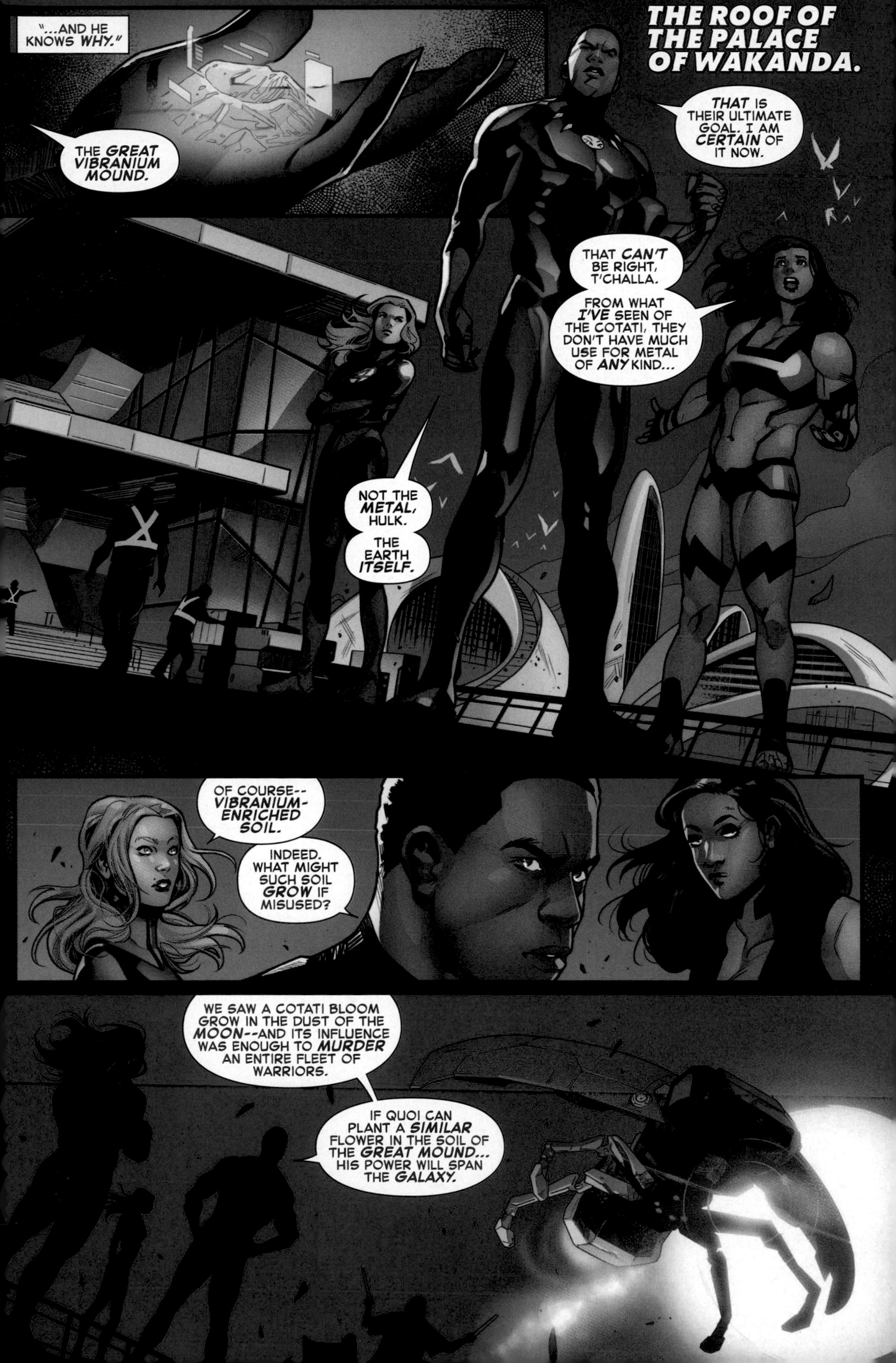
"...AND HE KNOWS WHY."
THE ROOF OF THE PALACE OF WAKANDA.
THE GREAT VIBRANIUM MOUND.
THAT IS THEIR ULTIMATE GOAL. I AM CERTAIN OF IT NOW.
THAT CAN'T BE RIGHT, T'CHALLA.
FROM WHAT I'VE SEEN OF THE COTATI, THEY DON'T HAVE MUCH USE FOR METAL OF ANY KIND...
NOT THE METAL, HULK.
THE EARTH ITSELF.
OF COURSE--VIBRANIUM-ENRICHED SOIL.
INDEED. WHAT MIGHT SUCH SOIL GROW IF MISUSED?
WE SAW A COTATI BLOOM GROW IN THE DUST OF THE MOON--AND ITS INFLUENCE WAS ENOUGH TO MURDER AN ENTIRE FLEET OF WARRIORS.
IF QUOI CAN PLANT A SIMILAR FLOWER IN THE SOIL OF THE GREAT MOUND... HIS POWER WILL SPAN THE GALAXY.

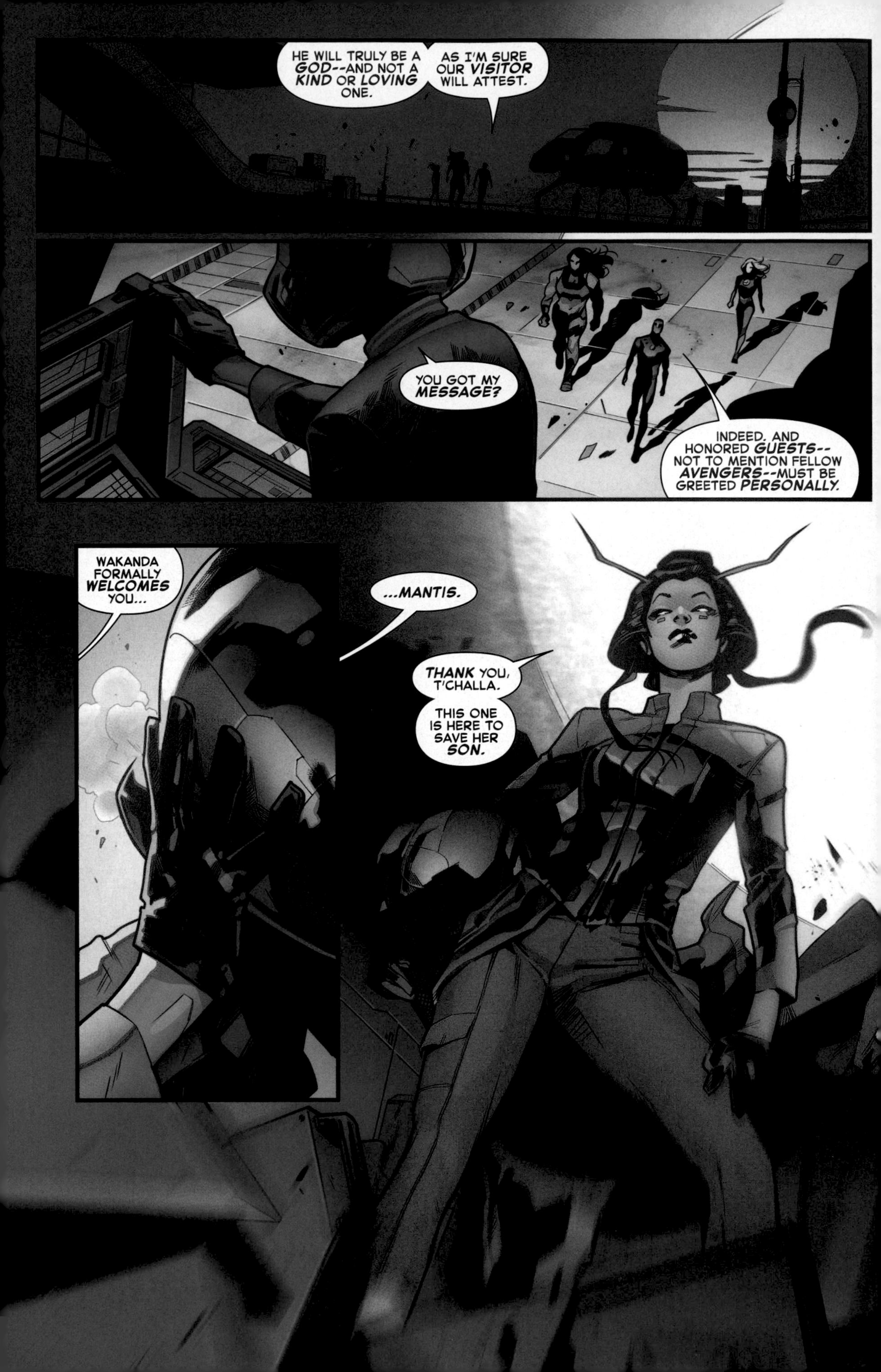
HE WILL TRULY BE A GOD--AND NOT A KIND OR LOVING ONE.
AS I'M SURE OUR VISITOR WILL ATTEST.
YOU GOT MY MESSAGE?
INDEED. AND HONORED GUESTS--NOT TO MENTION FELLOW AVENGERS--MUST BE GREETED PERSONALLY.
WAKANDA FORMALLY WELCOMES YOU...
...MANTIS.
THANK YOU, T'CHALLA.
THIS ONE IS HERE TO SAVE HER SON.

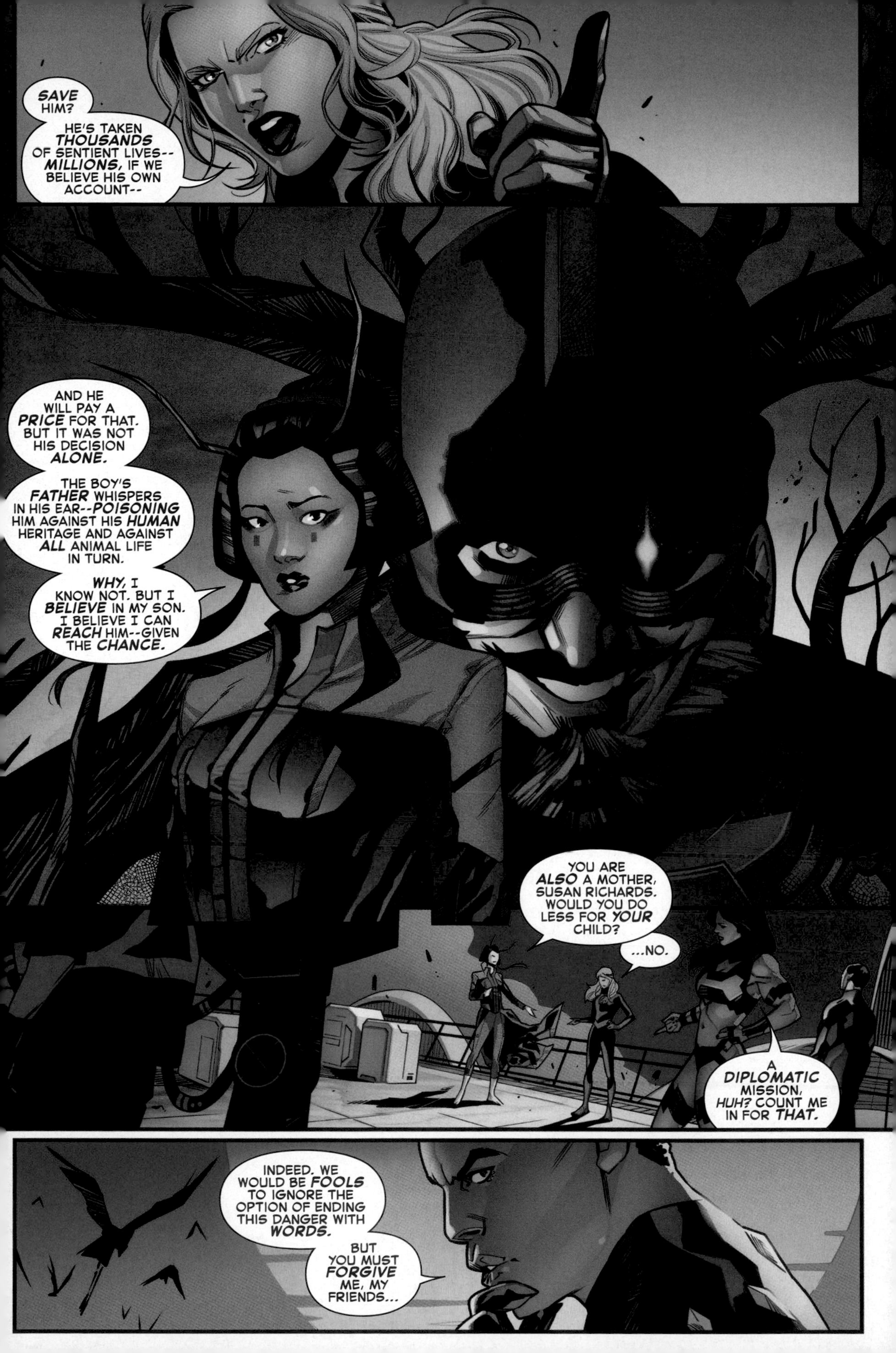
SAVE HIM?
HE'S TAKEN THOUSANDS OF SENTIENT LIVES-- MILLIONS, IF WE BELIEVE HIS OWN ACCOUNT--
AND HE WILL PAY A PRICE FOR THAT. BUT IT WAS NOT HIS DECISION ALONE.
THE BOY'S FATHER WHISPERS IN HIS EAR--POISONING HIM AGAINST HIS HUMAN HERITAGE AND AGAINST ALL ANIMAL LIFE IN TURN.
WHY, I KNOW NOT. BUT I BELIEVE IN MY SON. I BELIEVE I CAN REACH HIM--GIVEN THE CHANCE.
YOU ARE ALSO A MOTHER, SUSAN RICHARDS. WOULD YOU DO LESS FOR YOUR CHILD?
...NO.
A DIPLOMATIC MISSION, HUH? COUNT ME IN FOR THAT.
INDEED. WE WOULD BE FOOLS TO IGNORE THE OPTION OF ENDING THIS DANGER WITH WORDS.
BUT YOU MUST FORGIVE ME, MY FRIENDS...

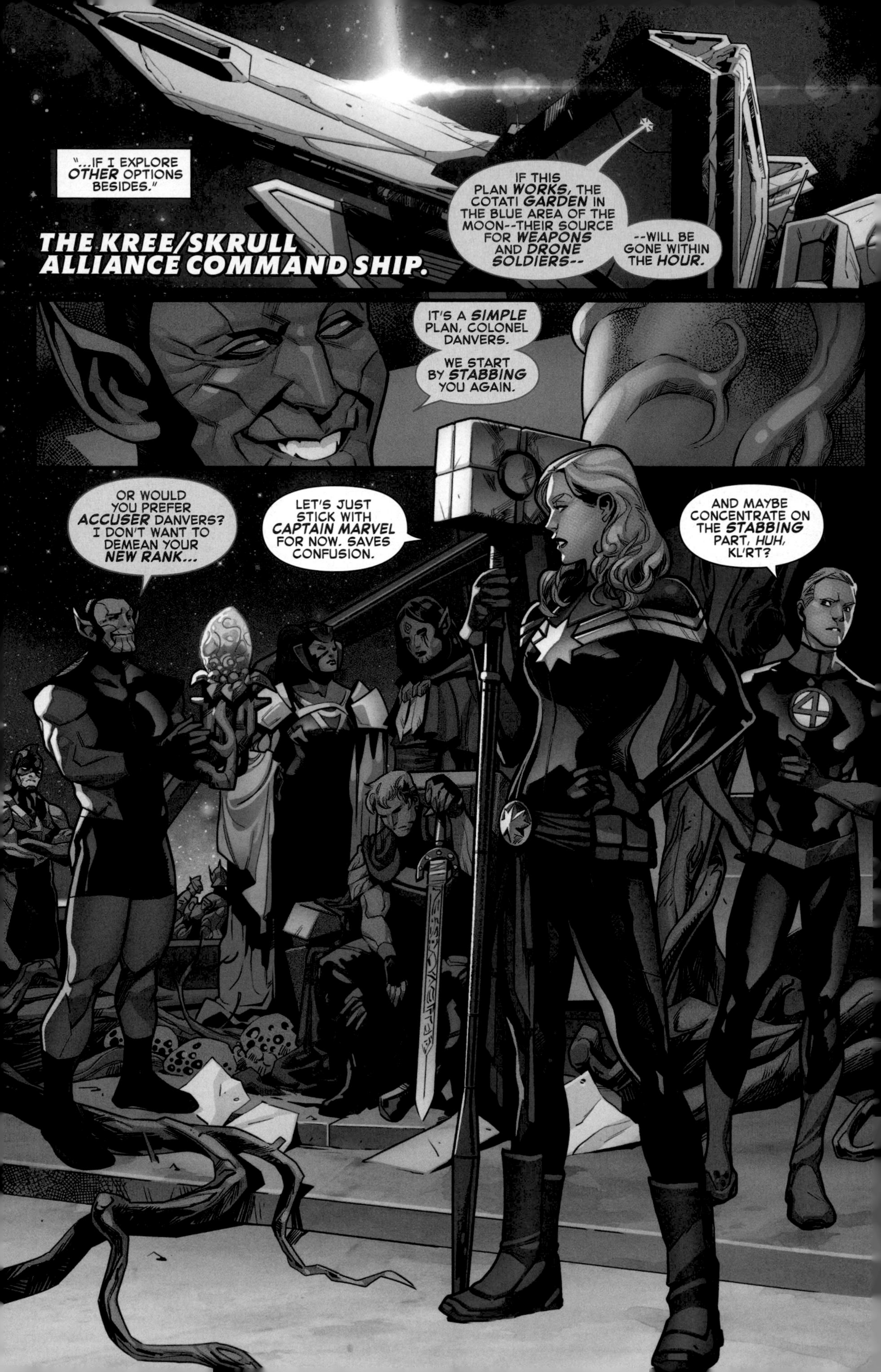
"...IF I EXPLORE OTHER OPTIONS BESIDES."
THE KREE/SKRULL ALLIANCE COMMAND SHIP.
IF THIS PLAN WORKS, THE COTATI GARDEN IN THE BLUE AREA OF THE MOON--THEIR SOURCE FOR WEAPONS AND DRONE SOLDIERS--
--WILL BE GONE WITHIN THE HOUR.
IT'S A SIMPLE PLAN, COLONEL DANVERS.
WE START BY STABBING YOU AGAIN.
OR WOULD YOU PREFER ACCUSER DANVERS? I DON'T WANT TO DEMEAN YOUR NEW RANK...
LET'S JUST STICK WITH CAPTAIN MARVEL FOR NOW. SAVES CONFUSION.
AND MAYBE CONCENTRATE ON THE STABBING PART, HUH, KL'RT?

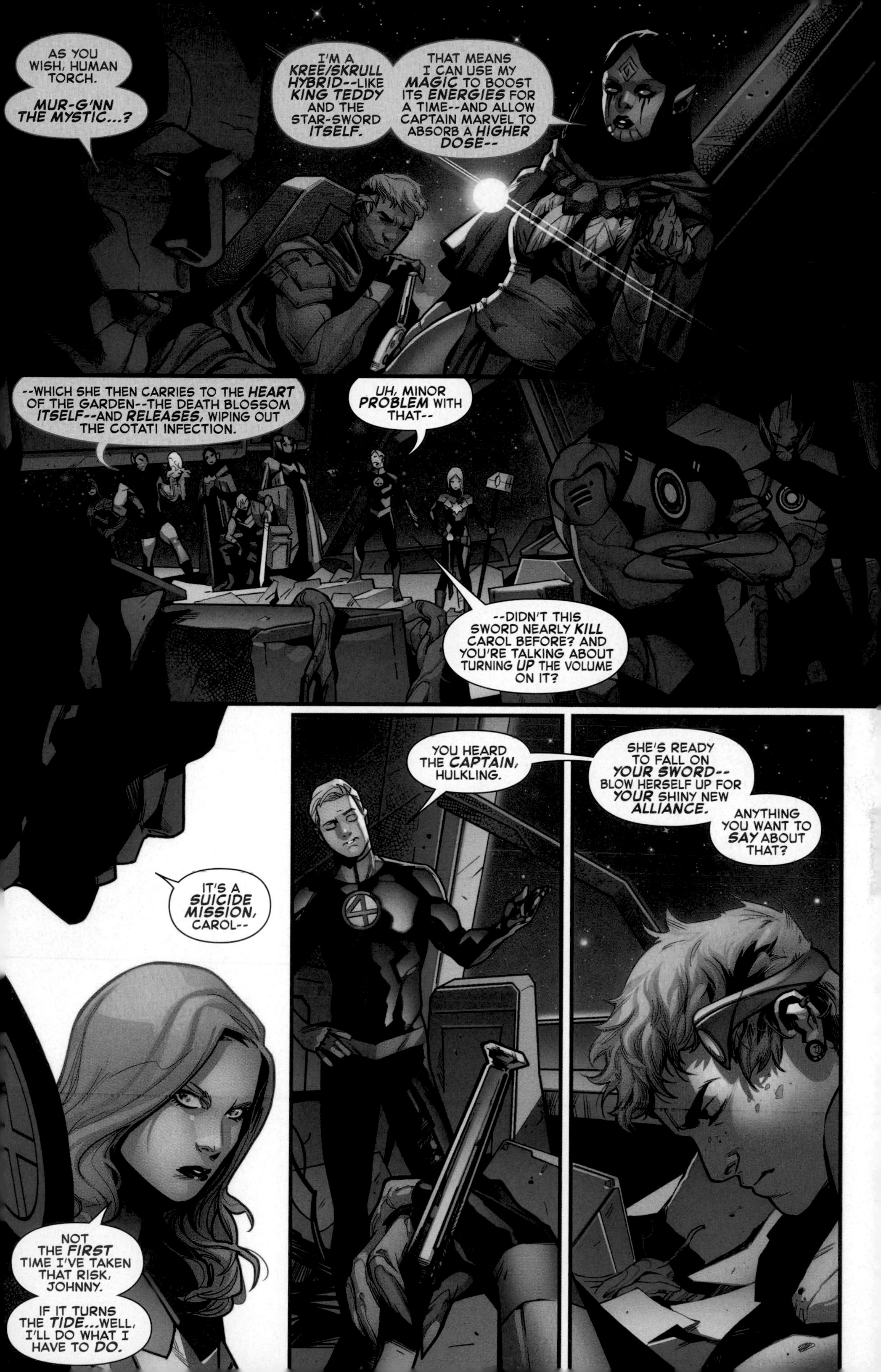
AS YOU WISH, HUMAN TORCH.
MUR-G'NN THE MYSTIC...?
I'M A KREE/SKRULL HYBRID--LIKE KING TEDDY AND THE STAR-SWORD ITSELF.
THAT MEANS I CAN USE MY MAGIC TO BOOST ITS ENERGIES FOR A TIME--AND ALLOW CAPTAIN MARVEL TO ABSORB A HIGHER DOSE--
--WHICH SHE THEN CARRIES TO THE HEART OF THE GARDEN--THE DEATH BLOSSOM ITSELF--AND RELEASES, WIPING OUT THE COTATI INFECTION.
UH, MINOR PROBLEM WITH THAT--
--DIDN'T THIS SWORD NEARLY KILL CAROL BEFORE? AND YOU'RE TALKING ABOUT TURNING UP THE VOLUME ON IT?
IT'S A SUICIDE MISSION, CAROL--
NOT THE FIRST TIME I'VE TAKEN THAT RISK, JOHNNY.
IF IT TURNS THE TIDE...WELL, I'LL DO WHAT I HAVE TO DO.
YOU HEARD THE CAPTAIN, HULKLING.
SHE'S READY TO FALL ON YOUR SWORD--BLOW HERSELF UP FOR YOUR SHINY NEW ALLIANCE.
ANYTHING YOU WANT TO SAY ABOUT THAT?

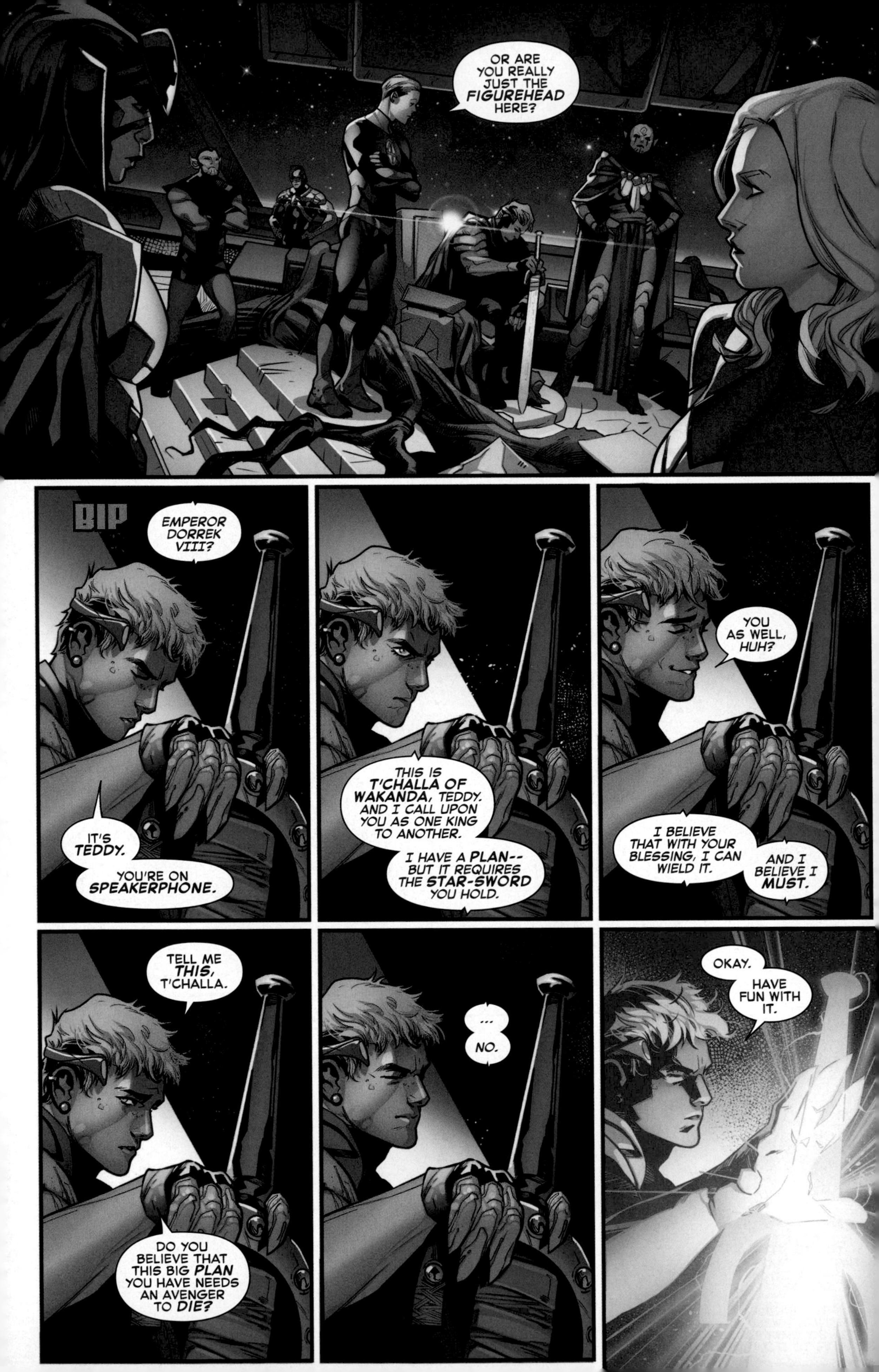

OR ARE YOU REALLY JUST THE FIGUREHEAD HERE?
BIP
EMPEROR DORREK VIII?
IT'S TEDDY.
YOU'RE ON SPEAKERPHONE.
THIS IS T'CHALLA OF WAKANDA, TEDDY. AND I CALL UPON YOU AS ONE KING TO ANOTHER.
I HAVE A PLAN-- BUT IT REQUIRES THE STAR-SWORD YOU HOLD.
YOU AS WELL, HUH?
I BELIEVE THAT WITH YOUR BLESSING, I CAN WIELD IT.
AND I BELIEVE I MUST.
TELL ME THIS, T'CHALLA.
DO YOU BELIEVE THAT THIS BIG PLAN YOU HAVE NEEDS AN AVENGER TO DIE?
...
NO.
OKAY.
HAVE FUN WITH IT.

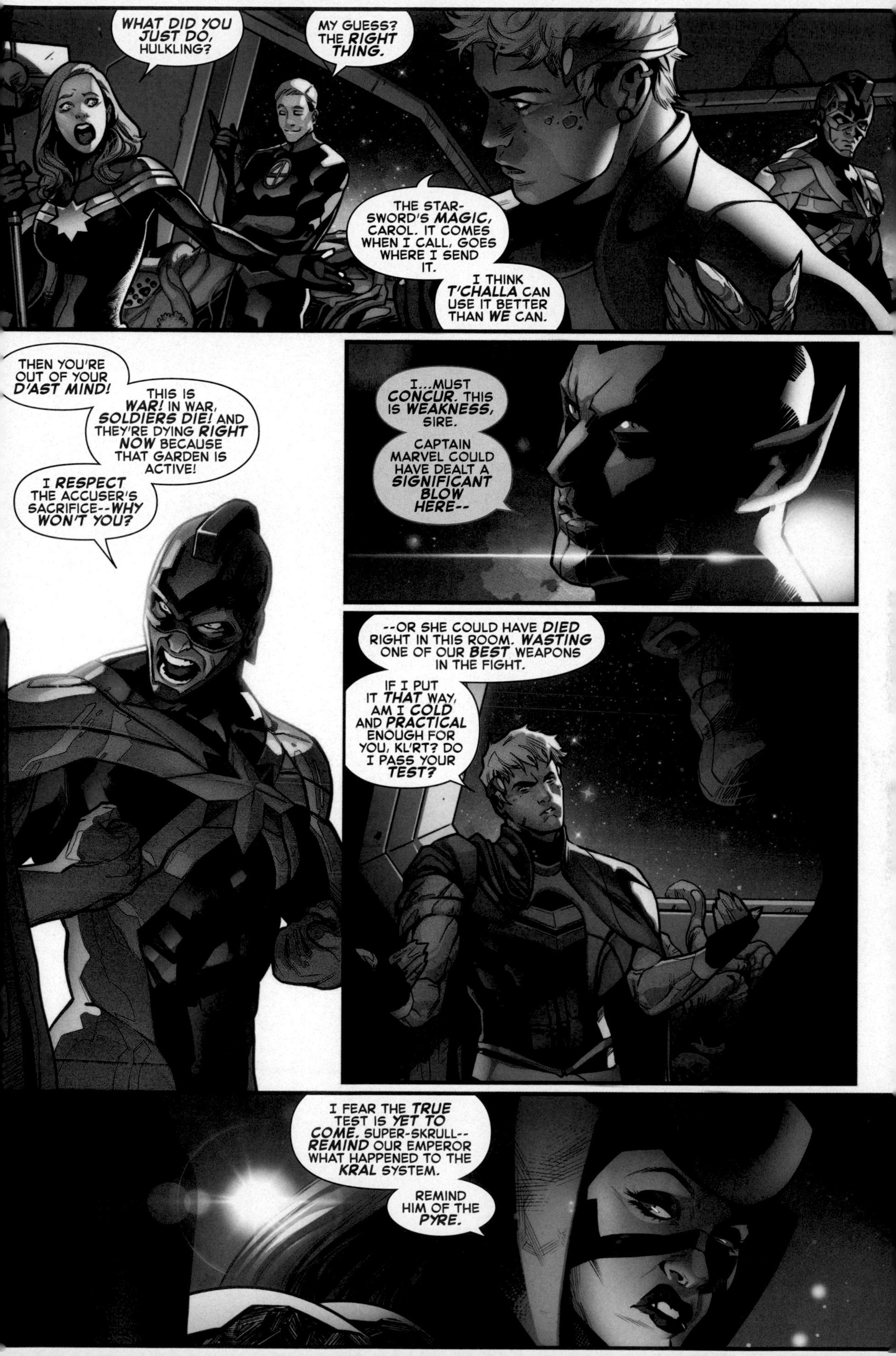
WHAT DID YOU JUST DO, HULKLING?
MY GUESS? THE RIGHT THING.
THE STAR-SWORD'S MAGIC, CAROL. IT COMES WHEN I CALL, GOES WHERE I SEND IT.
I THINK T'CHALLA CAN USE IT BETTER THAN WE CAN.
THEN YOU'RE OUT OF YOUR D'AST MIND!
THIS IS WAR! IN WAR, SOLDIERS DIE! AND THEY'RE DYING RIGHT NOW BECAUSE THAT GARDEN IS ACTIVE!
I RESPECT THE ACCUSER'S SACRIFICE--WHY WON'T YOU?
I...MUST CONCUR. THIS IS WEAKNESS, SIRE.
CAPTAIN MARVEL COULD HAVE DEALT A SIGNIFICANT BLOW HERE--
--OR SHE COULD HAVE DIED RIGHT IN THIS ROOM. WASTING ONE OF OUR BEST WEAPONS IN THE FIGHT.
IF I PUT IT THAT WAY, AM I COLD AND PRACTICAL ENOUGH FOR YOU, KL'RT? DO I PASS YOUR TEST?
I FEAR THE TRUE TEST IS YET TO COME. SUPER-SKRULL-- REMIND OUR EMPEROR WHAT HAPPENED TO THE KRAL SYSTEM.
REMIND HIM OF THE PYRE.

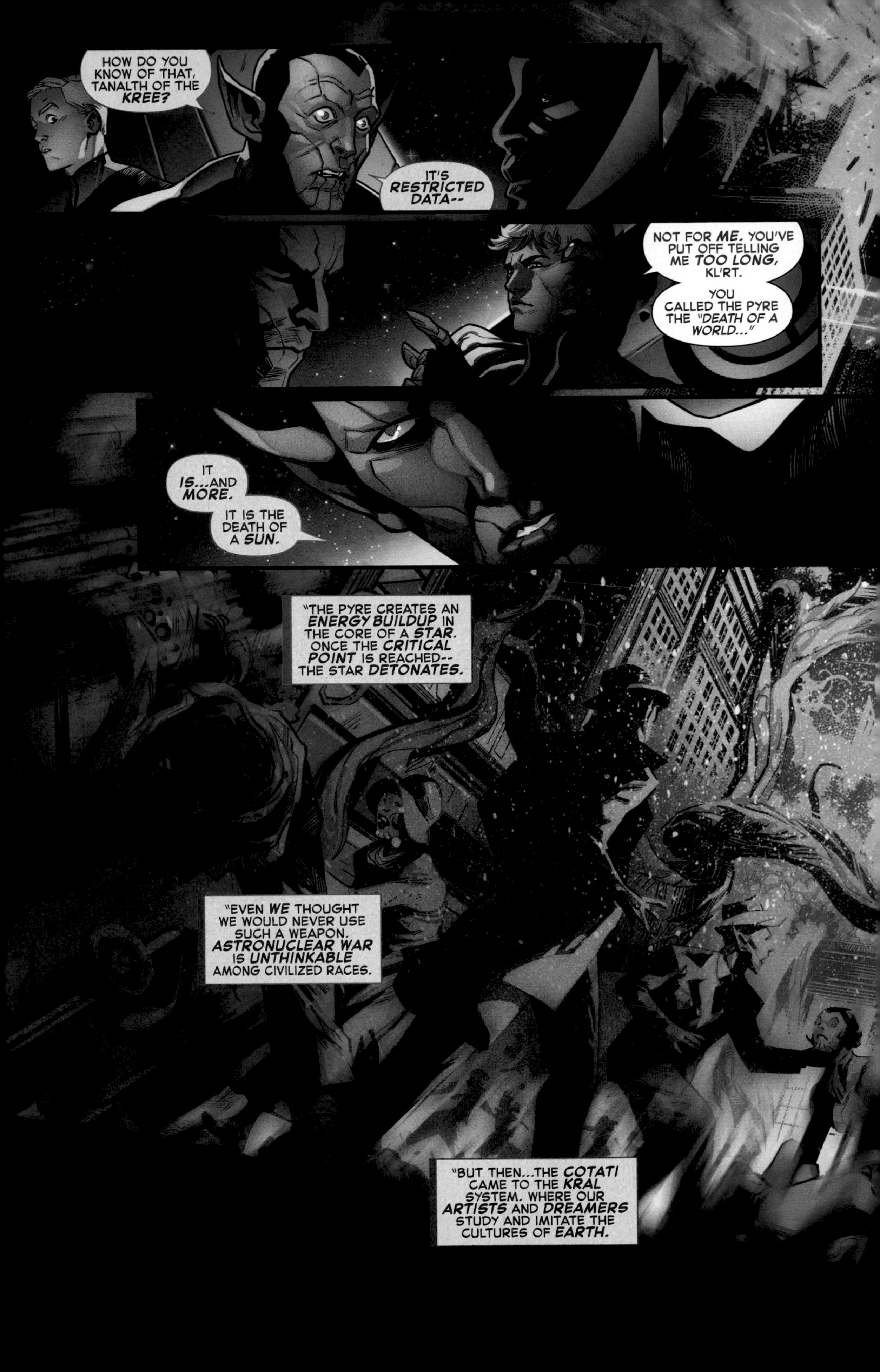
HOW DO YOU KNOW OF THAT, TANALTH OF THE KREE?
IT'S RESTRICTED DATA--
NOT FOR ME. YOU'VE PUT OFF TELLING ME TOO LONG, KL'RT.
YOU CALLED THE PYRE THE "DEATH OF A WORLD..."
IT IS...AND MORE.
IT IS THE DEATH OF A SUN.
"THE PYRE CREATES AN ENERGY BUILDUP IN THE CORE OF A STAR. ONCE THE CRITICAL POINT IS REACHED-- THE STAR DETONATES.
"EVEN WE THOUGHT WE WOULD NEVER USE SUCH A WEAPON. ASTRONUCLEAR WAR IS UNTHINKABLE AMONG CIVILIZED RACES.
"BUT THEN...THE COTATI CAME TO THE KRAL SYSTEM. WHERE OUR ARTISTS AND DREAMERS STUDY AND IMITATE THE CULTURES OF EARTH.

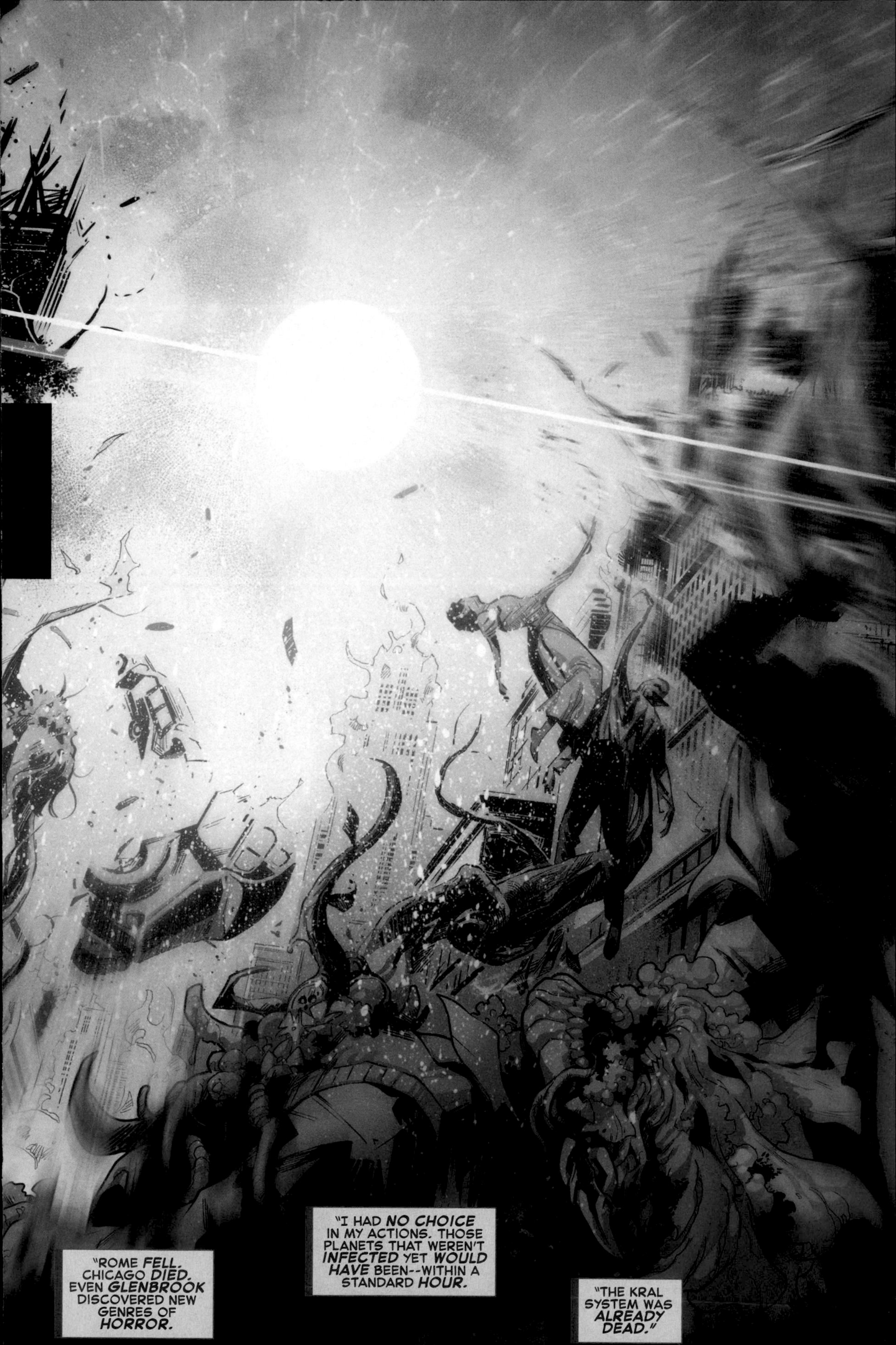
"ROME FELL. CHICAGO DIED. EVEN GLENBROOK DISCOVERED NEW GENRES OF HORROR.
"I HAD NO CHOICE IN MY ACTIONS. THOSE PLANETS THAT WEREN'T INFECTED YET WOULD HAVE BEEN--WITHIN A STANDARD HOUR.
"THE KRAL SYSTEM WAS ALREADY DEAD."

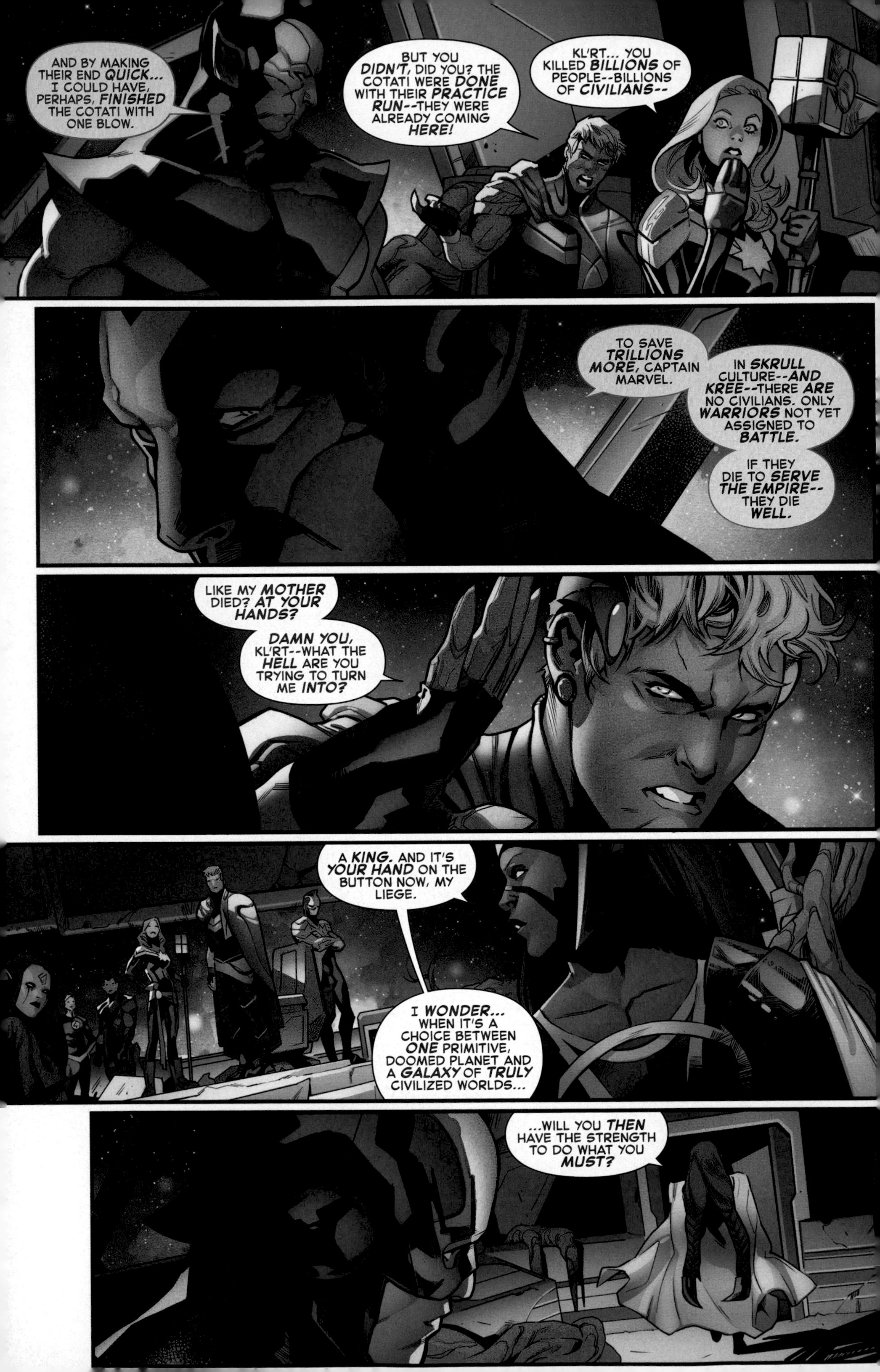
AND BY MAKING THEIR END QUICK... I COULD HAVE, PERHAPS, FINISHED THE COTATI WITH ONE BLOW.
BUT YOU DIDN'T, DID YOU? THE COTATI WERE DONE WITH THEIR PRACTICE RUN--THEY WERE ALREADY COMING HERE!
KL'RT... YOU KILLED BILLIONS OF PEOPLE--BILLIONS OF CIVILIANS--
TO SAVE TRILLIONS MORE, CAPTAIN MARVEL.
IN SKRULL CULTURE--AND KREE--THERE ARE NO CIVILIANS. ONLY WARRIORS NOT YET ASSIGNED TO BATTLE.
IF THEY DIE TO SERVE THE EMPIRE--THEY DIE WELL.
LIKE MY MOTHER DIED? AT YOUR HANDS?
DAMN YOU, KL'RT--WHAT THE HELL ARE YOU TRYING TO TURN ME INTO?
A KING. AND IT'S YOUR HAND ON THE BUTTON NOW, MY LIEGE.
I WONDER... WHEN IT'S A CHOICE BETWEEN ONE PRIMITIVE, DOOMED PLANET AND A GALAXY OF TRULY CIVILIZED WORLDS...
...WILL YOU THEN HAVE THE STRENGTH TO DO WHAT YOU MUST?

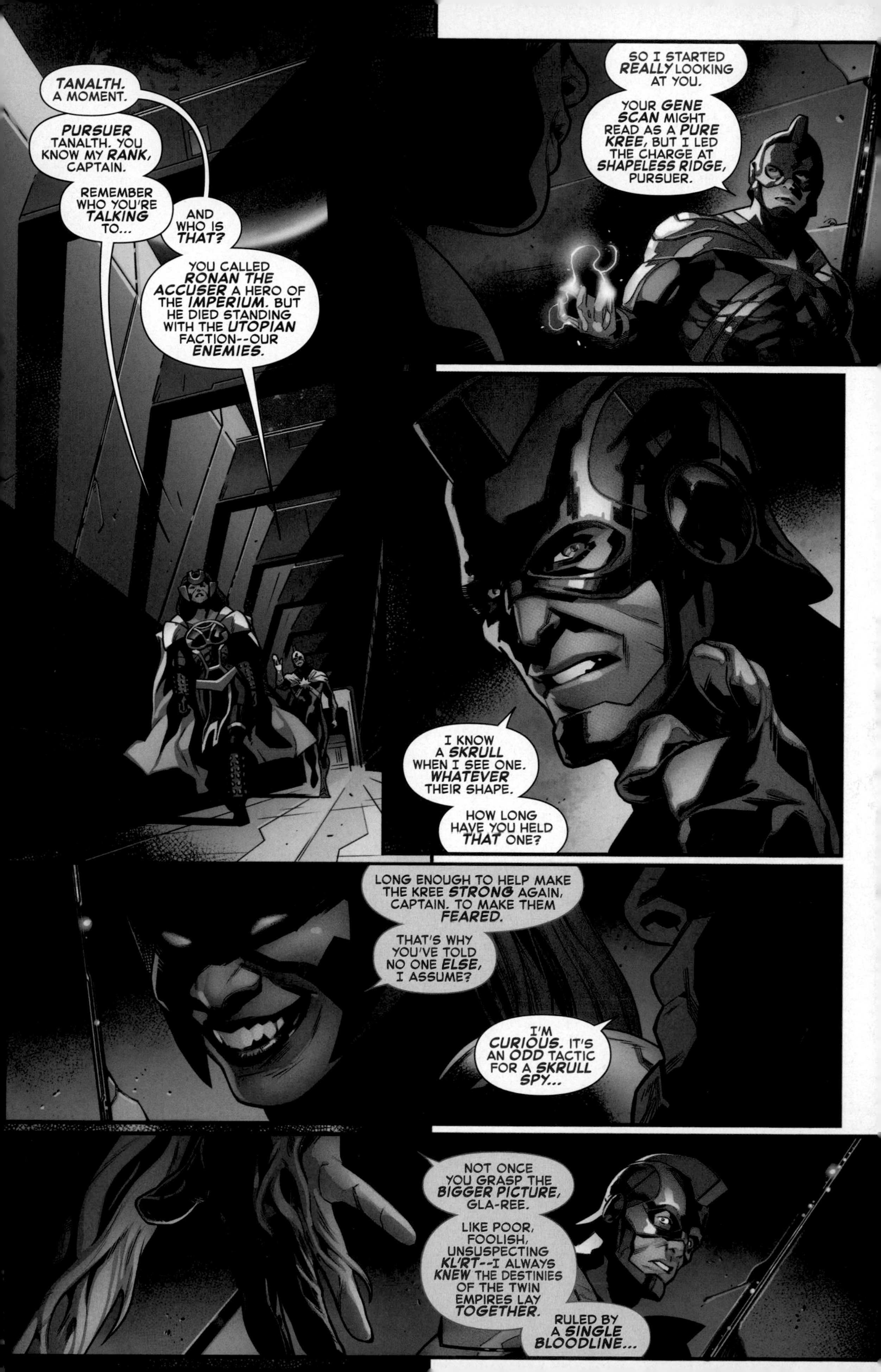
TANALTH. A MOMENT.
PURSUER TANALTH. YOU KNOW MY RANK, CAPTAIN.
REMEMBER WHO YOU'RE TALKING TO...
AND WHO IS THAT?
YOU CALLED RONAN THE ACCUSER A HERO OF THE IMPERIUM. BUT HE DIED STANDING WITH THE UTOPIAN FACTION--OUR ENEMIES.
SO I STARTED REALLY LOOKING AT YOU.
YOUR GENE SCAN MIGHT READ AS A PURE KREE, BUT I LED THE CHARGE AT SHAPELESS RIDGE, PURSUER.
I KNOW A SKRULL WHEN I SEE ONE. WHATEVER THEIR SHAPE.
HOW LONG HAVE YOU HELD THAT ONE?
LONG ENOUGH TO HELP MAKE THE KREE STRONG AGAIN, CAPTAIN. TO MAKE THEM FEARED.
THAT'S WHY YOU'VE TOLD NO ONE ELSE, I ASSUME?
I'M CURIOUS. IT'S AN ODD TACTIC FOR A SKRULL SPY...
NOT ONCE YOU GRASP THE BIGGER PICTURE, GLA-REE.
LIKE POOR, FOOLISH, UNSUSPECTING KL'RT--I ALWAYS KNEW THE DESTINIES OF THE TWIN EMPIRES LAY TOGETHER.
RULED BY A SINGLE BLOODLINE...

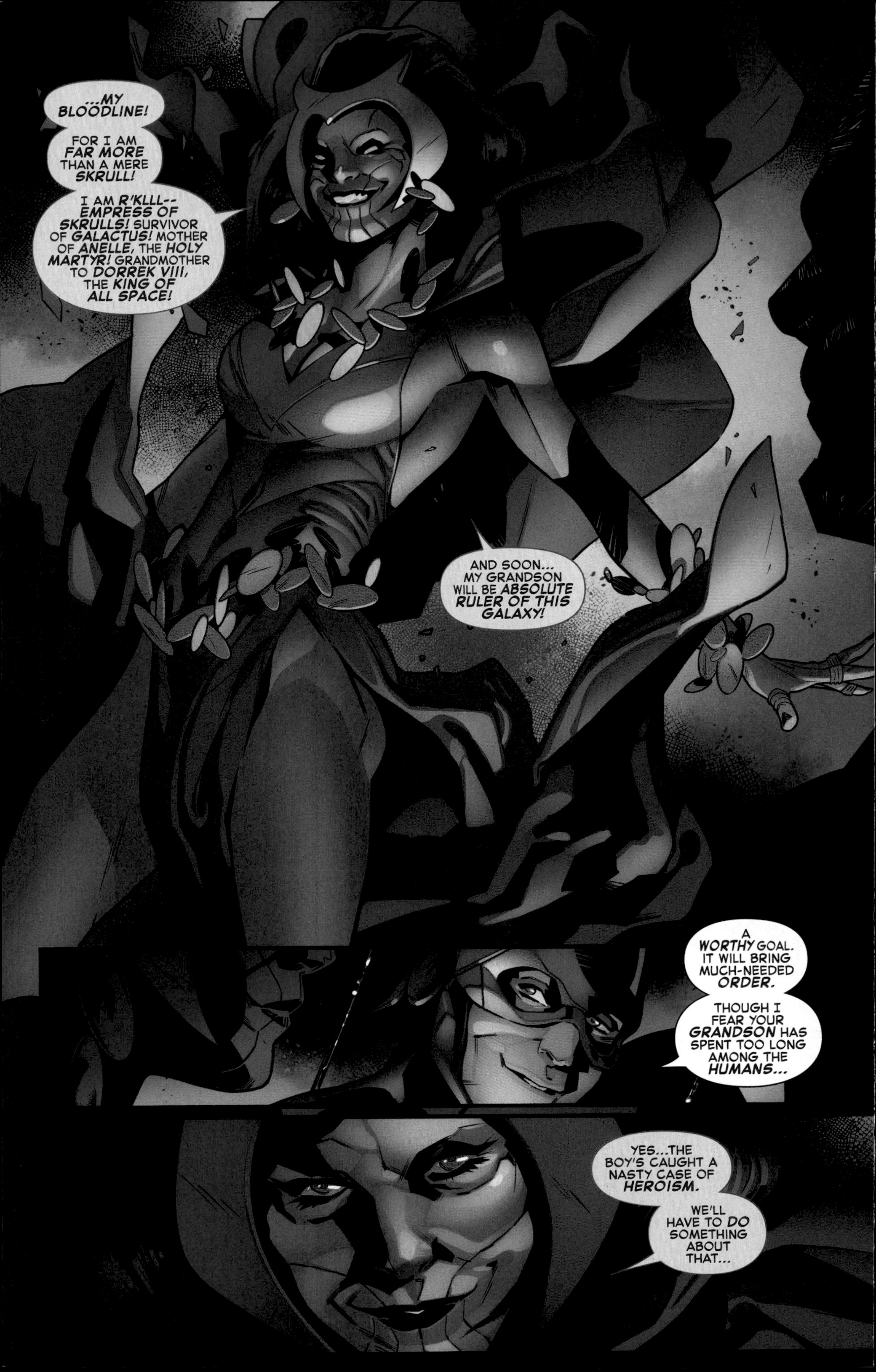
...MY BLOODLINE!
FOR I AM FAR MORE THAN A MERE SKRULL!
I AM R'KLLL-- EMPRESS OF SKRULLS! SURVIVOR OF GALACTUS! MOTHER OF ANELLE, THE HOLY MARTYR! GRANDMOTHER TO DORREK VIII, THE KING OF ALL SPACE!
AND SOON... MY GRANDSON WILL BE ABSOLUTE RULER OF THIS GALAXY!
A WORTHY GOAL. IT WILL BRING MUCH-NEEDED ORDER.
THOUGH I FEAR YOUR GRANDSON HAS SPENT TOO LONG AMONG THE HUMANS...
YES...THE BOY'S CAUGHT A NASTY CASE OF HEROISM.
WE'LL HAVE TO DO SOMETHING ABOUT THAT...

EMPYRE 4 SECOND-PRINTING VARIANT BY
Jamie McKelvie & **Rachelle Rosenberg**

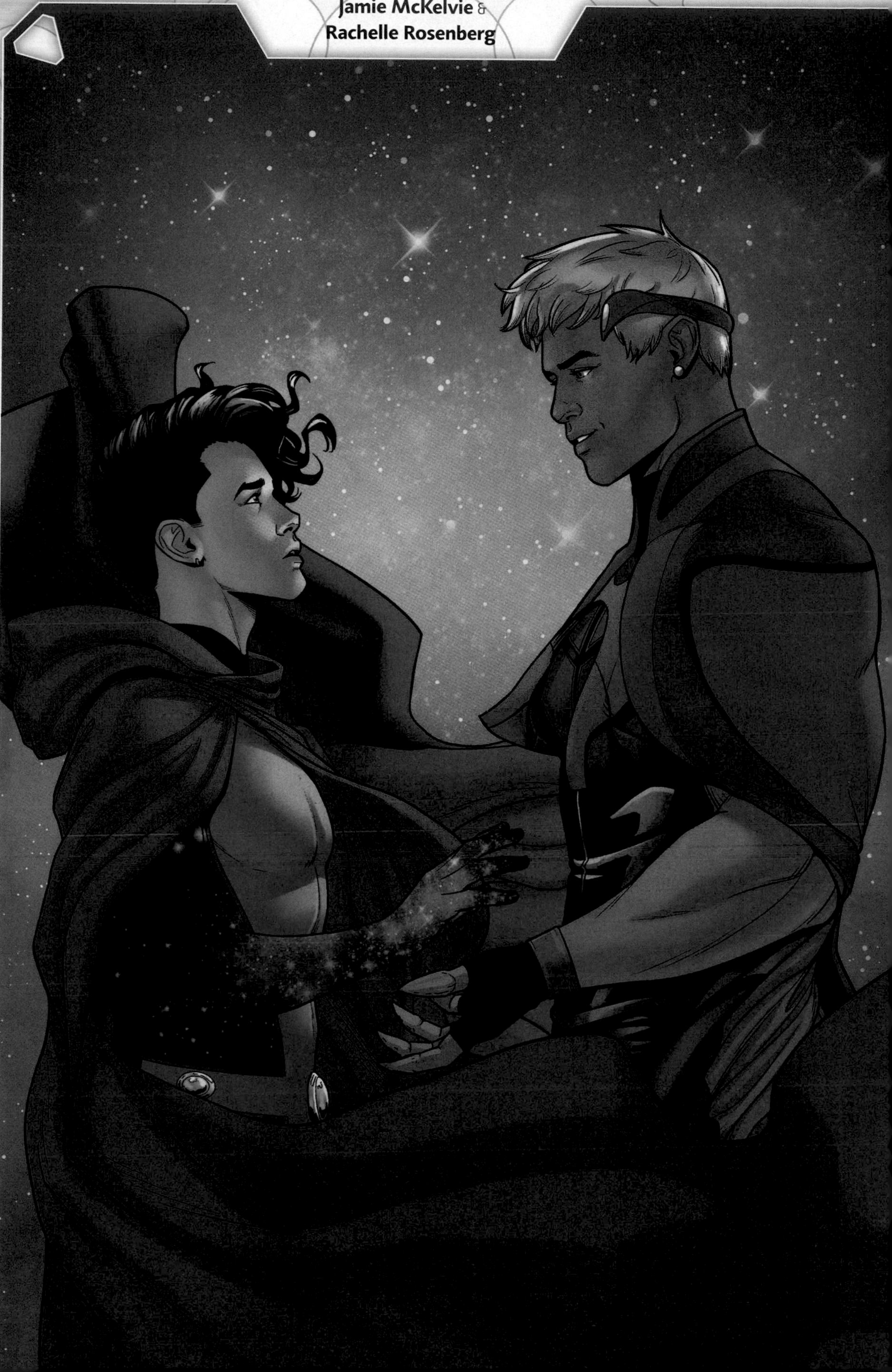

EMPYRE 4

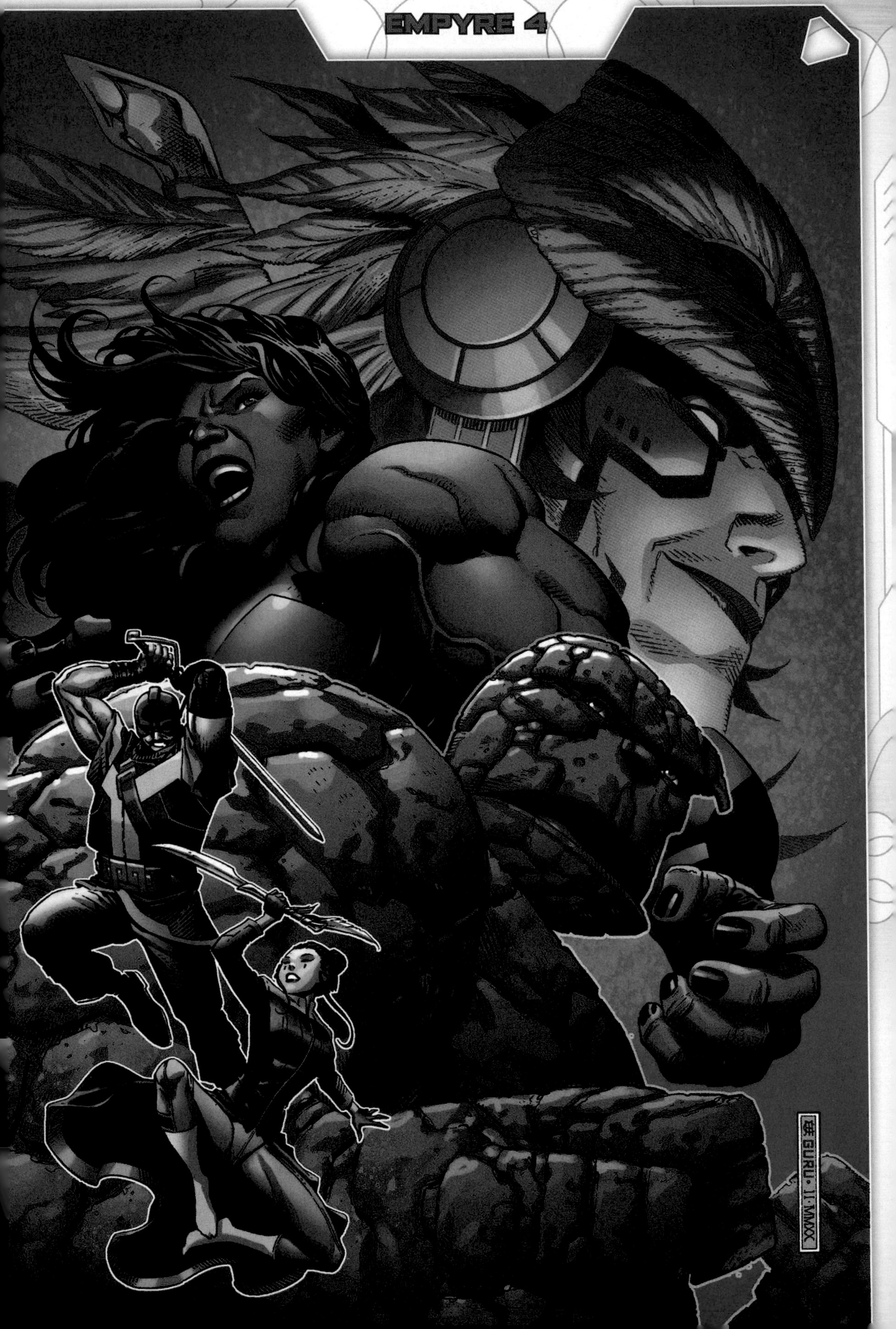
GURU • 11 • MMXX

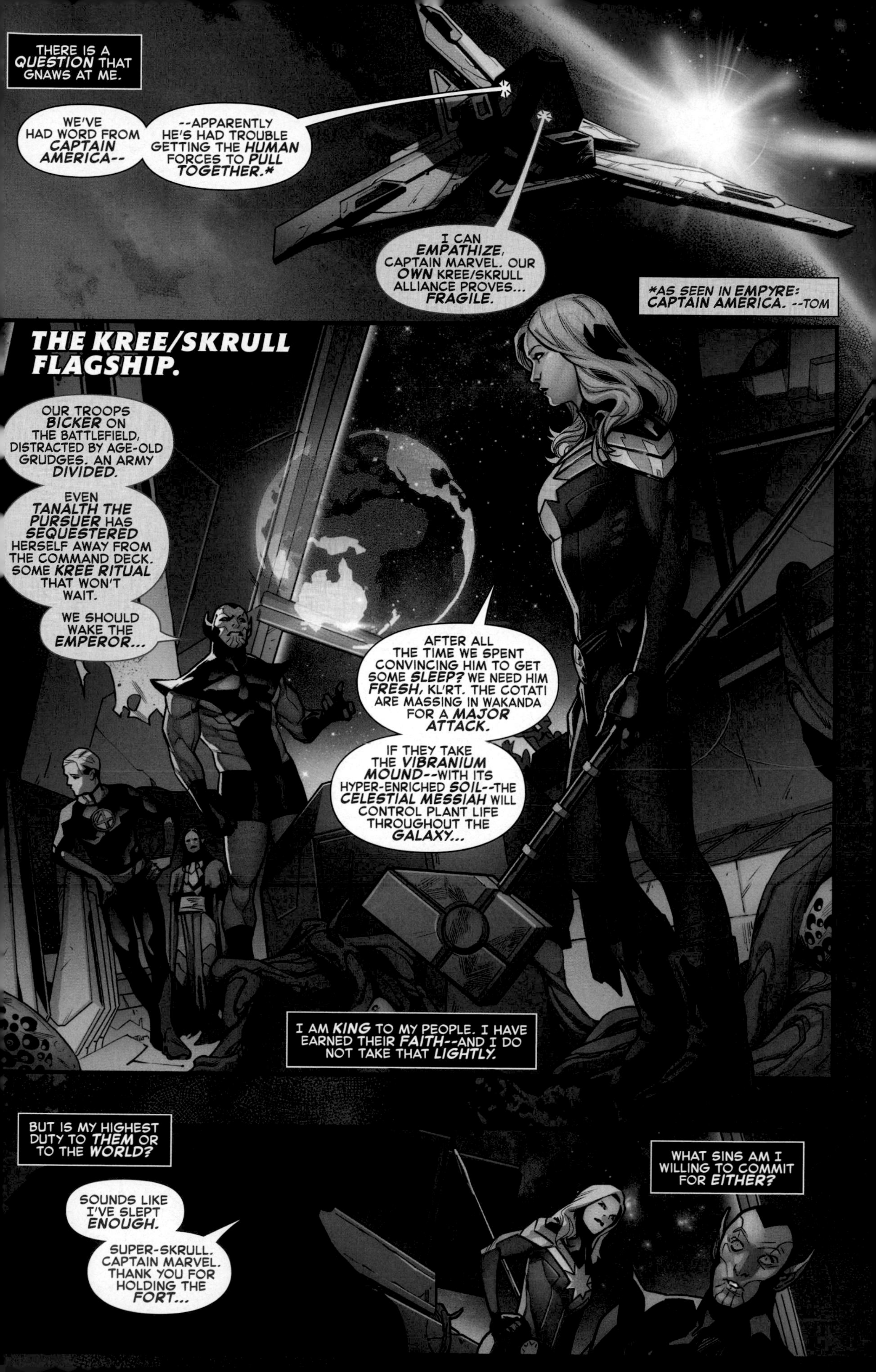
THERE IS A QUESTION THAT GNAWS AT ME.
WE'VE HAD WORD FROM CAPTAIN AMERICA--
--APPARENTLY HE'S HAD TROUBLE GETTING THE HUMAN FORCES TO PULL TOGETHER.*
I CAN EMPATHIZE, CAPTAIN MARVEL. OUR OWN KREE/SKRULL ALLIANCE PROVES... FRAGILE.
*AS SEEN IN EMPYRE: CAPTAIN AMERICA. --TOM
THE KREE/SKRULL FLAGSHIP.
OUR TROOPS BICKER ON THE BATTLEFIELD, DISTRACTED BY AGE-OLD GRUDGES. AN ARMY DIVIDED.
EVEN TANALTH THE PURSUER HAS SEQUESTERED HERSELF AWAY FROM THE COMMAND DECK. SOME KREE RITUAL THAT WON'T WAIT.
WE SHOULD WAKE THE EMPEROR...
AFTER ALL THE TIME WE SPENT CONVINCING HIM TO GET SOME SLEEP? WE NEED HIM FRESH, KL'RT. THE COTATI ARE MASSING IN WAKANDA FOR A MAJOR ATTACK.
IF THEY TAKE THE VIBRANIUM MOUND--WITH ITS HYPER-ENRICHED SOIL--THE CELESTIAL MESSIAH WILL CONTROL PLANT LIFE THROUGHOUT THE GALAXY...
I AM KING TO MY PEOPLE. I HAVE EARNED THEIR FAITH--AND I DO NOT TAKE THAT LIGHTLY.
BUT IS MY HIGHEST DUTY TO THEM OR TO THE WORLD?
WHAT SINS AM I WILLING TO COMMIT FOR EITHER?
SOUNDS LIKE I'VE SLEPT ENOUGH.
SUPER-SKRULL. CAPTAIN MARVEL. THANK YOU FOR HOLDING THE FORT...

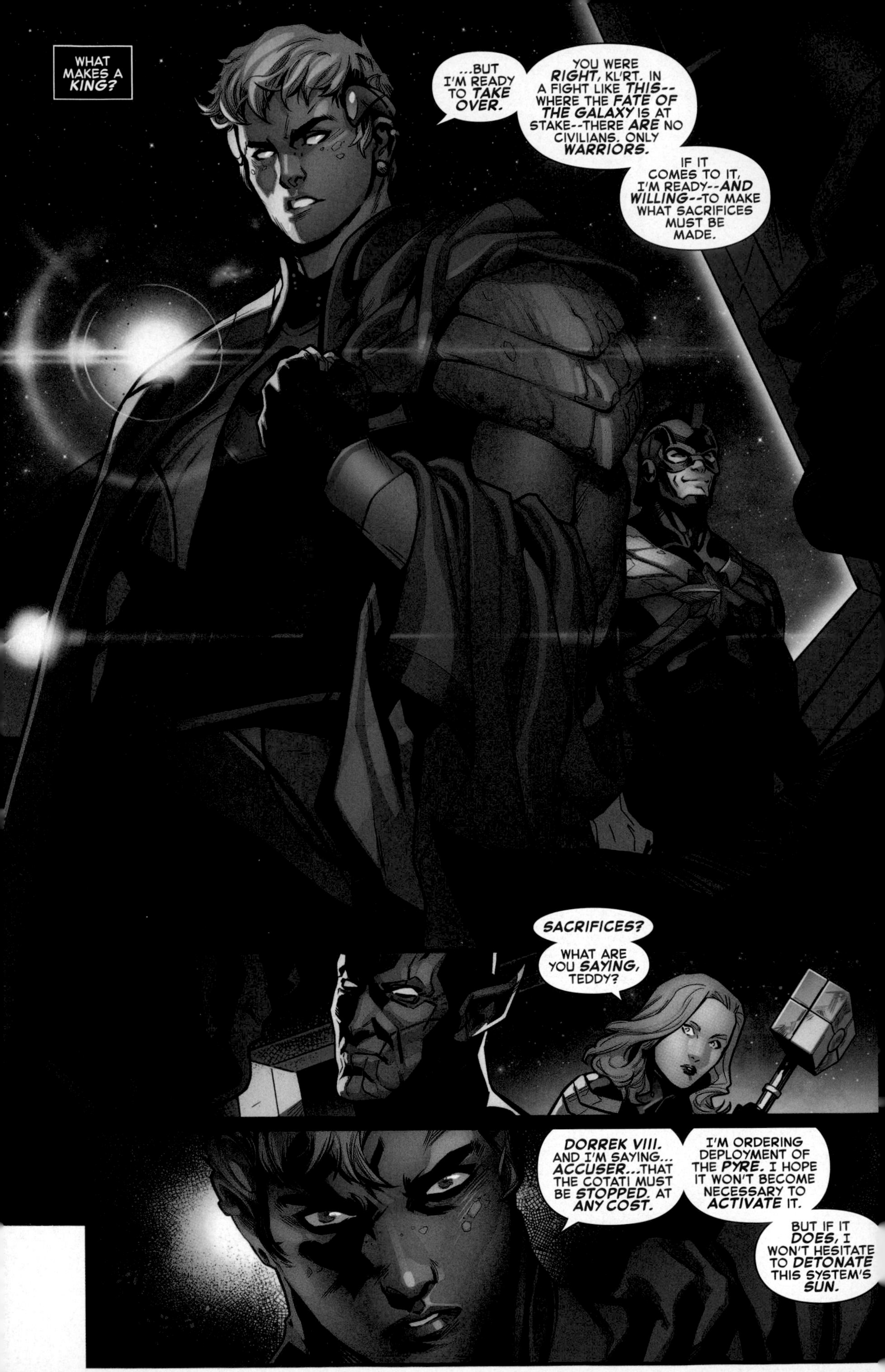
WHAT MAKES A KING?
...BUT I'M READY TO TAKE OVER.
YOU WERE RIGHT, KL'RT. IN A FIGHT LIKE THIS--WHERE THE FATE OF THE GALAXY IS AT STAKE--THERE ARE NO CIVILIANS. ONLY WARRIORS.
IF IT COMES TO IT, I'M READY--AND WILLING--TO MAKE WHAT SACRIFICES MUST BE MADE.
SACRIFICES?
WHAT ARE YOU SAYING, TEDDY?
DORREK VIII. AND I'M SAYING... ACCUSER...THAT THE COTATI MUST BE STOPPED. AT ANY COST.
I'M ORDERING DEPLOYMENT OF THE PYRE. I HOPE IT WON'T BECOME NECESSARY TO ACTIVATE IT.
BUT IF IT DOES, I WON'T HESITATE TO DETONATE THIS SYSTEM'S SUN.

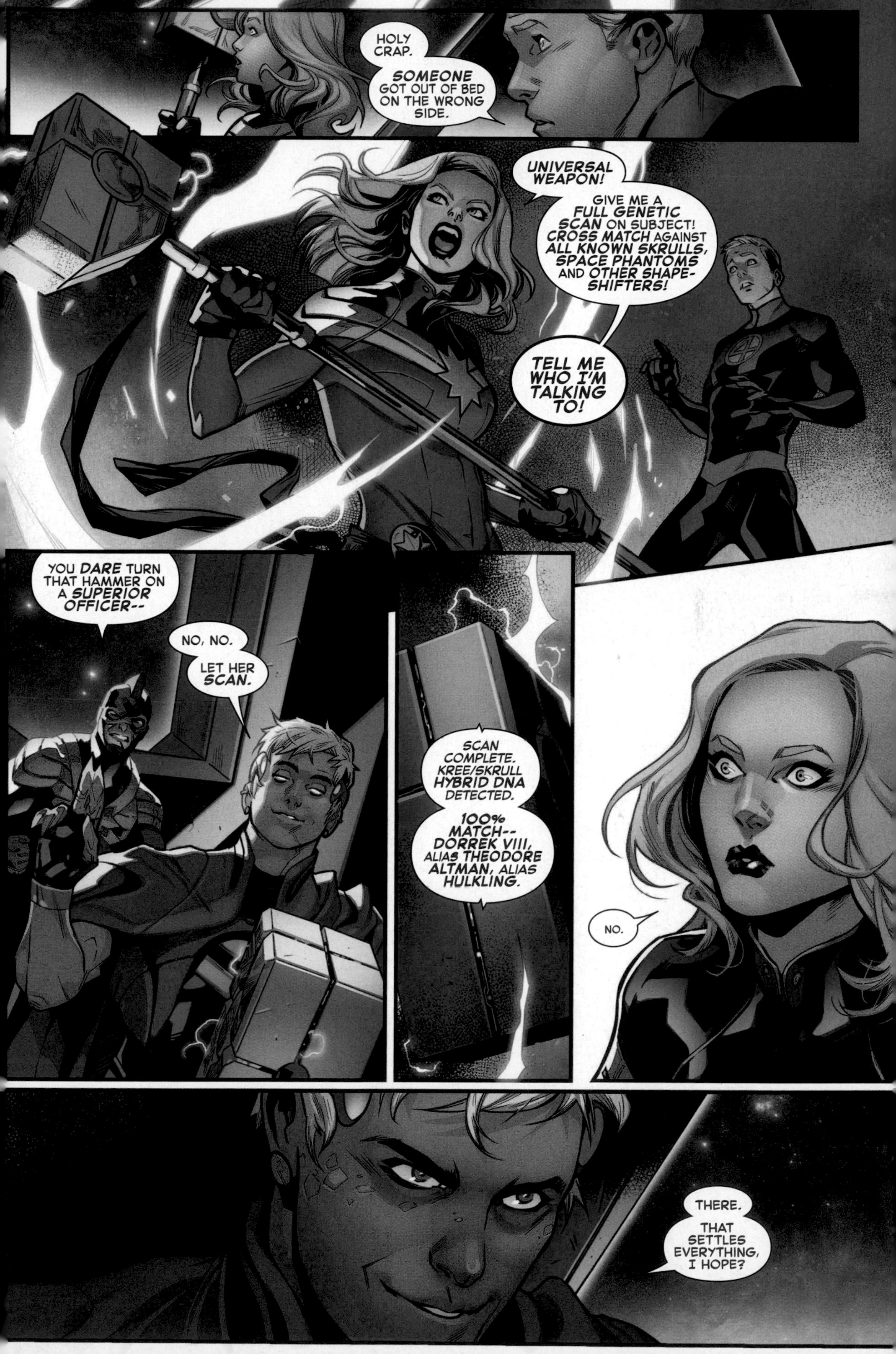
HOLY CRAP.
SOMEONE GOT OUT OF BED ON THE WRONG SIDE.
UNIVERSAL WEAPON!
GIVE ME A FULL GENETIC SCAN ON SUBJECT! CROSS MATCH AGAINST ALL KNOWN SKRULLS, SPACE PHANTOMS AND OTHER SHAPE-SHIFTERS!
TELL ME WHO I'M TALKING TO!
YOU DARE TURN THAT HAMMER ON A SUPERIOR OFFICER--
NO, NO.
LET HER SCAN.
SCAN COMPLETE. KREE/SKRULL HYBRID DNA DETECTED.
100% MATCH-- DORREK VIII, ALIAS THEODORE ALTMAN, ALIAS HULKLING.
NO.
THERE.
THAT SETTLES EVERYTHING, I HOPE?

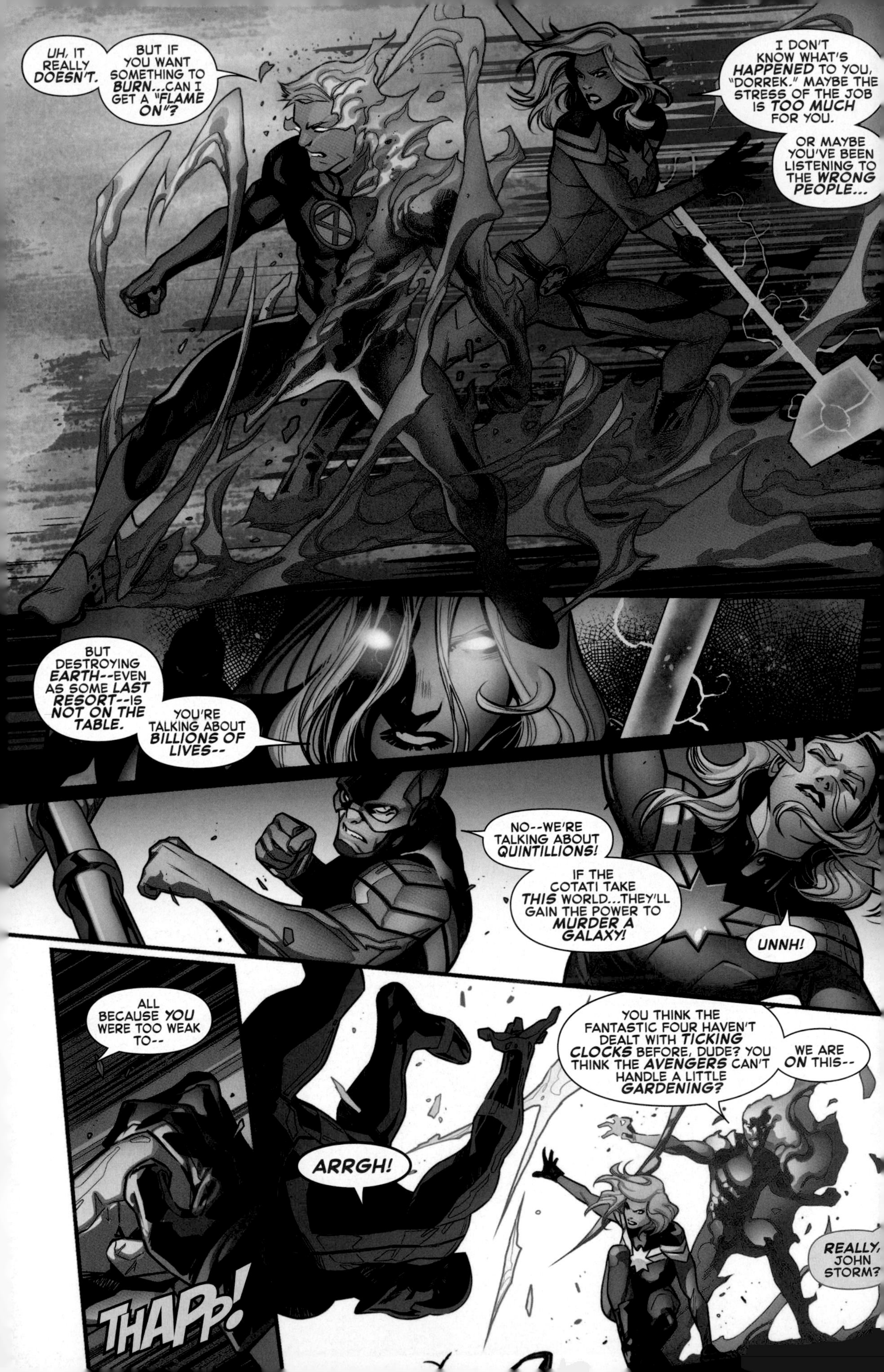
UH, IT REALLY DOESN'T.
BUT IF YOU WANT SOMETHING TO BURN...CAN I GET A "FLAME ON"?
I DON'T KNOW WHAT'S HAPPENED TO YOU, "DORREK." MAYBE THE STRESS OF THE JOB IS TOO MUCH FOR YOU.
OR MAYBE YOU'VE BEEN LISTENING TO THE WRONG PEOPLE...
BUT DESTROYING EARTH--EVEN AS SOME LAST RESORT--IS NOT ON THE TABLE.
YOU'RE TALKING ABOUT BILLIONS OF LIVES--
NO--WE'RE TALKING ABOUT QUINTILLIONS!
IF THE COTATI TAKE THIS WORLD...THEY'LL GAIN THE POWER TO MURDER A GALAXY!
UNNH!
ALL BECAUSE YOU WERE TOO WEAK TO--
ARRGH!
THAPP!
YOU THINK THE FANTASTIC FOUR HAVEN'T DEALT WITH TICKING CLOCKS BEFORE, DUDE? YOU THINK THE AVENGERS CAN'T HANDLE A LITTLE GARDENING?
WE ARE ON THIS--
REALLY, JOHN STORM?

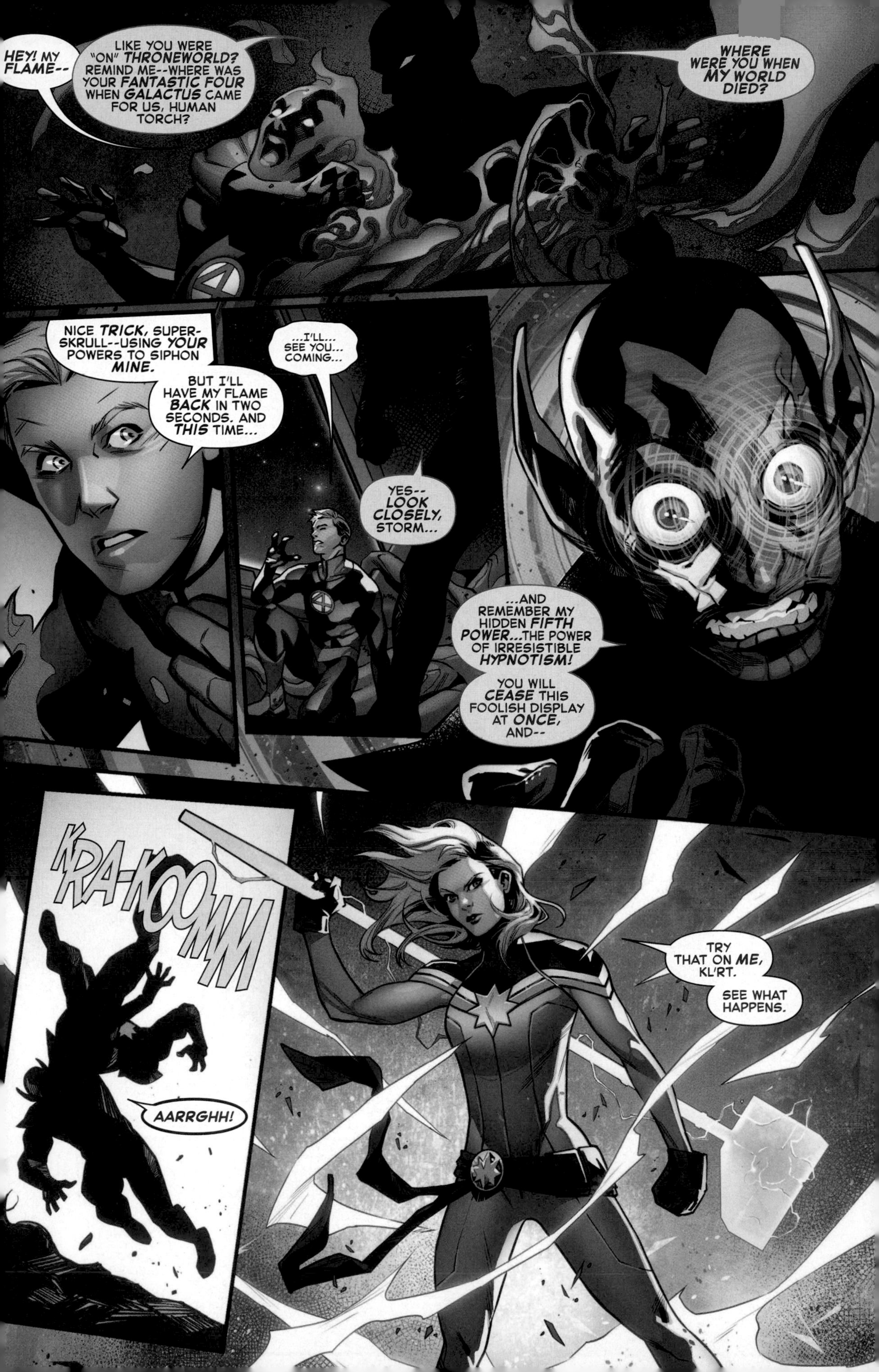
HEY! MY FLAME--
LIKE YOU WERE "ON" THRONEWORLD? REMIND ME--WHERE WAS YOUR FANTASTIC FOUR WHEN GALACTUS CAME FOR US, HUMAN TORCH?
WHERE WERE YOU WHEN MY WORLD DIED?
NICE TRICK, SUPER-SKRULL--USING YOUR POWERS TO SIPHON MINE.
BUT I'LL HAVE MY FLAME BACK IN TWO SECONDS. AND THIS TIME...
...I'LL... SEE YOU... COMING...
YES-- LOOK CLOSELY, STORM...
...AND REMEMBER MY HIDDEN FIFTH POWER...THE POWER OF IRRESISTIBLE HYPNOTISM!
YOU WILL CEASE THIS FOOLISH DISPLAY AT ONCE, AND--
KRA-KOOMM
AARRGHH!
TRY THAT ON ME, KL'RT.
SEE WHAT HAPPENS.

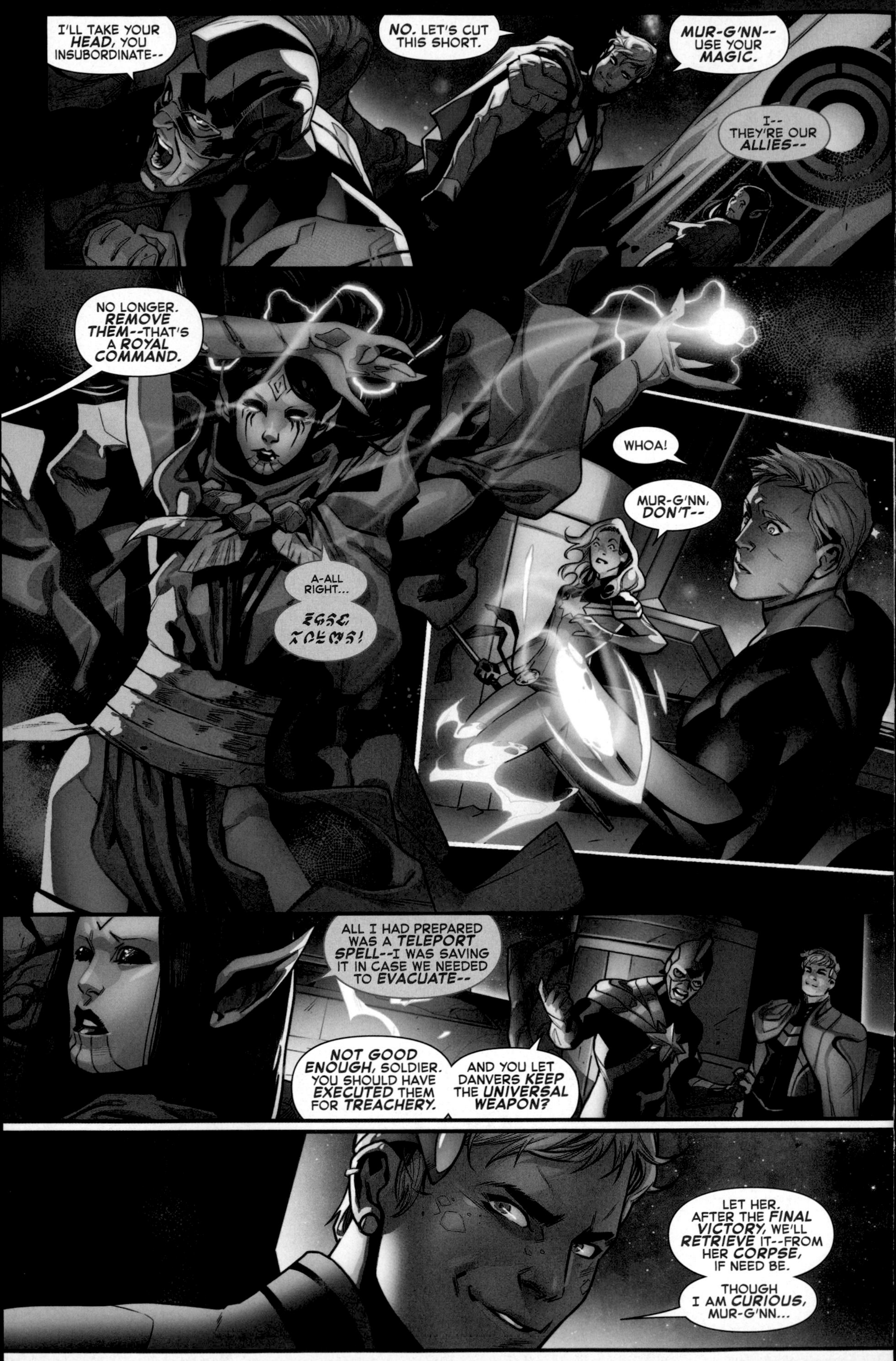
I'LL TAKE YOUR HEAD, YOU INSUBORDINATE--
NO. LET'S CUT THIS SHORT.
MUR-G'NN-- USE YOUR MAGIC.
I-- THEY'RE OUR ALLIES--
NO LONGER. REMOVE THEM--THAT'S A ROYAL COMMAND.
WHOA!
MUR-G'NN, DON'T--
A-ALL RIGHT...
ALL I HAD PREPARED WAS A TELEPORT SPELL--I WAS SAVING IT IN CASE WE NEEDED TO EVACUATE--
NOT GOOD ENOUGH, SOLDIER. YOU SHOULD HAVE EXECUTED THEM FOR TREACHERY.
AND YOU LET DANVERS KEEP THE UNIVERSAL WEAPON?
LET HER. AFTER THE FINAL VICTORY, WE'LL RETRIEVE IT--FROM HER CORPSE, IF NEED BE.
THOUGH I AM CURIOUS, MUR-G'NN...

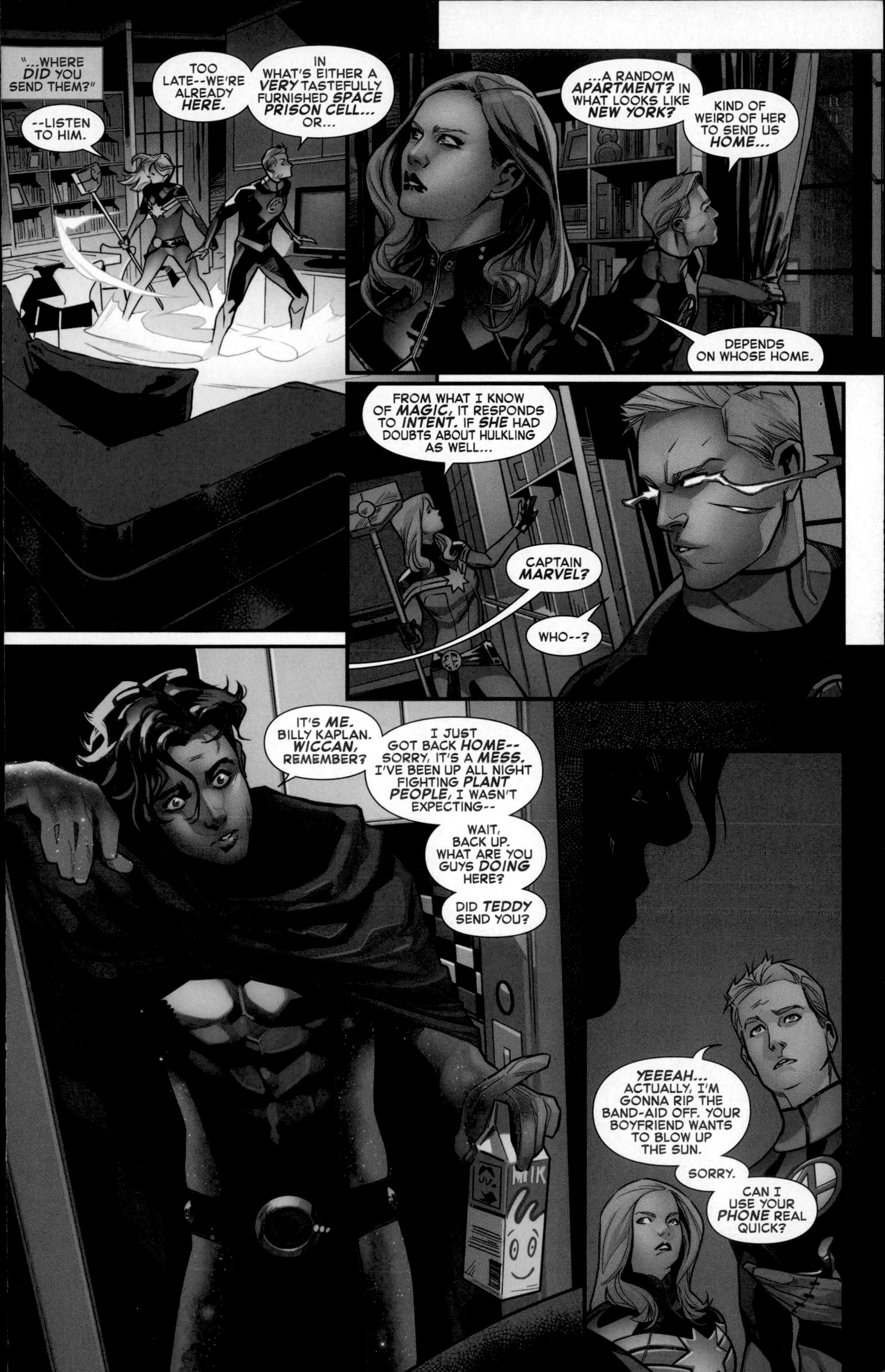

"...WHERE DID YOU SEND THEM?"
--LISTEN TO HIM.
TOO LATE--WE'RE ALREADY HERE.
IN WHAT'S EITHER A VERY TASTEFULLY FURNISHED SPACE PRISON CELL... OR...
...A RANDOM APARTMENT? IN WHAT LOOKS LIKE NEW YORK?
KIND OF WEIRD OF HER TO SEND US HOME...
DEPENDS ON WHOSE HOME.
FROM WHAT I KNOW OF MAGIC, IT RESPONDS TO INTENT. IF SHE HAD DOUBTS ABOUT HULKLING AS WELL...
CAPTAIN MARVEL?
WHO--?
IT'S ME. BILLY KAPLAN. WICCAN, REMEMBER?
I JUST GOT BACK HOME-- SORRY, IT'S A MESS. I'VE BEEN UP ALL NIGHT FIGHTING PLANT PEOPLE, I WASN'T EXPECTING--
WAIT, BACK UP. WHAT ARE YOU GUYS DOING HERE?
DID TEDDY SEND YOU?
YEEEAH... ACTUALLY, I'M GONNA RIP THE BAND-AID OFF. YOUR BOYFRIEND WANTS TO BLOW UP THE SUN.
SORRY.
CAN I USE YOUR PHONE REAL QUICK?

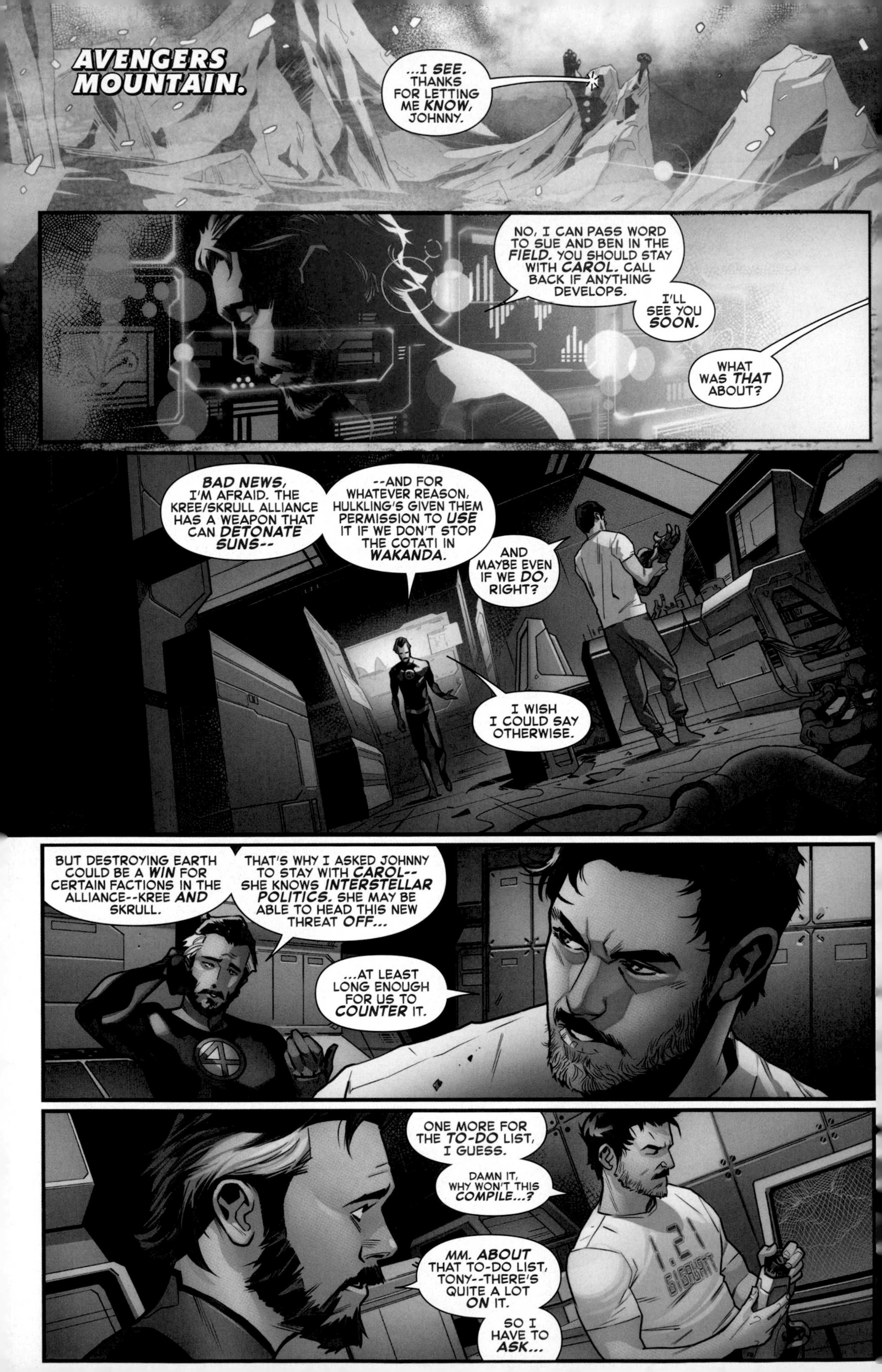
AVENGERS MOUNTAIN.
...I SEE. THANKS FOR LETTING ME KNOW, JOHNNY.
NO, I CAN PASS WORD TO SUE AND BEN IN THE FIELD. YOU SHOULD STAY WITH CAROL. CALL BACK IF ANYTHING DEVELOPS.
I'LL SEE YOU SOON.
WHAT WAS THAT ABOUT?
BAD NEWS, I'M AFRAID. THE KREE/SKRULL ALLIANCE HAS A WEAPON THAT CAN DETONATE SUNS--
--AND FOR WHATEVER REASON, HULKLING'S GIVEN THEM PERMISSION TO USE IT IF WE DON'T STOP THE COTATI IN WAKANDA.
AND MAYBE EVEN IF WE DO, RIGHT?
I WISH I COULD SAY OTHERWISE.
BUT DESTROYING EARTH COULD BE A WIN FOR CERTAIN FACTIONS IN THE ALLIANCE--KREE AND SKRULL.
THAT'S WHY I ASKED JOHNNY TO STAY WITH CAROL-- SHE KNOWS INTERSTELLAR POLITICS. SHE MAY BE ABLE TO HEAD THIS NEW THREAT OFF...
...AT LEAST LONG ENOUGH FOR US TO COUNTER IT.
ONE MORE FOR THE TO-DO LIST, I GUESS.
DAMN IT, WHY WON'T THIS COMPILE...?
1.21 GIGAWATT
MM. ABOUT THAT TO-DO LIST, TONY--THERE'S QUITE A LOT ON IT.
SO I HAVE TO ASK...

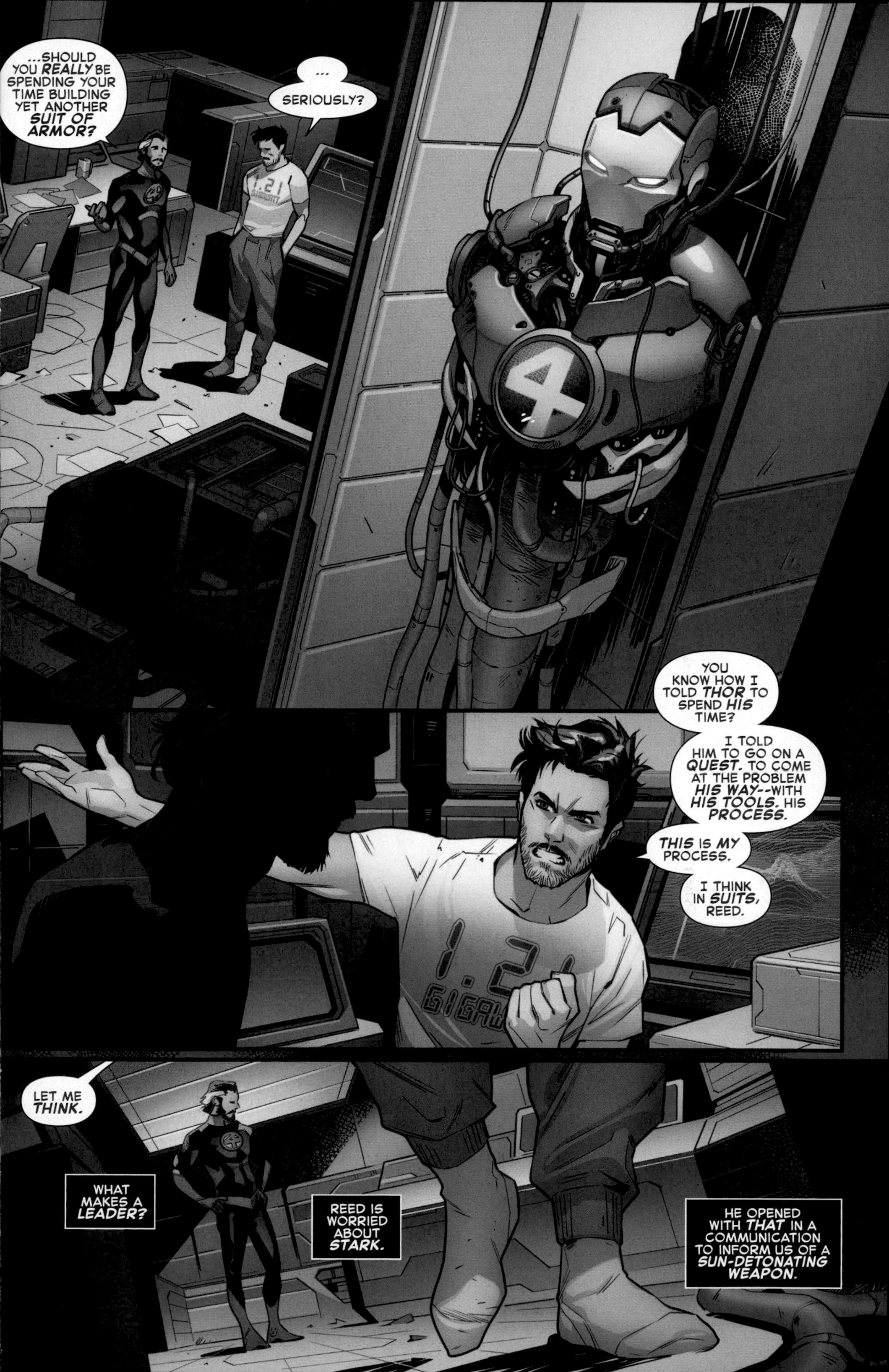
...SHOULD YOU REALLY BE SPENDING YOUR TIME BUILDING YET ANOTHER SUIT OF ARMOR?
...
SERIOUSLY?
YOU KNOW HOW I TOLD THOR TO SPEND HIS TIME?
I TOLD HIM TO GO ON A QUEST. TO COME AT THE PROBLEM HIS WAY--WITH HIS TOOLS. HIS PROCESS.
THIS IS MY PROCESS.
I THINK IN SUITS, REED.
LET ME THINK.
WHAT MAKES A LEADER?
REED IS WORRIED ABOUT STARK.
HE OPENED WITH THAT IN A COMMUNICATION TO INFORM US OF A SUN-DETONATING WEAPON.

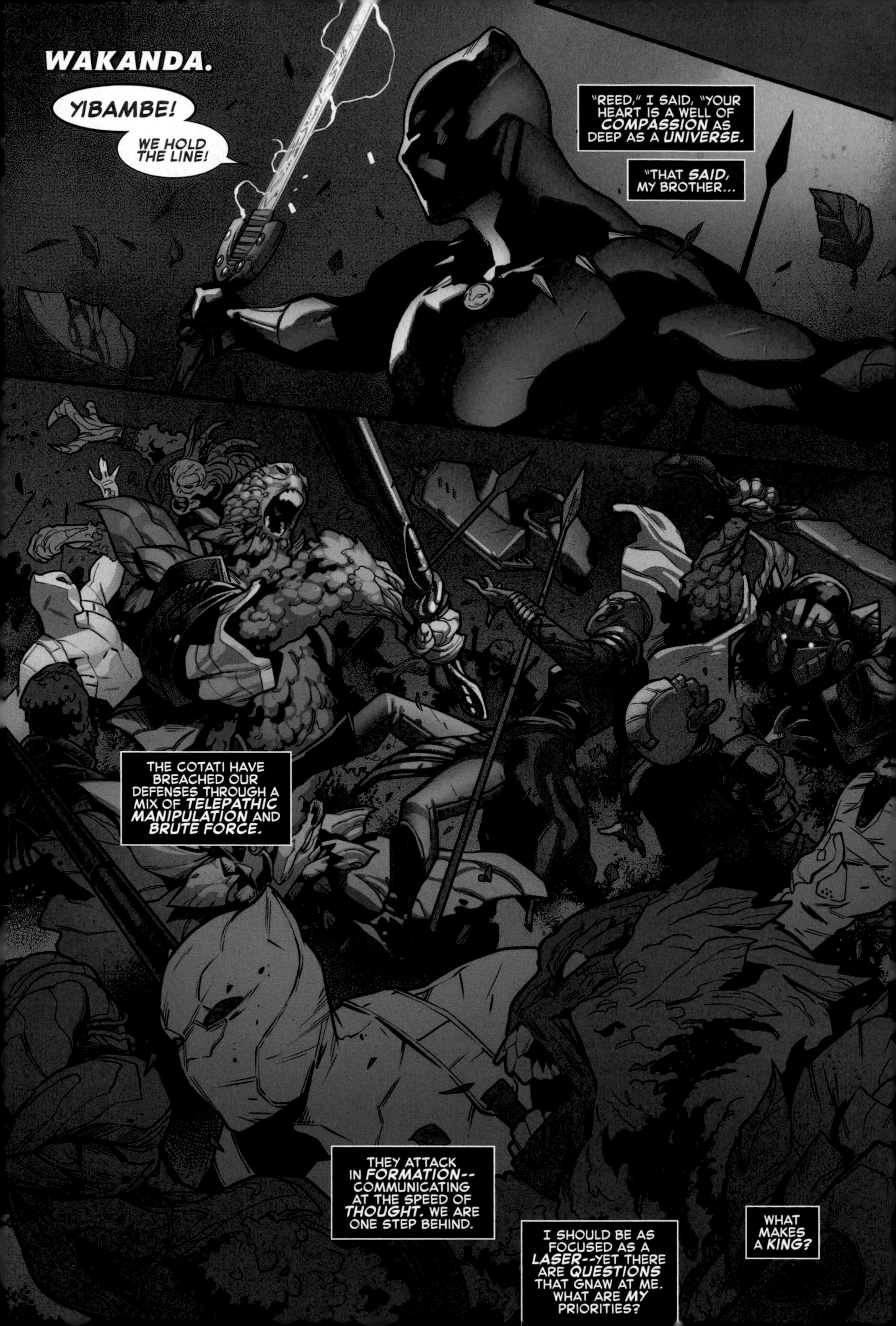
WAKANDA.
YIBAMBE!
WE HOLD THE LINE!
"REED," I SAID, "YOUR HEART IS A WELL OF COMPASSION AS DEEP AS A UNIVERSE.
"THAT SAID, MY BROTHER...
THE COTATI HAVE BREACHED OUR DEFENSES THROUGH A MIX OF TELEPATHIC MANIPULATION AND BRUTE FORCE.
THEY ATTACK IN FORMATION--COMMUNICATING AT THE SPEED OF THOUGHT. WE ARE ONE STEP BEHIND.
I SHOULD BE AS FOCUSED AS A LASER--YET THERE ARE QUESTIONS THAT GNAW AT ME. WHAT ARE MY PRIORITIES?
WHAT MAKES A KING?

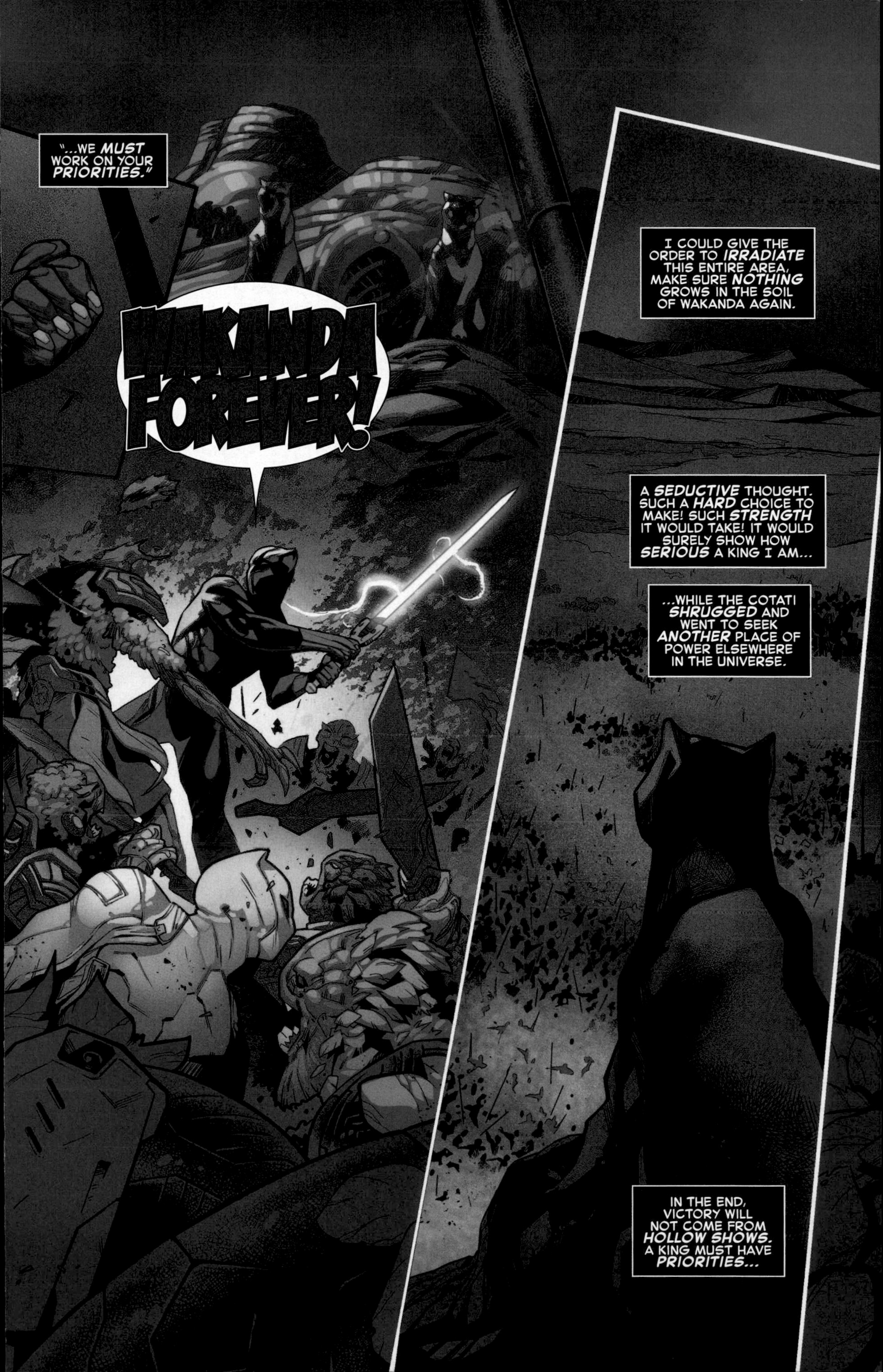
"...WE MUST WORK ON YOUR PRIORITIES."
WAKANDA FOREVER!
I COULD GIVE THE ORDER TO IRRADIATE THIS ENTIRE AREA, MAKE SURE NOTHING GROWS IN THE SOIL OF WAKANDA AGAIN.
A SEDUCTIVE THOUGHT. SUCH A HARD CHOICE TO MAKE! SUCH STRENGTH IT WOULD TAKE! IT WOULD SURELY SHOW HOW SERIOUS A KING I AM...
...WHILE THE COTATI SHRUGGED AND WENT TO SEEK ANOTHER PLACE OF POWER ELSEWHERE IN THE UNIVERSE.
IN THE END, VICTORY WILL NOT COME FROM HOLLOW SHOWS. A KING MUST HAVE PRIORITIES...

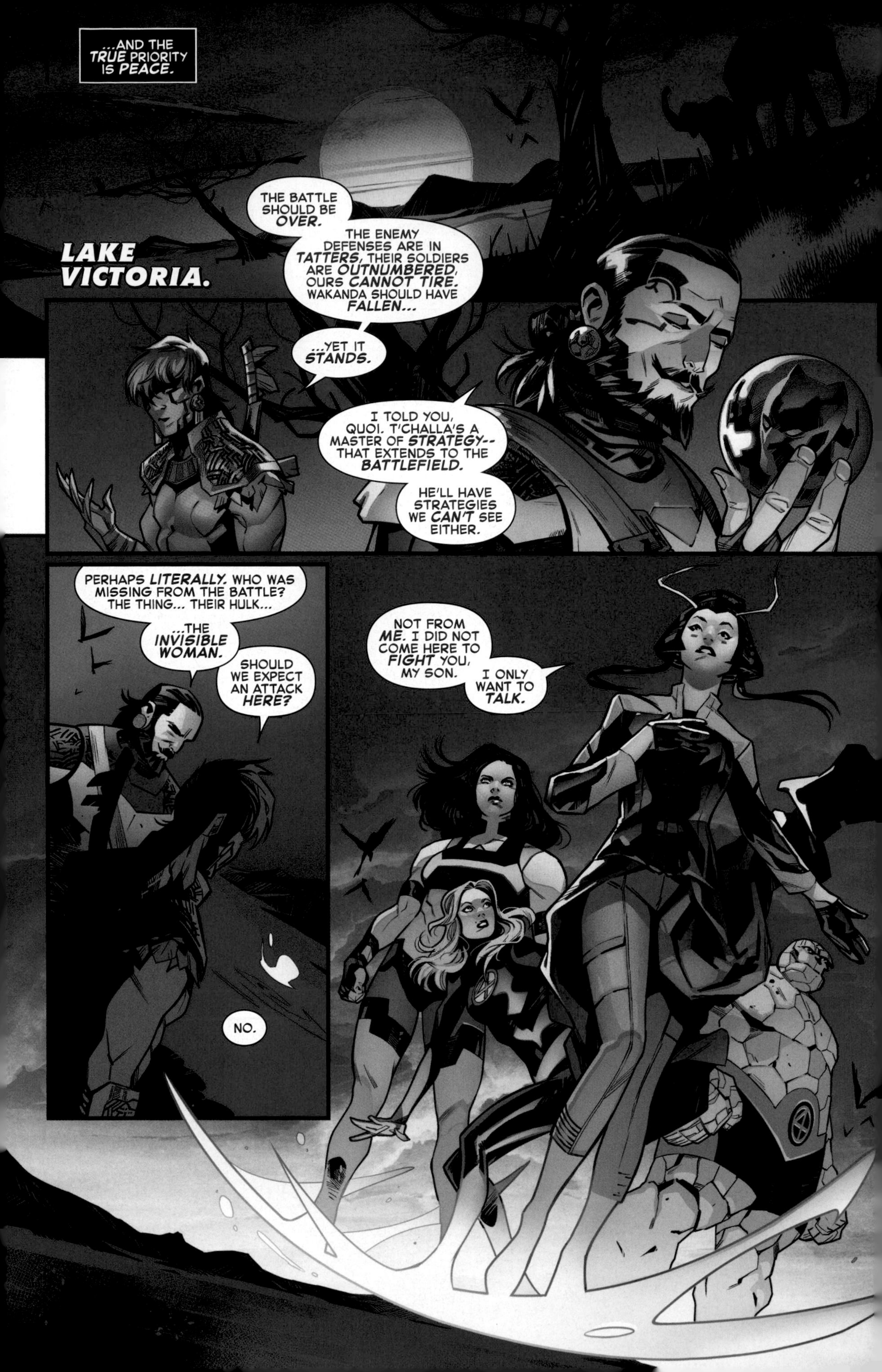
...AND THE TRUE PRIORITY IS PEACE.
LAKE VICTORIA.
THE BATTLE SHOULD BE OVER.
THE ENEMY DEFENSES ARE IN TATTERS, THEIR SOLDIERS ARE OUTNUMBERED, OURS CANNOT TIRE. WAKANDA SHOULD HAVE FALLEN...
...YET IT STANDS.
I TOLD YOU, QUOI. T'CHALLA'S A MASTER OF STRATEGY-- THAT EXTENDS TO THE BATTLEFIELD.
HE'LL HAVE STRATEGIES WE CAN'T SEE EITHER.
PERHAPS LITERALLY. WHO WAS MISSING FROM THE BATTLE? THE THING... THEIR HULK...
...THE INVISIBLE WOMAN.
SHOULD WE EXPECT AN ATTACK HERE?
NO.
NOT FROM ME. I DID NOT COME HERE TO FIGHT YOU, MY SON.
I ONLY WANT TO TALK.

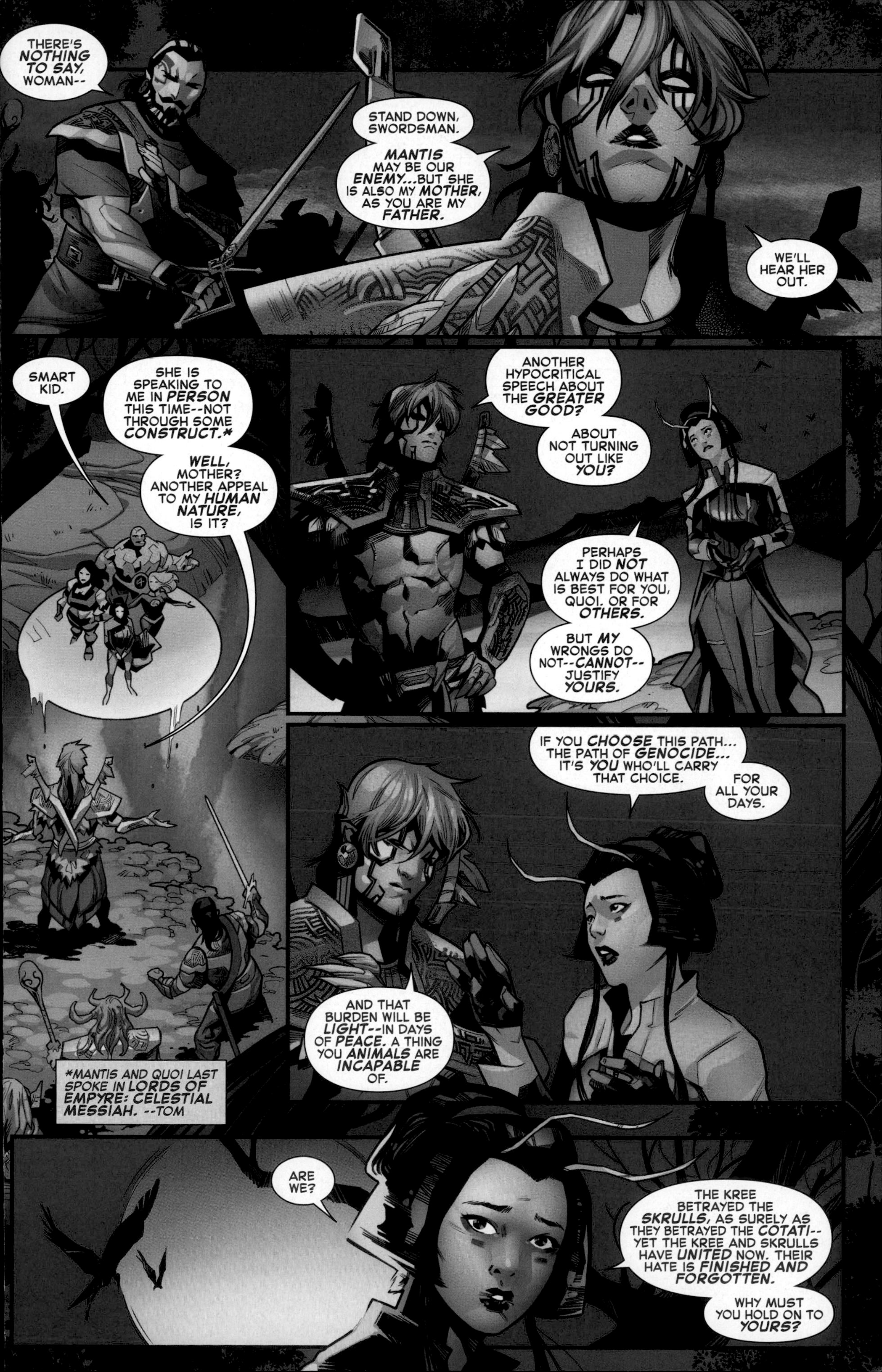
THERE'S NOTHING TO SAY, WOMAN--
STAND DOWN, SWORDSMAN.
MANTIS MAY BE OUR ENEMY...BUT SHE IS ALSO MY MOTHER, AS YOU ARE MY FATHER.
WE'LL HEAR HER OUT.
SMART KID.
SHE IS SPEAKING TO ME IN PERSON THIS TIME--NOT THROUGH SOME CONSTRUCT.*
WELL, MOTHER? ANOTHER APPEAL TO MY HUMAN NATURE, IS IT?
*MANTIS AND QUOI LAST SPOKE IN LORDS OF EMPYRE: CELESTIAL MESSIAH. --TOM
ANOTHER HYPOCRITICAL SPEECH ABOUT THE GREATER GOOD?
ABOUT NOT TURNING OUT LIKE YOU?
PERHAPS I DID NOT ALWAYS DO WHAT IS BEST FOR YOU, QUOI. OR FOR OTHERS.
BUT MY WRONGS DO NOT--CANNOT--JUSTIFY YOURS.
IF YOU CHOOSE THIS PATH... THE PATH OF GENOCIDE... IT'S YOU WHO'LL CARRY THAT CHOICE.
FOR ALL YOUR DAYS.
AND THAT BURDEN WILL BE LIGHT--IN DAYS OF PEACE. A THING YOU ANIMALS ARE INCAPABLE OF.
ARE WE?
THE KREE BETRAYED THE SKRULLS, AS SURELY AS THEY BETRAYED THE COTATI--YET THE KREE AND SKRULLS HAVE UNITED NOW. THEIR HATE IS FINISHED AND FORGOTTEN.
WHY MUST YOU HOLD ON TO YOURS?

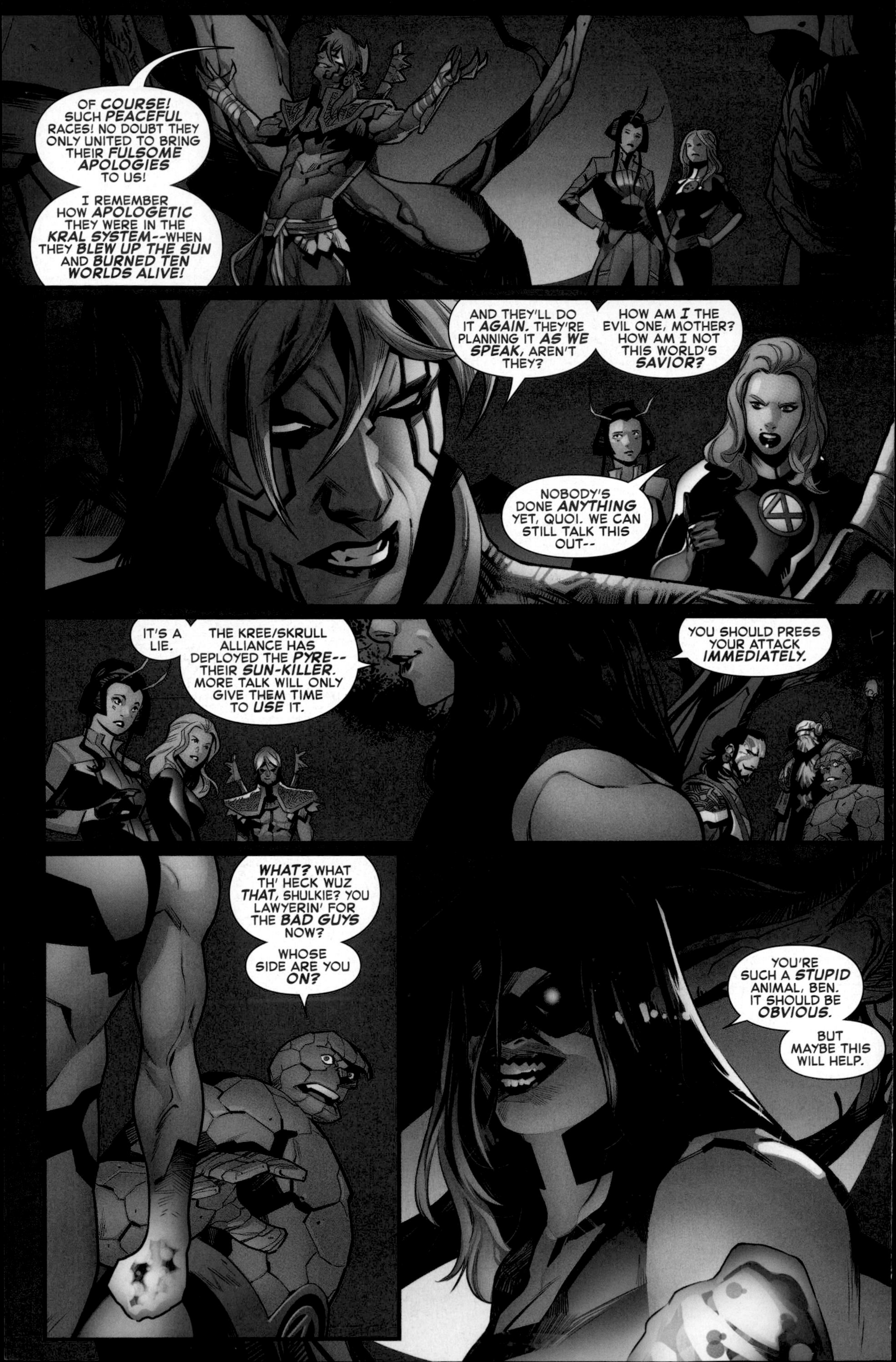
OF COURSE! SUCH PEACEFUL RACES! NO DOUBT THEY ONLY UNITED TO BRING THEIR FULSOME APOLOGIES TO US!
I REMEMBER HOW APOLOGETIC THEY WERE IN THE KRAL SYSTEM--WHEN THEY BLEW UP THE SUN AND BURNED TEN WORLDS ALIVE!
AND THEY'LL DO IT AGAIN. THEY'RE PLANNING IT AS WE SPEAK, AREN'T THEY?
HOW AM I THE EVIL ONE, MOTHER? HOW AM I NOT THIS WORLD'S SAVIOR?
NOBODY'S DONE ANYTHING YET, QUOI. WE CAN STILL TALK THIS OUT--
IT'S A LIE.
THE KREE/SKRULL ALLIANCE HAS DEPLOYED THE PYRE-- THEIR SUN-KILLER. MORE TALK WILL ONLY GIVE THEM TIME TO USE IT.
YOU SHOULD PRESS YOUR ATTACK IMMEDIATELY.
WHAT? WHAT TH' HECK WUZ THAT, SHULKIE? YOU LAWYERIN' FOR THE BAD GUYS NOW?
WHOSE SIDE ARE YOU ON?
YOU'RE SUCH A STUPID ANIMAL, BEN. IT SHOULD BE OBVIOUS.
BUT MAYBE THIS WILL HELP.

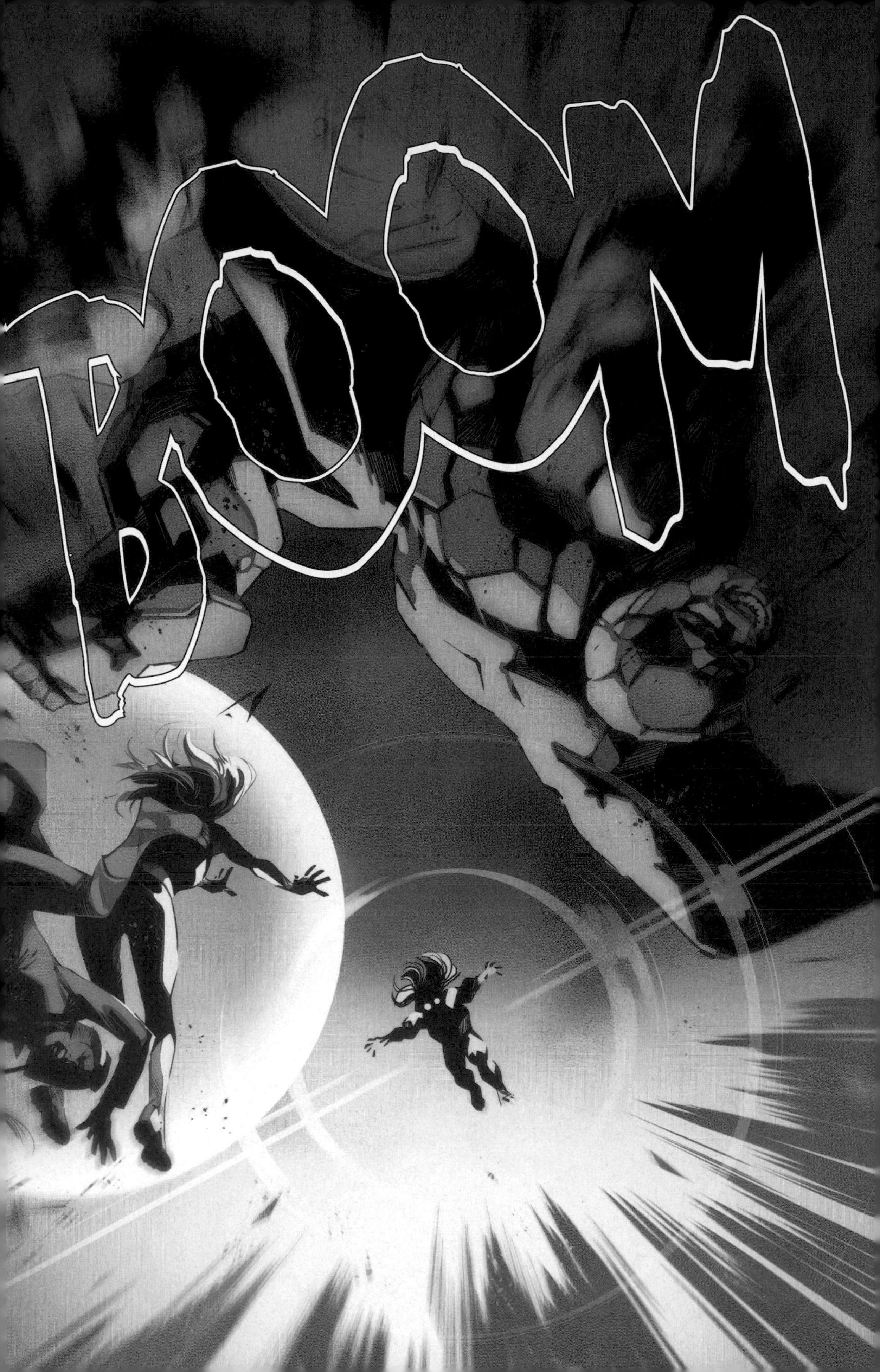
BOOM

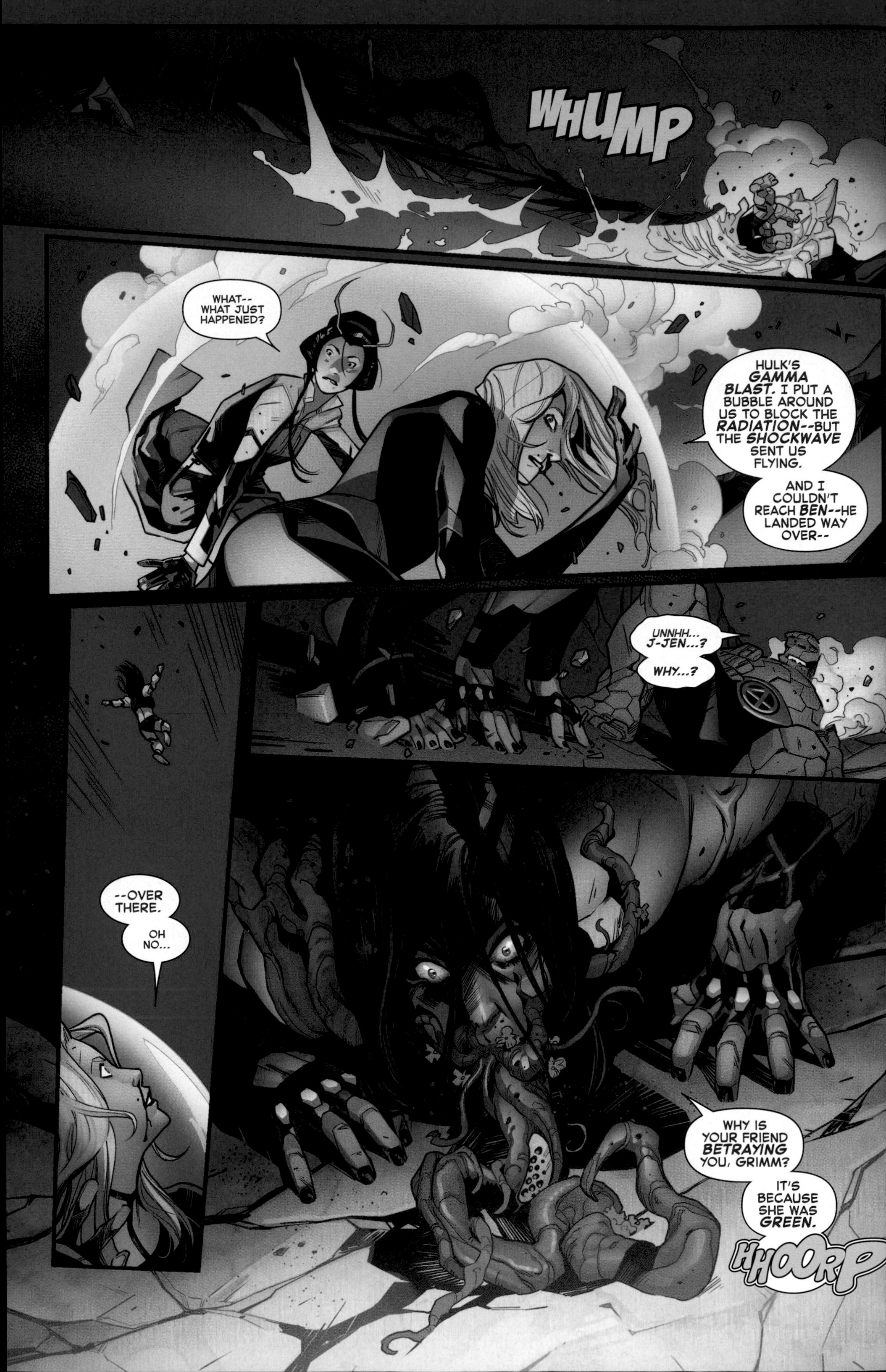
WHUMP
WHAT-- WHAT JUST HAPPENED?
HULK'S GAMMA BLAST. I PUT A BUBBLE AROUND US TO BLOCK THE RADIATION--BUT THE SHOCKWAVE SENT US FLYING.
AND I COULDN'T REACH BEN--HE LANDED WAY OVER--
UNNHH... J-JEN...?
WHY...?
--OVER THERE.
OH NO...
WHY IS YOUR FRIEND BETRAYING YOU, GRIMM?
IT'S BECAUSE SHE WAS GREEN.
HHOORP

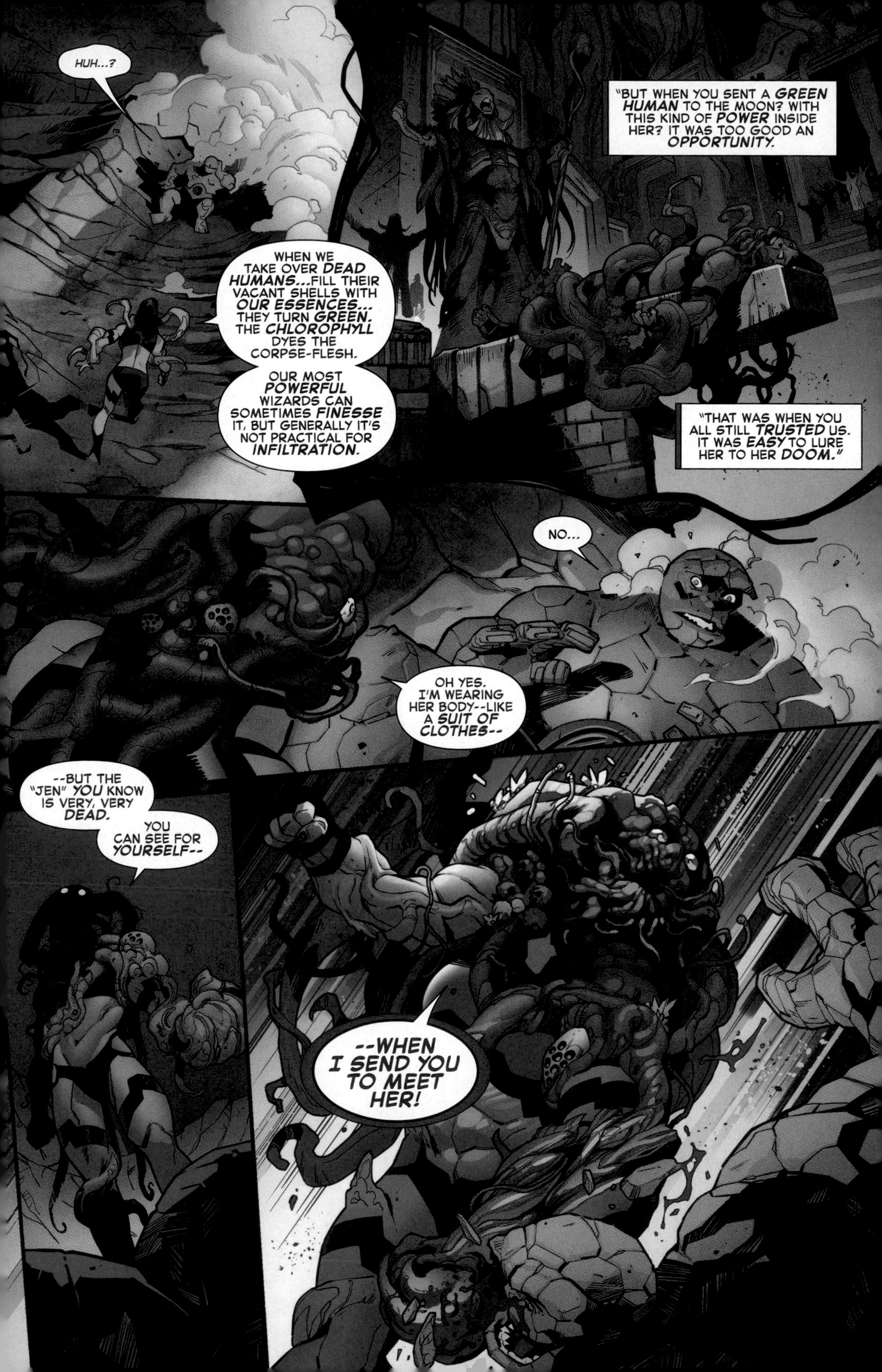
HUH...?
"BUT WHEN YOU SENT A GREEN HUMAN TO THE MOON? WITH THIS KIND OF POWER INSIDE HER? IT WAS TOO GOOD AN OPPORTUNITY.
WHEN WE TAKE OVER DEAD HUMANS...FILL THEIR VACANT SHELLS WITH OUR ESSENCES... THEY TURN GREEN. THE CHLOROPHYLL DYES THE CORPSE-FLESH.
OUR MOST POWERFUL WIZARDS CAN SOMETIMES FINESSE IT, BUT GENERALLY IT'S NOT PRACTICAL FOR INFILTRATION.
"THAT WAS WHEN YOU ALL STILL TRUSTED US. IT WAS EASY TO LURE HER TO HER DOOM."
NO...
OH YES. I'M WEARING HER BODY--LIKE A SUIT OF CLOTHES--
--BUT THE "JEN" YOU KNOW IS VERY, VERY DEAD.
YOU CAN SEE FOR YOURSELF--
--WHEN I SEND YOU TO MEET HER!

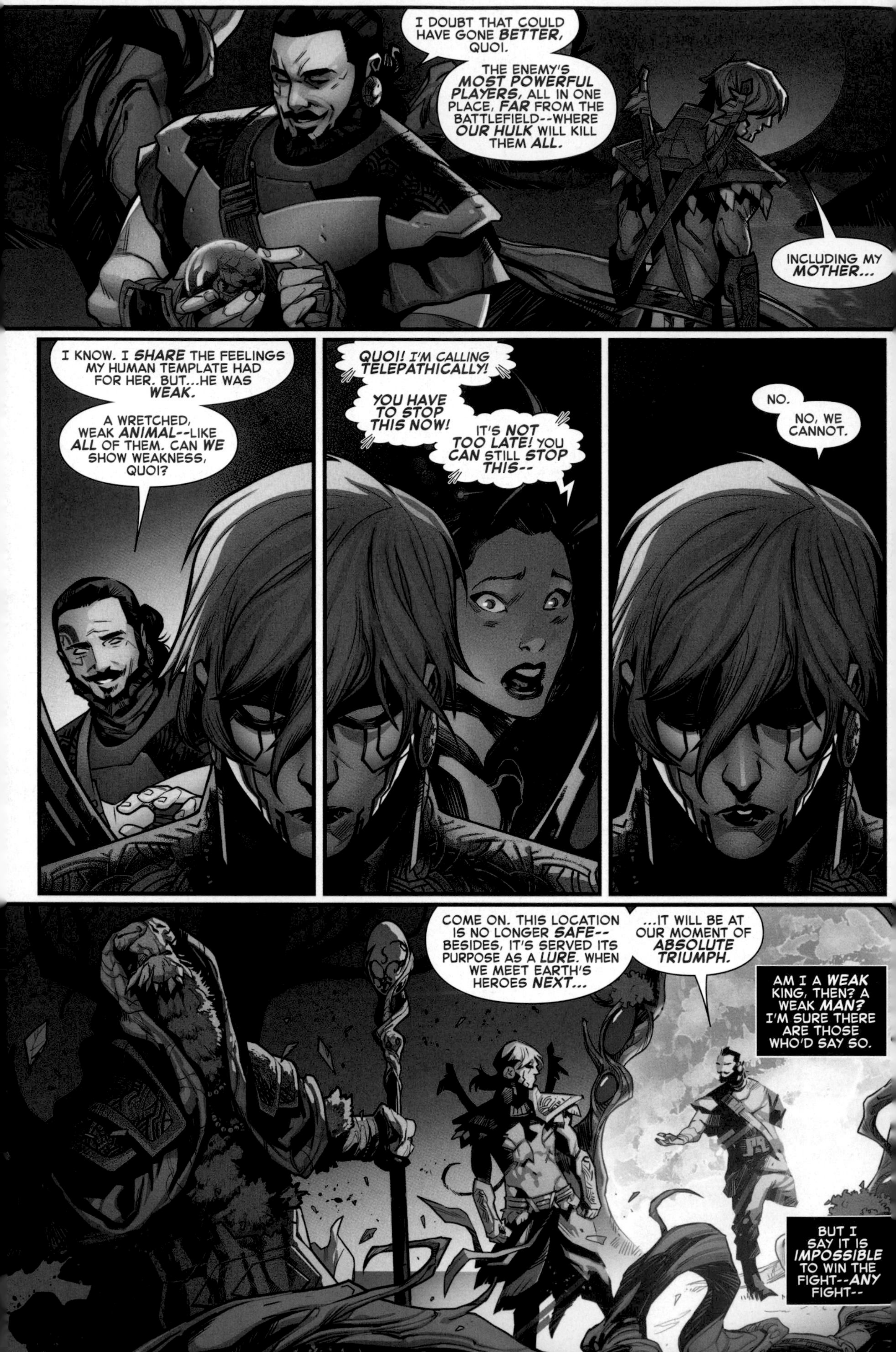
I DOUBT THAT COULD HAVE GONE BETTER, QUOI.
THE ENEMY'S MOST POWERFUL PLAYERS, ALL IN ONE PLACE, FAR FROM THE BATTLEFIELD--WHERE OUR HULK WILL KILL THEM ALL.
INCLUDING MY MOTHER...
I KNOW. I SHARE THE FEELINGS MY HUMAN TEMPLATE HAD FOR HER. BUT...HE WAS WEAK.
A WRETCHED, WEAK ANIMAL--LIKE ALL OF THEM. CAN WE SHOW WEAKNESS, QUOI?
QUOI! I'M CALLING TELEPATHICALLY!
YOU HAVE TO STOP THIS NOW!
IT'S NOT TOO LATE! YOU CAN STILL STOP THIS--
NO.
NO, WE CANNOT.
COME ON. THIS LOCATION IS NO LONGER SAFE-- BESIDES, IT'S SERVED ITS PURPOSE AS A LURE. WHEN WE MEET EARTH'S HEROES NEXT...
...IT WILL BE AT OUR MOMENT OF ABSOLUTE TRIUMPH.
AM I A WEAK KING, THEN? A WEAK MAN? I'M SURE THERE ARE THOSE WHO'D SAY SO.
BUT I SAY IT IS IMPOSSIBLE TO WIN THE FIGHT--ANY FIGHT--

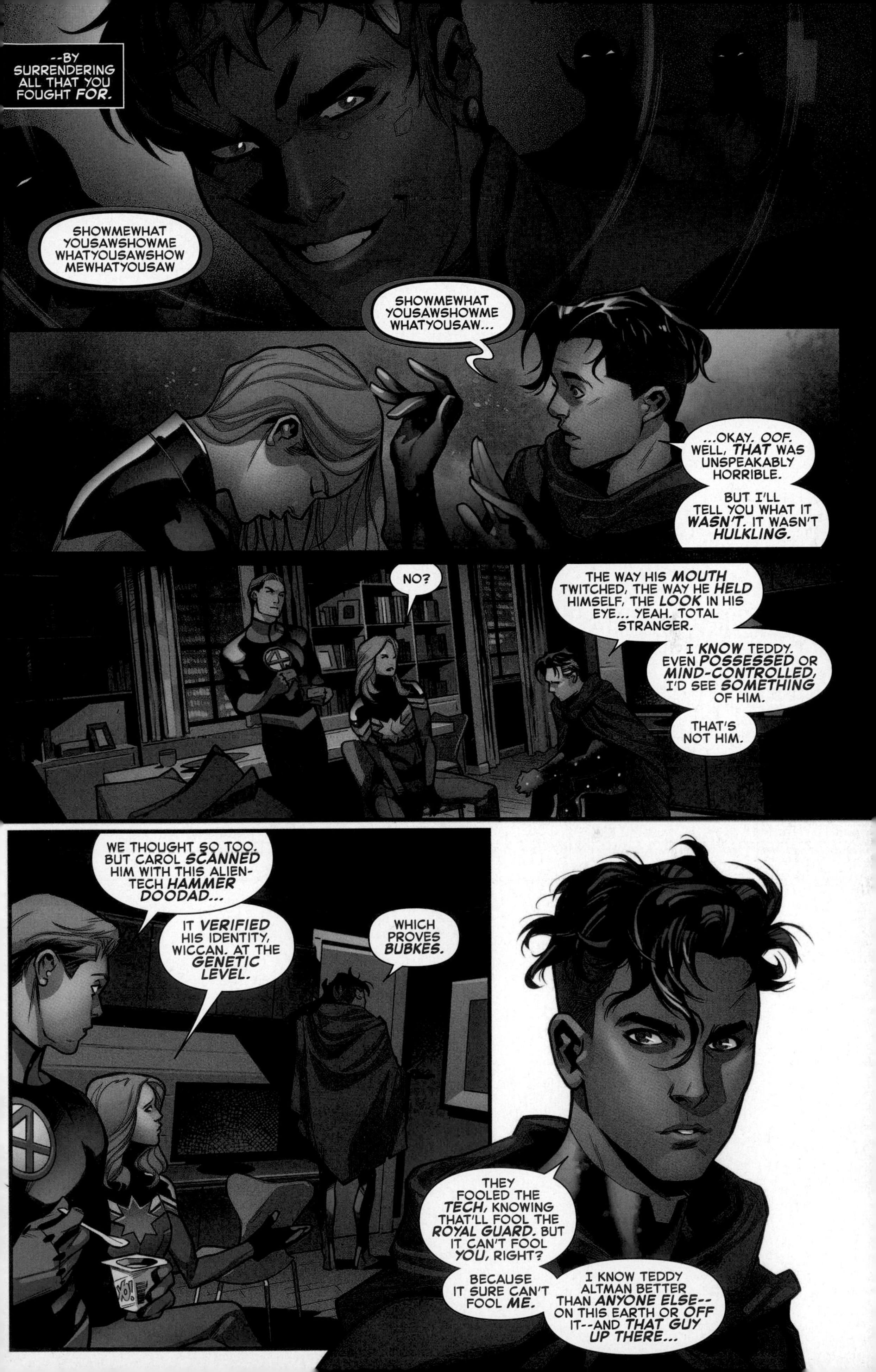
--BY SURRENDERING ALL THAT YOU FOUGHT *FOR.*
SHOWMEWHAT YOUSAWSHOWME WHATYOUSAWSHOW MEWHATYOUSAW
SHOWMEWHAT YOUSAWSHOWME WHATYOUSAW...
...OKAY. *OOF.* WELL, ***THAT*** WAS UNSPEAKABLY HORRIBLE.
BUT I'LL TELL YOU WHAT IT ***WASN'T.*** IT WASN'T ***HULKLING.***
NO?
THE WAY HIS ***MOUTH*** TWITCHED, THE WAY HE ***HELD*** HIMSELF, THE ***LOOK*** IN HIS EYE... YEAH. TOTAL STRANGER.
I ***KNOW*** TEDDY. EVEN ***POSSESSED*** OR ***MIND-CONTROLLED,*** I'D SEE ***SOMETHING*** OF HIM.
THAT'S NOT HIM.
WE THOUGHT SO TOO. BUT CAROL ***SCANNED*** HIM WITH THIS ALIEN-TECH ***HAMMER DOODAD...***
IT ***VERIFIED*** HIS IDENTITY, WICCAN. AT THE ***GENETIC LEVEL.***
WHICH PROVES ***BUBKES.***
THEY FOOLED THE ***TECH,*** KNOWING THAT'LL FOOL THE ***ROYAL GUARD.*** BUT IT CAN'T FOOL ***YOU,*** RIGHT?
BECAUSE IT SURE CAN'T FOOL ***ME.***
I KNOW TEDDY ALTMAN BETTER THAN ***ANYONE ELSE--*** ON THIS EARTH OR ***OFF*** IT--AND ***THAT GUY UP THERE...***
YO!

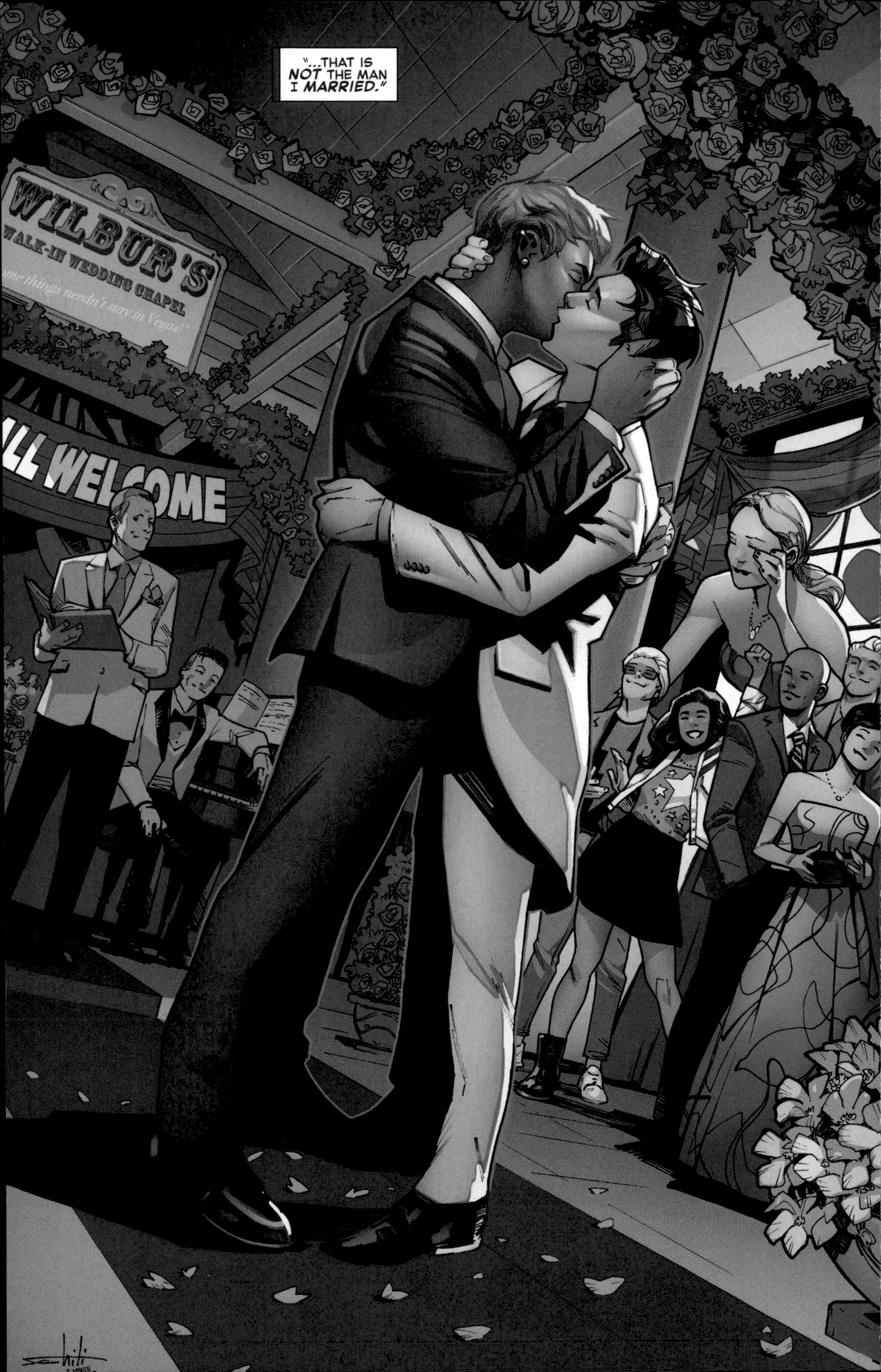
"...THAT IS NOT THE MAN I MARRIED."
WILBUR'S
WALK-IN WEDDING CHAPEL
ome things needn't stay in Vegas!"
LL WELCOME

EMPYRE 5 SECOND-PRINTING VARIANT BY
Valerio Schiti & **Rachelle Rosenberg**

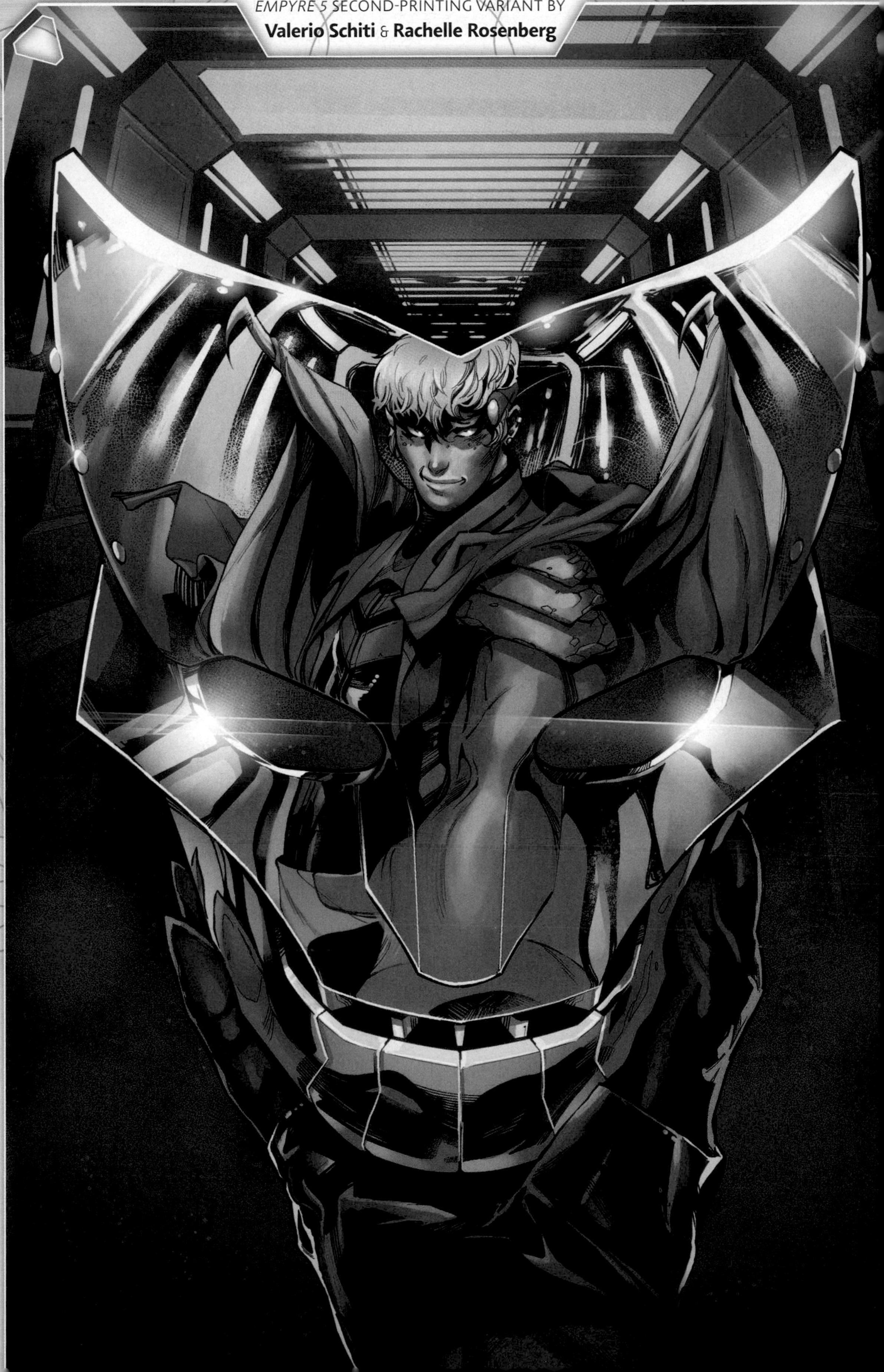

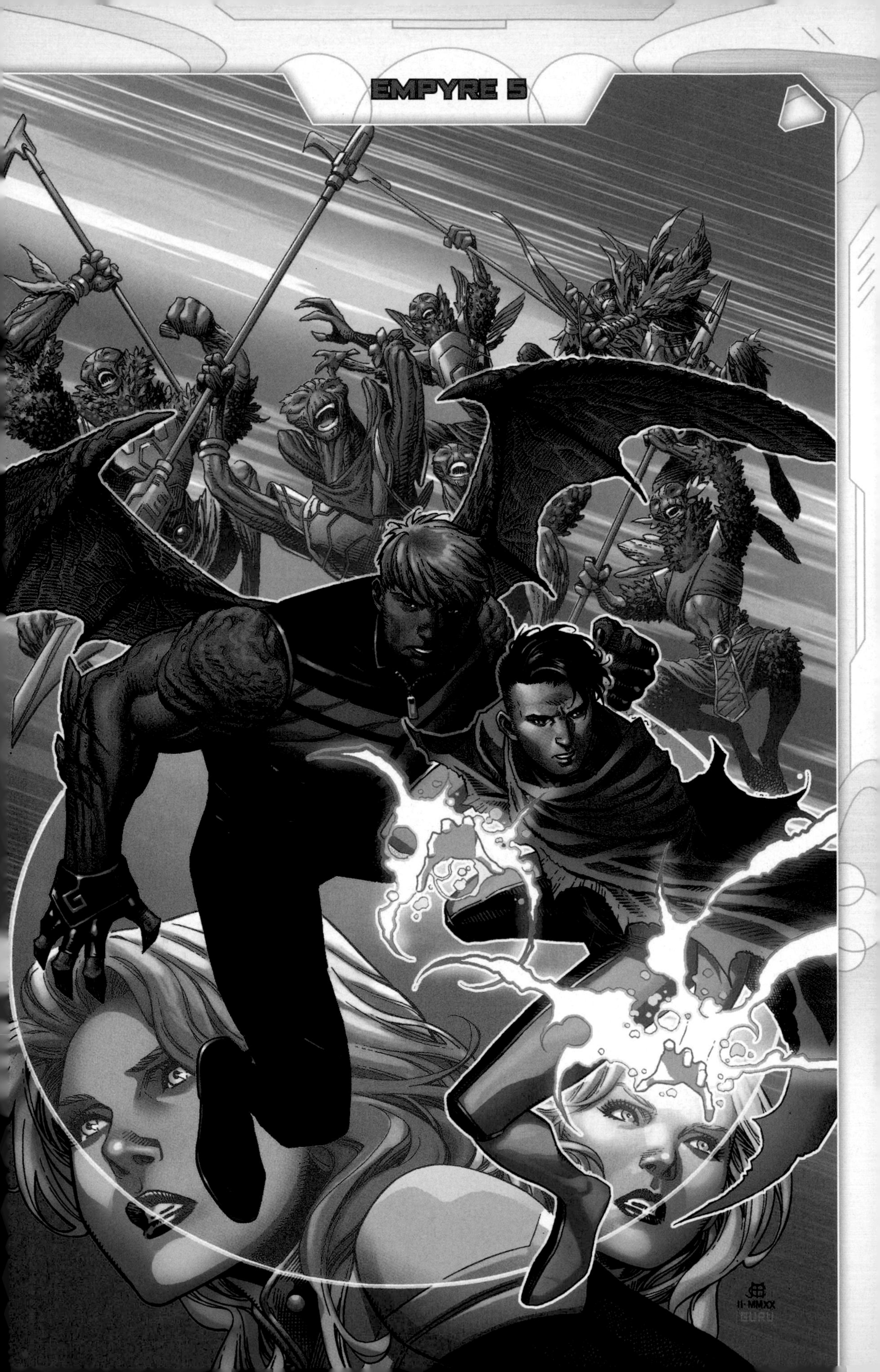
EMPYRE 5
II-MMXX

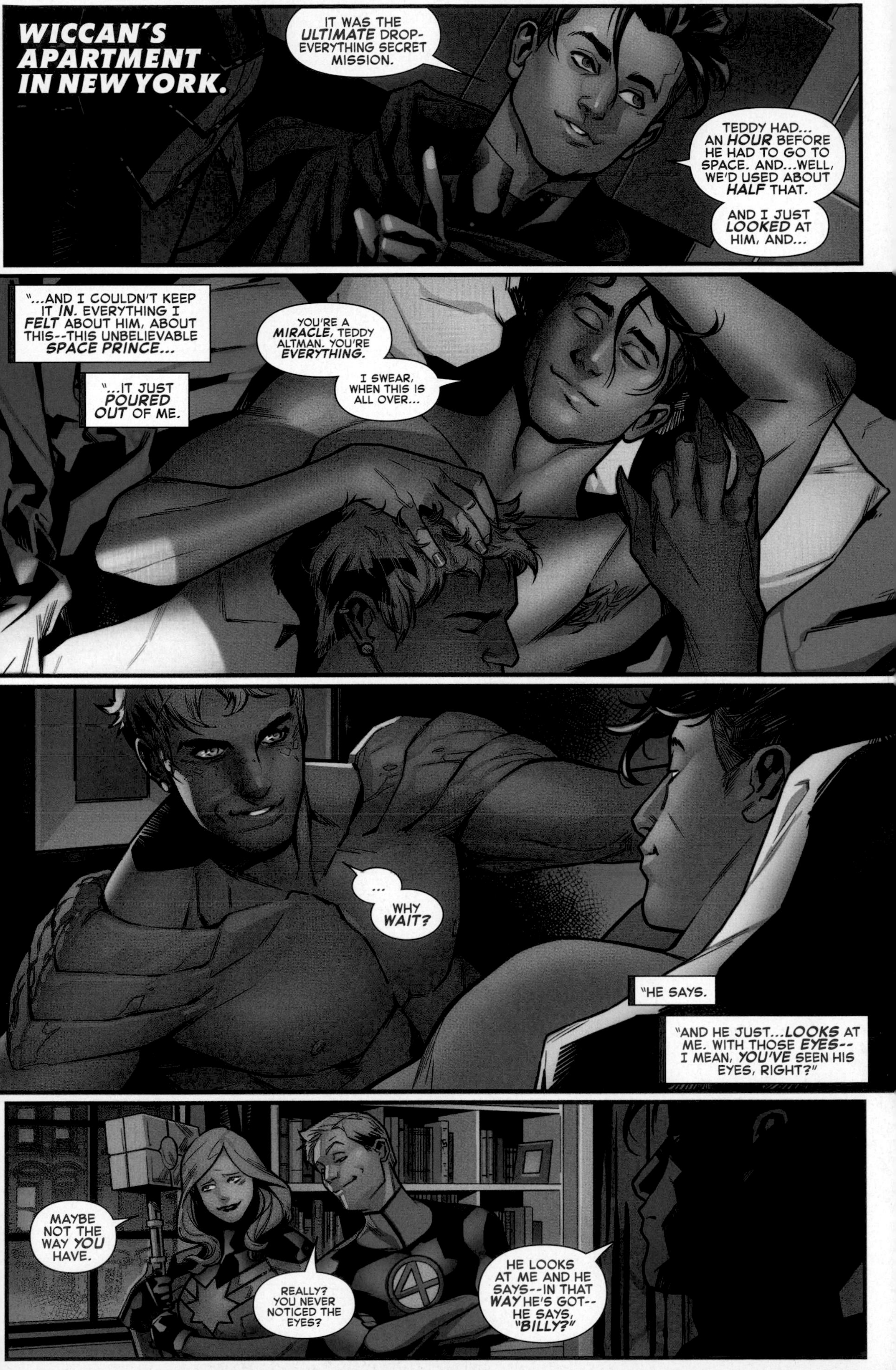
WICCAN'S APARTMENT IN NEW YORK.
IT WAS THE ULTIMATE DROP-EVERYTHING SECRET MISSION.
TEDDY HAD... AN HOUR BEFORE HE HAD TO GO TO SPACE. AND...WELL, WE'D USED ABOUT HALF THAT.
AND I JUST LOOKED AT HIM, AND...
"...AND I COULDN'T KEEP IT IN. EVERYTHING I FELT ABOUT HIM, ABOUT THIS--THIS UNBELIEVABLE SPACE PRINCE...
"...IT JUST POURED OUT OF ME.
YOU'RE A MIRACLE, TEDDY ALTMAN. YOU'RE EVERYTHING.
I SWEAR, WHEN THIS IS ALL OVER...
...
WHY WAIT?
"HE SAYS.
"AND HE JUST...LOOKS AT ME. WITH THOSE EYES-- I MEAN, YOU'VE SEEN HIS EYES, RIGHT?"
MAYBE NOT THE WAY YOU HAVE.
REALLY? YOU NEVER NOTICED THE EYES?
HE LOOKS AT ME AND HE SAYS--IN THAT WAY HE'S GOT-- HE SAYS, "BILLY?"

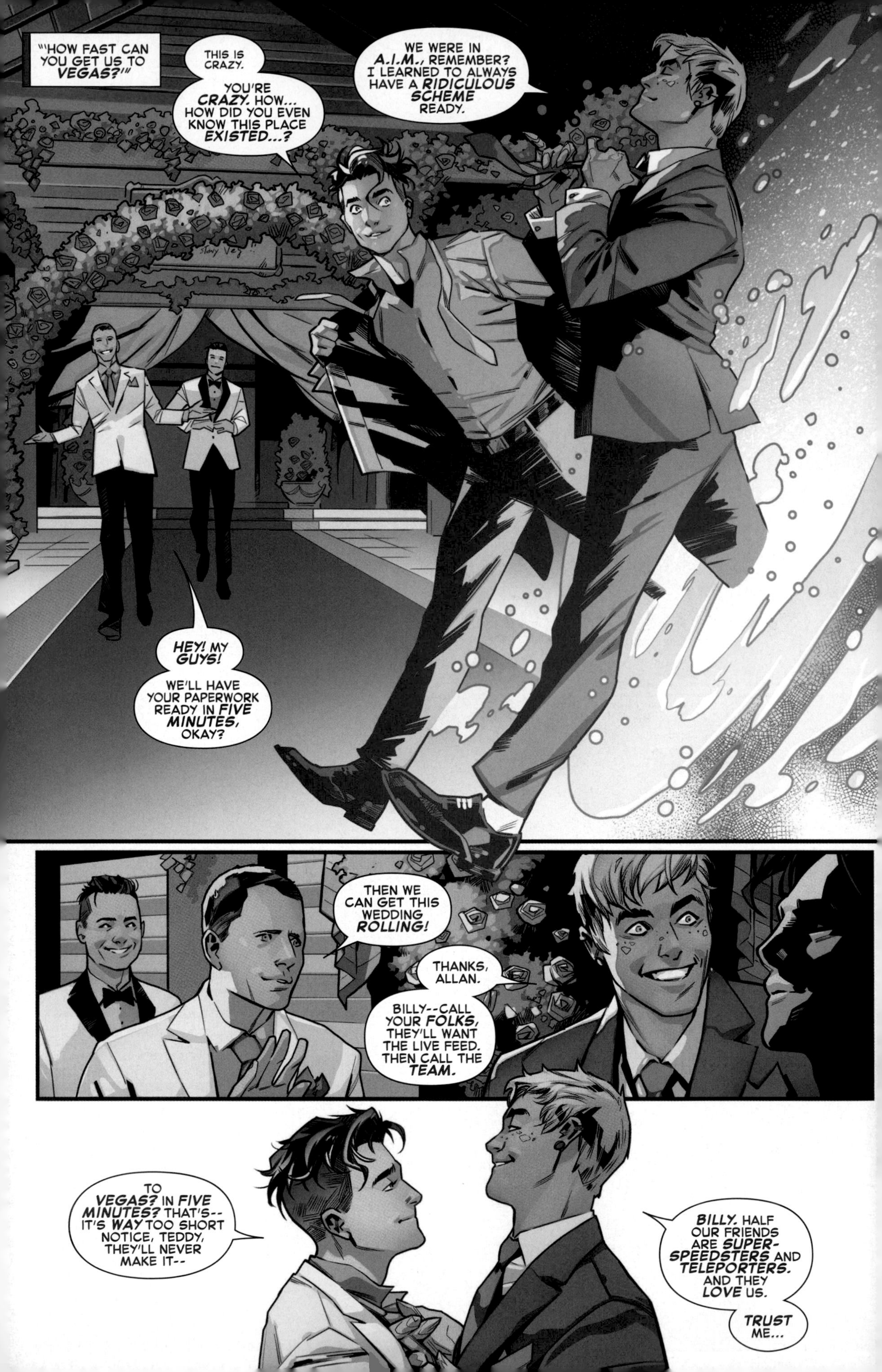
"HOW FAST CAN YOU GET US TO VEGAS?"
THIS IS CRAZY.
YOU'RE CRAZY. HOW... HOW DID YOU EVEN KNOW THIS PLACE EXISTED...?
WE WERE IN A.I.M., REMEMBER? I LEARNED TO ALWAYS HAVE A RIDICULOUS SCHEME READY.
HEY! MY GUYS!
WE'LL HAVE YOUR PAPERWORK READY IN FIVE MINUTES, OKAY?
THEN WE CAN GET THIS WEDDING ROLLING!
THANKS, ALLAN.
BILLY--CALL YOUR FOLKS, THEY'LL WANT THE LIVE FEED. THEN CALL THE TEAM.
TO VEGAS? IN FIVE MINUTES? THAT'S--IT'S WAY TOO SHORT NOTICE, TEDDY, THEY'LL NEVER MAKE IT--
BILLY. HALF OUR FRIENDS ARE SUPER-SPEEDSTERS AND TELEPORTERS. AND THEY LOVE US.
TRUST ME...

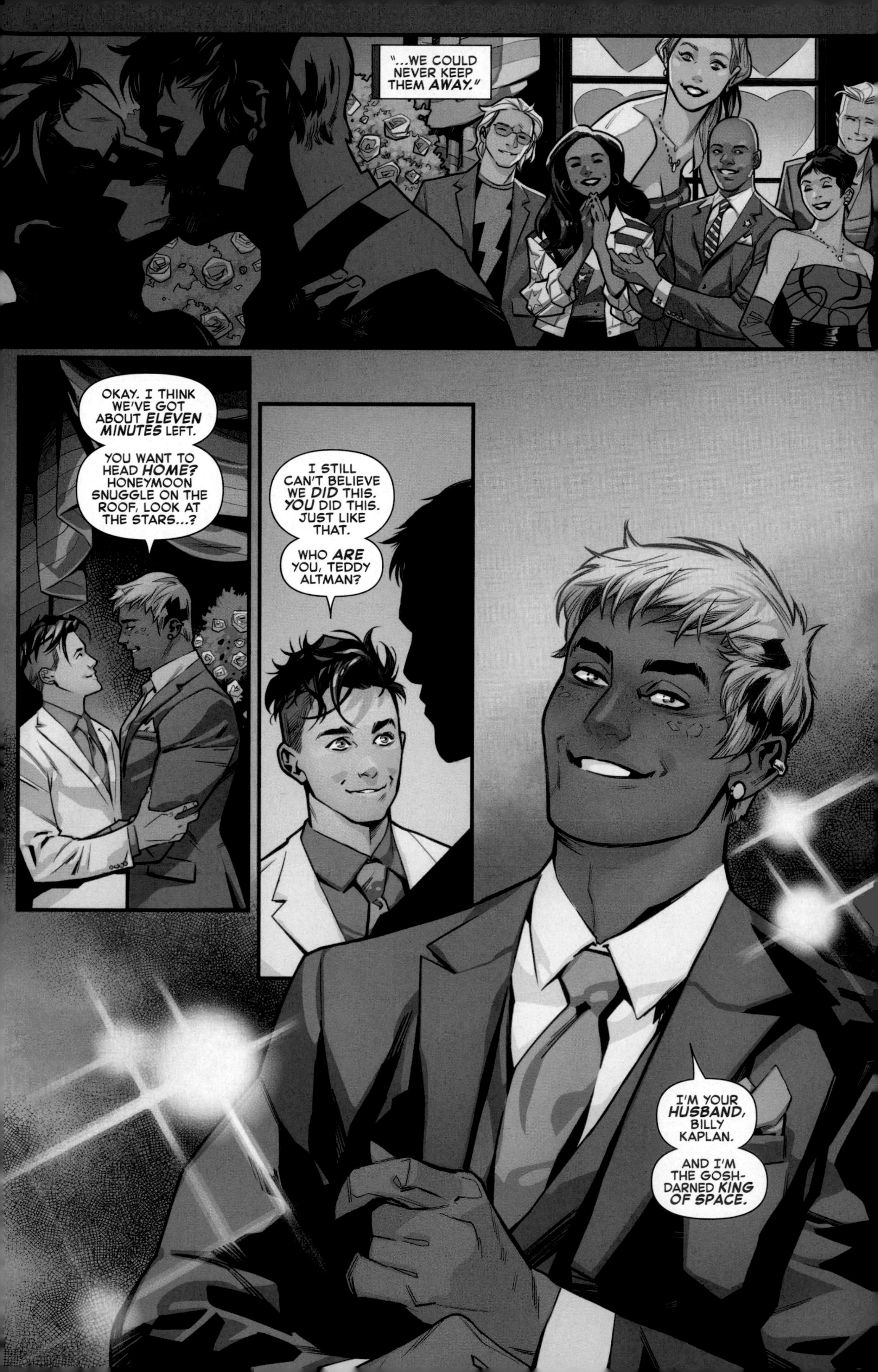
"...WE COULD NEVER KEEP THEM AWAY."
OKAY. I THINK WE'VE GOT ABOUT ELEVEN MINUTES LEFT.
YOU WANT TO HEAD HOME? HONEYMOON SNUGGLE ON THE ROOF, LOOK AT THE STARS...?
I STILL CAN'T BELIEVE WE DID THIS. YOU DID THIS. JUST LIKE THAT.
WHO ARE YOU, TEDDY ALTMAN?
I'M YOUR HUSBAND, BILLY KAPLAN.
AND I'M THE GOSH-DARNED KING OF SPACE.

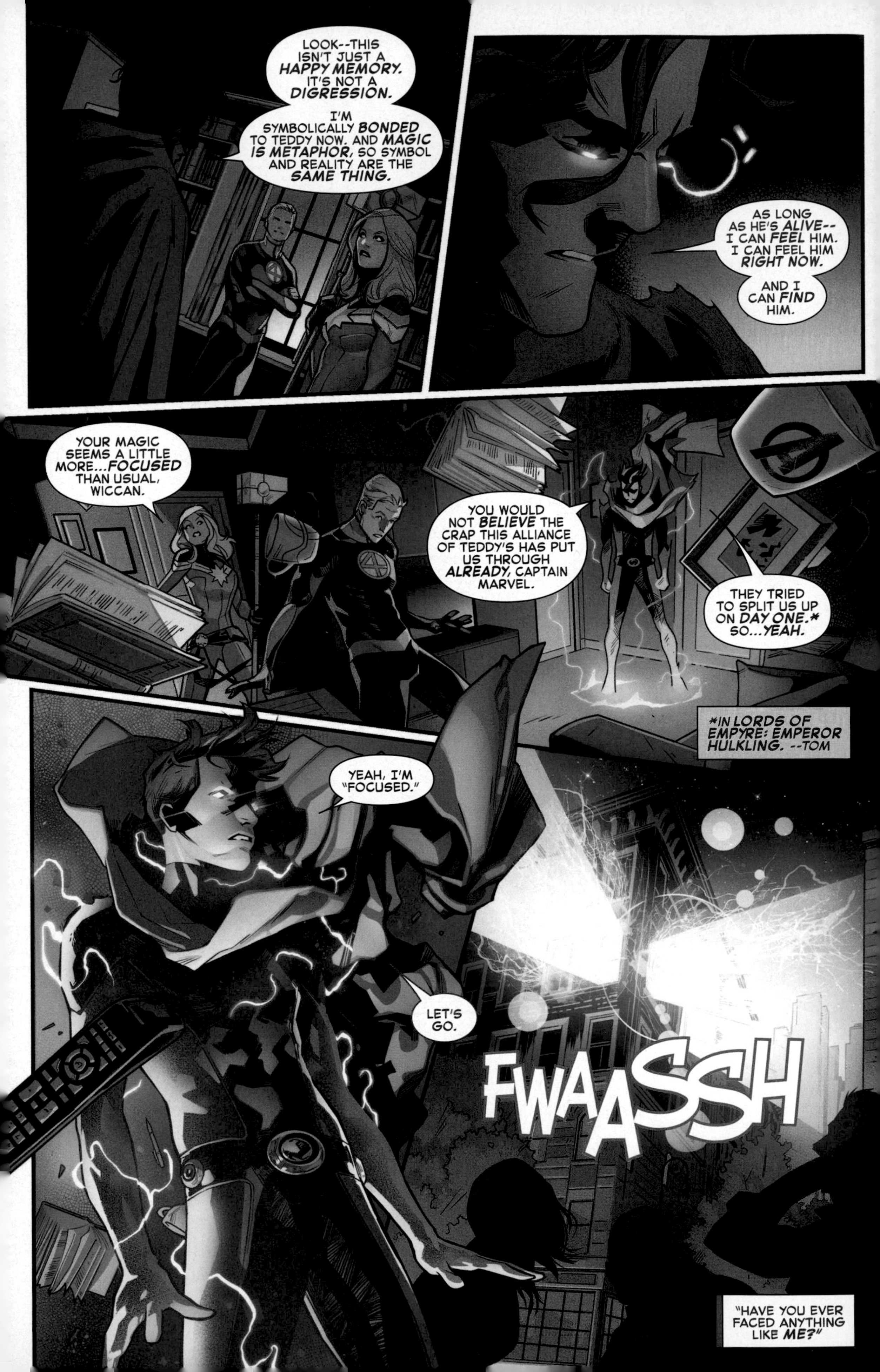
LOOK--THIS ISN'T JUST A HAPPY MEMORY. IT'S NOT A DIGRESSION.
I'M SYMBOLICALLY BONDED TO TEDDY NOW. AND MAGIC IS METAPHOR, SO SYMBOL AND REALITY ARE THE SAME THING.
AS LONG AS HE'S ALIVE-- I CAN FEEL HIM. I CAN FEEL HIM RIGHT NOW.
AND I CAN FIND HIM.
YOUR MAGIC SEEMS A LITTLE MORE...FOCUSED THAN USUAL, WICCAN.
YOU WOULD NOT BELIEVE THE CRAP THIS ALLIANCE OF TEDDY'S HAS PUT US THROUGH ALREADY, CAPTAIN MARVEL.
THEY TRIED TO SPLIT US UP ON DAY ONE.* SO...YEAH.
*IN LORDS OF EMPYRE: EMPEROR HULKLING. --TOM
YEAH, I'M "FOCUSED."
LET'S GO.
FWAASSH
"HAVE YOU EVER FACED ANYTHING LIKE ME?"

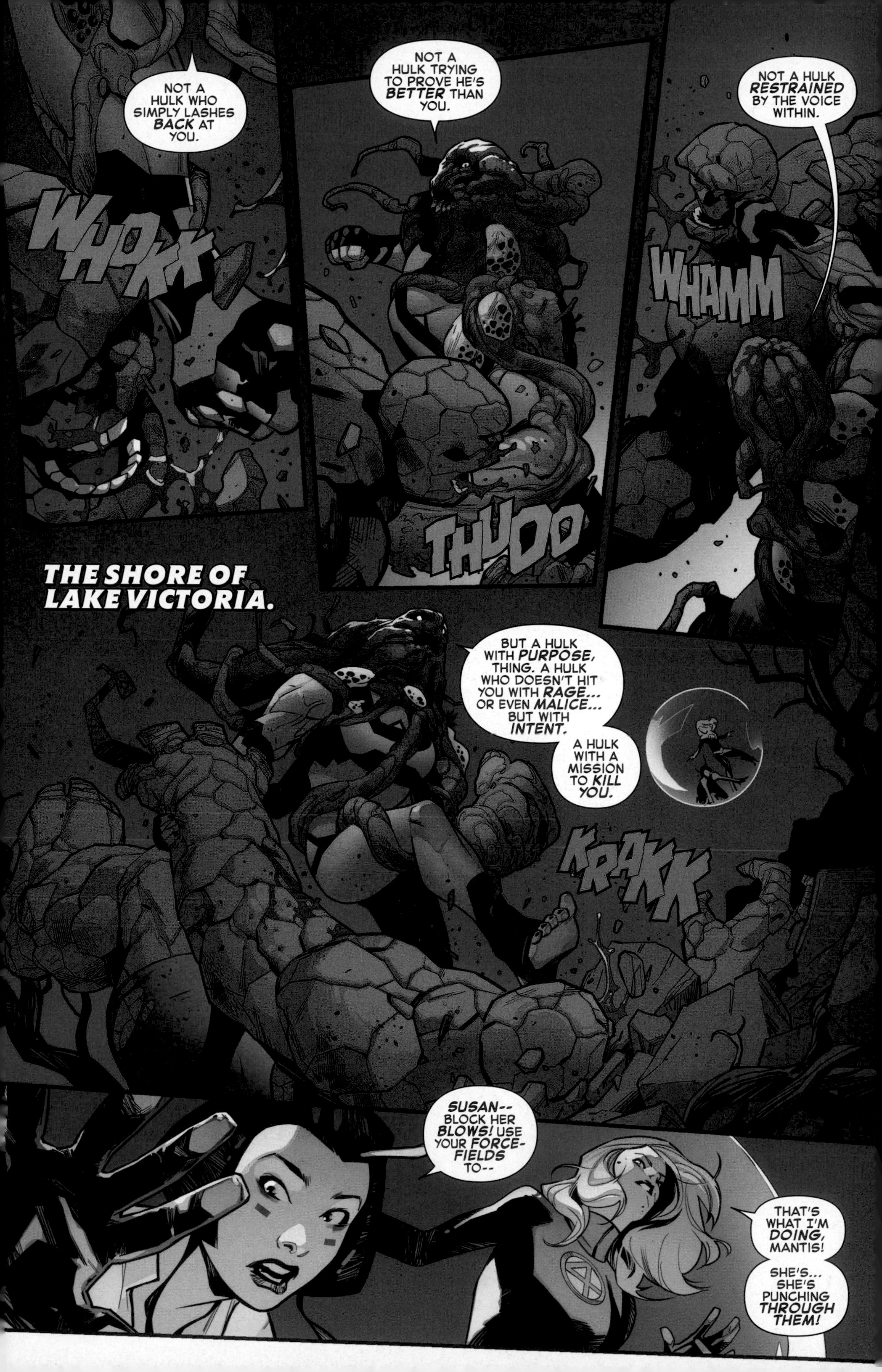
NOT A HULK WHO SIMPLY LASHES BACK AT YOU.
WHOKK
NOT A HULK TRYING TO PROVE HE'S BETTER THAN YOU.
THUDD
NOT A HULK RESTRAINED BY THE VOICE WITHIN.
WHAMM
THE SHORE OF LAKE VICTORIA.
BUT A HULK WITH PURPOSE, THING. A HULK WHO DOESN'T HIT YOU WITH RAGE... OR EVEN MALICE... BUT WITH INTENT.
A HULK WITH A MISSION TO KILL YOU.
KRAKK
SUSAN-- BLOCK HER BLOWS! USE YOUR FORCE-FIELDS TO--
THAT'S WHAT I'M DOING, MANTIS!
SHE'S... SHE'S PUNCHING THROUGH THEM!

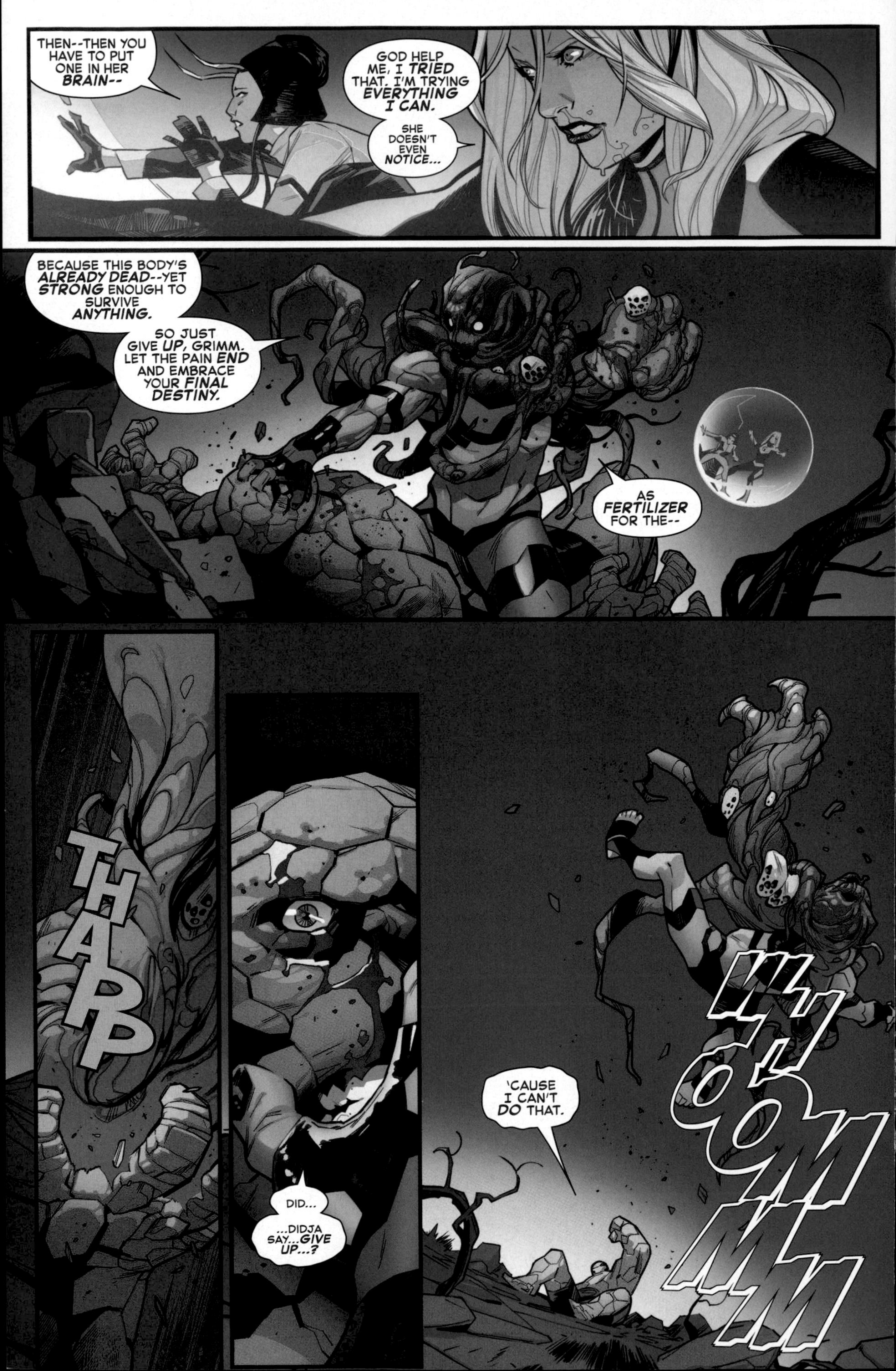
THEN--THEN YOU HAVE TO PUT ONE IN HER BRAIN--
GOD HELP ME, I TRIED THAT. I'M TRYING EVERYTHING I CAN.
SHE DOESN'T EVEN NOTICE...
BECAUSE THIS BODY'S ALREADY DEAD--YET STRONG ENOUGH TO SURVIVE ANYTHING.
SO JUST GIVE UP, GRIMM. LET THE PAIN END AND EMBRACE YOUR FINAL DESTINY.
AS FERTILIZER FOR THE--
THAPP
DID...
...DIDJA SAY...GIVE UP...?
'CAUSE I CAN'T DO THAT.
WHOOMM

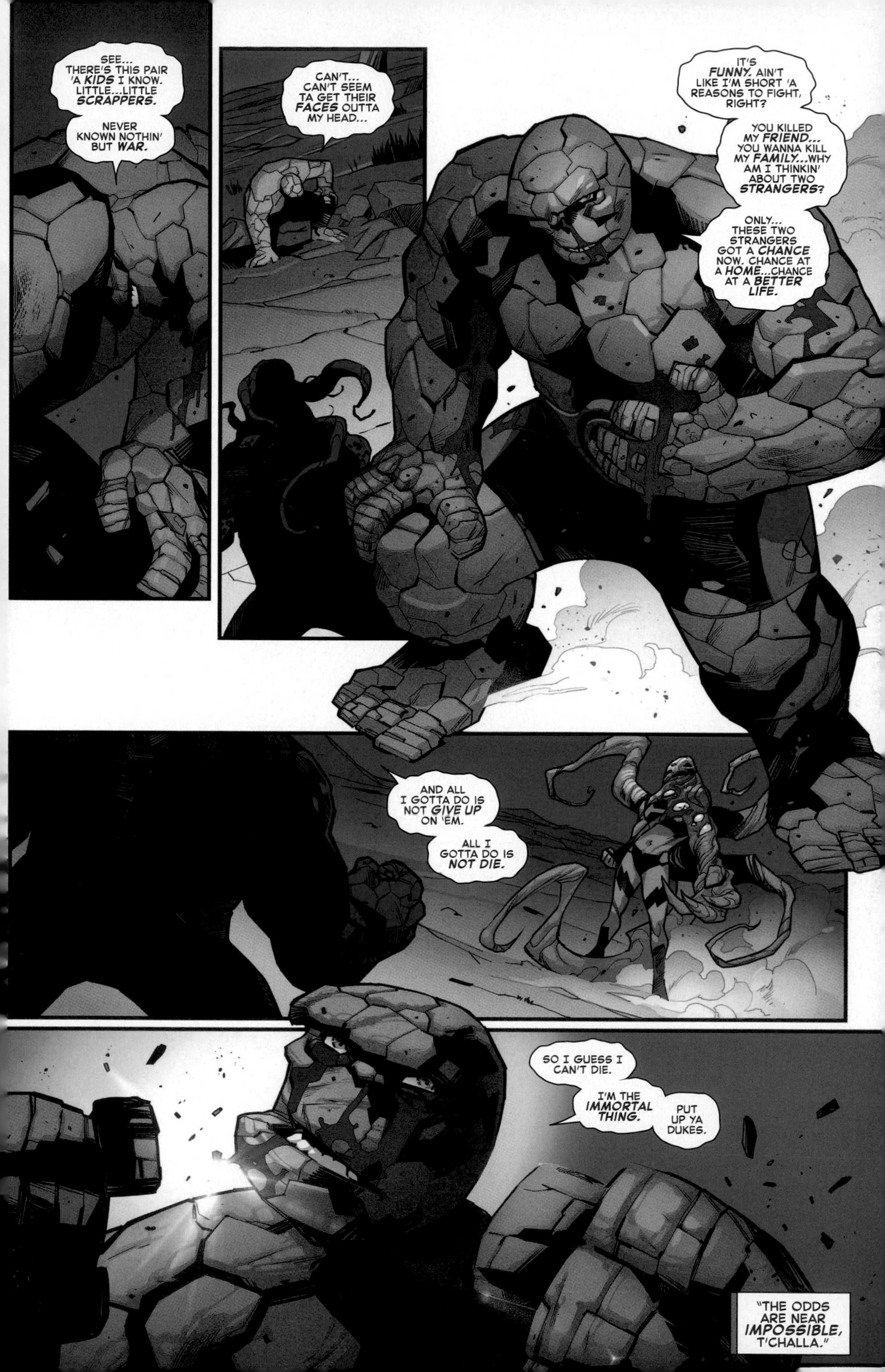
SEE... THERE'S THIS PAIR 'A KIDS I KNOW. LITTLE...LITTLE SCRAPPERS.
NEVER KNOWN NOTHIN' BUT WAR.
CAN'T... CAN'T SEEM TA GET THEIR FACES OUTTA MY HEAD...
IT'S FUNNY. AIN'T LIKE I'M SHORT 'A REASONS TO FIGHT, RIGHT?
YOU KILLED MY FRIEND... YOU WANNA KILL MY FAMILY...WHY AM I THINKIN' ABOUT TWO STRANGERS?
ONLY... THESE TWO STRANGERS GOT A CHANCE NOW. CHANCE AT A HOME...CHANCE AT A BETTER LIFE.
AND ALL I GOTTA DO IS NOT GIVE UP ON 'EM.
ALL I GOTTA DO IS NOT DIE.
SO I GUESS I CAN'T DIE.
I'M THE IMMORTAL THING.
PUT UP YA DUKES.
"THE ODDS ARE NEAR IMPOSSIBLE, T'CHALLA."

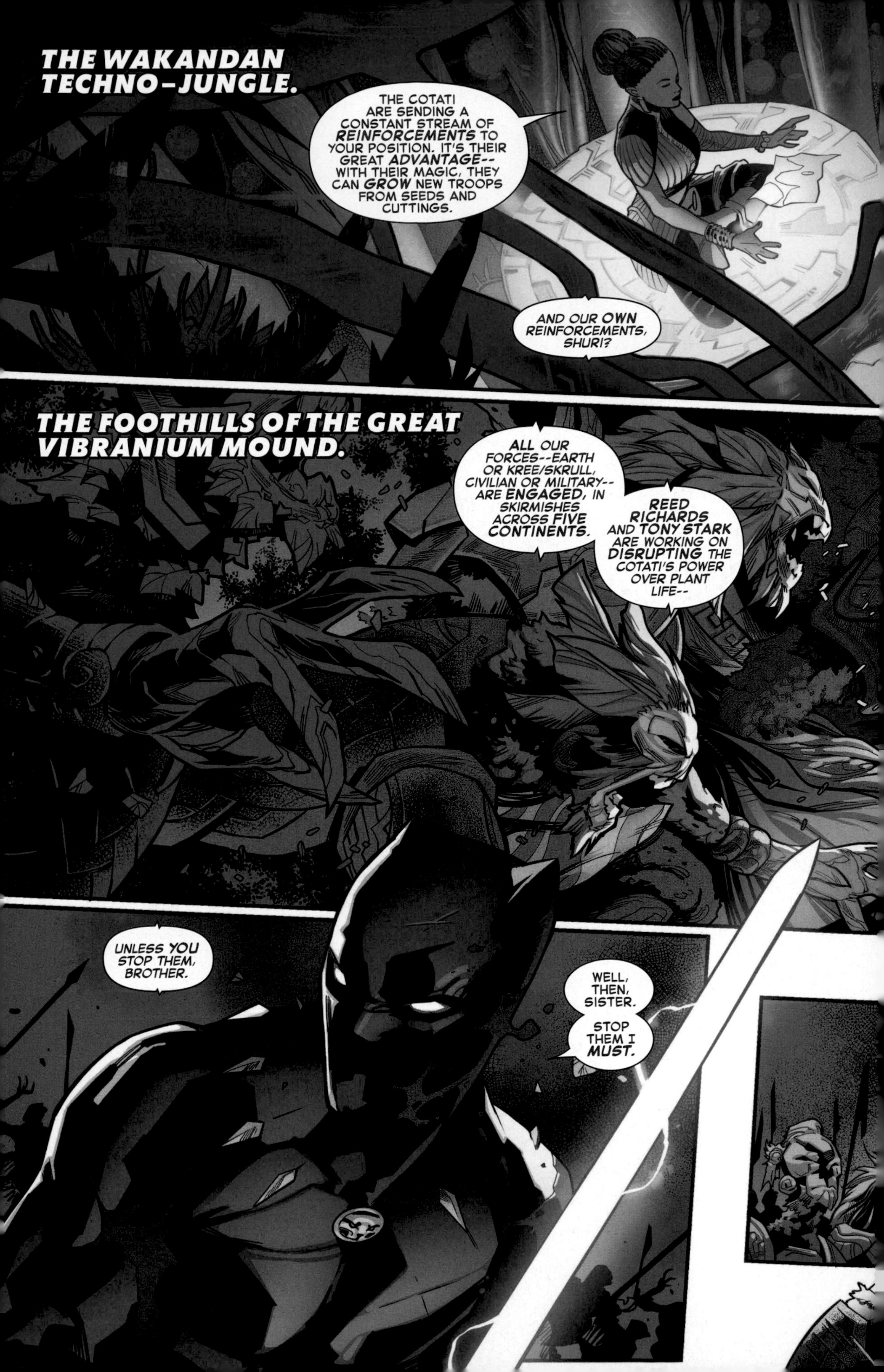
THE WAKANDAN TECHNO-JUNGLE.
THE COTATI ARE SENDING A CONSTANT STREAM OF REINFORCEMENTS TO YOUR POSITION. IT'S THEIR GREAT ADVANTAGE-- WITH THEIR MAGIC, THEY CAN GROW NEW TROOPS FROM SEEDS AND CUTTINGS.
AND OUR OWN REINFORCEMENTS, SHURI?
THE FOOTHILLS OF THE GREAT VIBRANIUM MOUND.
ALL OUR FORCES--EARTH OR KREE/SKRULL, CIVILIAN OR MILITARY--ARE ENGAGED, IN SKIRMISHES ACROSS FIVE CONTINENTS.
REED RICHARDS AND TONY STARK ARE WORKING ON DISRUPTING THE COTATI'S POWER OVER PLANT LIFE--
UNLESS YOU STOP THEM, BROTHER.
WELL, THEN, SISTER.
STOP THEM I MUST.

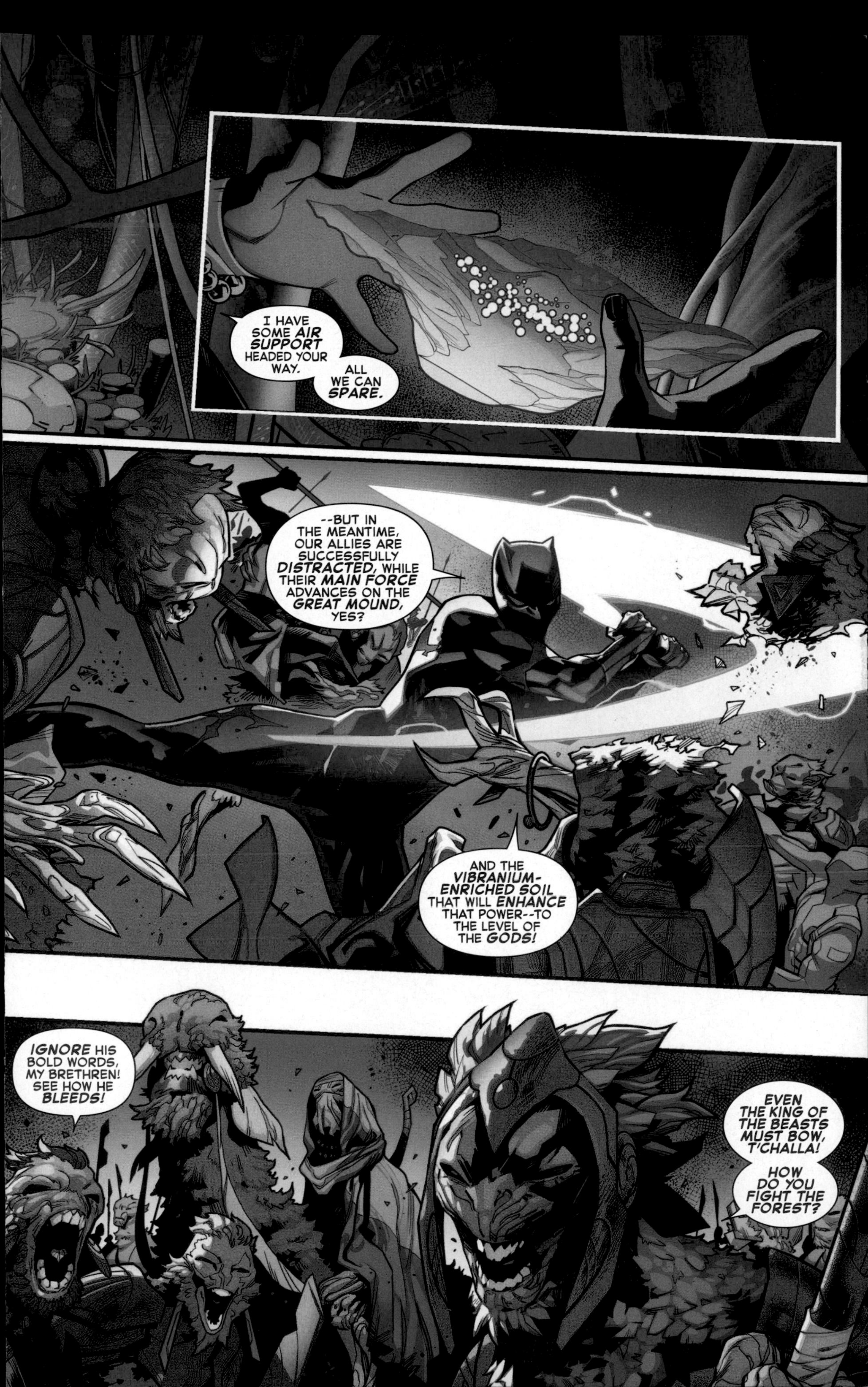

I HAVE SOME AIR SUPPORT HEADED YOUR WAY.
ALL WE CAN SPARE.
--BUT IN THE MEANTIME, OUR ALLIES ARE SUCCESSFULLY DISTRACTED, WHILE THEIR MAIN FORCE ADVANCES ON THE GREAT MOUND, YES?
AND THE VIBRANIUM-ENRICHED SOIL THAT WILL ENHANCE THAT POWER--TO THE LEVEL OF THE GODS!
IGNORE HIS BOLD WORDS, MY BRETHREN! SEE HOW HE BLEEDS!
EVEN THE KING OF THE BEASTS MUST BOW, T'CHALLA!
HOW DO YOU FIGHT THE FOREST?

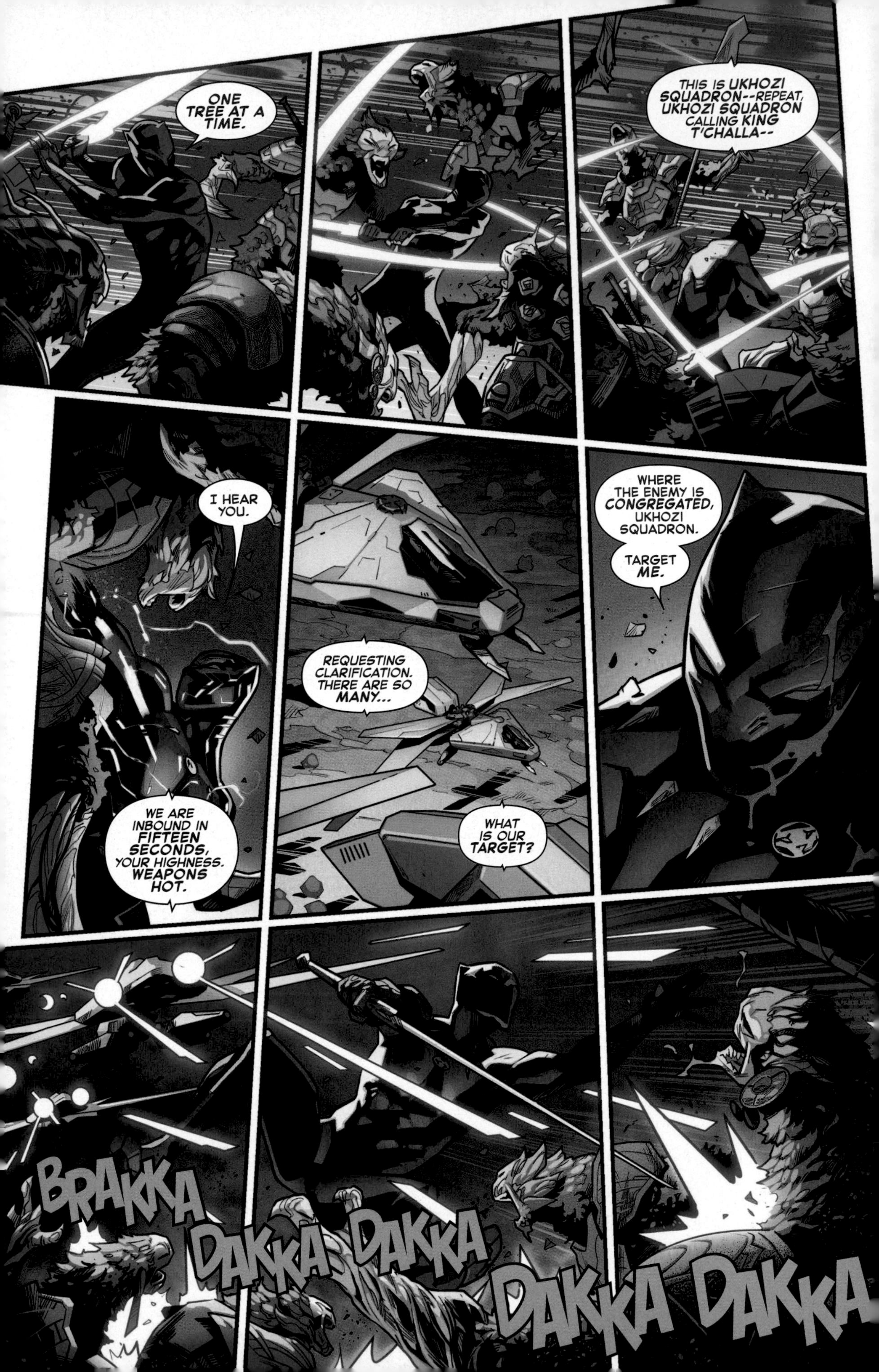
ONE TREE AT A TIME.
THIS IS UKHOZI SQUADRON--REPEAT, UKHOZI SQUADRON CALLING KING T'CHALLA--
I HEAR YOU.
WE ARE INBOUND IN FIFTEEN SECONDS, YOUR HIGHNESS. WEAPONS HOT.
REQUESTING CLARIFICATION. THERE ARE SO MANY...
WHAT IS OUR TARGET?
WHERE THE ENEMY IS CONGREGATED, UKHOZI SQUADRON.
TARGET ME.
BRAKKA
DAKKA DAKKA
DAKKA DAKKA

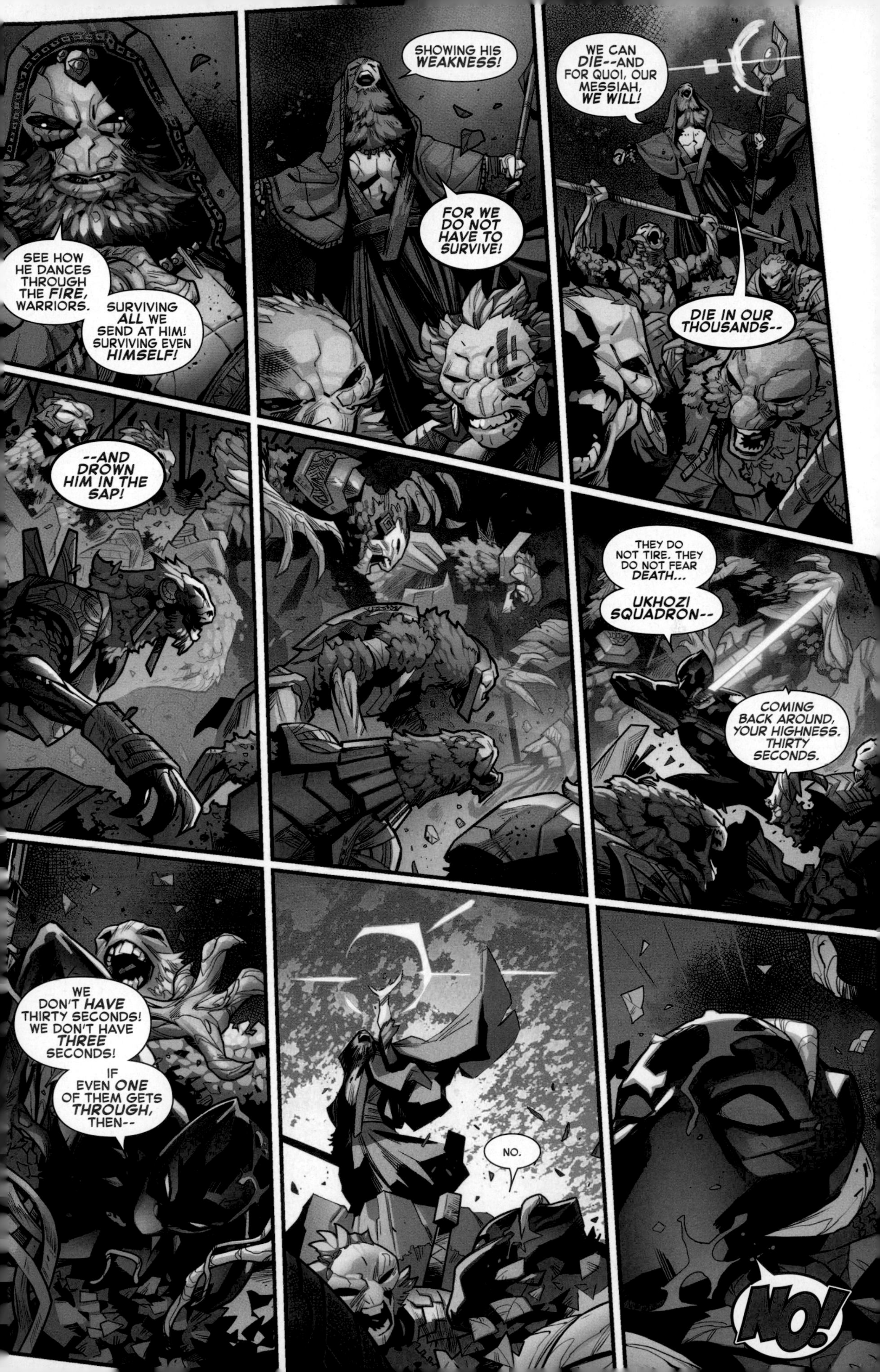
SEE HOW HE DANCES THROUGH THE FIRE, WARRIORS.
SURVIVING ALL WE SEND AT HIM! SURVIVING EVEN HIMSELF!
SHOWING HIS WEAKNESS!
FOR WE DO NOT HAVE TO SURVIVE!
WE CAN DIE--AND FOR QUOI, OUR MESSIAH, WE WILL!
DIE IN OUR THOUSANDS--
--AND DROWN HIM IN THE SAP!
THEY DO NOT TIRE. THEY DO NOT FEAR DEATH...
UKHOZI SQUADRON--
COMING BACK AROUND, YOUR HIGHNESS. THIRTY SECONDS.
WE DON'T HAVE THIRTY SECONDS! WE DON'T HAVE THREE SECONDS!
IF EVEN ONE OF THEM GETS THROUGH, THEN--
NO.
NO!

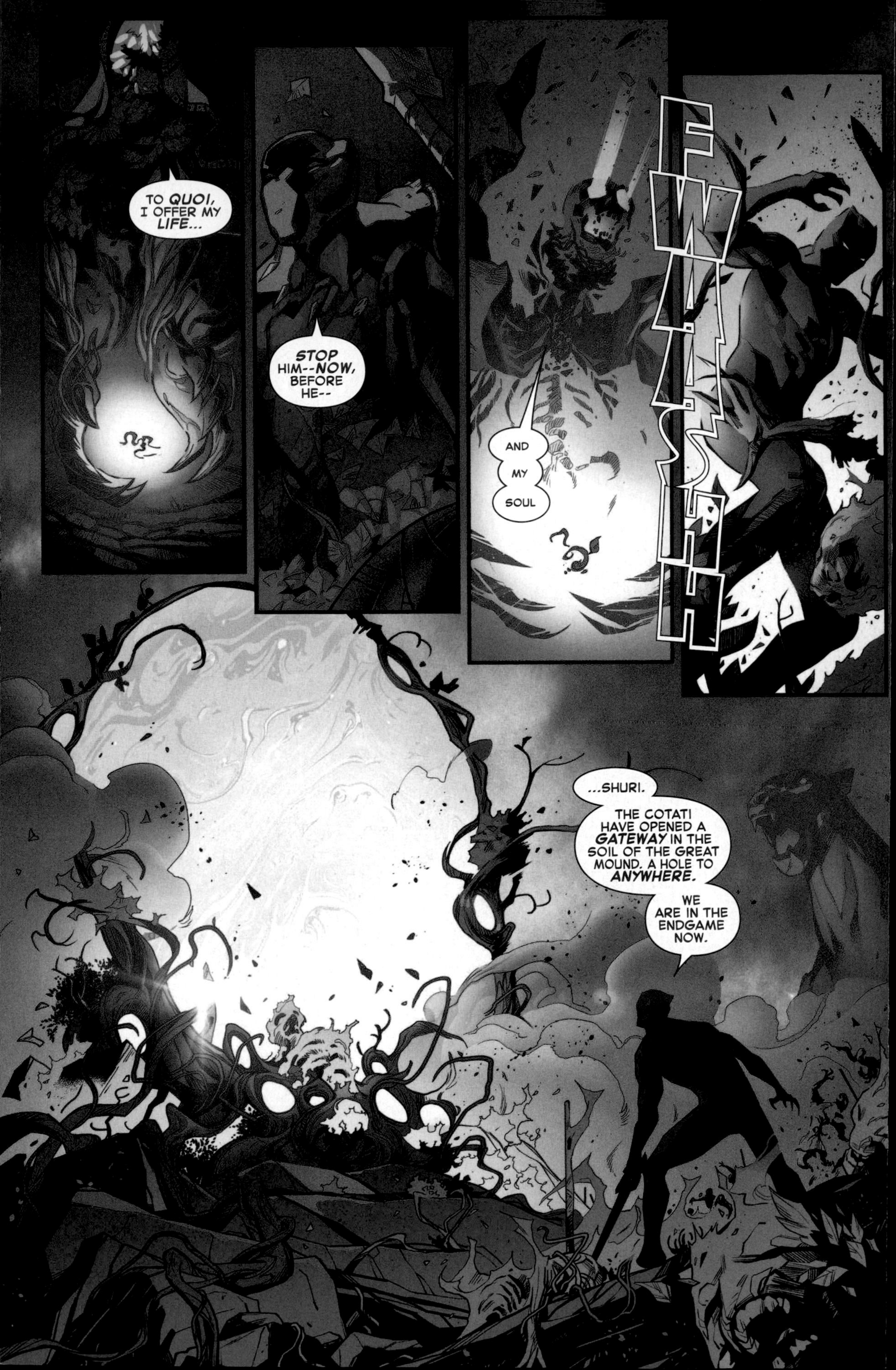
TO QUOI, I OFFER MY LIFE...
STOP HIM--NOW, BEFORE HE--
AND
MY
SOUL
FWAAASHH
...SHURI.
THE COTATI HAVE OPENED A GATEWAY IN THE SOIL OF THE GREAT MOUND. A HOLE TO ANYWHERE.
WE ARE IN THE ENDGAME NOW.

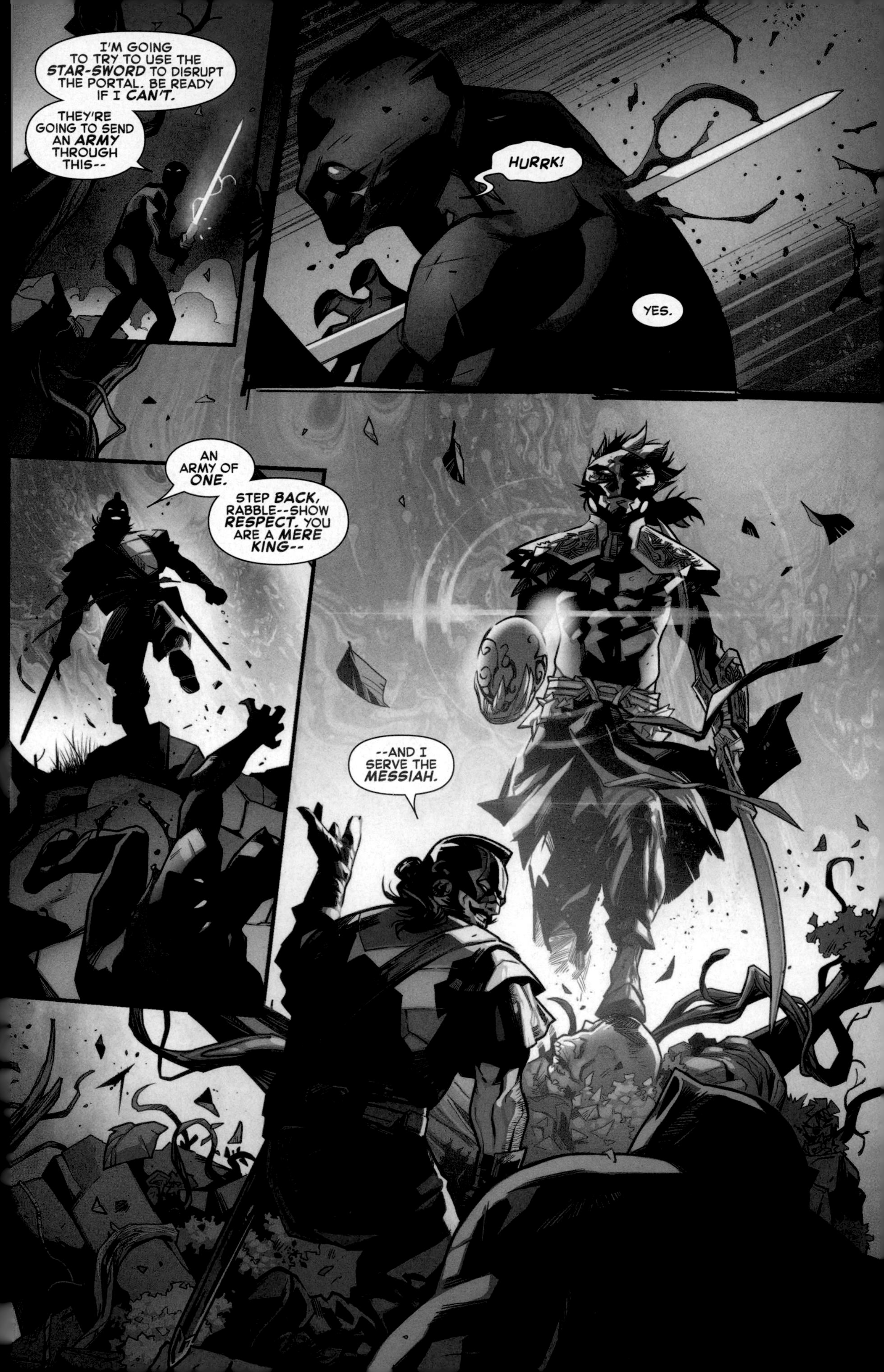
I'M GOING TO TRY TO USE THE STAR-SWORD TO DISRUPT THE PORTAL. BE READY IF I CAN'T.
THEY'RE GOING TO SEND AN ARMY THROUGH THIS--
HURRK!
YES.
AN ARMY OF ONE.
STEP BACK, RABBLE--SHOW RESPECT. YOU ARE A MERE KING--
--AND I SERVE THE MESSIAH.

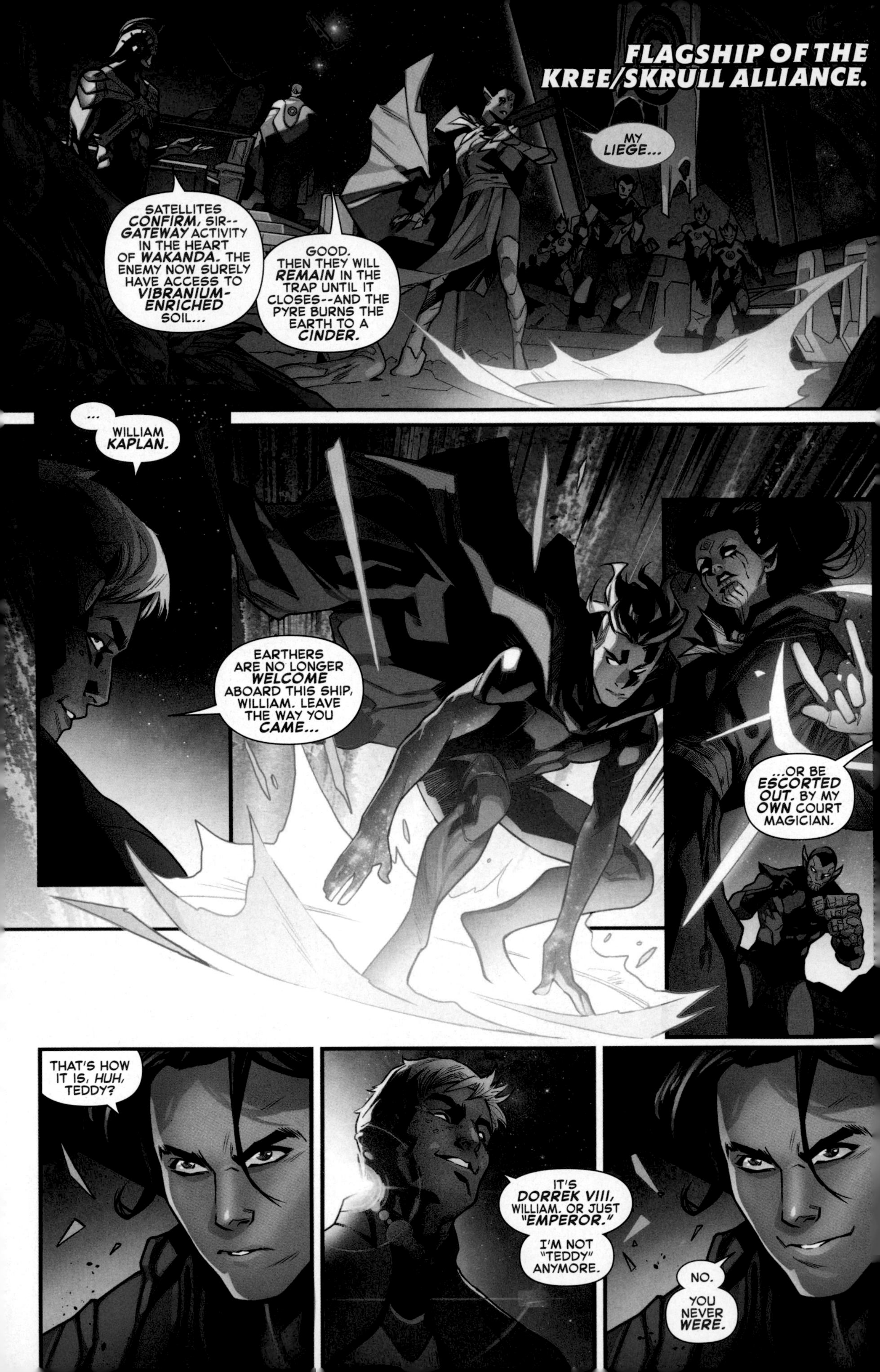

FLAGSHIP OF THE KREE/SKRULL ALLIANCE.
MY LIEGE...
SATELLITES CONFIRM, SIR-- GATEWAY ACTIVITY IN THE HEART OF WAKANDA. THE ENEMY NOW SURELY HAVE ACCESS TO VIBRANIUM-ENRICHED SOIL...
GOOD. THEN THEY WILL REMAIN IN THE TRAP UNTIL IT CLOSES--AND THE PYRE BURNS THE EARTH TO A CINDER.
... WILLIAM KAPLAN.
EARTHERS ARE NO LONGER WELCOME ABOARD THIS SHIP, WILLIAM. LEAVE THE WAY YOU CAME...
...OR BE ESCORTED OUT. BY MY OWN COURT MAGICIAN.
THAT'S HOW IT IS, HUH, TEDDY?
IT'S DORREK VIII, WILLIAM. OR JUST "EMPEROR."
I'M NOT "TEDDY" ANYMORE.
NO.
YOU NEVER WERE.

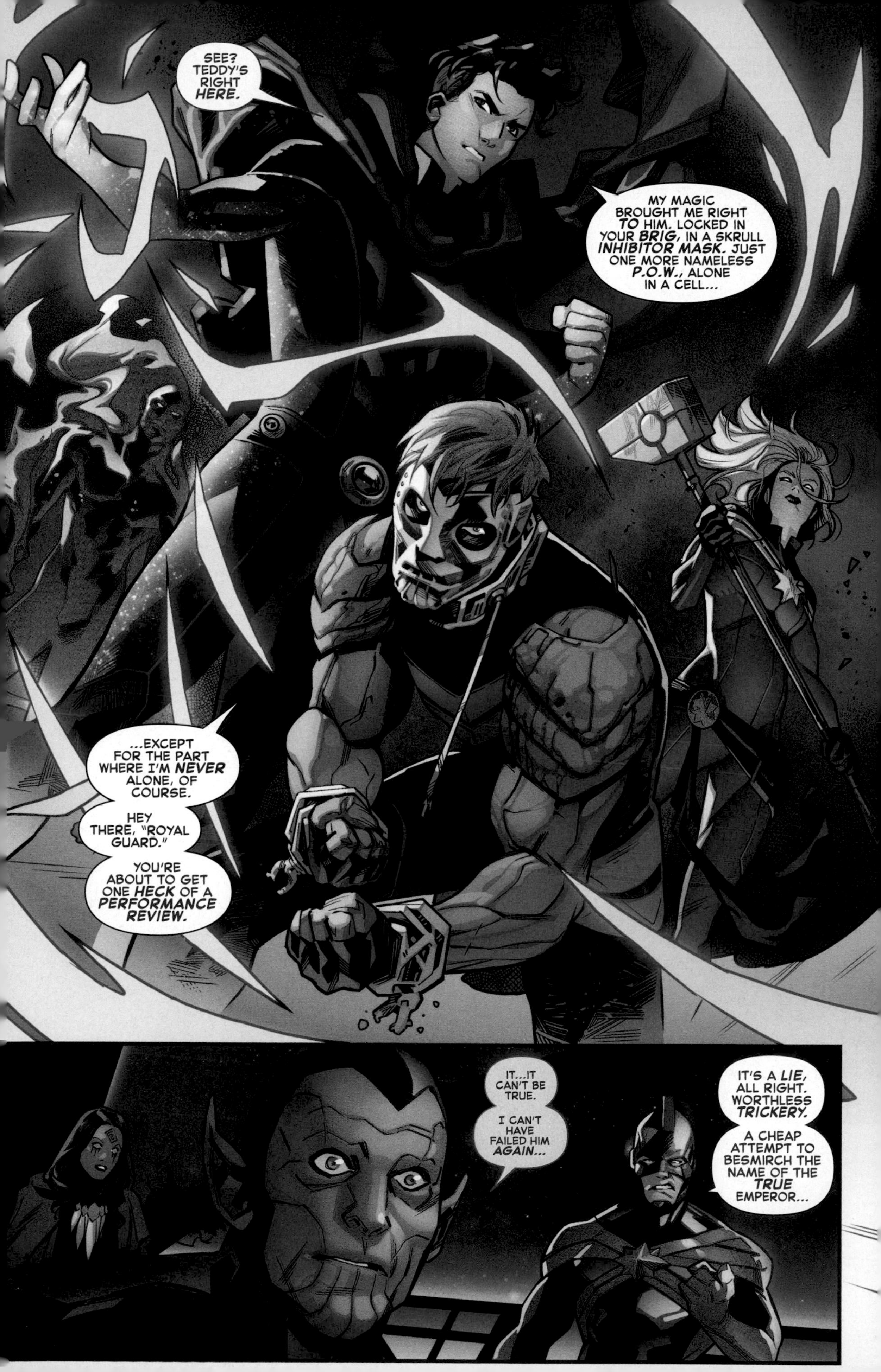
SEE? TEDDY'S RIGHT HERE.
MY MAGIC BROUGHT ME RIGHT TO HIM. LOCKED IN YOUR BRIG, IN A SKRULL INHIBITOR MASK. JUST ONE MORE NAMELESS P.O.W., ALONE IN A CELL...
...EXCEPT FOR THE PART WHERE I'M NEVER ALONE, OF COURSE.
HEY THERE, "ROYAL GUARD."
YOU'RE ABOUT TO GET ONE HECK OF A PERFORMANCE REVIEW.
IT...IT CAN'T BE TRUE.
I CAN'T HAVE FAILED HIM AGAIN...
IT'S A LIE, ALL RIGHT. WORTHLESS TRICKERY.
A CHEAP ATTEMPT TO BESMIRCH THE NAME OF THE TRUE EMPEROR...

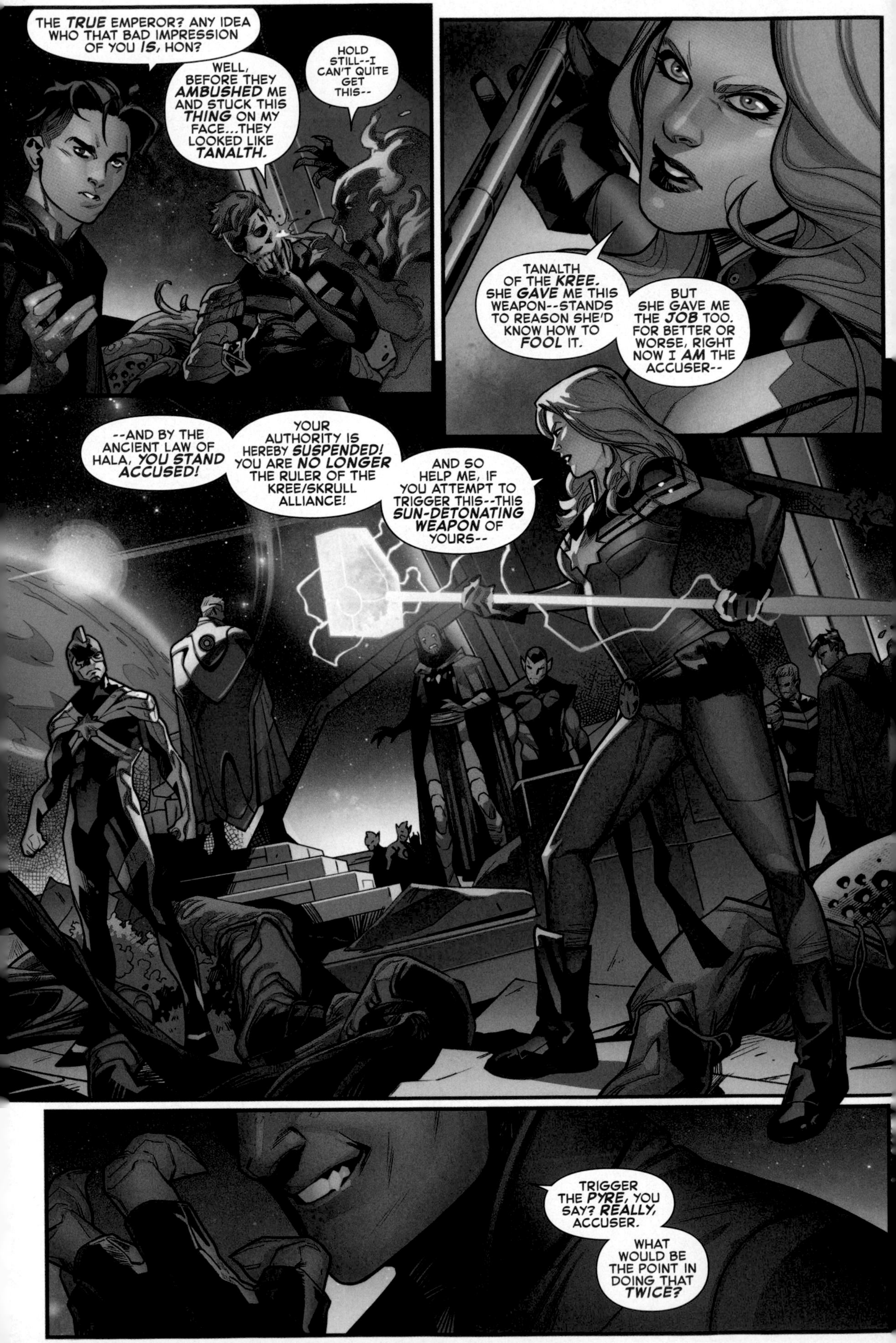
THE TRUE EMPEROR? ANY IDEA WHO THAT BAD IMPRESSION OF YOU IS, HON?
WELL, BEFORE THEY AMBUSHED ME AND STUCK THIS THING ON MY FACE...THEY LOOKED LIKE TANALTH.
HOLD STILL--I CAN'T QUITE GET THIS--
TANALTH OF THE KREE. SHE GAVE ME THIS WEAPON--STANDS TO REASON SHE'D KNOW HOW TO FOOL IT.
BUT SHE GAVE ME THE JOB TOO. FOR BETTER OR WORSE, RIGHT NOW I AM THE ACCUSER--
--AND BY THE ANCIENT LAW OF HALA, YOU STAND ACCUSED!
YOUR AUTHORITY IS HEREBY SUSPENDED! YOU ARE NO LONGER THE RULER OF THE KREE/SKRULL ALLIANCE!
AND SO HELP ME, IF YOU ATTEMPT TO TRIGGER THIS--THIS SUN-DETONATING WEAPON OF YOURS--
TRIGGER THE PYRE, YOU SAY? REALLY, ACCUSER.
WHAT WOULD BE THE POINT IN DOING THAT TWICE?

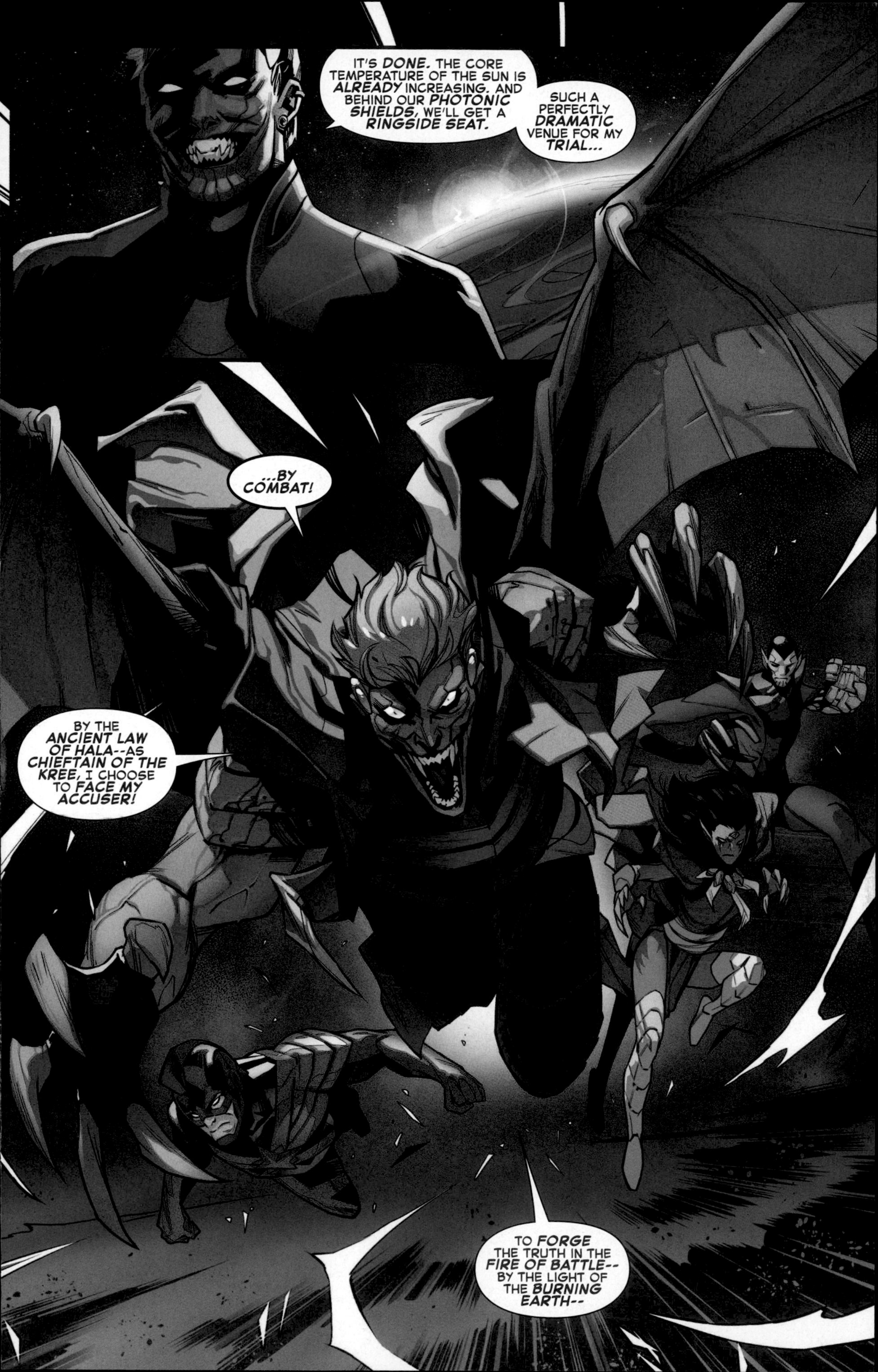
IT'S DONE. THE CORE TEMPERATURE OF THE SUN IS ALREADY INCREASING. AND BEHIND OUR PHOTONIC SHIELDS, WE'LL GET A RINGSIDE SEAT.
SUCH A PERFECTLY DRAMATIC VENUE FOR MY TRIAL...
...BY COMBAT!
BY THE ANCIENT LAW OF HALA--AS CHIEFTAIN OF THE KREE, I CHOOSE TO FACE MY ACCUSER!
TO FORGE THE TRUTH IN THE FIRE OF BATTLE--BY THE LIGHT OF THE BURNING EARTH--

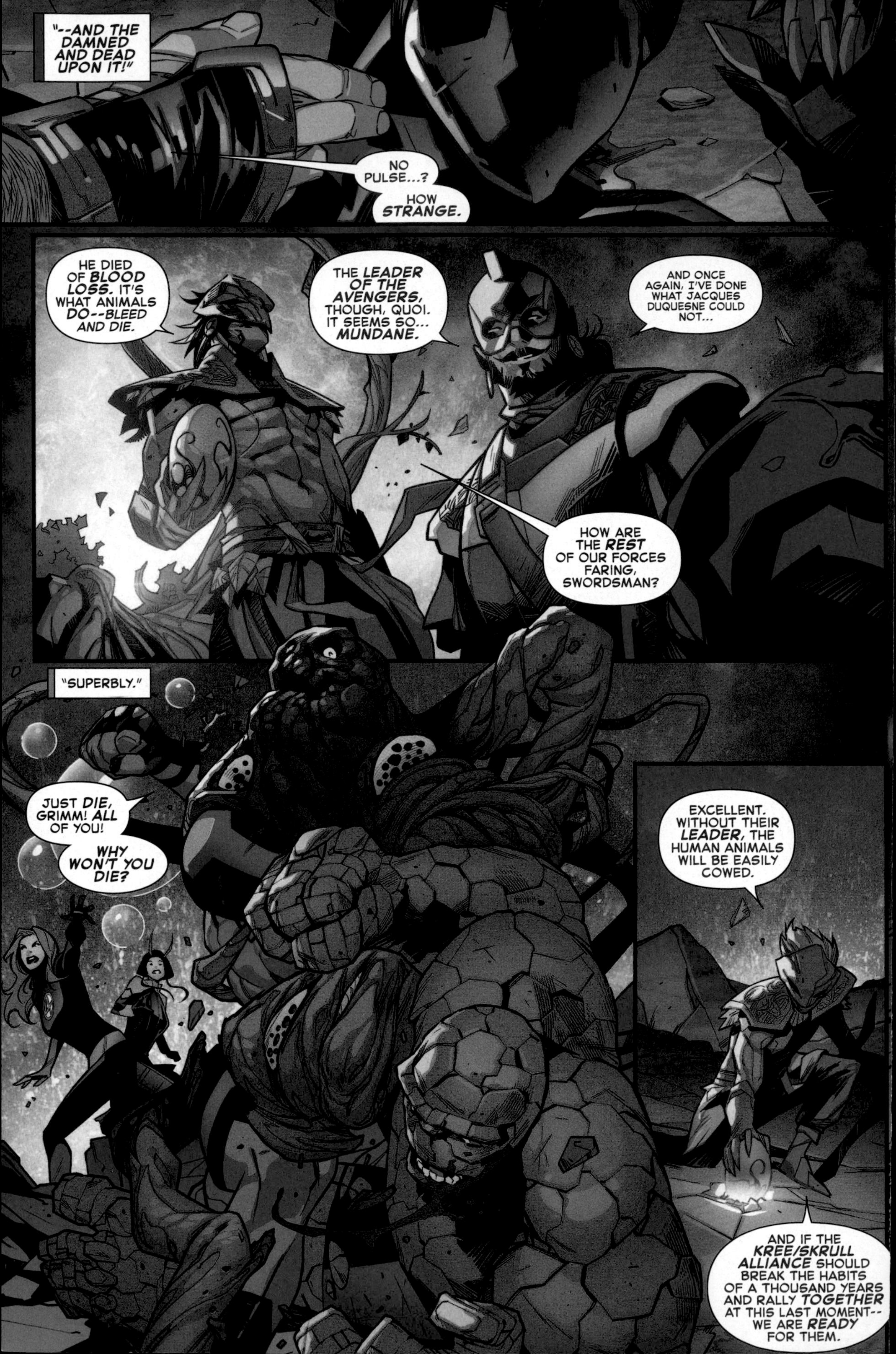
"--AND THE DAMNED AND DEAD UPON IT!"
NO PULSE...?
HOW STRANGE.
HE DIED OF BLOOD LOSS. IT'S WHAT ANIMALS DO--BLEED AND DIE.
THE LEADER OF THE AVENGERS, THOUGH, QUOI. IT SEEMS SO... MUNDANE.
AND ONCE AGAIN, I'VE DONE WHAT JACQUES DUQUESNE COULD NOT...
HOW ARE THE REST OF OUR FORCES FARING, SWORDSMAN?
"SUPERBLY."
JUST DIE, GRIMM! ALL OF YOU!
WHY WON'T YOU DIE?
EXCELLENT. WITHOUT THEIR LEADER, THE HUMAN ANIMALS WILL BE EASILY COWED.
AND IF THE KREE/SKRULL ALLIANCE SHOULD BREAK THE HABITS OF A THOUSAND YEARS AND RALLY TOGETHER AT THIS LAST MOMENT--WE ARE READY FOR THEM.

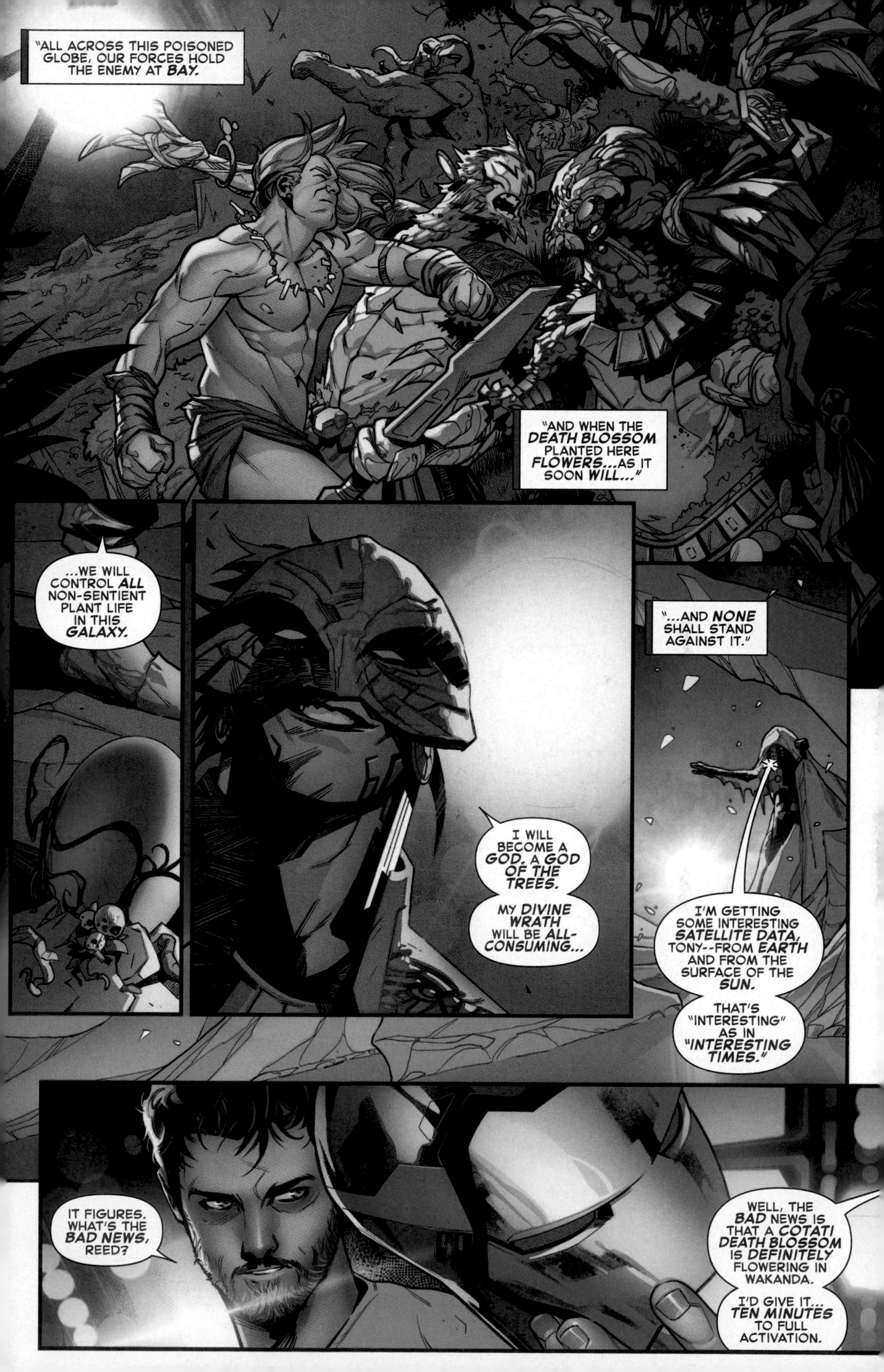
"ALL ACROSS THIS POISONED GLOBE, OUR FORCES HOLD THE ENEMY AT BAY.
"AND WHEN THE DEATH BLOSSOM PLANTED HERE FLOWERS...AS IT SOON WILL..."
...WE WILL CONTROL ALL NON-SENTIENT PLANT LIFE IN THIS GALAXY.
I WILL BECOME A GOD. A GOD OF THE TREES.
MY DIVINE WRATH WILL BE ALL-CONSUMING...
"...AND NONE SHALL STAND AGAINST IT."
I'M GETTING SOME INTERESTING SATELLITE DATA, TONY--FROM EARTH AND FROM THE SURFACE OF THE SUN.
THAT'S "INTERESTING" AS IN "INTERESTING TIMES."
IT FIGURES. WHAT'S THE BAD NEWS, REED?
WELL, THE BAD NEWS IS THAT A COTATI DEATH BLOSSOM IS DEFINITELY FLOWERING IN WAKANDA.
I'D GIVE IT... TEN MINUTES TO FULL ACTIVATION.

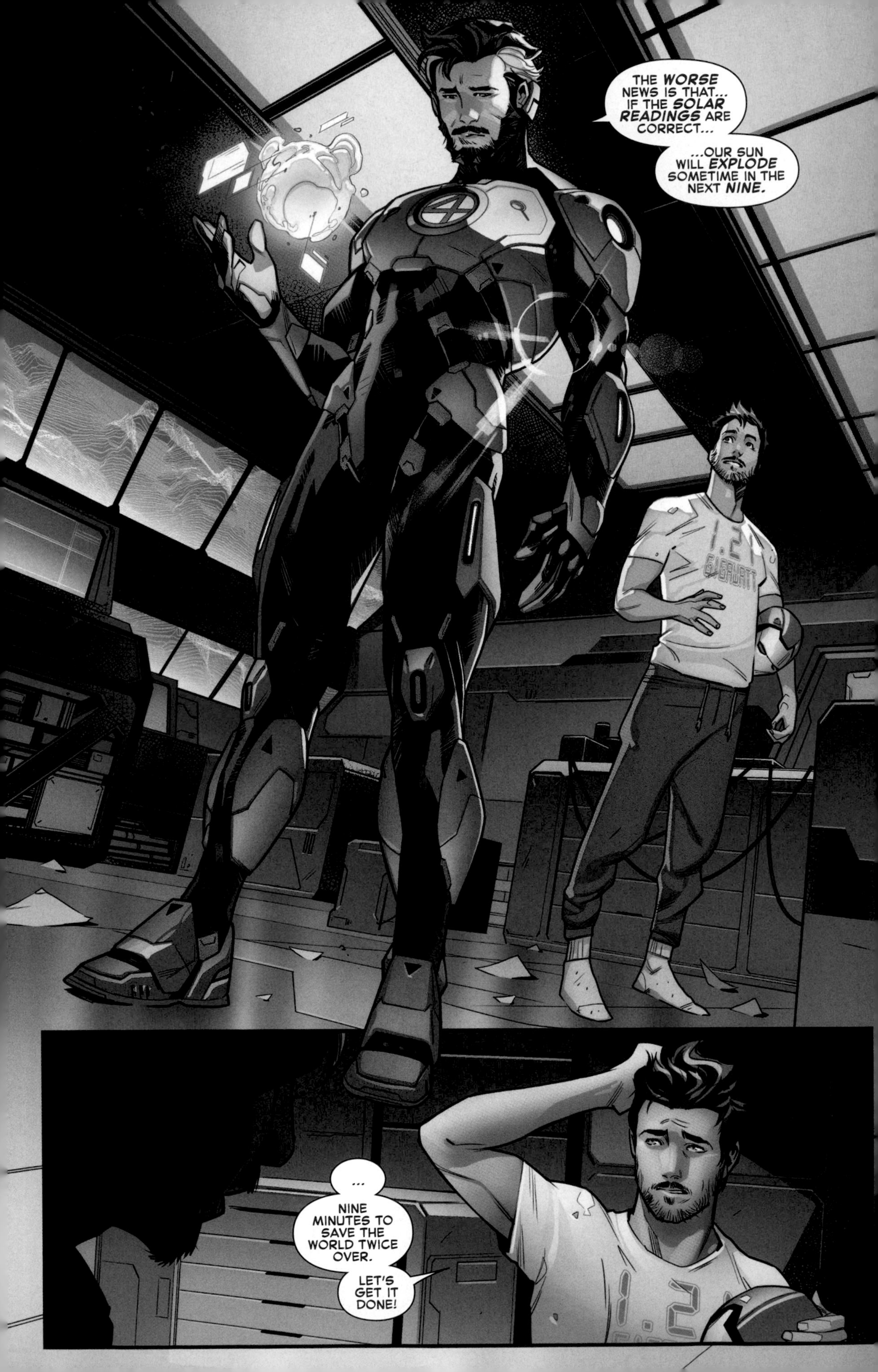
THE WORSE NEWS IS THAT... IF THE SOLAR READINGS ARE CORRECT...
...OUR SUN WILL EXPLODE SOMETIME IN THE NEXT NINE.
...
NINE MINUTES TO SAVE THE WORLD TWICE OVER.
LET'S GET IT DONE!

EMPYRE 6 SECRET VARIANT BY

Patrick Gleason & **Matthew Wilson**

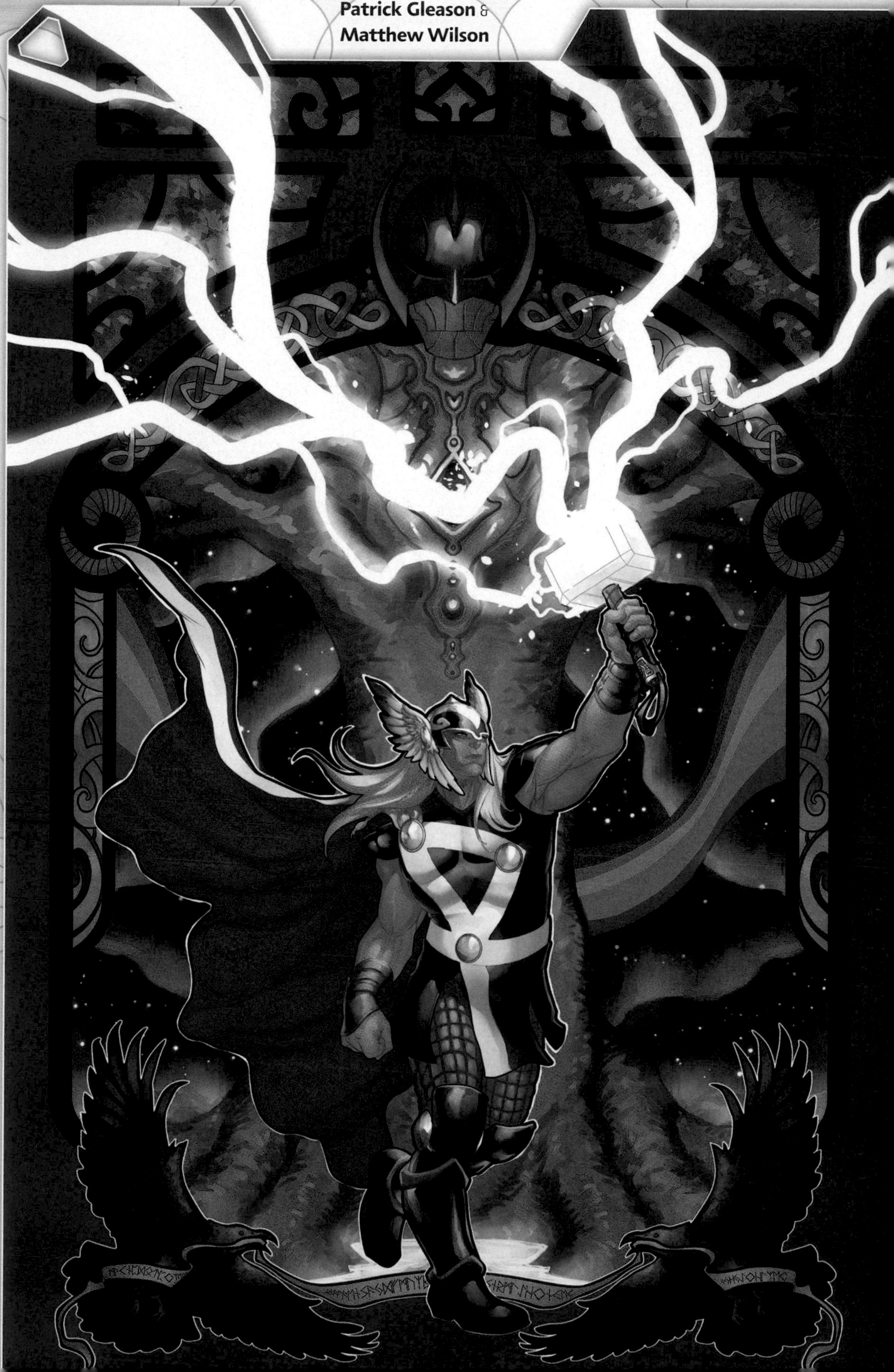

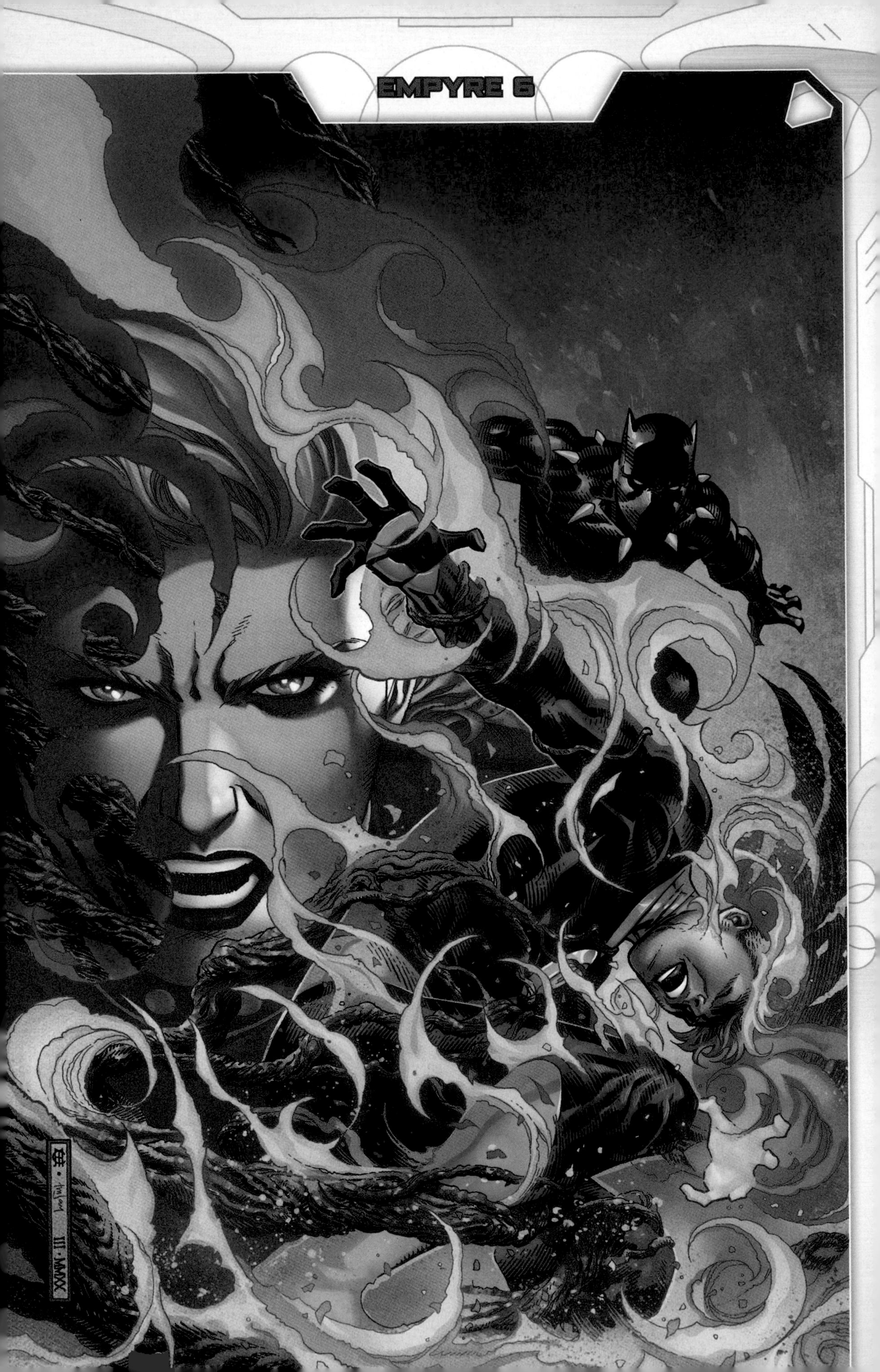
EMPYRE 6
III · MMXX

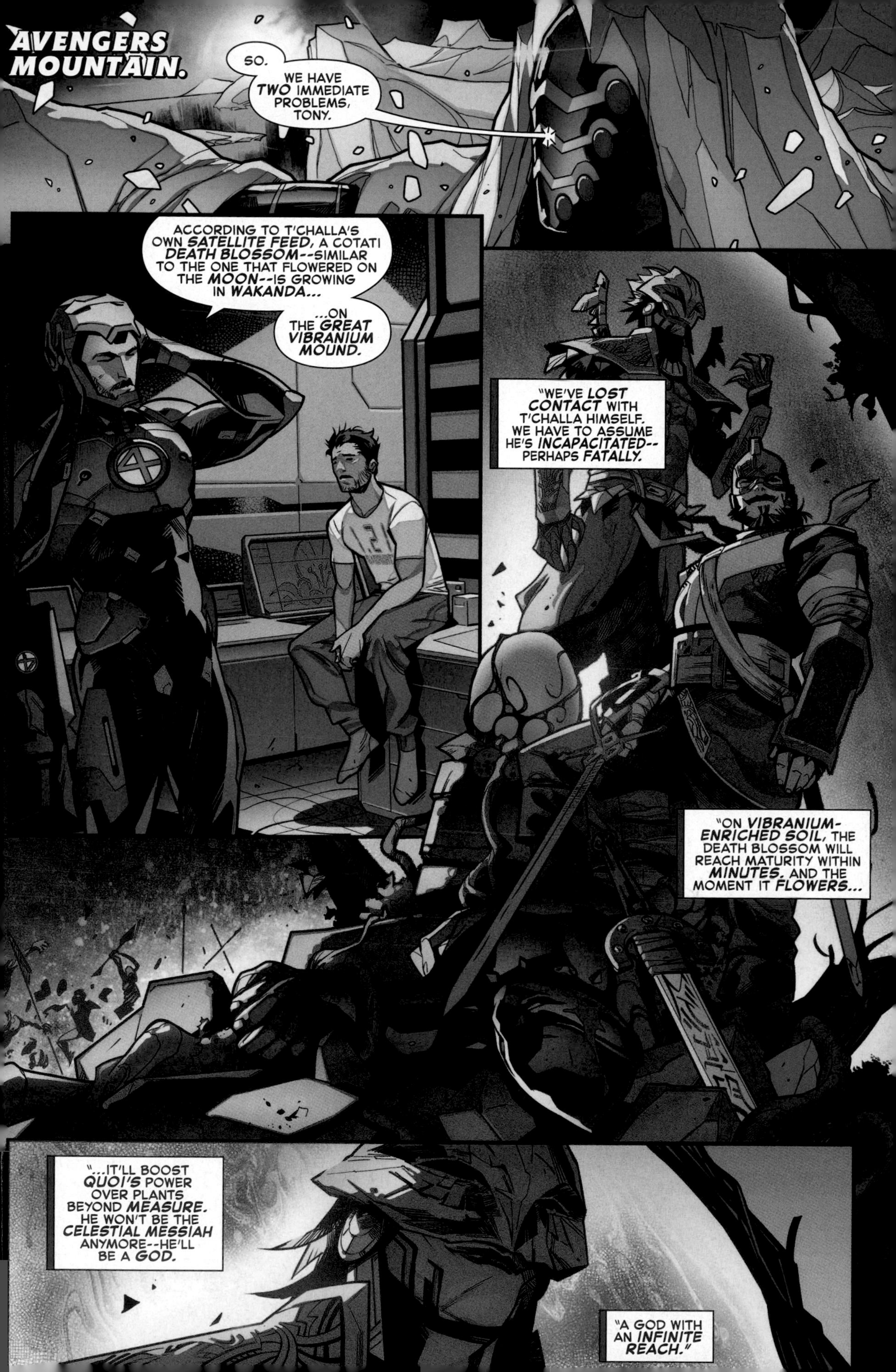
AVENGERS MOUNTAIN.
SO.
WE HAVE TWO IMMEDIATE PROBLEMS, TONY.
ACCORDING TO T'CHALLA'S OWN SATELLITE FEED, A COTATI DEATH BLOSSOM--SIMILAR TO THE ONE THAT FLOWERED ON THE MOON--IS GROWING IN WAKANDA...
...ON THE GREAT VIBRANIUM MOUND.
"WE'VE LOST CONTACT WITH T'CHALLA HIMSELF. WE HAVE TO ASSUME HE'S INCAPACITATED--PERHAPS FATALLY.
"ON VIBRANIUM-ENRICHED SOIL, THE DEATH BLOSSOM WILL REACH MATURITY WITHIN MINUTES. AND THE MOMENT IT FLOWERS...
"...IT'LL BOOST QUOI'S POWER OVER PLANTS BEYOND MEASURE. HE WON'T BE THE CELESTIAL MESSIAH ANYMORE--HE'LL BE A GOD.
"A GOD WITH AN INFINITE REACH."

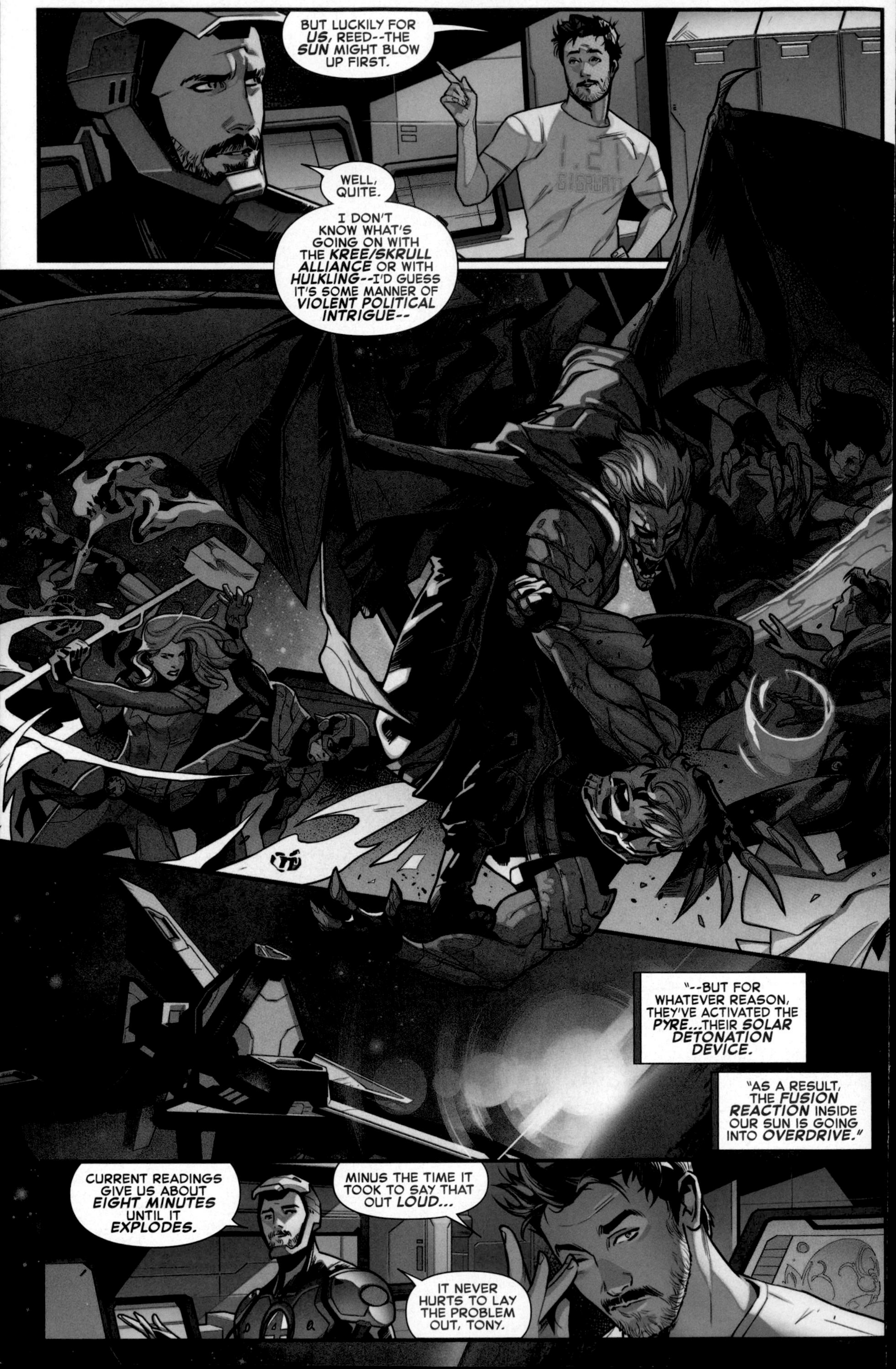
BUT LUCKILY FOR US, REED--THE SUN MIGHT BLOW UP FIRST.
1.21 GIGAWATTS
WELL, QUITE.
I DON'T KNOW WHAT'S GOING ON WITH THE KREE/SKRULL ALLIANCE OR WITH HULKLING--I'D GUESS IT'S SOME MANNER OF VIOLENT POLITICAL INTRIGUE--
"--BUT FOR WHATEVER REASON, THEY'VE ACTIVATED THE PYRE...THEIR SOLAR DETONATION DEVICE.
"AS A RESULT, THE FUSION REACTION INSIDE OUR SUN IS GOING INTO OVERDRIVE."
CURRENT READINGS GIVE US ABOUT EIGHT MINUTES UNTIL IT EXPLODES.
MINUS THE TIME IT TOOK TO SAY THAT OUT LOUD...
IT NEVER HURTS TO LAY THE PROBLEM OUT, TONY.

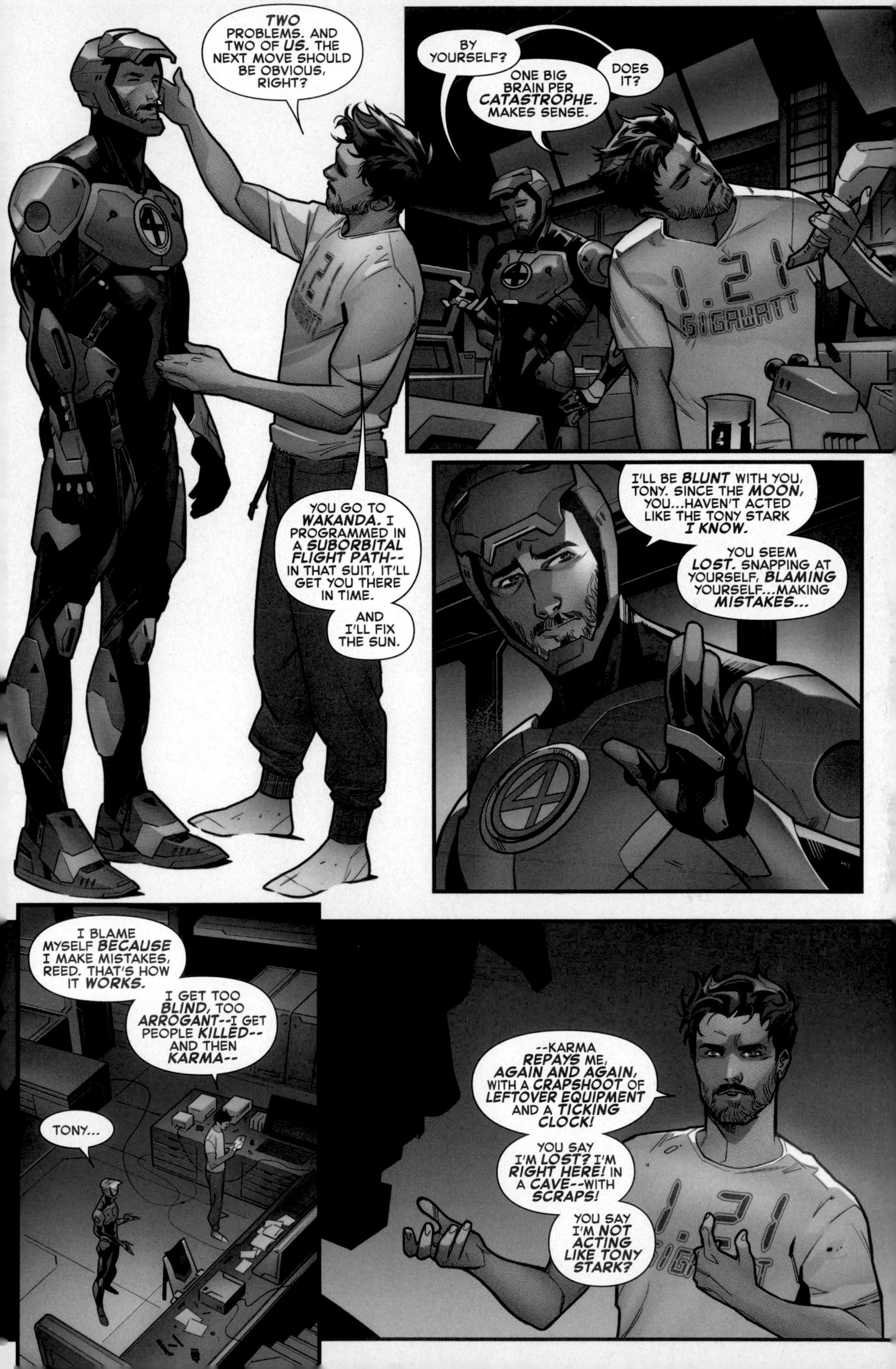
TWO PROBLEMS. AND TWO OF US. THE NEXT MOVE SHOULD BE OBVIOUS, RIGHT?
YOU GO TO WAKANDA. I PROGRAMMED IN A SUBORBITAL FLIGHT PATH-- IN THAT SUIT, IT'LL GET YOU THERE IN TIME.
AND I'LL FIX THE SUN.
BY YOURSELF?
ONE BIG BRAIN PER CATASTROPHE. MAKES SENSE.
DOES IT?
I'LL BE BLUNT WITH YOU, TONY. SINCE THE MOON, YOU...HAVEN'T ACTED LIKE THE TONY STARK I KNOW.
YOU SEEM LOST. SNAPPING AT YOURSELF, BLAMING YOURSELF...MAKING MISTAKES...
I BLAME MYSELF BECAUSE I MAKE MISTAKES, REED. THAT'S HOW IT WORKS.
I GET TOO BLIND, TOO ARROGANT--I GET PEOPLE KILLED-- AND THEN KARMA--
TONY...
--KARMA REPAYS ME, AGAIN AND AGAIN, WITH A CRAPSHOOT OF LEFTOVER EQUIPMENT AND A TICKING CLOCK!
YOU SAY I'M LOST? I'M RIGHT HERE! IN A CAVE--WITH SCRAPS!
YOU SAY I'M NOT ACTING LIKE TONY STARK?

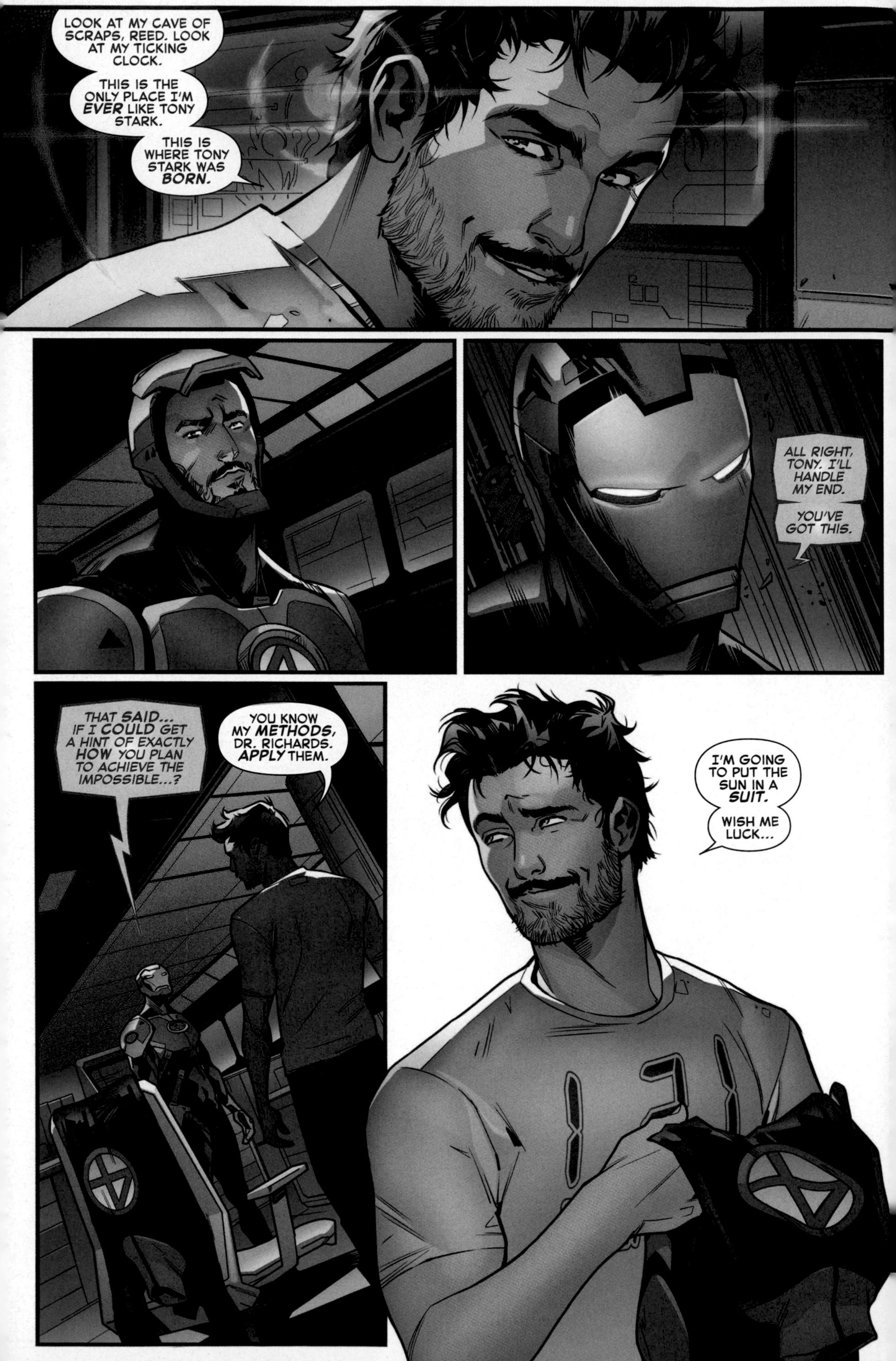
LOOK AT MY CAVE OF SCRAPS, REED. LOOK AT MY TICKING CLOCK.
THIS IS THE ONLY PLACE I'M *EVER* LIKE TONY STARK.
THIS IS WHERE TONY STARK WAS ***BORN.***
ALL RIGHT, TONY. I'LL HANDLE MY END.
YOU'VE GOT THIS.
THAT **SAID...** IF I **COULD** GET A HINT OF EXACTLY **HOW** YOU PLAN TO ACHIEVE THE IMPOSSIBLE...?
YOU KNOW MY ***METHODS,*** DR. RICHARDS. ***APPLY*** THEM.
I'M GOING TO PUT THE SUN IN A ***SUIT.***
WISH ME LUCK...

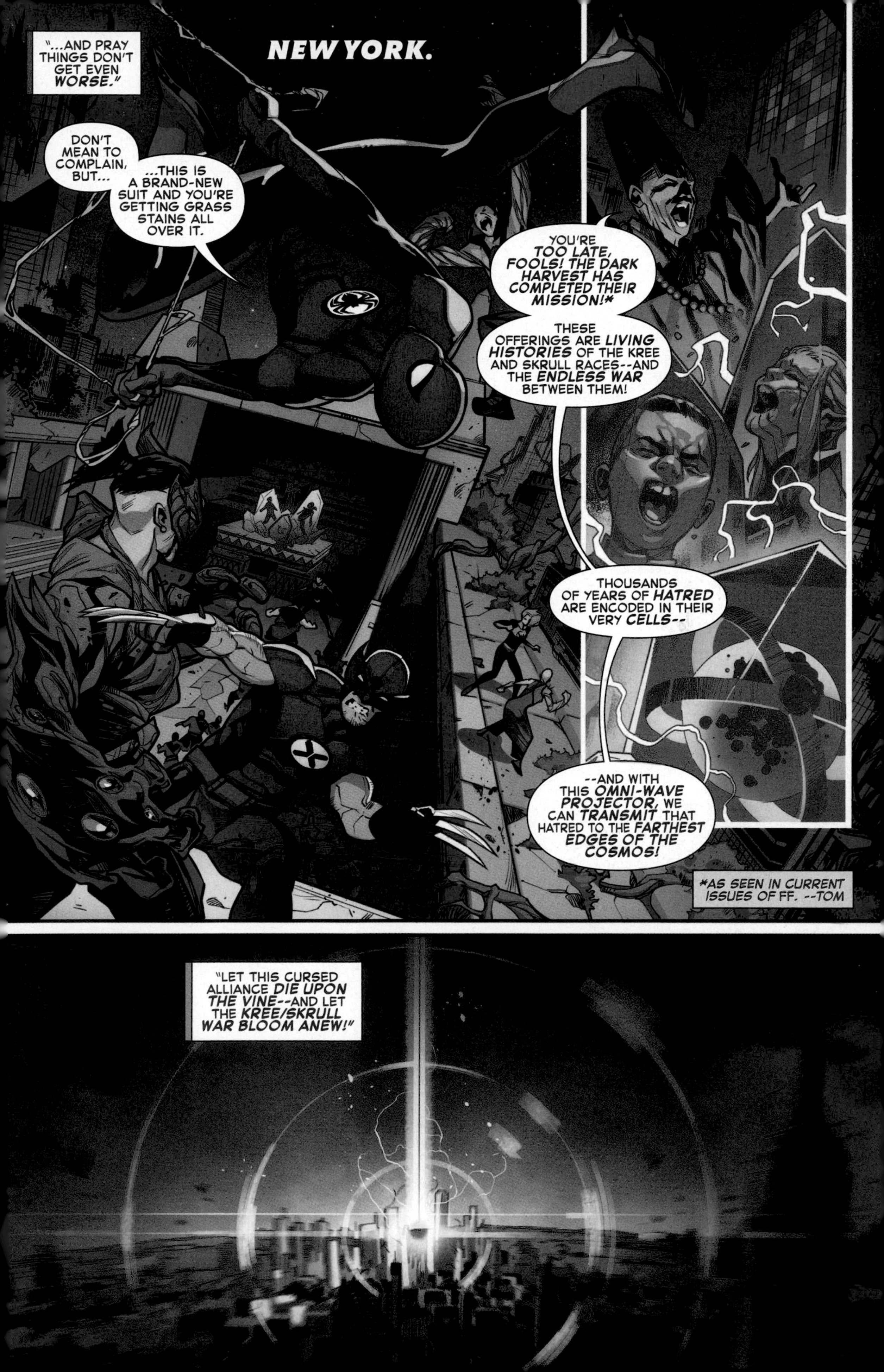
"...AND PRAY THINGS DON'T GET EVEN WORSE."
NEW YORK.
DON'T MEAN TO COMPLAIN, BUT...
...THIS IS A BRAND-NEW SUIT AND YOU'RE GETTING GRASS STAINS ALL OVER IT.
YOU'RE TOO LATE, FOOLS! THE DARK HARVEST HAS COMPLETED THEIR MISSION!*
THESE OFFERINGS ARE LIVING HISTORIES OF THE KREE AND SKRULL RACES--AND THE ENDLESS WAR BETWEEN THEM!
THOUSANDS OF YEARS OF HATRED ARE ENCODED IN THEIR VERY CELLS--
--AND WITH THIS OMNI-WAVE PROJECTOR, WE CAN TRANSMIT THAT HATRED TO THE FARTHEST EDGES OF THE COSMOS!
*AS SEEN IN CURRENT ISSUES OF FF. --TOM
"LET THIS CURSED ALLIANCE DIE UPON THE VINE--AND LET THE KREE/SKRULL WAR BLOOM ANEW!"

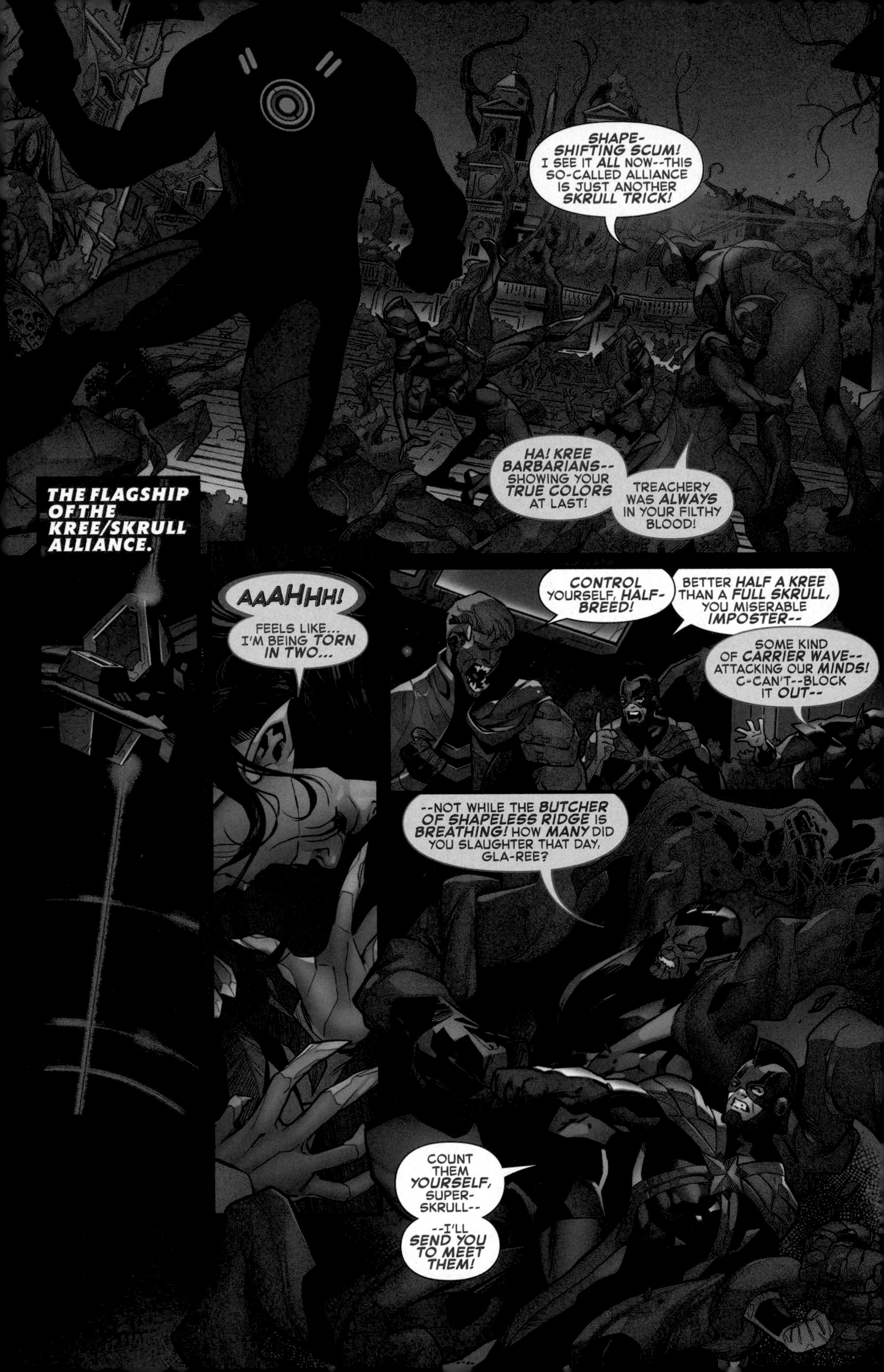
SHAPE-SHIFTING SCUM! I SEE IT ALL NOW--THIS SO-CALLED ALLIANCE IS JUST ANOTHER SKRULL TRICK!
HA! KREE BARBARIANS--SHOWING YOUR TRUE COLORS AT LAST!
TREACHERY WAS ALWAYS IN YOUR FILTHY BLOOD!
THE FLAGSHIP OF THE KREE/SKRULL ALLIANCE.
AAAHHH!
FEELS LIKE... I'M BEING TORN IN TWO...
CONTROL YOURSELF, HALF-BREED!
BETTER HALF A KREE THAN A FULL SKRULL, YOU MISERABLE IMPOSTER--
SOME KIND OF CARRIER WAVE--ATTACKING OUR MINDS! C-CAN'T--BLOCK IT OUT--
--NOT WHILE THE BUTCHER OF SHAPELESS RIDGE IS BREATHING! HOW MANY DID YOU SLAUGHTER THAT DAY, GLA-REE?
COUNT THEM YOURSELF, SUPER-SKRULL--
--I'LL SEND YOU TO MEET THEM!

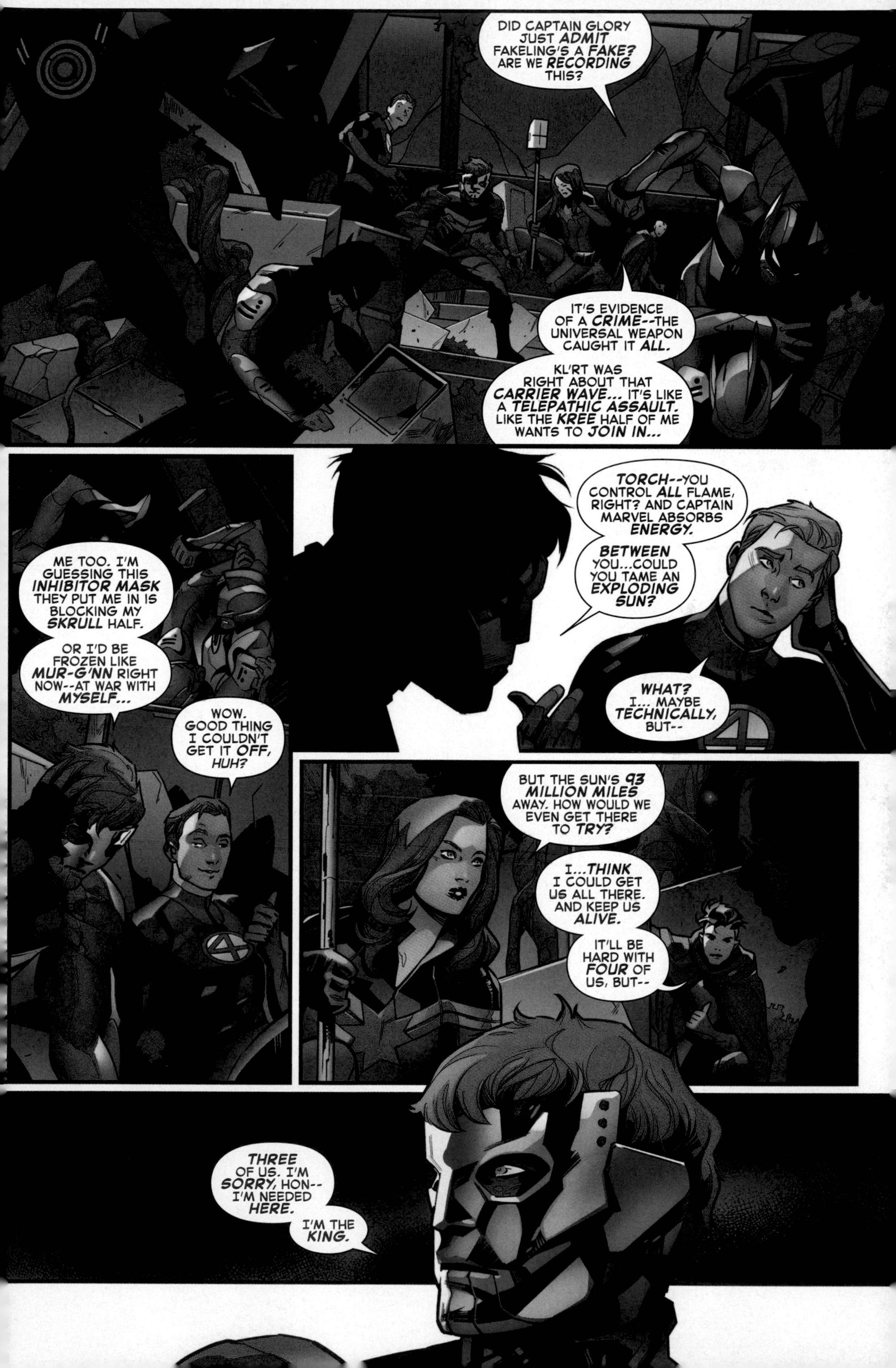

DID CAPTAIN GLORY JUST ADMIT FAKELING'S A FAKE? ARE WE RECORDING THIS?
IT'S EVIDENCE OF A CRIME--THE UNIVERSAL WEAPON CAUGHT IT ALL.
KL'RT WAS RIGHT ABOUT THAT CARRIER WAVE... IT'S LIKE A TELEPATHIC ASSAULT. LIKE THE KREE HALF OF ME WANTS TO JOIN IN...
ME TOO. I'M GUESSING THIS INHIBITOR MASK THEY PUT ME IN IS BLOCKING MY SKRULL HALF.
OR I'D BE FROZEN LIKE MUR-G'NN RIGHT NOW--AT WAR WITH MYSELF...
WOW. GOOD THING I COULDN'T GET IT OFF, HUH?
TORCH--YOU CONTROL ALL FLAME, RIGHT? AND CAPTAIN MARVEL ABSORBS ENERGY.
BETWEEN YOU...COULD YOU TAME AN EXPLODING SUN?
WHAT? I... MAYBE TECHNICALLY, BUT--
BUT THE SUN'S 93 MILLION MILES AWAY. HOW WOULD WE EVEN GET THERE TO TRY?
I...THINK I COULD GET US ALL THERE. AND KEEP US ALIVE.
IT'LL BE HARD WITH FOUR OF US, BUT--
THREE OF US. I'M SORRY, HON--I'M NEEDED HERE.
I'M THE KING.

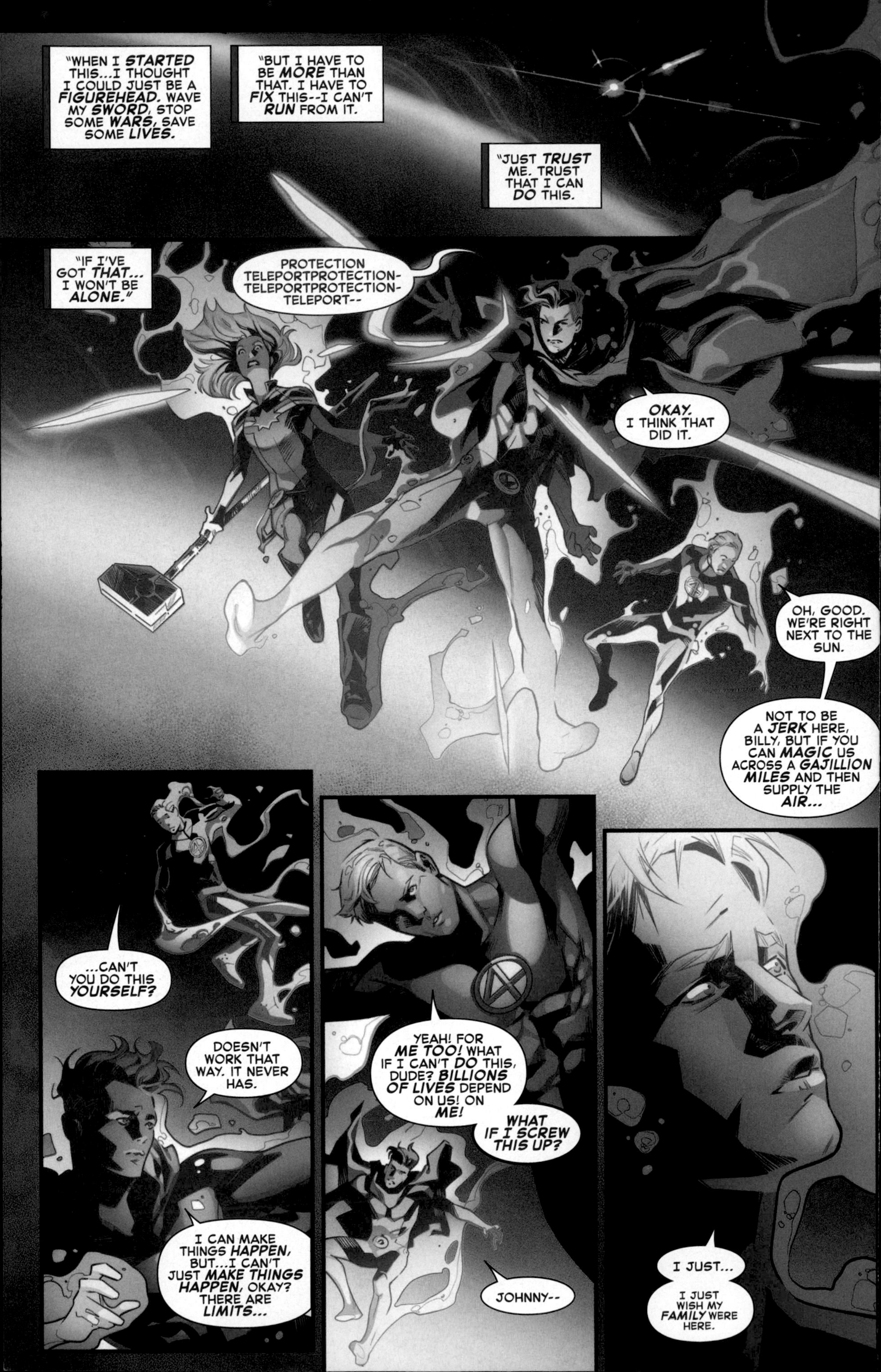
"WHEN I STARTED THIS...I THOUGHT I COULD JUST BE A FIGUREHEAD. WAVE MY SWORD, STOP SOME WARS, SAVE SOME LIVES.
"BUT I HAVE TO BE MORE THAN THAT. I HAVE TO FIX THIS--I CAN'T RUN FROM IT.
"JUST TRUST ME. TRUST THAT I CAN DO THIS.
"IF I'VE GOT THAT... I WON'T BE ALONE."
PROTECTION TELEPORTPROTECTION-TELEPORTPROTECTION-TELEPORT--
OKAY. I THINK THAT DID IT.
OH, GOOD. WE'RE RIGHT NEXT TO THE SUN.
NOT TO BE A JERK HERE, BILLY, BUT IF YOU CAN MAGIC US ACROSS A GAJILLION MILES AND THEN SUPPLY THE AIR...
...CAN'T YOU DO THIS YOURSELF?
DOESN'T WORK THAT WAY. IT NEVER HAS.
I CAN MAKE THINGS HAPPEN, BUT...I CAN'T JUST MAKE THINGS HAPPEN, OKAY? THERE ARE LIMITS...
YEAH! FOR ME TOO! WHAT IF I CAN'T DO THIS, DUDE? BILLIONS OF LIVES DEPEND ON US! ON ME!
WHAT IF I SCREW THIS UP?
JOHNNY--
I JUST...
I JUST WISH MY FAMILY WERE HERE.

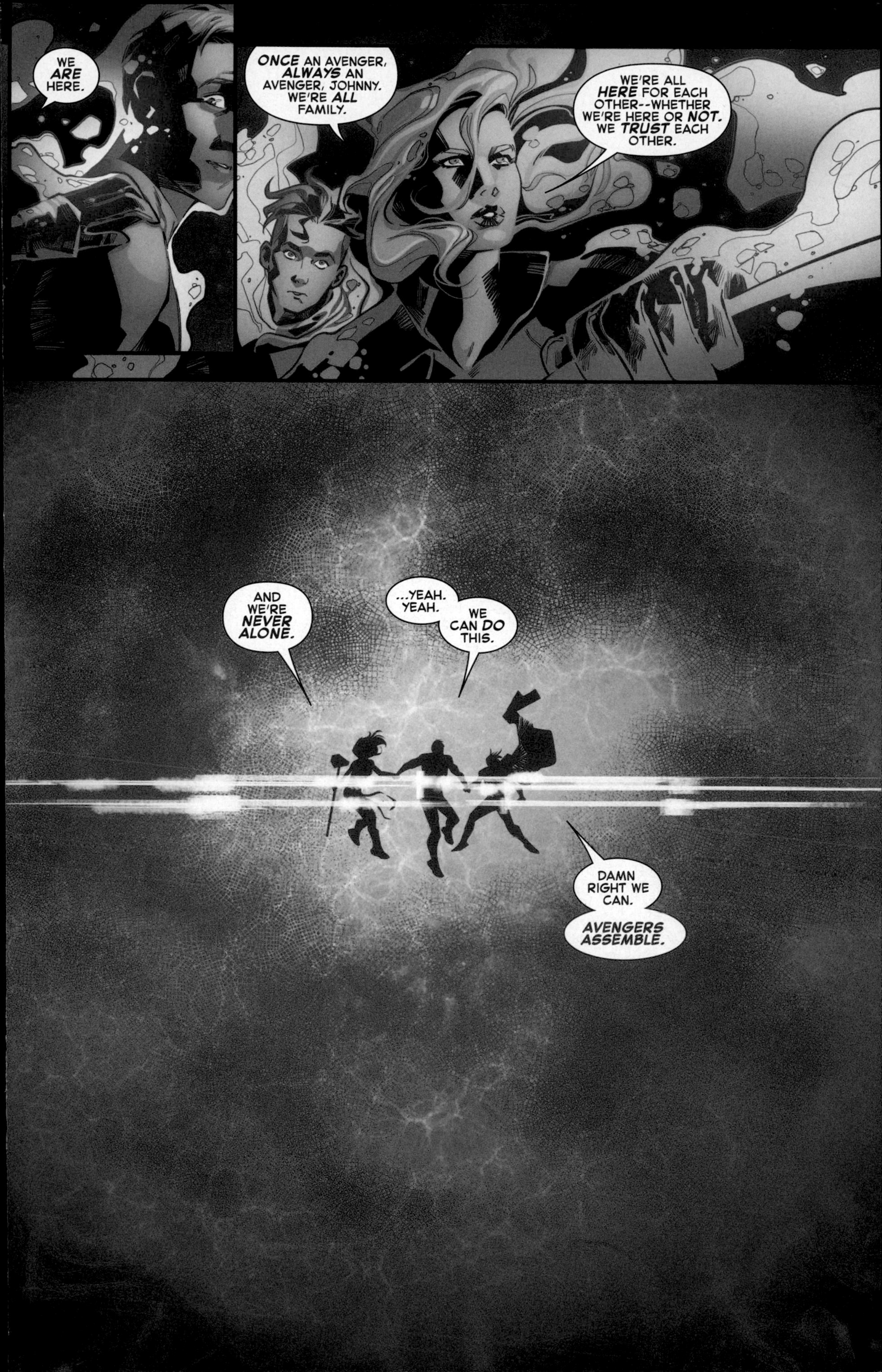
WE ARE HERE.
ONCE AN AVENGER, ALWAYS AN AVENGER, JOHNNY. WE'RE ALL FAMILY.
WE'RE ALL HERE FOR EACH OTHER--WHETHER WE'RE HERE OR NOT. WE TRUST EACH OTHER.
AND WE'RE NEVER ALONE.
...YEAH. YEAH.
WE CAN DO THIS.
DAMN RIGHT WE CAN.
AVENGERS ASSEMBLE.

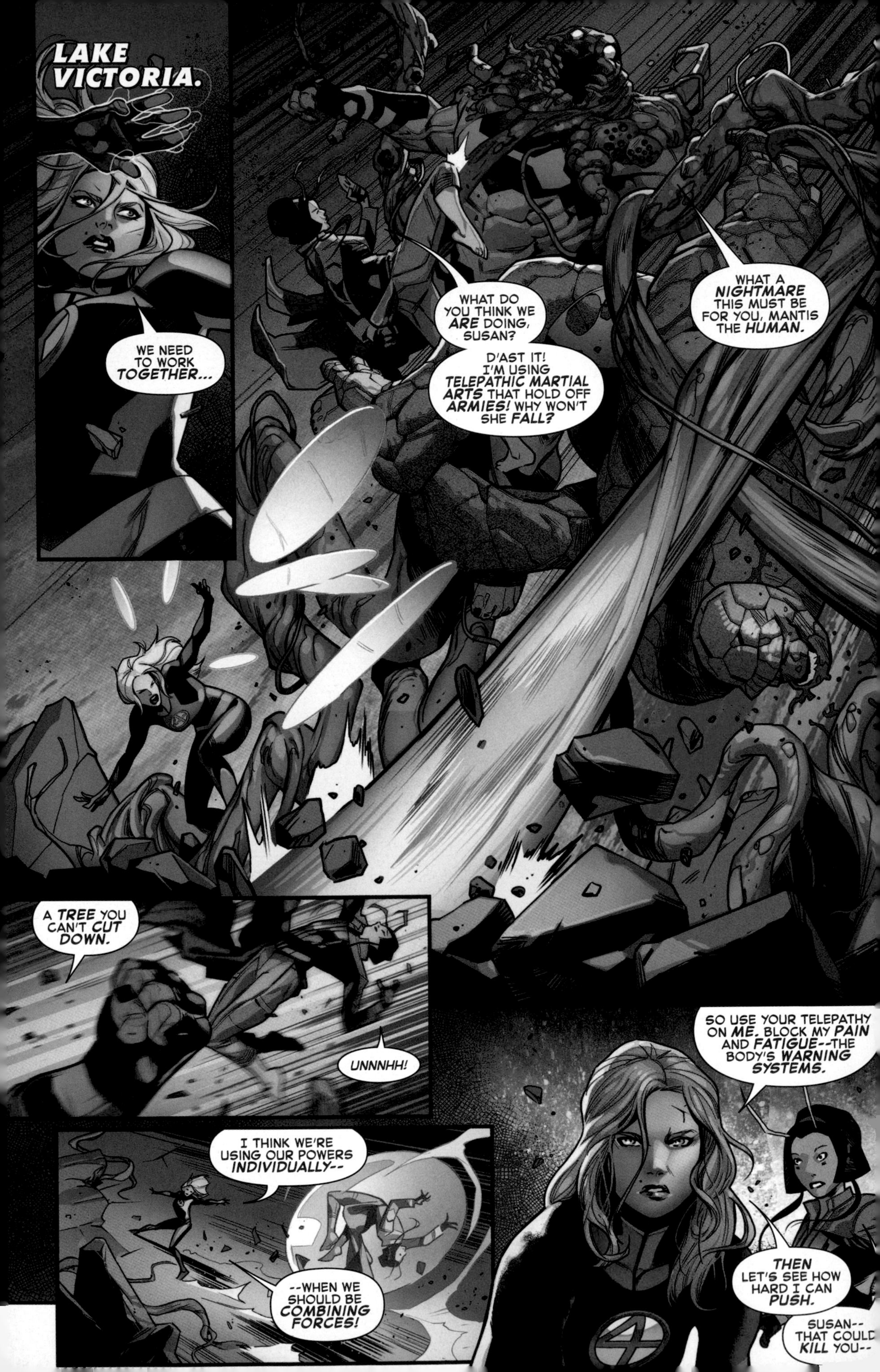
LAKE VICTORIA.
WE NEED TO WORK TOGETHER...
WHAT DO YOU THINK WE ARE DOING, SUSAN?
D'AST IT! I'M USING TELEPATHIC MARTIAL ARTS THAT HOLD OFF ARMIES! WHY WON'T SHE FALL?
WHAT A NIGHTMARE THIS MUST BE FOR YOU, MANTIS THE HUMAN.
A TREE YOU CAN'T CUT DOWN.
UNNNHH!
I THINK WE'RE USING OUR POWERS INDIVIDUALLY--
--WHEN WE SHOULD BE COMBINING FORCES!
SO USE YOUR TELEPATHY ON ME. BLOCK MY PAIN AND FATIGUE--THE BODY'S WARNING SYSTEMS.
THEN LET'S SEE HOW HARD I CAN PUSH.
SUSAN-- THAT COULD KILL YOU--

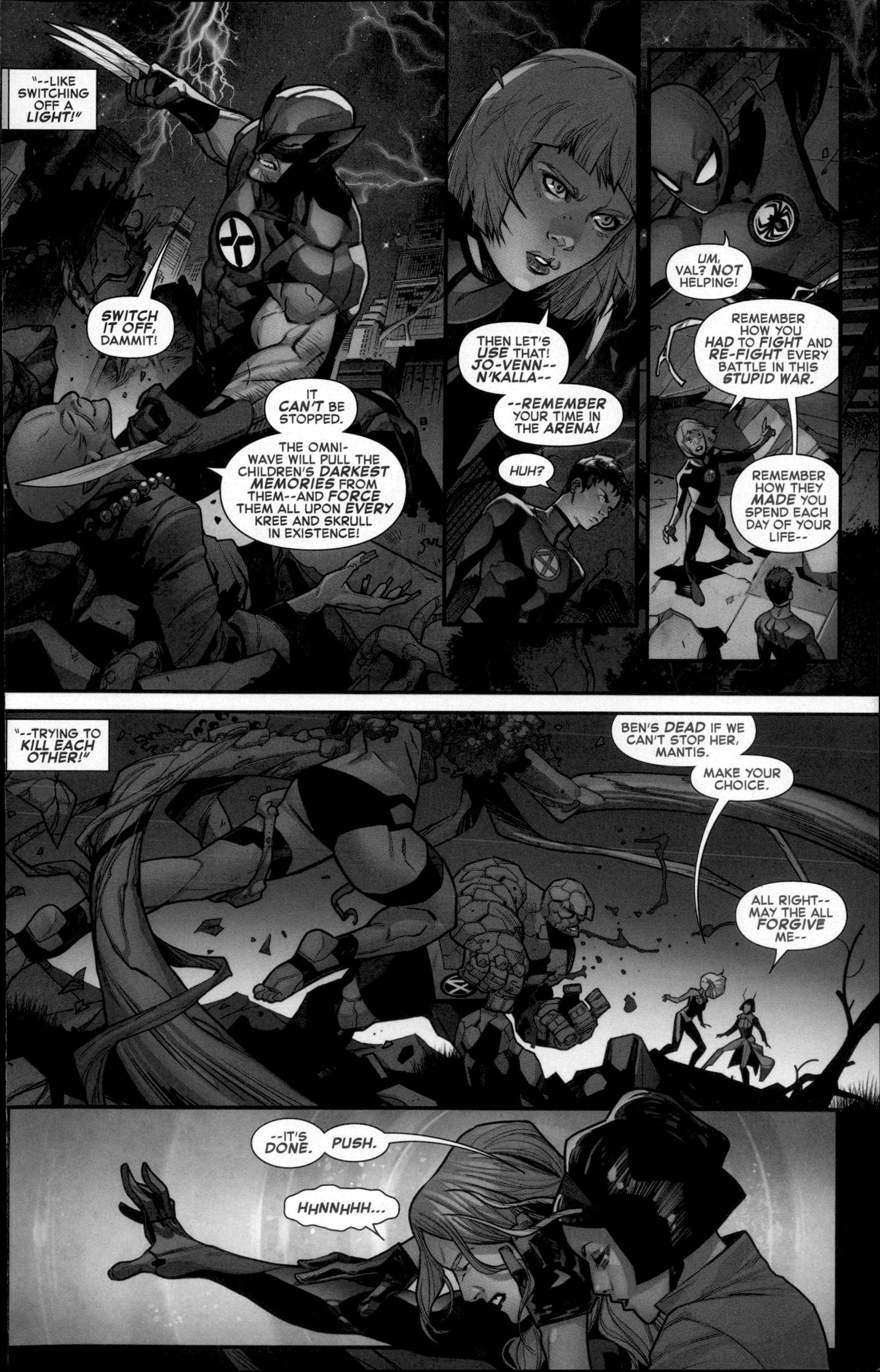
"--LIKE SWITCHING OFF A LIGHT!"
SWITCH IT OFF, DAMMIT!
IT CAN'T BE STOPPED.
THE OMNI-WAVE WILL PULL THE CHILDREN'S DARKEST MEMORIES FROM THEM--AND FORCE THEM ALL UPON EVERY KREE AND SKRULL IN EXISTENCE!
THEN LET'S USE THAT! JO-VENN--N'KALLA--
--REMEMBER YOUR TIME IN THE ARENA!
HUH?
UM, VAL? NOT HELPING!
REMEMBER HOW YOU HAD TO FIGHT AND RE-FIGHT EVERY BATTLE IN THIS STUPID WAR.
REMEMBER HOW THEY MADE YOU SPEND EACH DAY OF YOUR LIFE--
"--TRYING TO KILL EACH OTHER!"
BEN'S DEAD IF WE CAN'T STOP HER, MANTIS.
MAKE YOUR CHOICE.
ALL RIGHT--MAY THE ALL FORGIVE ME--
--IT'S DONE.
PUSH.
HHNNHHH...

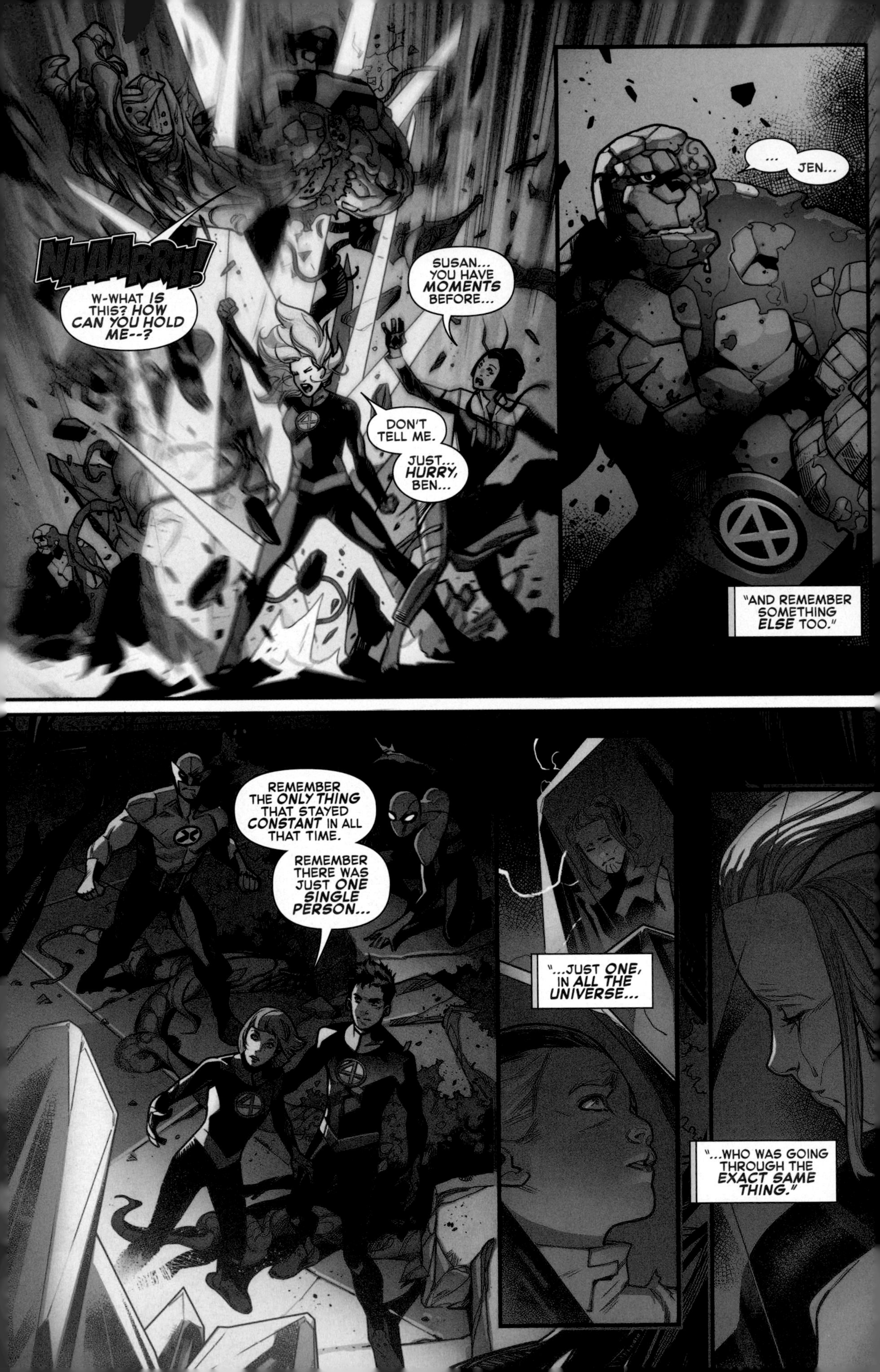

NAAARRGH!
W-WHAT IS THIS? HOW CAN YOU HOLD ME--?
SUSAN... YOU HAVE MOMENTS BEFORE...
DON'T TELL ME.
JUST... HURRY, BEN...
... JEN...
"AND REMEMBER SOMETHING ELSE TOO."
REMEMBER THE ONLY THING THAT STAYED CONSTANT IN ALL THAT TIME.
REMEMBER THERE WAS JUST ONE SINGLE PERSON...
"...JUST ONE, IN ALL THE UNIVERSE...
"...WHO WAS GOING THROUGH THE EXACT SAME THING."

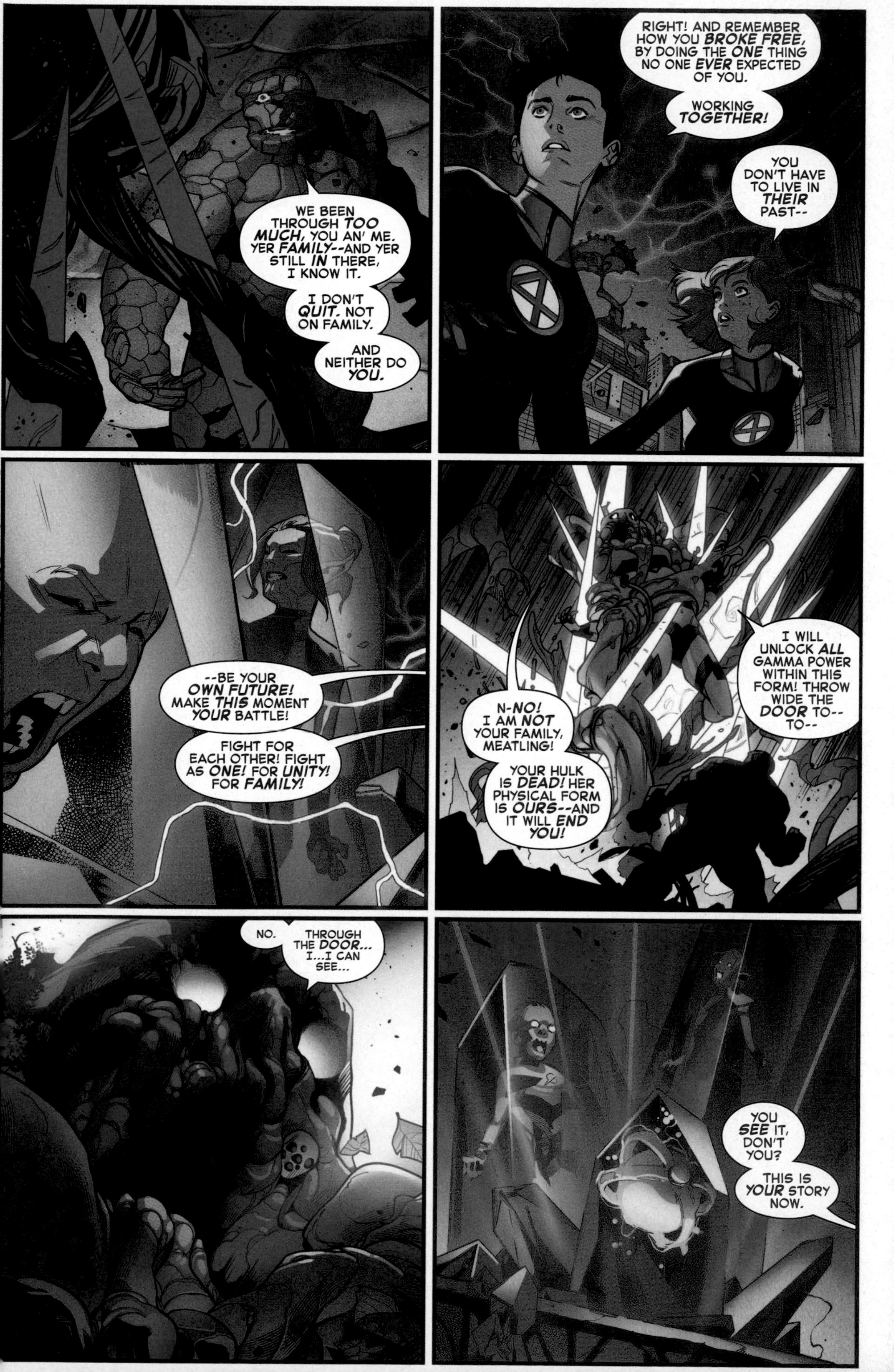
WE BEEN THROUGH TOO MUCH, YOU AN' ME. YER FAMILY--AND YER STILL IN THERE, I KNOW IT.
I DON'T QUIT. NOT ON FAMILY.
AND NEITHER DO YOU.
RIGHT! AND REMEMBER HOW YOU BROKE FREE, BY DOING THE ONE THING NO ONE EVER EXPECTED OF YOU.
WORKING TOGETHER!
YOU DON'T HAVE TO LIVE IN THEIR PAST--
--BE YOUR OWN FUTURE! MAKE THIS MOMENT YOUR BATTLE!
FIGHT FOR EACH OTHER! FIGHT AS ONE! FOR UNITY! FOR FAMILY!
I WILL UNLOCK ALL GAMMA POWER WITHIN THIS FORM! THROW WIDE THE DOOR TO--TO--
N-NO! I AM NOT YOUR FAMILY, MEATLING!
YOUR HULK IS DEAD! HER PHYSICAL FORM IS OURS--AND IT WILL END YOU!
NO.
THROUGH THE DOOR... I...I CAN SEE...
YOU SEE IT, DON'T YOU?
THIS IS YOUR STORY NOW.

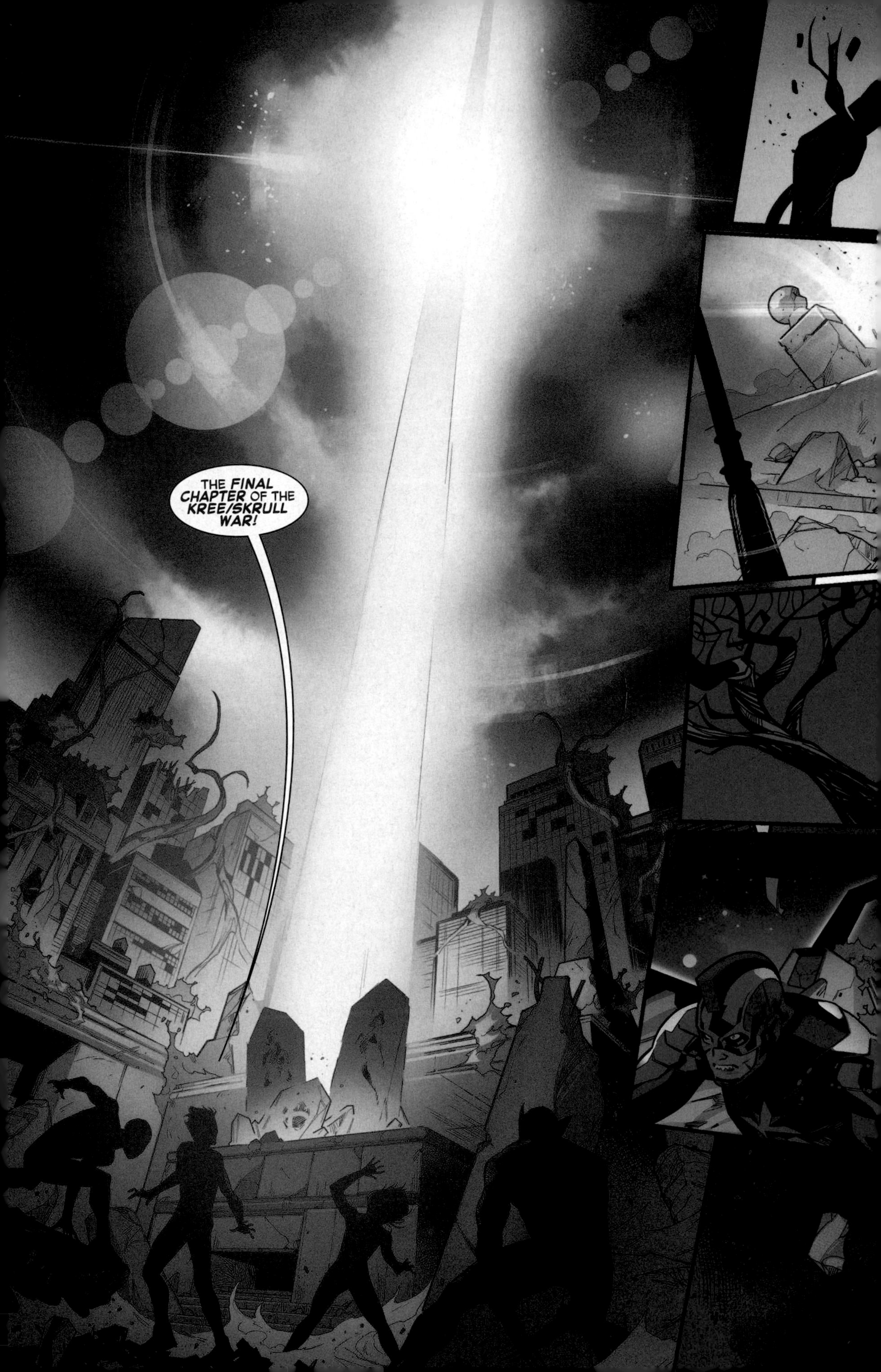
THE FINAL CHAPTER OF THE KREE/SKRULL WAR!

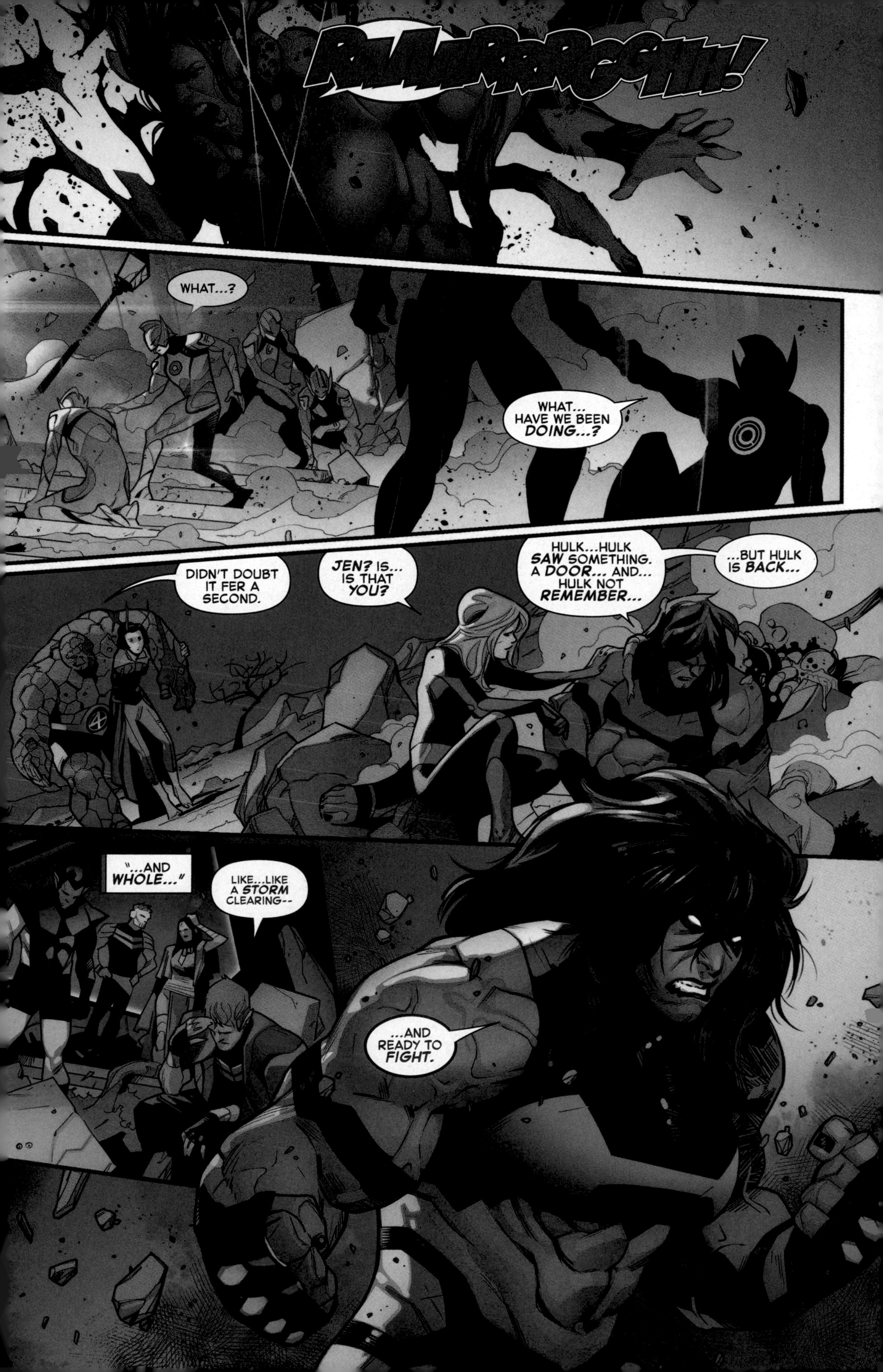

RAAARRRGGHH!
WHAT...?
WHAT... HAVE WE BEEN DOING...?
DIDN'T DOUBT IT FER A SECOND.
JEN? IS... IS THAT YOU?
HULK...HULK SAW SOMETHING. A DOOR... AND... HULK NOT REMEMBER...
...BUT HULK IS BACK...
"...AND WHOLE..."
LIKE...LIKE A STORM CLEARING--
...AND READY TO FIGHT.

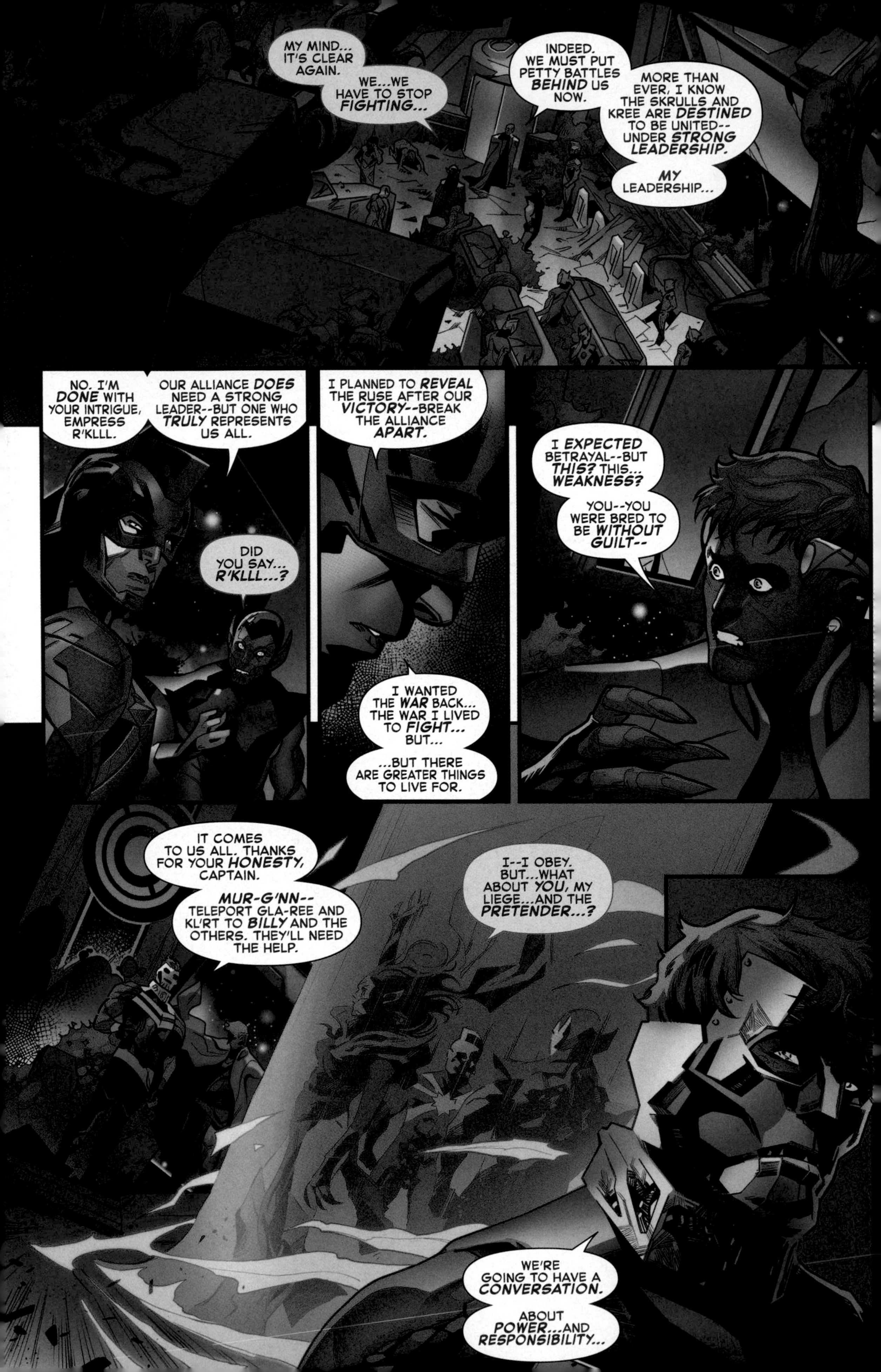

MY MIND... IT'S CLEAR AGAIN.
WE...WE HAVE TO STOP FIGHTING...
INDEED. WE MUST PUT PETTY BATTLES BEHIND US NOW.
MORE THAN EVER, I KNOW THE SKRULLS AND KREE ARE DESTINED TO BE UNITED--UNDER STRONG LEADERSHIP.
MY LEADERSHIP...
NO. I'M DONE WITH YOUR INTRIGUE, EMPRESS R'KLLL.
OUR ALLIANCE DOES NEED A STRONG LEADER--BUT ONE WHO TRULY REPRESENTS US ALL.
DID YOU SAY... R'KLLL...?
I PLANNED TO REVEAL THE RUSE AFTER OUR VICTORY--BREAK THE ALLIANCE APART.
I WANTED THE WAR BACK... THE WAR I LIVED TO FIGHT... BUT...
...BUT THERE ARE GREATER THINGS TO LIVE FOR.
I EXPECTED BETRAYAL--BUT THIS? THIS... WEAKNESS?
YOU--YOU WERE BRED TO BE WITHOUT GUILT--
IT COMES TO US ALL. THANKS FOR YOUR HONESTY, CAPTAIN.
MUR-G'NN--TELEPORT GLA-REE AND KL'RT TO BILLY AND THE OTHERS. THEY'LL NEED THE HELP.
I--I OBEY. BUT...WHAT ABOUT YOU, MY LIEGE...AND THE PRETENDER...?
WE'RE GOING TO HAVE A CONVERSATION.
ABOUT POWER...AND RESPONSIBILITY...

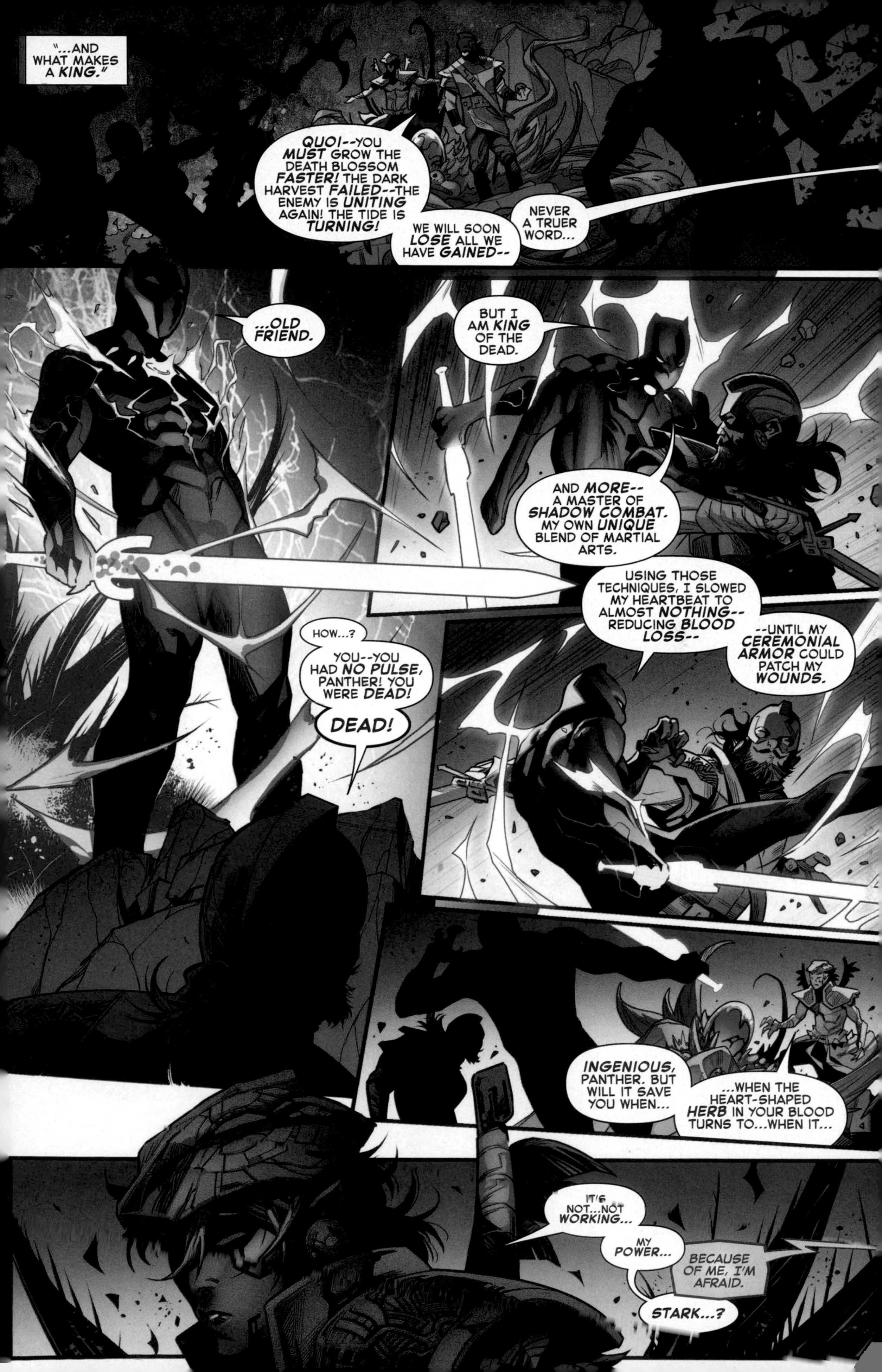
"...AND WHAT MAKES A KING."
QUOI--YOU MUST GROW THE DEATH BLOSSOM FASTER! THE DARK HARVEST FAILED--THE ENEMY IS UNITING AGAIN! THE TIDE IS TURNING!
WE WILL SOON LOSE ALL WE HAVE GAINED--
NEVER A TRUER WORD...
...OLD FRIEND.
BUT I AM KING OF THE DEAD.
AND MORE-- A MASTER OF SHADOW COMBAT. MY OWN UNIQUE BLEND OF MARTIAL ARTS.
USING THOSE TECHNIQUES, I SLOWED MY HEARTBEAT TO ALMOST NOTHING-- REDUCING BLOOD LOSS--
--UNTIL MY CEREMONIAL ARMOR COULD PATCH MY WOUNDS.
HOW...?
YOU--YOU HAD NO PULSE, PANTHER! YOU WERE DEAD!
DEAD!
INGENIOUS, PANTHER. BUT WILL IT SAVE YOU WHEN...
...WHEN THE HEART-SHAPED HERB IN YOUR BLOOD TURNS TO...WHEN IT...
IT'S NOT...NOT WORKING...
MY POWER...
BECAUSE OF ME, I'M AFRAID.
STARK...?

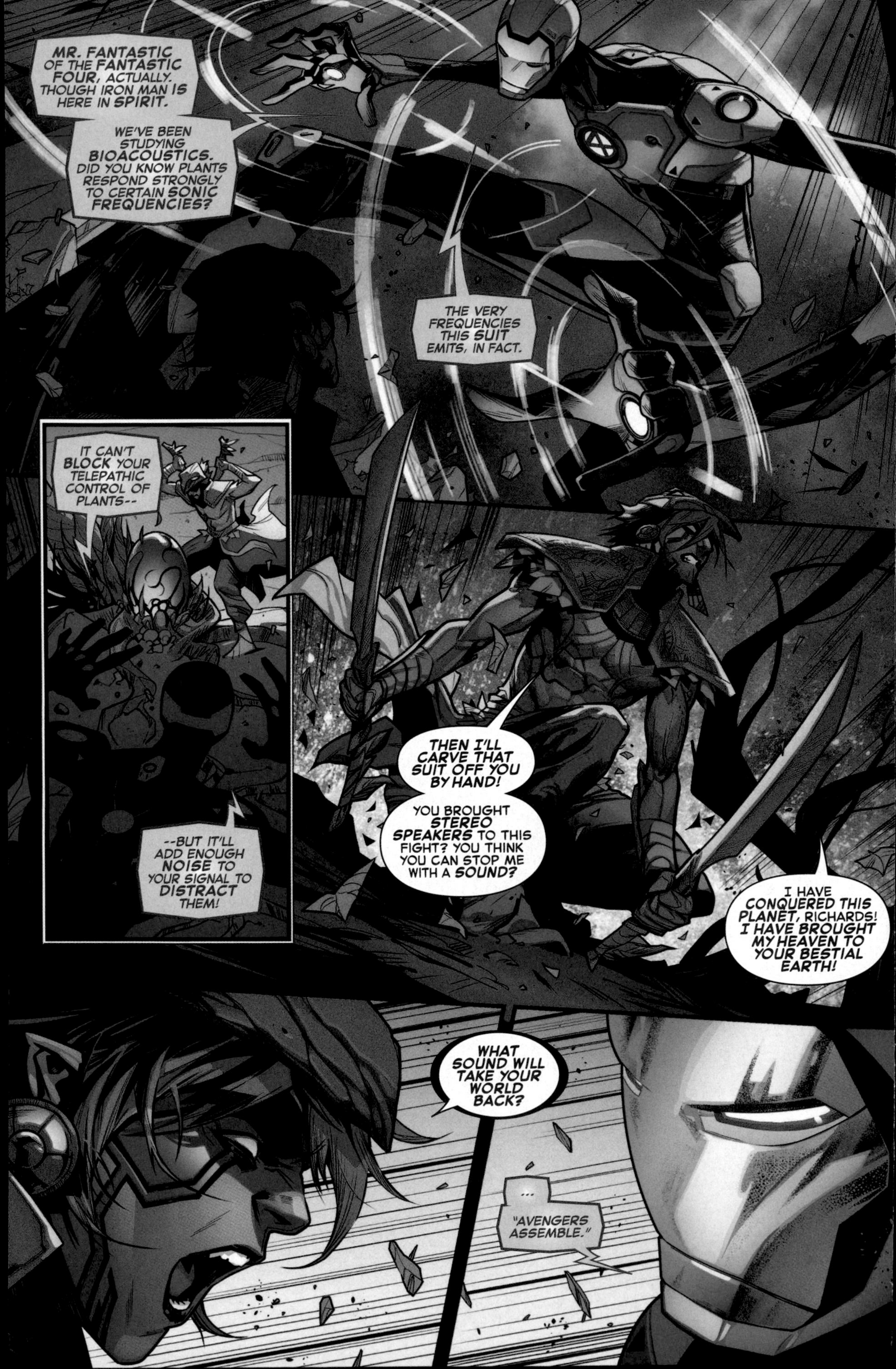
MR. FANTASTIC OF THE FANTASTIC FOUR, ACTUALLY. THOUGH IRON MAN IS HERE IN SPIRIT.
WE'VE BEEN STUDYING BIOACOUSTICS. DID YOU KNOW PLANTS RESPOND STRONGLY TO CERTAIN SONIC FREQUENCIES?
THE VERY FREQUENCIES THIS SUIT EMITS, IN FACT.
IT CAN'T BLOCK YOUR TELEPATHIC CONTROL OF PLANTS--
--BUT IT'LL ADD ENOUGH NOISE TO YOUR SIGNAL TO DISTRACT THEM!
THEN I'LL CARVE THAT SUIT OFF YOU BY HAND!
YOU BROUGHT STEREO SPEAKERS TO THIS FIGHT? YOU THINK YOU CAN STOP ME WITH A SOUND?
I HAVE CONQUERED THIS PLANET, RICHARDS! I HAVE BROUGHT MY HEAVEN TO YOUR BESTIAL EARTH!
WHAT SOUND WILL TAKE YOUR WORLD BACK?
...
"AVENGERS ASSEMBLE."

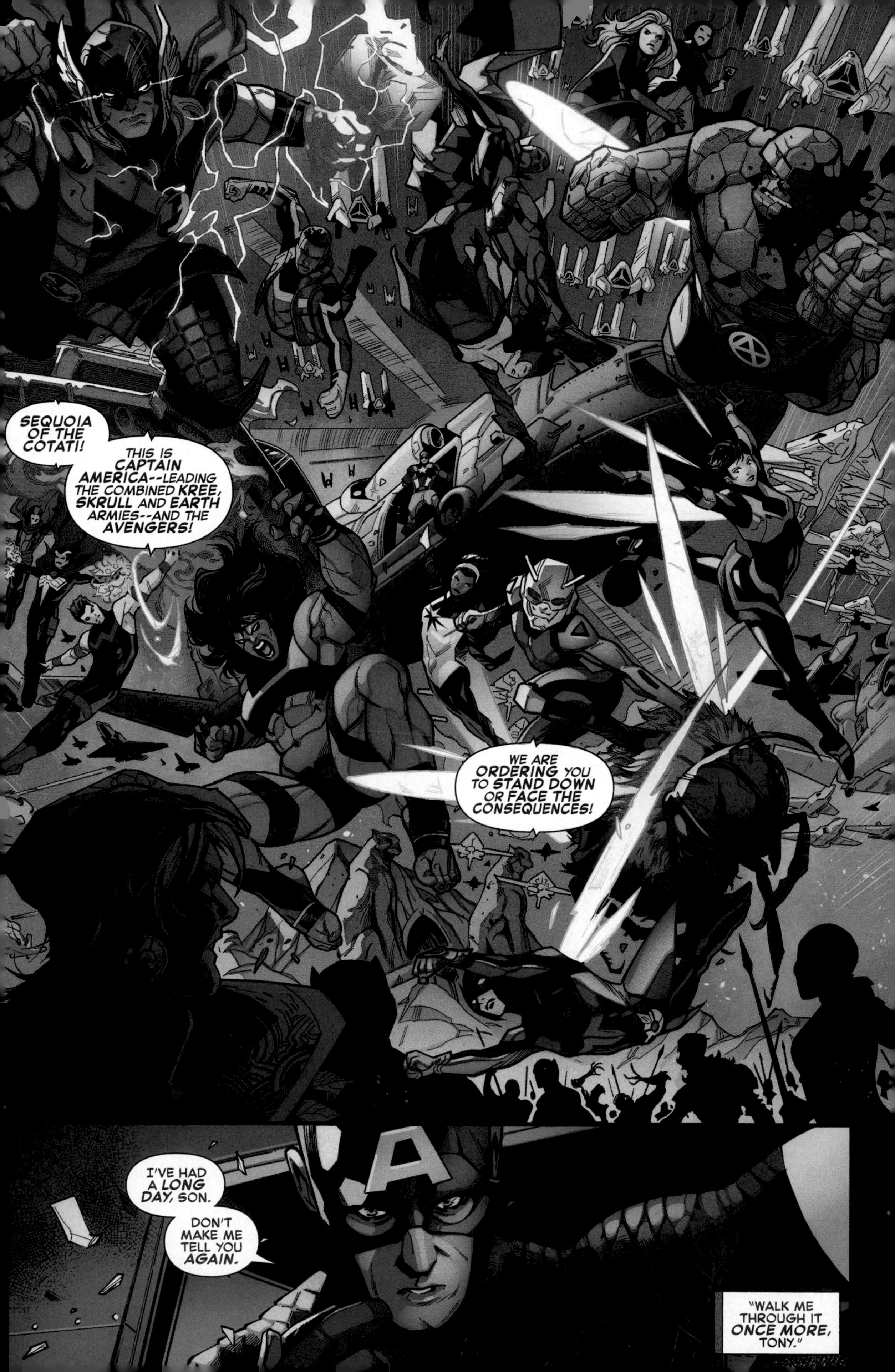

SEQUOIA OF THE COTATI!
THIS IS CAPTAIN AMERICA--LEADING THE COMBINED KREE, SKRULL AND EARTH ARMIES--AND THE AVENGERS!
WE ARE ORDERING YOU TO STAND DOWN OR FACE THE CONSEQUENCES!
I'VE HAD A LONG DAY, SON.
DON'T MAKE ME TELL YOU AGAIN.
"WALK ME THROUGH IT ONCE MORE, TONY."

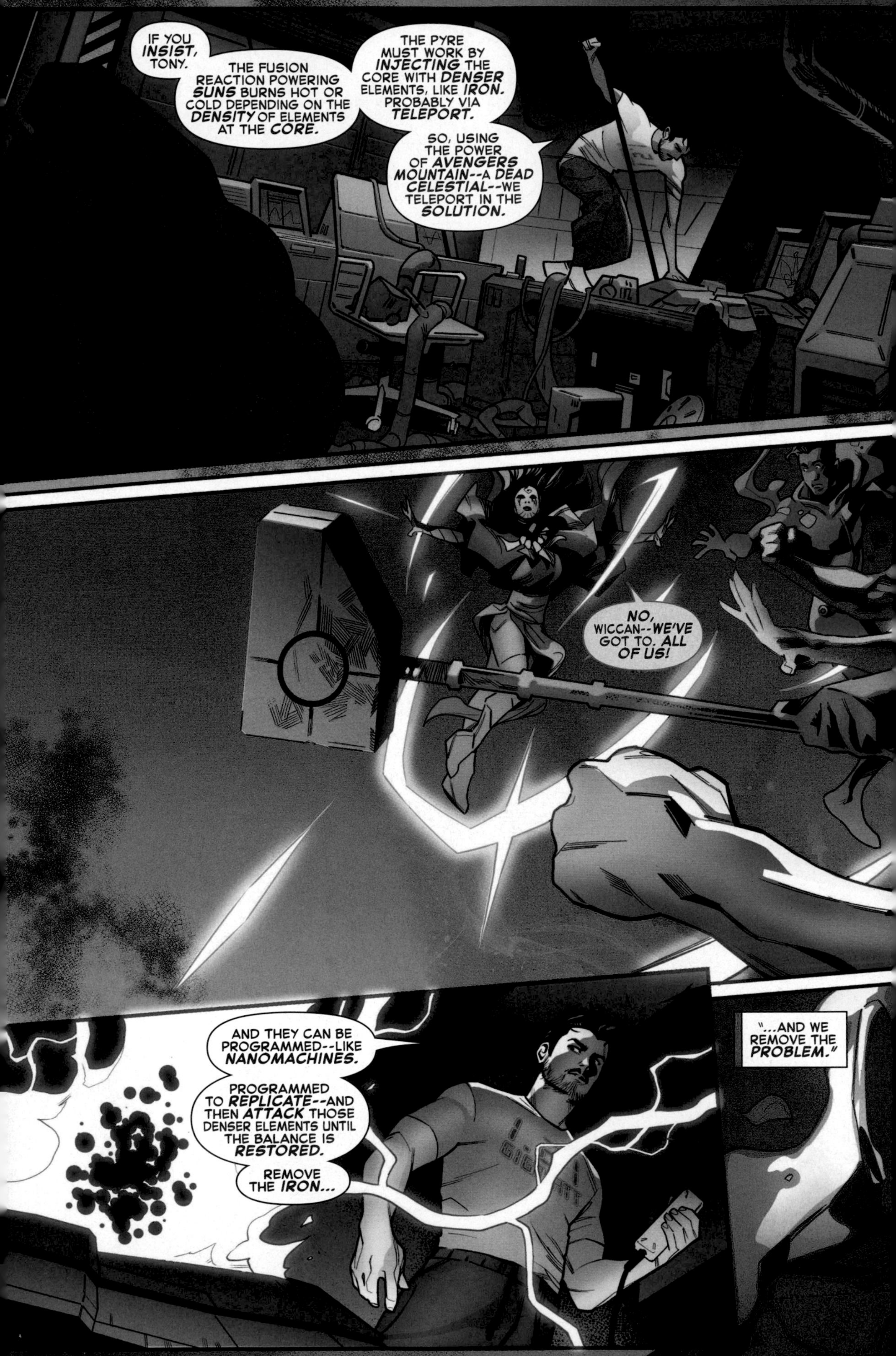
IF YOU INSIST, TONY.
THE FUSION REACTION POWERING SUNS BURNS HOT OR COLD DEPENDING ON THE DENSITY OF ELEMENTS AT THE CORE.
THE PYRE MUST WORK BY INJECTING THE CORE WITH DENSER ELEMENTS, LIKE IRON. PROBABLY VIA TELEPORT.
SO, USING THE POWER OF AVENGERS MOUNTAIN--A DEAD CELESTIAL--WE TELEPORT IN THE SOLUTION.
NO, WICCAN--WE'VE GOT TO. ALL OF US!
AND THEY CAN BE PROGRAMMED--LIKE NANOMACHINES.
PROGRAMMED TO REPLICATE--AND THEN ATTACK THOSE DENSER ELEMENTS UNTIL THE BALANCE IS RESTORED.
REMOVE THE IRON...
"...AND WE REMOVE THE PROBLEM."

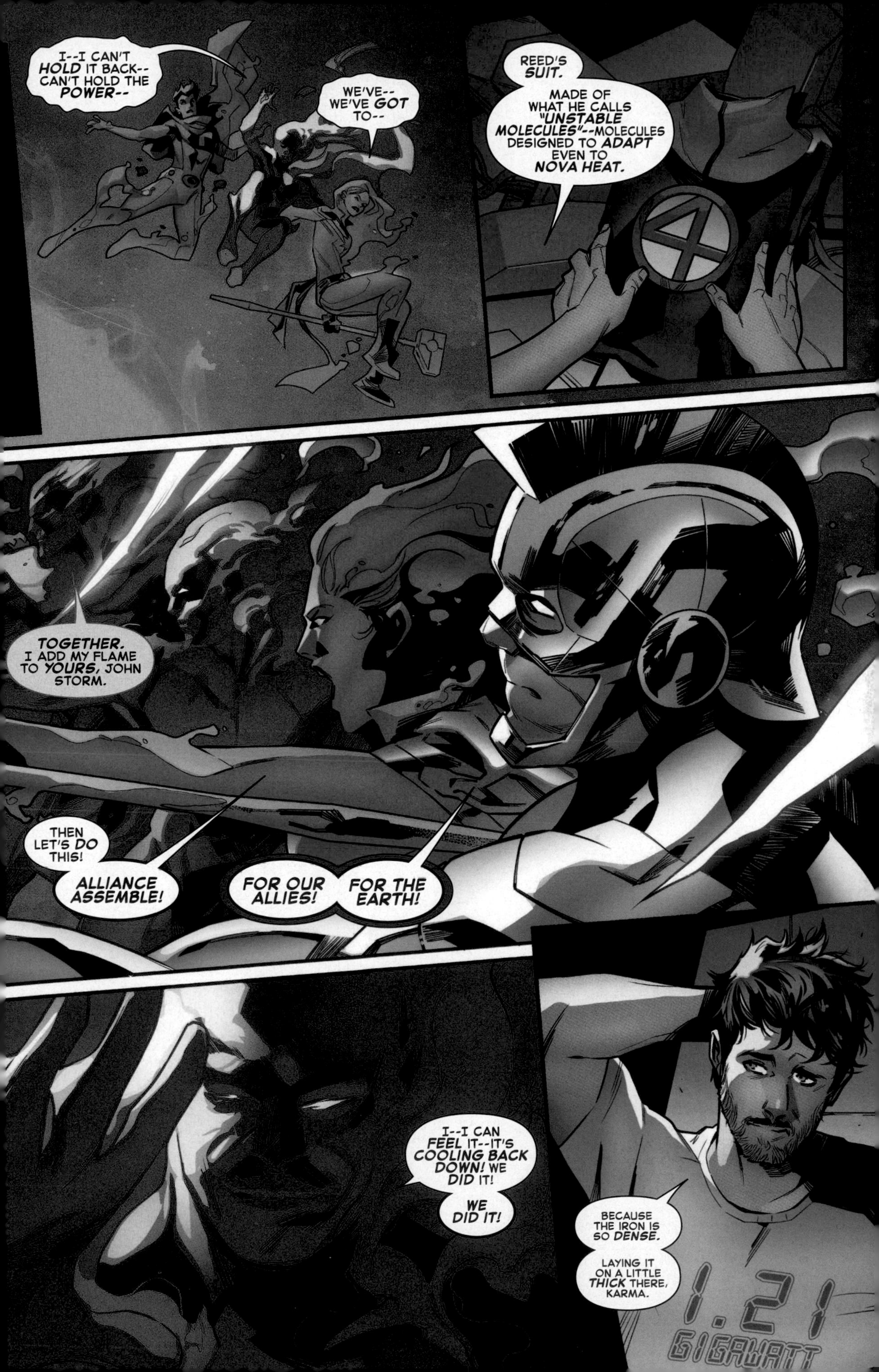
I--I CAN'T HOLD IT BACK-- CAN'T HOLD THE POWER--
WE'VE-- WE'VE GOT TO--
REED'S SUIT.
MADE OF WHAT HE CALLS "UNSTABLE MOLECULES"--MOLECULES DESIGNED TO ADAPT EVEN TO NOVA HEAT.
TOGETHER. I ADD MY FLAME TO YOURS, JOHN STORM.
THEN LET'S DO THIS!
ALLIANCE ASSEMBLE!
FOR OUR ALLIES!
FOR THE EARTH!
I--I CAN FEEL IT--IT'S COOLING BACK DOWN! WE DID IT!
WE DID IT!
BECAUSE THE IRON IS SO DENSE.
LAYING IT ON A LITTLE THICK THERE, KARMA.
1.21 GIGAWATT

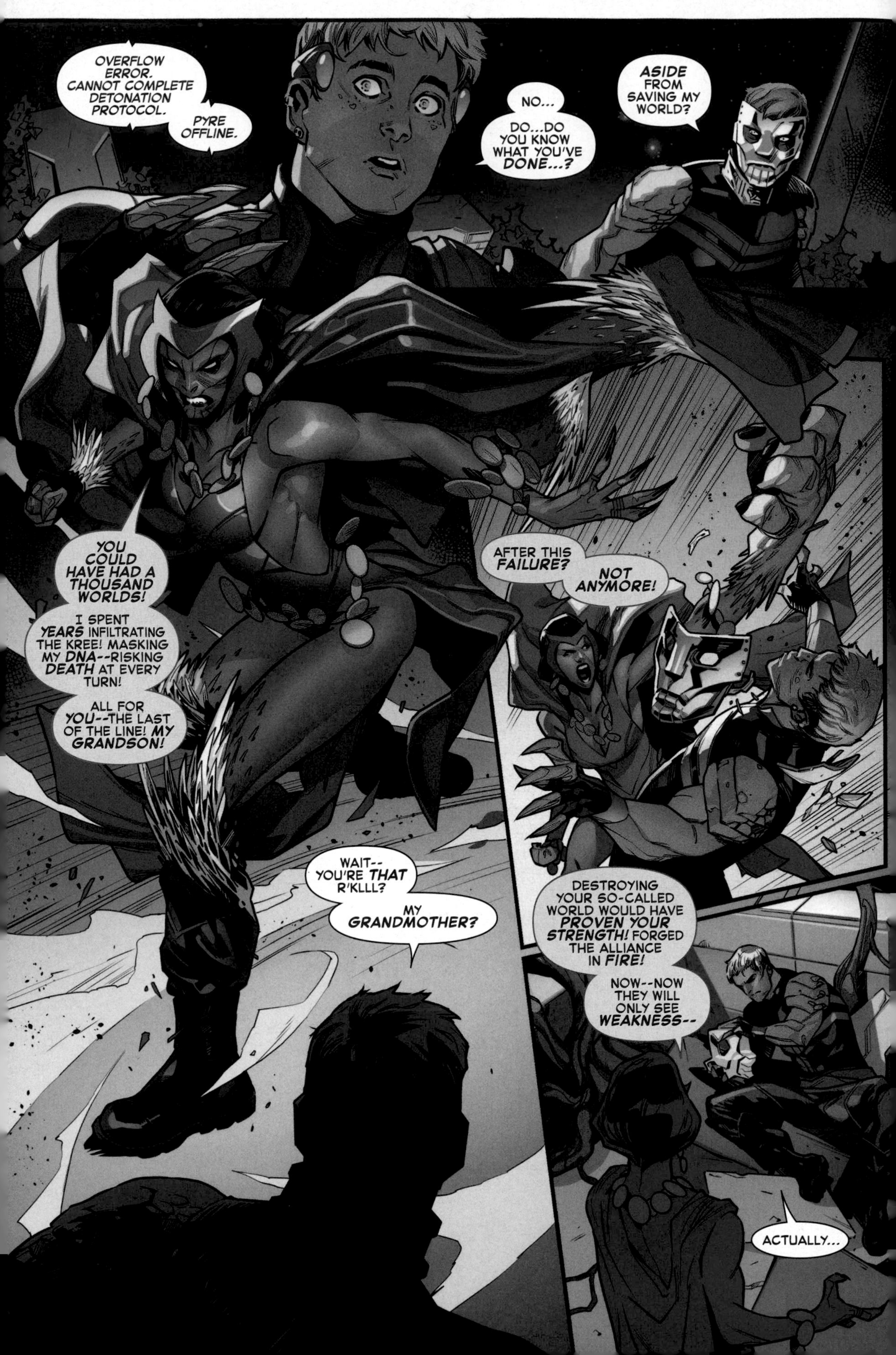

OVERFLOW ERROR. CANNOT COMPLETE DETONATION PROTOCOL.
PYRE OFFLINE.
NO...
DO...DO YOU KNOW WHAT YOU'VE DONE...?
ASIDE FROM SAVING MY WORLD?
YOU COULD HAVE HAD A THOUSAND WORLDS!
I SPENT YEARS INFILTRATING THE KREE! MASKING MY DNA--RISKING DEATH AT EVERY TURN!
ALL FOR YOU--THE LAST OF THE LINE! MY GRANDSON!
AFTER THIS FAILURE?
NOT ANYMORE!
WAIT--YOU'RE THAT R'KLLL?
MY GRANDMOTHER?
DESTROYING YOUR SO-CALLED WORLD WOULD HAVE PROVEN YOUR STRENGTH! FORGED THE ALLIANCE IN FIRE!
NOW--NOW THEY WILL ONLY SEE WEAKNESS--
ACTUALLY...

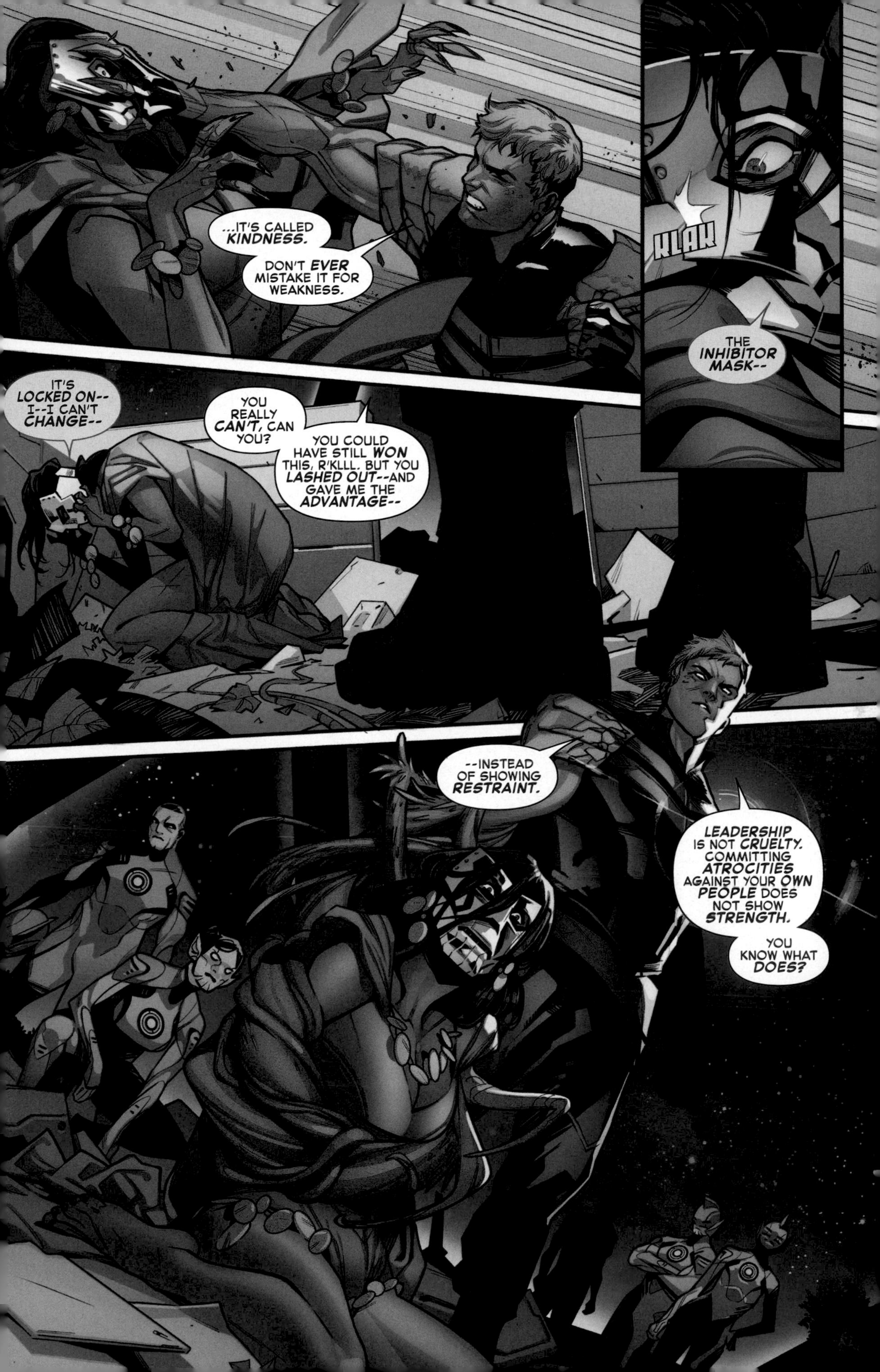
...IT'S CALLED KINDNESS.
DON'T EVER MISTAKE IT FOR WEAKNESS.
KLAK
THE INHIBITOR MASK--
IT'S LOCKED ON-- I--I CAN'T CHANGE--
YOU REALLY CAN'T, CAN YOU?
YOU COULD HAVE STILL WON THIS, R'KLLL. BUT YOU LASHED OUT--AND GAVE ME THE ADVANTAGE--
--INSTEAD OF SHOWING RESTRAINT.
LEADERSHIP IS NOT CRUELTY. COMMITTING ATROCITIES AGAINST YOUR OWN PEOPLE DOES NOT SHOW STRENGTH.
YOU KNOW WHAT DOES?

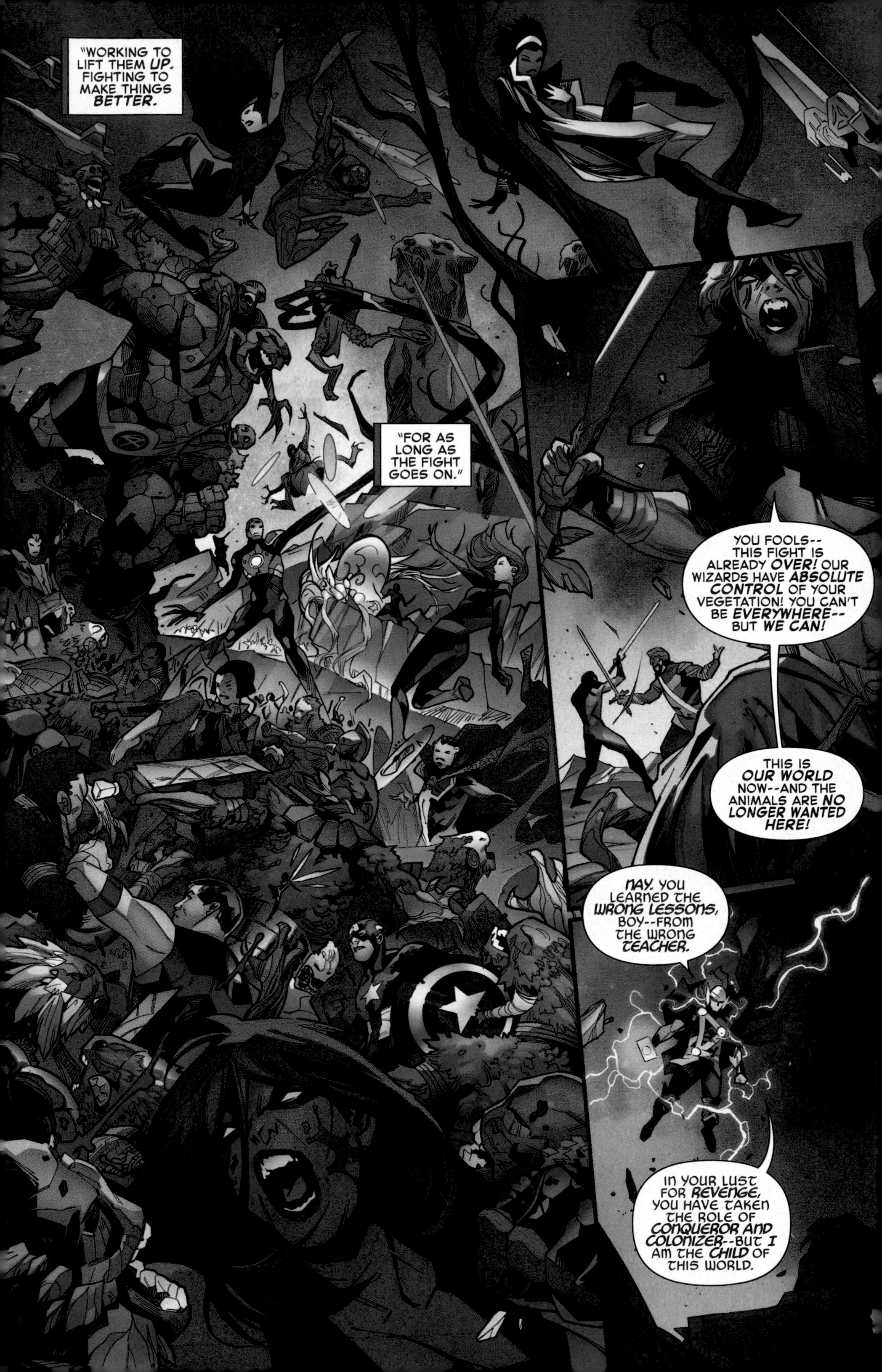

"WORKING TO LIFT THEM UP. FIGHTING TO MAKE THINGS BETTER.
"FOR AS LONG AS THE FIGHT GOES ON."
YOU FOOLS-- THIS FIGHT IS ALREADY OVER! OUR WIZARDS HAVE ABSOLUTE CONTROL OF YOUR VEGETATION! YOU CAN'T BE EVERYWHERE-- BUT WE CAN!
THIS IS OUR WORLD NOW--AND THE ANIMALS ARE NO LONGER WANTED HERE!
NAY. YOU LEARNED THE WRONG LESSONS, BOY--FROM THE WRONG TEACHER.
IN YOUR LUST FOR REVENGE, YOU HAVE TAKEN THE ROLE OF CONQUEROR AND COLONIZER--BUT I AM THE CHILD OF THIS WORLD.

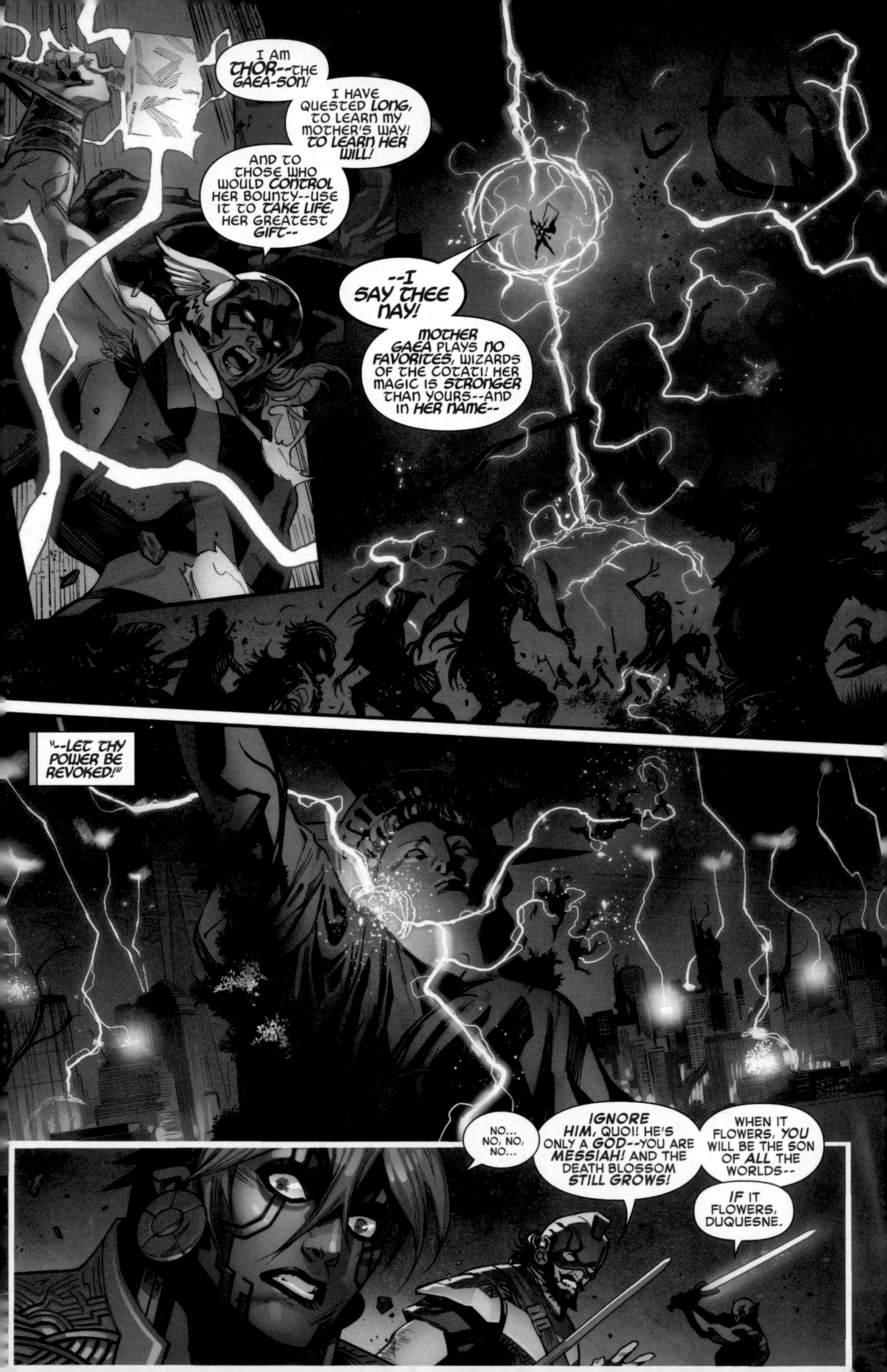
I AM THOR--THE GAEA-SON!
I HAVE QUESTED LONG, TO LEARN MY MOTHER'S WAY! TO LEARN HER WILL!
AND TO THOSE WHO WOULD CONTROL HER BOUNTY--USE IT TO TAKE LIFE, HER GREATEST GIFT--
--I SAY THEE NAY!
MOTHER GAEA PLAYS NO FAVORITES, WIZARDS OF THE COTATI! HER MAGIC IS STRONGER THAN YOURS--AND IN HER NAME--
"--LET THY POWER BE REVOKED!"
NO... NO, NO, NO...
IGNORE HIM, QUOI! HE'S ONLY A GOD--YOU ARE MESSIAH! AND THE DEATH BLOSSOM STILL GROWS!
WHEN IT FLOWERS, YOU WILL BE THE SON OF ALL THE WORLDS--
IF IT FLOWERS, DUQUESNE.

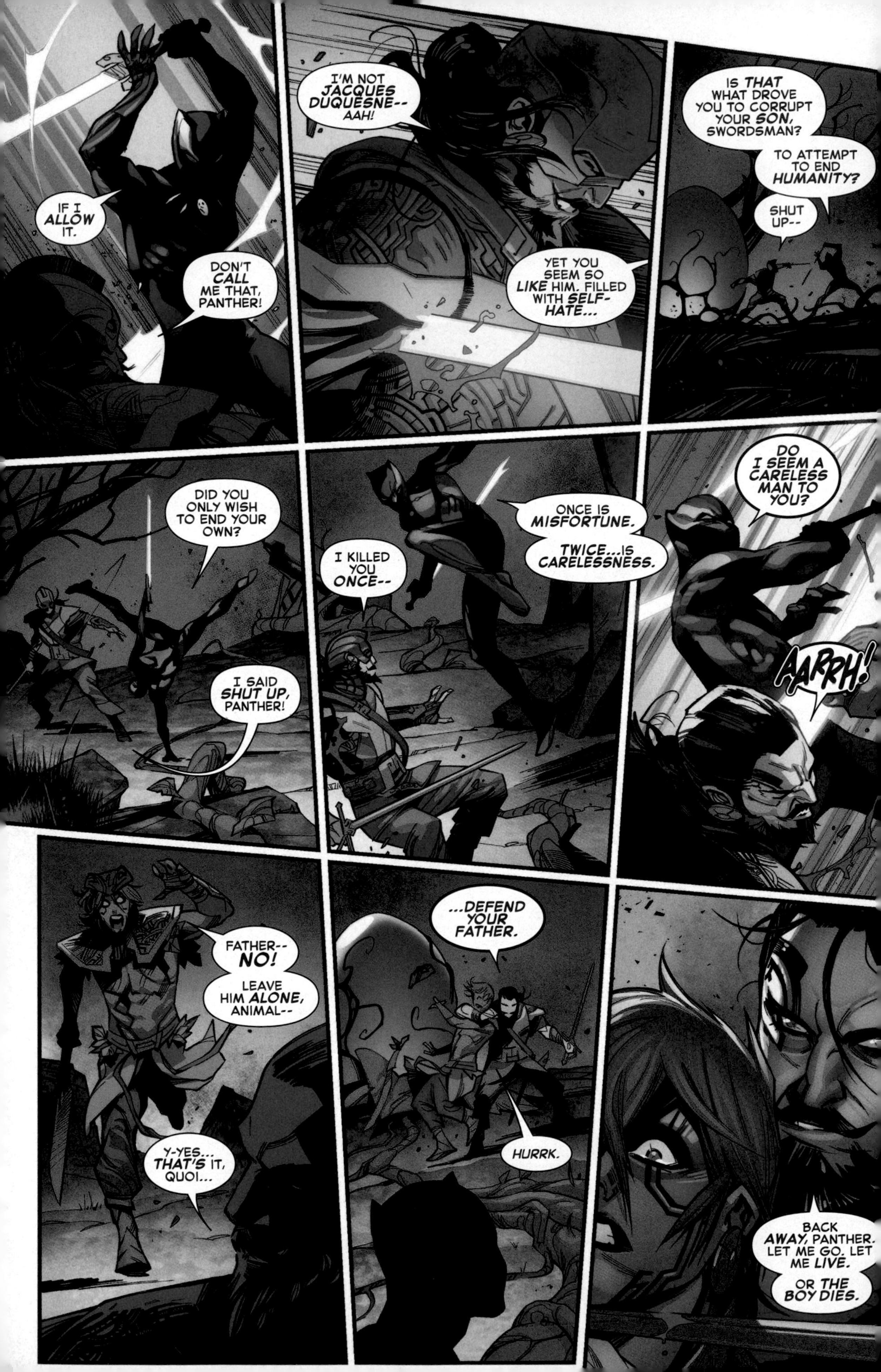
IF I ALLOW IT.
DON'T CALL ME THAT, PANTHER!
I'M NOT JACQUES DUQUESNE-- AAH!
YET YOU SEEM SO LIKE HIM. FILLED WITH SELF-HATE...
IS THAT WHAT DROVE YOU TO CORRUPT YOUR SON, SWORDSMAN?
TO ATTEMPT TO END HUMANITY?
SHUT UP--
DID YOU ONLY WISH TO END YOUR OWN?
I SAID SHUT UP, PANTHER!
I KILLED YOU ONCE--
ONCE IS MISFORTUNE.
TWICE...IS CARELESSNESS.
DO I SEEM A CARELESS MAN TO YOU?
AARRH!
FATHER-- NO!
LEAVE HIM ALONE, ANIMAL--
Y-YES... THAT'S IT, QUOI...
...DEFEND YOUR FATHER.
HURRK.
BACK AWAY, PANTHER. LET ME GO. LET ME LIVE.
OR THE BOY DIES.

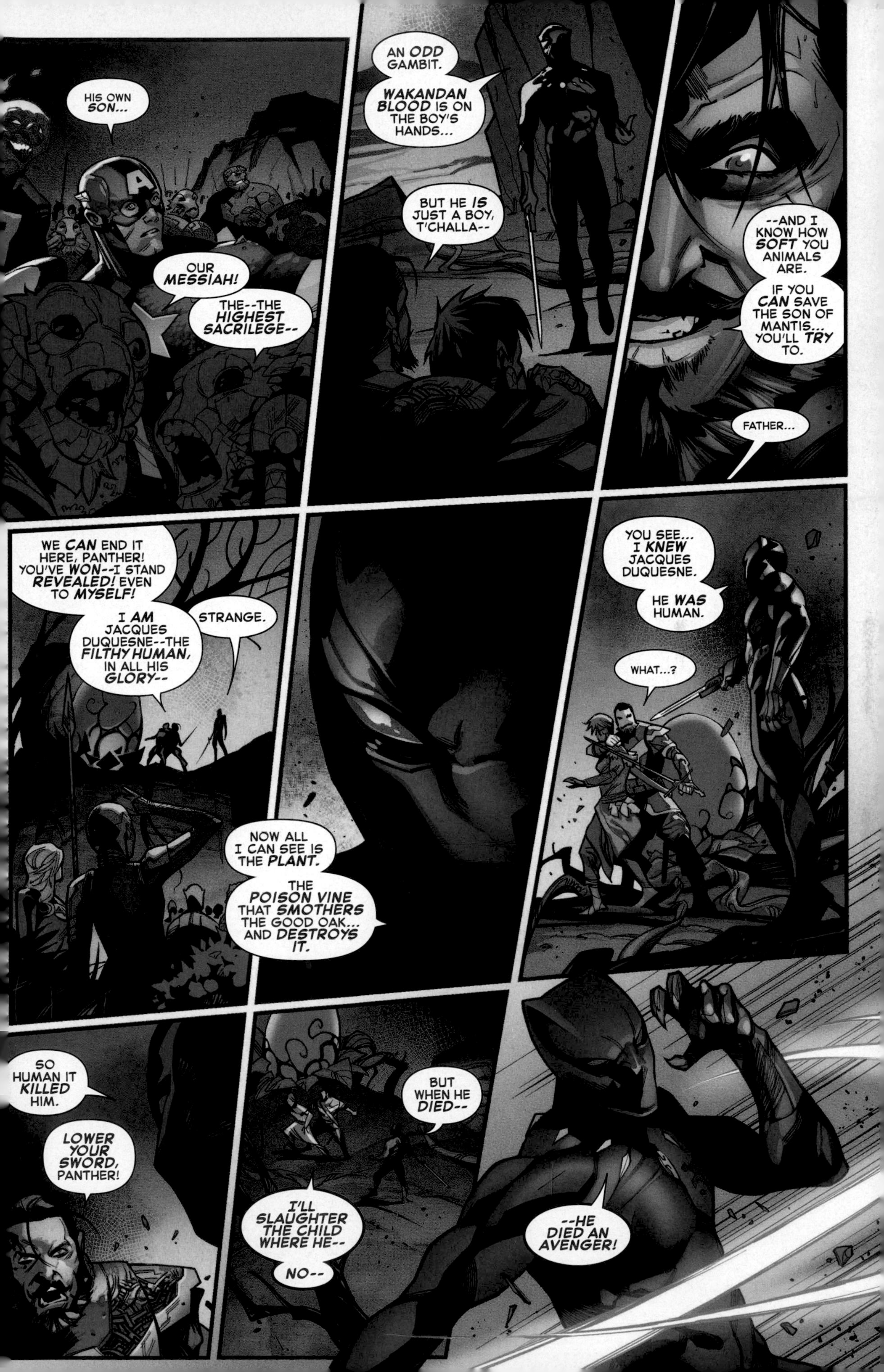
HIS OWN SON...
OUR MESSIAH!
THE--THE HIGHEST SACRILEGE--
AN ODD GAMBIT.
WAKANDAN BLOOD IS ON THE BOY'S HANDS...
BUT HE IS JUST A BOY, T'CHALLA--
--AND I KNOW HOW SOFT YOU ANIMALS ARE.
IF YOU CAN SAVE THE SON OF MANTIS... YOU'LL TRY TO.
FATHER...
WE CAN END IT HERE, PANTHER! YOU'VE WON--I STAND REVEALED! EVEN TO MYSELF!
I AM JACQUES DUQUESNE--THE FILTHY HUMAN, IN ALL HIS GLORY--
STRANGE.
NOW ALL I CAN SEE IS THE PLANT.
THE POISON VINE THAT SMOTHERS THE GOOD OAK... AND DESTROYS IT.
YOU SEE... I KNEW JACQUES DUQUESNE.
HE WAS HUMAN.
WHAT...?
SO HUMAN IT KILLED HIM.
LOWER YOUR SWORD, PANTHER!
BUT WHEN HE DIED--
I'LL SLAUGHTER THE CHILD WHERE HE--
NO--
--HE DIED AN AVENGER!

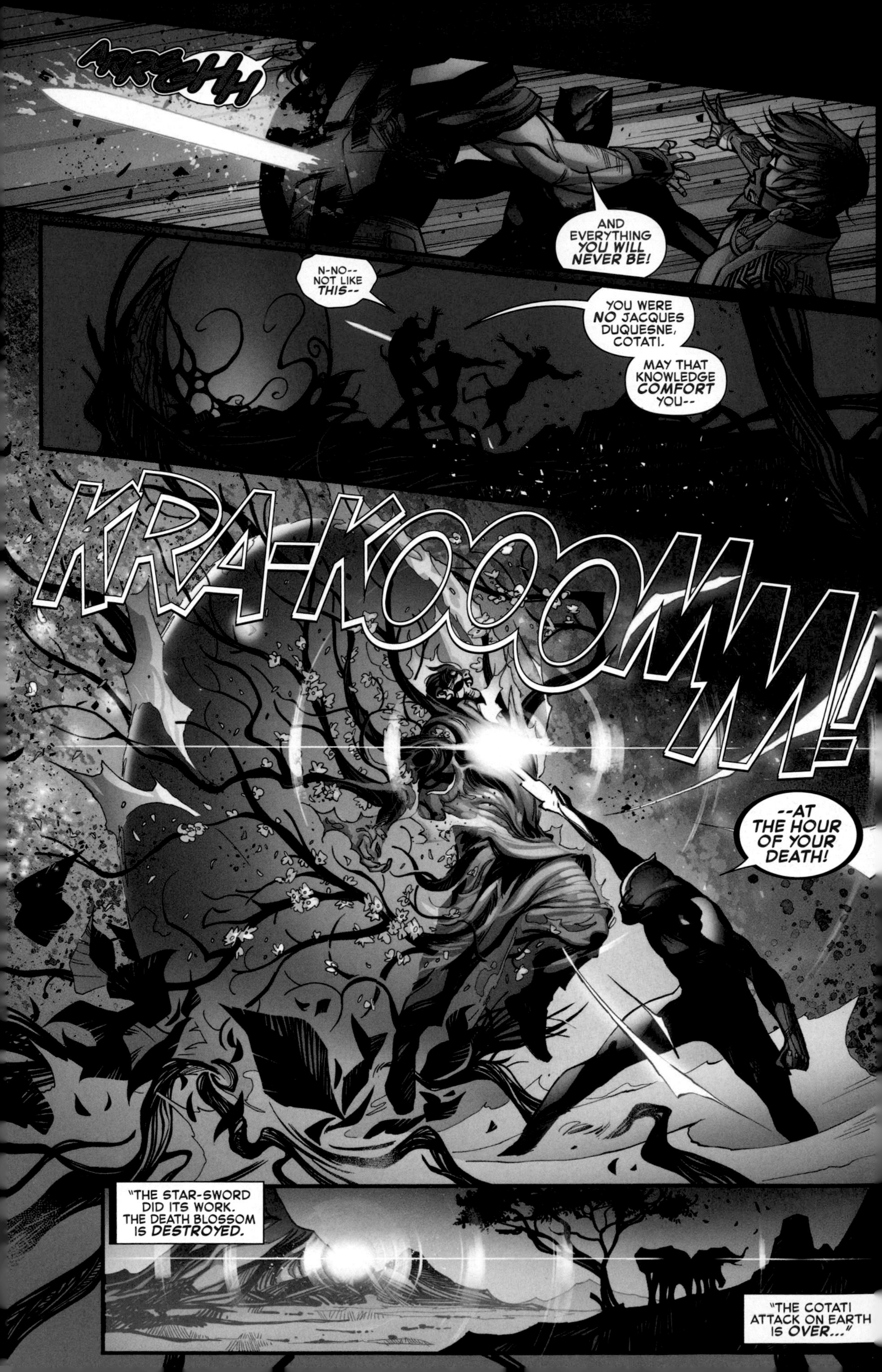
ARRGHH
AND EVERYTHING YOU WILL NEVER BE!
N-NO-- NOT LIKE THIS--
YOU WERE NO JACQUES DUQUESNE, COTATI.
MAY THAT KNOWLEDGE COMFORT YOU--
KRA-KOOOMM!!
--AT THE HOUR OF YOUR DEATH!
"THE STAR-SWORD DID ITS WORK. THE DEATH BLOSSOM IS DESTROYED.
"THE COTATI ATTACK ON EARTH IS OVER..."

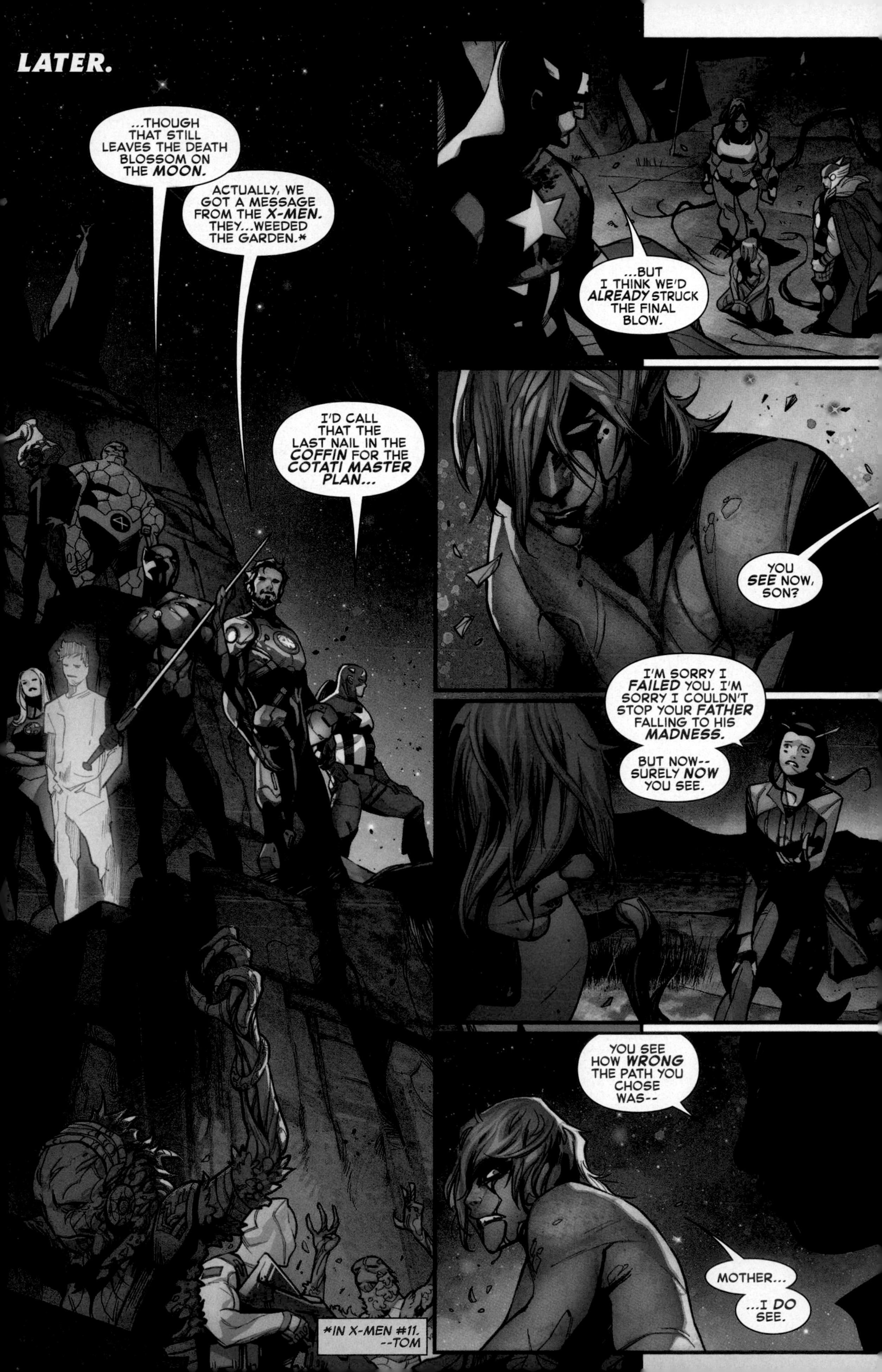
LATER.
...THOUGH THAT STILL LEAVES THE DEATH BLOSSOM ON THE MOON.
ACTUALLY, WE GOT A MESSAGE FROM THE X-MEN. THEY...WEEDED THE GARDEN.*
I'D CALL THAT THE LAST NAIL IN THE COFFIN FOR THE COTATI MASTER PLAN...
*IN X-MEN #11. --TOM
...BUT I THINK WE'D ALREADY STRUCK THE FINAL BLOW.
YOU SEE NOW, SON?
I'M SORRY I FAILED YOU. I'M SORRY I COULDN'T STOP YOUR FATHER FALLING TO HIS MADNESS.
BUT NOW-- SURELY NOW YOU SEE.
YOU SEE HOW WRONG THE PATH YOU CHOSE WAS--
MOTHER...
...I DO SEE.

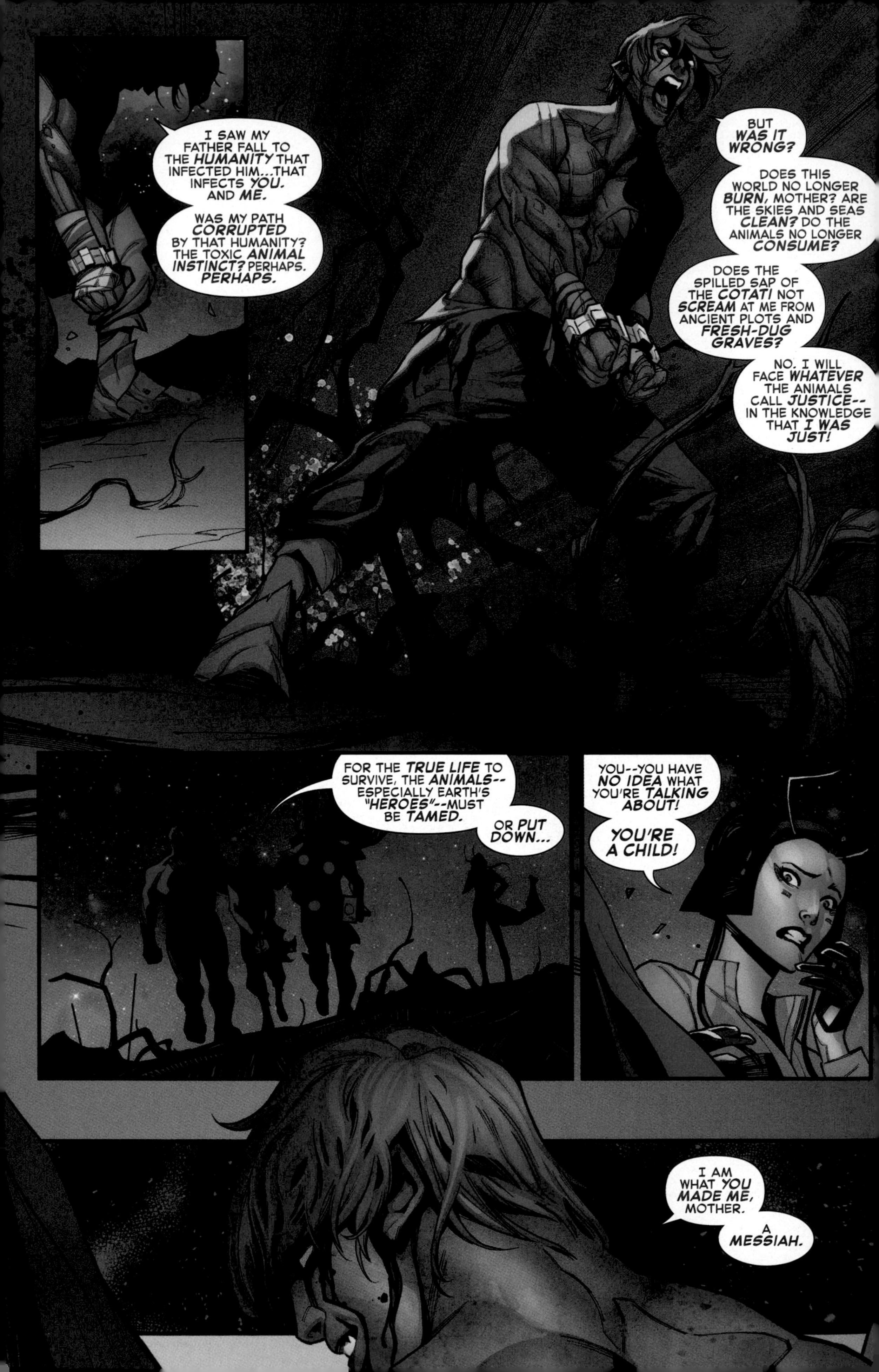
I SAW MY FATHER FALL TO THE HUMANITY THAT INFECTED HIM...THAT INFECTS YOU. AND ME.
WAS MY PATH CORRUPTED BY THAT HUMANITY? THE TOXIC ANIMAL INSTINCT? PERHAPS. PERHAPS.
BUT WAS IT WRONG?
DOES THIS WORLD NO LONGER BURN, MOTHER? ARE THE SKIES AND SEAS CLEAN? DO THE ANIMALS NO LONGER CONSUME?
DOES THE SPILLED SAP OF THE COTATI NOT SCREAM AT ME FROM ANCIENT PLOTS AND FRESH-DUG GRAVES?
NO. I WILL FACE WHATEVER THE ANIMALS CALL JUSTICE-- IN THE KNOWLEDGE THAT I WAS JUST!
FOR THE TRUE LIFE TO SURVIVE, THE ANIMALS-- ESPECIALLY EARTH'S "HEROES"--MUST BE TAMED.
OR PUT DOWN...
YOU--YOU HAVE NO IDEA WHAT YOU'RE TALKING ABOUT!
YOU'RE A CHILD!
I AM WHAT YOU MADE ME, MOTHER.
A MESSIAH.

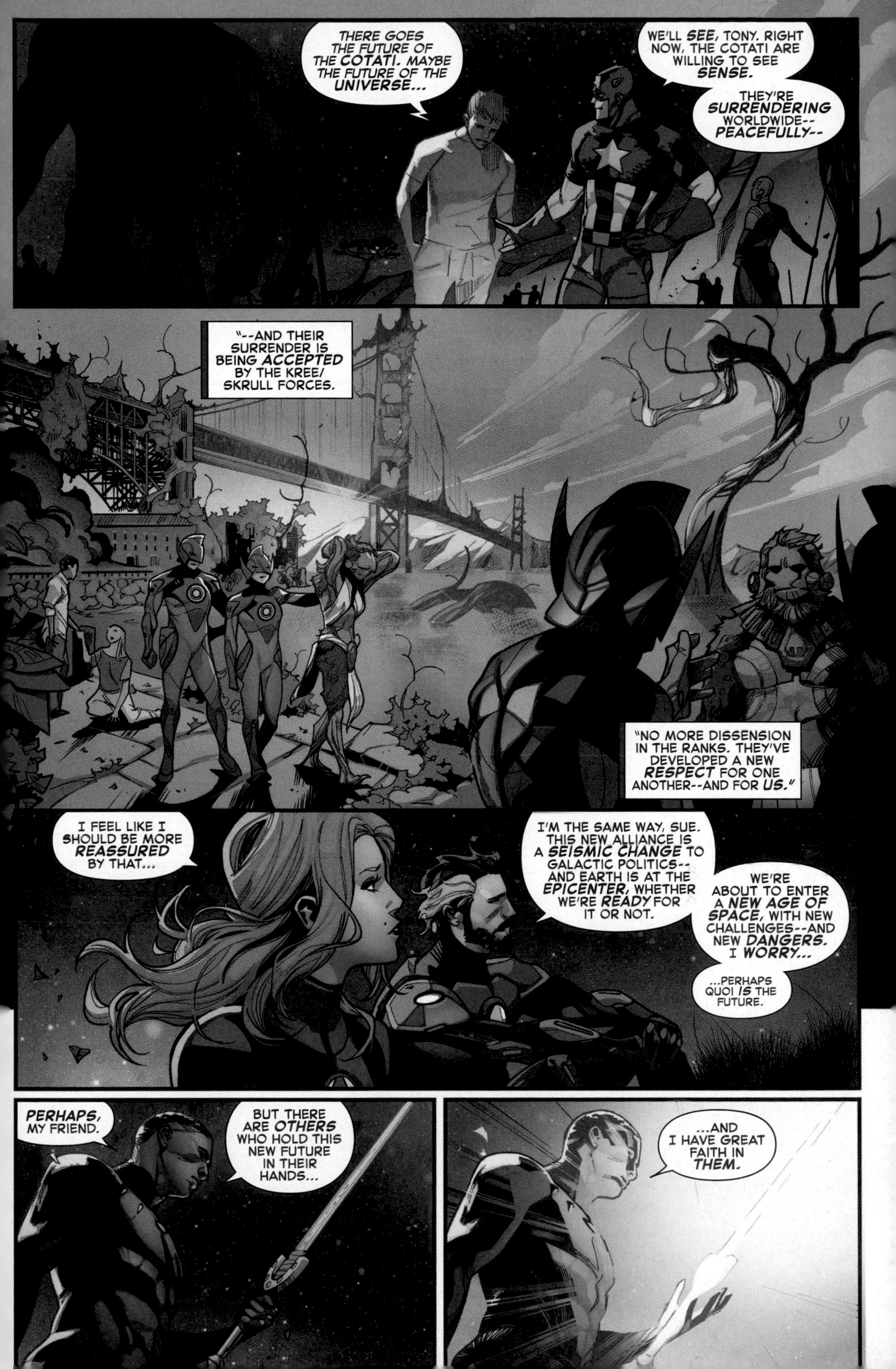
THERE GOES THE FUTURE OF THE COTATI. MAYBE THE FUTURE OF THE UNIVERSE...
WE'LL SEE, TONY. RIGHT NOW, THE COTATI ARE WILLING TO SEE SENSE.
THEY'RE SURRENDERING WORLDWIDE--PEACEFULLY--
"--AND THEIR SURRENDER IS BEING ACCEPTED BY THE KREE/SKRULL FORCES.
"NO MORE DISSENSION IN THE RANKS. THEY'VE DEVELOPED A NEW RESPECT FOR ONE ANOTHER--AND FOR US."
I FEEL LIKE I SHOULD BE MORE REASSURED BY THAT...
I'M THE SAME WAY, SUE. THIS NEW ALLIANCE IS A SEISMIC CHANGE TO GALACTIC POLITICS--AND EARTH IS AT THE EPICENTER, WHETHER WE'RE READY FOR IT OR NOT.
WE'RE ABOUT TO ENTER A NEW AGE OF SPACE, WITH NEW CHALLENGES--AND NEW DANGERS. I WORRY...
...PERHAPS QUOI IS THE FUTURE.
PERHAPS, MY FRIEND.
BUT THERE ARE OTHERS WHO HOLD THIS NEW FUTURE IN THEIR HANDS...
...AND I HAVE GREAT FAITH IN THEM.

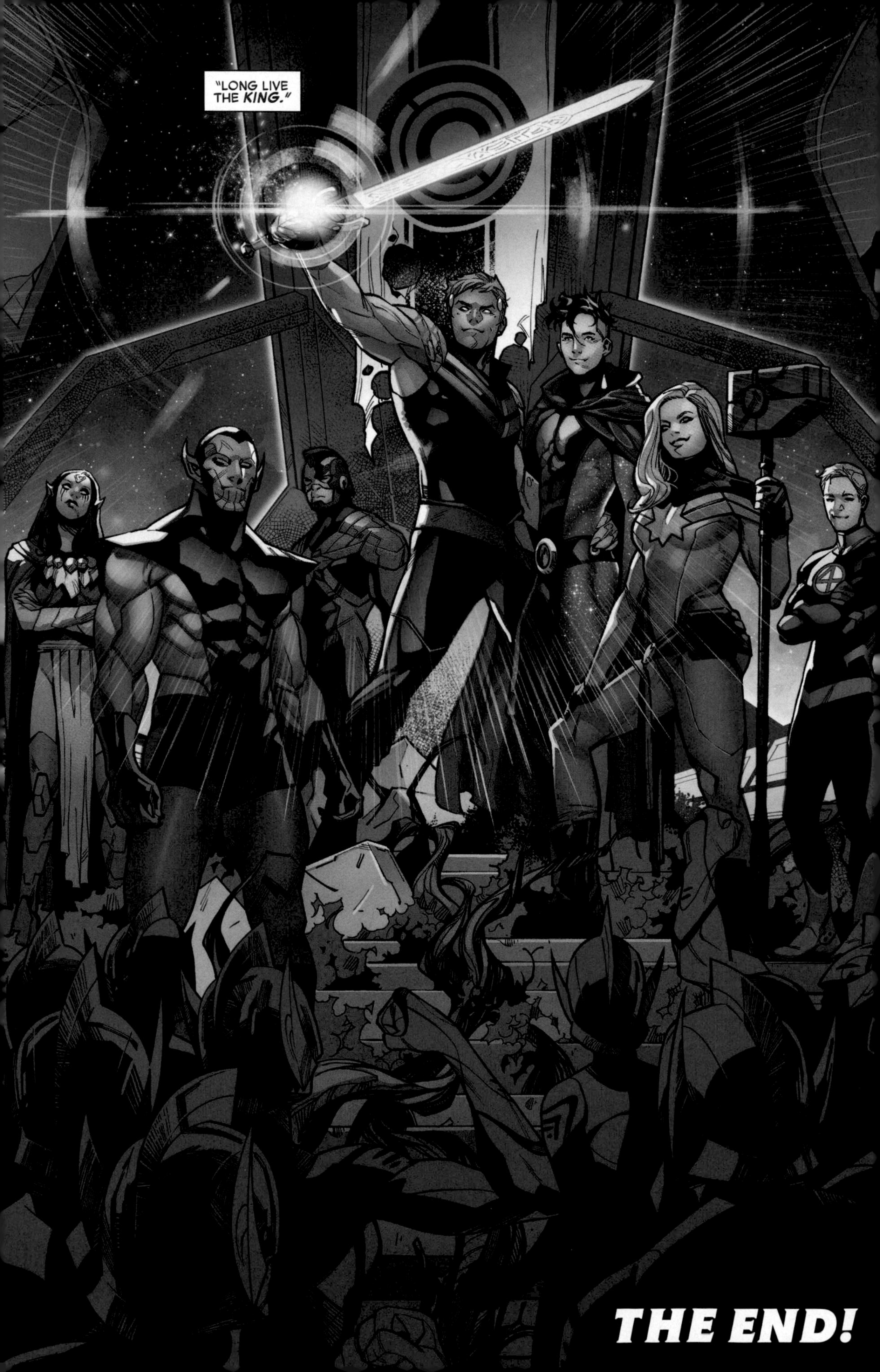
"LONG LIVE THE KING."
THE END!

EMPYRE: AFTERMATH — AVENGERS
SECRET VARIANT BY
Jim Cheung & **Marcelo Maiolo**

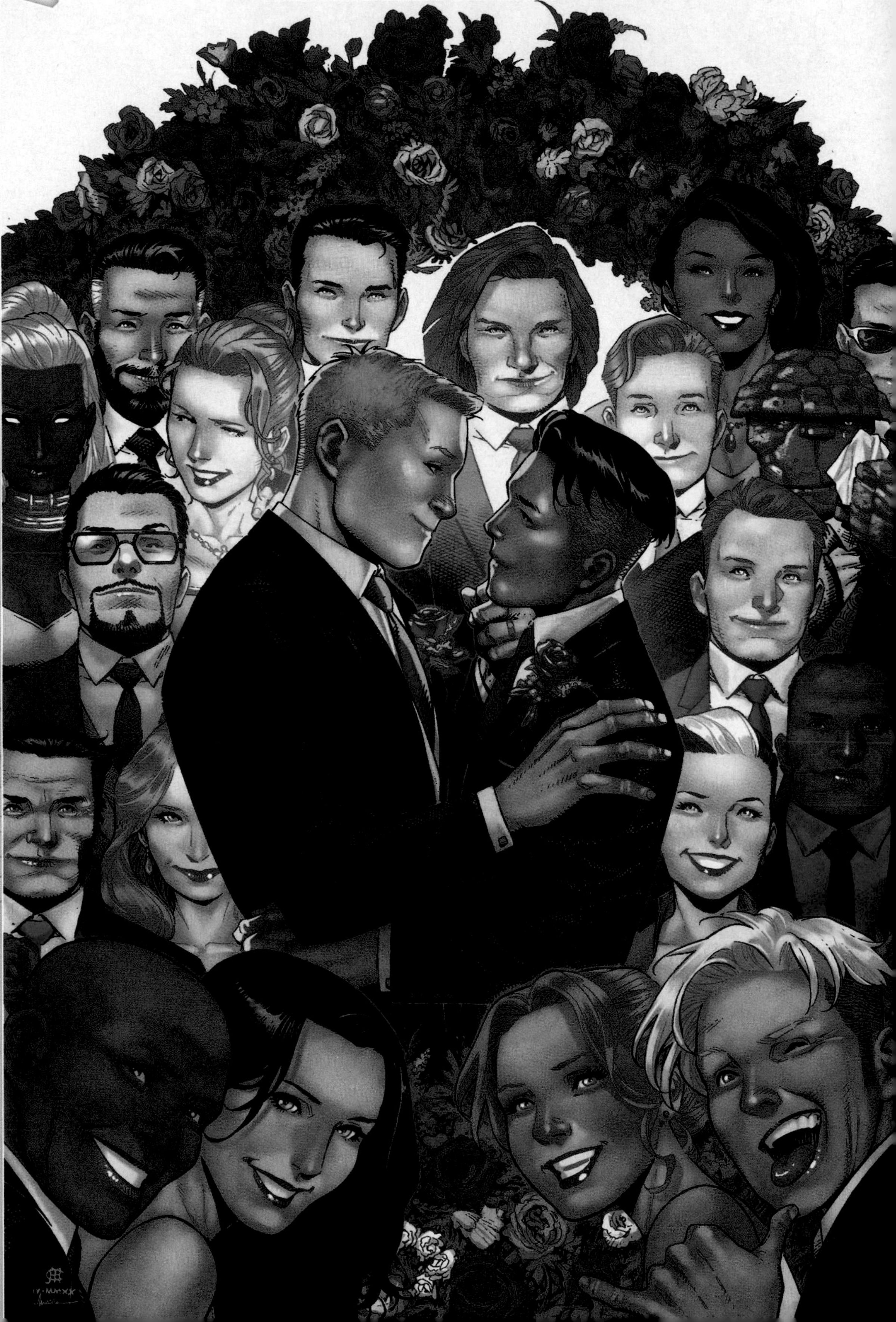

EMPYRE: AFTERMATH – AVENGERS

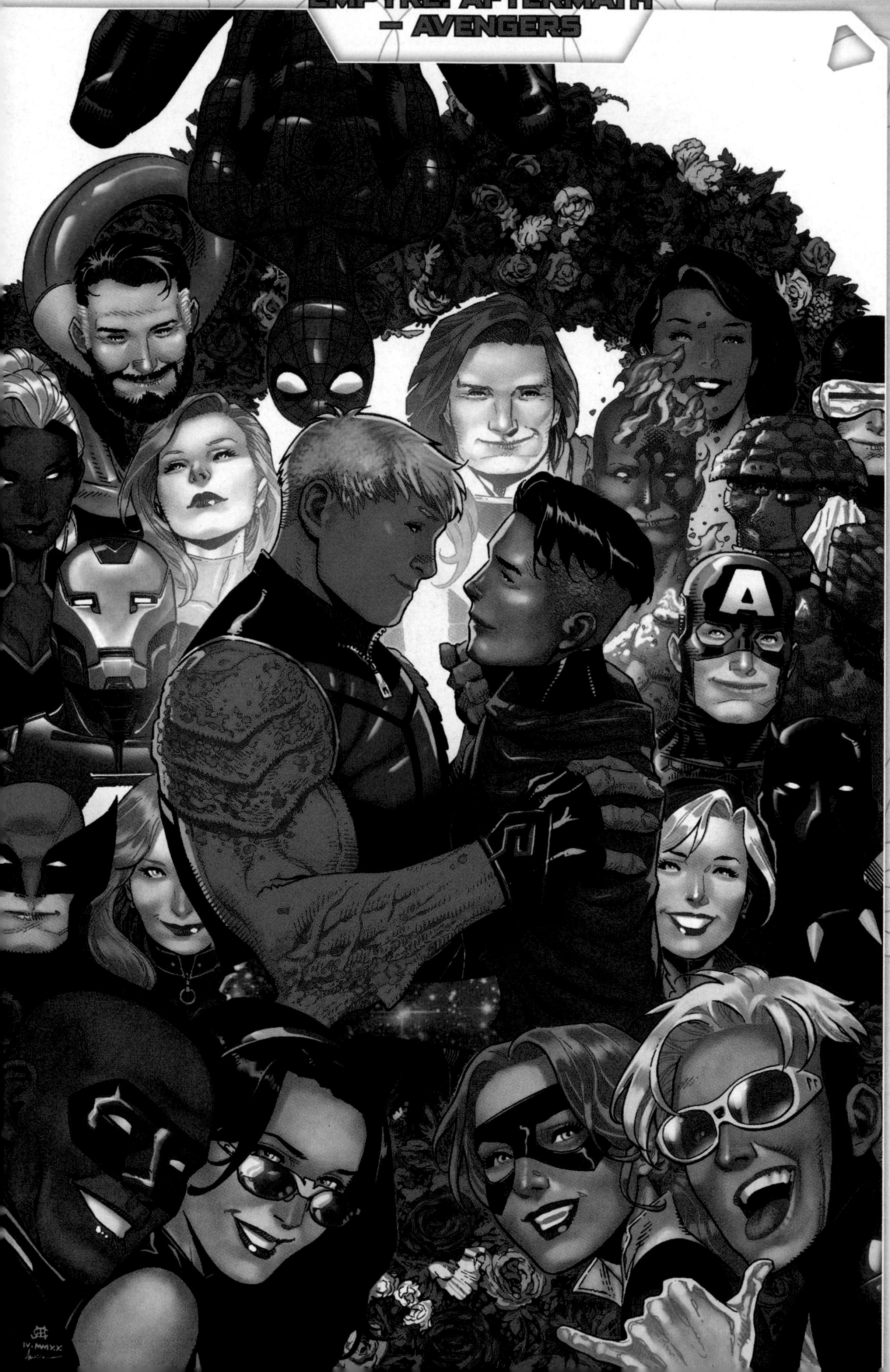

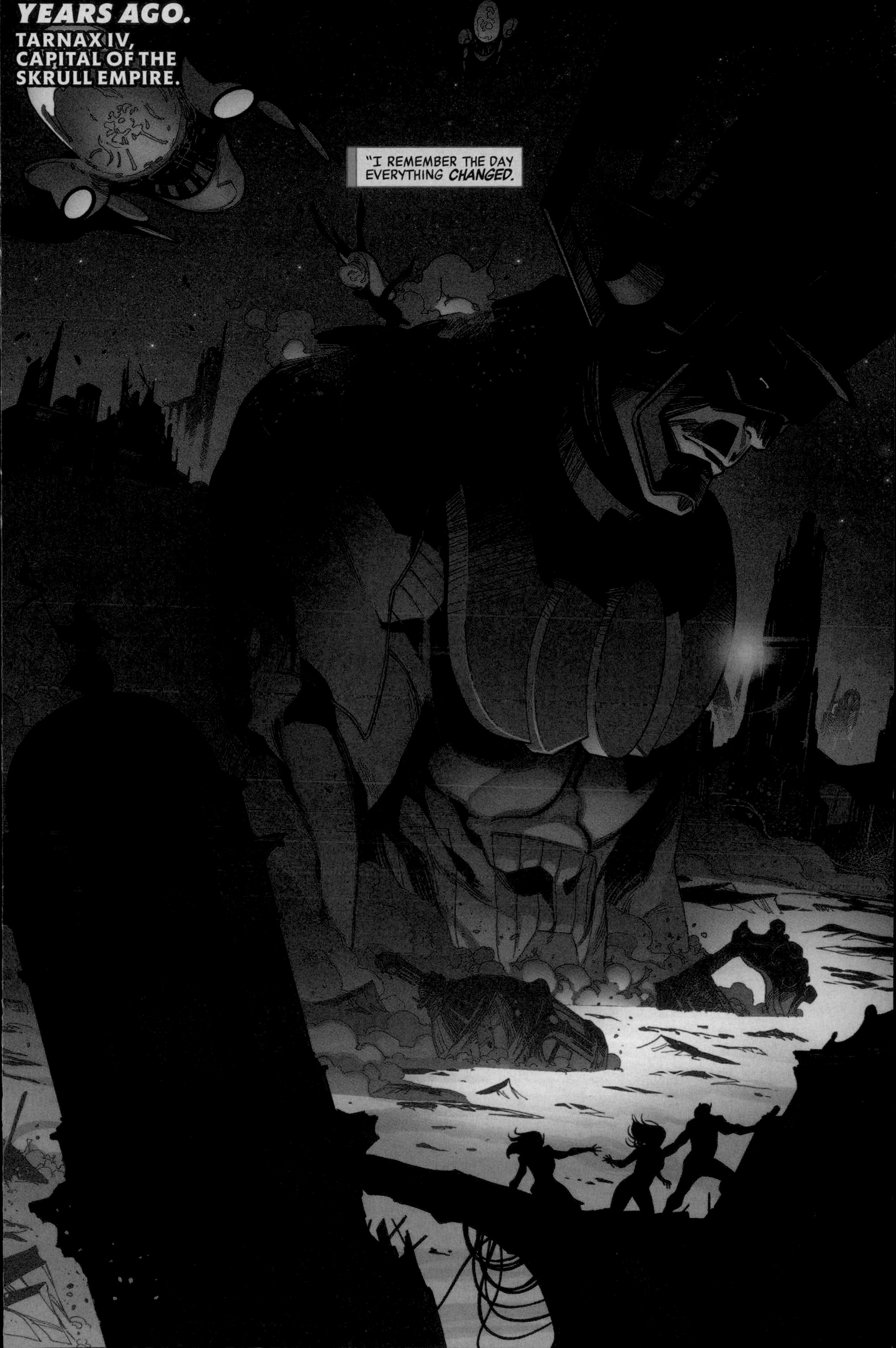
YEARS AGO.
TARNAX IV, CAPITAL OF THE SKRULL EMPIRE.
"I REMEMBER THE DAY EVERYTHING CHANGED.

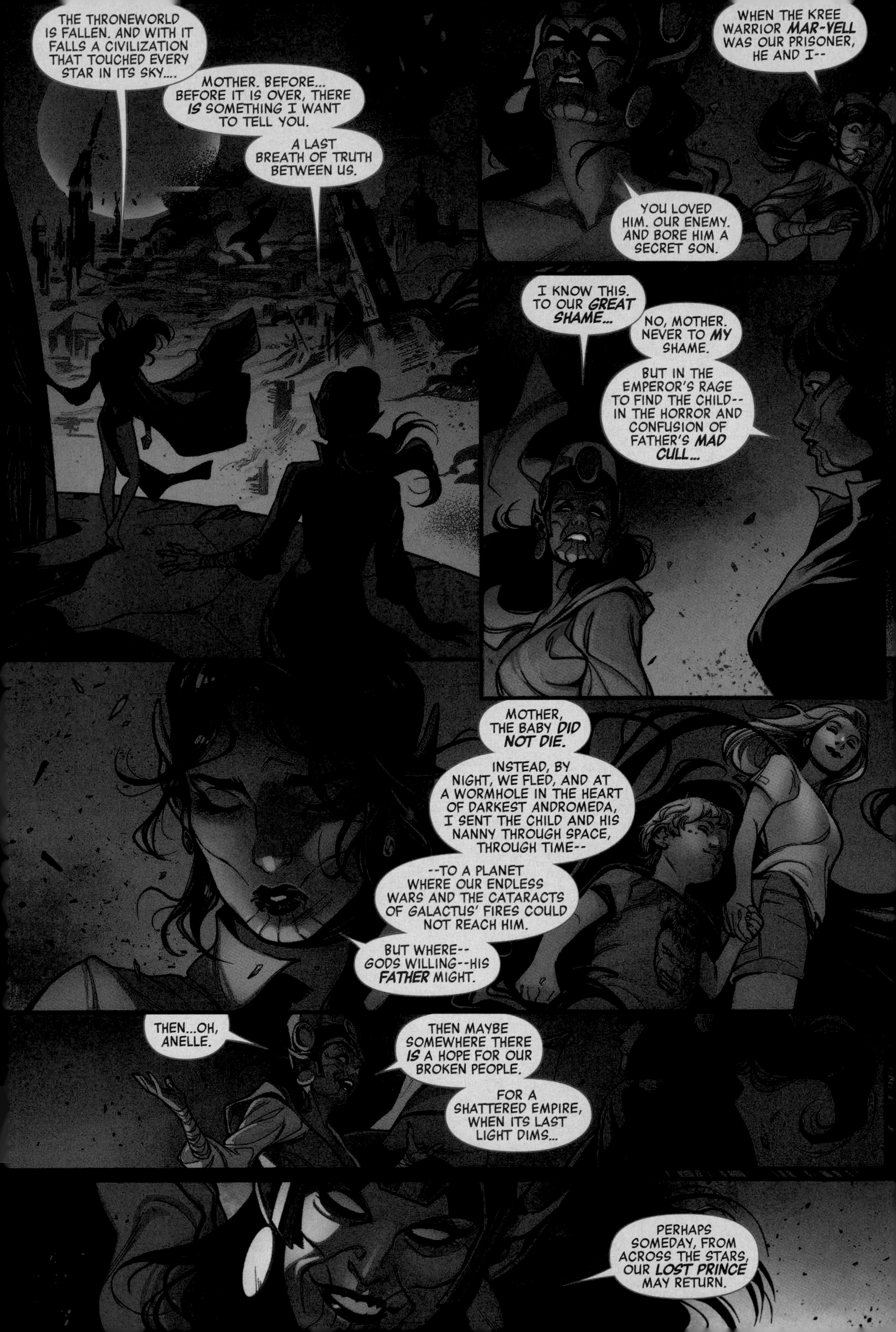
THE THRONEWORLD IS FALLEN. AND WITH IT FALLS A CIVILIZATION THAT TOUCHED EVERY STAR IN ITS SKY....
MOTHER. BEFORE... BEFORE IT IS OVER, THERE *IS* SOMETHING I WANT TO TELL YOU.
A LAST BREATH OF TRUTH BETWEEN US.
WHEN THE KREE WARRIOR **MAR-VELL** WAS OUR PRISONER, HE AND I--
YOU LOVED HIM. OUR ENEMY. AND BORE HIM A SECRET SON.
I KNOW THIS. TO OUR ***GREAT SHAME...***
NO, MOTHER. NEVER TO ***MY*** SHAME.
BUT IN THE EMPEROR'S RAGE TO FIND THE CHILD-- IN THE HORROR AND CONFUSION OF FATHER'S ***MAD CULL...***
MOTHER, THE BABY ***DID NOT DIE.***
INSTEAD, BY NIGHT, WE FLED, AND AT A WORMHOLE IN THE HEART OF DARKEST ANDROMEDA, I SENT THE CHILD AND HIS NANNY THROUGH SPACE, THROUGH TIME--
--TO A PLANET WHERE OUR ENDLESS WARS AND THE CATARACTS OF GALACTUS' FIRES COULD NOT REACH HIM.
BUT WHERE-- GODS WILLING--HIS ***FATHER*** MIGHT.
THEN...OH, ANELLE.
THEN MAYBE SOMEWHERE THERE ***IS*** A HOPE FOR OUR BROKEN PEOPLE.
FOR A SHATTERED EMPIRE, WHEN ITS LAST LIGHT DIMS...
PERHAPS SOMEDAY, FROM ACROSS THE STARS, OUR ***LOST PRINCE*** MAY RETURN.

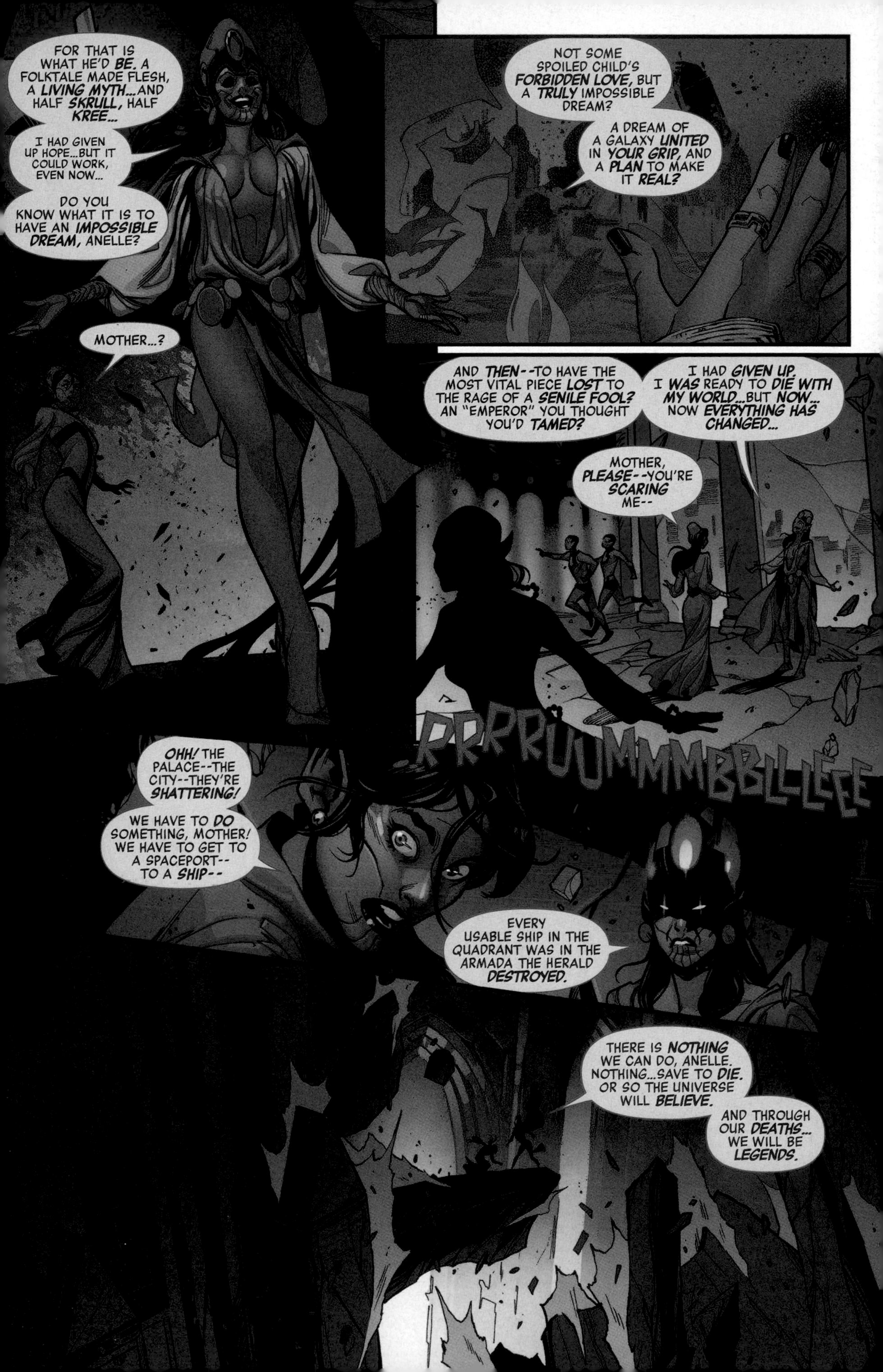
FOR THAT IS WHAT HE'D BE. A FOLKTALE MADE FLESH, A LIVING MYTH...AND HALF SKRULL, HALF KREE...
I HAD GIVEN UP HOPE...BUT IT COULD WORK, EVEN NOW...
DO YOU KNOW WHAT IT IS TO HAVE AN IMPOSSIBLE DREAM, ANELLE?
NOT SOME SPOILED CHILD'S FORBIDDEN LOVE, BUT A TRULY IMPOSSIBLE DREAM?
A DREAM OF A GALAXY UNITED IN YOUR GRIP, AND A PLAN TO MAKE IT REAL?
MOTHER...?
AND THEN--TO HAVE THE MOST VITAL PIECE LOST TO THE RAGE OF A SENILE FOOL? AN "EMPEROR" YOU THOUGHT YOU'D TAMED?
I HAD GIVEN UP. I WAS READY TO DIE WITH MY WORLD...BUT NOW... NOW EVERYTHING HAS CHANGED...
MOTHER, PLEASE--YOU'RE SCARING ME--
RRRRUUMMMBBLLLEEE
OHH! THE PALACE--THE CITY--THEY'RE SHATTERING!
WE HAVE TO DO SOMETHING, MOTHER! WE HAVE TO GET TO A SPACEPORT--TO A SHIP--
EVERY USABLE SHIP IN THE QUADRANT WAS IN THE ARMADA THE HERALD DESTROYED.
THERE IS NOTHING WE CAN DO, ANELLE. NOTHING...SAVE TO DIE. OR SO THE UNIVERSE WILL BELIEVE.
AND THROUGH OUR DEATHS... WE WILL BE LEGENDS.

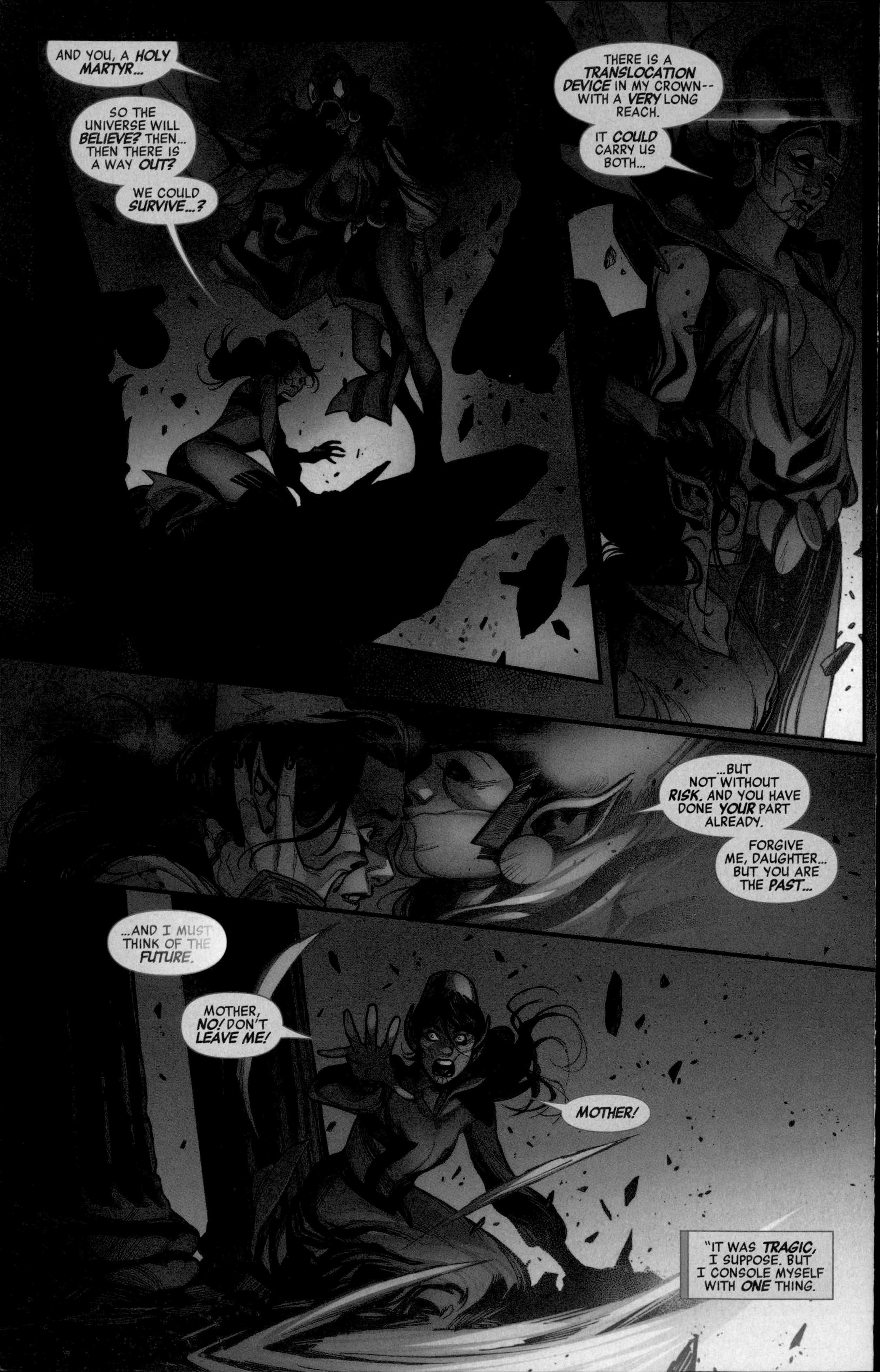
AND YOU, A HOLY MARTYR...
SO THE UNIVERSE WILL BELIEVE? THEN... THEN THERE IS A WAY OUT?
WE COULD SURVIVE...?
THERE IS A TRANSLOCATION DEVICE IN MY CROWN-- WITH A VERY LONG REACH.
IT COULD CARRY US BOTH...
...BUT NOT WITHOUT RISK. AND YOU HAVE DONE YOUR PART ALREADY.
FORGIVE ME, DAUGHTER... BUT YOU ARE THE PAST...
...AND I MUST THINK OF THE FUTURE.
MOTHER, NO! DON'T LEAVE ME!
MOTHER!
"IT WAS TRAGIC, I SUPPOSE. BUT I CONSOLE MYSELF WITH ONE THING.

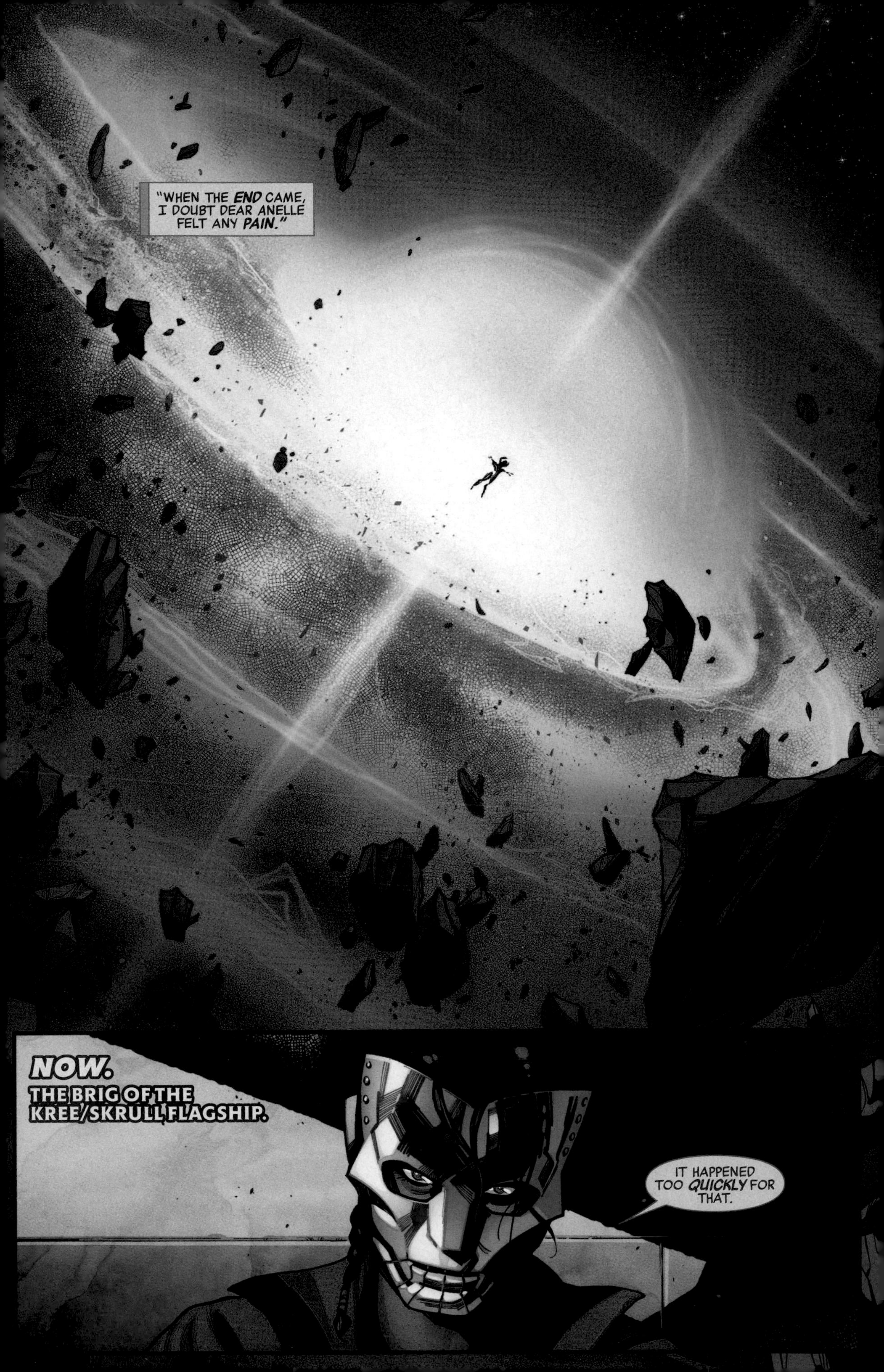
"WHEN THE END CAME, I DOUBT DEAR ANELLE FELT ANY PAIN."
NOW.
THE BRIG OF THE KREE/SKRULL FLAGSHIP.
IT HAPPENED TOO QUICKLY FOR THAT.

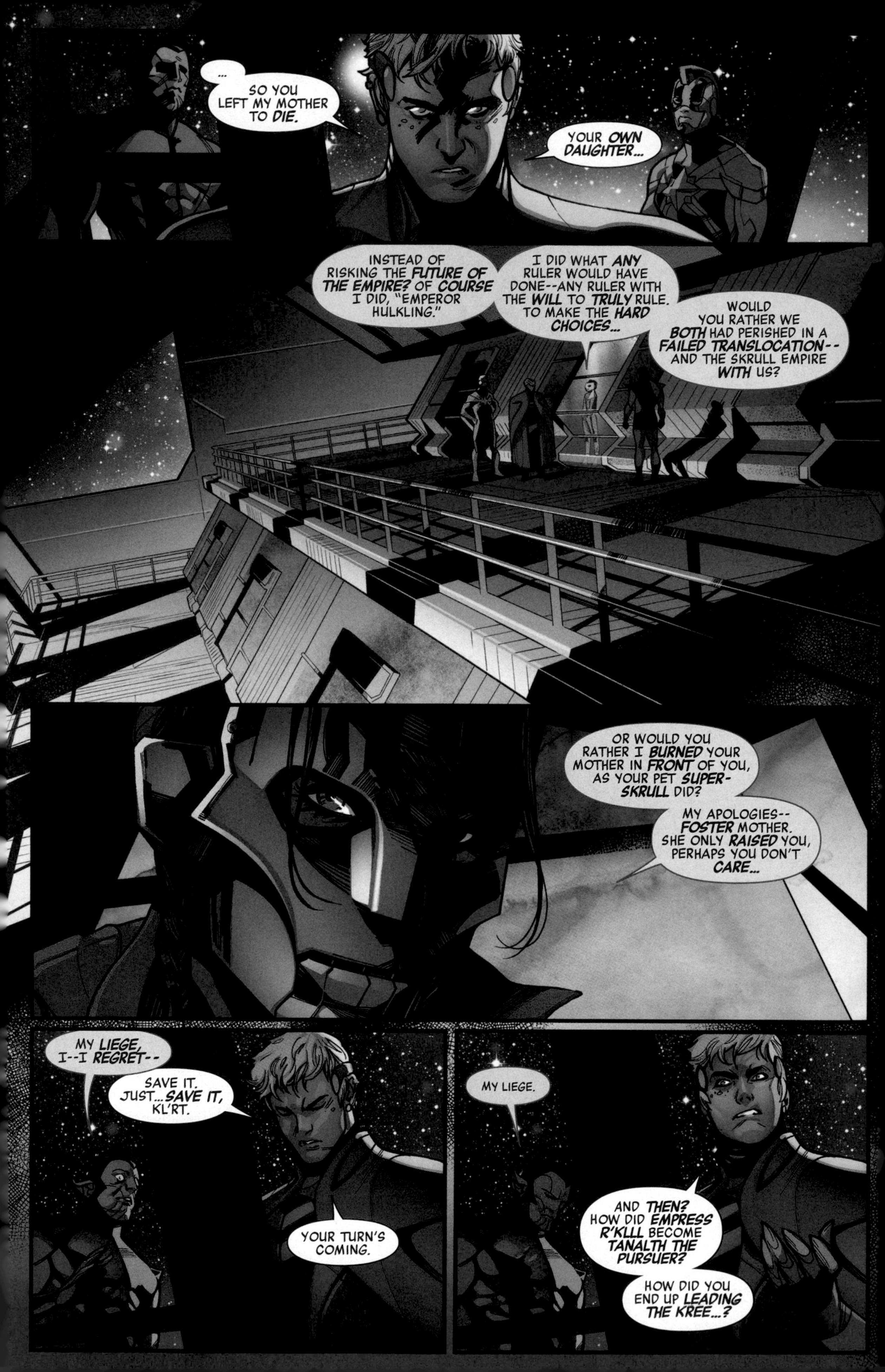
...
SO YOU LEFT MY MOTHER TO DIE.
YOUR OWN DAUGHTER...
INSTEAD OF RISKING THE FUTURE OF THE EMPIRE? OF COURSE I DID, "EMPEROR HULKLING."
I DID WHAT ANY RULER WOULD HAVE DONE--ANY RULER WITH THE WILL TO TRULY RULE. TO MAKE THE HARD CHOICES...
WOULD YOU RATHER WE BOTH HAD PERISHED IN A FAILED TRANSLOCATION--AND THE SKRULL EMPIRE WITH US?
OR WOULD YOU RATHER I BURNED YOUR MOTHER IN FRONT OF YOU, AS YOUR PET SUPER-SKRULL DID?
MY APOLOGIES--FOSTER MOTHER. SHE ONLY RAISED YOU, PERHAPS YOU DON'T CARE...
MY LIEGE, I--I REGRET--
SAVE IT. JUST...SAVE IT, KL'RT.
YOUR TURN'S COMING.
MY LIEGE.
AND THEN? HOW DID EMPRESS R'KLLL BECOME TANALTH THE PURSUER?
HOW DID YOU END UP LEADING THE KREE...?

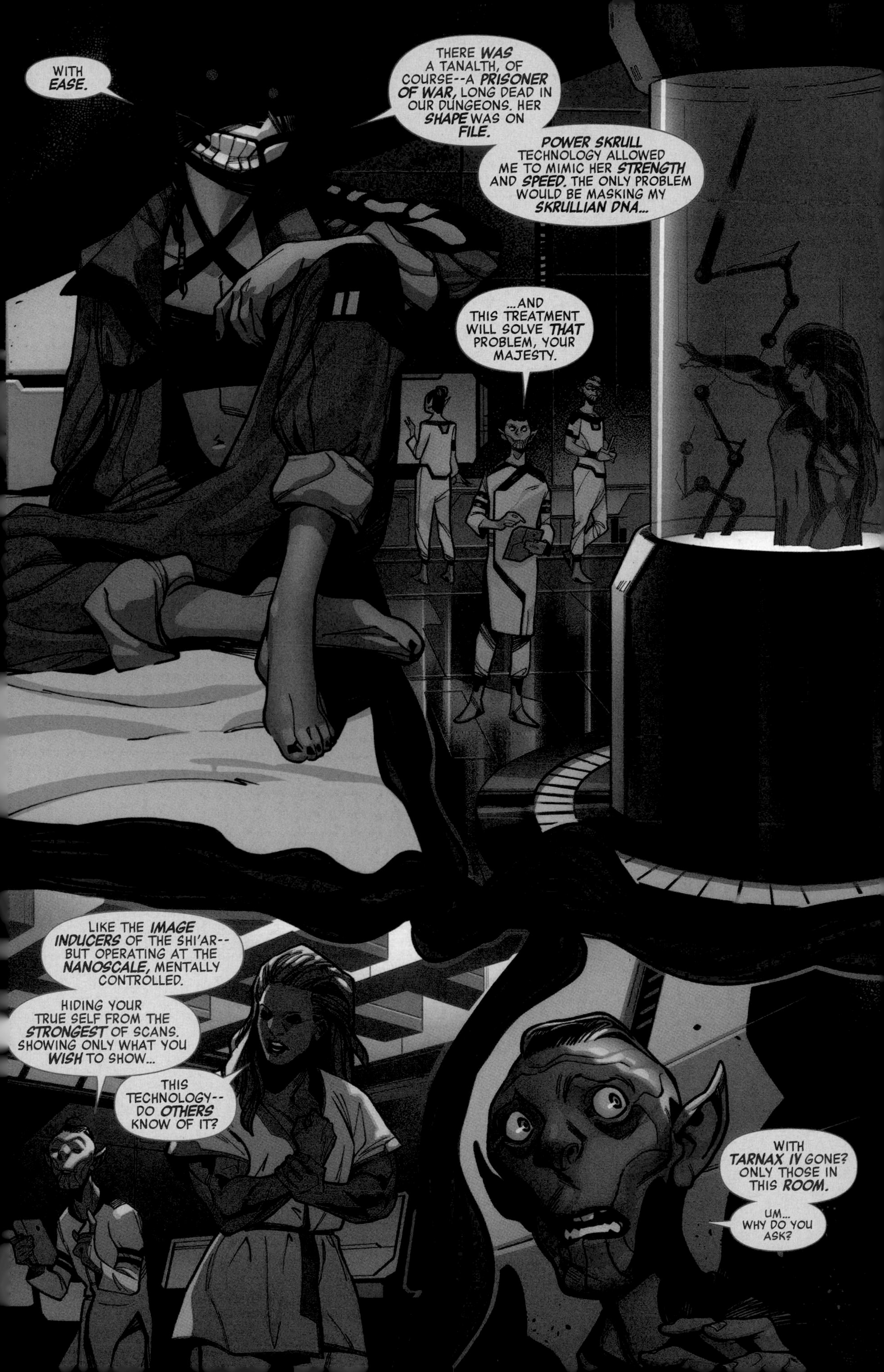
WITH EASE.
THERE WAS A TANALTH, OF COURSE--A PRISONER OF WAR, LONG DEAD IN OUR DUNGEONS. HER SHAPE WAS ON FILE.
POWER SKRULL TECHNOLOGY ALLOWED ME TO MIMIC HER STRENGTH AND SPEED. THE ONLY PROBLEM WOULD BE MASKING MY SKRULLIAN DNA...
...AND THIS TREATMENT WILL SOLVE THAT PROBLEM, YOUR MAJESTY.
LIKE THE IMAGE INDUCERS OF THE SHI'AR--BUT OPERATING AT THE NANOSCALE, MENTALLY CONTROLLED.
HIDING YOUR TRUE SELF FROM THE STRONGEST OF SCANS. SHOWING ONLY WHAT YOU WISH TO SHOW...
THIS TECHNOLOGY--DO OTHERS KNOW OF IT?
WITH TARNAX IV GONE? ONLY THOSE IN THIS ROOM.
UM... WHY DO YOU ASK?

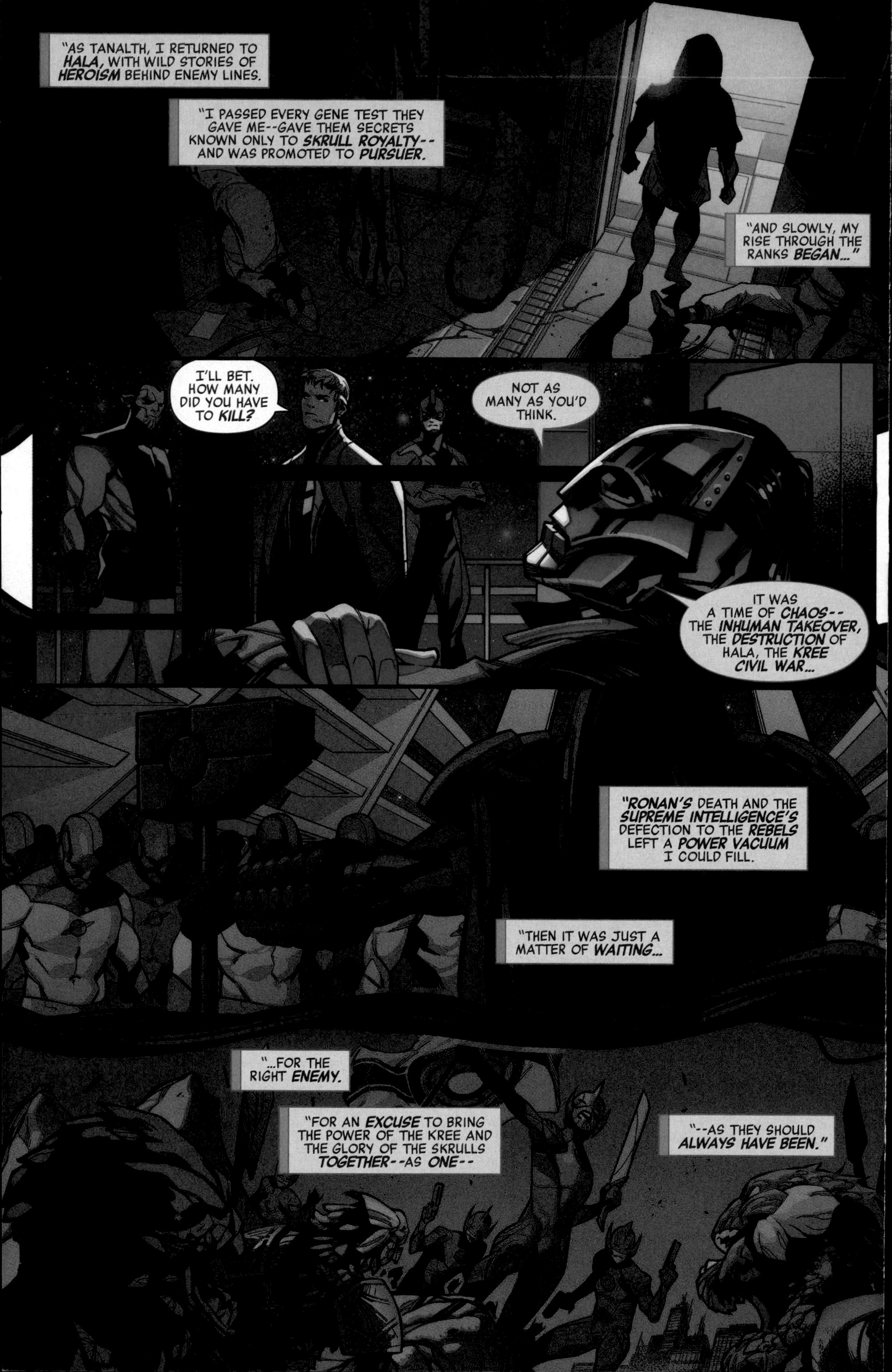
"AS TANALTH, I RETURNED TO HALA, WITH WILD STORIES OF HEROISM BEHIND ENEMY LINES.
"I PASSED EVERY GENE TEST THEY GAVE ME--GAVE THEM SECRETS KNOWN ONLY TO SKRULL ROYALTY--AND WAS PROMOTED TO PURSUER.
"AND SLOWLY, MY RISE THROUGH THE RANKS BEGAN..."
I'LL BET. HOW MANY DID YOU HAVE TO KILL?
NOT AS MANY AS YOU'D THINK.
IT WAS A TIME OF CHAOS--THE INHUMAN TAKEOVER, THE DESTRUCTION OF HALA, THE KREE CIVIL WAR...
"RONAN'S DEATH AND THE SUPREME INTELLIGENCE'S DEFECTION TO THE REBELS LEFT A POWER VACUUM I COULD FILL.
"THEN IT WAS JUST A MATTER OF WAITING...
"...FOR THE RIGHT ENEMY.
"FOR AN EXCUSE TO BRING THE POWER OF THE KREE AND THE GLORY OF THE SKRULLS TOGETHER--AS ONE--
"--AS THEY SHOULD ALWAYS HAVE BEEN."

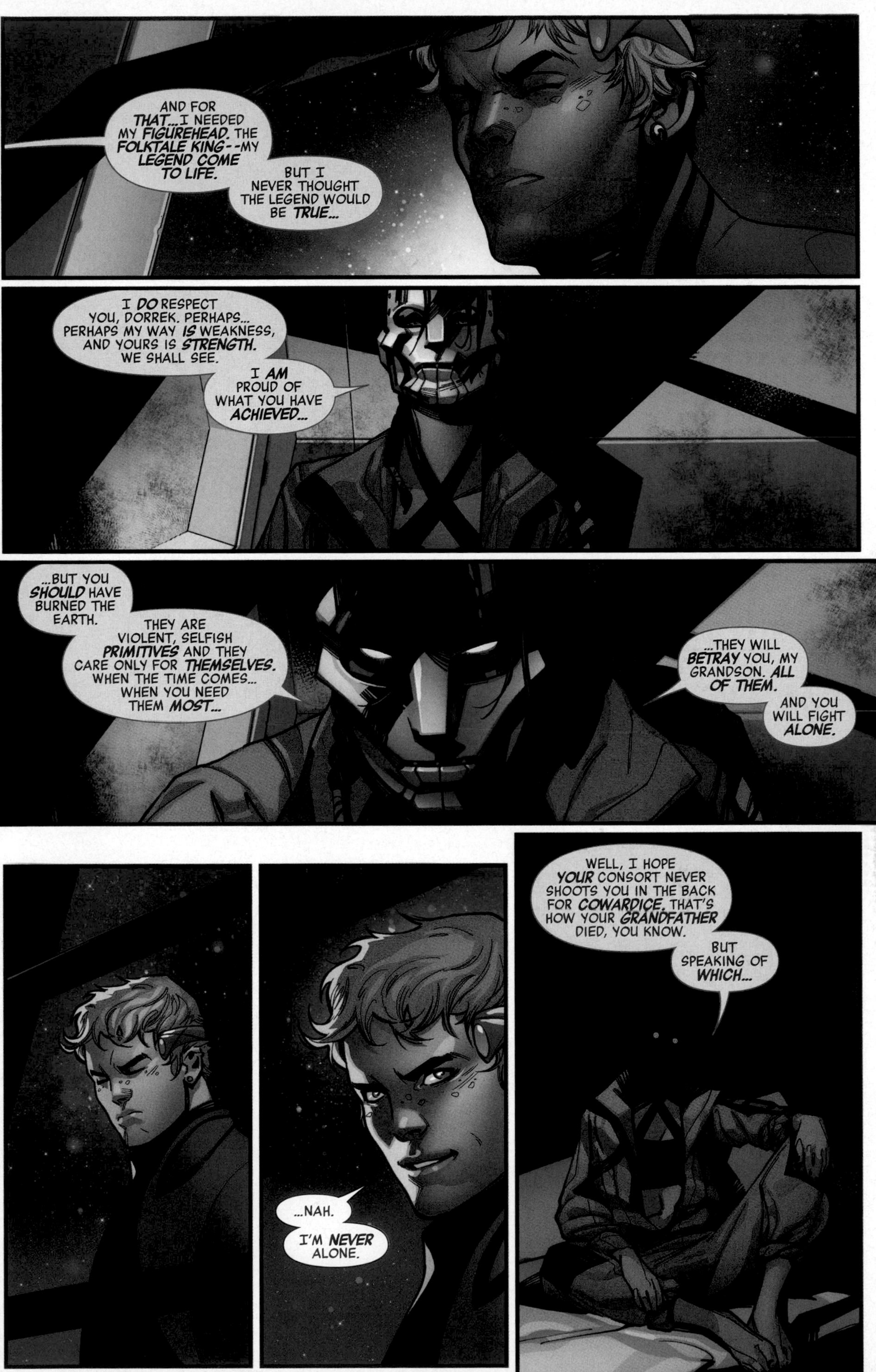
AND FOR THAT...I NEEDED MY FIGUREHEAD. THE FOLKTALE KING--MY LEGEND COME TO LIFE.
BUT I NEVER THOUGHT THE LEGEND WOULD BE TRUE...
I DO RESPECT YOU, DORREK. PERHAPS... PERHAPS MY WAY IS WEAKNESS, AND YOURS IS STRENGTH. WE SHALL SEE.
I AM PROUD OF WHAT YOU HAVE ACHIEVED...
...BUT YOU SHOULD HAVE BURNED THE EARTH.
THEY ARE VIOLENT, SELFISH PRIMITIVES AND THEY CARE ONLY FOR THEMSELVES. WHEN THE TIME COMES... WHEN YOU NEED THEM MOST...
...THEY WILL BETRAY YOU, MY GRANDSON. ALL OF THEM.
AND YOU WILL FIGHT ALONE.
...NAH.
I'M NEVER ALONE.
WELL, I HOPE YOUR CONSORT NEVER SHOOTS YOU IN THE BACK FOR COWARDICE. THAT'S HOW YOUR GRANDFATHER DIED, YOU KNOW.
BUT SPEAKING OF WHICH...

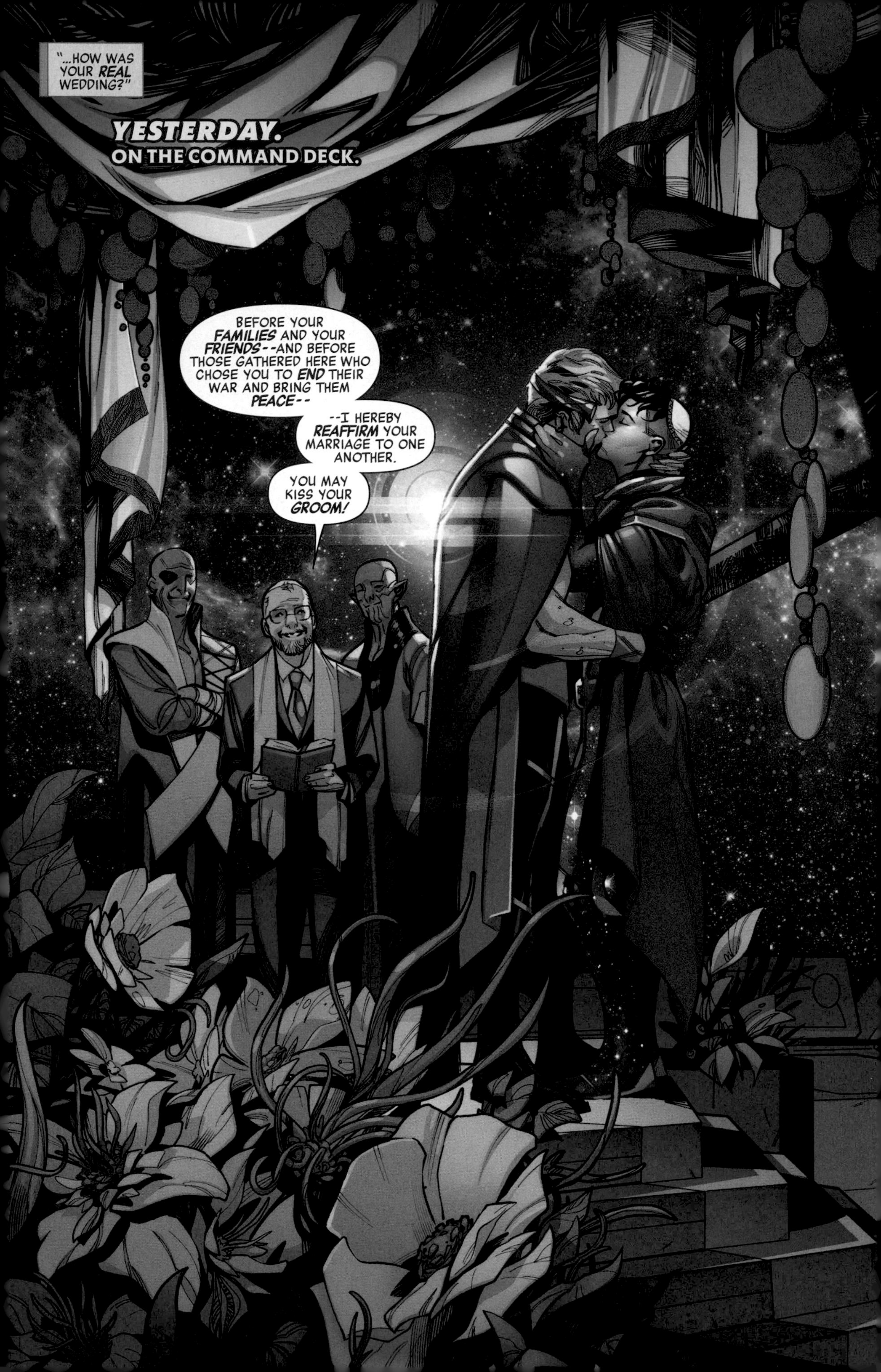
"...HOW WAS YOUR REAL WEDDING?"
YESTERDAY.
ON THE COMMAND DECK.
BEFORE YOUR FAMILIES AND YOUR FRIENDS--AND BEFORE THOSE GATHERED HERE WHO CHOSE YOU TO END THEIR WAR AND BRING THEM PEACE--
--I HEREBY REAFFIRM YOUR MARRIAGE TO ONE ANOTHER.
YOU MAY KISS YOUR GROOM!

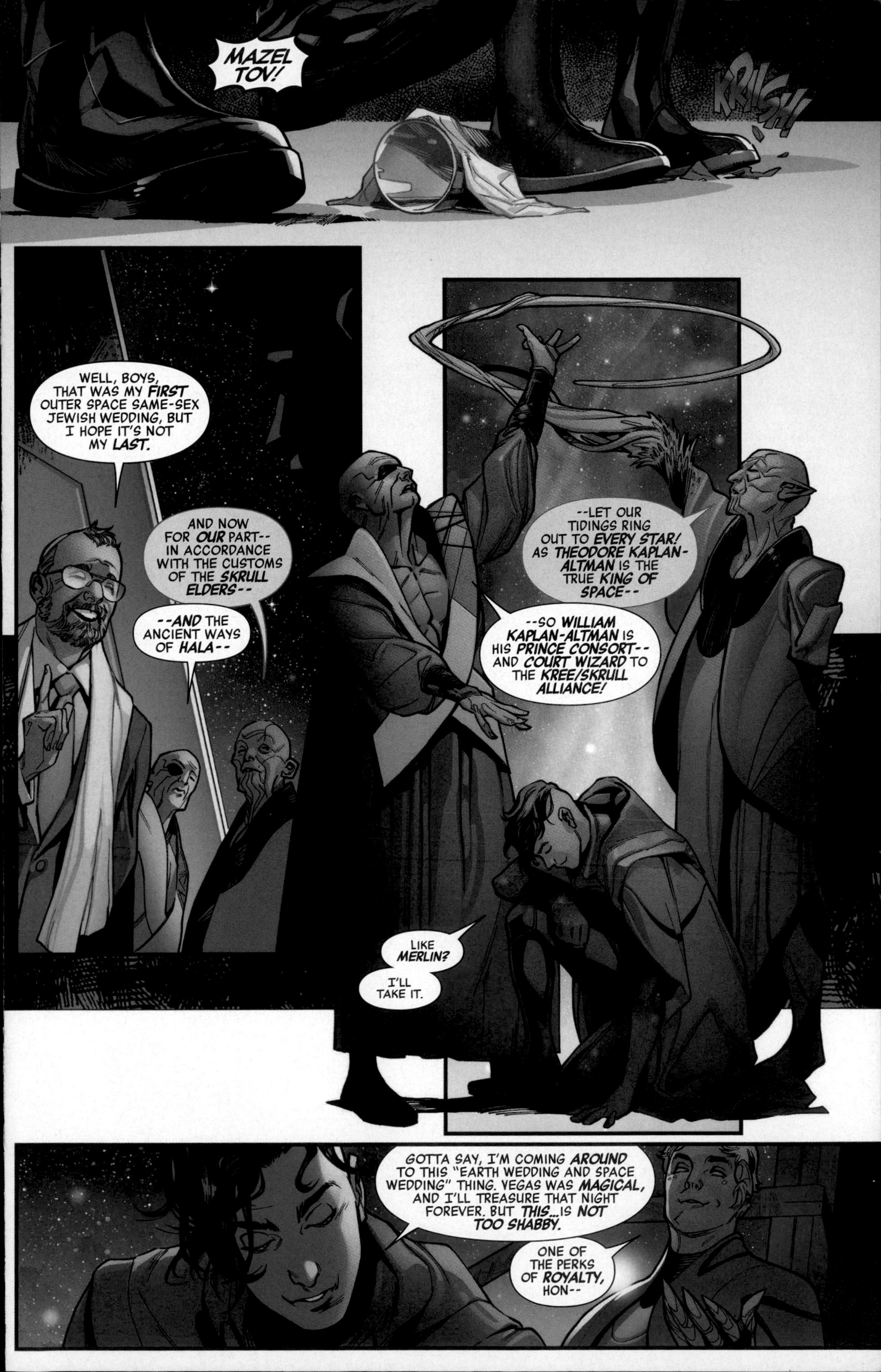
MAZEL TOV!
KRISH!
WELL, BOYS, THAT WAS MY FIRST OUTER SPACE SAME-SEX JEWISH WEDDING, BUT I HOPE IT'S NOT MY LAST.
AND NOW FOR OUR PART-- IN ACCORDANCE WITH THE CUSTOMS OF THE SKRULL ELDERS--
--AND THE ANCIENT WAYS OF HALA--
--LET OUR TIDINGS RING OUT TO EVERY STAR! AS THEODORE KAPLAN-ALTMAN IS THE TRUE KING OF SPACE--
--SO WILLIAM KAPLAN-ALTMAN IS HIS PRINCE CONSORT-- AND COURT WIZARD TO THE KREE/SKRULL ALLIANCE!
LIKE MERLIN?
I'LL TAKE IT.
GOTTA SAY, I'M COMING AROUND TO THIS "EARTH WEDDING AND SPACE WEDDING" THING. VEGAS WAS MAGICAL, AND I'LL TREASURE THAT NIGHT FOREVER. BUT THIS...IS NOT TOO SHABBY.
ONE OF THE PERKS OF ROYALTY, HON--

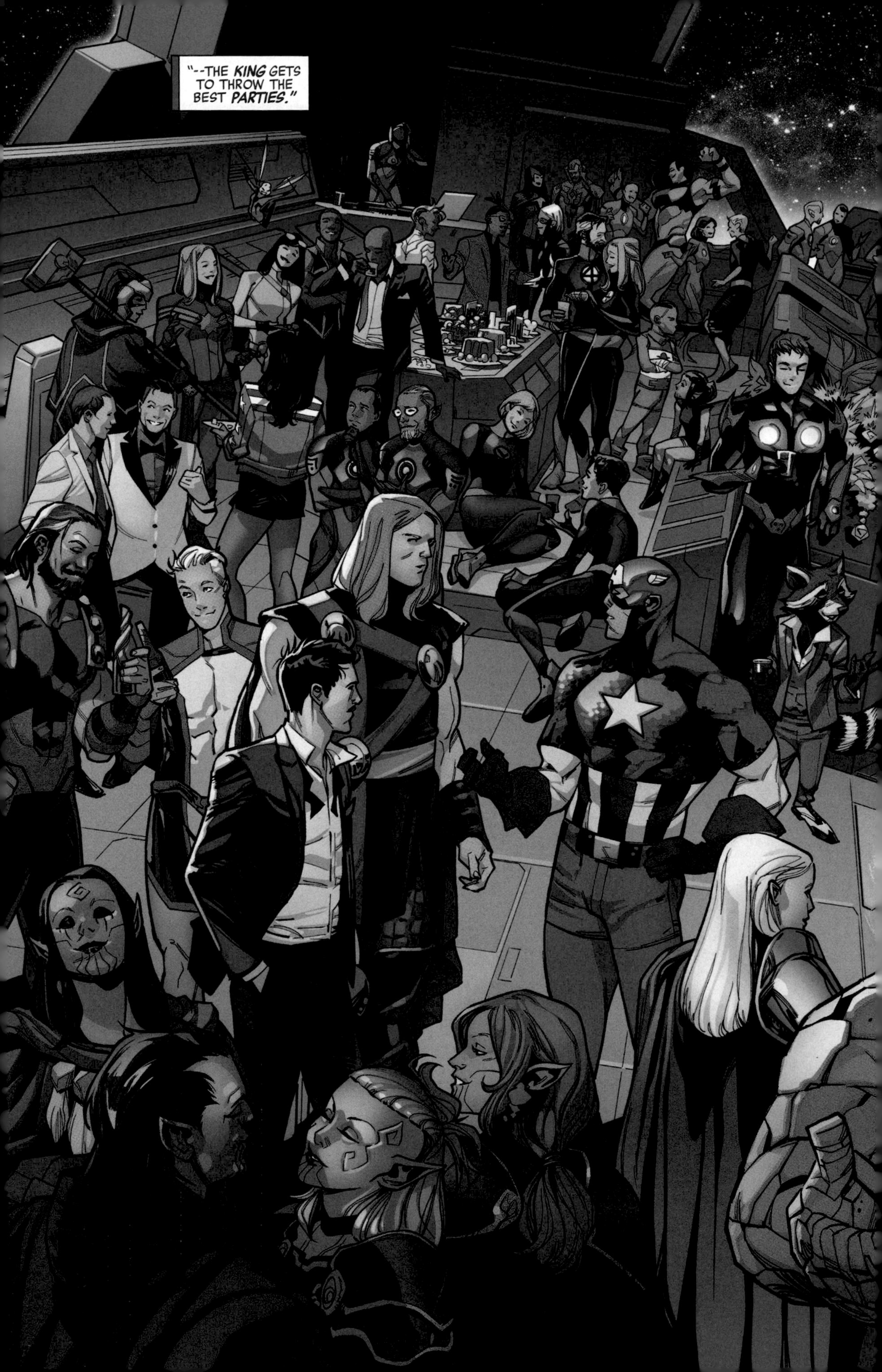
"--THE KING GETS TO THROW THE BEST PARTIES."

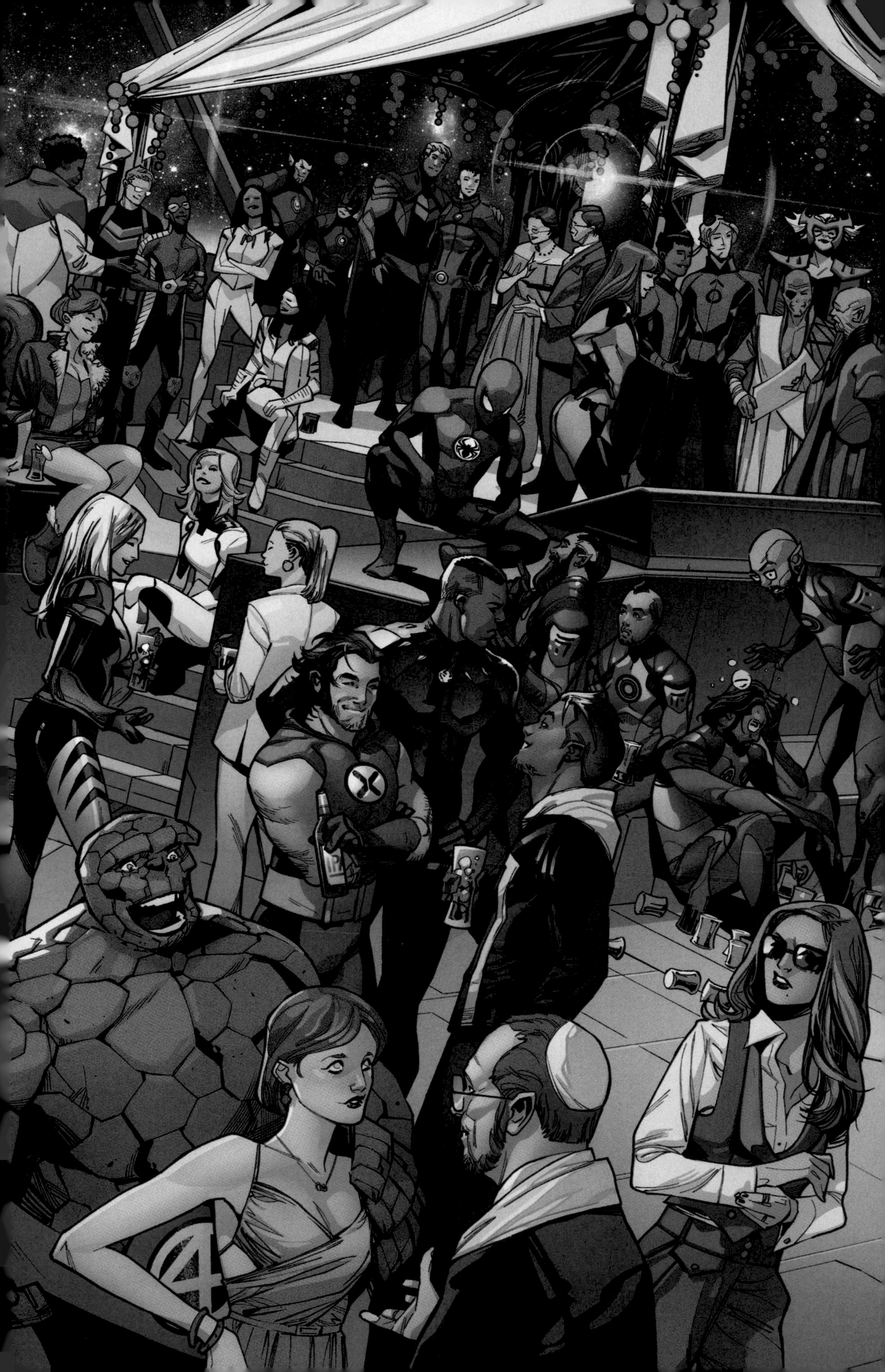

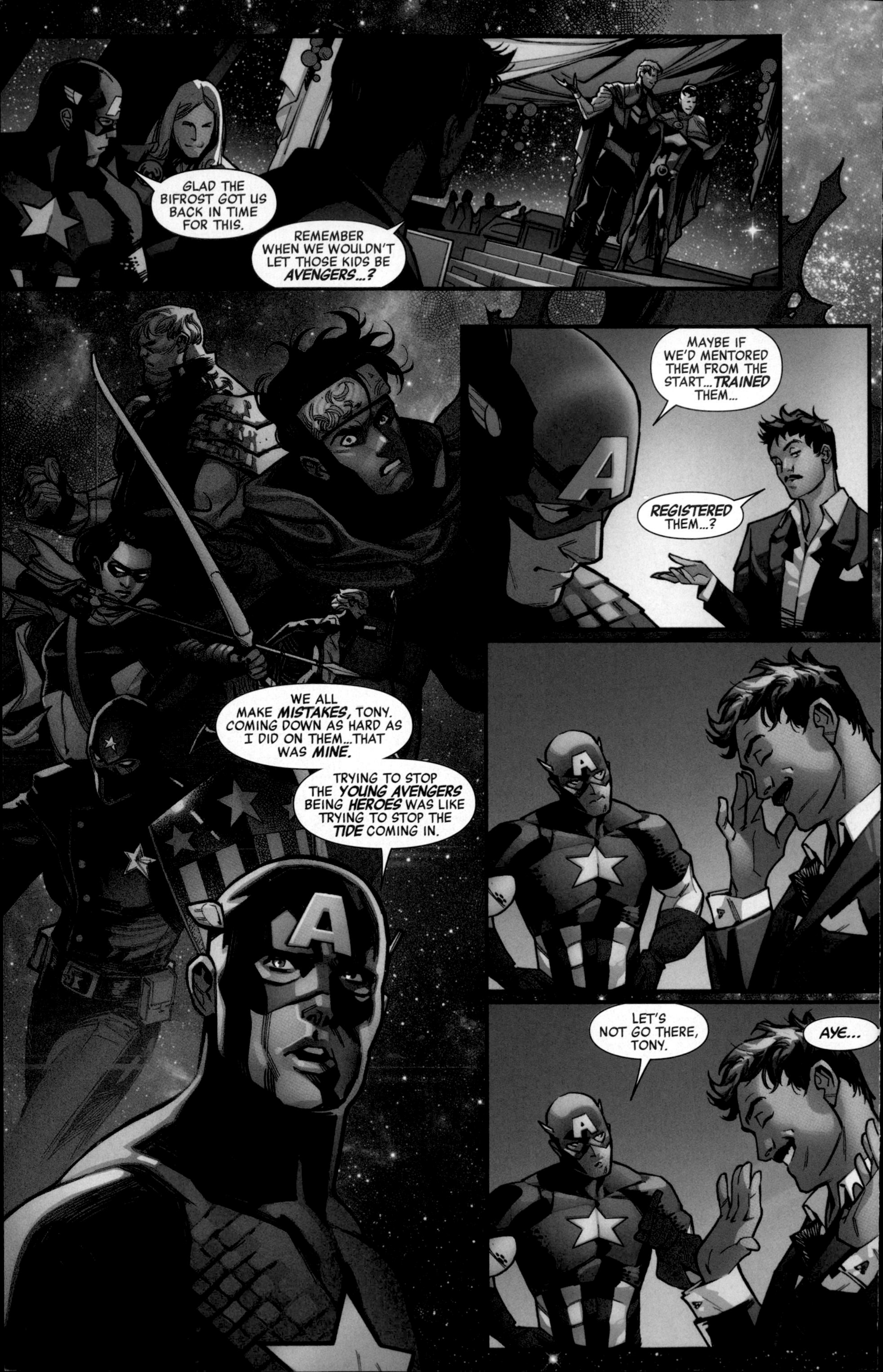

GLAD THE BIFROST GOT US BACK IN TIME FOR THIS.
REMEMBER WHEN WE WOULDN'T LET THOSE KIDS BE AVENGERS...?
MAYBE IF WE'D MENTORED THEM FROM THE START...TRAINED THEM...
REGISTERED THEM...?
WE ALL MAKE MISTAKES, TONY. COMING DOWN AS HARD AS I DID ON THEM...THAT WAS MINE.
TRYING TO STOP THE YOUNG AVENGERS BEING HEROES WAS LIKE TRYING TO STOP THE TIDE COMING IN.
LET'S NOT GO THERE, TONY.
AYE...

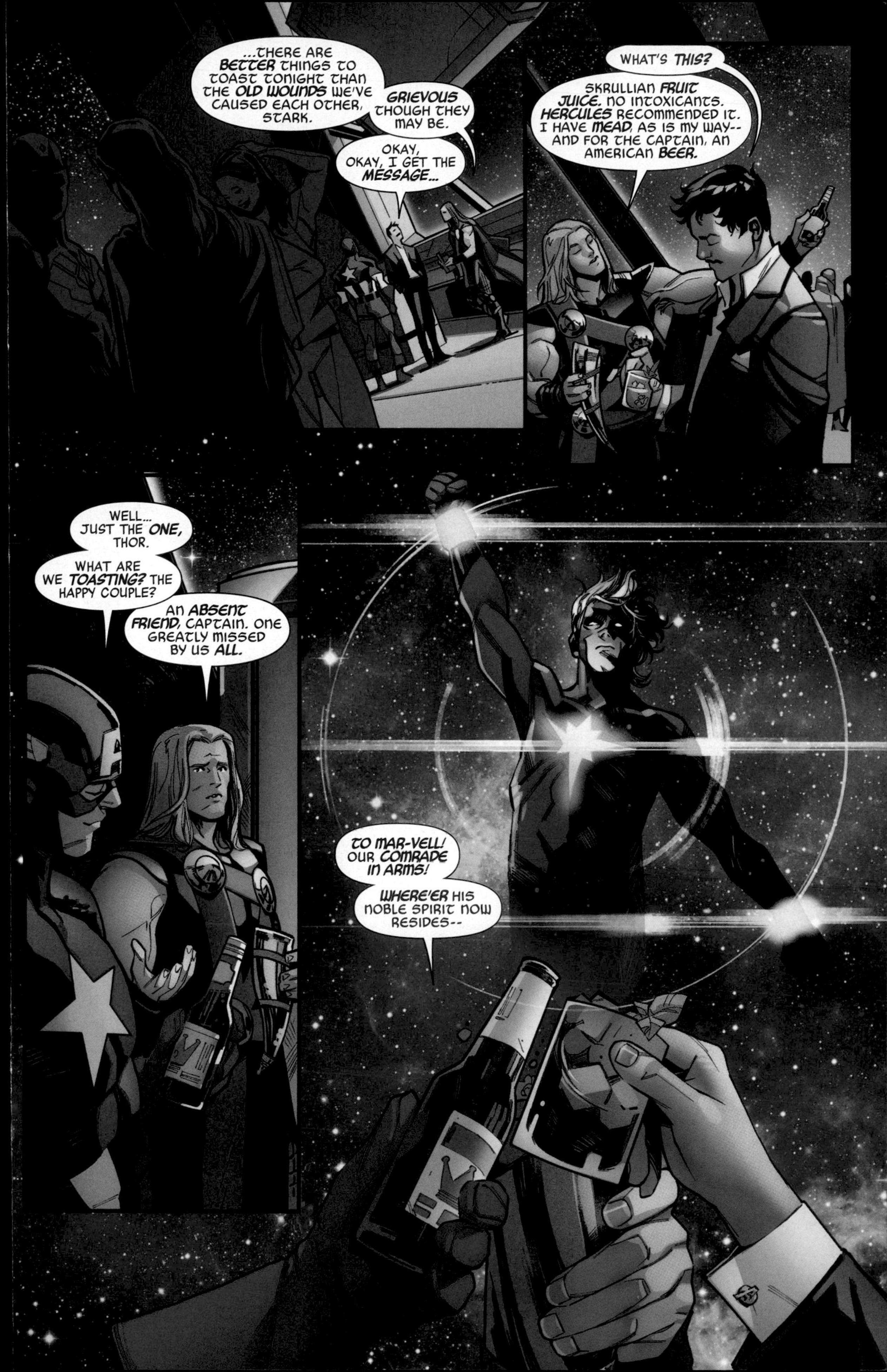
...THERE ARE BETTER THINGS TO TOAST TONIGHT THAN THE OLD WOUNDS WE'VE CAUSED EACH OTHER, STARK.
GRIEVOUS THOUGH THEY MAY BE.
OKAY, OKAY, I GET THE MESSAGE...
WHAT'S THIS?
SKRULLIAN FRUIT JUICE. NO INTOXICANTS. HERCULES RECOMMENDED IT. I HAVE MEAD, AS IS MY WAY-- AND FOR THE CAPTAIN, AN AMERICAN BEER.
WELL... JUST THE ONE, THOR.
WHAT ARE WE TOASTING? THE HAPPY COUPLE?
AN ABSENT FRIEND, CAPTAIN. ONE GREATLY MISSED BY US ALL.
TO MAR-VELL! OUR COMRADE IN ARMS!
WHERE'ER HIS NOBLE SPIRIT NOW RESIDES--

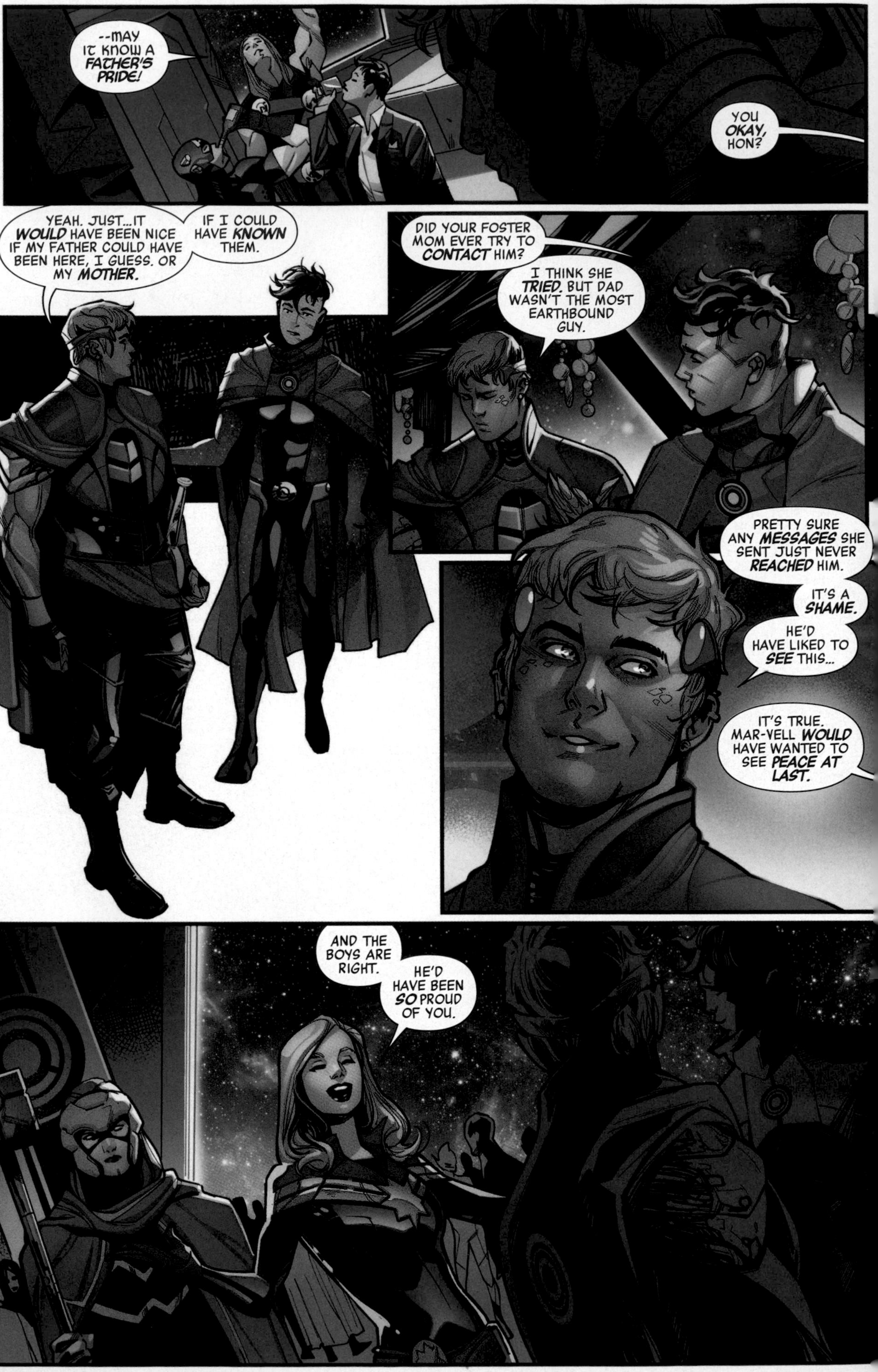
--MAY IT KNOW A FATHER'S PRIDE!
YOU OKAY, HON?
YEAH. JUST...IT WOULD HAVE BEEN NICE IF MY FATHER COULD HAVE BEEN HERE, I GUESS. OR MY MOTHER.
IF I COULD HAVE KNOWN THEM.
DID YOUR FOSTER MOM EVER TRY TO CONTACT HIM?
I THINK SHE TRIED. BUT DAD WASN'T THE MOST EARTHBOUND GUY.
PRETTY SURE ANY MESSAGES SHE SENT JUST NEVER REACHED HIM.
IT'S A SHAME.
HE'D HAVE LIKED TO SEE THIS...
IT'S TRUE. MAR-VELL WOULD HAVE WANTED TO SEE PEACE AT LAST.
AND THE BOYS ARE RIGHT.
HE'D HAVE BEEN SO PROUD OF YOU.

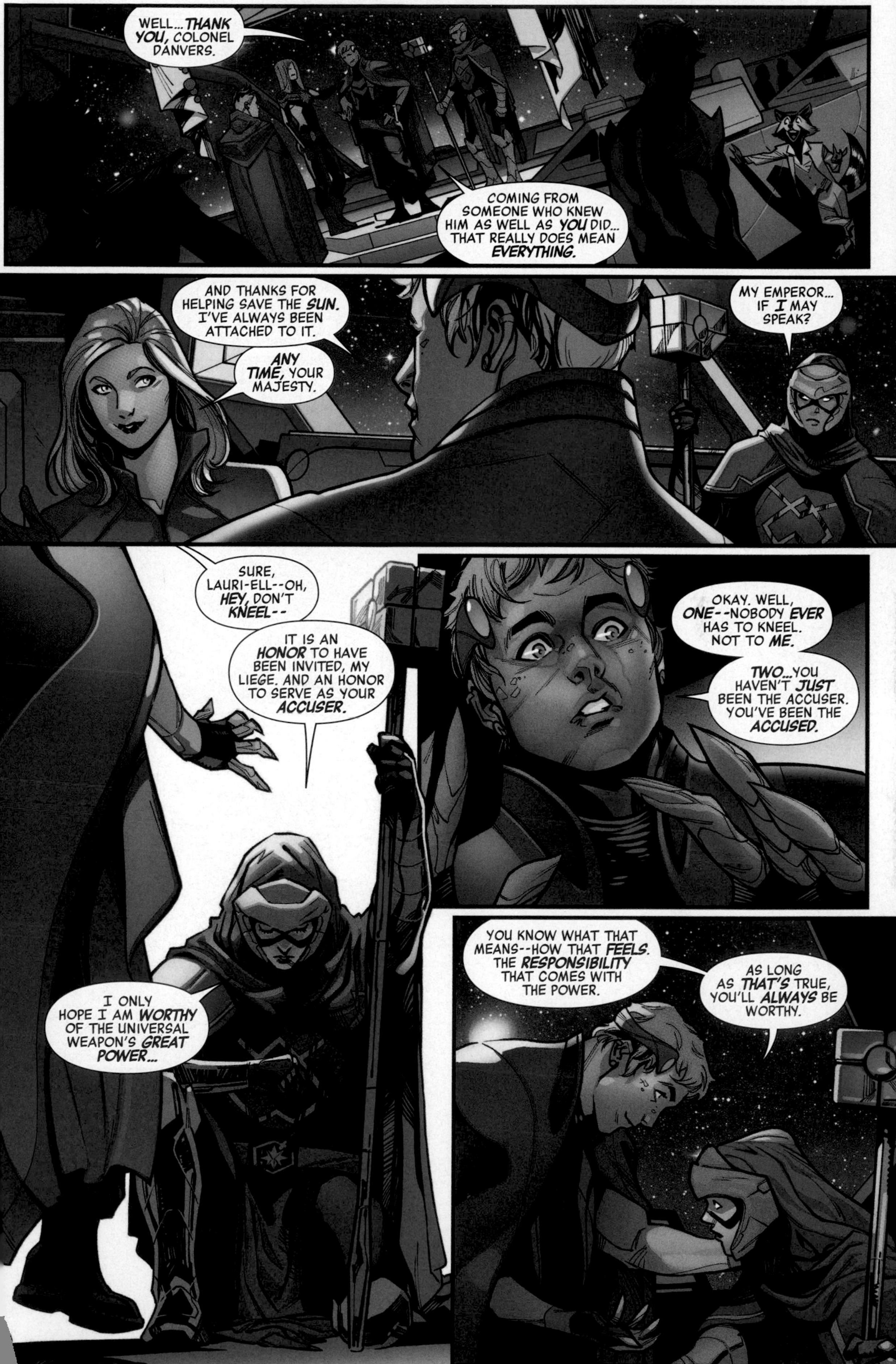
WELL... THANK YOU, COLONEL DANVERS.
COMING FROM SOMEONE WHO KNEW HIM AS WELL AS YOU DID... THAT REALLY DOES MEAN EVERYTHING.
AND THANKS FOR HELPING SAVE THE SUN. I'VE ALWAYS BEEN ATTACHED TO IT.
ANY TIME, YOUR MAJESTY.
MY EMPEROR... IF I MAY SPEAK?
SURE, LAURI-ELL--OH, HEY, DON'T KNEEL--
IT IS AN HONOR TO HAVE BEEN INVITED, MY LIEGE. AND AN HONOR TO SERVE AS YOUR ACCUSER.
OKAY. WELL, ONE--NOBODY EVER HAS TO KNEEL. NOT TO ME.
TWO... YOU HAVEN'T JUST BEEN THE ACCUSER. YOU'VE BEEN THE ACCUSED.
I ONLY HOPE I AM WORTHY OF THE UNIVERSAL WEAPON'S GREAT POWER...
YOU KNOW WHAT THAT MEANS--HOW THAT FEELS. THE RESPONSIBILITY THAT COMES WITH THE POWER.
AS LONG AS THAT'S TRUE, YOU'LL ALWAYS BE WORTHY.

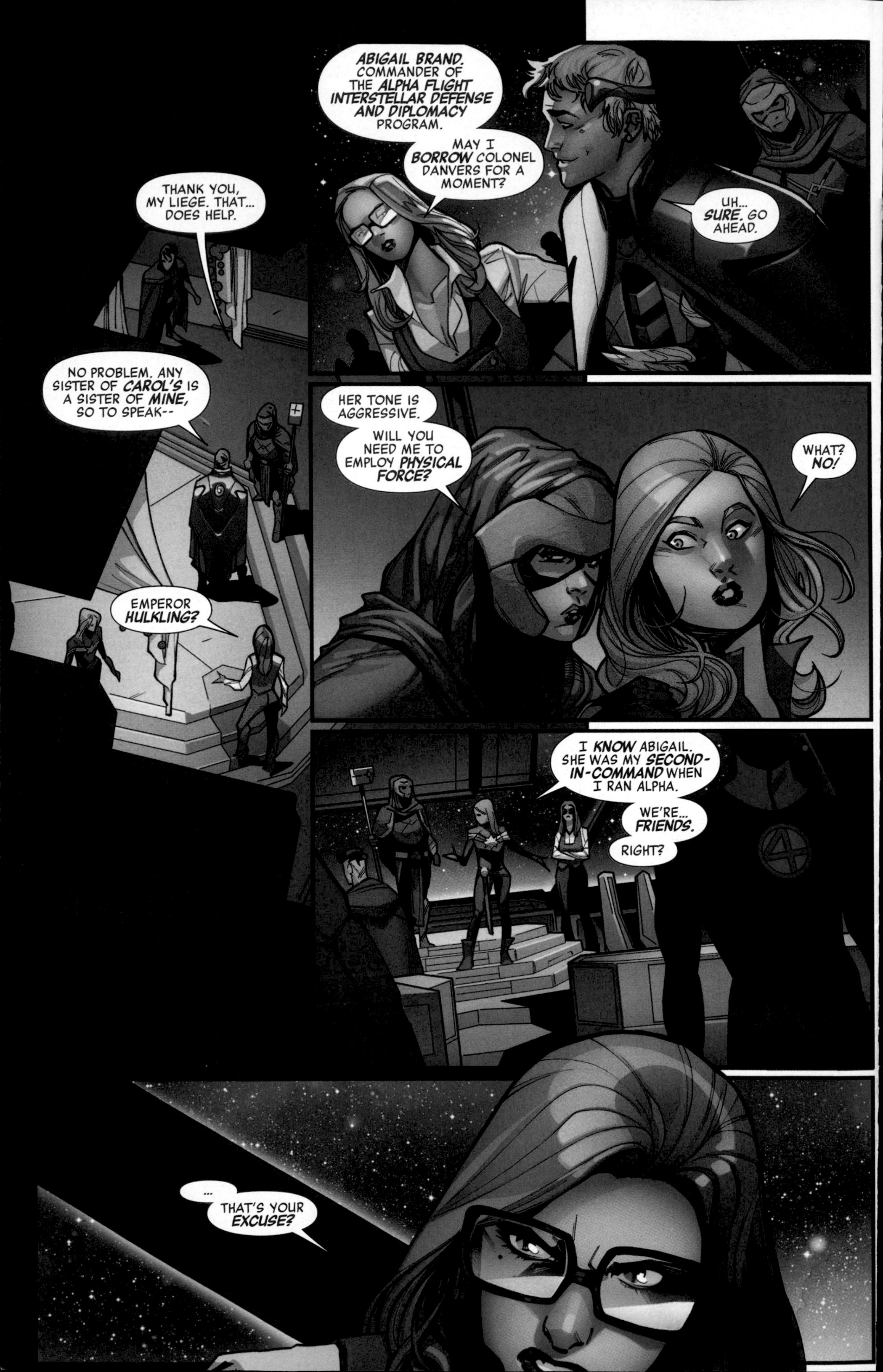
ABIGAIL BRAND. COMMANDER OF THE ALPHA FLIGHT INTERSTELLAR DEFENSE AND DIPLOMACY PROGRAM.
MAY I BORROW COLONEL DANVERS FOR A MOMENT?
UH... SURE. GO AHEAD.
THANK YOU, MY LIEGE. THAT... DOES HELP.
NO PROBLEM. ANY SISTER OF CAROL'S IS A SISTER OF MINE, SO TO SPEAK--
EMPEROR HULKLING?
HER TONE IS AGGRESSIVE.
WILL YOU NEED ME TO EMPLOY PHYSICAL FORCE?
WHAT? NO!
I KNOW ABIGAIL. SHE WAS MY SECOND-IN-COMMAND WHEN I RAN ALPHA.
WE'RE... FRIENDS.
RIGHT?
...
THAT'S YOUR EXCUSE?

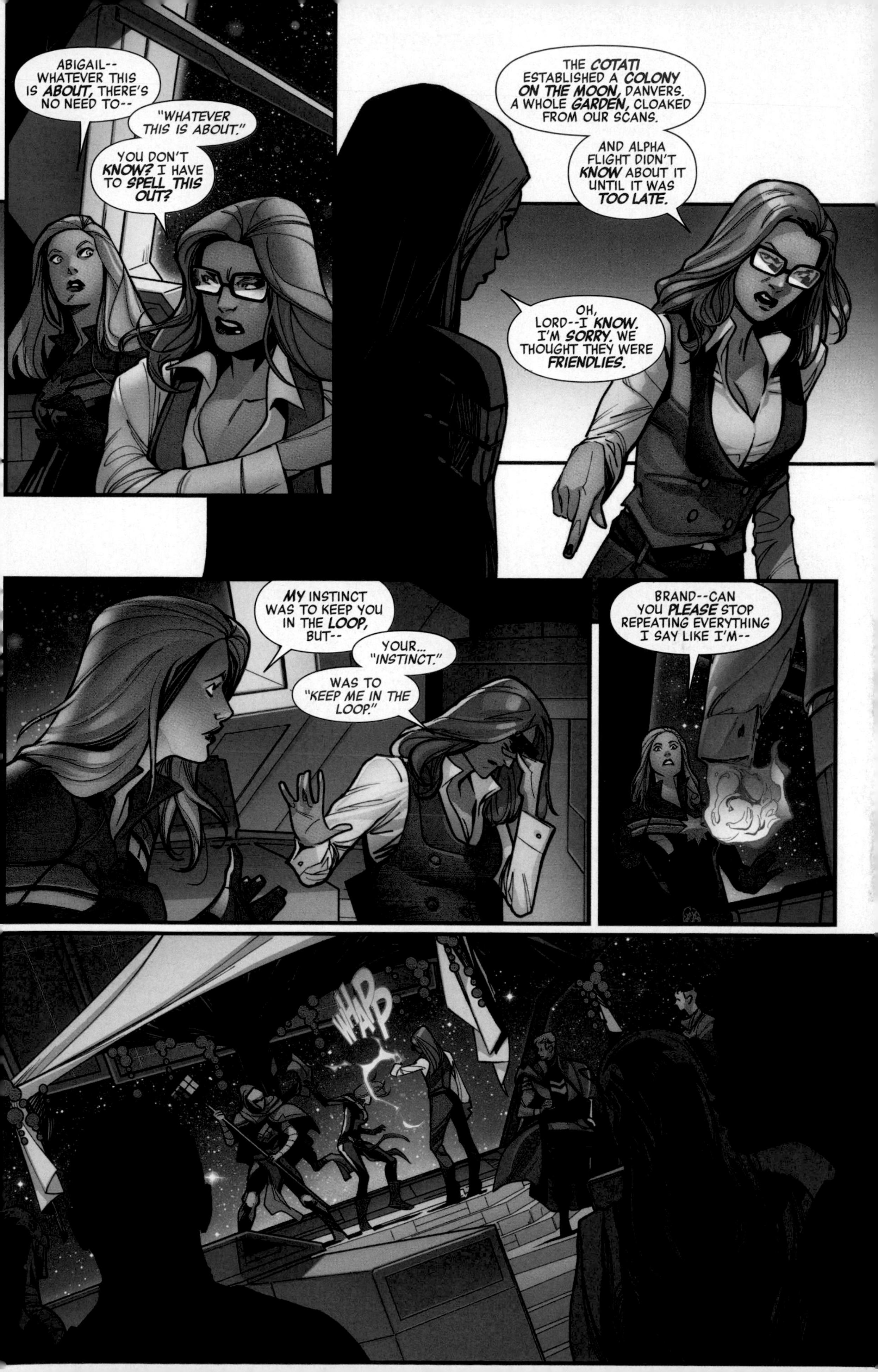
ABIGAIL-- WHATEVER THIS IS ABOUT, THERE'S NO NEED TO--
"WHATEVER THIS IS ABOUT."
YOU DON'T KNOW? I HAVE TO SPELL THIS OUT?
THE COTATI ESTABLISHED A COLONY ON THE MOON, DANVERS. A WHOLE GARDEN, CLOAKED FROM OUR SCANS.
AND ALPHA FLIGHT DIDN'T KNOW ABOUT IT UNTIL IT WAS TOO LATE.
OH, LORD--I KNOW. I'M SORRY. WE THOUGHT THEY WERE FRIENDLIES.
MY INSTINCT WAS TO KEEP YOU IN THE LOOP, BUT--
YOUR... "INSTINCT."
WAS TO "KEEP ME IN THE LOOP."
BRAND--CAN YOU PLEASE STOP REPEATING EVERYTHING I SAY LIKE I'M--
WHAP

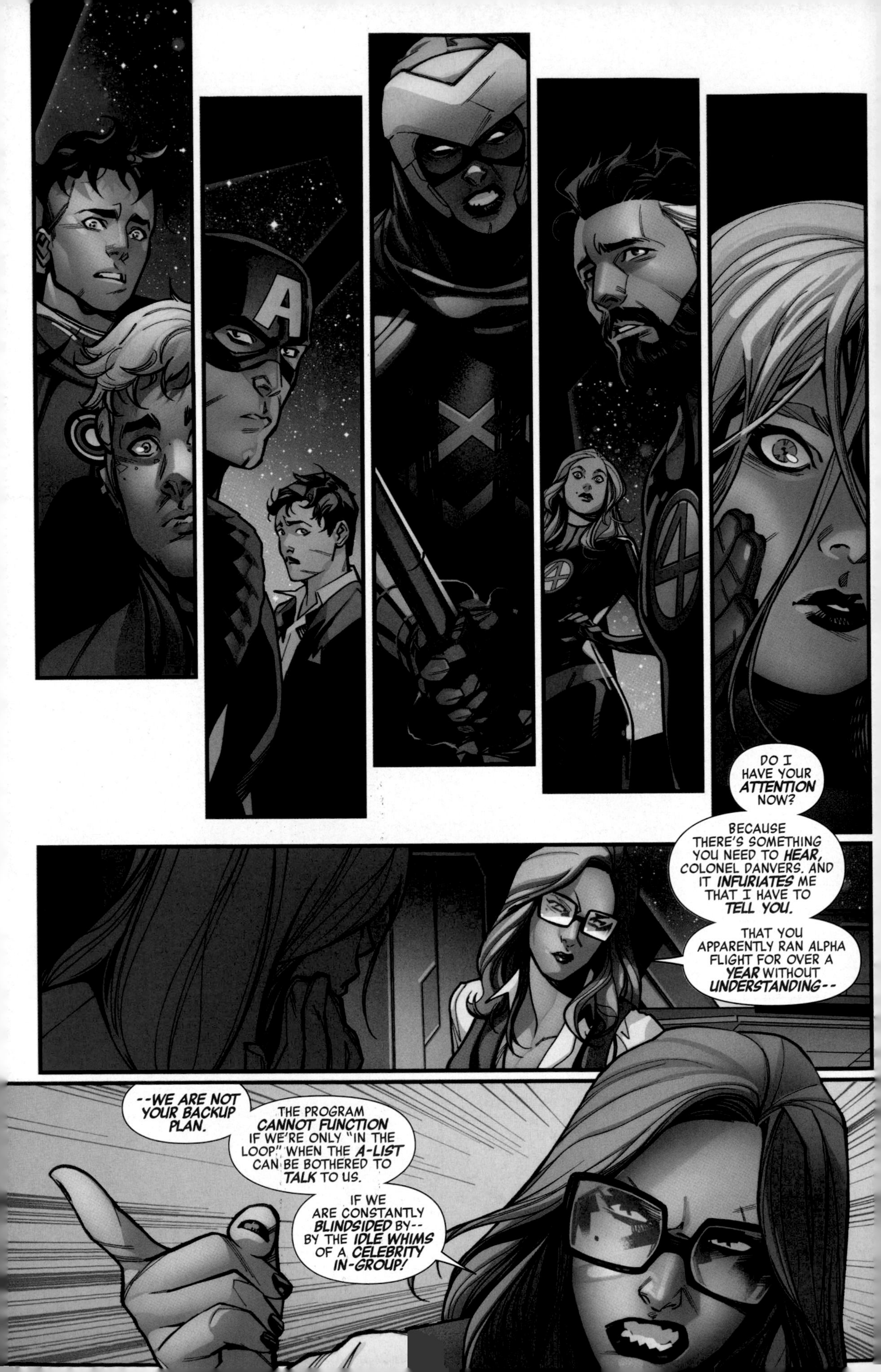
DO I HAVE YOUR ATTENTION NOW?
BECAUSE THERE'S SOMETHING YOU NEED TO HEAR, COLONEL DANVERS. AND IT INFURIATES ME THAT I HAVE TO TELL YOU.
THAT YOU APPARENTLY RAN ALPHA FLIGHT FOR OVER A YEAR WITHOUT UNDERSTANDING--
--WE ARE NOT YOUR BACKUP PLAN.
THE PROGRAM CANNOT FUNCTION IF WE'RE ONLY "IN THE LOOP" WHEN THE A-LIST CAN BE BOTHERED TO TALK TO US.
IF WE ARE CONSTANTLY BLINDSIDED BY-- BY THE IDLE WHIMS OF A CELEBRITY IN-GROUP!

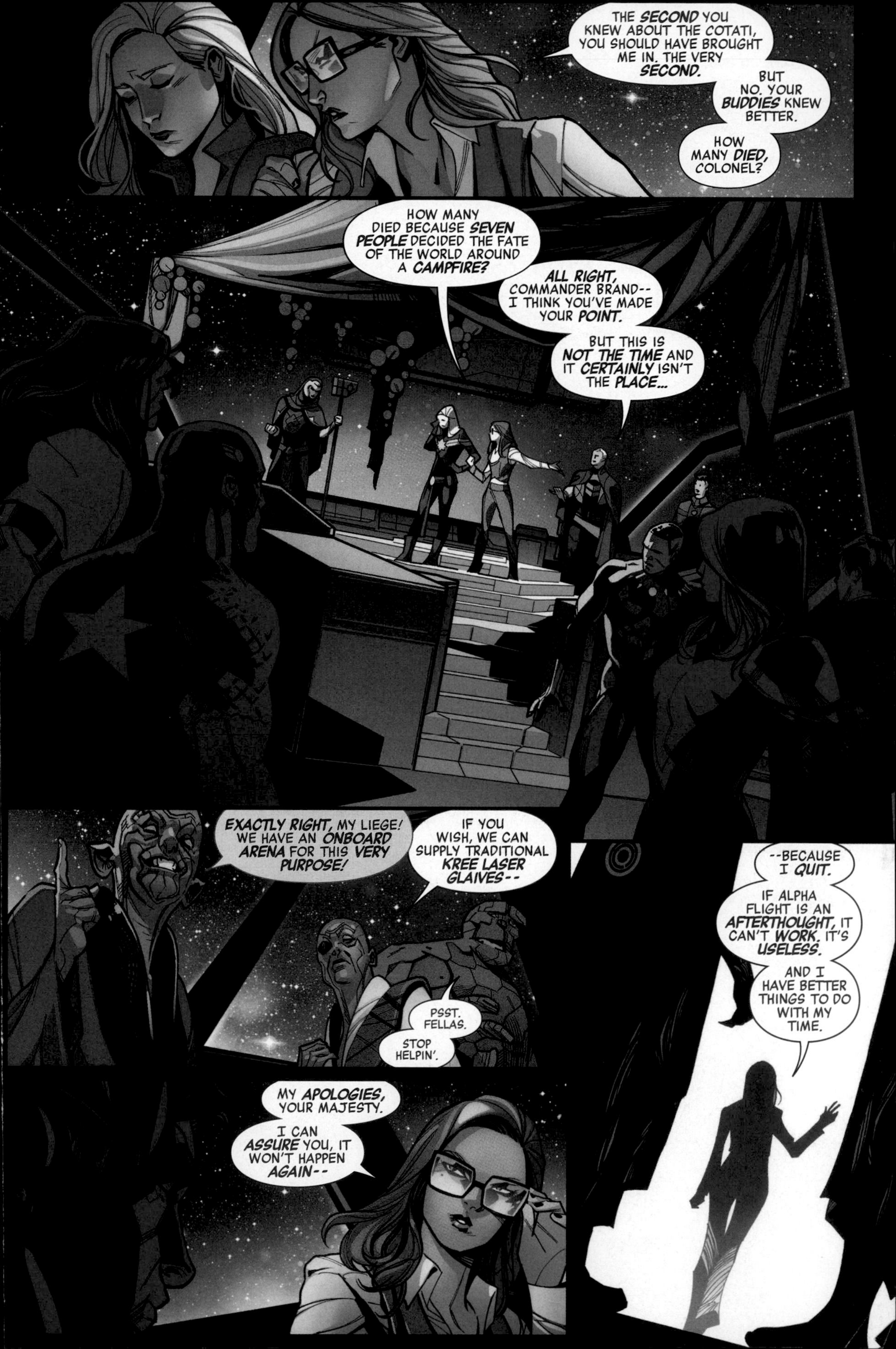
THE SECOND YOU KNEW ABOUT THE COTATI, YOU SHOULD HAVE BROUGHT ME IN. THE VERY SECOND.
BUT NO. YOUR BUDDIES KNEW BETTER.
HOW MANY DIED, COLONEL?
HOW MANY DIED BECAUSE SEVEN PEOPLE DECIDED THE FATE OF THE WORLD AROUND A CAMPFIRE?
ALL RIGHT, COMMANDER BRAND-- I THINK YOU'VE MADE YOUR POINT.
BUT THIS IS NOT THE TIME AND IT CERTAINLY ISN'T THE PLACE...
EXACTLY RIGHT, MY LIEGE! WE HAVE AN ONBOARD ARENA FOR THIS VERY PURPOSE!
IF YOU WISH, WE CAN SUPPLY TRADITIONAL KREE LASER GLAIVES--
PSST. FELLAS.
STOP HELPIN'.
MY APOLOGIES, YOUR MAJESTY.
I CAN ASSURE YOU, IT WON'T HAPPEN AGAIN--
--BECAUSE I QUIT.
IF ALPHA FLIGHT IS AN AFTERTHOUGHT, IT CAN'T WORK. IT'S USELESS.
AND I HAVE BETTER THINGS TO DO WITH MY TIME.

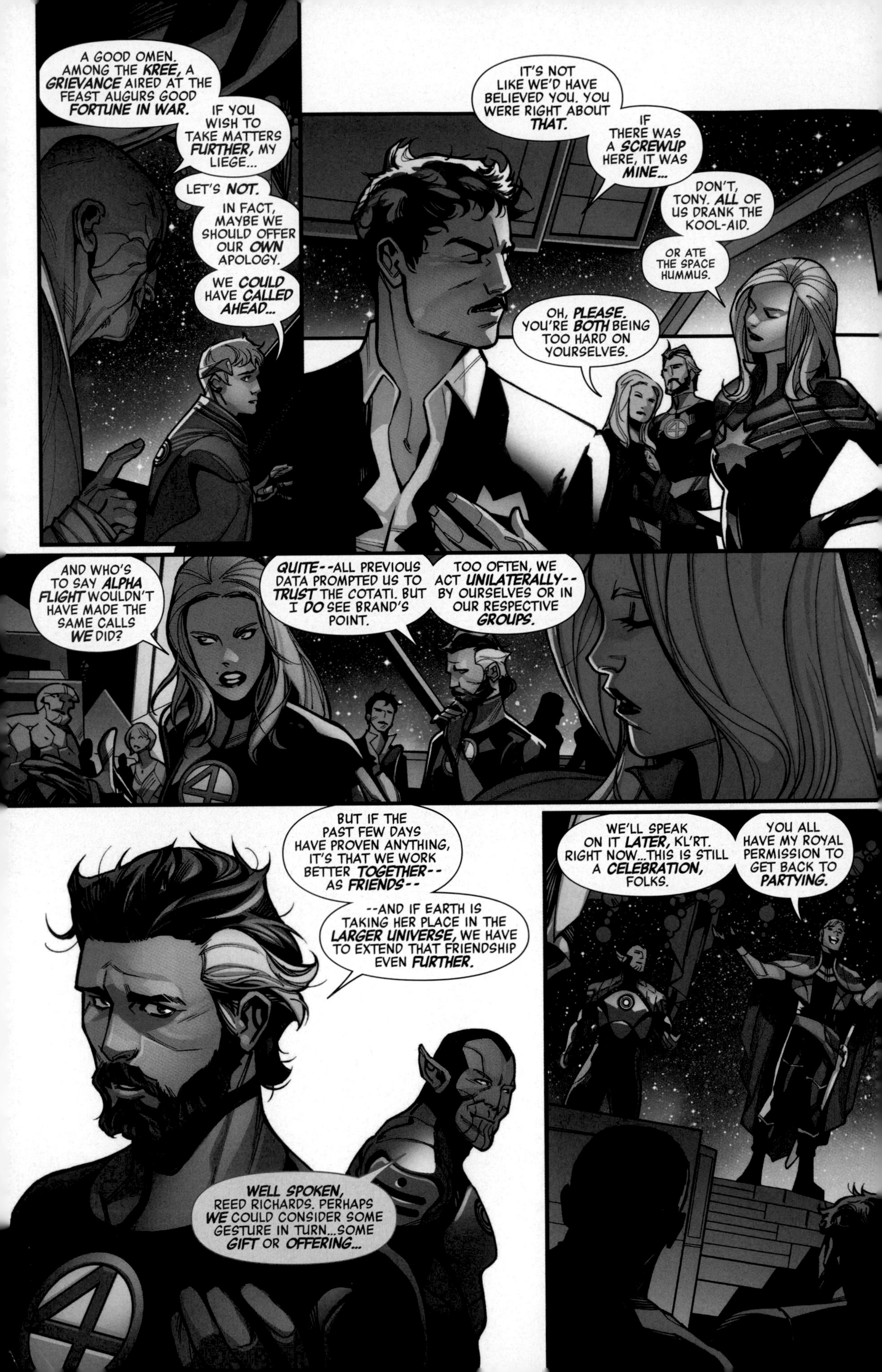
A GOOD OMEN. AMONG THE KREE, A GRIEVANCE AIRED AT THE FEAST AUGURS GOOD FORTUNE IN WAR.
IF YOU WISH TO TAKE MATTERS FURTHER, MY LIEGE...
LET'S NOT.
IN FACT, MAYBE WE SHOULD OFFER OUR OWN APOLOGY.
WE COULD HAVE CALLED AHEAD...
IT'S NOT LIKE WE'D HAVE BELIEVED YOU. YOU WERE RIGHT ABOUT THAT.
IF THERE WAS A SCREWUP HERE, IT WAS MINE...
DON'T, TONY. ALL OF US DRANK THE KOOL-AID.
OR ATE THE SPACE HUMMUS.
OH, PLEASE. YOU'RE BOTH BEING TOO HARD ON YOURSELVES.
AND WHO'S TO SAY ALPHA FLIGHT WOULDN'T HAVE MADE THE SAME CALLS WE DID?
QUITE--ALL PREVIOUS DATA PROMPTED US TO TRUST THE COTATI. BUT I DO SEE BRAND'S POINT.
TOO OFTEN, WE ACT UNILATERALLY--BY OURSELVES OR IN OUR RESPECTIVE GROUPS.
BUT IF THE PAST FEW DAYS HAVE PROVEN ANYTHING, IT'S THAT WE WORK BETTER TOGETHER--AS FRIENDS--
--AND IF EARTH IS TAKING HER PLACE IN THE LARGER UNIVERSE, WE HAVE TO EXTEND THAT FRIENDSHIP EVEN FURTHER.
WELL SPOKEN, REED RICHARDS. PERHAPS WE COULD CONSIDER SOME GESTURE IN TURN...SOME GIFT OR OFFERING...
WE'LL SPEAK ON IT LATER, KL'RT. RIGHT NOW...THIS IS STILL A CELEBRATION, FOLKS.
YOU ALL HAVE MY ROYAL PERMISSION TO GET BACK TO PARTYING.

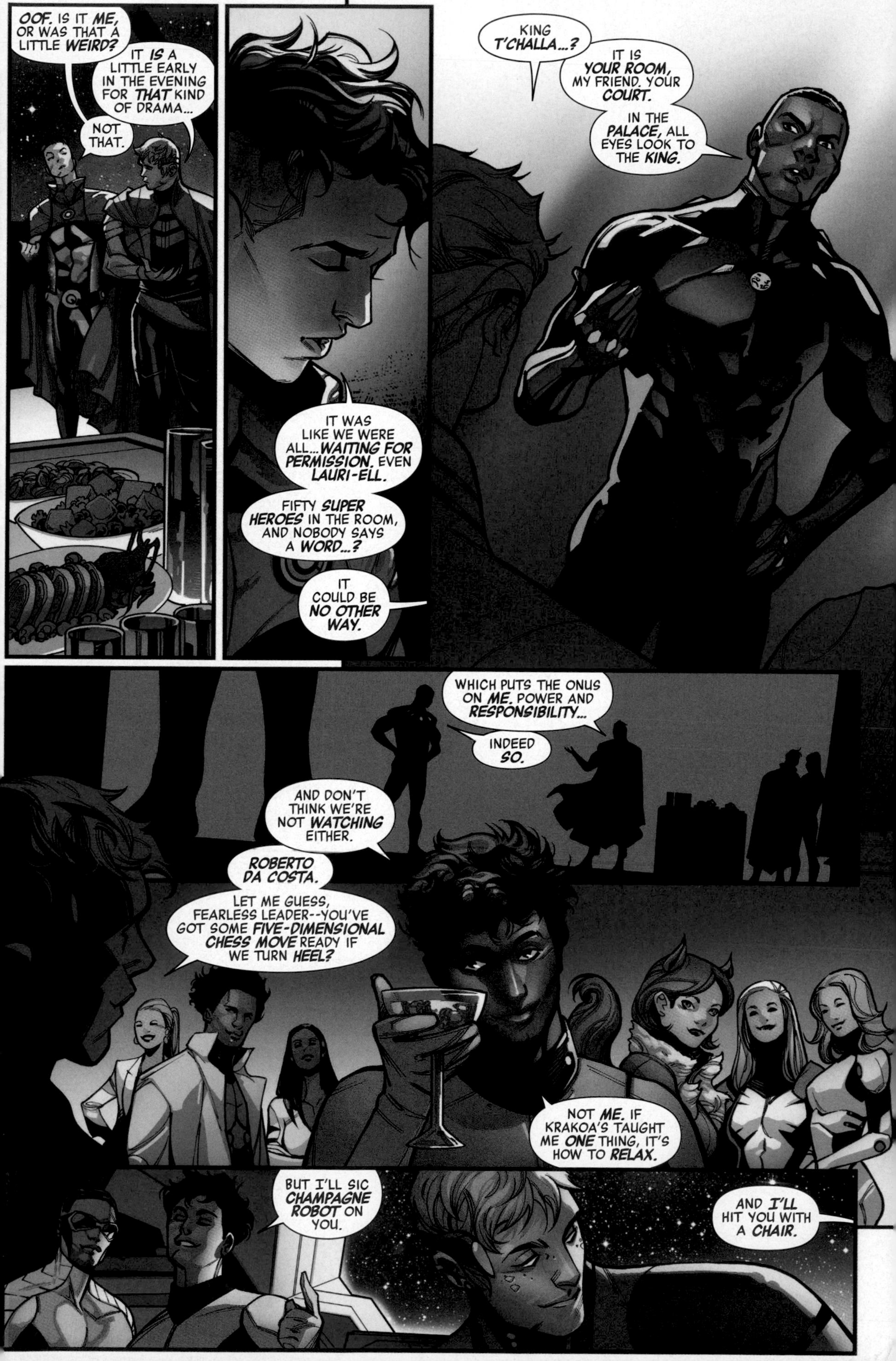
OOF. IS IT ME, OR WAS THAT A LITTLE WEIRD?
IT IS A LITTLE EARLY IN THE EVENING FOR THAT KIND OF DRAMA...
NOT THAT.
IT WAS LIKE WE WERE ALL...WAITING FOR PERMISSION. EVEN LAURI-ELL.
FIFTY SUPER HEROES IN THE ROOM, AND NOBODY SAYS A WORD...?
KING T'CHALLA...?
IT IS YOUR ROOM, MY FRIEND. YOUR COURT.
IN THE PALACE, ALL EYES LOOK TO THE KING.
IT COULD BE NO OTHER WAY.
WHICH PUTS THE ONUS ON ME. POWER AND RESPONSIBILITY...
INDEED SO.
AND DON'T THINK WE'RE NOT WATCHING EITHER.
ROBERTO DA COSTA.
LET ME GUESS, FEARLESS LEADER--YOU'VE GOT SOME FIVE-DIMENSIONAL CHESS MOVE READY IF WE TURN HEEL?
NOT ME. IF KRAKOA'S TAUGHT ME ONE THING, IT'S HOW TO RELAX.
BUT I'LL SIC CHAMPAGNE ROBOT ON YOU.
AND I'LL HIT YOU WITH A CHAIR.

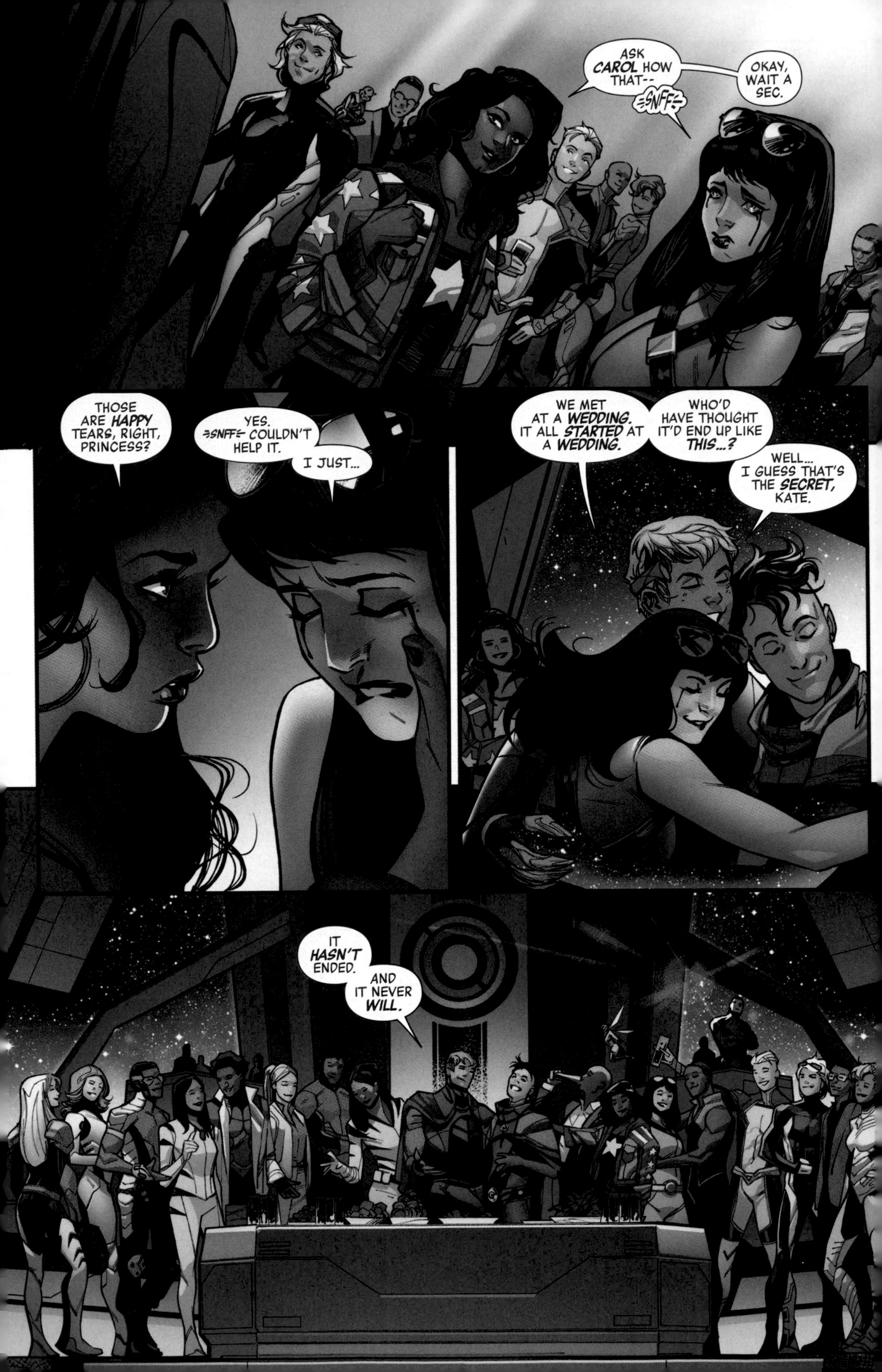

ASK CAROL HOW THAT--
SNFF
OKAY, WAIT A SEC.
THOSE ARE HAPPY TEARS, RIGHT, PRINCESS?
SNFF YES. COULDN'T HELP IT.
I JUST...
WE MET AT A WEDDING. IT ALL STARTED AT A WEDDING.
WHO'D HAVE THOUGHT IT'D END UP LIKE THIS...?
WELL... I GUESS THAT'S THE SECRET, KATE.
IT HASN'T ENDED.
AND IT NEVER WILL.

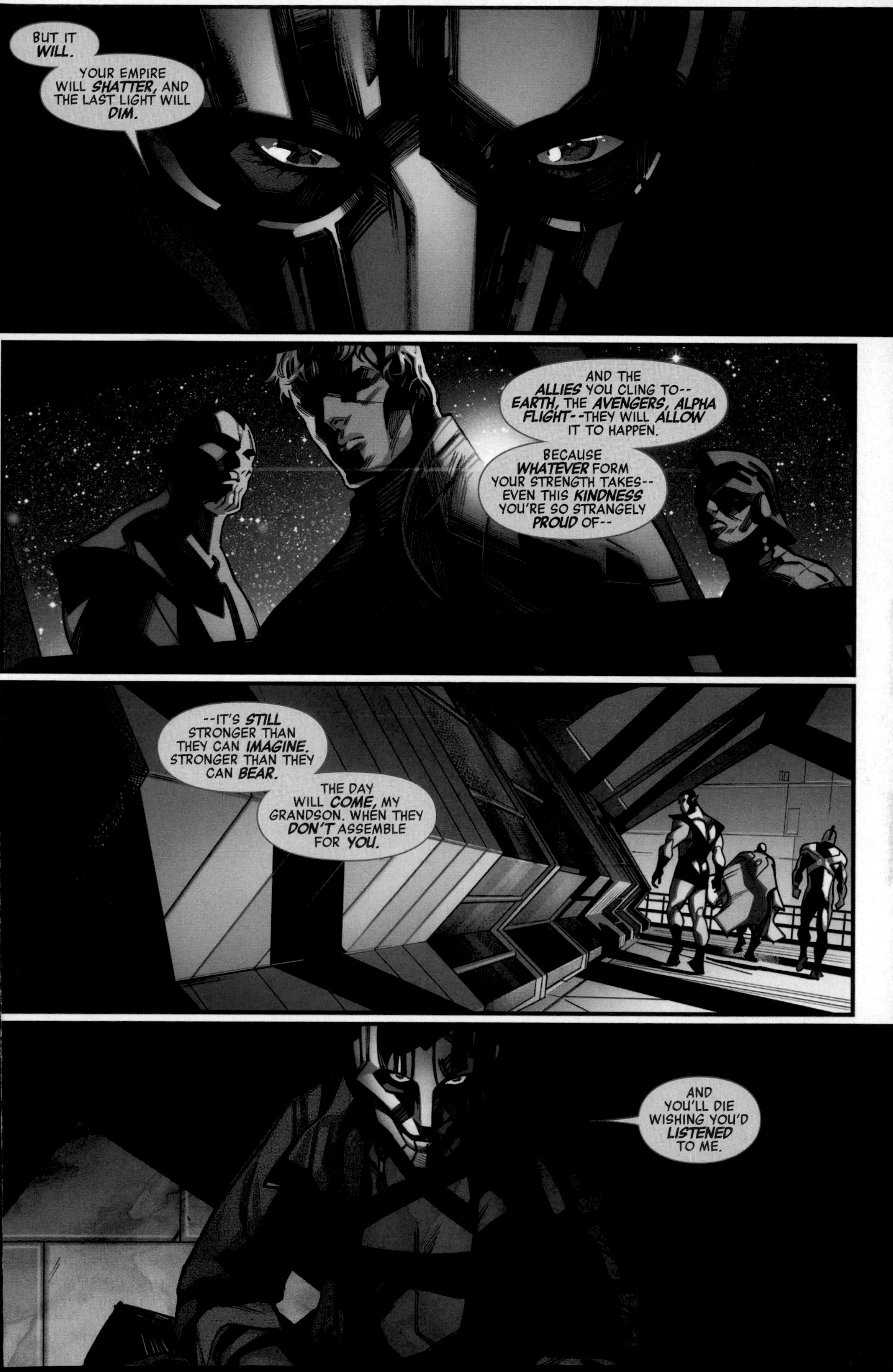
BUT IT WILL.
YOUR EMPIRE WILL SHATTER, AND THE LAST LIGHT WILL DIM.
AND THE ALLIES YOU CLING TO--EARTH, THE AVENGERS, ALPHA FLIGHT--THEY WILL ALLOW IT TO HAPPEN.
BECAUSE WHATEVER FORM YOUR STRENGTH TAKES--EVEN THIS KINDNESS YOU'RE SO STRANGELY PROUD OF--
--IT'S STILL STRONGER THAN THEY CAN IMAGINE. STRONGER THAN THEY CAN BEAR.
THE DAY WILL COME, MY GRANDSON. WHEN THEY DON'T ASSEMBLE FOR YOU.
AND YOU'LL DIE WISHING YOU'D LISTENED TO ME.

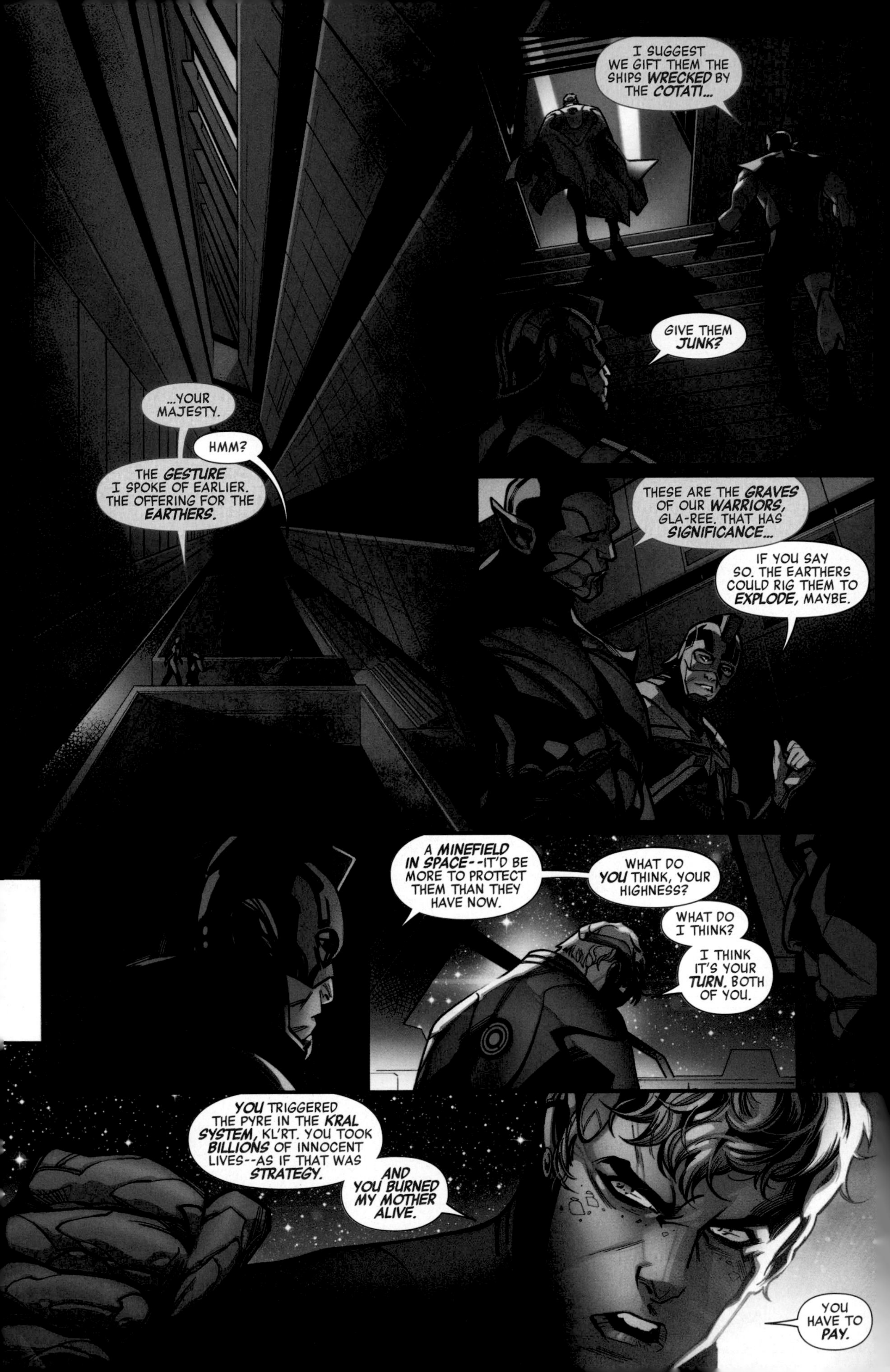

I SUGGEST WE GIFT THEM THE SHIPS WRECKED BY THE COTATI...
GIVE THEM JUNK?
...YOUR MAJESTY.
HMM?
THE GESTURE I SPOKE OF EARLIER. THE OFFERING FOR THE EARTHERS.
THESE ARE THE GRAVES OF OUR WARRIORS, GLA-REE. THAT HAS SIGNIFICANCE...
IF YOU SAY SO. THE EARTHERS COULD RIG THEM TO EXPLODE, MAYBE.
A MINEFIELD IN SPACE--IT'D BE MORE TO PROTECT THEM THAN THEY HAVE NOW.
WHAT DO YOU THINK, YOUR HIGHNESS?
WHAT DO I THINK?
I THINK IT'S YOUR TURN. BOTH OF YOU.
YOU TRIGGERED THE PYRE IN THE KRAL SYSTEM, KL'RT. YOU TOOK BILLIONS OF INNOCENT LIVES--AS IF THAT WAS STRATEGY.
AND YOU BURNED MY MOTHER ALIVE.
YOU HAVE TO PAY.

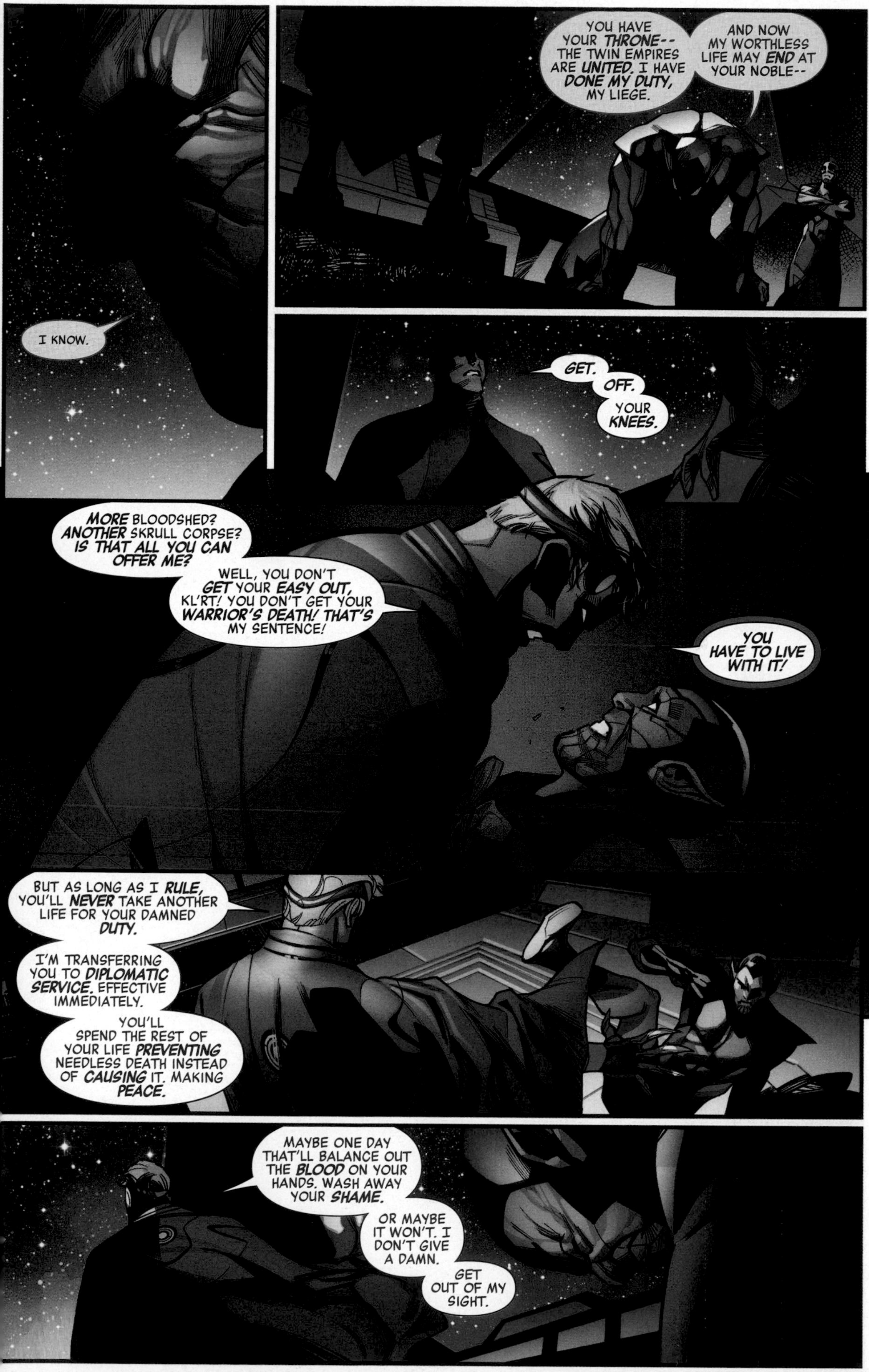
YOU HAVE YOUR THRONE-- THE TWIN EMPIRES ARE UNITED. I HAVE DONE MY DUTY, MY LIEGE.
AND NOW MY WORTHLESS LIFE MAY END AT YOUR NOBLE--
I KNOW.
GET.
OFF.
YOUR KNEES.
MORE BLOODSHED? ANOTHER SKRULL CORPSE? IS THAT ALL YOU CAN OFFER ME?
WELL, YOU DON'T GET YOUR EASY OUT, KL'RT! YOU DON'T GET YOUR WARRIOR'S DEATH! THAT'S MY SENTENCE!
YOU HAVE TO LIVE WITH IT!
BUT AS LONG AS I RULE, YOU'LL NEVER TAKE ANOTHER LIFE FOR YOUR DAMNED DUTY.
I'M TRANSFERRING YOU TO DIPLOMATIC SERVICE. EFFECTIVE IMMEDIATELY.
YOU'LL SPEND THE REST OF YOUR LIFE PREVENTING NEEDLESS DEATH INSTEAD OF CAUSING IT. MAKING PEACE.
MAYBE ONE DAY THAT'LL BALANCE OUT THE BLOOD ON YOUR HANDS. WASH AWAY YOUR SHAME.
OR MAYBE IT WON'T. I DON'T GIVE A DAMN.
GET OUT OF MY SIGHT.

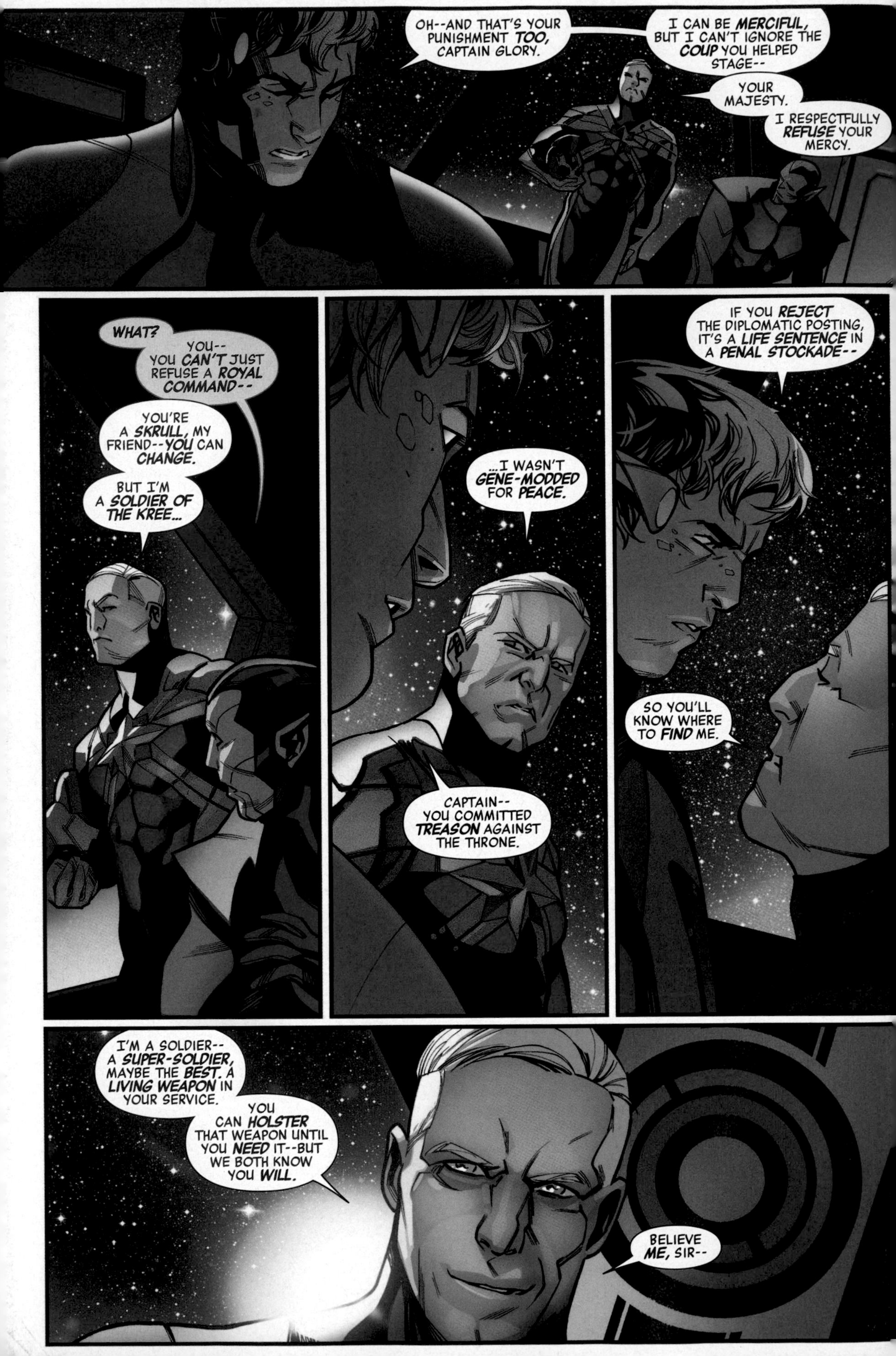
OH--AND THAT'S YOUR PUNISHMENT TOO, CAPTAIN GLORY.
I CAN BE MERCIFUL, BUT I CAN'T IGNORE THE COUP YOU HELPED STAGE--
YOUR MAJESTY.
I RESPECTFULLY REFUSE YOUR MERCY.
WHAT?
YOU-- YOU CAN'T JUST REFUSE A ROYAL COMMAND--
YOU'RE A SKRULL, MY FRIEND--YOU CAN CHANGE.
BUT I'M A SOLDIER OF THE KREE...
...I WASN'T GENE-MODDED FOR PEACE.
CAPTAIN-- YOU COMMITTED TREASON AGAINST THE THRONE.
IF YOU REJECT THE DIPLOMATIC POSTING, IT'S A LIFE SENTENCE IN A PENAL STOCKADE--
SO YOU'LL KNOW WHERE TO FIND ME.
I'M A SOLDIER-- A SUPER-SOLDIER, MAYBE THE BEST. A LIVING WEAPON IN YOUR SERVICE.
YOU CAN HOLSTER THAT WEAPON UNTIL YOU NEED IT--BUT WE BOTH KNOW YOU WILL.
BELIEVE ME, SIR--

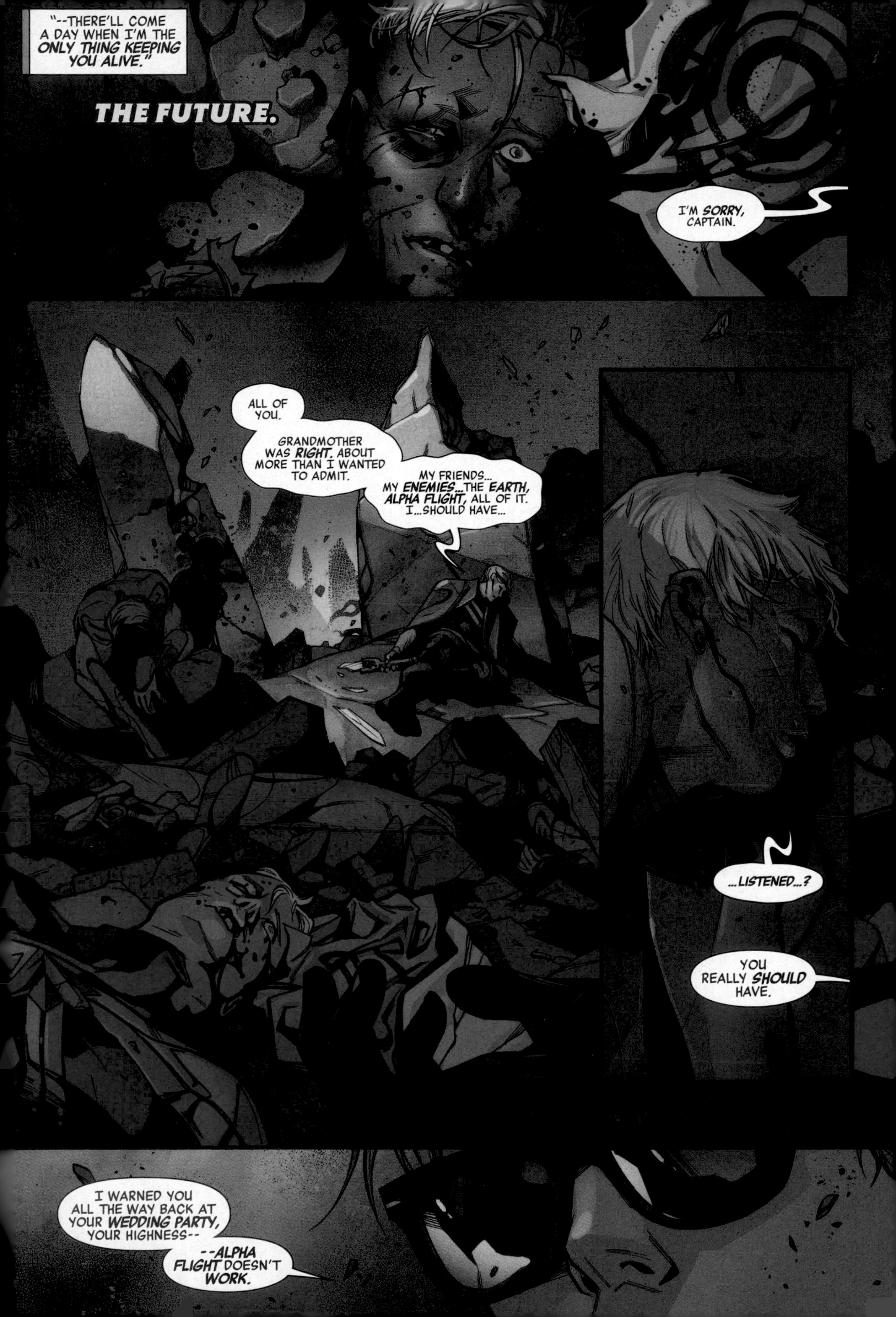
"--THERE'LL COME A DAY WHEN I'M THE ONLY THING KEEPING YOU ALIVE."
THE FUTURE.
I'M SORRY, CAPTAIN.
ALL OF YOU.
GRANDMOTHER WAS RIGHT. ABOUT MORE THAN I WANTED TO ADMIT.
MY FRIENDS... MY ENEMIES...THE EARTH, ALPHA FLIGHT, ALL OF IT. I...SHOULD HAVE...
...LISTENED...?
YOU REALLY SHOULD HAVE.
I WARNED YOU ALL THE WAY BACK AT YOUR WEDDING PARTY, YOUR HIGHNESS--
--ALPHA FLIGHT DOESN'T WORK.

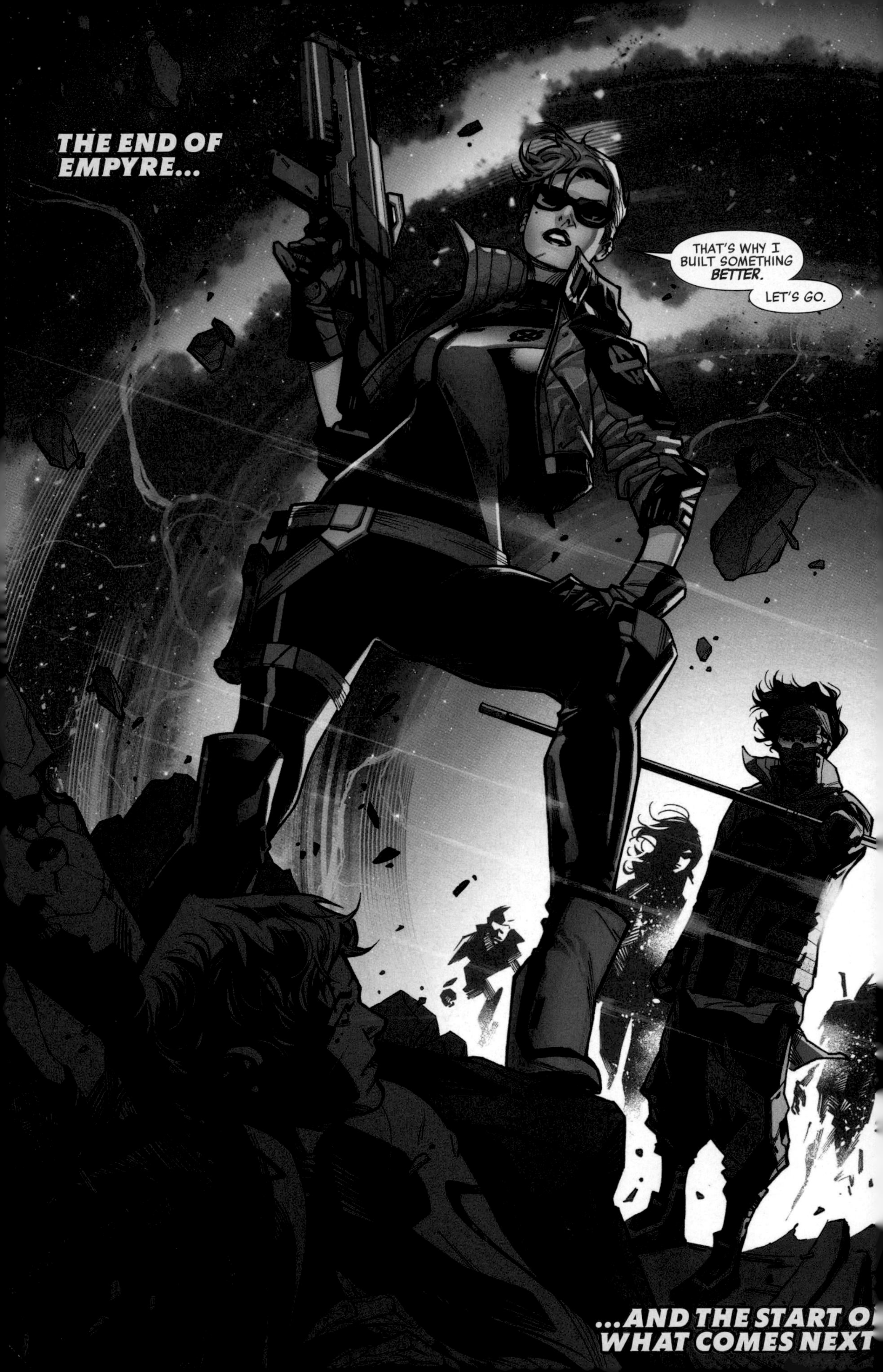
THE END OF EMPYRE...
THAT'S WHY I BUILT SOMETHING BETTER.
LET'S GO.
...AND THE START OF WHAT COMES NEXT

EMPYRE: FALLOUT — FANTASTIC FOUR VARIANT BY
Carmen Carnero & **Rachelle Rosenberg**

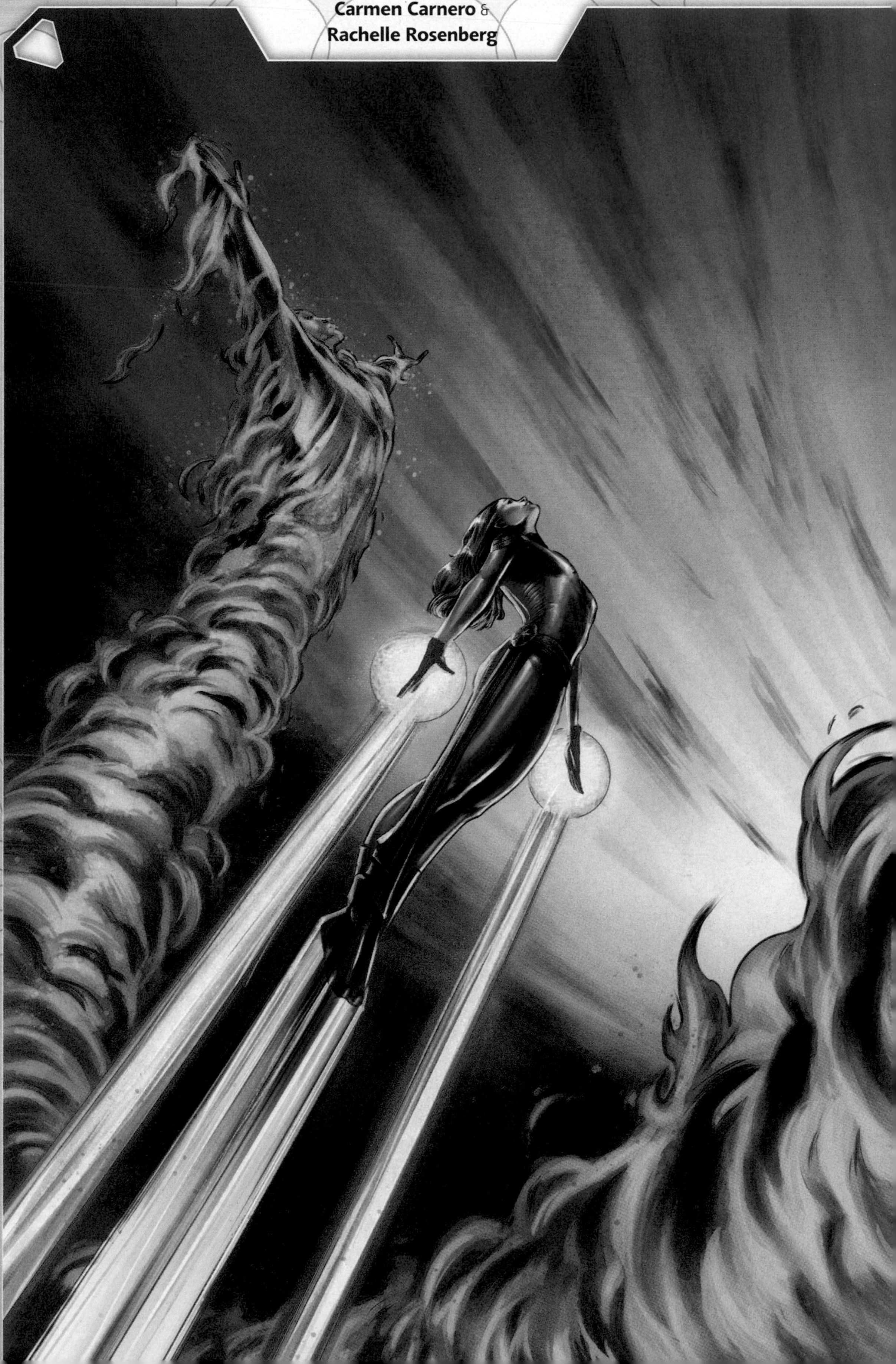

EMPYRE: FALLOUT – FANTSTIC FOUR

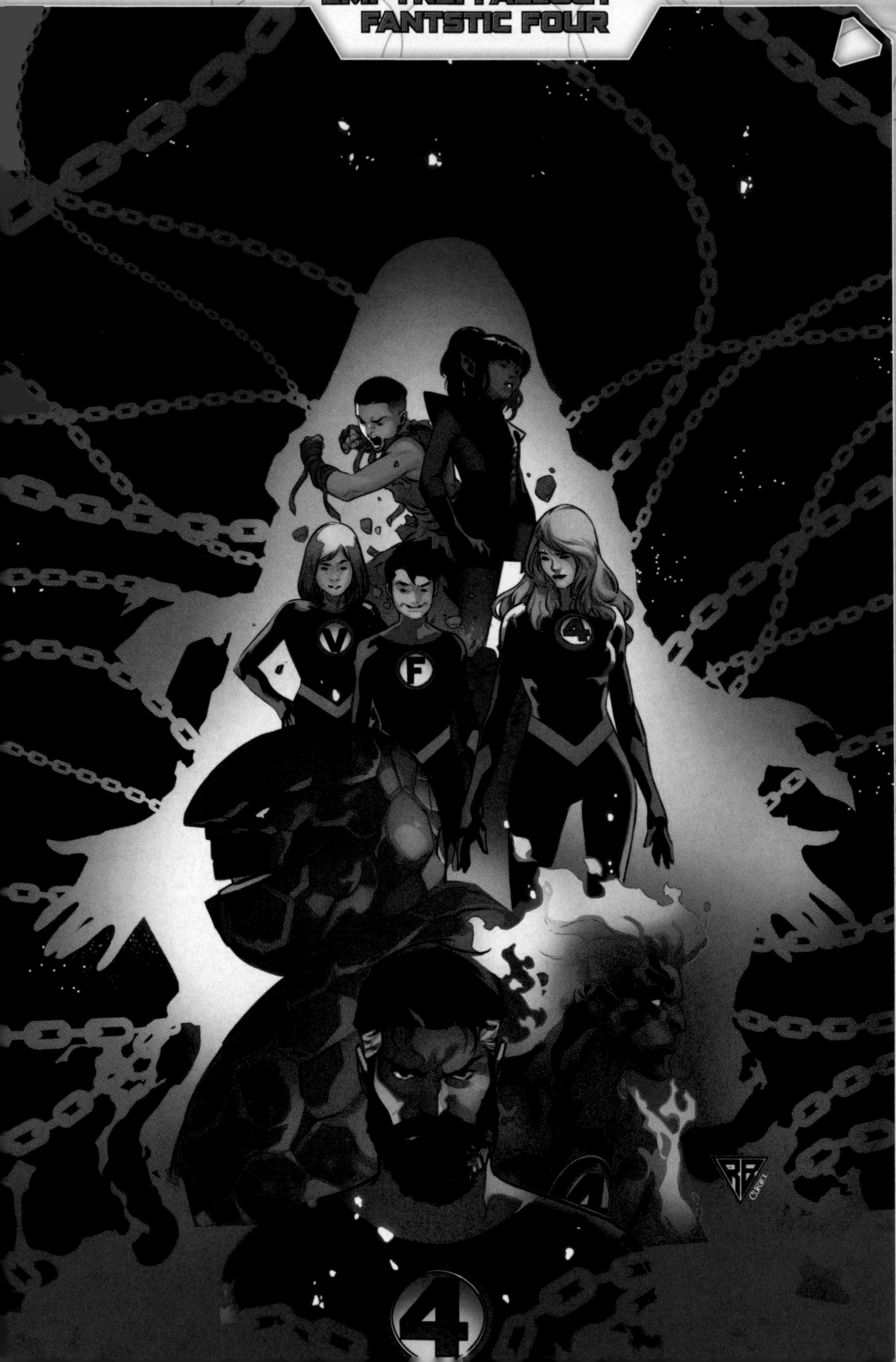

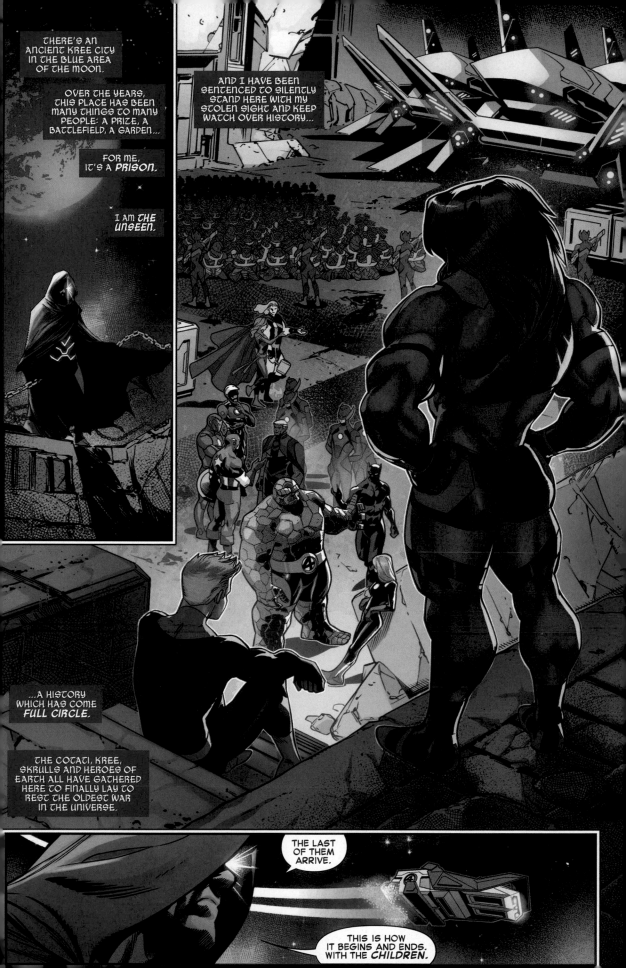

THERE'S AN ANCIENT KREE CITY IN THE BLUE AREA OF THE MOON.

OVER THE YEARS, THIS PLACE HAS BEEN MANY THINGS TO MANY PEOPLE: A PRIZE, A BATTLEFIELD, A GARDEN...

FOR ME, IT'S A *PRISON*.

I AM *THE UNSEEN*.

AND I HAVE BEEN SENTENCED TO SILENTLY STAND HERE WITH MY STOLEN SIGHT AND KEEP WATCH OVER HISTORY...

...A HISTORY WHICH HAS COME *FULL CIRCLE*.

THE COTATI, KREE, SKRULLS AND HEROES OF EARTH ALL HAVE GATHERED HERE TO FINALLY LAY TO REST THE OLDEST WAR IN THE UNIVERSE.

THE LAST OF THEM ARRIVE.

THIS IS HOW IT BEGINS AND ENDS. WITH THE *CHILDREN*.

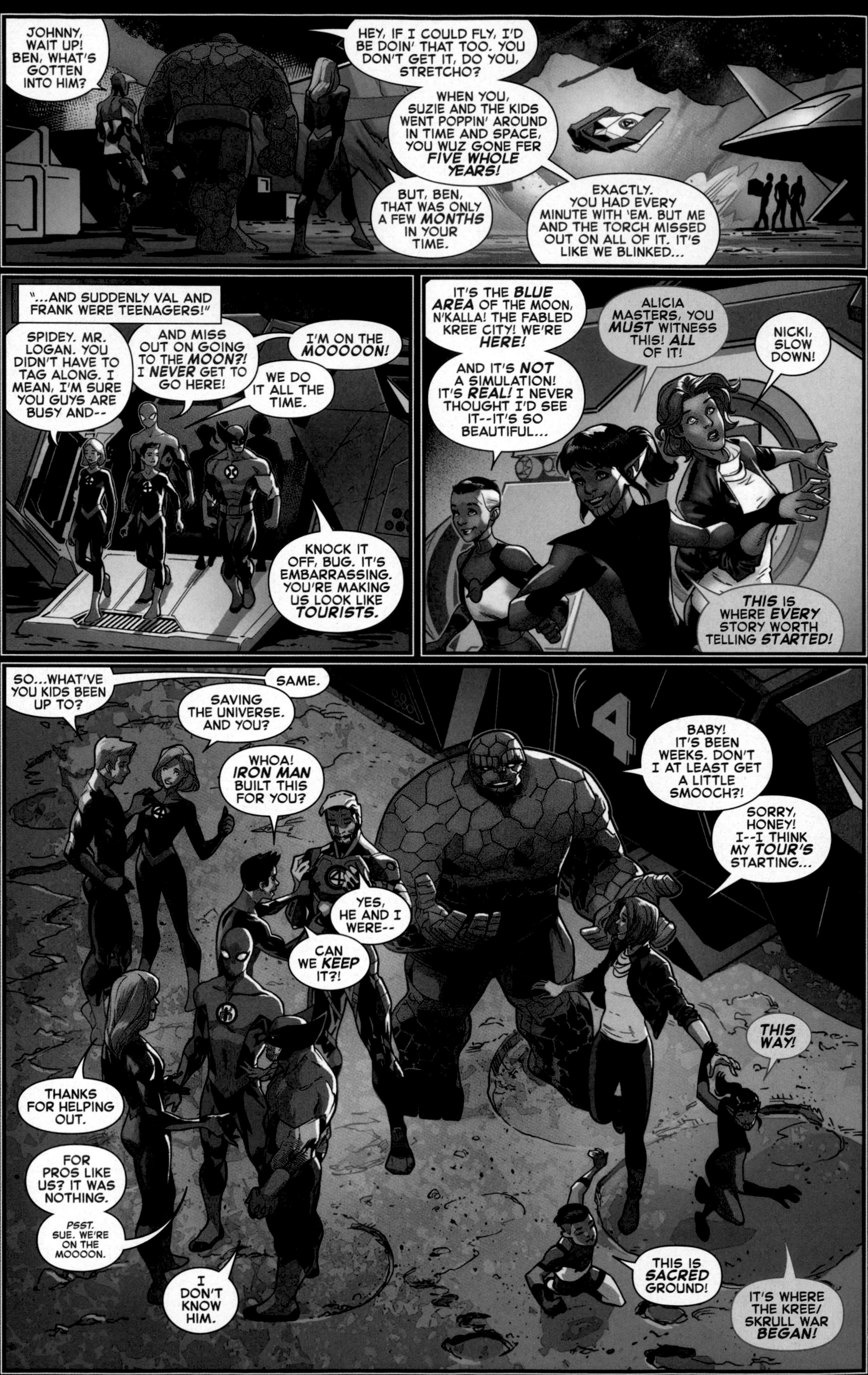
JOHNNY, WAIT UP! BEN, WHAT'S GOTTEN INTO HIM?
HEY, IF I COULD FLY, I'D BE DOIN' THAT TOO. YOU DON'T GET IT, DO YOU, STRETCHO?
WHEN YOU, SUZIE AND THE KIDS WENT POPPIN' AROUND IN TIME AND SPACE, YOU WUZ GONE FER FIVE WHOLE YEARS!
BUT, BEN, THAT WAS ONLY A FEW MONTHS IN YOUR TIME.
EXACTLY. YOU HAD EVERY MINUTE WITH 'EM. BUT ME AND THE TORCH MISSED OUT ON ALL OF IT. IT'S LIKE WE BLINKED...
"...AND SUDDENLY VAL AND FRANK WERE TEENAGERS!"
SPIDEY. MR. LOGAN. YOU DIDN'T HAVE TO TAG ALONG. I MEAN, I'M SURE YOU GUYS ARE BUSY AND--
AND MISS OUT ON GOING TO THE MOON?! I NEVER GET TO GO HERE!
I'M ON THE MOOOOON!
WE DO IT ALL THE TIME.
KNOCK IT OFF, BUG. IT'S EMBARRASSING. YOU'RE MAKING US LOOK LIKE TOURISTS.
IT'S THE BLUE AREA OF THE MOON, N'KALLA! THE FABLED KREE CITY! WE'RE HERE!
AND IT'S NOT A SIMULATION! IT'S REAL! I NEVER THOUGHT I'D SEE IT--IT'S SO BEAUTIFUL...
ALICIA MASTERS, YOU MUST WITNESS THIS! ALL OF IT!
NICKI, SLOW DOWN!
THIS IS WHERE EVERY STORY WORTH TELLING STARTED!
SO...WHAT'VE YOU KIDS BEEN UP TO?
SAVING THE UNIVERSE. AND YOU?
SAME.
WHOA! IRON MAN BUILT THIS FOR YOU?
YES, HE AND I WERE--
CAN WE KEEP IT?!
BABY! IT'S BEEN WEEKS. DON'T I AT LEAST GET A LITTLE SMOOCH?!
SORRY, HONEY! I--I THINK MY TOUR'S STARTING...
THIS WAY!
THANKS FOR HELPING OUT.
FOR PROS LIKE US? IT WAS NOTHING.
PSST. SUE. WE'RE ON THE MOOOON.
I DON'T KNOW HIM.
THIS IS SACRED GROUND!
IT'S WHERE THE KREE/SKRULL WAR BEGAN!

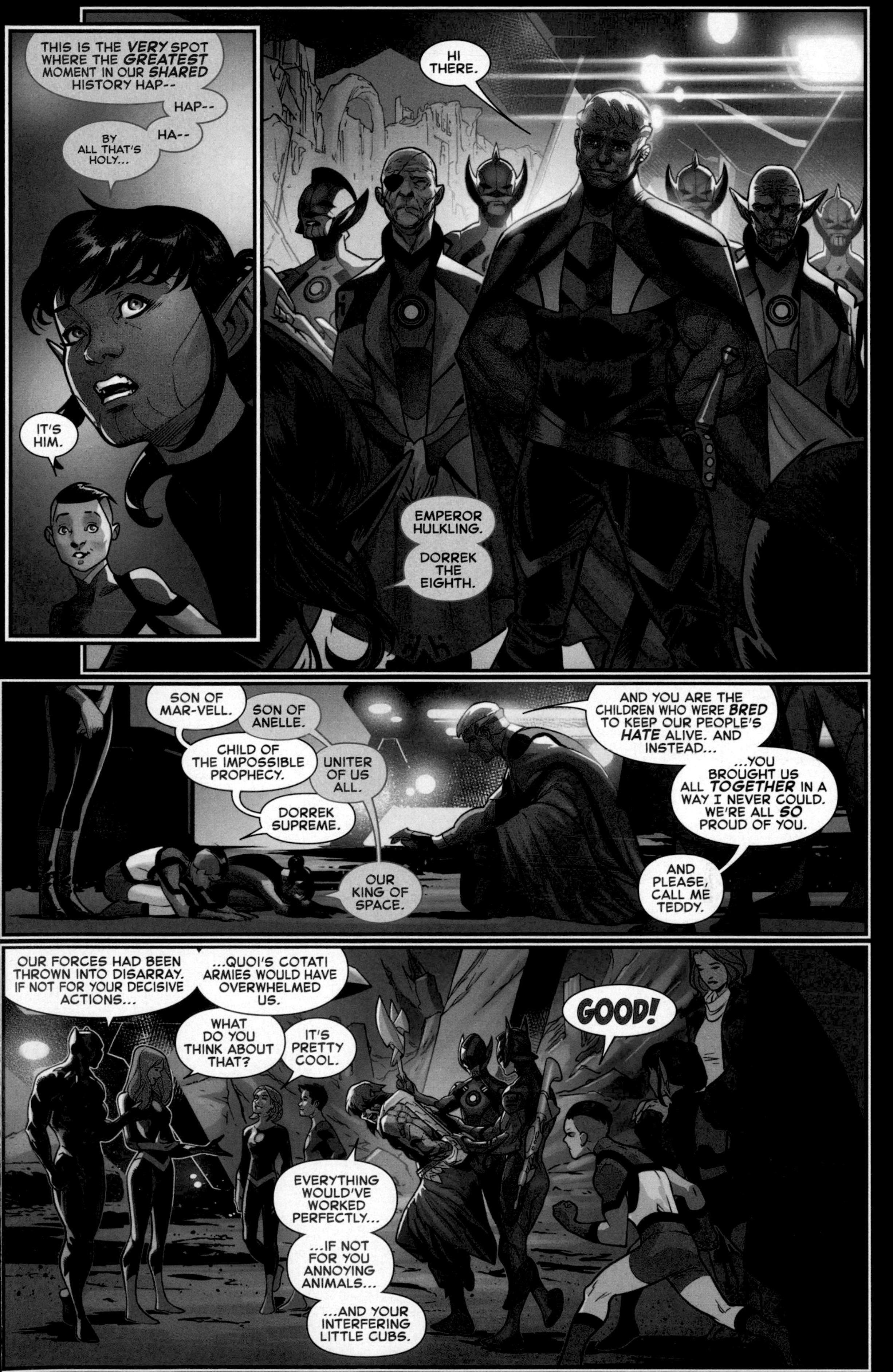
THIS IS THE VERY SPOT WHERE THE GREATEST MOMENT IN OUR SHARED HISTORY HAP--
HAP--
HA--
BY ALL THAT'S HOLY...
IT'S HIM.
HI THERE.
EMPEROR HULKLING.
DORREK THE EIGHTH.
SON OF MAR-VELL.
SON OF ANELLE.
CHILD OF THE IMPOSSIBLE PROPHECY.
UNITER OF US ALL.
DORREK SUPREME.
OUR KING OF SPACE.
AND YOU ARE THE CHILDREN WHO WERE BRED TO KEEP OUR PEOPLE'S HATE ALIVE. AND INSTEAD...
...YOU BROUGHT US ALL TOGETHER IN A WAY I NEVER COULD. WE'RE ALL SO PROUD OF YOU.
AND PLEASE, CALL ME TEDDY.
OUR FORCES HAD BEEN THROWN INTO DISARRAY. IF NOT FOR YOUR DECISIVE ACTIONS...
...QUOI'S COTATI ARMIES WOULD HAVE OVERWHELMED US.
WHAT DO YOU THINK ABOUT THAT?
IT'S PRETTY COOL.
GOOD!
EVERYTHING WOULD'VE WORKED PERFECTLY...
...IF NOT FOR YOU ANNOYING ANIMALS...
...AND YOUR INTERFERING LITTLE CUBS.

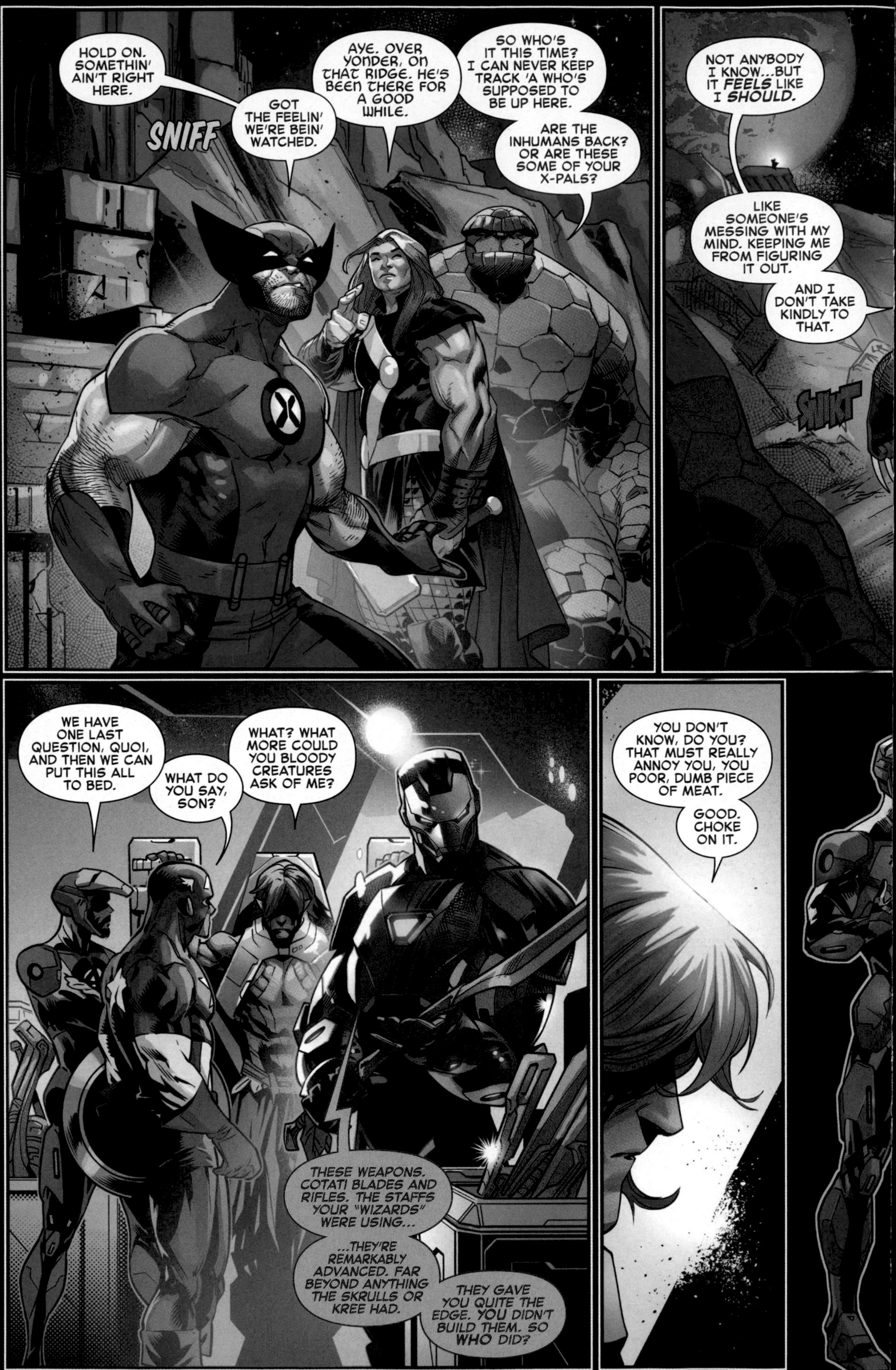
HOLD ON. SOMETHIN' AIN'T RIGHT HERE.
SNIFF
GOT THE FEELIN' WE'RE BEIN' WATCHED.
AYE. OVER YONDER, ON THAT RIDGE. HE'S BEEN THERE FOR A GOOD WHILE.
SO WHO'S IT THIS TIME? I CAN NEVER KEEP TRACK 'A WHO'S SUPPOSED TO BE UP HERE.
ARE THE INHUMANS BACK? OR ARE THESE SOME OF YOUR X-PALS?
NOT ANYBODY I KNOW...BUT IT FEELS LIKE I SHOULD.
LIKE SOMEONE'S MESSING WITH MY MIND. KEEPING ME FROM FIGURING IT OUT.
AND I DON'T TAKE KINDLY TO THAT.
SNIKT
WE HAVE ONE LAST QUESTION, QUOI, AND THEN WE CAN PUT THIS ALL TO BED.
WHAT DO YOU SAY, SON?
WHAT? WHAT MORE COULD YOU BLOODY CREATURES ASK OF ME?
THESE WEAPONS. COTATI BLADES AND RIFLES. THE STAFFS YOUR "WIZARDS" WERE USING...
...THEY'RE REMARKABLY ADVANCED. FAR BEYOND ANYTHING THE SKRULLS OR KREE HAD.
THEY GAVE YOU QUITE THE EDGE. YOU DIDN'T BUILD THEM. SO WHO DID?
YOU DON'T KNOW, DO YOU? THAT MUST REALLY ANNOY YOU, YOU POOR, DUMB PIECE OF MEAT.
GOOD. CHOKE ON IT.

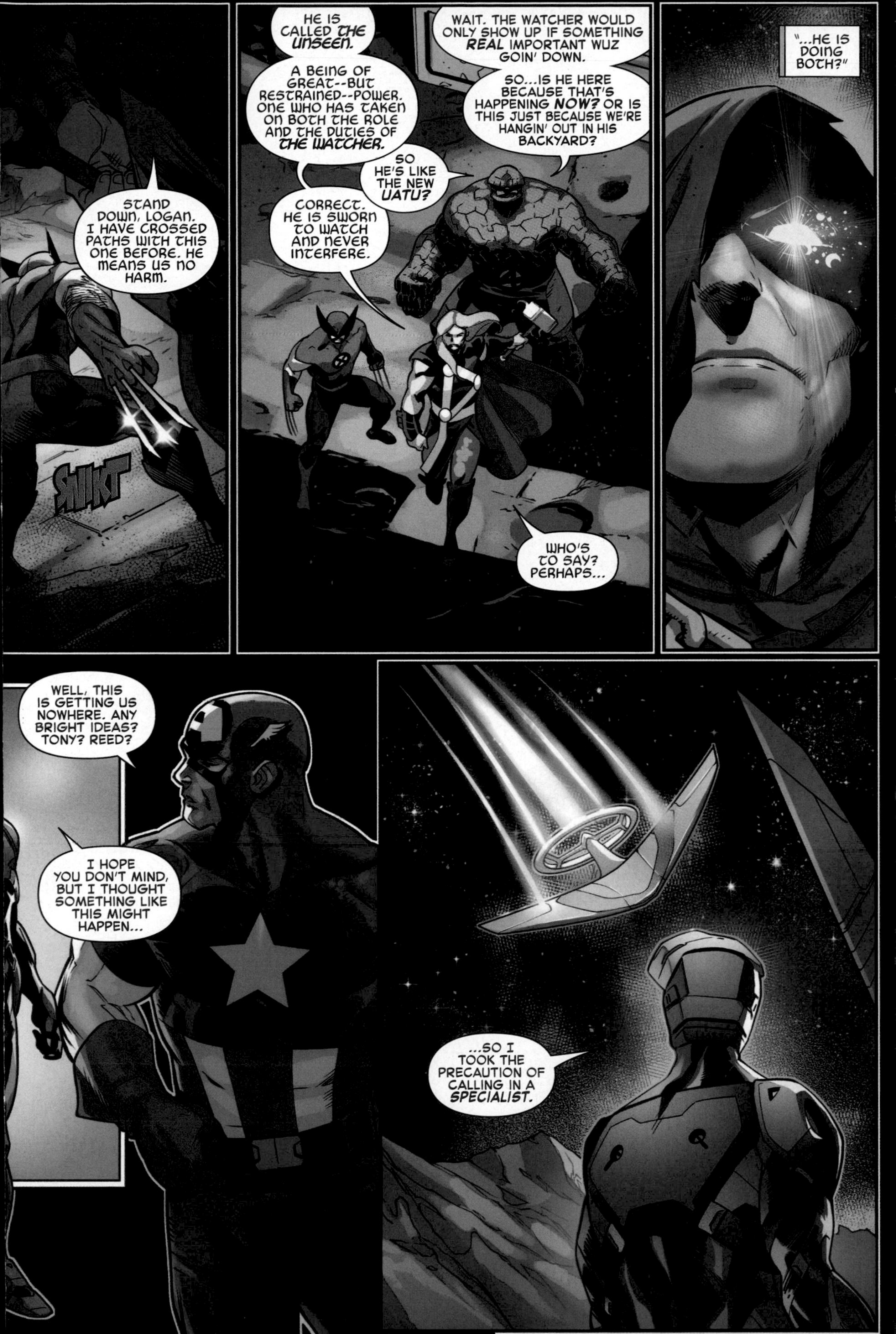
STAND DOWN, LOGAN. I HAVE CROSSED PATHS WITH THIS ONE BEFORE. HE MEANS US NO HARM.
SNIKT
HE IS CALLED THE UNSEEN.
A BEING OF GREAT--BUT RESTRAINED--POWER. ONE WHO HAS TAKEN ON BOTH THE ROLE AND THE DUTIES OF THE WATCHER.
SO HE'S LIKE THE NEW UATU?
CORRECT. HE IS SWORN TO WATCH AND NEVER INTERFERE.
WAIT. THE WATCHER WOULD ONLY SHOW UP IF SOMETHING REAL IMPORTANT WUZ GOIN' DOWN.
SO...IS HE HERE BECAUSE THAT'S HAPPENING NOW? OR IS THIS JUST BECAUSE WE'RE HANGIN' OUT IN HIS BACKYARD?
WHO'S TO SAY? PERHAPS...
"...HE IS DOING BOTH?"
WELL, THIS IS GETTING US NOWHERE. ANY BRIGHT IDEAS? TONY? REED?
I HOPE YOU DON'T MIND, BUT I THOUGHT SOMETHING LIKE THIS MIGHT HAPPEN...
...SO I TOOK THE PRECAUTION OF CALLING IN A SPECIALIST.

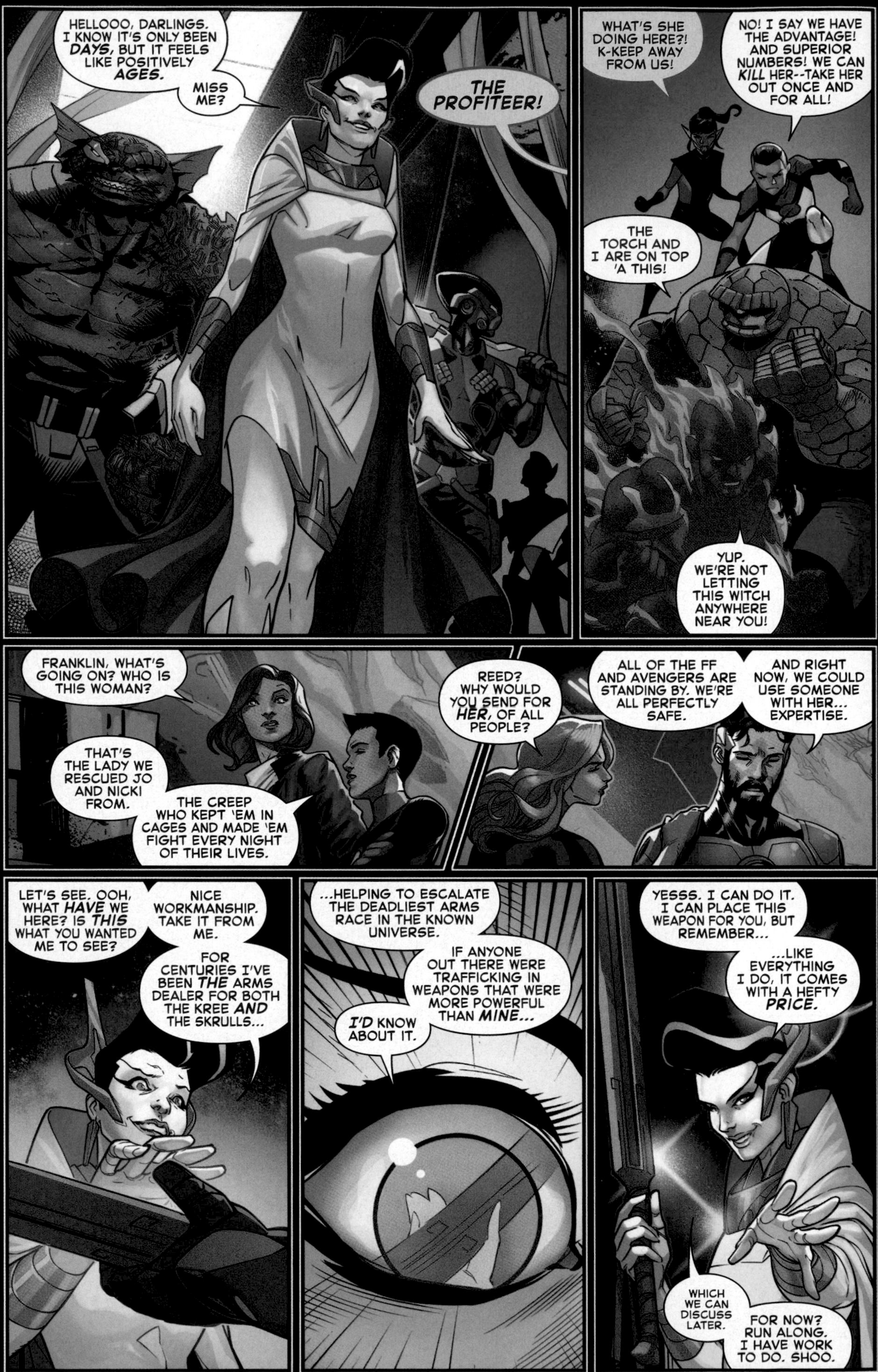
HELLOOO, DARLINGS. I KNOW IT'S ONLY BEEN DAYS, BUT IT FEELS LIKE POSITIVELY AGES.
MISS ME?
THE PROFITEER!
WHAT'S SHE DOING HERE?! K-KEEP AWAY FROM US!
NO! I SAY WE HAVE THE ADVANTAGE! AND SUPERIOR NUMBERS! WE CAN KILL HER--TAKE HER OUT ONCE AND FOR ALL!
THE TORCH AND I ARE ON TOP 'A THIS!
YUP. WE'RE NOT LETTING THIS WITCH ANYWHERE NEAR YOU!
FRANKLIN, WHAT'S GOING ON? WHO IS THIS WOMAN?
THAT'S THE LADY WE RESCUED JO AND NICKI FROM.
THE CREEP WHO KEPT 'EM IN CAGES AND MADE 'EM FIGHT EVERY NIGHT OF THEIR LIVES.
REED? WHY WOULD YOU SEND FOR HER, OF ALL PEOPLE?
ALL OF THE FF AND AVENGERS ARE STANDING BY. WE'RE ALL PERFECTLY SAFE.
AND RIGHT NOW, WE COULD USE SOMEONE WITH HER... EXPERTISE.
LET'S SEE. OOH, WHAT HAVE WE HERE? IS THIS WHAT YOU WANTED ME TO SEE?
NICE WORKMANSHIP. TAKE IT FROM ME.
FOR CENTURIES I'VE BEEN THE ARMS DEALER FOR BOTH THE KREE AND THE SKRULLS...
...HELPING TO ESCALATE THE DEADLIEST ARMS RACE IN THE KNOWN UNIVERSE.
IF ANYONE OUT THERE WERE TRAFFICKING IN WEAPONS THAT WERE MORE POWERFUL THAN MINE...
I'D KNOW ABOUT IT.
YESSS. I CAN DO IT. I CAN PLACE THIS WEAPON FOR YOU, BUT REMEMBER...
...LIKE EVERYTHING I DO, IT COMES WITH A HEFTY PRICE.
WHICH WE CAN DISCUSS LATER.
FOR NOW? RUN ALONG. I HAVE WORK TO DO. SHOO.

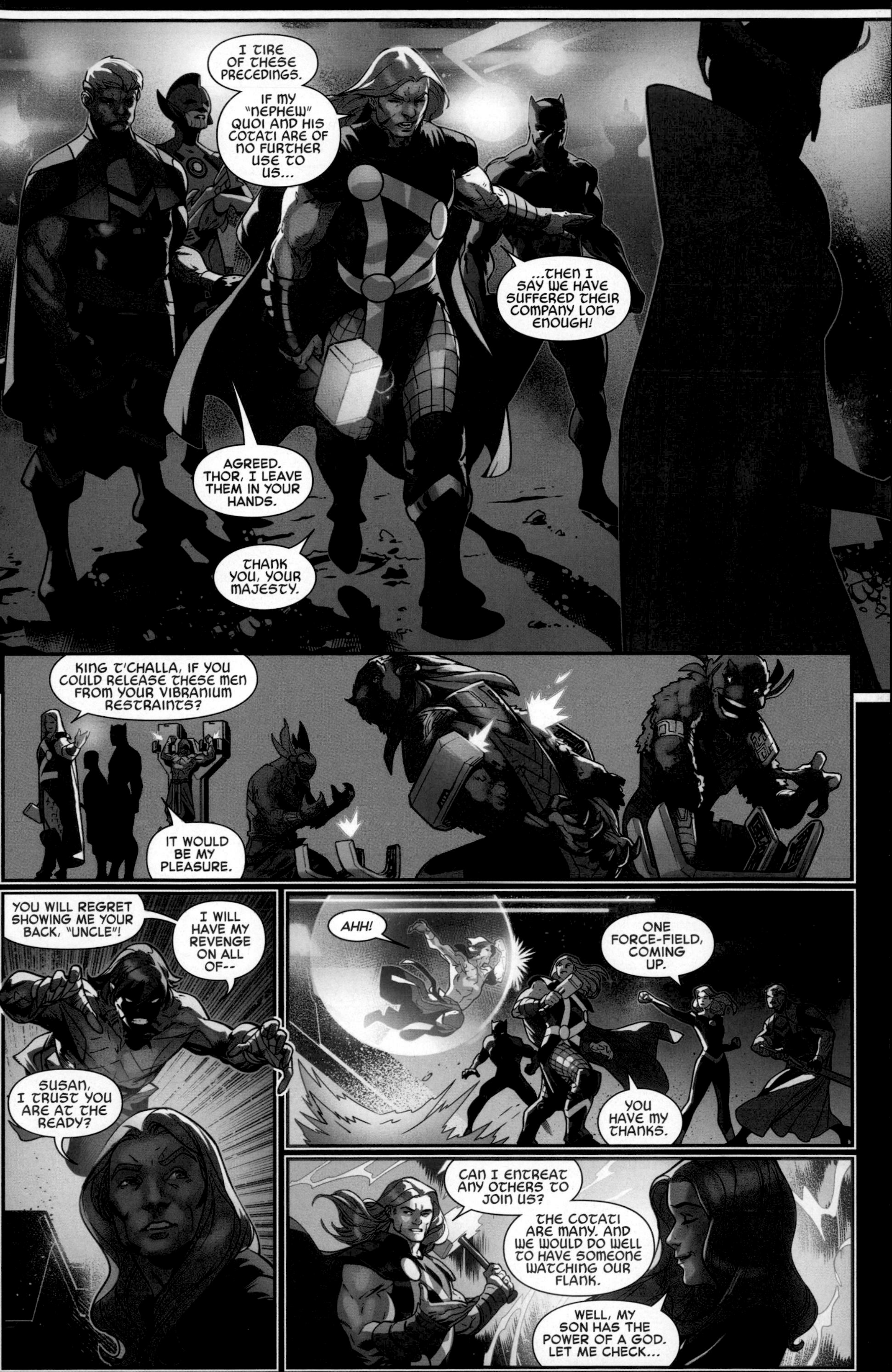
I TIRE OF THESE PRECEDINGS.
IF MY "NEPHEW" QUOI AND HIS COTATI ARE OF NO FURTHER USE TO US...
...THEN I SAY WE HAVE SUFFERED THEIR COMPANY LONG ENOUGH!
AGREED. THOR, I LEAVE THEM IN YOUR HANDS.
THANK YOU, YOUR MAJESTY.
KING T'CHALLA, IF YOU COULD RELEASE THESE MEN FROM YOUR VIBRANIUM RESTRAINTS?
IT WOULD BE MY PLEASURE.
YOU WILL REGRET SHOWING ME YOUR BACK, "UNCLE"!
I WILL HAVE MY REVENGE ON ALL OF--
SUSAN, I TRUST YOU ARE AT THE READY?
AHH!
ONE FORCE-FIELD, COMING UP.
YOU HAVE MY THANKS.
CAN I ENTREAT ANY OTHERS TO JOIN US?
THE COTATI ARE MANY. AND WE WOULD DO WELL TO HAVE SOMEONE WATCHING OUR FLANK.
WELL, MY SON HAS THE POWER OF A GOD. LET ME CHECK...

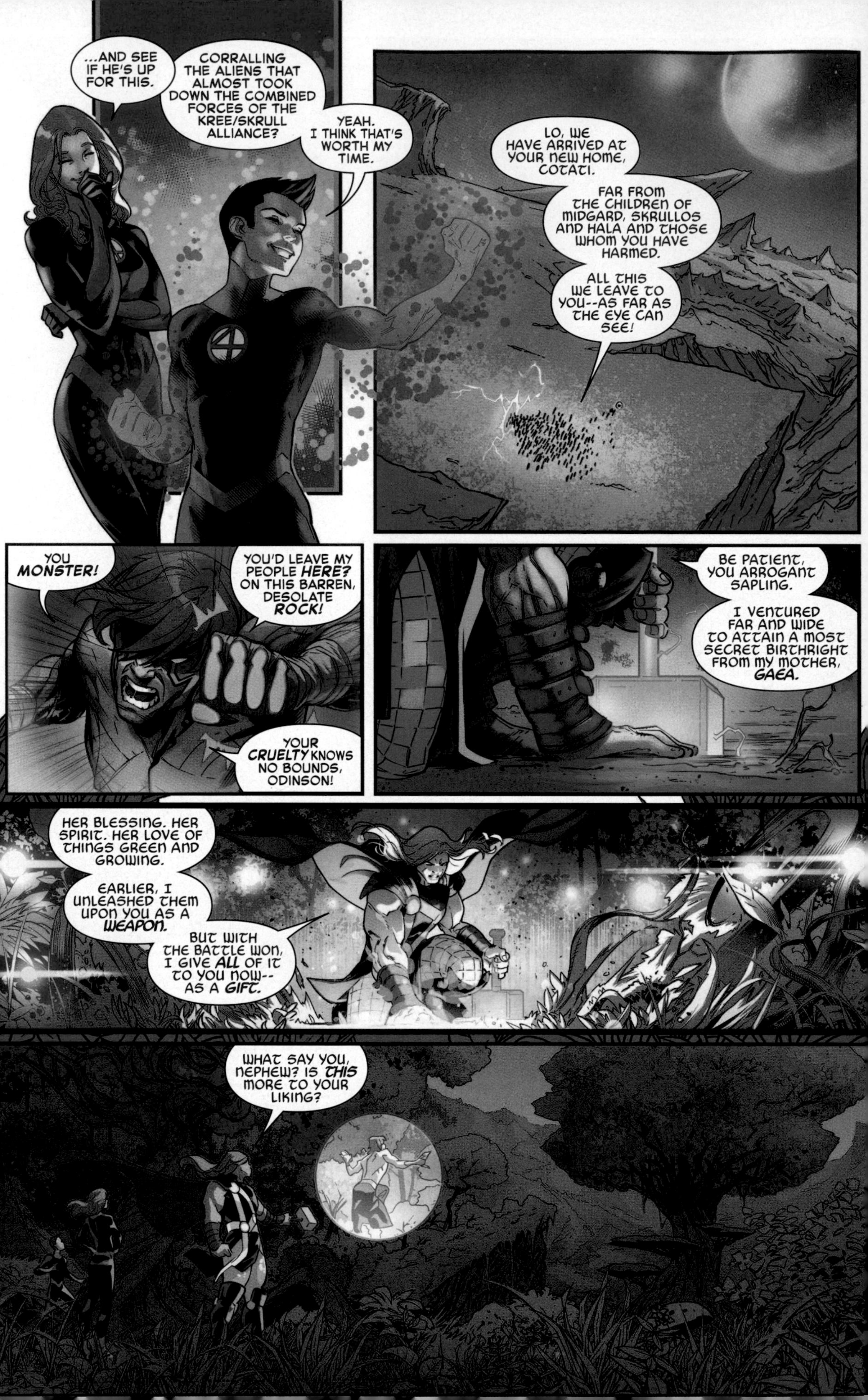
...AND SEE IF HE'S UP FOR THIS.
CORRALLING THE ALIENS THAT ALMOST TOOK DOWN THE COMBINED FORCES OF THE KREE/SKRULL ALLIANCE?
YEAH. I THINK THAT'S WORTH MY TIME.
LO, WE HAVE ARRIVED AT YOUR NEW HOME, COTATI.
FAR FROM THE CHILDREN OF MIDGARD, SKRULLOS AND HALA AND THOSE WHOM YOU HAVE HARMED.
ALL THIS WE LEAVE TO YOU--AS FAR AS THE EYE CAN SEE!
YOU MONSTER!
YOU'D LEAVE MY PEOPLE HERE? ON THIS BARREN, DESOLATE ROCK!
YOUR CRUELTY KNOWS NO BOUNDS, ODINSON!
BE PATIENT, YOU ARROGANT SAPLING.
I VENTURED FAR AND WIDE TO ATTAIN A MOST SECRET BIRTHRIGHT FROM MY MOTHER, GAEA.
HER BLESSING. HER SPIRIT. HER LOVE OF THINGS GREEN AND GROWING.
EARLIER, I UNLEASHED THEM UPON YOU AS A WEAPON.
BUT WITH THE BATTLE WON, I GIVE ALL OF IT TO YOU NOW--AS A GIFT.
WHAT SAY YOU, NEPHEW? IS THIS MORE TO YOUR LIKING?

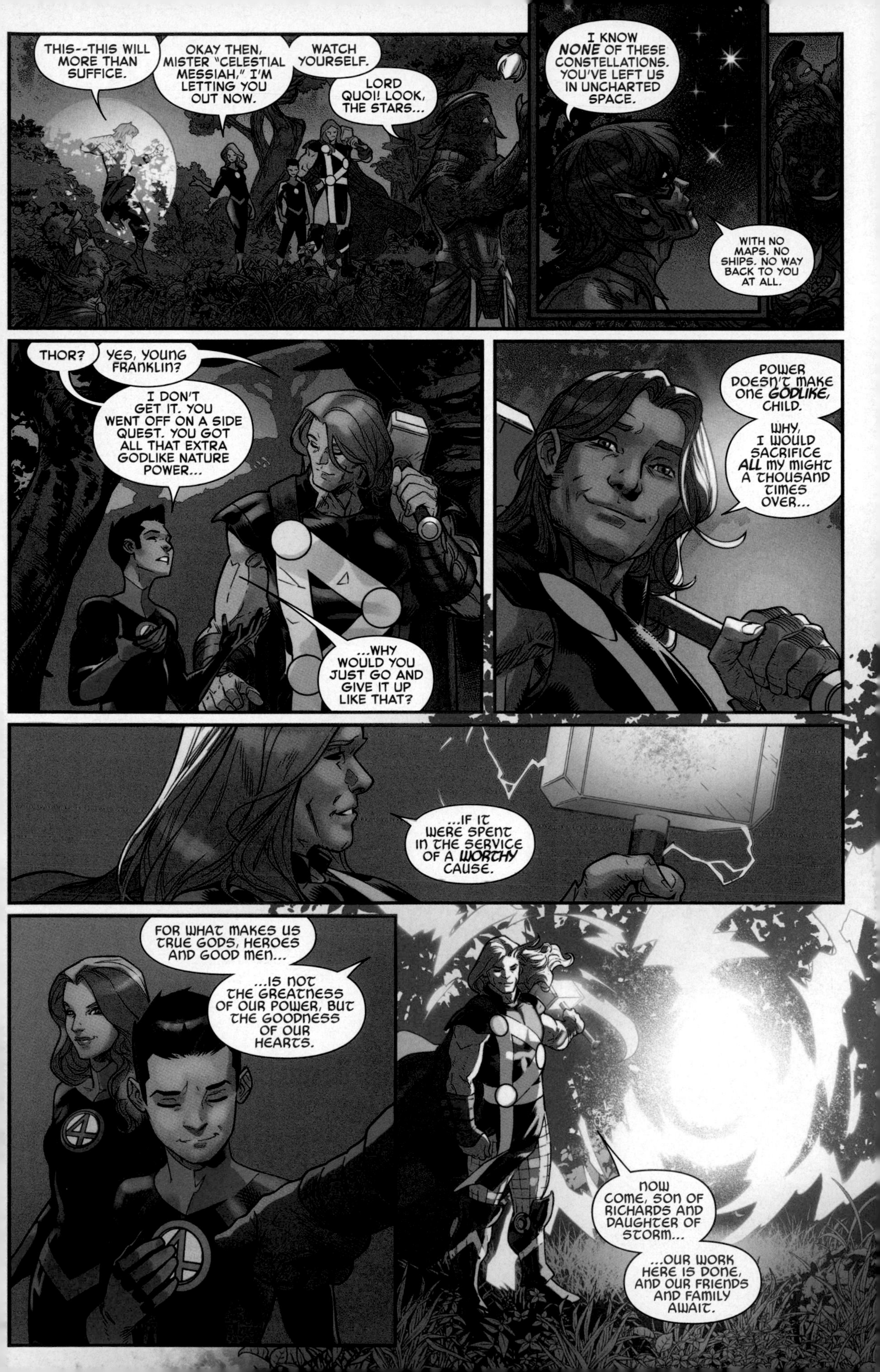
THIS--THIS WILL MORE THAN SUFFICE.
OKAY THEN, MISTER "CELESTIAL MESSIAH," I'M LETTING YOU OUT NOW.
WATCH YOURSELF.
LORD QUOI! LOOK, THE STARS...
I KNOW NONE OF THESE CONSTELLATIONS. YOU'VE LEFT US IN UNCHARTED SPACE.
WITH NO MAPS. NO SHIPS. NO WAY BACK TO YOU AT ALL.
THOR?
YES, YOUNG FRANKLIN?
I DON'T GET IT. YOU WENT OFF ON A SIDE QUEST. YOU GOT ALL THAT EXTRA GODLIKE NATURE POWER...
...WHY WOULD YOU JUST GO AND GIVE IT UP LIKE THAT?
POWER DOESN'T MAKE ONE GODLIKE, CHILD.
WHY, I WOULD SACRIFICE ALL MY MIGHT A THOUSAND TIMES OVER...
...IF IT WERE SPENT IN THE SERVICE OF A WORTHY CAUSE.
FOR WHAT MAKES US TRUE GODS, HEROES AND GOOD MEN...
...IS NOT THE GREATNESS OF OUR POWER, BUT THE GOODNESS OF OUR HEARTS.
NOW COME, SON OF RICHARDS AND DAUGHTER OF STORM...
...OUR WORK HERE IS DONE, AND OUR FRIENDS AND FAMILY AWAIT.

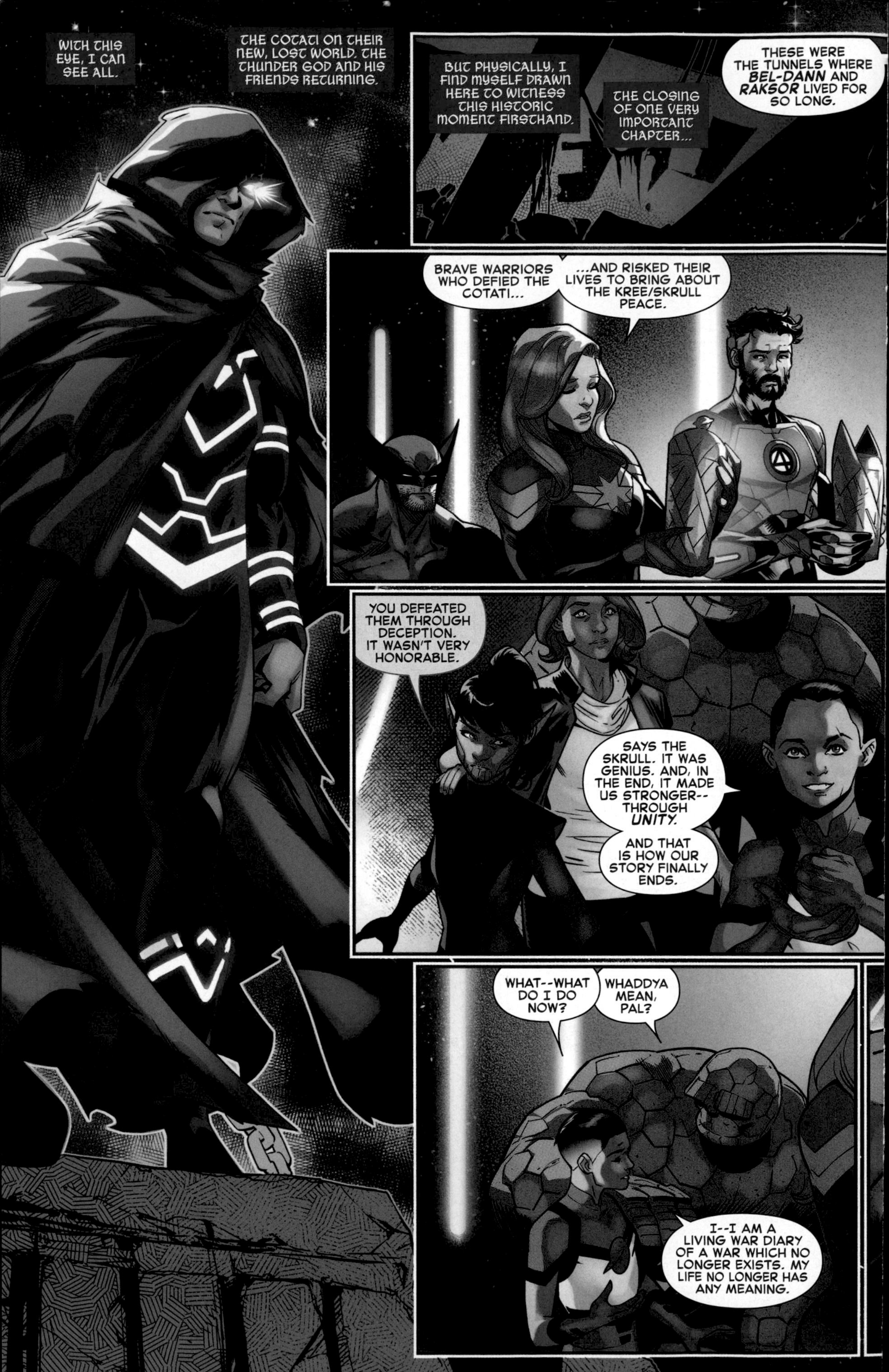
WITH THIS EYE, I CAN SEE ALL.
THE COTATI ON THEIR NEW, LOST WORLD. THE THUNDER GOD AND HIS FRIENDS RETURNING.
BUT PHYSICALLY, I FIND MYSELF DRAWN HERE TO WITNESS THIS HISTORIC MOMENT FIRSTHAND.
THE CLOSING OF ONE VERY IMPORTANT CHAPTER...
THESE WERE THE TUNNELS WHERE BEL-DANN AND RAKSOR LIVED FOR SO LONG.
BRAVE WARRIORS WHO DEFIED THE COTATI...
...AND RISKED THEIR LIVES TO BRING ABOUT THE KREE/SKRULL PEACE.
YOU DEFEATED THEM THROUGH DECEPTION. IT WASN'T VERY HONORABLE.
SAYS THE SKRULL. IT WAS GENIUS. AND, IN THE END, IT MADE US STRONGER--THROUGH UNITY.
AND THAT IS HOW OUR STORY FINALLY ENDS.
WHAT--WHAT DO I DO NOW?
WHADDYA MEAN, PAL?
I--I AM A LIVING WAR DIARY OF A WAR WHICH NO LONGER EXISTS. MY LIFE NO LONGER HAS ANY MEANING.

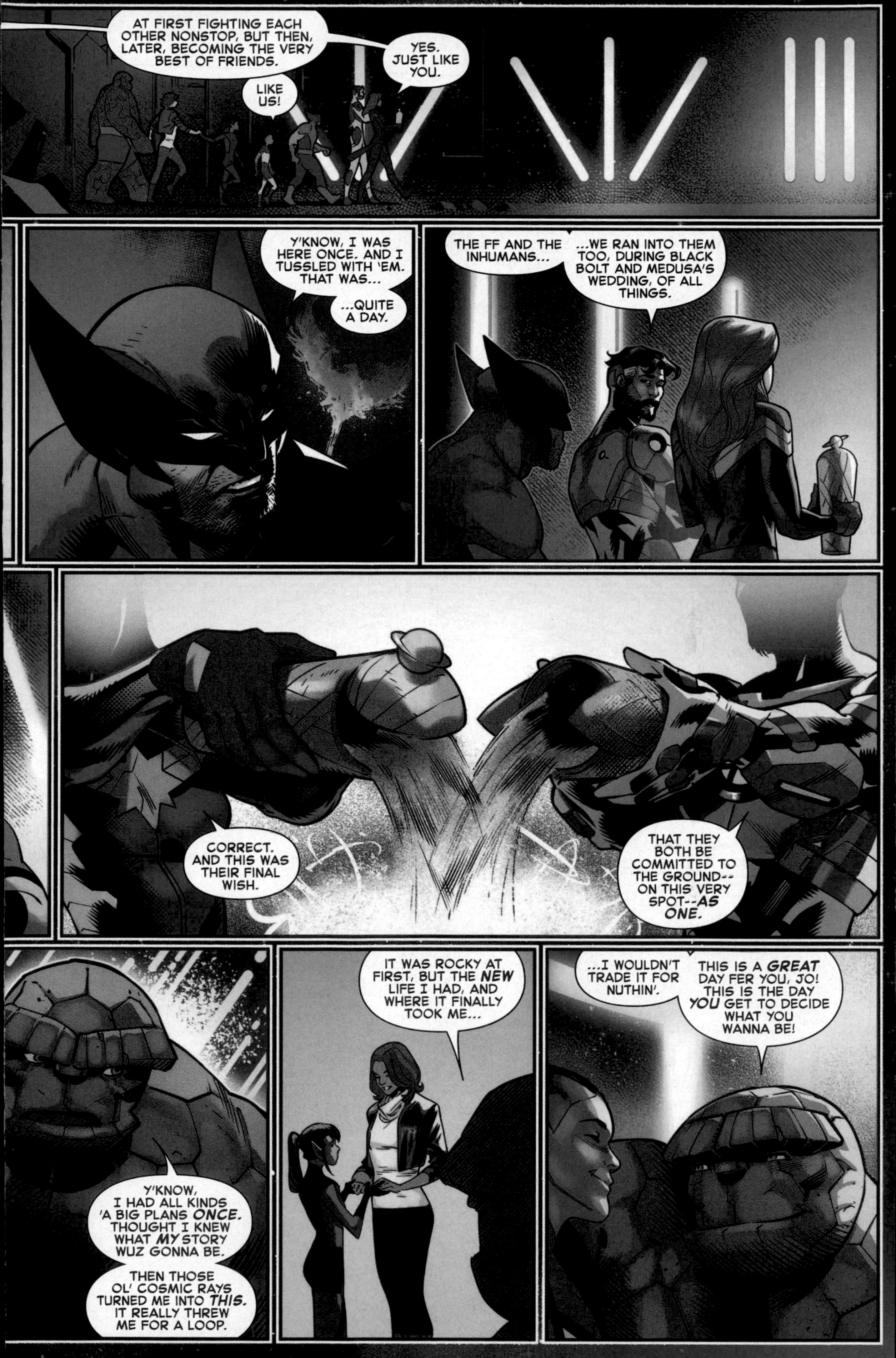

AT FIRST FIGHTING EACH OTHER NONSTOP, BUT THEN, LATER, BECOMING THE VERY BEST OF FRIENDS.
LIKE US!
YES. JUST LIKE YOU.
Y'KNOW, I WAS HERE ONCE. AND I TUSSLED WITH 'EM. THAT WAS...
...QUITE A DAY.
THE FF AND THE INHUMANS...
...WE RAN INTO THEM TOO, DURING BLACK BOLT AND MEDUSA'S WEDDING, OF ALL THINGS.
CORRECT. AND THIS WAS THEIR FINAL WISH.
THAT THEY BOTH BE COMMITTED TO THE GROUND-- ON THIS VERY SPOT--AS ONE.
Y'KNOW, I HAD ALL KINDS 'A BIG PLANS ONCE. THOUGHT I KNEW WHAT MY STORY WUZ GONNA BE.
THEN THOSE OL' COSMIC RAYS TURNED ME INTO THIS. IT REALLY THREW ME FOR A LOOP.
IT WAS ROCKY AT FIRST, BUT THE NEW LIFE I HAD, AND WHERE IT FINALLY TOOK ME...
...I WOULDN'T TRADE IT FOR NUTHIN'.
THIS IS A GREAT DAY FER YOU, JO! THIS IS THE DAY YOU GET TO DECIDE WHAT YOU WANNA BE!

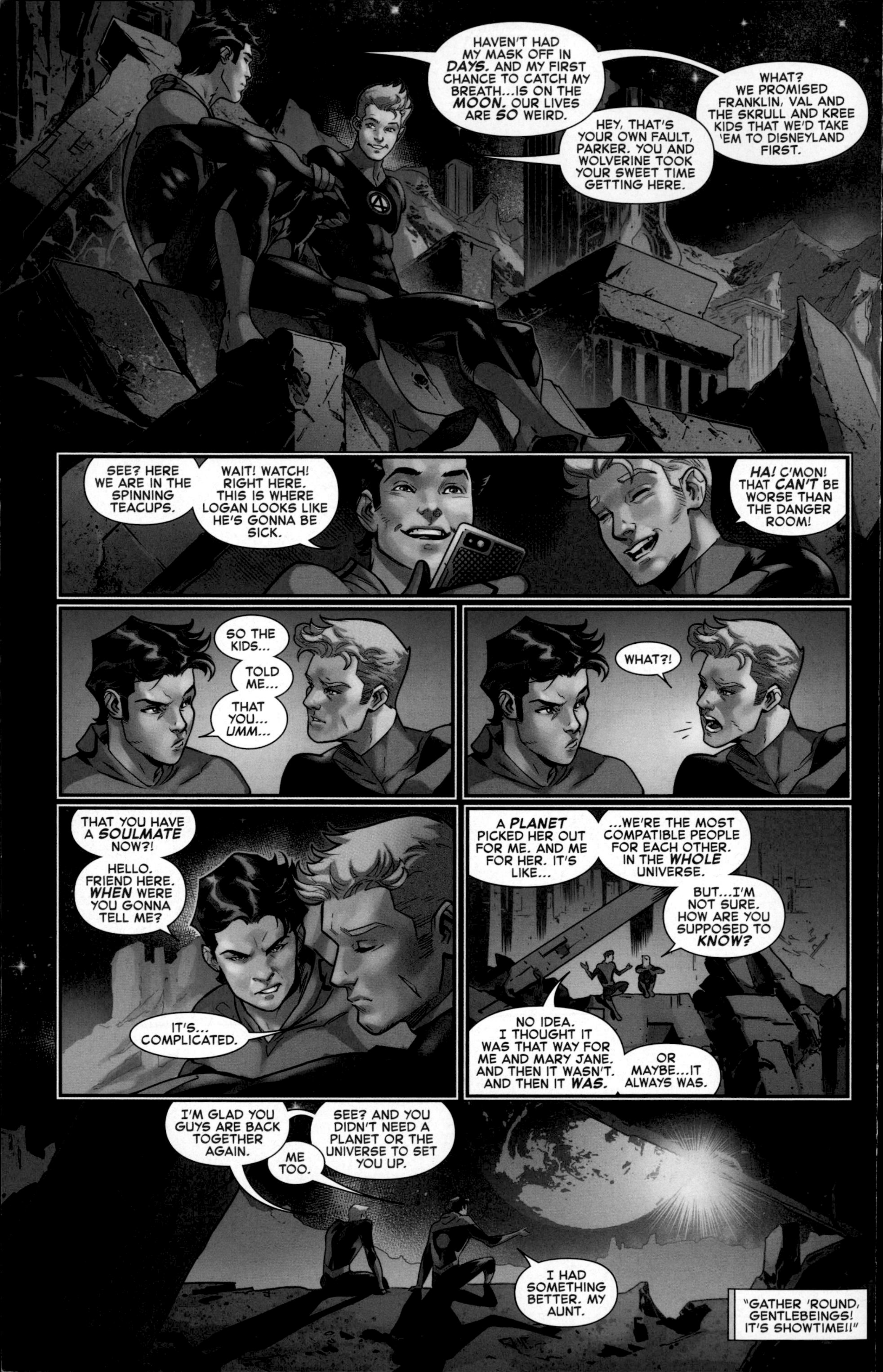
HAVEN'T HAD MY MASK OFF IN DAYS. AND MY FIRST CHANCE TO CATCH MY BREATH...IS ON THE MOON. OUR LIVES ARE SO WEIRD.
HEY, THAT'S YOUR OWN FAULT, PARKER. YOU AND WOLVERINE TOOK YOUR SWEET TIME GETTING HERE.
WHAT? WE PROMISED FRANKLIN, VAL AND THE SKRULL AND KREE KIDS THAT WE'D TAKE 'EM TO DISNEYLAND FIRST.
SEE? HERE WE ARE IN THE SPINNING TEACUPS.
WAIT! WATCH! RIGHT HERE. THIS IS WHERE LOGAN LOOKS LIKE HE'S GONNA BE SICK.
HA! C'MON! THAT CAN'T BE WORSE THAN THE DANGER ROOM!
SO THE KIDS...
TOLD ME...
THAT YOU... UMM...
WHAT?!
THAT YOU HAVE A SOULMATE NOW?!
HELLO. FRIEND HERE. WHEN WERE YOU GONNA TELL ME?
IT'S... COMPLICATED.
A PLANET PICKED HER OUT FOR ME. AND ME FOR HER. IT'S LIKE...
...WE'RE THE MOST COMPATIBLE PEOPLE FOR EACH OTHER. IN THE WHOLE UNIVERSE.
BUT...I'M NOT SURE. HOW ARE YOU SUPPOSED TO KNOW?
NO IDEA. I THOUGHT IT WAS THAT WAY FOR ME AND MARY JANE. AND THEN IT WASN'T. AND THEN IT WAS.
OR MAYBE...IT ALWAYS WAS.
I'M GLAD YOU GUYS ARE BACK TOGETHER AGAIN.
ME TOO.
SEE? AND YOU DIDN'T NEED A PLANET OR THE UNIVERSE TO SET YOU UP.
I HAD SOMETHING BETTER. MY AUNT.
"GATHER 'ROUND, GENTLEBEINGS! IT'S SHOWTIME!!"

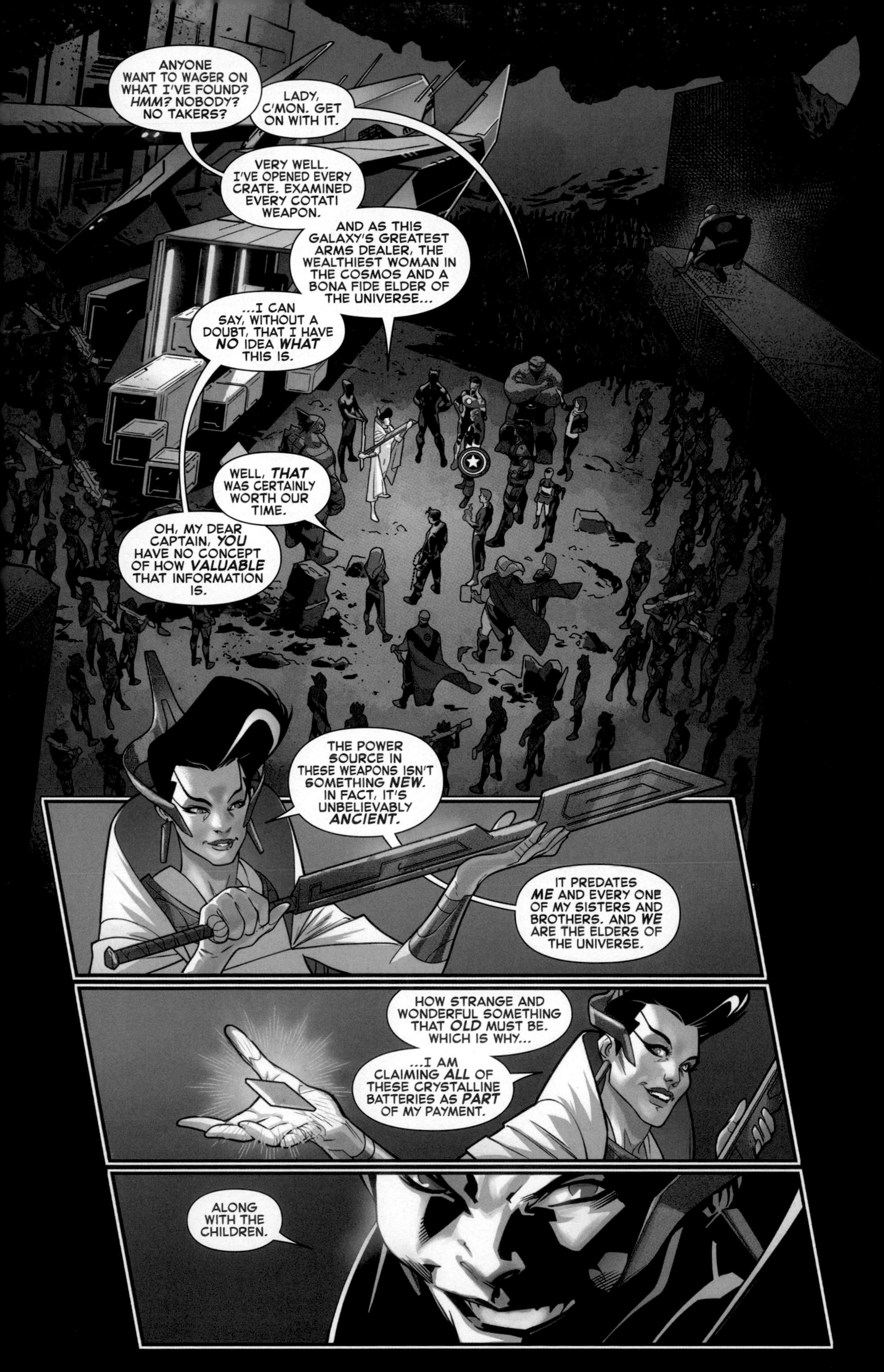
ANYONE WANT TO WAGER ON WHAT I'VE FOUND? HMM? NOBODY? NO TAKERS?
LADY, C'MON. GET ON WITH IT.
VERY WELL. I'VE OPENED EVERY CRATE. EXAMINED EVERY COTATI WEAPON.
AND AS THIS GALAXY'S GREATEST ARMS DEALER, THE WEALTHIEST WOMAN IN THE COSMOS AND A BONA FIDE ELDER OF THE UNIVERSE...
...I CAN SAY, WITHOUT A DOUBT, THAT I HAVE NO IDEA WHAT THIS IS.
WELL, THAT WAS CERTAINLY WORTH OUR TIME.
OH, MY DEAR CAPTAIN, YOU HAVE NO CONCEPT OF HOW VALUABLE THAT INFORMATION IS.
THE POWER SOURCE IN THESE WEAPONS ISN'T SOMETHING NEW. IN FACT, IT'S UNBELIEVABLY ANCIENT.
IT PREDATES ME AND EVERY ONE OF MY SISTERS AND BROTHERS. AND WE ARE THE ELDERS OF THE UNIVERSE.
HOW STRANGE AND WONDERFUL SOMETHING THAT OLD MUST BE. WHICH IS WHY...
...I AM CLAIMING ALL OF THESE CRYSTALLINE BATTERIES AS PART OF MY PAYMENT.
ALONG WITH THE CHILDREN.

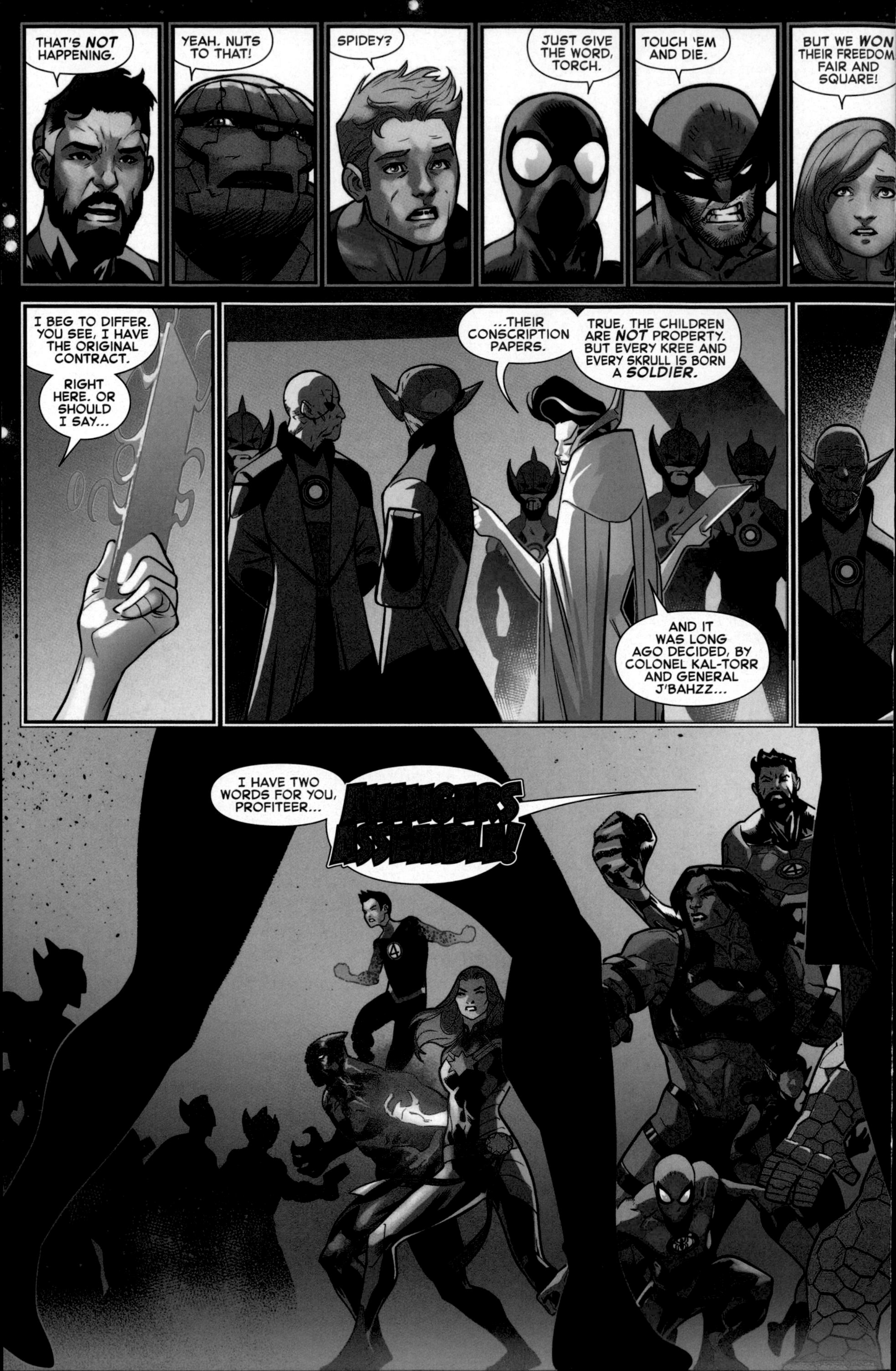
THAT'S NOT HAPPENING.
YEAH. NUTS TO THAT!
SPIDEY?
JUST GIVE THE WORD, TORCH.
TOUCH 'EM AND DIE.
BUT WE WON THEIR FREEDOM FAIR AND SQUARE!
I BEG TO DIFFER. YOU SEE, I HAVE THE ORIGINAL CONTRACT.
RIGHT HERE. OR SHOULD I SAY...
...THEIR CONSCRIPTION PAPERS.
TRUE, THE CHILDREN ARE NOT PROPERTY. BUT EVERY KREE AND EVERY SKRULL IS BORN A SOLDIER.
AND IT WAS LONG AGO DECIDED, BY COLONEL KAL-TORR AND GENERAL J'BAHZZ...
I HAVE TWO WORDS FOR YOU, PROFITEER...
AVENGERS ASSEMBLE!

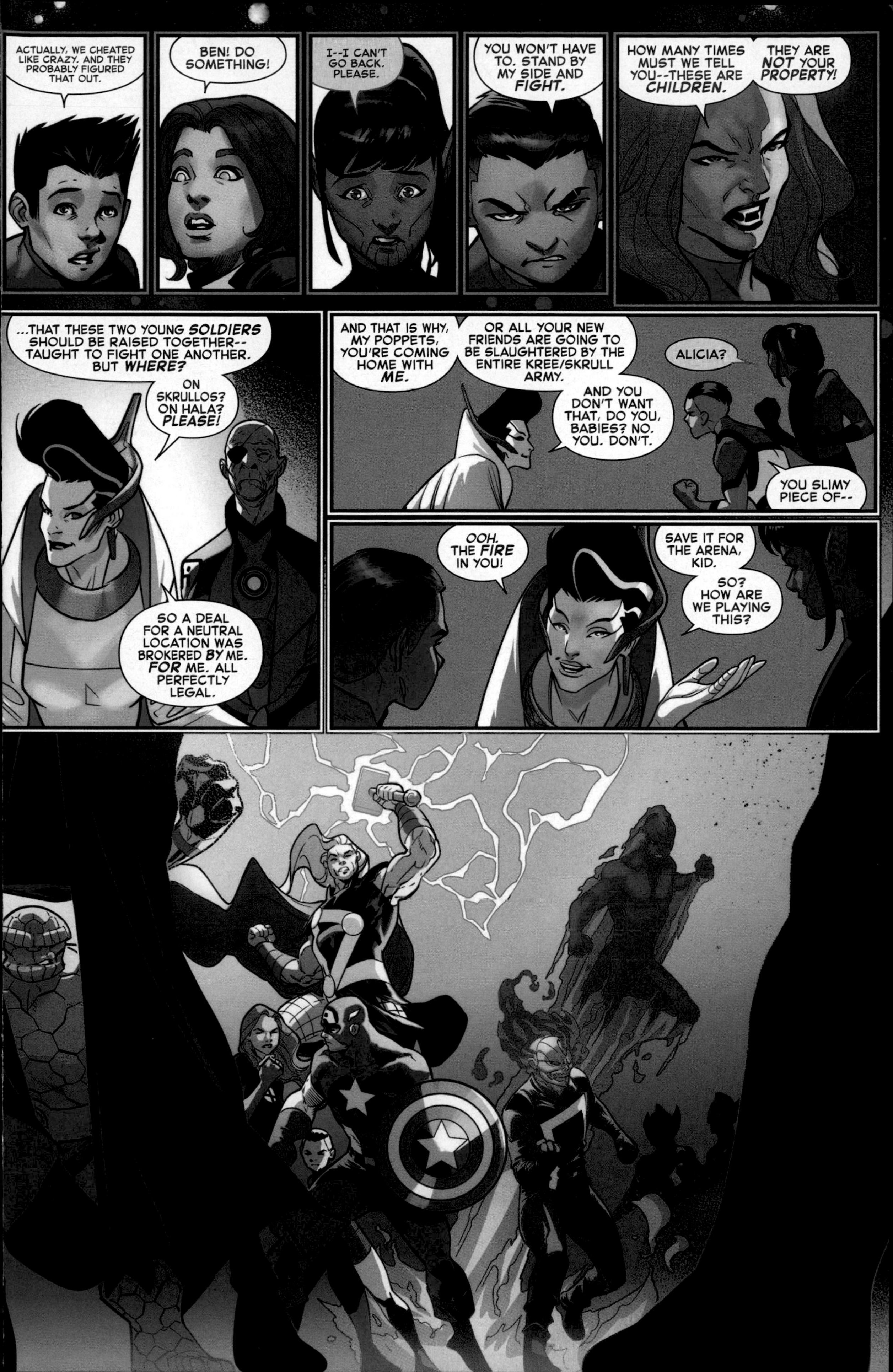

ACTUALLY, WE CHEATED LIKE CRAZY. AND THEY PROBABLY FIGURED THAT OUT.
BEN! DO SOMETHING!
I--I CAN'T GO BACK. PLEASE.
YOU WON'T HAVE TO. STAND BY MY SIDE AND FIGHT.
HOW MANY TIMES MUST WE TELL YOU--THESE ARE CHILDREN.
THEY ARE NOT YOUR PROPERTY!
...THAT THESE TWO YOUNG SOLDIERS SHOULD BE RAISED TOGETHER--TAUGHT TO FIGHT ONE ANOTHER. BUT WHERE?
ON SKRULLOS? ON HALA? PLEASE!
SO A DEAL FOR A NEUTRAL LOCATION WAS BROKERED BY ME. FOR ME. ALL PERFECTLY LEGAL.
AND THAT IS WHY, MY POPPETS, YOU'RE COMING HOME WITH ME.
OR ALL YOUR NEW FRIENDS ARE GOING TO BE SLAUGHTERED BY THE ENTIRE KREE/SKRULL ARMY.
AND YOU DON'T WANT THAT, DO YOU, BABIES? NO. YOU. DON'T.
ALICIA?
YOU SLIMY PIECE OF--
OOH. THE FIRE IN YOU!
SAVE IT FOR THE ARENA, KID.
SO? HOW ARE WE PLAYING THIS?

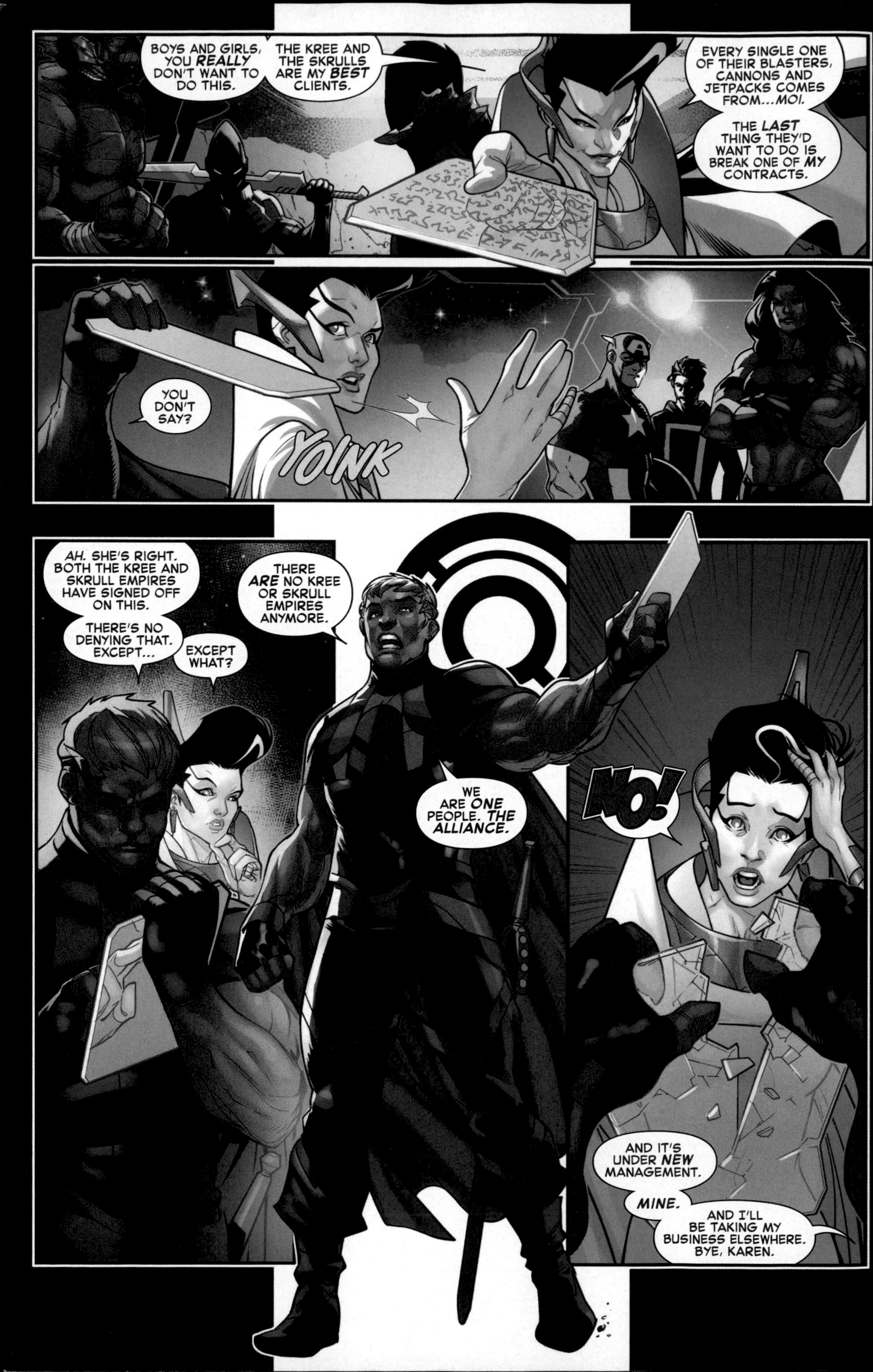

BOYS AND GIRLS, YOU REALLY DON'T WANT TO DO THIS.
THE KREE AND THE SKRULLS ARE MY BEST CLIENTS.
EVERY SINGLE ONE OF THEIR BLASTERS, CANNONS AND JETPACKS COMES FROM...MOI.
THE LAST THING THEY'D WANT TO DO IS BREAK ONE OF MY CONTRACTS.
YOU DON'T SAY?
YOINK
AH. SHE'S RIGHT. BOTH THE KREE AND SKRULL EMPIRES HAVE SIGNED OFF ON THIS.
THERE'S NO DENYING THAT. EXCEPT...
EXCEPT WHAT?
THERE ARE NO KREE OR SKRULL EMPIRES ANYMORE.
WE ARE ONE PEOPLE. THE ALLIANCE.
NO!
AND IT'S UNDER NEW MANAGEMENT.
MINE.
AND I'LL BE TAKING MY BUSINESS ELSEWHERE. BYE, KAREN.

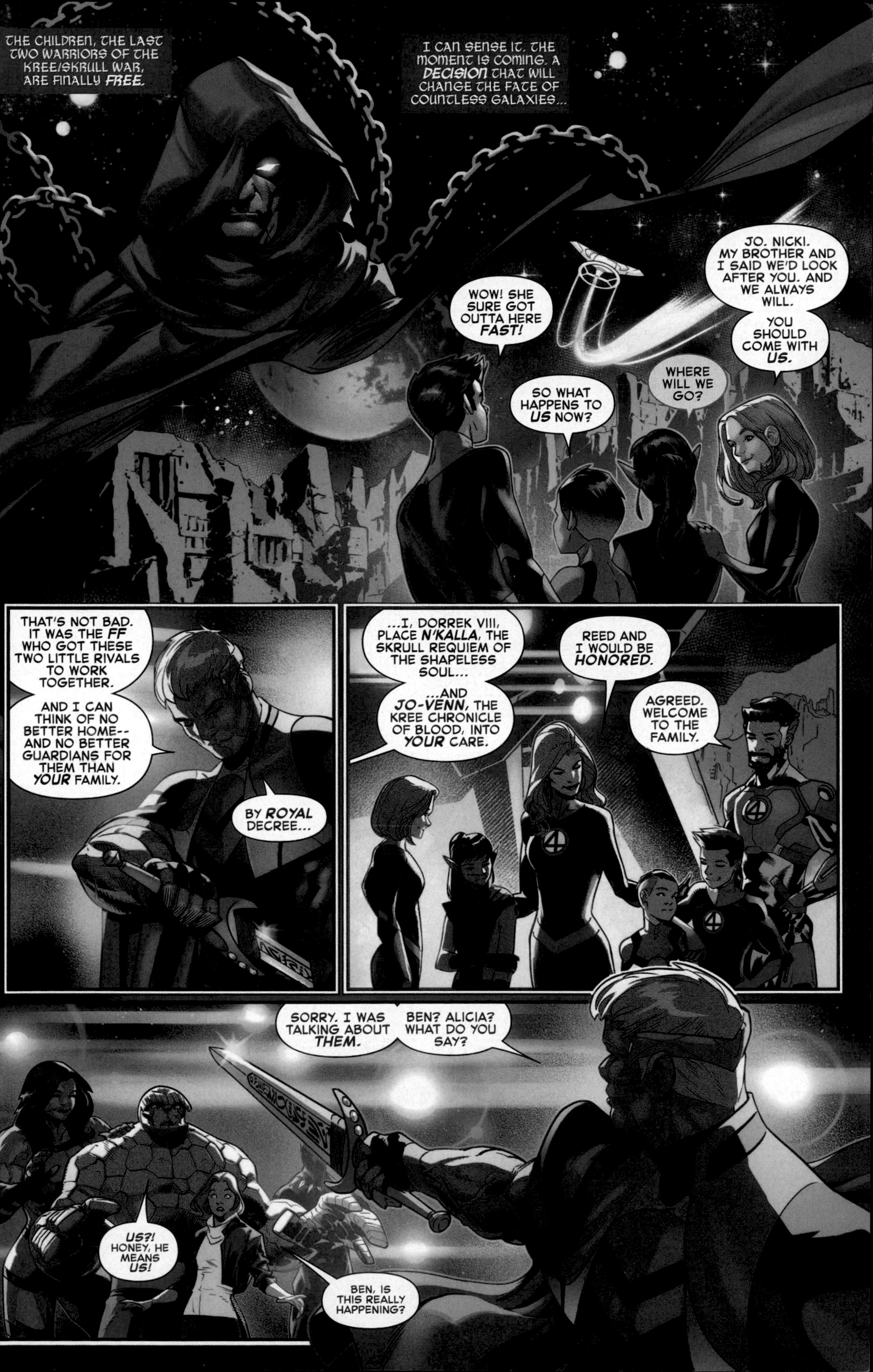
THE CHILDREN, THE LAST TWO WARRIORS OF THE KREE/SKRULL WAR, ARE FINALLY FREE.
I CAN SENSE IT. THE MOMENT IS COMING. A DECISION THAT WILL CHANGE THE FATE OF COUNTLESS GALAXIES...
WOW! SHE SURE GOT OUTTA HERE FAST!
JO. NICKI. MY BROTHER AND I SAID WE'D LOOK AFTER YOU. AND WE ALWAYS WILL.
YOU SHOULD COME WITH US.
WHERE WILL WE GO?
SO WHAT HAPPENS TO US NOW?
THAT'S NOT BAD. IT WAS THE FF WHO GOT THESE TWO LITTLE RIVALS TO WORK TOGETHER.
AND I CAN THINK OF NO BETTER HOME-- AND NO BETTER GUARDIANS FOR THEM THAN YOUR FAMILY.
BY ROYAL DECREE...
...I, DORREK VIII, PLACE N'KALLA, THE SKRULL REQUIEM OF THE SHAPELESS SOUL...
...AND JO-VENN, THE KREE CHRONICLE OF BLOOD, INTO YOUR CARE.
REED AND I WOULD BE HONORED.
AGREED. WELCOME TO THE FAMILY.
SORRY. I WAS TALKING ABOUT THEM.
BEN? ALICIA? WHAT DO YOU SAY?
US?! HONEY, HE MEANS US!
BEN, IS THIS REALLY HAPPENING?

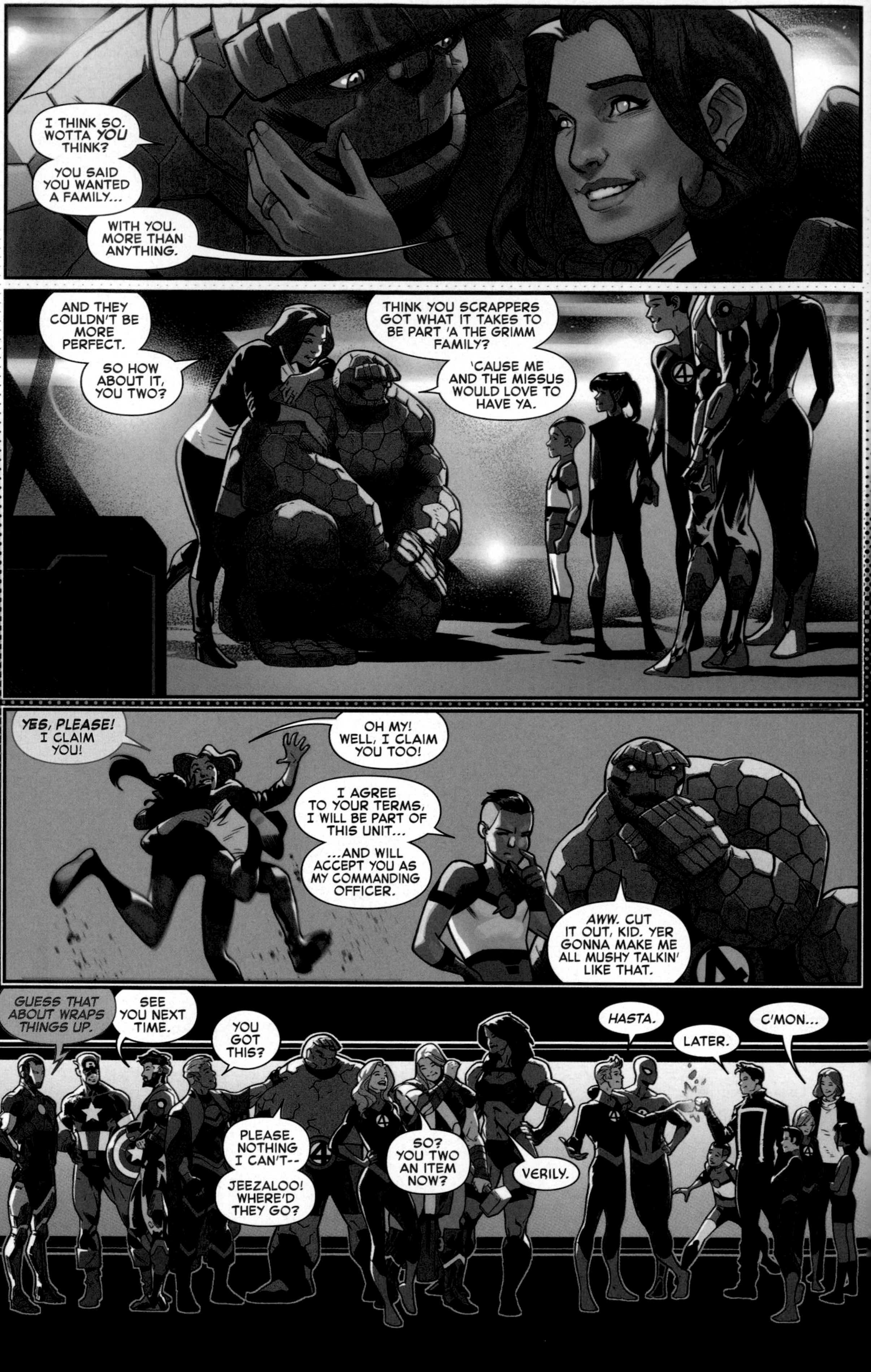
I THINK SO. WOTTA *YOU* THINK?
YOU SAID YOU WANTED A FAMILY...
WITH YOU. MORE THAN ANYTHING.
AND THEY COULDN'T BE MORE PERFECT.
SO HOW ABOUT IT, YOU TWO?
THINK YOU SCRAPPERS GOT WHAT IT TAKES TO BE PART 'A THE GRIMM FAMILY?
'CAUSE ME AND THE MISSUS WOULD LOVE TO HAVE YA.
YES, PLEASE! I CLAIM YOU!
OH MY! WELL, I CLAIM YOU TOO!
I AGREE TO YOUR TERMS, I WILL BE PART OF THIS UNIT...
...AND WILL ACCEPT YOU AS MY COMMANDING OFFICER.
AWW. CUT IT OUT, KID. YER GONNA MAKE ME ALL MUSHY TALKIN' LIKE THAT.
GUESS THAT ABOUT WRAPS THINGS UP.
SEE YOU NEXT TIME.
YOU GOT THIS?
PLEASE. NOTHING I CAN'T--
JEEZALOO! WHERE'D THEY GO?
SO? YOU TWO AN ITEM NOW?
VERILY.
HASTA.
LATER.
C'MON...

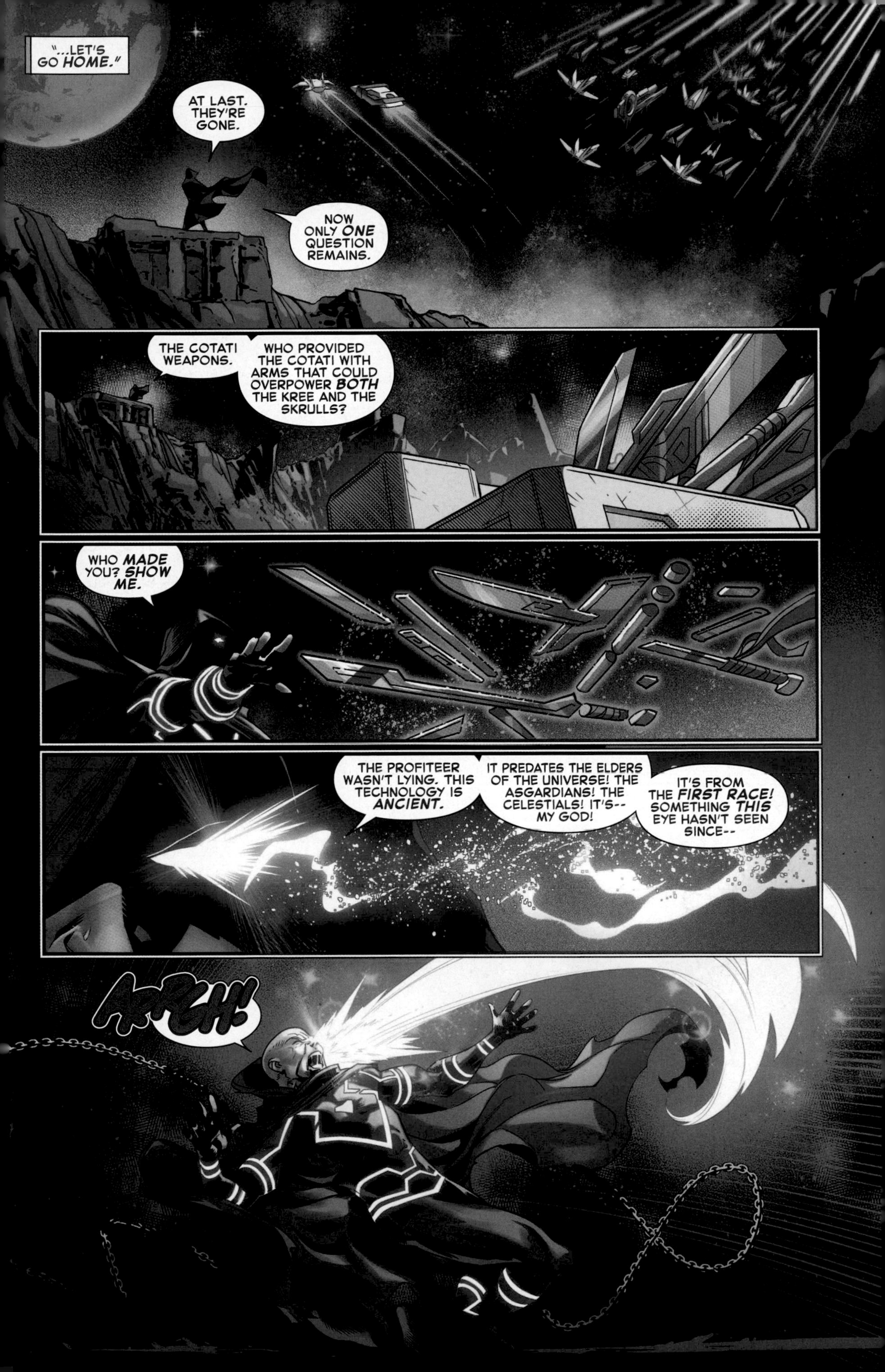
"...LET'S GO HOME."
AT LAST. THEY'RE GONE.
NOW ONLY ONE QUESTION REMAINS.
THE COTATI WEAPONS.
WHO PROVIDED THE COTATI WITH ARMS THAT COULD OVERPOWER BOTH THE KREE AND THE SKRULLS?
WHO MADE YOU? SHOW ME.
THE PROFITEER WASN'T LYING. THIS TECHNOLOGY IS ANCIENT.
IT PREDATES THE ELDERS OF THE UNIVERSE! THE ASGARDIANS! THE CELESTIALS! IT'S-- MY GOD!
IT'S FROM THE FIRST RACE! SOMETHING THIS EYE HASN'T SEEN SINCE--
ARRGH!

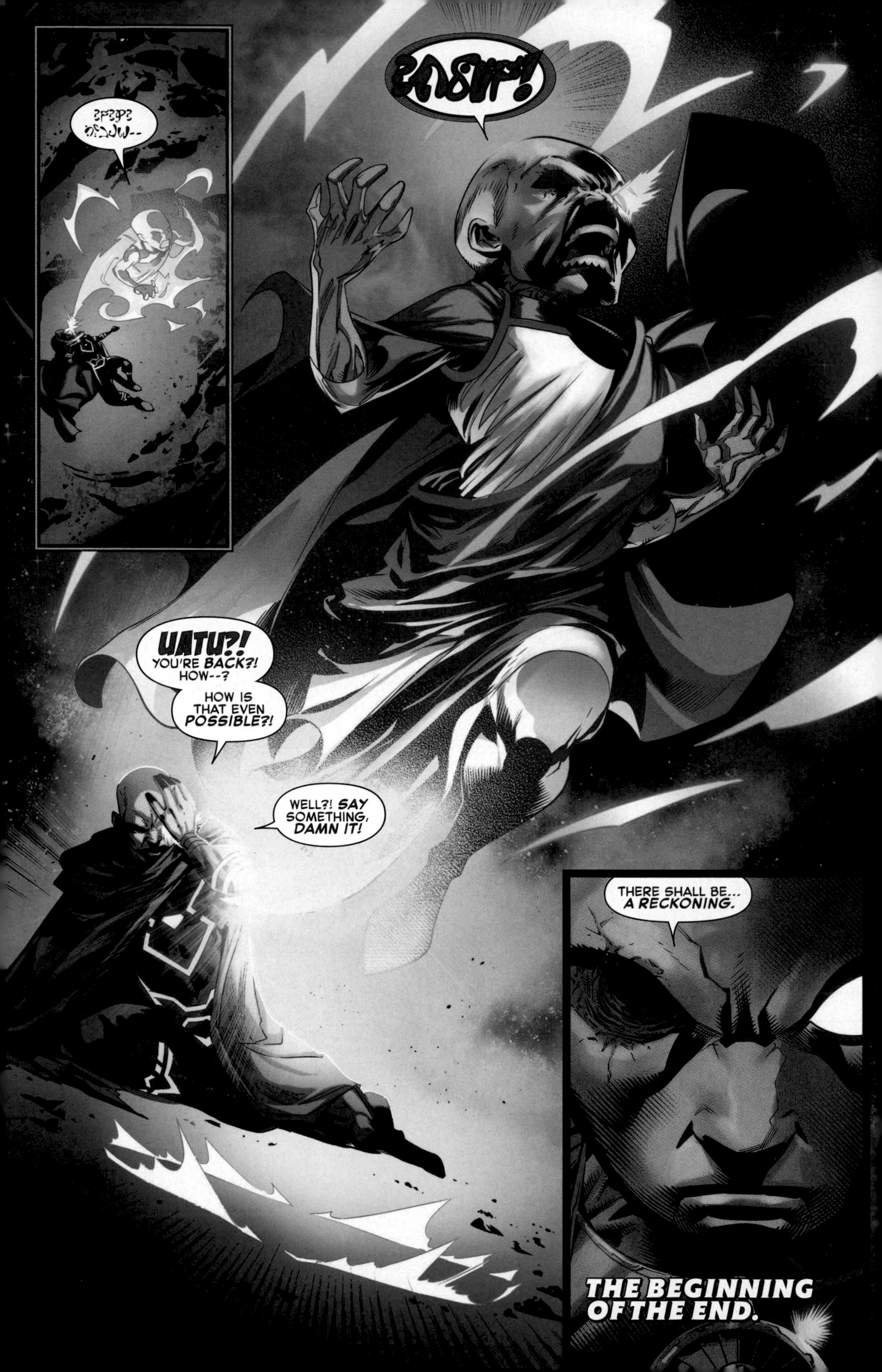
UATU?! YOU'RE BACK?! HOW--?
HOW IS THAT EVEN POSSIBLE?!
WELL?! SAY SOMETHING, DAMN IT!
THERE SHALL BE... A RECKONING.
THE BEGINNING OF THE END.

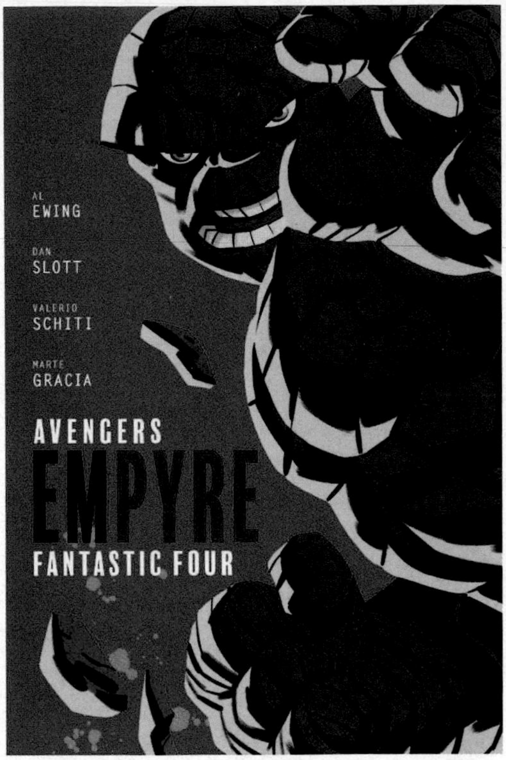
AL
EWING
DAN
SLOTT
VALERIO
SCHITI
MARTE
GRACIA
AVENGERS
EMPYRE
FANTASTIC FOUR

EMPYRE 1 FANTASTIC FOUR VARIANT BY
Michael Cho

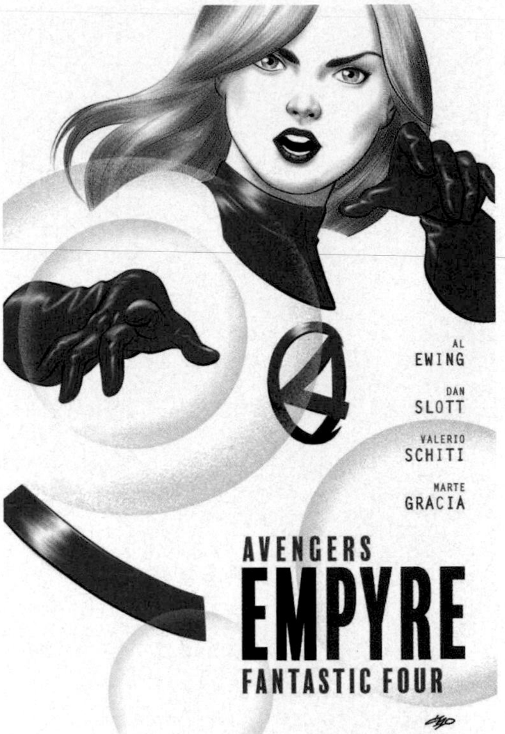
AL
EWING
DAN
SLOTT
VALERIO
SCHITI
MARTE
GRACIA
AVENGERS
EMPYRE
FANTASTIC FOUR

EMPYRE 2 FANTASTIC FOUR VARIANT BY
Michael Cho

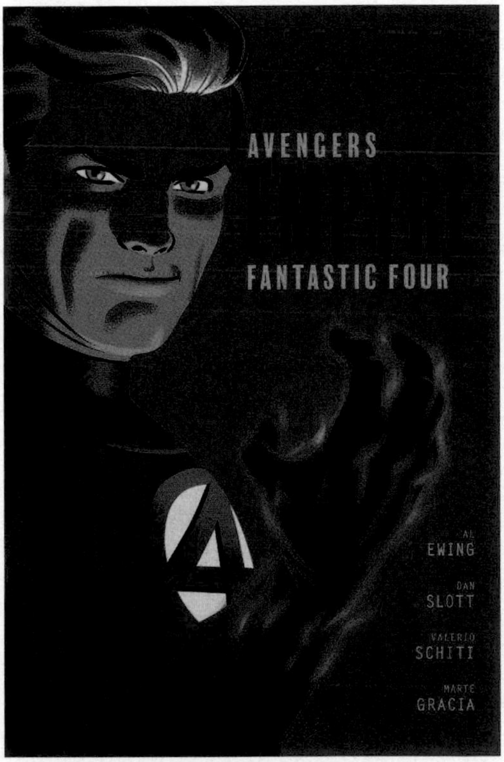
AVENGERS
FANTASTIC FOUR
AL
EWING
DAN
SLOTT
VALERIO
SCHITI
MARTE
GRACIA

EMPYRE 3 FANTASTIC FOUR VARIANT BY
Michael Cho

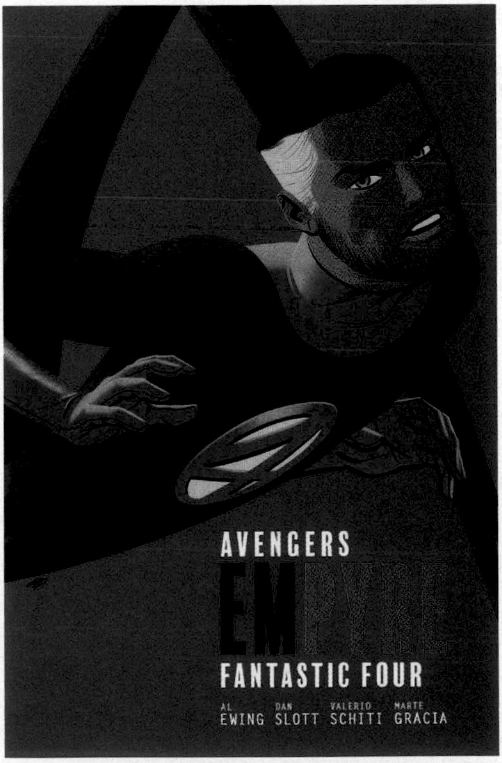
AVENGERS
FANTASTIC FOUR
AL EWING DAN SLOTT VALERIO SCHITI MARTE GRACIA

EMPYRE 4 FANTASTIC FOUR VARIANT BY
Michael Cho

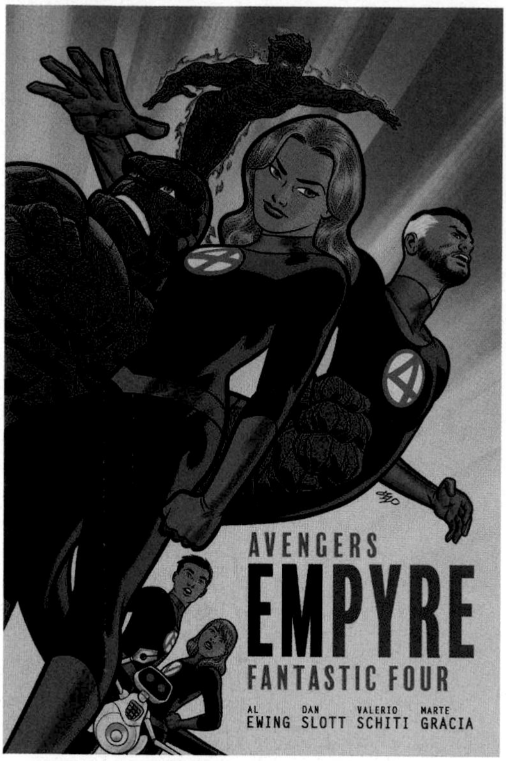
AVENGERS
EMPYRE
FANTASTIC FOUR
AL EWING
DAN SLOTT
VALERIO SCHITI
MARTE GRACIA

EMPYRE 5 FANTASTIC FOUR VARIANT BY
Michael Cho

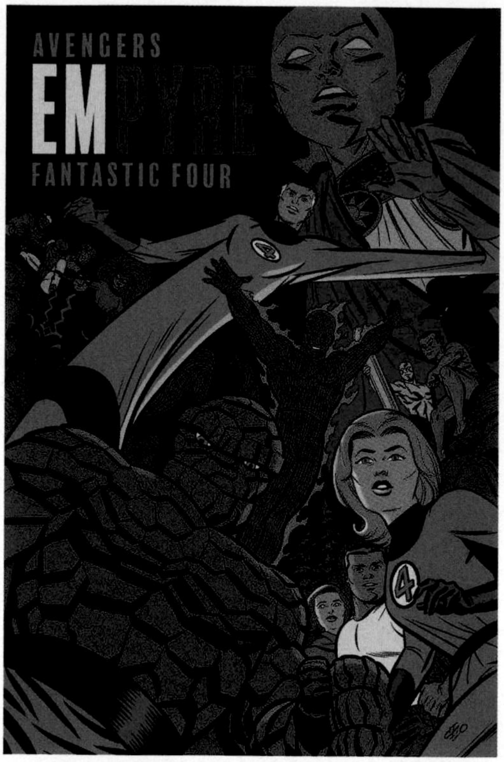
AVENGERS
EMPYRE
FANTASTIC FOUR

EMPYRE 6 FANTASTIC FOUR VARIANT BY
Michael Cho

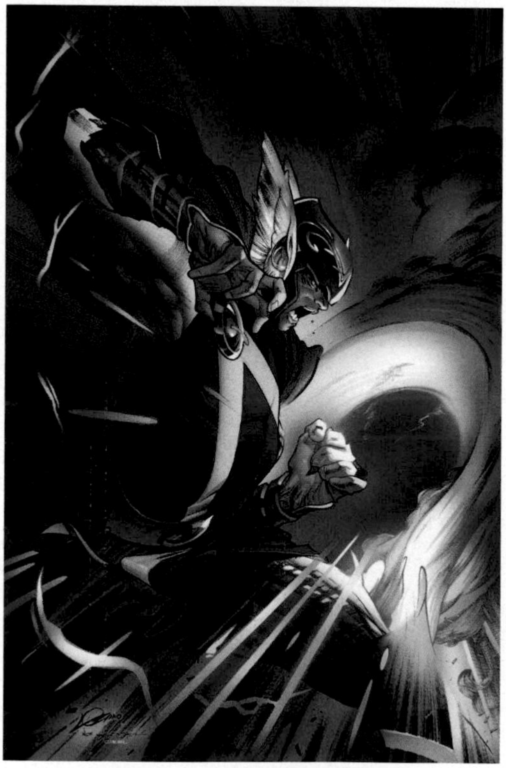

EMPYRE 1 AVENGERS VARIANT BY
Alexander Lozano,
Wade von Grawbadger & **Rain Beredo**

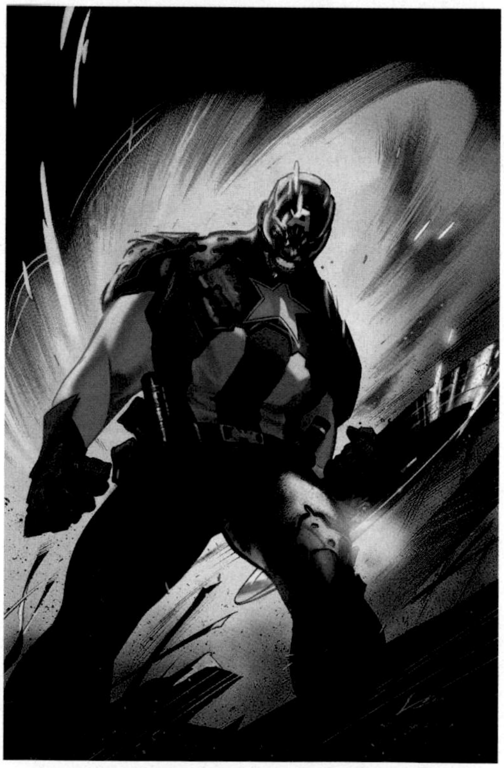

EMPYRE 2 AVENGERS VARIANT BY
Alexander Lozano,
Wade von Grawbadger & **Rain Beredo**

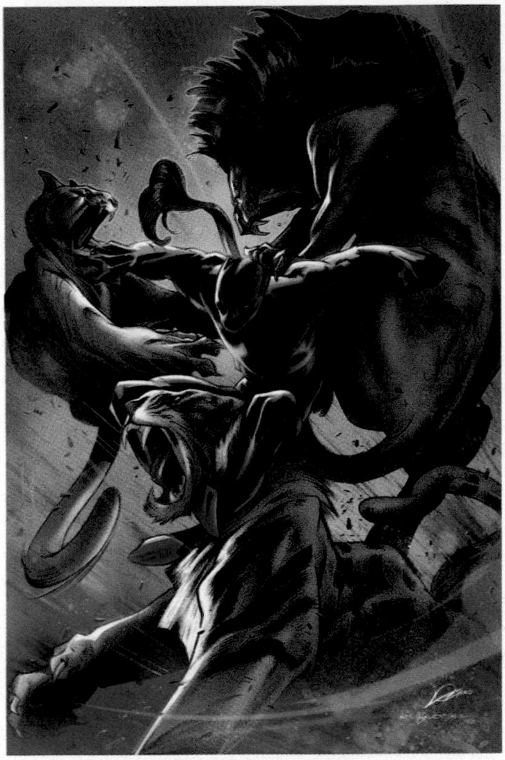

EMPYRE 3 AVENGERS VARIANT BY
Alexander Lozano, Wade von Grawbadger & Rain Beredo

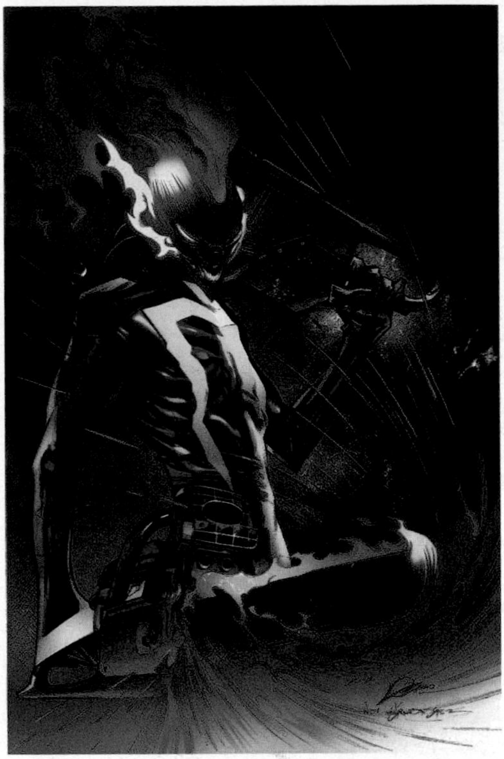

EMPYRE 4 AVENGERS VARIANT BY
Alexander Lozano, Wade von Grawbadger & Rain Beredo

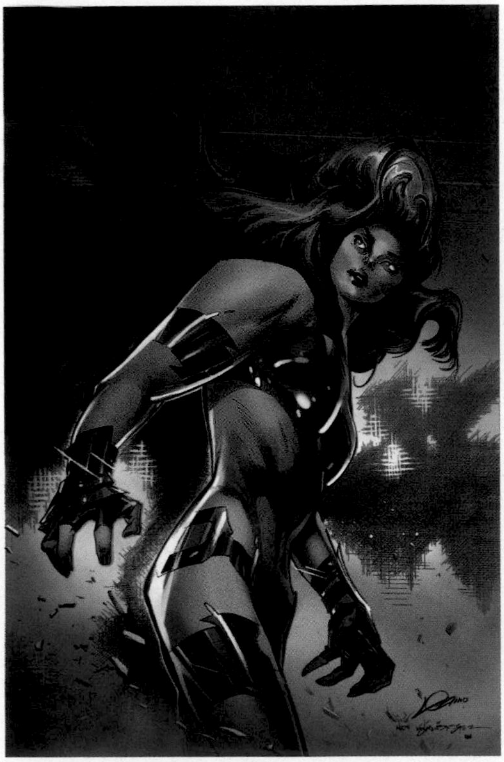

EMPYRE 5 AVENGERS VARIANT BY
Alexander Lozano, Wade von Grawbadger & Rain Beredo

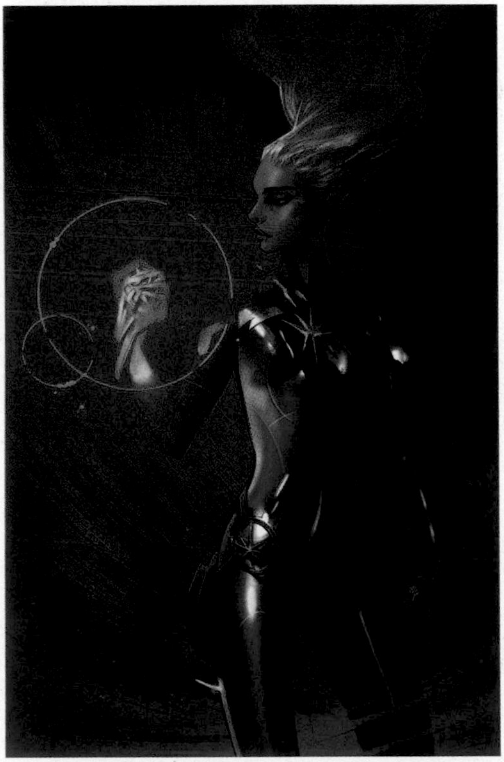

EMPYRE 6 AVENGERS VARIANT BY
Alexander Lozano, Wade von Grawbadger & Rain Beredo

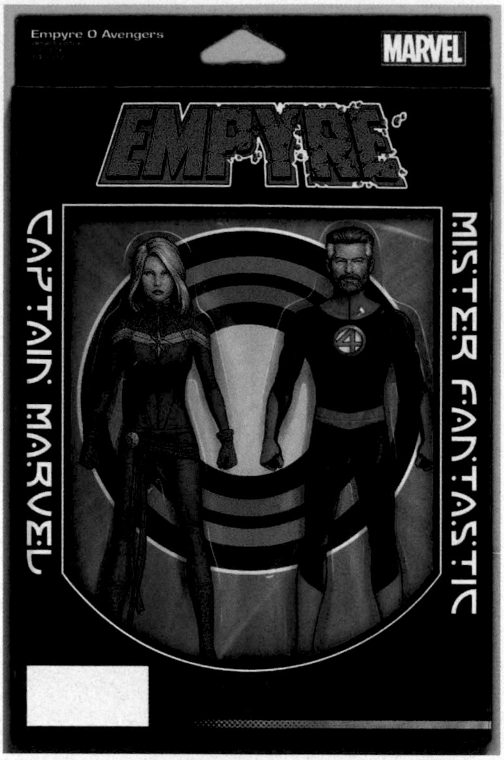
Empyre 0 Avengers
MARVEL
EMPYRE
CAPTAIN MARVEL
MISTER FANTASTIC

EMPYRE: AVENGERS 0 ACTION FIGURE VARIANT BY **John Tyler Christopher**

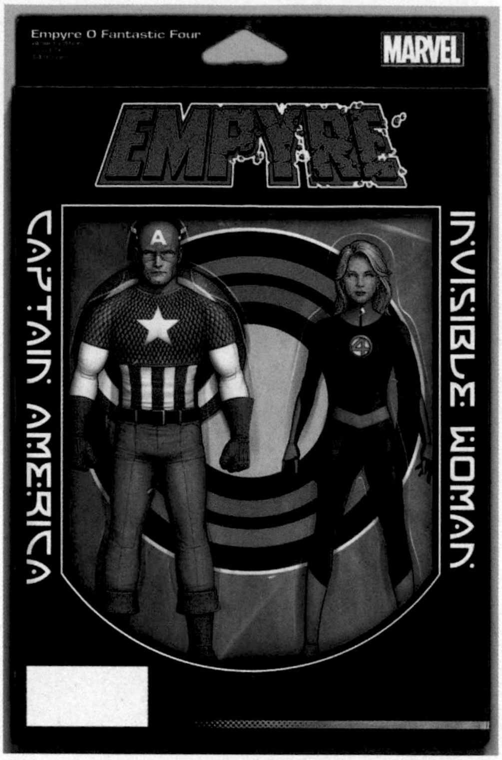
Empyre 0 Fantastic Four
MARVEL
EMPYRE
CAPTAIN AMERICA
INVISIBLE WOMAN

EMPYRE: FANTASTIC FOUR 0 ACTION FIGURE VARIANT BY **John Tyler Christopher**

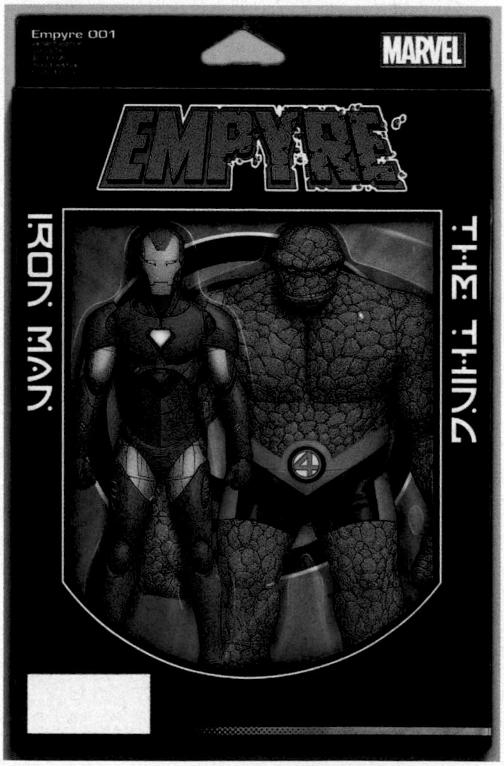
Empyre 001
MARVEL
EMPYRE
IRON MAN
THE THING

EMPYRE 1 ACTION FIGURE VARIANT BY **John Tyler Christopher**

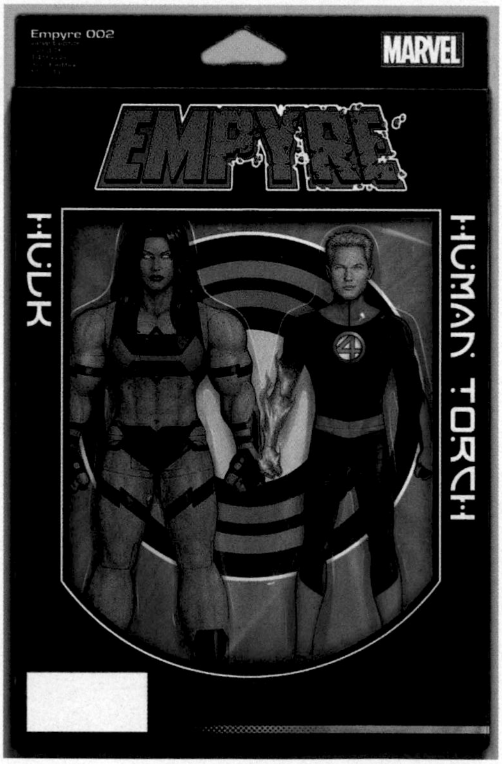
Empyre 002
MARVEL
EMPYRE
HULK
HUMAN TORCH

EMPYRE 2 ACTION FIGURE VARIANT BY **John Tyler Christopher**

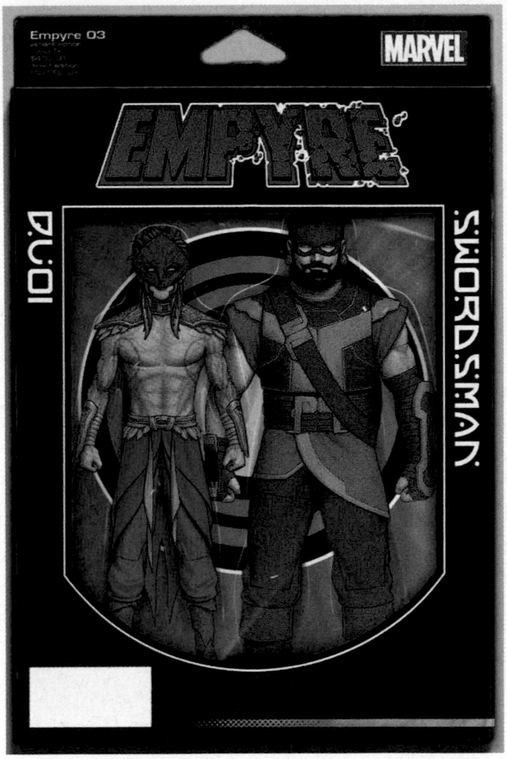

Empyre 03
MARVEL
EMPYRE
QUOI
SWORDSMAN

EMPYRE 3 ACTION FIGURE VARIANT BY
John Tyler Christopher

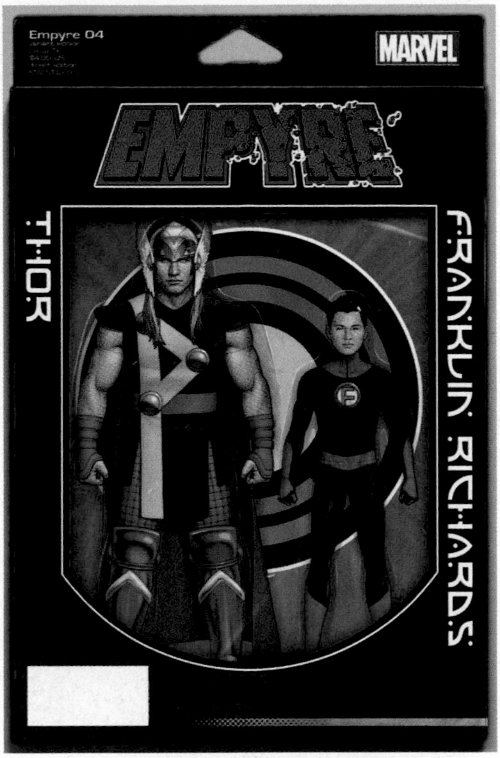

Empyre 04
MARVEL
EMPYRE
THOR
FRANKLIN RICHARDS

EMPYRE 4 ACTION FIGURE VARIANT BY
John Tyler Christopher

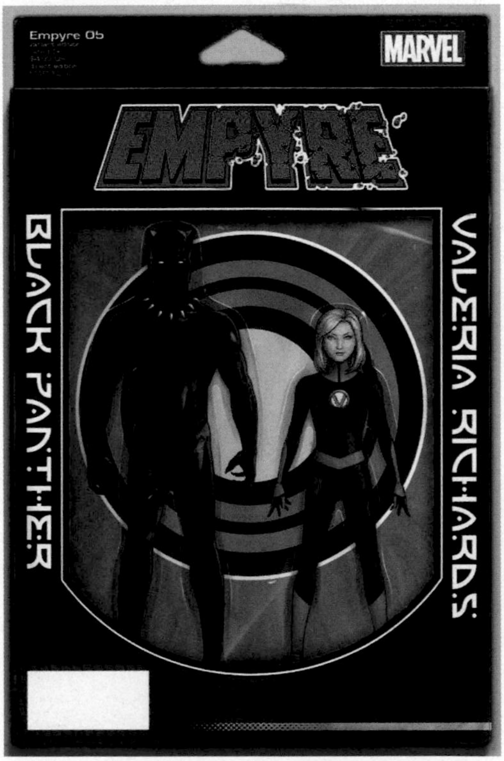

Empyre 05
MARVEL
EMPYRE
BLACK PANTHER
VALERIA RICHARDS

EMPYRE 5 ACTION FIGURE VARIANT BY
John Tyler Christopher

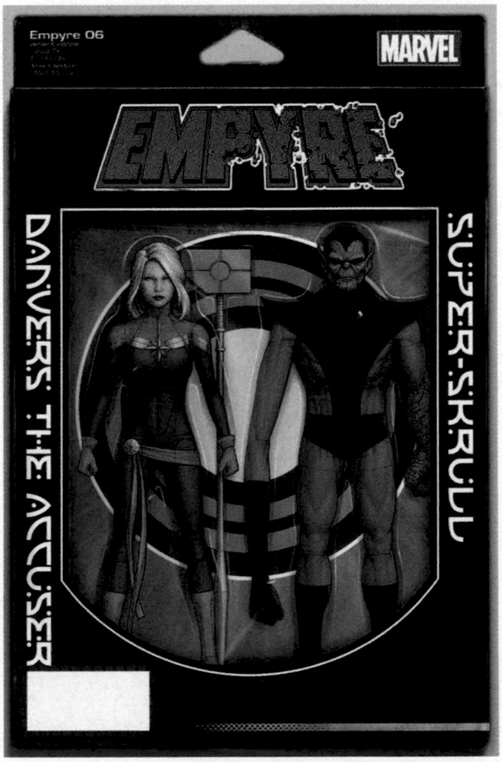

Empyre 06
MARVEL
EMPYRE
DANVERS THE ACCUSER
SUPER-SKRULL

EMPYRE 6 ACTION FIGURE VARIANT BY
John Tyler Christopher

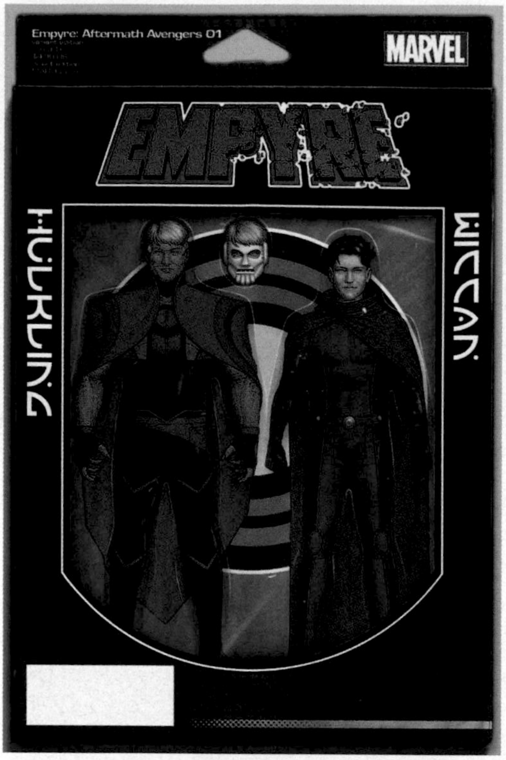
Empyre: Aftermath Avengers 01
MARVEL
EMPYRE
HULKLING
WICCAN

EMPYRE: AFTERMATH — AVENGERS ACTION FIGURE VARIANT BY **John Tyler Christopher**

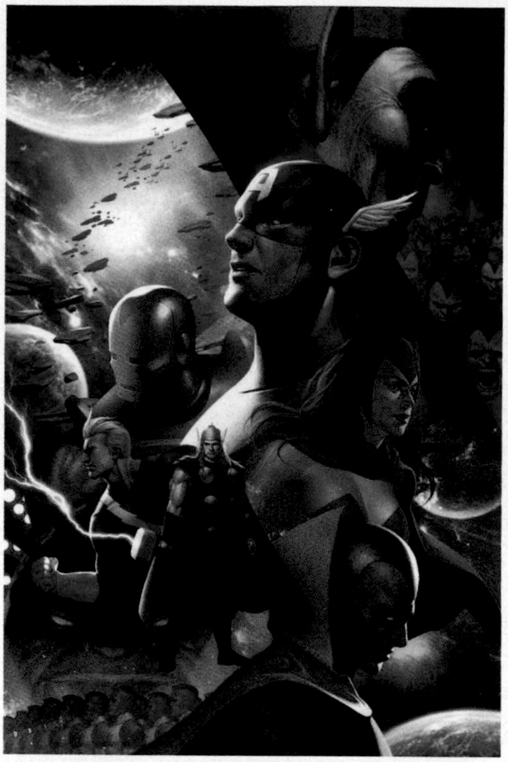

EMPYRE 1 SECOND-PRINTING VARIANT BY **InHyuk Lee**

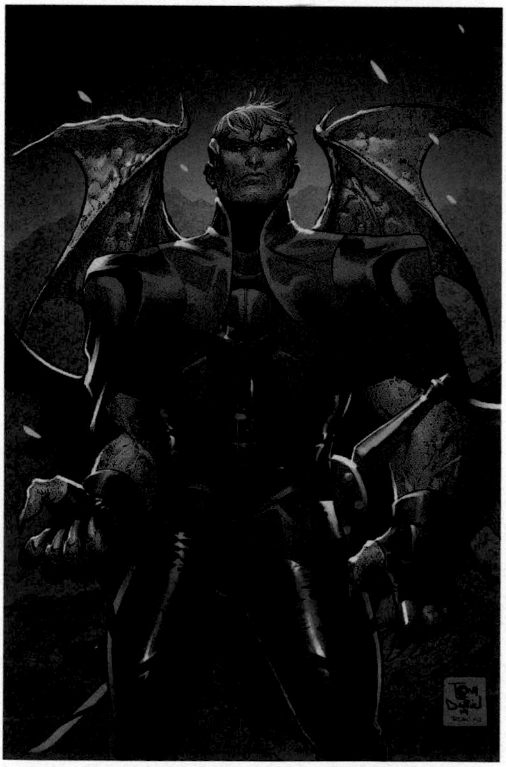

EMPYRE 1 KREE/SKRULL VARIANT BY **Tony Daniel & Rain Beredo**

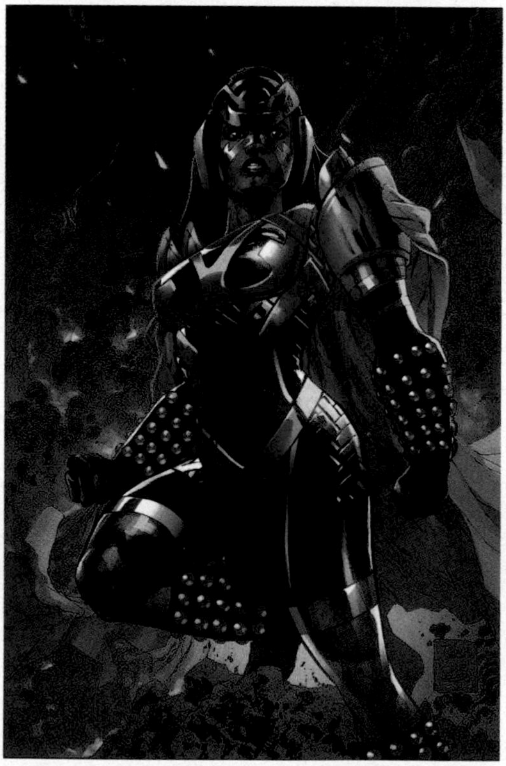

EMPYRE 2 KREE/SKRULL VARIANT BY **Tony Daniel & Rain Beredo**

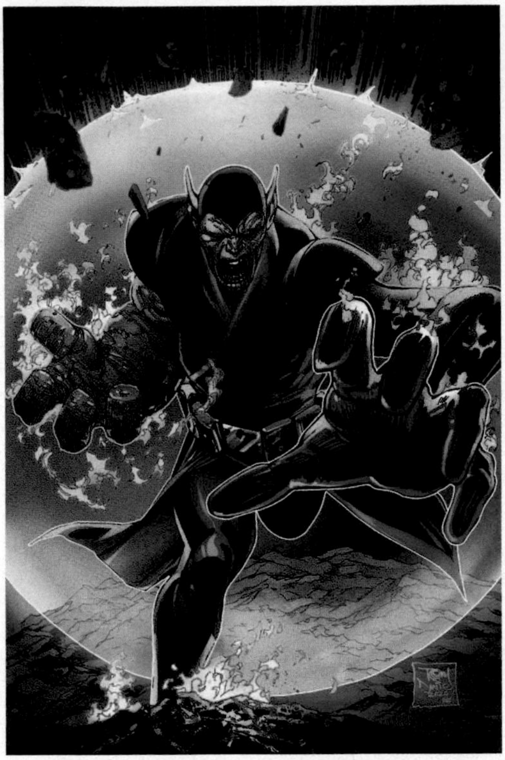

EMPYRE 3 KREE/SKRULL VARIANT BY
Tony Daniel & **Frank D'Armata**

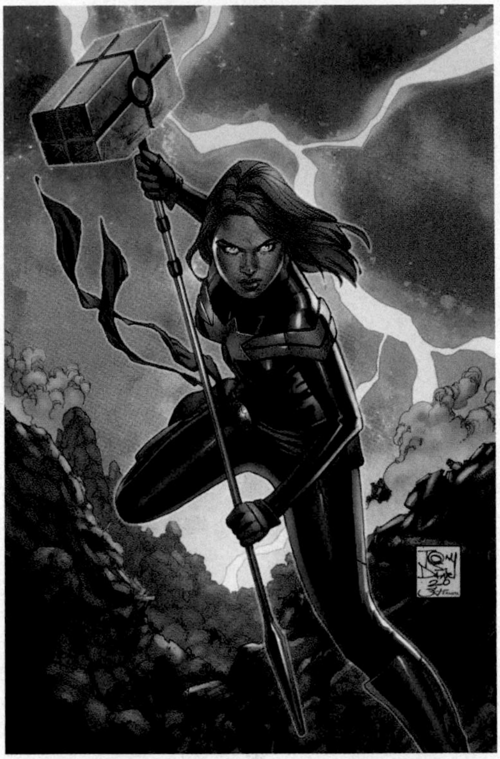

EMPYRE 4 KREE/SKRULL VARIANT BY
Tony Daniel & **Dono Sánchez-Almara**

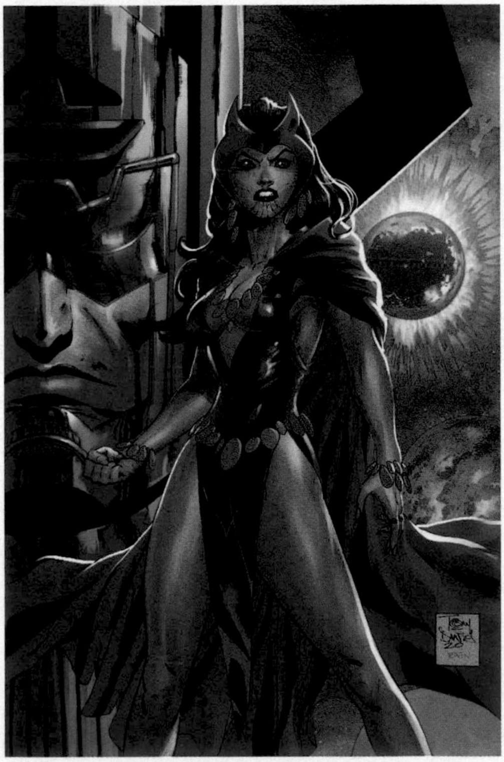

EMPYRE 5 KREE/SKRULL VARIANT BY
Tony Daniel & **Rain Beredo**

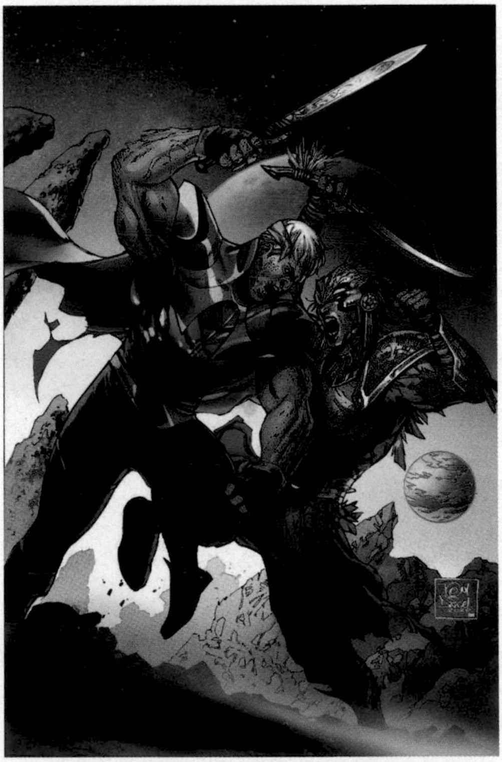

EMPYRE 6 KREE/SKRULL VARIANT BY
Tony Daniel & **Frank D'Armata**

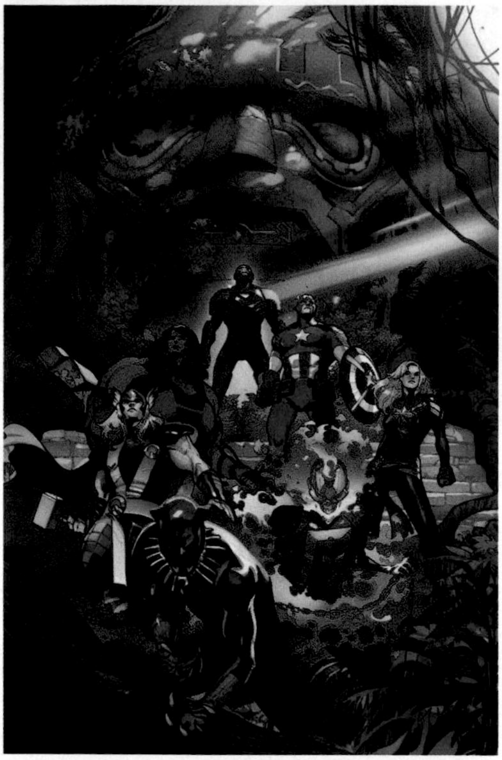

EMPYRE: AVENGERS 0 VARIANT BY
Pepe Larraz & **David Curiel**

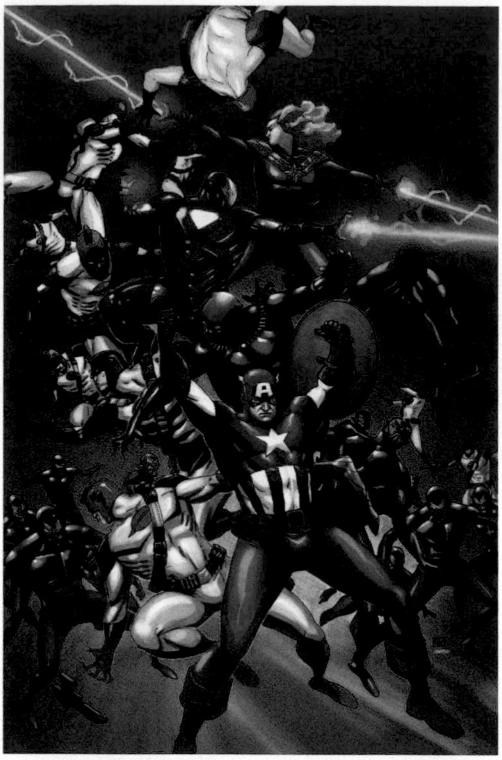

EMPYRE: AVENGERS 0 VARIANT BY
Khoi Pham & **Chris Sotomayor**

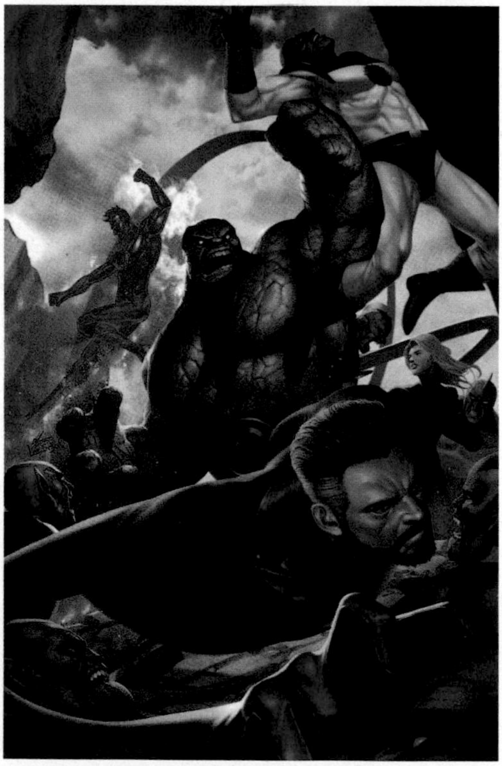

EMPYRE: FANTASTIC FOUR 0 VARIANT BY
InHyuk Lee

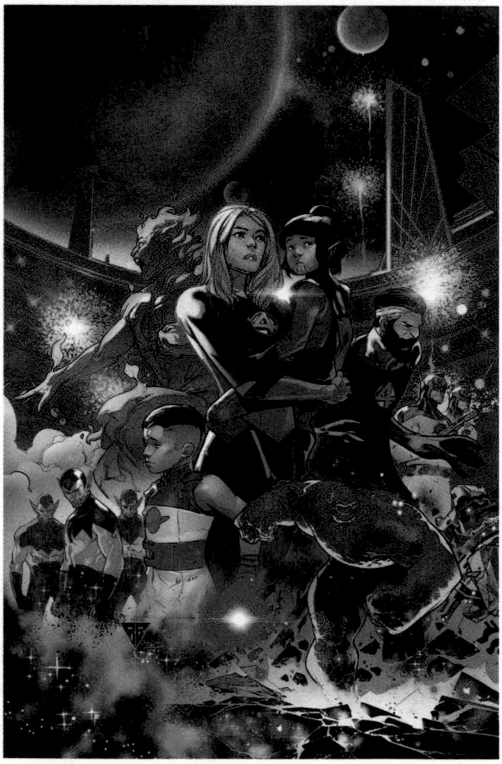

EMPYRE: FANTASTIC FOUR 0 VARIANT BY
R.B. Silva & **Marte Gracia**

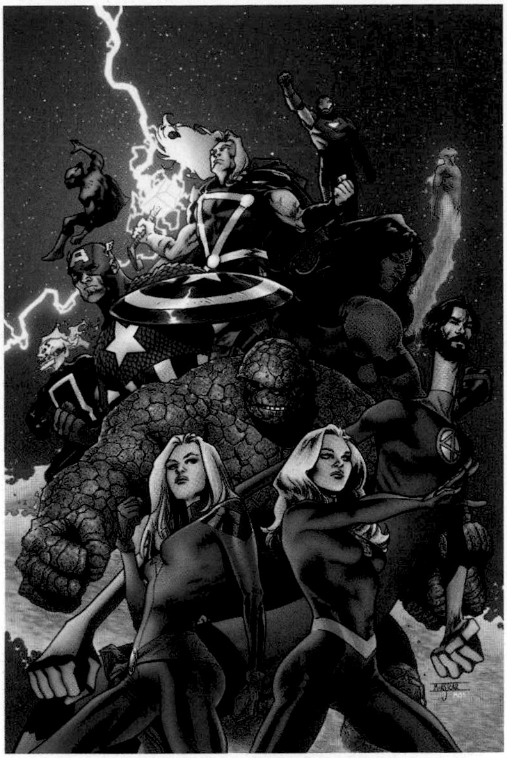

EMPYRE 1 VARIANT BY
Mahmud Asrar & Morry Hollowell

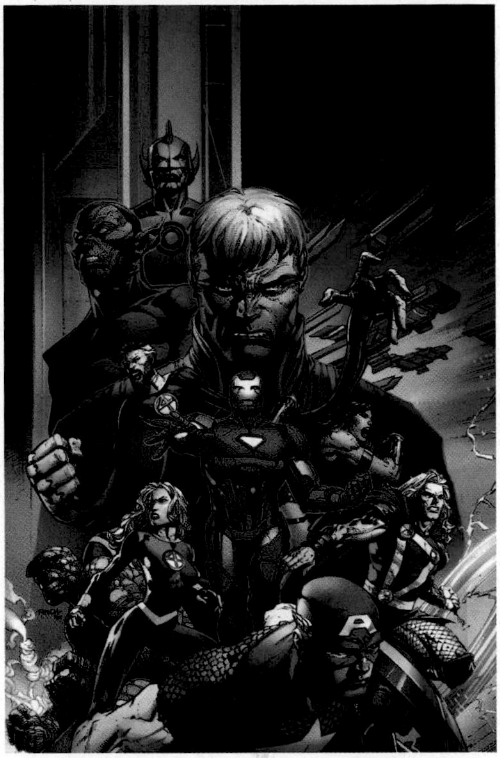

EMPYRE 1 VARIANT BY
David Finch & Frank D'Armata

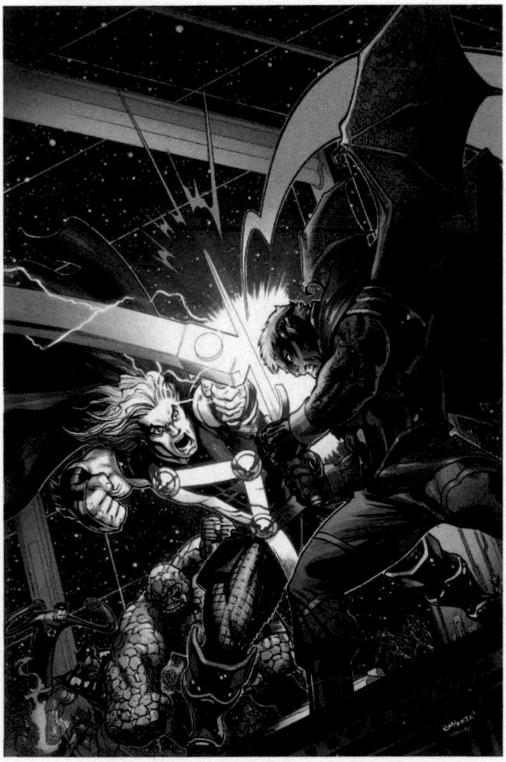

EMPYRE 1 PARTY VARIANT BY
Ed McGuinness & Jason Keith

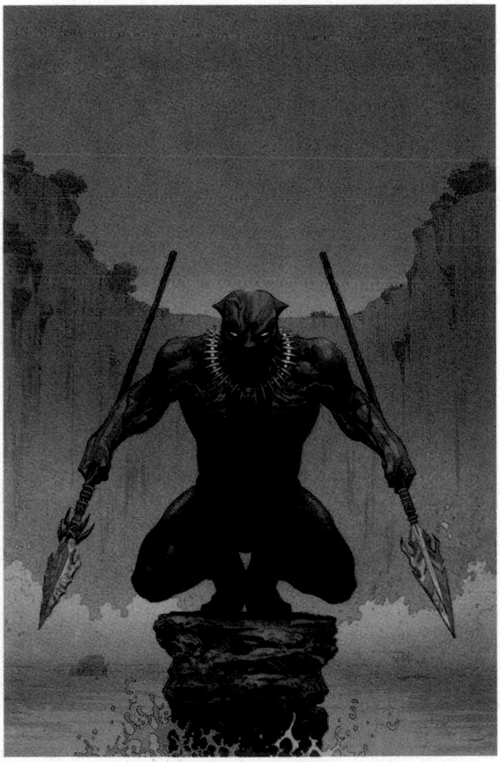

EMPYRE 1 SECRET VARIANT BY
Joshua Cassara & Matthew Wilson

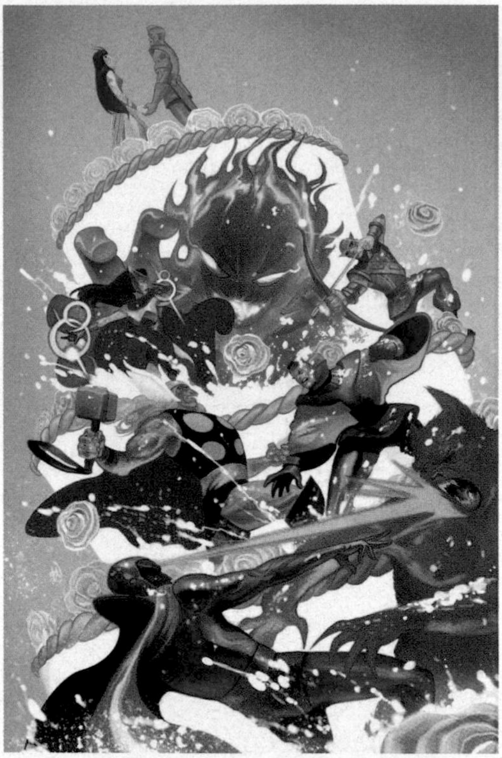

EMPYRE 2 SECOND-PRINTING VARIANT BY
Mike del Mundo

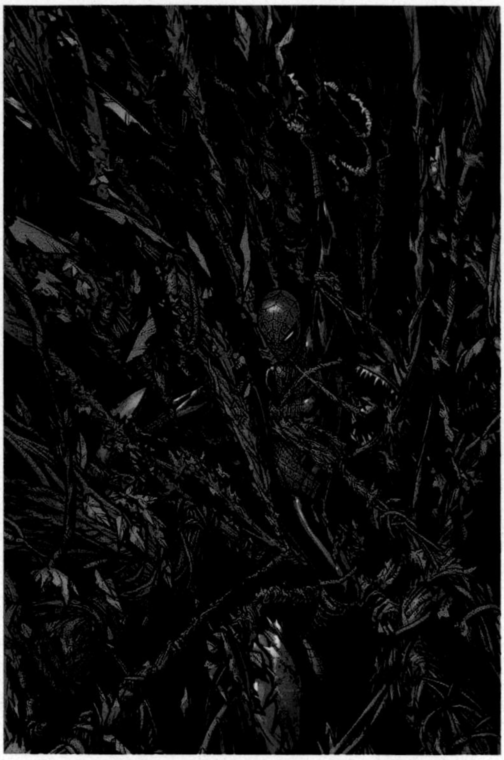

EMPYRE 2 SECRET VARIANT BY
Humberto Ramos & **Edgar Delgado**

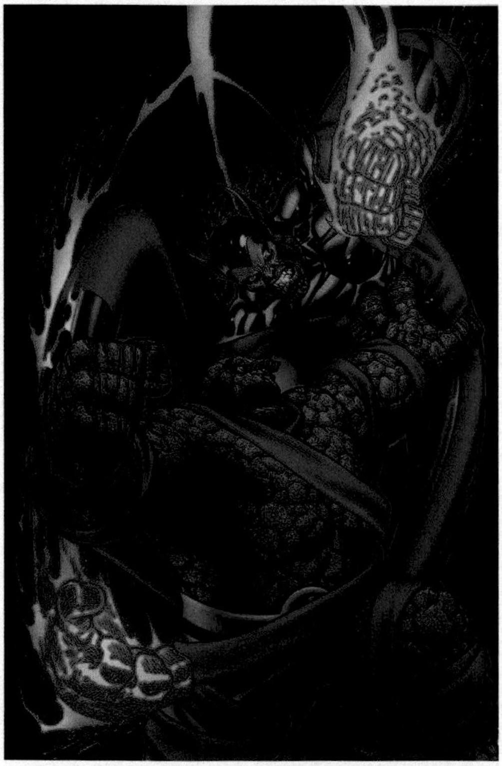

EMPYRE 3 VARIANT BY
Ed McGuinness & **Morry Hollowell**

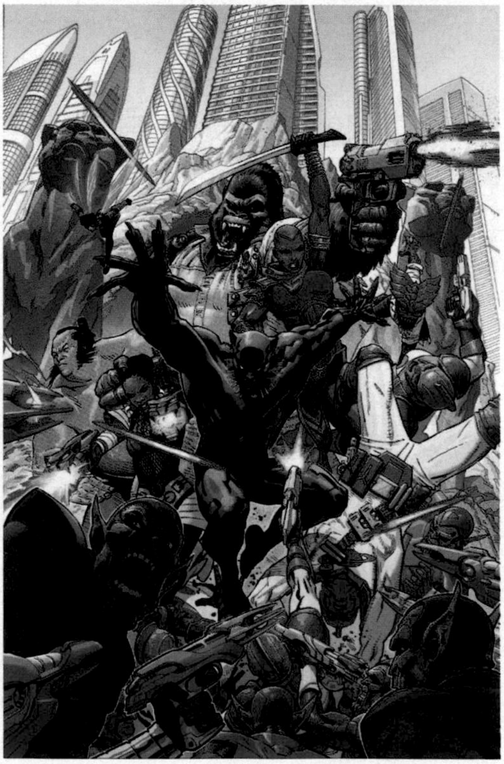

EMPYRE 3 SECRET VARIANT BY
Iban Coello & **Matthew Wilson**

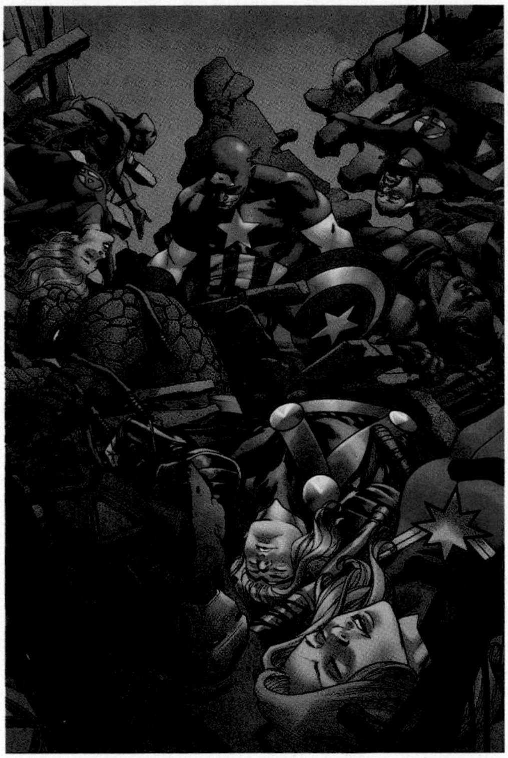

EMPYRE 4 SECRET VARIANT BY
R.B. Silva & **Matthew Wilson**

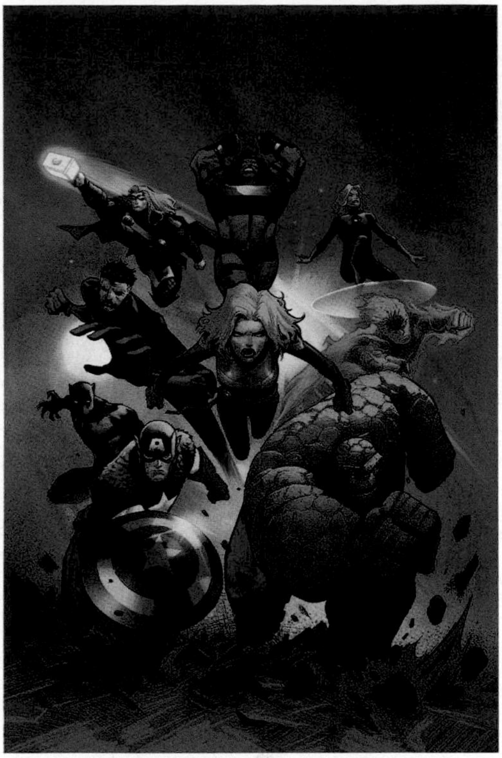

EMPYRE 4 SECRET VARIANT BY
Lee Garbett & **Frank Martin**

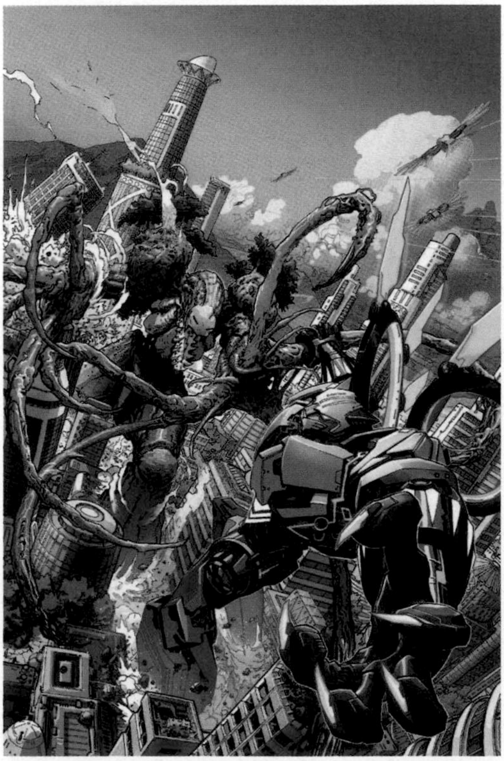

EMPYRE 5 SECRET VARIANT BY
Juann Cabal & **Matthew Wilson**

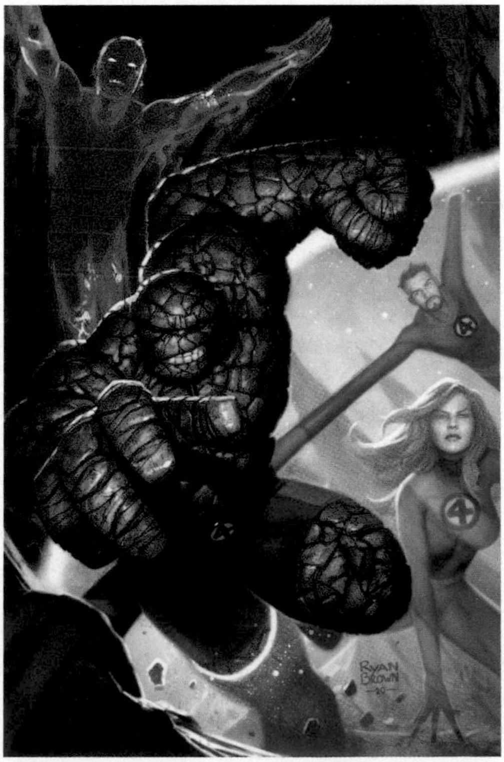
RYAN BROWN

EMPYRE 5 VARIANT BY
Ryan Brown

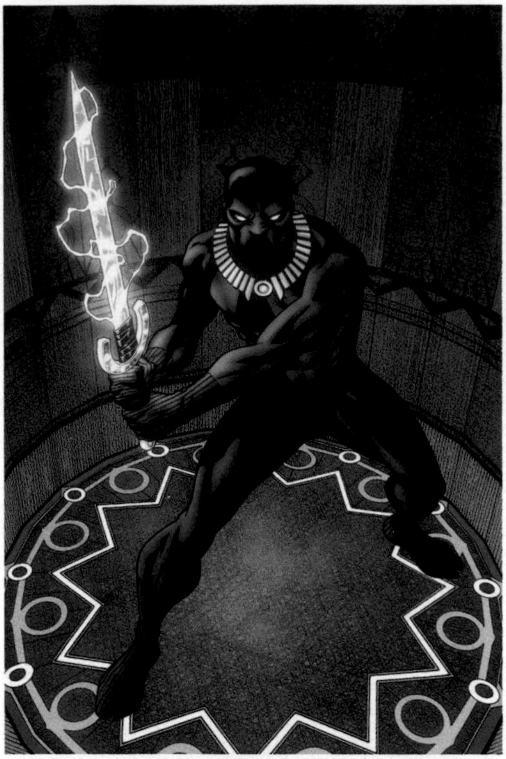

EMPYRE 6 VARIANT BY
Mike McKone & Morry Hollowell

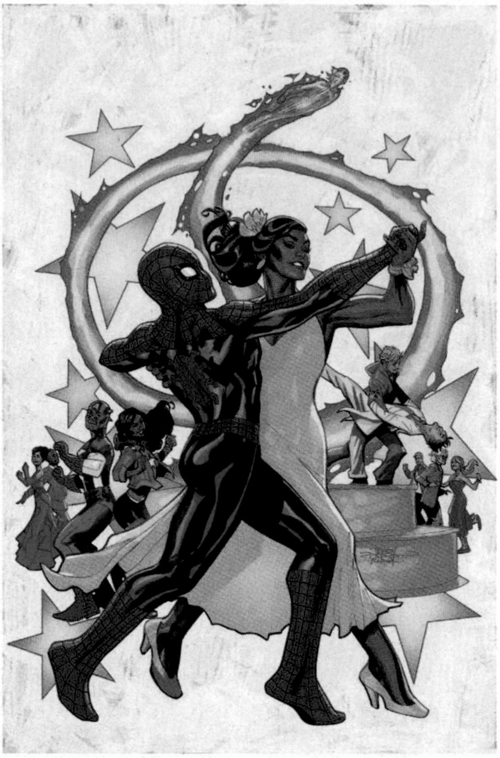

EMPYRE: AFTERMATH — AVENGERS VARIANT BY
Terry Dodson & Rachel Dodson

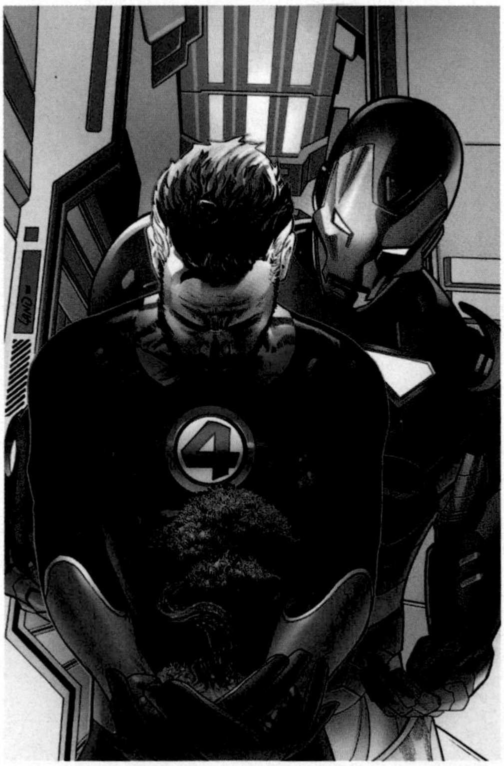

EMPYRE: AFTERMATH — AVENGERS VARIANT BY
Greg Land

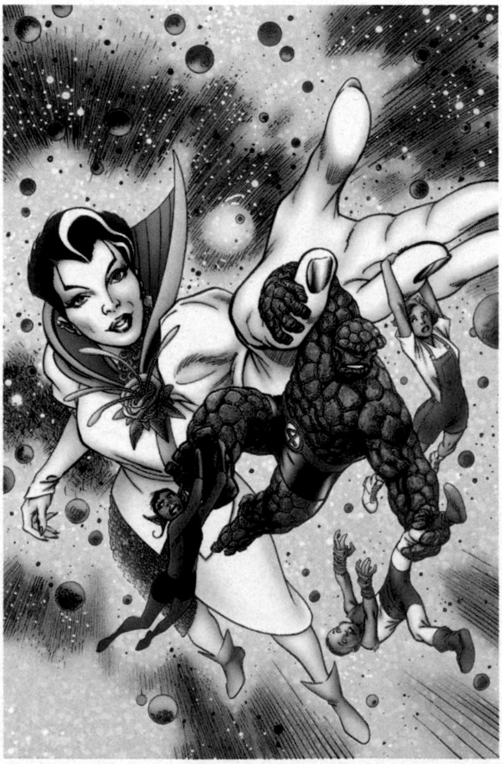

EMPYRE: FALLOUT — FANTASTIC FOUR VARIANT BY
Alan Davis & Morry Hollowell

DESIGNS BY

Valerio Schiti

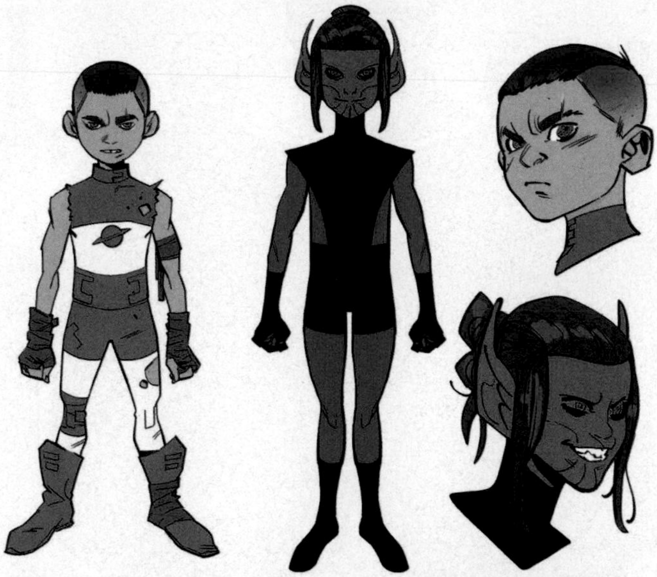

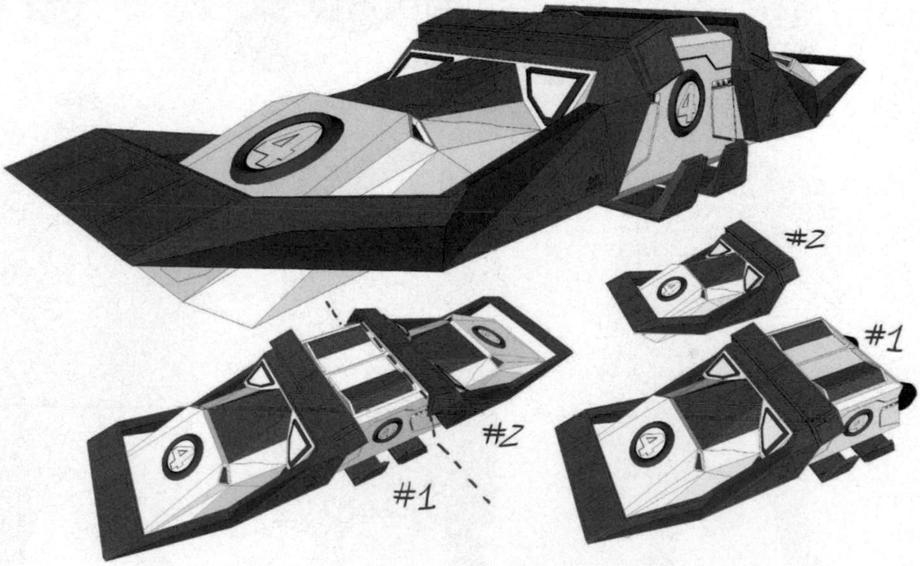
#2
#1
#2
#1

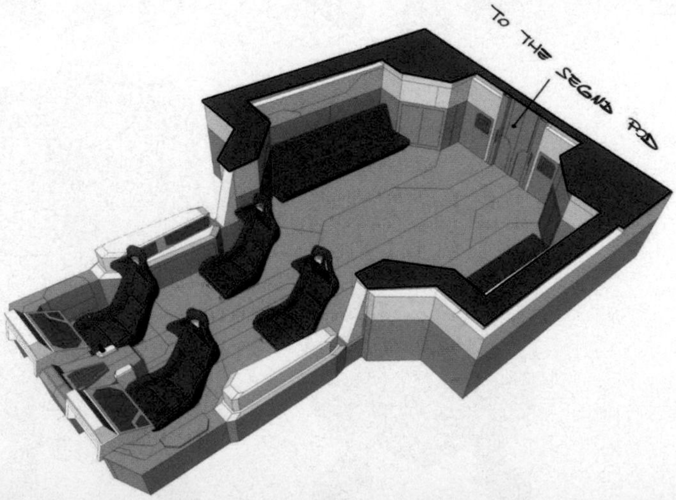
TO THE SEGND POD

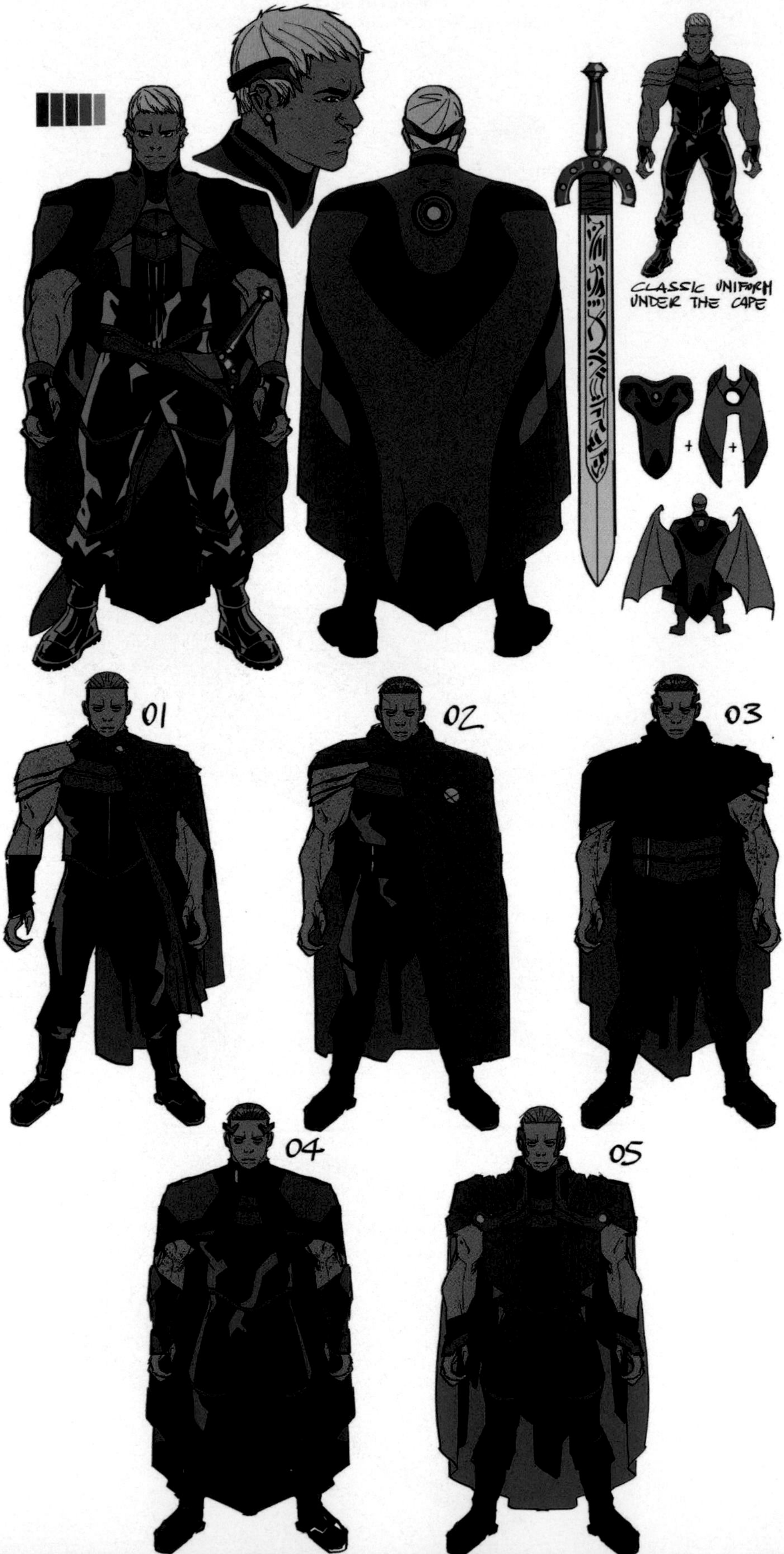
CLASSIC UNIFORM
UNDER THE CAPE
01
02
03
04
05

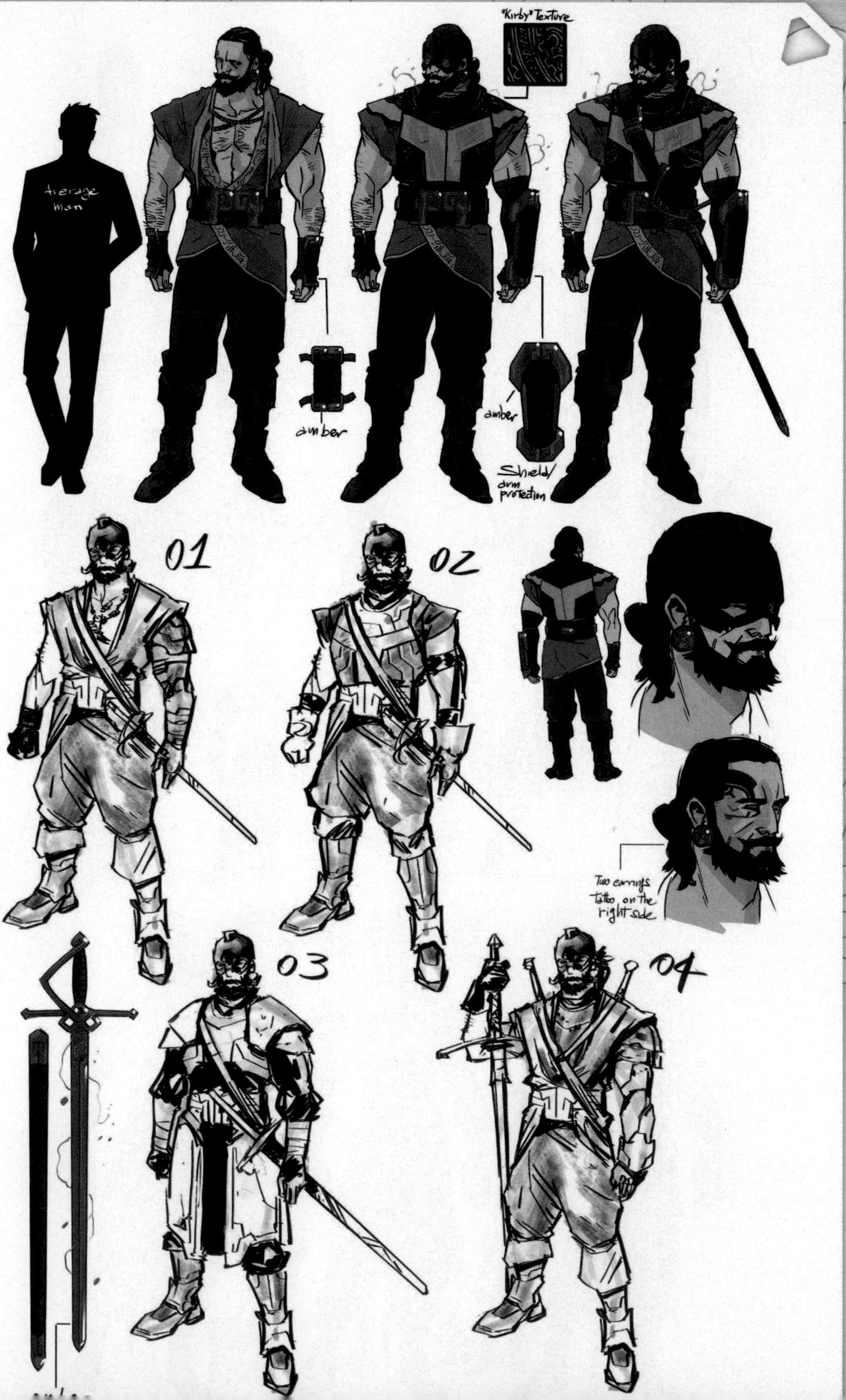

"Kirby" Texture
Average Man
amber
amber
Shield/ arm protection
01
02
Two earrings tattoo on the right side
03
04

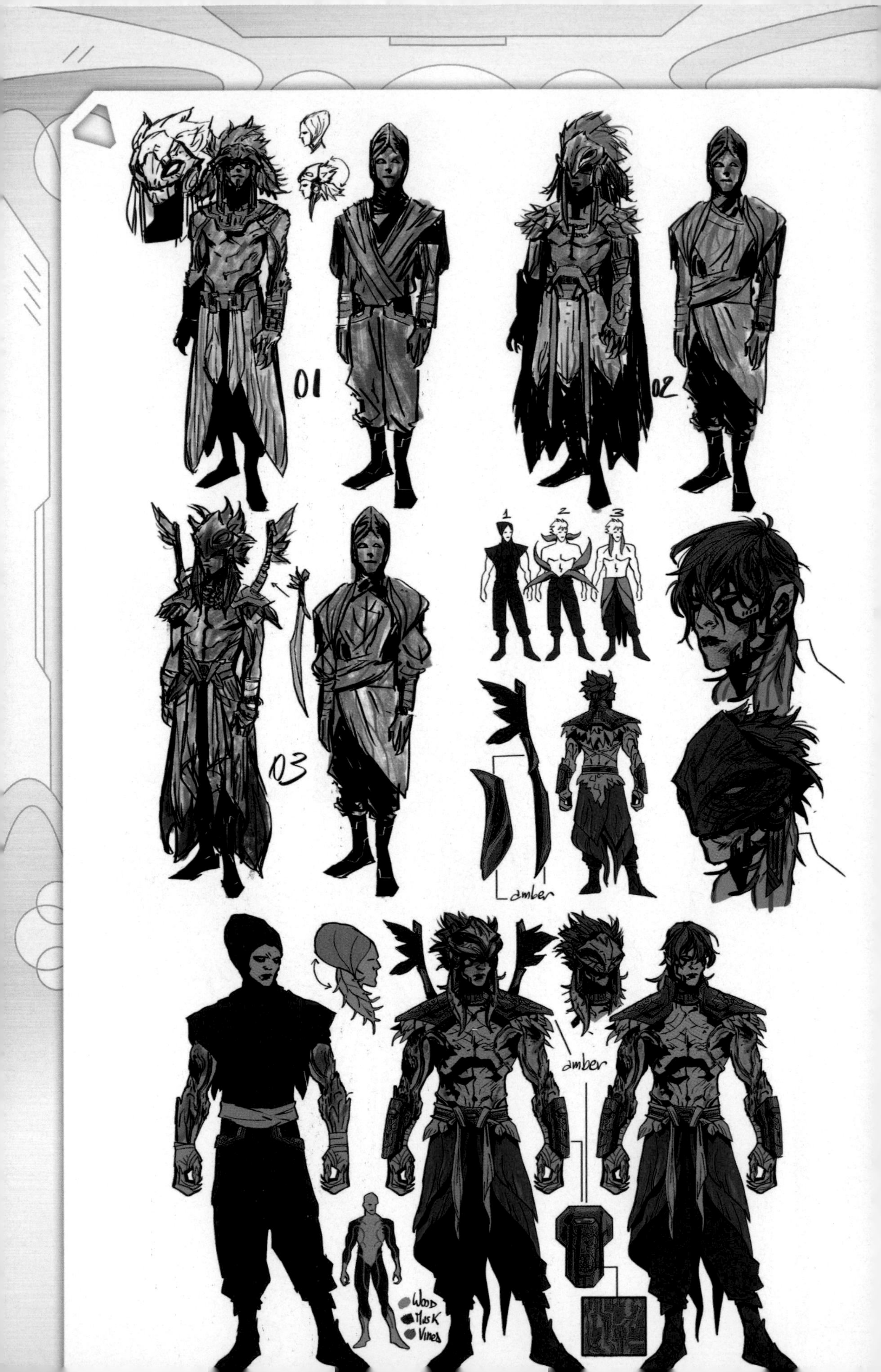

01
02
03
1
2
3
amber
amber
Wood
Mask
Vines

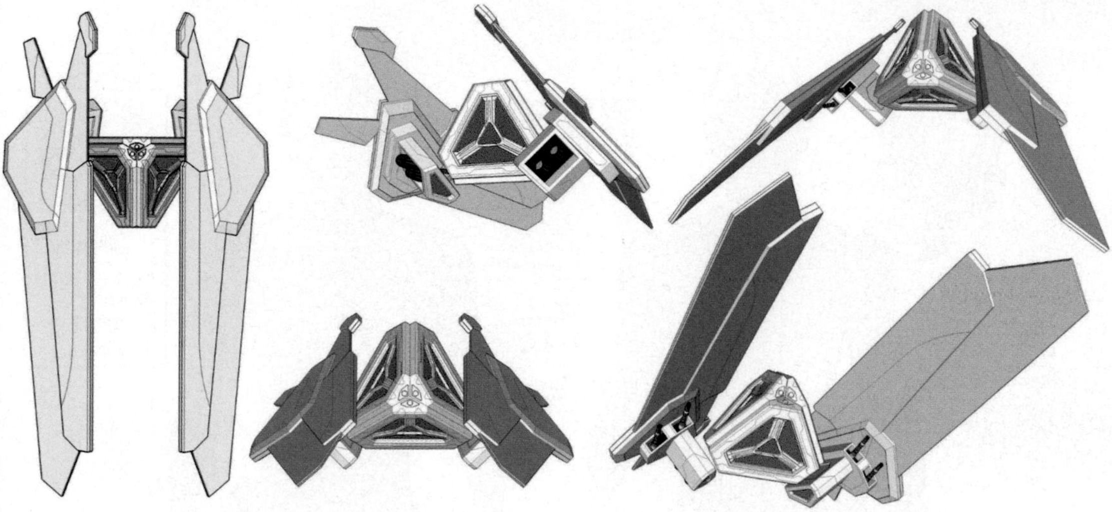

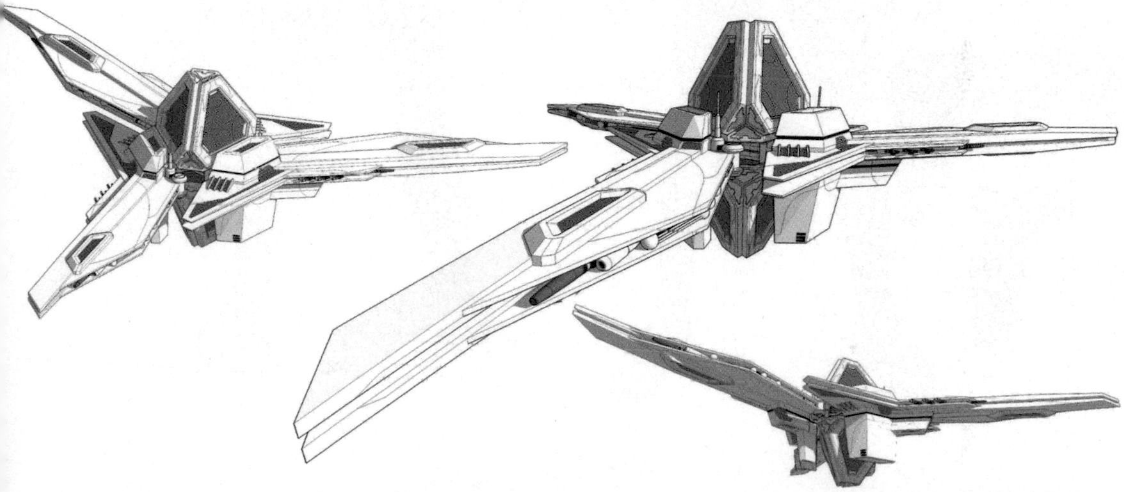

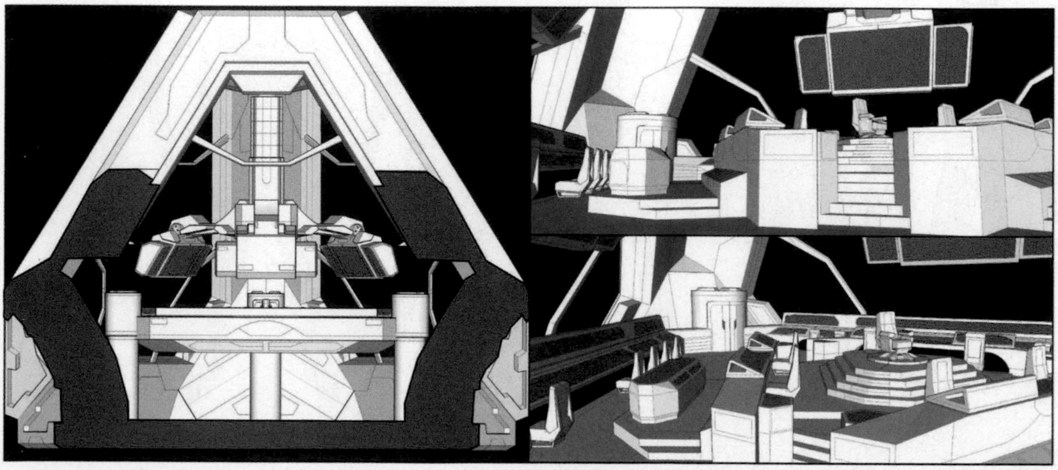

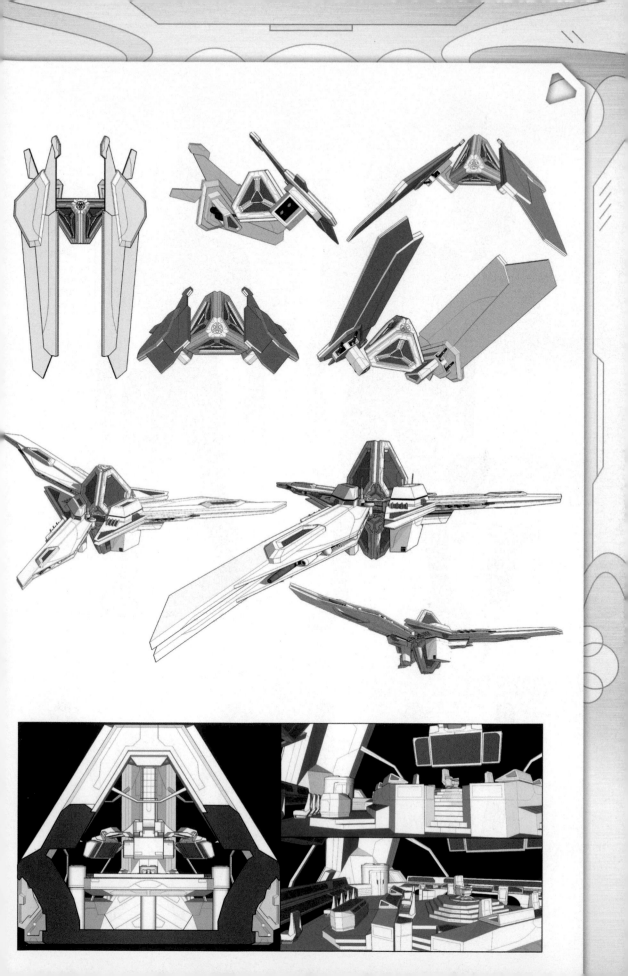

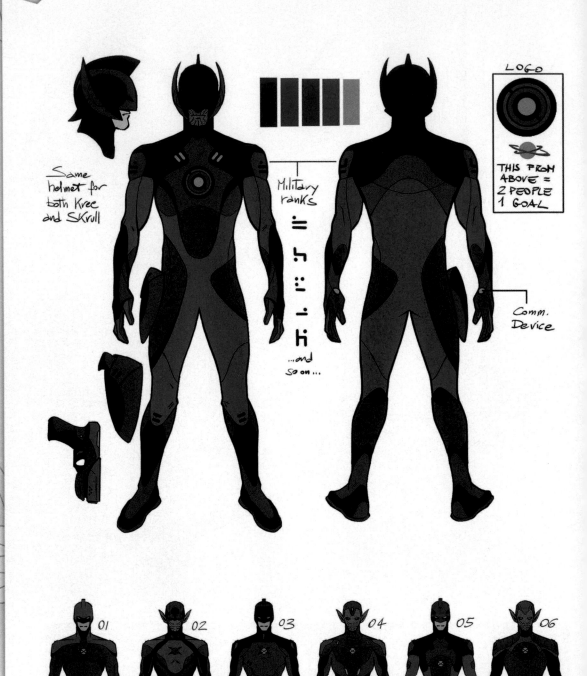

Same helmet for both Kree and Skrull

Military ranks

= ⼘ ⼘⼘ ⼘⼘⼘

...and so on...

LOGO

THIS FROM ABOVE = 2 PEOPLE 1 GOAL

Comm. Device

01 02 03 04 05 06

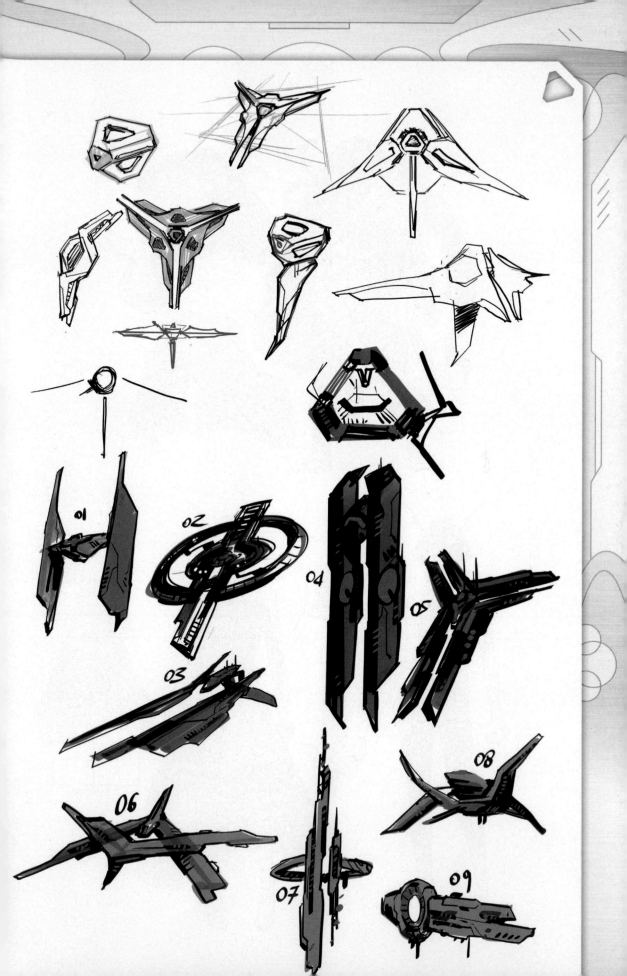

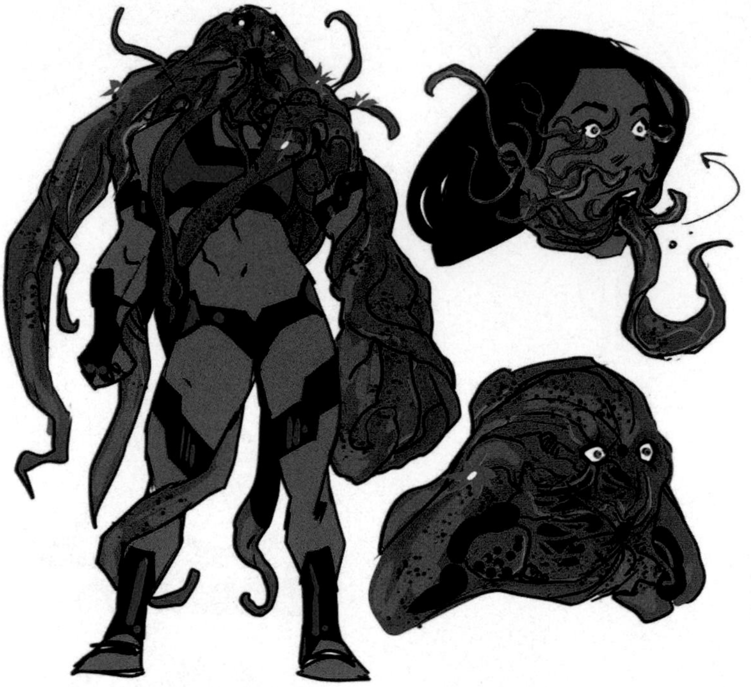

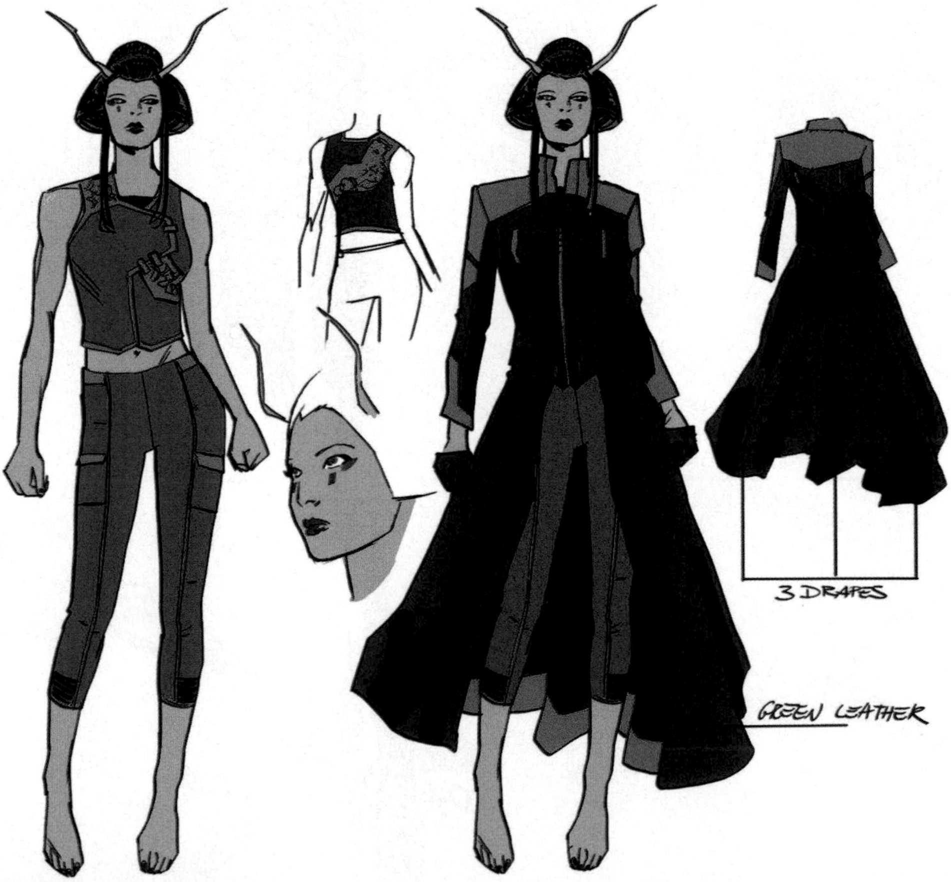
3 DRAPES
GREEN LEATHER

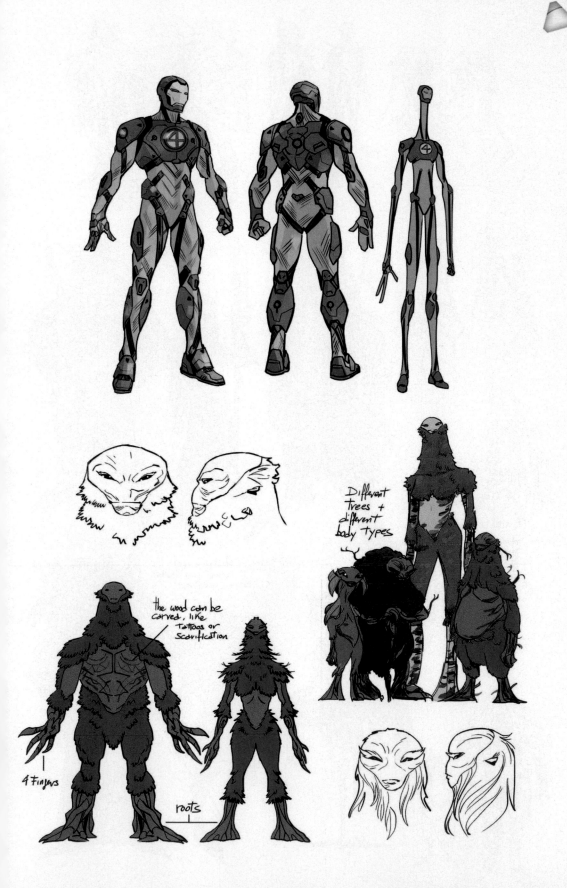

Different Trees + different body types

the wood can be carved, like Tattoos or Scarification

4 Fingers

roots

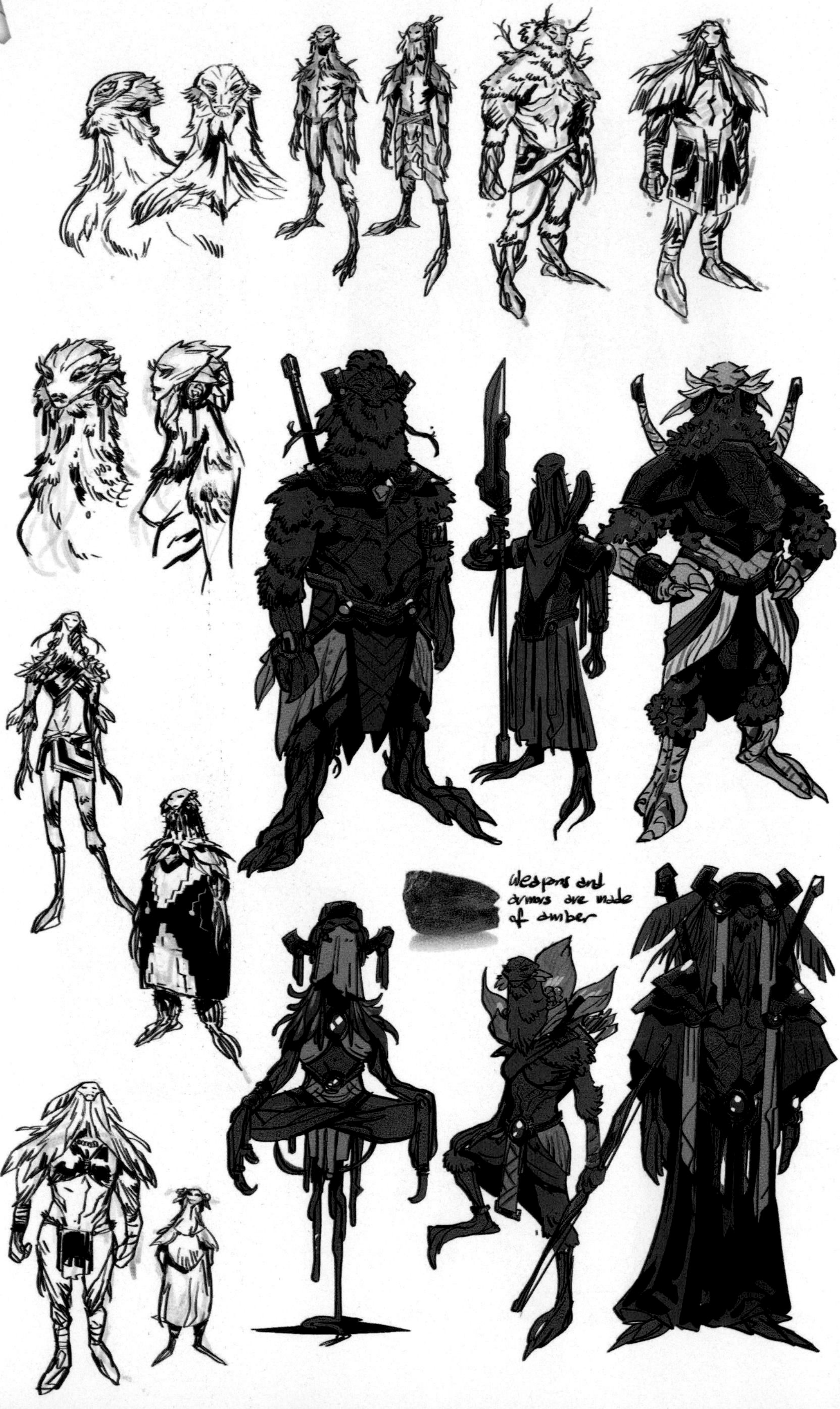
Weapons and armors are made of amber

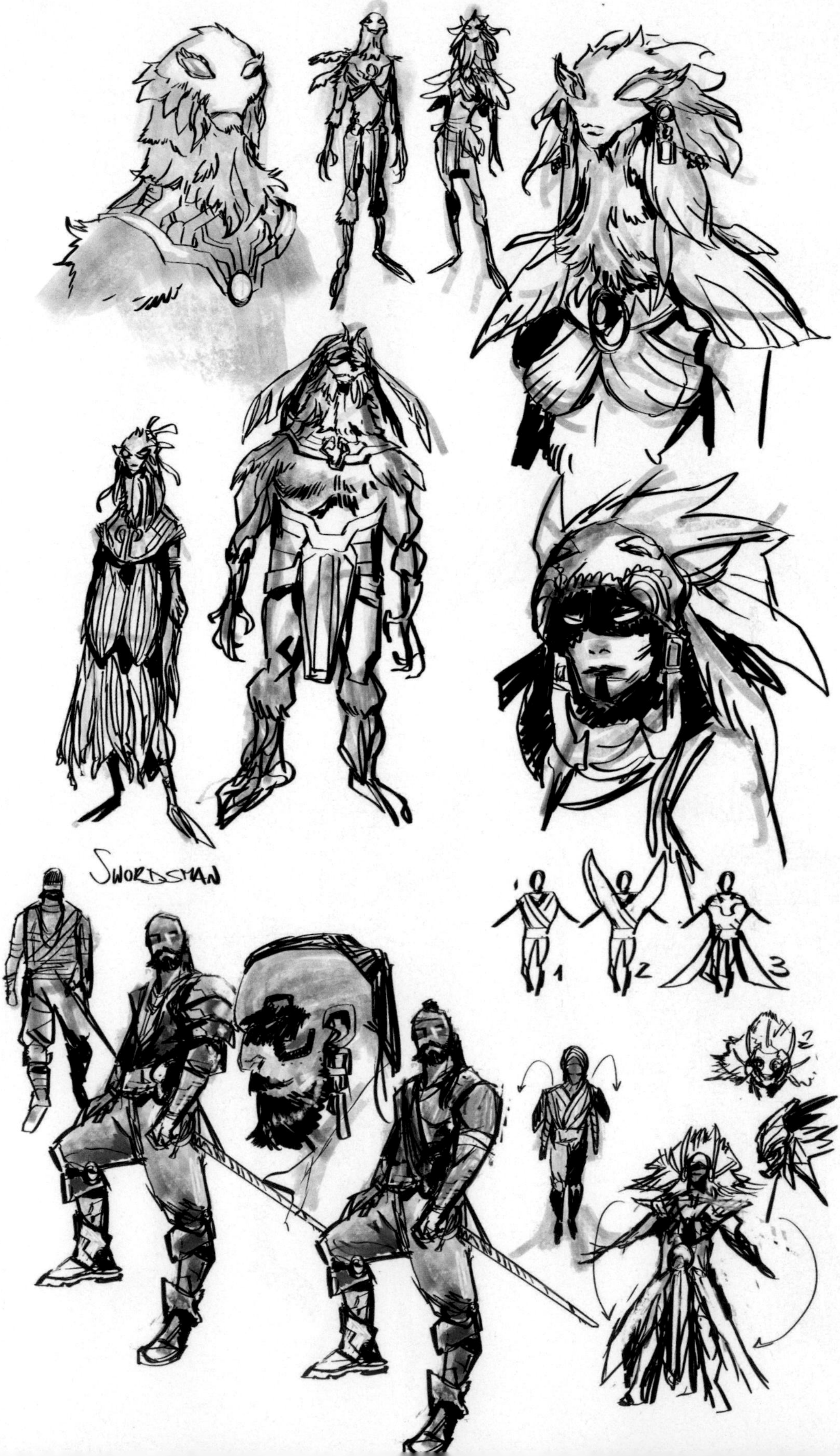
SWORDSMAN
1
2
3

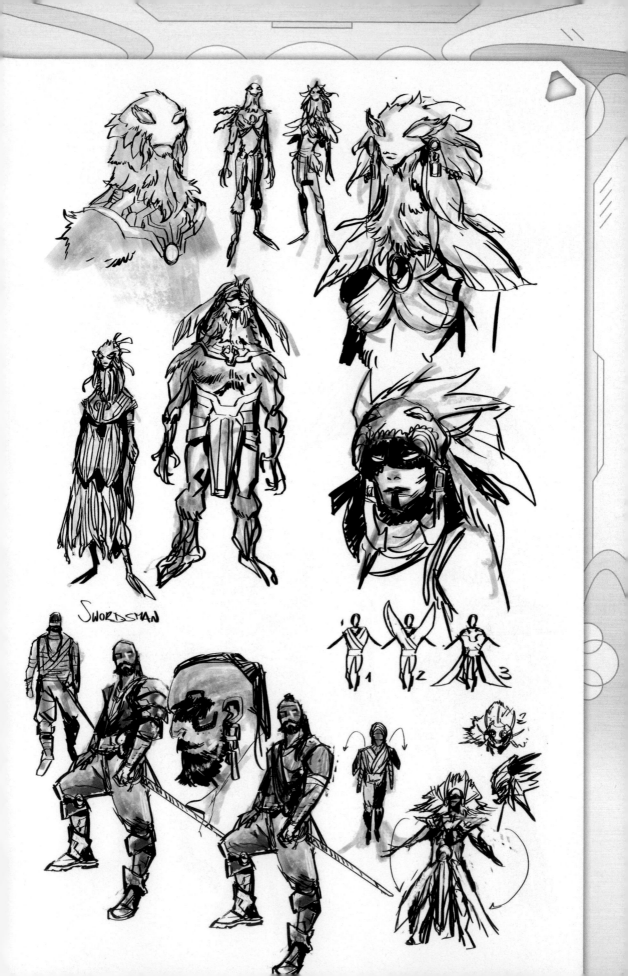

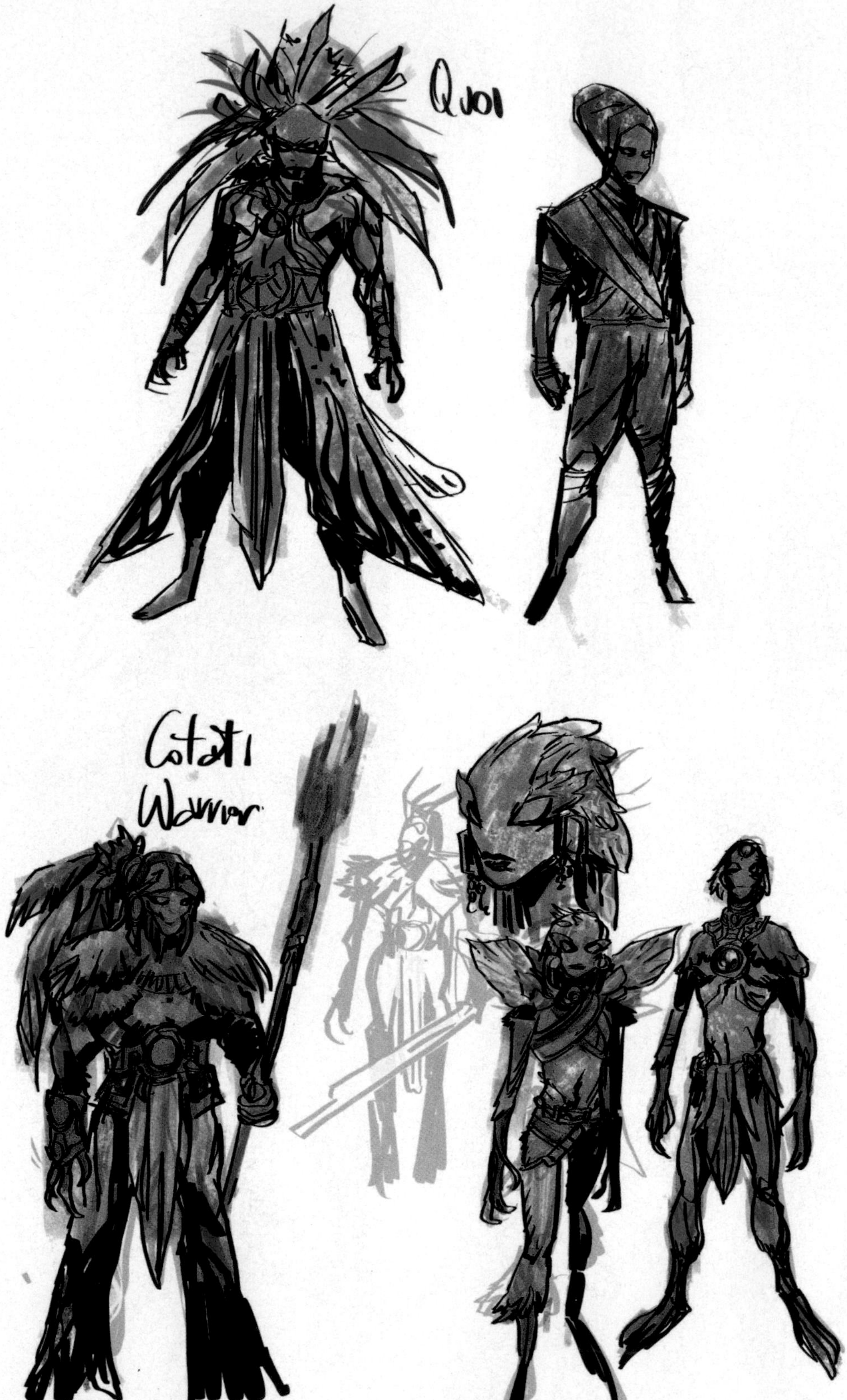
Quoi
Cotati Warrior